THE WORKS OF
GEORGE FARQUHAR

George Farquhar was the most popular and perhaps the best playwright to grace the stage at the turn of the eighteenth century, and he dominated the repertory for the next fifty years. The Irish-born actor and military officer arrived in London before he was twenty, captivated audiences with his lively, good-natured comedy, philandered with the leading actresses and female playwrights, married a widow with children, and wrote, besides the eight plays, many poems, letters, prologues, and epilogues, an epic, and a miscellany—all before his untimely death in 1707, when he had not yet turned thirty.

Shirley Strum Kenny has provided the first scholarly edition of the works since Stonehill's edition of 1930, in a reliable old-spelling text. She has added to the canon materials not printed since the beginning of the eighteenth century, some of which have never before been identified as Farquhar's.

Each play has an introduction describing its sources and composition, theatrical and publication history, influence, and textual problems. The introductions of the non-dramatic works contain similar information and relate the works to the contemporary events which occasioned them. Questions of authorship for newly identified works and possible or doubtful attributions are carefully considered.

Professor Kenny is President of Queen's College, Flushing, New York, and editor of *The Plays of Richard Steele*, among other books.

Portrait of George Farquhar. Frontispiece, *The Works of George Farquhar*, Dublin, 1775. By permission of the University of Chicago.

THE WORKS OF
GEORGE FARQUHAR

EDITED IN TWO VOLUMES BY
SHIRLEY STRUM KENNY

VOLUME II

CLARENDON PRESS · OXFORD
1988

Oxford University Press, Walton Street, Oxford OX2 6DP

Oxford New York Toronto
Delhi Bombay Calcutta Madras Karachi
Petaling Jaya Singapore Hong Kong Tokyo
Nairobi Dar es Salaam Cape Town
Melbourne Auckland

and associated companies in
Berlin Ibadan

Oxford is a trade mark of Oxford University Press

Published in the United States
by Oxford University Press, New York

© Oxford University Press, 1988

British Library Cataloguing in Publication Data
Farquhar, George
The works of George Farquhar.
I. Title.   II. Kenny, Shirley Strum
822'.4   PR3435
ISBN 0–19–811858–9 v.1
ISBN 0–19–812342–6 v.2

Library of Congress Cataloging in Publication Data
Farquhar, George, 1677?–1707.
The works of George Farquhar.
Includes indexes.
1. Kenny, Shirley Strum.   II. Title.
PR3435.A5K44   1986   822'.4   85–25942
ISBN 0–19–811858–9 (v. 1)
ISBN 0–19–812342–6 (v. 2)

Set by Hope Services, Abingdon
Printed in Great Britain
at the University Printing House, Oxford
by David Stanford
Printer to the University

CONTENTS

VOLUME II

LIST OF ILLUSTRATIONS

VOLUME II

ABBREVIATIONS FOR
FREQUENTLY QUOTED SOURCES

Archer	William Archer, ed. *George Farquhar*. Mermaid Series. Rept. London, 1959.
Biographia Dramatica	*Biographia Dramatica; or a Companion to the Playhouse*, David Erskine Baker (to 1764) and Isaac Reed (to 1782) and Stephen Jones (to 1811). 3 vols., London, 1812.
Biographical Dictionary	Philip H. Highfill, Jr., Kalman A. Burnim, and Edward A. Langhans. *A Biographical Dictionary of Actors, Actresses, Musicians, Dancers, Managers, and Other Stage Personnel in London, 1660–1800*. Carbondale, 1973–.
Churchill	Winston S. Churchill. *Marlborough His Life and Times*. 6 vols. London and New York, 1933–8.
Cibber	Colley Cibber. *An Apology for the Life of Colley Cibber*, ed. B. R. S. Fone, Ann Arbor, 1968.
Cunnington, Eighteenth	C. Willett and Phillis Cunnington, *Handbook of English Costume in the Eighteenth Century*. London, 1957.
Cunnington, Seventeenth	C. Willett and Phillis Cunnington, *Handbook of English Costume in the Seventeenth Century*. London, 1955.
Genest	John Genest. *Some Account of the English Stage*. 10 vols. Bath, 1832.
Hume	Robert D. Hume. *The Development of English Drama in the Late Seventeenth Century*. Oxford, 1976.
Hunt	Leigh Hunt, ed. *The Dramatic Works of Wycherley, Congreve, Vanbrugh, and Farquhar*. London, 1840.
James	Eugene Nelson James. *The Development of George Farquhar as a Comic Dramatist*. The Hague, 1972.
Jordan	Robert John Jordan. 'George Farquhar's Military Career', *Huntington Library Quarterly*, 37 (1973–4), 251–64.
Lawrence	W. J. Lawrence, 'The Mystery of "The Stage Coach"', *Modern Language Review*, 27 (1932), 392–7.

London Stage	*The London Stage 1660–1800*, ed. William Van Lennep, Emmett L. Avery, Arthur H. Scouten, G. W. Stone, Jr., and Charles Beecher Hogan, 5 Parts in 11 vols., Carbondale, Ill., 1960–8.
Military Dictionary	*A Military Dictionary Explaining All Difficult Terms in Martial Discipline, Fortification, and Gunnery.* 3rd edn. London, 1708.
Misson	*M. Misson's Memoirs and Observations in his Travels over England.* London, 1719.
NDCC	*B. E. Gent. A New Dictionary of the Terms Ancient and Modern of the Canting Crew.* London, [1690].
N&Q	*Notes and Queries.*
OED	*Oxford English Dictionary.*
Price	Curtis A. Price. *Music in the Restoration Theatre.* Ann Arbor, 1979.
Rothstein	Eric Rothstein. *George Farquhar.* Twayne English Authors Series. New York, 1967.
Scouller	R. E. Scouller. *The Armies of Queen Anne.* Oxford, 1966.
Spectator	*The Spectator*, ed. Donald F. Bond 5 vols. Oxford, 1965.
Stonehill	Charles Stonehill, ed. *The Complete Works of George Farquhar.* 2 vols. 1930, rept. New York, 1967.
TLS	*Times Literary Supplement.*
Wheatley	Henry B. Wheatley. *London, Past and Present: Its History, Associations, and Traditions.* 3 vols. London, 1891.
Wilkes	*The Works of George Farquhar.* Dublin, 1775.

CHRONOLOGY

1677 (?)		Farquhar born.
1694	17 July	Farquhar matriculated, Trinity College Dublin, at age 17.
1696–8		Farquhar performed at Smock Alley Theatre.
1698		Farquhar arrived in London(?).
	December (?)	*Love and a Bottle* opened at Drury Lane.
	15 (?) December	*The Adventures of Covent-Garden* published.
	29 December	*Love and a Bottle* published.
1699	Autumn (?)	'An Epilogue, spoken by Mr. Wilks at his first Appearance upon the English Stage' spoken at Drury Lane.
	28 November	First known performance of *The Constant Couple* at Drury Lane.
	11 December	*The Constant Couple* published.
1700	1 February	Second edition of *The Constant Couple* published.
	On or before 19 February	Epilogue to Oldmixon's *The Grove* spoken at Drury Lane.
	11 May	*Familiar and Courtly Letters* published.
	9 July	Prologue to Crauford's *Courtship A-la-Mode* spoken at Drury Lane.
	13 July	The New Prologue to *The Constant Couple* spoken at Drury Lane.
	7 August	Farquhar left England for the Netherlands.
	20 August	Third edition of *The Constant Couple* published.
	After 23 October	Farquhar returned to England.
1701	April (?)	*Sir Harry Wildair* opened at Drury Lane.
	3 May	Second volume of *Familiar and Courtly Letters* published.

1701	13 May	*Sir Harry Wildair* published.
	24 July	*Letters of Wit, Politicks and Morality* published.
	?	'A Prologue on the propos'd Union of the Two Houses' spoken.
	22 November	*Love and Business* published.
1701–2	Winter 1701– February 1702	*The Stage-Coach* opened at Lincoln's Inn Fields.
1702	February (?)	*The Inconstant* opened at Drury Lane.
	28 February	Second issue of *Love and Business* published.
	11 March	*The Inconstant* published.
	October–November	Prologue to Manning's *All for the Better* spoken at Drury Lane.
	November–December	Epilogue to Gildon's *The Patriot* spoken at Drury Lane.
	14 December	*The Twin-Rivals* opened at Drury Lane.
	22 December	Lintott bought copyright to it.
	29 December	*The Twin-Rivals* published.
1703 (?)		Farquhar married Margaret Pemell.
1704		Fourth edition of *The Constant Couple* published.
		The Stage-Coach published in Dublin.
	March (?)	Farquhar became a recruiting officer.
	14 June–20 October (?)	Farquhar served on recruiting duty, perhaps in Shrewsbury.
1704–5	October 1704– July 1705	Farquhar continued military service in Ireland.
	Between 15 November and 10 April (probably in March)	Benefit performance of *The Constant Couple* given in Dublin, with Farquhar as Sir Harry Wildair.
1705	3 or 4 May	*The Stage-Coach* published in London.
	12 June–10 July	Farquhar's regiment at encampment at the Curragh of Kildare.
	27 July	Farquhar sat in judgement at court martial in Dublin Castle.
	After August–before November	Farquhar departed Dublin, perhaps recruited in Lichfield.

1706	12 February	Lintott bought copyright to *The Recruiting Officer*.
	Before 1 March	Farquhar left his regiment.
	8 April	*The Recruiting Officer* opened at the Queen's Theatre in the Haymarket.
	25 April (or shortly before)	*The Recruiting Officer* published.
	15 October	'The Prologue Spoken by Mr. Wilks, At the Opening of the Theatre in the Hay Market' spoken.
	26 October	Second edition of *The Recruiting Officer* published.
	25 November	Prologue to Centlivre's *The Platonick Lady* spoken at the Queen's Theatre in the Haymarket.
	6 December	Third edition of *The Recruiting Officer* published.
1707	27 January	Lintott bought copyright to *The Beaux Stratagem*.
	8 March	*The Beaux Stratagem* opened at the Queen's Theatre in the Haymarket.
	27 March	*The Beaux Stratagem* published.
	23 May	Farquhar buried at St. Martin's-in-the-Fields.
	4 December	Lintott bought half rights to *Love and a Bottle* from Francis Coggen.
1708	27 March	First edition of *The Comedies* published.
1710		*Barcellona* published.
1711	18 January	'Second edition' of *Works* published.

INTRODUCTION

I HAVE tried to make Farquhar's works readily and reliably available to modern readers in an old-spelling text. The text includes revisions which are demonstrably Farquhar's and corrections of obvious errors, some caught by eighteenth-century printing-house employees, some by me. Corrections arising from the performance texts are noted and occasionally included in this edition. Although routine emendations in early editions have no authorial basis, I have accepted them if they satisfactorily correct errors; if they do not, I have followed copy-text or substituted more appropriate emendations.

For simplicity in reading, I have regularly standardized characters' names when more than one name or spelling occurs in the speech prefixes and stage directions, following Farquhar's intentions when they can be determined and arbitrarily choosing a single form when they can not. I have also added necessary stage directions, recording those from early editions in the footnotes and identifying those new to this edition by square brackets. With these few exceptions, the edition adheres as closely as possible to the copy-text.

Accidentals as well as substantives follow the copy-text very closely. My criterion is spelling and punctuation which is neither confusing nor misleading to readers familiar with eighteenth-century texts. Therefore pointing acceptable in Farquhar's time but not now (for example, a question mark used for a mild exclamation) stands. But since I do not consider compositorial foibles sacrosanct, I have freely changed obvious errors, such as a lower-case initial beginning a speech or the omission of punctuation at the end of one.

Typography and some accidentals are silently regularized. The edition neither reproduces nor notes initials, factotums, display capitals, swash letters, long _s_s, ligatures, _v_s used for _u_s _vv_s used for _w_s, wrong-fount letters and italics used in shortages, turned letters except _u_ and _n_, lost letters, or words jammed together in tight lines. Regardless of the copy-text, rhymed poetry, quotations, and letters are indented and italicized. Also italicized are characters' names in roman passages, but not accompanying titles such as 'Sir' or 'Mr.' unless they are part of a speech prefix. Characters' names in italic passages and stage directions appear in roman type. Proper nouns are regularly italicized in roman passages, and romanized in italic passages. Speech prefixes and stage directions, consistently italicized, begin with capitals, end with periods or dashes, and contain corrections of obvious misspellings. Entrances are centred, exits are set flush right, major stage directions between speeches centred, those within speeches enclosed in parentheses, and those incorrectly placed in the text positioned properly. The changes of typography and accidentals in speech prefixes and stage directions do not affect the lines written for the stage, but simplify the mechanical elements of the texts for which compositors were responsible. Lineation takes note of speech only; stage directions are not included in it.

The introduction to each play briefly treats the composition, sources, first production, theatrical history, critical reception, influence, textual problems, and history of publication. Farquhar well knew the traditions of English comedy, but few direct debts can be proved. I also hesitate to claim specific influences on later works, unless there is strong evidence of a specific relationship. The bibliographical section of each introduction describes the printing of the first edition and other significant ones to explain textual cruces. It develops the rationale for editorial decisions in each case. Textual notes record all substantive emendations of the copy-text and any debatable refusals to emend. Explanations provide information on textual decisions about which questions can reasonably arise. In *The Recruiting Officer* and *The Beaux Stratagem* in particular, I have also listed important theatrical revisions not included in the present text. Emendations of accidentals list all changes from copy-text in punctuation and spelling, except silent alterations; to prevent misunderstanding of the original accidentals. I include hyphenations of compound words at the ends of lines in both the copy-text and the present edition unless the second part of the compound is capitalized. The abbreviation 'ed.' stands for 'editor', and 'om.' for 'omitted'. The Commentary provides the reader with the necessary background of topical and literary allusions, sources, and occasionally relations to works by Farquhar or others.

The treatment of the non-dramatic works differs only in a few details. Introductions treat when possible the composition and sources, critical reception, influence, textual problems, and publication history; however, information is sparse for some minor works. Spelling of proper nouns is not regularized. For works published in a single edition, Textual Notes and Emendations of Accidentals do not include a siglum since they are invariably editorial corrections.

THE RECRUITING OFFICER

INTRODUCTION

SOURCES AND COMPOSITION

AFTER the disappointing reception of *The Twin-Rivals*, Farquhar produced no other known works until *The Recruiting Officer* opened in the spring of 1706. By 1704 he had married a widow with three children. The marriage, as it has traditionally been depicted, is proper material for an eighteenth-century novel: Farquhar, believing he could salvage his fortune by marrying a wealthy woman, proposed to a widow, Margaret Pemell, who must have been at least ten years his senior.[1] Because she was passionately enamoured of him, she led him to believe she was rich, but after vows were exchanged, he discovered his mistake. Nevertheless, he remained loyal to her and her children until he died in 1707. Most scholars have estimated the date of the wedding as 1703; a poem in 1704 referred to it:

Bid *F—r* (tho' bit) to his Consort be just, . . .[2]

The other known activity in Farquhar's life in the period between *The Twin-Rivals* and *The Recruiting Officer* was his military service. Having acquired a lieutenant's commission through either the Duke of Ormonde or the Earl of Orrery,[3] Farquhar became an officer in a regiment first constituted in March 1704. Because of shortages of funds, the recruiting campaign was deferred until 14 June, and the pay saved thereby was used for levy money.[4] The Earl of Orrery was to raise eleven companies, 'to Rendezvous at Shrewsbury, Whitchurch, Namptwich, Wrexham, Chester, Leverpoole and Whitehaven, and to Embarke on or before the 14th of September next. for Ireland'.[5] Orrery later claimed that Farquhar performed with great diligence in 'raising and Recruteing yᵉ sd. Reigmt.', an indication that he was involved in raising the company as well as subsequent recruitment;[6] Jordan believes the reference to raising the regiment indicates that he was on duty, perhaps in Shrewsbury, in the summer of 1704.[7] The fact that Farquhar did not publish new works during 1704–5 lends credence to the theory that he had embarked on his military career.

Farquhar's perception of the difficulties and injustices of recruiting date from this service. Employment was readily available in the countryside, and as a result the officers could not raise sufficient recruits to fulfil their needs; the recruitment period had to be extended for five weeks. Further, the standard rate of £3 per recruit for levy money did not prove sufficient incentive to entice men to join the army, and some officers found themselves having to supplement it out of their own pockets. In addition, if recruits deserted, the recruiting officer was personally liable for the levy money lost thereby. Farquhar apparently suffered such financial losses from his recruitment ventures that he put his own money into the effort 'to ye great prejudice of his family'.[8]

In October 1704 Orrery's troops were moving to Ireland; Farquhar went there some time between October and the following March. He was stationed in Dublin with his regiment at least until the end of July 1705 when he sat in judgement on a trooper named James Lloyd in Dublin Castle.[9] There is no known data on when Farquhar left military service, although he was back in London by 12 February when he signed the publication agreement with Lintott.[10]

Nothing is known about the time and place of composition of the play. The period between his departure from military service some time after August 1705 and his contract with Lintott in February 1706 seems a likely period. The dialogue mentions no events later than the victory at Blenheim in August 1704.

The chief source for the characterizations and the provincial setting so often discussed by critics was his own recruiting experience, as he says in the Dedication. The specific models for characters have been identified as local citizens, although scholars have not always agreed on which local citizens. Thomas Wilkes said in his *Life* (I. x–xi) that Ballance was based on Alderman Gosnell, once mayor of Shrewsbury and one of three senior aldermen elected to be a justice of the peace for life. Sylvia, according to Wilkes, was modelled on his daughter, and Kite on a sergeant from Farquhar's regiment.

A more convincing if equally unprovable case is made by
H. Owen and J. B. Blakeway in *A History of Shrewsbury*,
published in London in 1825; they based their attributions on
information imparted by Anne Blakeway of Shrewsbury, who
died in 1766. They claim Francis Berkeley, Esq., barrister and
recorder of Shrewsbury and Bridgenorth, who died in 1710,
was the model for Justice Ballance; John Hill, Esq., of
Shrewsbury, the model for one of the other justices; a Mr
Owens, probably Athlestane Owens of Rhiwsaison in
Montgomeryshire, for Worthy; a Miss Harnage, probably
Dorothy Harnage of Belsadine, for Melinda; Laconia Berkeley,
daughter of the recorder, for Sylvia. The same list appeared in
a piece in the *St. James's Chronicle*, supposedly procedured from
an old lady in Shrewsbury, conceivably Mrs Blakeway, and
communicated to the Bishop of Dromore.[11] The *Biographia
Dramatica* (III. 195) lists the same sources for the characters,
as does William Cooke in his *Memoirs of Samuel Foote, Esq.*
published in 1805, except that Cooke calls Berkeley by the
name Beverley. Plume is consistently identified as a self-
portrait, although, as Leigh Hunt pointed out, 'the gay
Captain could only have been the imaginary Farquhar;—gay
enough, we doubt not, while so imagining, but in his own
person, an anxious married man'.[12]

An amusing, if perhaps apochryphal, account of the
original of Kite is provided by Thomas Wilkes in *A General
View of the Stage*. Wilkes claims that a sergeant named Jones in
Farquhar's regiment on a recruiting mission fell into company
with a fellow sergeant who had recruited fourteen men in
Yorkshire. Instead of beating for volunteers of his own, Jones
ingratiated himself with the recruits by his 'agreeable drollery
and humorous songs' until they left their recruiter to go with
Jones to Ireland. Ormonde, receiving a complaint about the
'robbery', ordered Jones into custody, but Farquhar prevailed
upon him and obtained Jones's enlargement. Jones later
entertained Ormonde so delightfully that he received money
and promise of a commission. His tricks 'procured him the
nickname of Kite ever after'.[13]

Whether any of these attributions is accurate will probably
never be proven; moreover, since all the alleged models are
unknowns, acquisition of such information would add little to

an understanding of the play. Farquhar was not writing a *drame à clef*; there would have been little point in specifically drawing Shrewsbury characters for a London audience. But surely the experience in Shrewsbury contributed to his portrayals.

Although Farquhar once again wrote a strikingly original play, critics have traditionally foraged dramatic literature for sources for characters and scenes. Hunt admired Farquhar's originality, claiming he 'went only upon grounds of truth and observation, and his own impulses',[14] but most editors and critics have not been so generous, pointing instead to analogues in prior literature. Stonehill, for example, recalls that recruits appear on stage in Shadwell's *The Woman-Captain* (1679); he might well have added Steele's *The Funeral* (1701), which remained popular on stage during the time Farquhar was writing plays. He notes that astrologers appear in several plays, including Congreve's *Love for Love*, Wilson's *The Cheat's*, and Orrery's *Guzman*, and that in *The Astrologer* (1668) there is a scene 'quite suggestive of that between Kite and Melinda'. He also attributes to Shadwell's play 'the barest hint of Sylvia'.[15] Kavanagh finds the influence of Ben Jonson on Brazen and Worthy and the influence of Shakespeare, particularly *Twelfth Night*, on the play as a whole.[16] Rothstein finds that Farquhar's characters 'come directly from contemporary fiction. They are intricate developments of well-tried prototypes'. He mentions Scarron's *Comical Romance*, the model for Farquhar's *Adventures of Covent-Garden*, as a source for Sylvia's military disguise; in it Sophia disguises herself as Don Hernando and becomes Viceroy of Valencia. He finds predecessors to the astrologer in Jonson's Face and Subtle as well as Congreve's Foresight in *Love for Love*. Brazen and Ballance are stock Restoration characters.[17]

John Ross mentions a precedent for the court-room impressment scene in Shakespeare's *2 Henry IV*, III.ii, one for the use of an astrologer in a love affair in Dryden's *An Evening's Love: or, the Mock Astrologer*, and one for the astrological jargon in Foresight's verbiage.[18]

Critics generally agree that in forsaking the London drawing-room for the country air of Shrewsbury, Farquhar was introducing a new kind of atmosphere into comedy which was to affect not only *The Beaux Stratagem* but other subsequent comedy as well.

On Saturday, 6 April 1706, the *Daily Courant* followed its advertisement for a performance of *Camilla* with the notation that on Monday, 8 April, 'will be presented a Comedy, never Acted before, call'd, The Recruiting Officer'. Oddly enough, that advertisement and the fourteen that followed during the first season never mentioned that George Farquhar, once the darling of the theatre, had written the play. Whether the string of only mildly successful comedies had erased the magic of his name or whether his more than three-year absence had obscured his glory, his authorship was not touted. Things were to change in a year, for *The Beaux Stratagem* was regularly advertised as 'Written by the Author of the Recruiting Officer'.

No indications of unusual theatrical preparations exist. The scenes included the market-place, the walk by the Severn side, and the fields in which the duel was to be fought, as well as the usual set of rooms and apartments. Of these, only the walk by the Severn side was unusual and localized 'and may perhaps have had a specially painted scene'.[19] Costuming was routine. An overture and act-tunes were composed, and Leveridge wrote a long song, 'Come fair one be kind'.

The casting was almost completely traditional. Wilks played Plume, as he had played his forebears Sir Harry, Mirabel, and Elder Wou'dbe, and Cibber took the foppish braggart Brazen. Mills surprisingly did not take the role of Worthy, although with the exception of playing Vizard in *The Constant Couple*, he had always played the hero's friend in Farquhar's full-length plays, from Lovewell to Standard, Dugard, and Trueman; Williams was cast in the role of Worthy. Bullock played the lout's role named for him, 'Jubilee Dicky' Norris took Costar Pearmain, and Estcourt delighted audiences with his delightful portrayal of Kite. For the first time Anne Oldfield played opposite Wilks in one of Farquhar's plays, although the author had supposedly been her discoverer years before, and she had regularly played leads in other

comedies. Jane Rogers, who had played Lucinda, Angelica,
Oriana, and Constance, now took the role of Melinda.
Susannah Mountfort played Rose.

The comedy opened at Drury Lane on 8 April 1706, the
night of the benefit performance of D'Urfey's *Wonders in the Sun*
at the new Queen's Theatre, a conflict that stirred some
criticism. By the fourth performance on 12 April, singing and
dancing had been added to the programme. The heavy
competition from Betterton's troupe at the elegant new
theatre designed by Vanbrugh must have encouraged the
manager Rich to add *entr'acte* entertainment; Rich was, if we
may believe Cibber, totally enamoured of extraneous entertainment anyway.[20] But the immediate popularity of the new
play suggests that such measures were not really necessary.
By the fifth performance, it ran 'At the Desire of several
Persons of Quality'. The *Daily Courant* advertisement did not
mention a third-night benefit, although there probably was
one; Farquhar definitely received benefits at the sixth and
eighth performances, on 15 and 20 April.[21] All in all, the new
comedy ran ten times during its first season, with eight
performances in April and two in June. Had it opened in the
autumn, it might well have challenged the still unbroken
record of performances within the first season set by *The
Constant Couple* in 1699–1700.

As the 1706–7 season opened, many of the Drury Lane
actors joined Owen Swiny at the new Queen's Theatre in the
Haymarket, apparently with the blessing of Rich. Of the
original cast of *The Recruiting Officer*, the actors who played
Plume, Brazen, Silvia, Ballance, Scruple, Bullock, Pearmain,
and Appletree moved to the Queen's Theatre; those who
played Melinda, Lucy, and Scale appeared on neither roster;
and only Worthy, Kite, and Rose remained at Drury Lane.
The result was a battle for audiences altogether unusual in the
second year of a play in this period. On 24 October the Drury
Lane company advertised a performance of the play at Dorset
Garden, 'By the *deserted Company* of Comedians of the Theatre
Royal'. No mention of the cast appears in the advertisement,
but singing and dancing were announced for that performance
and the one that followed on 1 November. On 14 November
the Queen's Theatre countered with a production featuring

the original Plume, Silvia, Brazen, Ballance, Bullock, Pearmain, and Appletree; Mills, who probably should have had the role in the first place, took Worthy, Kite was played by the comedian Pack, and Margaret Bicknell played Rose. By 30 November both houses ran productions of *The Recruiting Officer* simultaneously; the Drury Lane advertisement sought playgoers with the notice 'The true Sergeant Kite is perform'd in Drury Lane'. Estcourt's Kite had been so admired and enjoyed that he alone was considered competitive with the majority of the cast, including the most popular actors once housed at Drury Lane. That season several Kites swooped on to the stage: Fairbank tried the role at Queen's and Pinkethman at Drury Lane, perhaps at a time when Estcourt was unable to perform. In all, the play ran twelve times at Drury Lane and nine at Queen's, for a total of twenty-one performances.

That season provided a preview of the continuing popularity that made *The Recruiting Officer* one of the most frequently performed plays throughout the century. According to the listings in *The London Stage, The Recruiting Officer* was performed in London a total of 512 times by the end of the century. A tally of the performances by decade produces a slight variation on the curve expected for humane comedies in the century,[22] with strong growth in the 1720s, followed by the expected development in the 1730s and 1740s and a gradual decline thereafter except for a flare of activity in the last decade of the century:

Decade	Performance-count
1705–10	55 performances
1710–20	51 performances
1720–30	71 performances
1730–40	81 performances
1740–50	108 performances[23]
1750–60	53 performances
1760–70	32 performances
1770–80	18 performances
1780–90	15 performances
1790–1800	28 performances

Of the total number of performances, the Drury Lane Company accounted for 185 and Covent Garden another 119.

The comedy was also performed at Queen's 18 times, Lincoln's Inn Fields 77, Goodman's Fields 45, Haymarket 33, Southwark 10, and various other places 25.

Of the 512 performances, more than one-quarter were benefit performances, about half for performers, about a third for other theatre functionaries, and the rest, more than twenty, for various gentlemen, gentlewomen, and orphan children in distress as well as lying-in hospitals and other charitable endeavours. Farquhar's own children benefited on 29 May 1717 and 16 May 1729; his wife Margaret, having lost her husband at so young an age, seems to have been industrious in trying to profit from his service in the theatre as well as the army. Pinkethman's widow was another recipient, on 19 May 1726. Moreover, the piece was performed by royal command on thirteen occasions, and was twice acted for Tunisian dignitaries. The Freemasons requested it as well.

Perhaps because from the very beginning *The Recruiting Officer* played at more than one house and because the original cast was split the autumn after the comedy opened, no one seemed really to 'own' the roles in the way Wilks 'owned' Sir Harry, and Norris Jubilee Dicky. Wilks played Plume throughout his career, but even during his lifetime the role was taken by many others, including Powell, Bickerstaff, Elrington, Leigh, Orfeur, Ryan, Smith, Ray, Giffard, and Wignell, and after he died, by Kelly, Harrison, Marshall, W. Mills, 'Fielding of the Buffalo Tavern in Bloomsbury', Mullart, 'a Young Gentleman of the Temple', Havard, Wright, a 'Gentleman from Oxford', Garrick, Bransby, Mrs Charke, Cushing, Oates, another 'Gentleman', Bates, Williams, Jackson, Palmer, Quelch, Smith, Ross, yet another gentleman, Cautherly, Lewis, Comerford, Stokes, Crawford, Bannister Junior, Holman, Wroughton, Barrymore, and Charles Kemble. The mere list evokes all the trends and quirks of the eighteenth-century stage, from the delight in amateurs to the admiration for the great, the vogue for females in male roles, and the selection of vehicles to introduce newly acquired actors to a theatre. A list of similar length is required to name all the Kites or the Silvias of the eighteenth century. Estcourt, so famous for his original portrayal, was challenged immediately by Pack, Fairbank, and Pinkethman. He left the theatre after the 1711–12 season and died in 1712. Silvia was a vehicle for leading actresses including Peg Woffington, who had triumphed in the role in Dublin before coming to London to shine not only as Silvia but as Farquhar's Sir Harry. The smaller roles were, like the bigger ones, passed around. Garrick at one point chose to play Costar Pearmain, a whim that irritated the Revd T. Newton, who wrote to him:

I was almost angry with you, to see your name last week in the bills for Costar Pearmain. . . . You who are equal to the greatest parts, strangely demean yourself in acting any thing that is low and little. . .[24]

The vast number of actors who took roles in *The Recruiting Officer*, was, of course, a result of the fact that the play ran in so many different theatres. Drury Lane and Queen's competed with it regularly until the companies merged in 1710–11; Drury Lane and Lincoln's Inn Fields competed from 1714–15 through 1729–30, with only five performances given elsewhere in that period. By 1730 others were joining the competition. In 1729–30 Goodman's Fields vigorously entered the market with this play as with others, and Covent Garden began performances in 1732–3. By that season, in fact, the play was running at five houses, and it continued to play at four to six houses for several years. Then competition settled down primarily to performances at Drury Lane and Covent Garden, both of which regularly ran it most seasons until 1760; Covent Garden continued regular performances until 1774 and revived it during eleven more seasons before the end of the century.

London, in fact, never had a season without at least one performance until 1779–80, and there were only five other seasons in the century in which no productions occurred. The popularity of the play continued in the nineteenth century, and even today *The Recruiting Officer* is revived more than most comedies of the period.

Theatrical records are, of course, full of additions to the play and anecdotes about productions. For example, when the news of the victory of the Duke of Savoy and Prince Eugene at Turin was reported on 16 September 1706, in a performance

at Bath, Estcourt added to 'Over the hills and far away' the
following verse:

> The Noble Captain Prince Eugene,
> Has beat French, Orleans, and Marsin,
> And march'd up and reliev'd Turin,
> Over the Hills and far away.[25]

On 2 January 1707 'a new Prologue and a Dialogue between
the English and the Paris Gazetteers treating of the Victory of
Ramilly' was performed by Leveridge and others.[26] On
13 July 1710 at a benefit for Estcourt, a 'prodigiously satirical
Interscenium' was introduced in which a troop of soldiers
sang a song highly derogatory toward the Duke of Marlborough
while praising Prince Eugene.[27] Steele wrote a prologue for a
Drury Lane performance on 21 September 1714, spoken by
Wilks, to celebrate King George's landing at Greenwich on
18 September and his first royal entry into London on 20
September.[28] On 16 November 1747 when Garrick was
playing Plume, a song and chorus on the victory of 25 October
over the French fleet at Cape Finisterre was added. *The
Recruiting Officer* was the first play performed when the newly
built theatre at Lincoln's Inn Fields opened in 1714, and
Drury Lane opened with it, having redecorated, 'new Gilt,
Painted and ornamented with Festoons &c.' on 13 September
1755. The play was, all in all, deeply imbedded in the
theatrical history and tradition of the period.

Nor was its popularity limited to London. It was a piece
frequently performed in Dublin and was chosen to open the
Aungier Street theatre in March 1734.[29] Garrick played
Plume at Smock Alley, and he was one of many in the role
during the century.[30] There were also performances at Tralee,
Cork, Belfast, Kilkenny, and Londonderry.[31] Productions are,
of course, recorded at many English, Scottish, and Welsh towns,
and the comedy travelled well to the colonies. Archer reports
that it was 'the first play ever seen in Australia', a group of
convicts having acted it at Sydney on 4 June 1789.[32]

REPUTATION AND INFLUENCE

Farquhar had, as the stage history indicates, struck a design that proved enormously appealing to audiences. Here was a play that became so well known that one might merely mention Kite and evoke instant recognition. Moreover, the play was immediately popular with readers as well as viewers.

Whether educated people knew *The Recruiting Officer* from the stage or the printed text, clearly they knew it well enough to refer easily to it in casual conversation. James Boswell's familiarity provides a good example, one of many that could be cited. Boswell had, in fact, developed a passion in 1759, when only nineteen, for a much older actress named Mrs Cowper, who had played Silvia at Drury Lane a couple of times in 1753. One must assume, however, that he would have known the play regardless of his romantic inclinations. He casually refers to it on several occasions in his journal. He records a dinner conversation in 1762 with Thomas Sheridan, who said that bishops were enemies of merit: 'If a man could write well, they were of Captain Plume's opinion about the attorney: "A dangerous man; discharge him, discharge him."' He describes in his journal a man who 'strutted with the step of Costar Pearmain in *The Recruiting Officer*', and he comments on his amour with Louisa, 'As Captain Plume says, the best security for a woman's mind is her body'.[33]

Garrick knew the play long before he came to London: Thomas Davies recorded that the budding actor at the age of eleven decided to stage *The Recruiting Officer* at Gilbert Walmesley's house in Lichfield; he held auditions for the roles, distributed the parts to 'young gentlemen and ladies', chose Kite for himself, and mounted such a fine performance 'that the audience at Lichfield remembered it for years afterward'.[34] Dr Johnson of course knew the play, not only from Garrick's precocious performance in Lichfield but from the London stage, and no doubt from reading as well; Boswell relates that Johnson told Charles Holland, in the green room at a performance of *The Recruiting Officer*, that he thought Farquhar 'a man whose writings have considerable merit'.[35]

Johnson's remark is indicative not only of the familiarity created by the frequency of performance and publication but

also of the esteem in which Farquhar was held after he had
written *The Recruiting Officer* and a year later *The Beaux
Stratagem*. Few critics have ever spoken of him as brilliant;
most have rated him below Etherege, Wycherley, and
Congreve. But finally, with the instant and lasting success of
The Recruiting Officer, Farquhar began to receive the praise,
albeit sometimes still grudging, denied him throughout most
of his career; unfortunately, he only had one more year in
which to enjoy his revived recognition and appreciation. The
Muses Mercury mourned his death by presenting a balanced,
certainly not altogether commendatory, but doubtless re-
presentative view of his contribution to the stage:

All that love Comedy will be sorry to hear of the Death of Mr.
Farquhar, whose two last Plays had something in them that was truly
humorous and *diverting*. 'Tis true the Criticks will not allow any Part of
them to be regular; but Mr. *Farquhar* had a Genius for Comedy, of
which one may say, that it was rather above Rules than below them.
His *Conduct*, tho not *Artful*, was *surprizing*: His *Characters*, tho not
Great, were Just: His Humour, tho *low*, *diverting*: His *Dialogue*, tho
loose and *incorrect*, *gay* and *agreeable*; and his *Wit*, tho not *super-abundant*,
pleasant. In a word, his Plays have in the *toute ensemble*, as the Painters
phrase it, a certain Air of *Novelty* and *Mirth*, which pleas'd the
Audience every time they were represented: And such as love to
laugh at the *Theater*, will probably miss him more than they now
imagine.[36]

Four months later, the *Muses Mercury* seemed even gloomier
about the loss of Farquhar's 'Genius for Comedy':

As for *Comedies*, there's no great Expectation of any thing of that
kind, since Mr. *Farquehar's* Death. The two Gentlemen, who would
probably always succeed in the *Comick* Vein, Mr. *Congreve* and Capt.
Steel, having Affairs of much greater Importance to take up their
Time and Thoughts. And unless the *Players* write themselves, the
Town must wait for Comedy till another *Genius* appears.[37]

More traditional commentators on literature could not
bring themselves to praise the play or the author. Although
Steele never showed Pope's contempt for Farquhar, he
repeatedly attributed his contemporary's success to good
acting rather than good writing. For example, in *Tatler*, no. 20
(26 May 1709) he wrote:

This evening was acted, 'The Recruiting Officer', in which Mr. Estcourt's proper sense and observation is what supports the play. There is not, in my humble opinion, the humour hit in Sergeant Kite; but it is admirably supplied by his action. If I have skill to judge, that man is an excellent actor; but the crowd of the audience are fitter for representations at Mayfair, than a theatre royal.

Critics generally held to the reluctant admission that Farquhar played well on stage, unwilling to acknowledge any literary merit. They did admit that he had a pleasurable naturalness and ease.

The evaluation in *A Companion to the Theatre* was far more generous than Steele or in fact most evaluators would allow. The design of the play and the incidents, and writer said:

. . . are extremely diverting in the representation, and altogether serve to render this comedy as entertaining as any I know of, that the stage for many years has had to boast of; and I believe will always continue to be so; at least while there are military gentlemen in the kingdom; ladies who delight in a red coat and feather; or, in fact, while there remain any lovers of true nature in a dramatic performance.[38]

An essay in *Pasquin*, no. 75, on 22 October 1723, gave a comparable evaluation:

. . . no one will deny but that the late Mr. *Farquhar* had a great Share of Merit. The uncommon Vivacity of his Genius, the happy Sprightliness of his Fancy, the Easiness of his Stile, the unforc'd Pleasantry and natural Humours of his Characters, will remain I doubt long unmatch'd upon the *British* Stage. Had this Gentleman been as happy in his Fortune as he was in his Genius, he might perhaps have been thought one of those Poetick Comets which are seen scarce in an Age:

The *Dramatic Censor* (ii. 468) found *The Recruiting Officer* and *The Beaux Stratagem* Farquhar's best work, and believed his plays 'not so laboured and correct' as Congreve's but fully as agreeable. Farquhar's characters are 'well selected from the volume of life, pleasingly grouped, and well disposed of at the catastrophes'. Generally, criticism in the eighteenth century ran along the lines of *Pasquin* and the *Dramatic Censor*. Farquhar lacked correctness and regularity, but he had pleasing, lifelike characters, amusing plots, and brisk dialogue.

If one sought actors' reactions rather than literary critics', however, a quite different attitude prevailed. Farquhar's plays worked on stage; audiences came to see them. If one wanted a crowded hall, for a benefit or any other performance, *The Recruiting Officer* was a crowd-pleaser.

Later critics have not veered far from the earliest evaluations. Critics in general do not admire *The Recruiting Officer*, but they like it. They speak of its freshness: from the beginning critics have commented on the breath of country air admitted to the theatre when Farquhar turned from London to Shrewsbury, and they write of the natural liveliness of the characters as though it were a result of their healthy provincial setting. The critics of the twentieth century have not, in fact, significantly deviated from the eighteenth-century evaluations of the play.

But popularity does not necessarily indicate significant influence on later works. Like other plays of the period, *The Recruiting Officer* had some impact on the German theatre. Stonehill mentions several German adaptations, including Gottlieb Stephanie's *Abgedankte Offiziere* and a year later *Die Werber*. He also attributes to Lessing the development of a tradition imitative of Farquhar which introduced a 'whole school of German Drama'.[39]

But to prove influence on the London stage is difficult. One would expect the kind of rush to imitate that had followed the creation of Sir Harry Wildair and the enviable success of *The Constant Couple*: plays about recruiting officers or at least military men, plays set in the country, plays with spirited, lively heroines like Silvia, most of all, perhaps, imitations of Kite. One does not find the expected evidence.

The lack is explicable in two ways: first the efflorescence of humane comedy at the turn of the century was beginning to fade. Congreve had left the theatre years before; by 1705 Vanbrugh was occupied with Blenheim and Steele had turned to government service and journalism; both became less involved with the theatre after producing plays that year; Cibber grew so busy with acting and managerial duties that he had little time for writing. Susanna Centlivre wrote comedies, as did Charles Shadwell, Thomas Baker, and a few others, but in general comedy was not as prominent in the schedule of *premières* as it had been a few years earlier.

Moreover, the Queen's Theatre opened, the management structures were frequently revised, the troupes briefly merged, and opera captured the hearts of audiences. The resultant upheaval greatly reduced the attention paid to comedy. When comedy competed with comedy, as it had in the late 1690s, a play such as *The Constant Couple* promised success to clever imitators; when comedy competed with opera, as it did in the 1710s, the managerial instinct was to stick with old favourites. The number of new comedies produced fell from something like eight a year to three or four. The theatres mounted ruinously expensive operas, imported singers and dancers to embellish dramatic programmes, strove in every way for novelty. The focus simply did not fall on new comedy.

Even had it done so, Farquhar had not, in fact, provided a pattern for a new kind of comedy; he had fashioned of the old, well-known materials a piece of unusual quality. But he had years before prefigured Plume in Sir Harry; Silvia, extraordinary in her vitality, belongs to a tradition of energetic heroines disguised as boys that Farquhar knew well from Shakespeare and that he used earlier in Leanthe, Angelica, and Oriana. Kite, the audience's favourite character, was heightened from earlier clever servants, but he was not cut from new cloth. The loving but hard-nosed father, the faithful friend, the *miles gloriosus* turned fop, the country bumpkins—all were exquisitely crafted from traditions that pre-dated *The Recruiting Officer*. Rose, with her country earthiness and yet the delicate bloom of youth, was new, a crude forerunner in some ways for Cherry in *The Beaux Stratagem*. The characters as a group were delightfully impregnated with life and spirit, but they were scarcely innovative.

The same can be said for the plot of tricks and disguises, deceits and counter-deceits, all in the spirit of fun. Farquhar worked with the stuff of comedy that he well knew. The laughter may have been more uproarious than in earlier plays, the stage business more boisterous; but the basic structure of romantic pairs and humorous triangles, of disguised trickery of one's intended and one's parent, of witty repartee above stairs and earthy, sparkling good humour below stairs, could not be considered new. *The Recruiting Officer* enriched the stage immeasurably, but it is difficult to argue that it reshaped it.

THE TEXT

On 12 February 1705, two months before the *première* performance, Bernard Lintott purchased publication rights for *The Recruiting Officer* for £16. 2s. 6d. He got good value, for he published three quarto editions within seven months of the *première* and a fourth a year later. The immediate and lasting stage popularity assured his success; in all, Lintott was publisher or partner in more than twenty editions.

The first quarto appeared on or conceivably shortly before 25 April 1706, seventeen days after the play opened and five days after the author's benefit on the eighth night. The advertisement in the *Daily Courant* on 25 April reads 'There is now publish'd' rather than 'This day is publish'd'; the wording suggests that publication may have slightly preceded the advertisement. Michael Shugrue in the Introduction to the Regents edition of the play incorrectly cites the date of publication as 12 April, the day of the fourth performance, because the Drury Lane advertisement for that night carried the usual notice 'This Play, is Sold by J. Knapton . . . and B. Lintott', a formula repeated daily with theatrical advertisements.[40] However, actual publication occurred after the first run ended.

The quarto has the collational formula A–K⁴. After printing began, an effort was made to save paper. Sheets B and C contain pages of no more than thirty-eight lines, but sheets D–I contain forty-line pages. Even so, the compositors of K reduced the type size significantly and printed forty-six-line pages in order to prevent the need for sheet L. Oddly enough, K was printed after the prelims; K4ᵛ contains errata for the title-page and the Dedication. In some copies of Q1 the title-page reads '*Æolis*' and 'is Acted', and A3 l. 2 uses italics for '*Woodcocks*' (copies at the British Library, Clark, University of Texas); other copies exhibit '*eolis*', 'was Acted', and 'Woodcocks' (copies at Harvard, University of Texas).

The composition is unusually neat and seemingly unrushed. The text was set *seriatim*. There is no evidence of a second compositor except in K2ᵛ–K4ᵛ, pp. 68–72. The usual signs— different abbreviations for speech prefixes, different compositorial habits concerning stage directions, dashes, and other punctuation, different handling of act and scene notations—do not occur throughout the rest of the text. But in $K2^v$–$K4^v$ (not in $K1$–$K2$), speech prefixes which are spelt out are followed by commas rather than periods, and on $K3$ the speech prefix for the maid Lucy is misspelt '*Lucia*'. Clearly even K, although partially set by a different compositor, was set *seriatim*.

Running-title evidence does not indicate a volume split in half and imposed on two sets of formes as is often the case for first editions. A single skeleton can be identified for inner B, C, D, E, F, and I, and outer G and K. One skeleton was used for outer B, C, and E, and inner G and H. One possibility is that Lintott's February purchase of the rights resulted in his receiving the manuscript early; but even if it arrived at any time during rehearsals, the length of the run still provided an opportunity to avoid rush.

The 'Second Edition Corrected' was published by Lintott on 23 May, less than a month after the first. The quarto has the collational formula A–K^4; A contains the prelims, page by page as they appear in the original; the text is printed on $B1^r$–$K4^r$, and $K4^v$, p. 72, contains an advertisement for books printed for Lintott, including four comedies by Farquhar, *The Recruiting Officer*, *The Inconstant*, *The Twin-Rivals*, and *The Trip to the Jubilee*.

The title-page reads 'Corrected' but not 'Corrected by the Author', and the revisions themselves are most unusual for the period. Shugrue believes they are the work of a copy editor 'consciously regularizing, normalizing, and, indeed, bowdlerizing the first quarto',[41] an opinion with which I totally disagree. John Ross believes that compositors corrected minor misprints, normalized spelling and punctuation, and substituted 'more formal or common alternatives for Farquhar's vigorous, colloquial dialect, word-forms, and phrases'. Changes in stage directions, he believes, might be Farquhar's since they concern staging; at least they were made with his approval. The major revisions were made for reasons of 'theatrical effectiveness' rather than the demands of propriety. Ross follows a rather eclectic pattern of accepting some revisions, refusing others.[42] I cannot subscribe to his conclusions either. A. Norman Jeffares adheres primarily to the text of Q1, with some minor revisions from Q2.[43]

Ordinarily, after the first edition printers used as copy-text a printed copy marked with emendations, perhaps interlineated or interleaved with new or revised materials, or perhaps merely marked for deletions. The copy-text is easily recognizable behind the new edition. Certain categories of changes are introduced habitually: spellings and punctuation are regularized, obvious misspellings and mispunctuation are corrected, capitalization and italics are standardized and usually increased (for example, proper nouns that have escaped italics in the first edition are often italicized in the second), contractions are expanded or phrases contracted ('you're' becomes 'you are' or alternatively 'you are' becomes 'you're'). Ross is right in concluding that compositors might well be responsible for such usual procedures.

But Q2 contains far more frequent variations in accidentals than one usually finds in second editions, even those with authorial revisions. For example, Plume's verse in 1.i, 129–30, is italicized in Q1:

> *Spleen, thou worst of Fiends below,*
> *Fly, I conjure thee by this Magick Blow.*

In Q2 the lines are printed in roman. Even more surprising is the fact that Silvia's lines in 1.ii. 38–9, printed as two lines of italicized verse in Q1, are printed as prose, in roman, in Q2.[44] Those variants are not the result of literary decisions, or, in fact, even a shortage of italic type. They speak of different copy-text.

A short passage picked at random and printed here in parallel texts will demonstrate the frequency and indifference of variations in accidentals:

Q1	Q2
Mob. Brother! Hold there	*Mob.* Brother! hold there,
Friend, I'm no Kindred to you that	Friend; I am no Kindred to you that
I know of, as yet—Lookye Serjeant,	I know of yet—Look'ee Serjeant,
no coaxing, no wheedling d'ye'see;	no Coaxing, no Wheedling, d'ye see—
if I have a mind to list, why so—	If I have a mind to list, why so—
If not, why 'tis not so—Therefore	If not, why, 'tis not so—therefore
take your Cap and your Brothership	take your Cap and your Brothership

back again, for I ain't dispos'd at	back again, for I am not dispos'd at
this present Writing—No coaxing,	this present Writing—No Coaxing,
no Brothering me, Faith.	no Brothering me, faith.

This single speech, only six lines in the quarto texts, contains eighteen variants, including seven punctuation changes, seven changes in capitalization, one spelling, two contractions, and one variant in wording. By no means unusual in Q2, such numerous revisions are strikingly odd in second editions of play texts of the period whether they are revised or not. Compositors tend to follow the accidentals of the printed copy-text fairly closely. Dramatists do not introduce the kind of insignificant revisions made in this speech. Typical of multiple editions of this period, the third quarto contains no revisions from Q2 in the passage, and Q4 contains none from Q3. The first edition of the *Comedies*, O1, introduces two, a capital H in 'Hold' and a period after 'yet'; O2 introduces no revisions into its copy-text, O1.

Minor substantive variants support the theory that Q1 was not the copy-text for Q2. Contractions in Q1 are frequently replaced by fully spelt words in Q2. The contractions 'you're' and 'I'm', for example, often become 'you are' and 'I am'. However, within fourteen lines on p. 4 of Q1, 'I am' becomes 'I'm' (l. 5) and 'I'm' becomes 'I am' (l. 19). Similarly on p. 53 of Q1 'let us' (l. 3), 'I'm' (l. 5), and 'cannot' (l. 16) become 'let's', 'I am', and 'can't'. A compositor's tendency toward consistency cannot explain such inconsistency. The text is riddled with inconsistencies of that kind.

Q2 also contains many variations that one does not expect from either a compositor or an author. For example, indifferent changes in stage directions are highly unlikely, but such variants occur with surprising frequency in Q2. A few examples will illustrate:

Q1	Q2
[*Exeunt, Drum beating the Granadeer-March*	[*Exit Drum beating a Granadeers March.*
[*Takes up a piece of the Letter.*]	[*Takes up a Bit.*]
[*Looking at it.*	[*Looking earnestly upon the Piece.*]

Enter Rose *and her Brother* Bullock,
Rose *with a Basket on her Arm,*
crying chickens.   *Enter* Rose *and her Brother*
                                             Bullock, *and Chickens on her*
[*All this while* Bullock *whistles*   *Arms in a Basket,* &c.
about the Stage.
                                             [*Whistles about the Stage.*
[*He tips the wink upon* Kite, *who*
returns it.]   [*Tips him the wink, he*
                                             returns it.]

The variations in stage directions in the two texts matter not a
whit. The action on stage in each case is identical regardless of
the phrasing. Moreover, since stage directions are sub-
literary, such revisions do not in the least affect the quality of
the literary text. There would be nothing for either compositor
or author to gain by introducing such indifferent variants into
stage directions.

A few of the stage directions have a conceivable rationale
for compositorial revision because in some cases a shorter
direction in Q2 saves a line of type. For example, when the
stage direction is omitted from the line, '*Bull.* [*Crying.*] Pray,
Captain, don't send *Ruose* to the West-Indies.', one line rather
than two is required to set the speech. Because Q2 included an
advertisement on p. 72, such economies could matter. On the
other hand, the substitution of '[*Unmasks.*' for '[*Pulls off her*
mask.' does not save a line. That compositors reduced some
stage directions to save lines is possible but not provable.

In a number of instances a stage direction is moved from
before to after a line of dialogue or vice versa. Again, there can
be little literary or theatrical motive for the move, for in most
cases the action accompanies the line in question, and in any
event the match of dialogue to stage business is not difficult.
Compositors traditionally did not show much concern for
placement of stage directions; nor did Farquhar.

The kind of variants in the stage directions resembles those
in the Q1, Q2, and 1736 editions of *The Stage-Coach.* That is,
the differences are those one finds when texts are set from two
different manuscripts, perhaps a manuscript and a promptbook. If stage directions were written in the margin, as they
were in the playhouse and in manuscripts, the exact placement
would be decided by the compositor as he set type, and

placement by two different compositors might well vary slightly. Also, if stage directions were abbreviated or cryptically terse, the enlargements might vary slightly. For example, 'Ex. Drum bt. Grndr Mrch' might well engender either of the readings reproduced above. Similarly, other condensed directions could produce more than one reading just as setting from two different manuscripts might.

The line lengths also suggest the possibility of a copy-text other than Q1 for Q2 except for the prelims. Q2 is only one page shorter than Q1 and a song plus an entire scene (v.i) are excised. One would expect in such a case a line-for-line or page-for-page reproduction with perhaps the possibility of some crowding to save a little space. This occurs in the prelims. The Dedication in Q2 largely follows the line length in Q1, except that in the course of long paragraphs the line endings begin to vary, as could be expected. Moreover, accidental variants in the prelims are comparable in number to those in other second editions. Line length, of course, does not vary in the verse of the Prologue; the prose of the Epilogue has a few differences. Accidental variants are also at expected levels. Q1 was obviously the copy-text for the Dramatis Personae. But as soon as the text of Act I begins, remarkable variations occur. For example, Kite's first speech is set in two paragraphs in Q1, one in Q2; accidental variants immediately are noticeably frequent. Except for the prelims, the evidence suggests that the copy-text was not Q1. It was probably the playhouse copy.

When Q2 was published, the play had run eight times, but it had not run for the past month; there was time in that month for the printer to borrow the stage copy. Moreover, the prompter would have preferred to use a printed copy; therefore, the manuscript theatrical copy might be lent as copy-text for Q2. *The Recruiting Officer* played twice more in June, after the second edition was published. Q1 had been advertised in the *Daily Courant* as recently as 20 May, three days before the new edition appeared. If revisions had occurred on stage in such a popular play, Farquhar or Lintott might well have wanted to introduce them into Q2. Puzzling substantive revisions become comprehensible if, in fact, the playhouse copy served as copy-text.

First of all, the categories of indifferent minor substantive and accidental variants would be explained simply through the natural evolution from manuscript to print. If two manuscript copies were made from Farquhar's foul papers, one for Lintott, one for Rich, variants could have been introduced just through mistakes in reading the manuscript and copying it. Certainly slight variations in stage directions would exist. Paragraphing, end punctuation, placement of stage directions, varying treatments of contractions would not be at all unusual. In particular, authors were careless of accidentals, expecting compositors to introduce or correct punctuation and capitalization, so the striking number of variants in accidentals would be entirely ordinary. Spelling and other habits ('Wauns' versus 'Wounds', 'Pound' or 'Pounds') might consistently vary.

But significant substantive revisions in Q2 raise questions: why should one manuscript carry the word 'famous', for example, and the other 'faithful', or why should one read 'confided' and the other 'trusted'? The same question can arise for 'you' and 'thou', 'Advices' and 'Letters', 'advis'd' and 'persuaded', 'War' and 'Victory'. Some of these changes might well have evolved on stage, but it seems surprising for so many to be found even in the playhouse copy.

Another category which at first seems surprising is perhaps less so. A number of Farquhar's earthy colloquialisms in Q1 are toned down in Q2, a fact that has always pained editors, who prefer the Q1 version. The usual explanation is that Farquhar tried to make a more 'literary' text by substituting less colloquial language. For example, in Q1 Plume asks Worthy if love can 'bring you into this Pickle?', but in Q2 the pickle becomes a 'Condition'. In Q1 Silvia reminds Melinda of how the cold sharp air used to make their 'Noses drop', but in Q2 it only made their 'Fingers ake'. In Q1 Worthy would not 'give a Fig for' the conquest of Melinda, and in Q2 he would not 'value' it. Although scholars assume that the more vital language occurred on stage, the more sedate or 'literary' on the page, conceivably players would not have been eager to talk of dripping noses and pickles; conceivably the revisions were those of the playhouse, not of the author. Similarly, some kinds of cuts could be results of stage experience, either the difficulty of saying certain combinations of words or the decision that some lines retard the pace. For example, in Q1 Silvia says:

As you say, Cosin *Melinda*, there are several sorts of Airs, Airs in Conversation, Airs in Behaviour, Airs in Dress; then we have our Quality Airs, our sickly Airs, our reserv'd Airs, and sometimes our impudent Airs.

In Q2 the speech is reduced to 'As you say, Cousin *Melinda*, there are several sorts of Airs.' The lines in Q1, amusing to read, could in fact have seemed static on stage and therefore they might have been deleted; extant promptbooks with cuts marked in them often reflect exactly that kind of deletion.

In some instances suggestive lines were omitted. Rose's reference to 'an ugly Song of Chickens and Sparragus', her line 'But I hope, Captin, you won't part with me', and other suggestive dialogue is cut. Scholars have assumed the deletions resulted from an attempt to clean up the printed copy. In fact, nobody was making much of a stir about bawdy on the printed page. The reformers wielded their power over the stage, not the book trade. Performances, therefore, were more liable to expurgation than printed texts. A few texts were cleaned up; Steele, for example, provided prim revisions for the second edition of *The Funeral*.[45] But by and large playwrights of the period did not revise later editions at all; they were paid a fee for the purchase of the copyright of the first edition; few showed interest in later sales, which did not fatten their purses. However, the reformers remained insistent in the theatres, and therefore, playwrights, Farquhar included, eschewed the bawdy or even suggestive. Farquhar, fresh from the army, might well have written mildly suggestive lines, deemed expendable in production, including the entire first scene of Act V, which does not appear in Q2.

The song by Leveridge was also omitted in Q2. Ross believes it was deleted because it was extraneous dramatically and the words were 'at best mediocre' and concludes, 'It was probably not well enough liked to have lasting-power.'[46] I suspect it simply was not reproduced in the playhouse manuscript. Obviously added during rehearsal by the playhouse musician, it might well have been delivered to Lintott to insert in Q1; yet it would not necessarily have been included in the Drury Lane copy. Printed texts sometimes included the lyrics of songs, sometimes only the first line or two. In *Love and a Bottle* the songs added in rehearsal were not even noted in the printed text (see Introduction, *Love and a Bottle* i. 11–13, 16–17). Songs printed in plays often appear to be discrete copy: they tend to be headed by the name of the composer and performer, and stiffly titled 'Song' or in this case 'A Song'. Publishers must have perceived them as attractive additions to the text. But the many published texts which do not carry the words of songs indicate that the entire song was not necessarily part of the dramatic manuscript unless perhaps the author wrote the lyrics, which was not always the case. There is no reason to believe that Farquhar decided to delete the song; the fact that Q1 was not copy-text explains why it disappeared in Q2.

Another cut deletes the farcical stage business in iv.iii in which Kite as the conjuror puts his hand under the table. Plume grabs it, and Melinda and Lucy shriek and run into a corner. One can only speculate on the reasons for the cut. Perhaps the staging did not work effectively; perhaps the audience did not respond with hilarity. At any rate, one must surmise that Q2 reflects the stage version.

Finally there are revised passages, in ii.i at the point that Plume greets Silvia and in iv.i when Plume and Silvia bandy Rose about. Scholars, even though not realizing the theatrical copy probably served as copy-text, have generally assumed these revisions reflect the stage version. The identification of the underlying manuscript certainly adds weight to the attribution. Other revisions also suggest theatrical experience. The revision of '*Cacodemon del Fuego*' to '*Cacodemon del Plumo*' is exactly the kind of change that would happen in rehearsal. In iii.i of Q1 Rose exits and then, without re-entering, continues to speak later in the scene; in Q2 the exit and accompanying lines are omitted so that she is properly on stage for her later lines. However, even in Q2 the crux of Silvia's identification in disguise both as Jack Wilfull and as Captain Pinch, a double identity that Plume does not even react to, is never clarified. Nor are the speech prefixes for Costar Pearmain and Thomas

Appletree (1st and 2nd Mob), although obviously the prompt copy should carry the proper speech prefixes.

The weight of evidence shows, then, that the 'Second Edition Corrected' was corrected not by the author marking a copy of Q1 but rather by the importation of a second manuscript; the most likely possibility is that the manuscript was the playhouse copy, sent to Lintott during a period in which no performances were scheduled. Less than three weeks later, the play was back on stage.

The 'Third Edition Corrected' (Q3) was advertised by Lintott on 28 and 29 November 1706 for publication on 3 December; on 6 December the *Daily Courant* advertisement read 'This Day is publish'd'. Pre-publication advertisements for a third edition speak of a lively continuing demand for copies. Page by page, Q3 adheres to its copy-text, Q2, except for the addition of the last word 'and' on p. 2, inadvertently omitted in Q2. No additional revisions were made. The only variants are the usual kind of corrections of errors and introduction of new errors typical of multiple editions.

Lintott advertised in the *Post-Man*, 13–16 December 1707, the publication 'in a few Days' of the fourth quarto. The 'Fourth Edition Corrected' (Q4), some seven months after Farquhar's death, was a line-by-line reprint of Q3 with a few very minor variants. The advertisement on p. 72, however, listed six of Farquhar's plays rather than four, *Love and a Bottle* and *The Beaux Stratagem* having been added to Lintott's list.

The only other edition that need be discussed individually is the 1728 duodecimo printed as part of the *Works*. Like *The Twin-Rivals* of 1728, this edition seems to have ties with the theatre. In particular, the scenes involving Costar Pearmain and Thomas Appletree show attention to the prompt copy. The speech prefixes in II.iii (1st *Mob* and 2nd *Mob* in earlier texts) are assigned to *Tho.* and *Cost.* Some of Costar's and Thomas's lines are revised. Given the number of actors that appeared in these roles between 1706 and 1728, however, one cannot assume that the revised lines date from Farquhar's time. The authenticity of Q2 as a stage text for the original performance seems far more likely.

In all, more than fifty editions of *The Recruiting Officer*

appeared during the eighteenth century, including at least
seven published in Dublin, three in Edinburgh, two in Belfast,
and one in Glasgow. Besides the frequent reprints sold by
Lintott and his partners in editions of the *Works*,[17] there were
two editions (1710, 1720) by Thomas Johnson, who imported
copies printed at The Hague, a piracy by the mysterious
duplicator who almost invisibly produced carefully imitative
editions in the 1730s,[48] editions more blatantly published by
the 'Booksellers in Town and Country', editions marked with
the corrections in the manager's book. As the comedy was
perenially popular on stage, it continued to sell with great
regularity in the bookstalls.

After the third performance of *The Recruiting Officer*,
Leveridge's song 'Come Fair One Be Kind' was advertised by
Walsh in the *Monthly Mask of Vocal Music*.[49] Two copies of the
Walsh half-sheet engraving are in the British Library collection,
one in the Folger. The song continued to be published later,
for example in *Pills to Purge Melancholy* (1706) and in *Songs
Compleat, Pleasant and Divertive* (1719). 'Over the Hills and Far
Away', sung to an old tune also used in 'Jockey's Lamentation',
was published in *Pills to Purge Melancholy* in 1706 as 'The
Recruiting Officer; Or, The Merry Volunteers'. The tune had
also been used earlier by D'Urfey in 'The Hubble Bubbles'
(copy in the Folger) in *The Campaigners* (1698). The overture
and four airs were advertised by Walsh and Hare in the *Daily
Courant* on 5 June 1706 for 1*s.* 6*d.* I have found no extant copy
of the act music.

For the present edition, I have used Q1 as copy-text, and I
have introduced the revised scenes from Q2. I have not,
however, revised the minor changes in wording that occur in
Q2; nor have I omitted the song, v.i, or other deletions except
for the one that keeps Rose on stage to say her lines. The
decision on treatment of the text has, perhaps, been arbitrary:
if Q1 and Q2 derive from two manuscripts, one sent to
Lintott, the other to Rich, one might certainly argue for
greater validity for the manuscript that went to the theatre
and was revised as it was readied for performance. Earlier
editors have found various rationalizations for using the more
appealing Q1 version, and I admit a reluctance to relinquish
the best version on the grounds of logical consistency. But in

any case, the decision on copy-text is a close judgement call. Textual notes will apprise the reader of important decisions not to revise as well as of revisions in the text. I have also followed the 1728 duodecimo and introduced some of my own corrections in the speech prefixes *Costar Pearmain* and *Thomas Appletree* in ii.iii, simply to make the text more readable.

I have collated the following copies: Q1, British Library, Harvard, Huntington, Clark, University of Texas (three copies); Q2, Bodleian, Harvard; Q3, Folger; Q4, Bodleian; *Comedies*, first edition, Clark; second edition, Library of Congress, personal copy; third edition, Folger; 1728, Library of Congress; 1733, personal copy; 1736, Folger.

Two songs of which snatches are sung, are printed in full in the Appendix.

NOTES

1. James R. Sutherland, 'New Light on George Farquhar', Correspondence in *TLS*, 6 Mar. 1937, p. 171. Sutherland points out that Farquhar was about 25 and his bride had a son who was old enough for military service in 1709, thus probably 15 or so in 1704.
2. *Memoirs Relating to the Late Famous Mr. Tho. Brown.*
3. Jordan, pp. 251–3.
4. Bodley MS Eng. Hist. b. 124, fol. 43, noted in Jordan, p. 253.
5. PRO, WO 25/3149, fol. 29, cited in Jordan, p. 253.
6. Sutherland, p. 171.
7. Jordan, p. 253; Farquhar speaks in the Dedication to *The Recruiting Officer* of being in Shrewsbury 'some time ago'; he may have served there in summer 1704.
8. Orrery's statement, in Sutherland, p. 171.
9. Jordan, pp. 257–60.
10. Nichols, viii. 296.
11. H. Owen and J. B. Blakeway, *A History of Shrewsbury* (2 vols., London 1825), i. 501. W. F. Prideaux, 'The Recruiting Officer', *N&Q*, 9th ser. 1 (1898), 241–2.
12. Hunt, p. lxxiv.
13. Thomas Wilkes, *A General View of the Stage* (London, 1759), pp. 275–6.
14. Hunt, p. lxxiv.
15. Stonehill, ii. 35.
16. Kavanagh, pp. 223–5.
17. Rothstein, pp. 129–30.
18. *The Recruiting Officer*, ed. John Ross, The New Mermaids (London and New York, 1977), p. xvii.
19. Sybil Rosenfeld, 'Notes on *The Recruiting Officer*', *Theatre Notebook*, 18 (1963–4), 47–8.
20. Cibber, *Apology*, p. 180.
21. Advertisements, *Daily Courant*, 6–20 Apr.
22. See Shirley Strum Kenny, 'Perennial Favorites: Congreve, Vanbrugh, Cibber,

Farquhar, and Steele', Friedman Festschrift, Supplement to *Modern Philology*, 73 (1976), S4–S11.

23. The count includes performances of a French translation at the Haymarket.

24. *London Stage*, Part 3, ii. 959.

25. *Daily Courant*, 24 September 1706. Also Genest, ii. 340.

26. Advertisement, *Daily Courant*, 31 Dec. 1706.

27. *London in 1710: From the Travels of Zacharias Conrad von Uffenbach*, trans. and ed. W. H. Quarrell and Margaret Mare (London, 1934), p. 138. *London Stage*, Part 2, ii. 227.

28. *The Occasional Verse of Richard Steele*, ed. Rae Blanchard (Oxford, 1952), p. 93.

29. Hitchcock, i. 86.

30. Sheldon, pp. 453–4.

31. Smith, *1720–1800*, p. 308.

32. Archer, p. 244, citing Collins's *History of New South Wales*.

33. *Boswell's London Journal, 1762–1763*, ed. Frederick A. Pottle (New York, 1951), pp. 91, 140; *Boswell in Search of a Wife, 1766–1769*, ed. Frederick A. Pottle (New York, 1956), p. 173; cited in Kenny, 'Perennial Favorites', p. S10.

34. Thomas Davies, *Memoir of the Life of David Garrick* (4th edn. London, 1784), i. 4–6, cited in W. Jackson Bate, *Samuel Johnson* (New York and London, 1977), pp. 81–2. Bate believes that Davies must have heard the anecdote from Samuel Johnson.

35. *Boswell's Life of Johnson*, ed. George Birkbeck Hill, rev. L. F. Powell (Oxford, 1934), iv. 7.

36. *Muses Mercury*, May 1707, pp. 123–4.

37. *Muses Mercury*, Sept. 1707, p. 218.

38. *A Companion to the Theatre* (2nd edn., London, 1740), ii. 206, cited in *Biographia Britannica*, p. 694.

39. Stonehill, i, p. xix. See Introduction, *The Constant Couple*, vol. i, pp. 138–9.

40. *The Recruiting Officer*, ed. Michael Shugrue, Regents Restoration Drama series (Lincoln, Neb., 1965), p. ix.

41. Shugrue, p. x.

42. Ross, pp. xxxiv–xl.

43. A. Norman Jeffares (ed.), *Restoration Comedy* (4 vols., London, 1974), p. 399.

44. The lines, a quotation from Dryden's *The Spanish Friar*, appear as poetry in the original.

45. Steele, pp. 9–13.

46. Ross, p. xxxix.

47. See Kenny, 'The Publication of Plays', pp. 330–1.

48. See Shirley Strum Kenny, 'Piracies of Two Plays by Farquhar', *Studies in Bibliography*, 28 (1975), 297–305.

49. Advertisement, *Daily Courant*, 11 Apr. 1706.

Composite scene. Foreground: Kite recruiting the mob. Background:
Kite as conjurer, advising Melinda and Lucy. Frontispiece, *The Recruiting
Officer, The Comedies of George Farquhar*, [1711]. Act I, Scene i, and Act IV,
Scene iii.

THE RECRUITING OFFICER

A COMEDY

Captique dolis, donisque coacti.
Virg. Lib. II Æneid.

ABBREVIATIONS USED IN THE NOTES

Q1   First edition. London: Lintott, 1706.

Q2   Second edition. London: Lintott, 1706.

Q4   Fourth edition. London: Lintott, 1707.

1728   Sixth edition, *Works*, London: Lintott, 1728. (Vol. II labelled Fifth Edition.)

Broadside   Half-sheet broadside engraving, 'A Song Set by Mr. Leveridge Sung by Mr. Wilks in the Comedy call'd the Recruiting Officer' [London: 1706].

TO

All Friends round
THE
WREKIN.

My Lords and Gentlemen,
 Instead of the mercenary Expectations that attend Addresses
of this nature, I humbly beg, that this may be received as an
Acknowledgment for the Favours you have already confer'd;
I have transgress'd the Rules of Dedication in offering you any
thing in that style, without first asking your leave: But the
Entertainment I found in *Shropshire* commands me to be
grateful, and that's all I intend.
 Twas my good fortune to be order'd some time ago into the
Place which is made the Scene of this Comedy; I was a perfect 10
Stranger to every thing in *Salop*, but its Character of Loyalty,
the Number of its Inhabitants, the Alacrity of the Gentlemen
in recruiting the Army, with their generous and hospitable
Reception of Strangers.
 This Character I found so amply verify'd in every Particular,
that you made Recruiting, which is the greatest Fatigue upon
Earth to others, to be the greatest Pleasure in the World to
me.
 The Kingdom cannot shew better Bodies of Men, better
Inclinations for the Service, more Generosity, more good 20
Understanding, nor more Politeness than is to be found at the
Foot of the *Wrekin*.
 Some little Turns of Humour that I met with almost within
the Shade of that famous Hill, gave the rise to this Comedy,
and People were apprehensive, that, by the Example of some
others, I would make the Town merry at the expence of the
Country Gentlemen: But they forgot that I was to write a
Comedy, not a Libel; and that whilst I held to Nature, no
Person of any Character in your Country could suffer by being

30 expos'd. I have drawn the Justice and the Clown in their *puris Naturalibus*; the one an apprehensive, sturdy, brave Blockhead; and the other a worthy, honest, generous Gentleman, hearty in his Country's Cause, and of as good an Understanding as I could give him, which I must confess is far short of his own.

I humbly beg leave to interline a Word or two of the Adventures of the *Recruiting Officer* upon the Stage. Mr. *Rich*, who commands the Company for which those Recruits were rais'd, has desir'd me to acquit him before the World of a Charge which he thinks lyes heavy upon him for acting this
40 Play on Mr. *Durfey*'s Third Night.

Be it known unto all Men by these Presents, that it was my Act and Deed, or rather Mr. *Durfey's*; for he *wou'd* play his Third Night against the First of mine. He brought down a huge Flight of frightful Birds upon me, when (Heaven knows) I had not a Feather'd Fowl in my Play, except one single *Kite*: But I presently made *Plume* a Bird, because of his Name, and *Brazen* another, because of the Feather in his Hat; and with these three I engag'd his whole Empire, which I think was as great a *Wonder* as any *in the Sun*.

50 But to answer his Complaints more gravely, the Season was far advanc'd; the Officers that made the greatest Figures in my Play were all commanded to their Posts abroad, and waited only for a Wind, which might possibly turn in less time than a Day: And I know none of Mr. *Durfey*'s Birds that had Posts abroad but his Woodcocks, and their Season is over; so that he might put off a Day with less Prejudice than the Recruiting Officer cou'd, who has this farther to say for himself, that he was posted before the other spoke, and could not with Credit recede from his Station.

60 These and some other Rubs this Comedy met with before it appear'd. But on the other hand, it had powerful Helps to set it forward: The Duke of *Ormond* encourag'd the Author, and the Earl of *Orrery* approv'd the Play—My *Recruits* were *reviewed* by my *General* and my *Collonel*, and could not fail to *pass Muster*; and still to add to my success, they were rais'd among my *Friends round the Wrekin*.

This Health has the advantage over our other celebrated Toasts, never to grow worse for the wearing: 'Tis a lasting Beauty, old without Age, and common without Scandal. That

you may live long to set it cheerfully round, and to enjoy the 70
abundant Pleasures of your fair and plentiful Country, is the
hearty Wish of,

My Lords and Gentlemen,
Your most Obliged,
and most Obedient Servant,
Geo. Farquhar.

Dramatis Personæ.

[MEN.]

Mr. *Ballance,* ⎫
Mr. *Scale,* ⎬ Three Justices, ⎧ Mr. *Keen.*
Mr. *Scruple,* ⎭ ⎨ Mr. *Phillips.*
  ⎩ Mr. *Kent.*
Mr. *Worthy,* a Gentleman of *Shropshire.* Mr. Williams.
Captain *Plume,* ⎫ Two Recruiting ⎧ Mr. *Wilks.*
Captain *Brazen,* ⎭ Officers, ⎨ Mr. *Cibber.*
Kite, Serjeant to *Plume,* Mr. *Estcourt.*
Bullock, a Countrey Clown, Mr. *Bullock.*
Costar Pearmain, ⎫ ⎧ Mr. *Norris.*
Thomas Appletree, ⎬ Two Recruits, ⎨ Mr. *Fairbank.*

WOMEN.

Melinda, a Lady of Fortune, Mrs. *Rogers,*
Silvia, Daughter to *Ballance,* in Love with
   Plume, Mrs. *Oldfield.*
Lucy, Melinda's Maid, Mrs. *Sapsford.*
Rose, a Countrey Wench, Mrs. *Mountfort.*
[*Drum*], Constable, *Recruits, Mob, Smith, Butcher, Prisoners,*
   Servants and Attendants.

SCENE *Shrewsbury.*

THE
PROLOGUE

In Antient Times, when Hellen's fatal Charms
Rous'd the contending Universe to Arms,
The Græcian Council happily deputes
The Sly Ulysses forth—to raise Recruits.
The Artful Captain found, without delay,
Where Great Achilles, a Deserter, lay.
Him Fate had warn'd to shun the Trojan Blows:
Him Greece requir'd—against their Trojan Foes.
All the Recruiting Arts were needful here
To raise this Great, this tim'rous Volunteer.   10
Ulysses well could talk—He stirs, he warms
The warlike Youth—He listens to the Charms
Of Plunder, fine Lac'd Coats, and glitt'ring Arms.
Ulysses caught the Young Aspiring Boy,
And listed him who wrought the Fate of Troy.
Thus by Recruiting was bold Hector slain:
Recruiting thus Fair Hellen did regain.
If for One Hellen such prodigious things
Were acted, that they ev'n listed Kings;
If for one Hellen's artful vicious Charms   20
Half the transported World was found in Arms;
What for so Many Hellens may We dare,
Whose Minds, as well as Faces, are so Fair?
If, by One Hellen's Eyes, Old Greece cou'd find
It's Homer fir'd to write—Ev'n Homer Blind;
The Britains sure beyond compare may write,
That view so many Hellens every Night.

THE
Recruiting Officer.

ACT I. Scene i.

SCENE, *the Market-Place—Drum beats the Granadeer-March.*

Enter Serjeant Kite, *follow'd by the Mob.*

Kite. (*Making a Speech.*) If any Gentlemen Soldiers, or others, have a mind to serve her Majesty, and pull down the *French* King, if any Prentices have severe Masters, any Children have undutiful Parents; if any Servants have too little Wages, or any Husband too much Wife, let them repair to the Noble Serjeant *Kite*, at the Sign of the *Raven*, In this good Town of *Shrewsbury*, and they shall receive present Relief and Entertainment.—

Gentlemen, I don't beat my Drums here to insnare or
10 inveigle any Man; for you must know, Gentlemen, that I am a Man of Honour: Besides, I don't beat up for common Soldiers; no, I list only Granadeers, Granadeers, Gentlemen —Pray Gentlemen observe this Cap—This is the Cap of Honour, it dubs a Man a Gentleman in the drawing of a Tricker; and he that has the good Fortune to be born six Foot high, was born to be a Great Man–Sir, (*To one of the Mob.*) Will you give me leave to try this Cap upon your Head?

Mob. Is there no harm in't? Won't the Cap list me?

Kite. No, no, no more than I can,—Come, let me see how it
20 becomes you.

Mob. Are you sure there be no Conjuration in it, no Gunpowder-plot upon me?

Kite. —No, no, Friend; don't fear, Man.

Mob. My mind misgives me plaguely—Let me see it—(*Going to put it on.*) It smells woundily of Sweat and Brimstone; pray, Serjeant, what Writing is this upon the Face of it?

Kite. The Crown, or the Bed of Honour.

Mob. Pray now, what may be that same *Bed of Honour*?

Kite. O, a mighty large Bed, bigger than half than the great Bed of *Ware*, ten thousand People may lie in't together, and 30 never feel one another.

Mob. My Wife and I wou'd do well to lie in't, for we don't care for feeling one another—But do Folk sleep sound in this same *Bed of Honour*?

Kite. Sound! Ay, so sound that they never wake.

Mob. Wauns! I wish again that my Wife lay there.

Kite. Say you so? Then I find Brother—

Mob. Brother! Hold there Friend, I'm no Kindred to you that I know of, as yet—Lookye Serjeant, no coaxing, no wheedling d'ye'see; if I have a mind to list, why so— If not, 40 why 'tis not so—Therefore take your Cap and your Brothership back again, for I an't dispos'd at this present Writing—No coaxing, no Brothering me, Faith.

Kite. I coax! I wheedle! I'm above it. Sir, I have serv'd twenty Campaigns—But, Sir, you talk well, and I must own that you are a Man every Inch of you, a pretty young sprightly Fellow—I love a Fellow with a Spirit, but I scorn to coax, 'tis base; tho' I must say, that never in my Life have I seen a better built Man: How firm and strong he treads, he steps like a Castle! But I scorn to wheedle any Man—Come, honest 50 Lad, will you take share of a Pot?

Mob. Nay, for that matter, I'll spend my Penny with the best he that wears a Head, that is, begging your Pardon Sir, and in a fair way.

Kite. Give me your hand then, and now Gentlemen, I have no more to say but this—Here's a Purse of Gold, and there is a Tub of humming Ale at my Quarters, 'this the Queen's Money, and the Queen's Drink; She's a generous Queen, and loves her Subjects—I hope, Gentlemen, you won't refuse the Queen's Health.   60

All Mob. No, no, no.

Kite. Huzza, then, huzza for the Queen, and the Honour of *Shropshire*.

All Mob. Huzza.

I.i. 27, 29, 35, 37 *Kite.*] Q2; *Serj.*

Kite. Beat Drum—

> *Exeunt, Drum beating the Granadeer-March.*
> *Enter* Plume *in a Riding Habit.*

Plume. By the Granadeer-March that shou'd be my Drum, and by that Shout it shou'd beat with Success—Let me see—(*Looks on his Watch.*) Four a Clock—at ten Yesterday Morning I left *London*—A hundred and twenty Miles in thirty
70 Hours, is pretty smart riding, but nothing to the Fatigue of Recruiting.

Enter Kite.

Kite. Welcome to *Shrewsbury*, noble Captain, from the Banks of the *Danube* to the *Severn* side, noble Captain you are welcome.

Plume. A very elegant Reception indeed, Mr. *Kite*, I find you are failry enter'd into your Recruiting Strain—Pray what Success?

Kite. I have been here but a Week, and I have recruited five.

80   *Plume.* Five! Pray, What are they?

Kite. I have listed the strong Man of *Kent*, the King of the Gypsies, a *Scotch* Pedlar, a Scoundrel Attorney, and a *Welsh* Parson.

Plume. An Attorney! Wer't thou mad? List a Lawyer! Discharge him, discharge him this Minute.

Kite. Why Sir?

Plume. Because I will have no Body in my Company that can write; a Fellow that can write, can draw Petitions—I say, this Minute discharge him.

90   *Kite.* And what shall I do with the Parson?

Plume. Can he write?

Kite. Umh—He plays rarely upon the Fiddle.

Plume. Keep him by all means—But how stands the Country affected? Were the People pleas'd with the News of my coming to Town?

Kite. Sir, the Mob are so pleas'd with your Honour, and the Justices and better sort of People are so delighted with me, that we shall soon do our Business—But, Sir, you have got a Recruit here that you little think of.

100   *Plume.* Who?

Kite. One that you beat up for last time you were in the

Country; you remember your old Friend *Molly* at the *Castle*.

Plume. She's not with Child, I hope.

Kite. No, no, Sir;—She was brought to Bed Yesterday.

Plume. Kite, you must Father the Child.

Kite. Humph—And so her Friends will oblige me to marry the Mother.

Plume. If they shou'd, we'll take her with us, she can wash you know, and make a Bed upon occasion.

Kite. Ay, or unmake it upon Occasion, but your Honour 110 knows that I'm marry'd already.

Plume. To how many?

Kite. I can't tell readily—I have set them down here upon the back of the Muster-Roll. (*Draws out the Muster-Roll.*) Let me see—*Imprimis*, Mrs. *Sheely Snickereyes*, she sells Potatoes upon *Ormond-Key* in *Dublin*—*Peggy Guzzle*, the Brandy Woman at the Horse-Guard at *Whitehall*—*Dolly Waggon*, the Carrier's Daughter in *Hull*—Madamoseille *Van-Bottomflat* at the *Buss*—Then *Jenny Okam* the Ship-Carpenter's Widow at *Portsmouth*; but I don't reckon upon her, for she was marry'd at the same 120 time to two Lieutenants of Marines, and a Man of War's Boatswain.

Plume. A full Company, you have nam'd five—Come, make 'em half a Dozen, *Kite*—Is the Child a Boy or a Girl?

Kite. A Chopping Boy.

Plume. Then set the Mother down in your List, and the Boy in mine; enter him a Granadeer by the Name of *Francis Kite*, absent upon *Furlow*—I'll allow you a Man's Pay for his Subsistence, and now go comfort the Wench in the Straw.

Kite. I shall, Sir.   130

Plume. But hold, have you made any Use of your *German* Doctor's Habit since you arriv'd?

Kite. Yes, yes, Sir; and my Fame's all about the Country, for the most famous Fortune-teller that ever told a Lye; I was oblig'd to let my Landlord into the Secret for the Convenience of keeping it so; but he's an honest Fellow, and will be trusty to any Roguery that is confided to him: This Device, Sir, will get you Men, and me Money, which I think is all we want at

present—But yonder comes your Friend, Mr. *Worthy*—Has
140 your Honour any farther Commands?

    Plume. None at present.

Exit Kite.

'Tis indeed the Picture of *Worthy*, but the Life's departed.

Enter Worthy.

    Plume. What! Arms a-cross, *Worthy*! Methinks you shou'd
hold 'em open when a Friend's so near—The Man has got the
Vapours in his Ears I believe. I must expel this melancholy
Spirit.

Spleen, thou worst of Fiends below,
Fly, I conjure thee by this Magick Blow.
(*Slaps* Worthy *on the Shoulder.*)

    Worthy. *Plume*! My dear Captain, welcome, safe and sound
150 return'd!

    Plume. I 'scap'd safe from *Germany*, and sound I hope from
London, you see I have lost neither Leg, Arm, nor Nose—Then
for my inside, 'tis neither troubled with Sympathies nor
Antipathies, and I have an excellent Stomach for roast Beef.

    Worthy. Thou art a happy Fellow, once I was so.

    Plume. What ails thee, Man? No Inundations nor Earth-
quakes in *Wales*, I hope? Has your Father rose from the dead,
and reassum'd his Estate?

    Worthy. No.

160   *Plume.* Then, you are marry'd surely.

    Worthy. No.

    Plume. Then you are mad, or turning *Quaker*.

    Worthy. Come, I must out with it—Your once gay roving
Friend is dwindled into an obsequious, thoughtful, romantick,
constant Coxcomb.

    Plume. And pray, What is all this for?

    Worthy. For a Woman.

    Plume. Shake hands Brother, if you go to that—Behold me
as obsequious, as thoughtful, and as constant a Coxcomb as
170 your Worship.

    Worthy. For whom?

    Plume. For a Regiment—But for a Woman, 'sdeath, I have
been constant to fifteen at a time, but never melancholy for
one; and can the Love of one bring you into this Pickle? Pray,

174 Pickle] Q2 reads 'Condition'

who is this miraculous *Hellen*?

Worthy. A *Hellen* indeed, not to be won under a ten Year's Siege, as great a Beauty, and as great a Jilt.

Plume. A Jilt! Pho—Is she as great a Whore?

Worthy. No, no.

Plume. 'Tis ten thousand pities—But who is she? Do I know 180 her?

Worthy. Very well.

Plume. Impossible—I know no Woman that will hold out a ten Year's Siege.

Worthy. What think you of *Melinda*?

Plume. Melinda! Why she began to capitulate this time Twelve-month, and offer'd to surrender upon honourable Terms; and I advis'd you to propose a Settlement of five hundred Pound a Year to her, before I went last abroad.

Worthy. I did, and she hearken'd to't, desiring only one 190 Week to consider; when, beyond her Hopes, the Town was reliev'd, and I forc'd to turn my Siege into a Blockade.

Plume. Explain, explain.

Worthy. My Lady *Richly*, her Aunt in *Flintshire* dies, and leaves her at this critical time twenty thousand Pound.

Plume. Oh the Devil, what a delicate Woman was there spoil'd: But by the Rules of War now, *Worthy*, your Blockade was foolish—After such a Convoy of Provisions was enter'd the Place, you cou'd have no thought of reducing it by Famine—You shou'd have redoubled your Attacks, taken the 200 Town by Storm, or have dy'd upon the Breach.

Worthy. I did make one general Assault, and push'd it with all my Forces; but I was so vigorously repuls'd, that despairing of ever gaining her for a Mistress, I have alter'd my Conduct, given my Addresses the obsequious and distant turn, and court her now for a Wife.

Plume. So, as you grew obsequious, she grew haughty, and because you approach'd her as a Goddess, she us'd you like a Dog.

Worthy. Exactly.   210

Plume. 'Tis the way of 'em all—Come *Worthy*, your obsequious and distant Airs will never bring you together; you must not

---

175 miraculous] Q2 reads 'wonderful'   183 Impossible] Q2 reads 'That's impossible'   197 your Blockade] Q2 reads 'Blockade'

think to surmount her Pride by your Humility—Wou'd you
bring her to better Thoughts of you, she must be reduc'd to a
meaner Opinion of her self—Let me see—The very first thing
that I wou'd do, shou'd be to lie with her Chamber-maid, and
hire three or four Wenches in the Neighbourhood to report
that I had got them with Child. Suppose we lampoon'd all the
pretty Women in Town, and left her out? Or what if we made
220 a Ball, and forgot to invite her, with one or two of the Ugliest.

Worthy. These wou'd be Mortifications, I must confess,—
But we live in such a precise, dull Place, that we can have no
Balls, no Lampoons, no—

Plume. What! No Bastards! And so many Recruiting
Officers in Town; I thought 'twas a Maxim among them to
leave as many Recruits in the Country as they carry'd out.

Worthy. No body doubts your Good-will, Noble Captain, in
serving your Country with your best Blood—Witness our
Friend *Molly* at the *Castle*—There have been Tears in Town
230 about that Business, Captain.

Plume. I hope *Silvia* has not heard of 't.

Worthy. O Sir, have you thought of her? I began to fancy
you had forgot poor *Silvia.*

Plume. Your Affairs had put my own quite out of my Head:
'Tis true, *Sylvia* and I had once agreed to go to Bed together,
cou'd we have adjusted Preliminaries; but she wou'd have the
Wedding before Consummation, and I was for Consummation
before the Wedding—We cou'd not agree, she was a pert
obstinate Fool, and wou'd lose her Maidenhead her own way,
240 so she may keep it for *Plume.*

Worthy. But do you intend to marry upon no other
Conditions.

Plume. Your Pardon, Sir, I'll marry upon no Conditions at
all, if I shou'd, I'm resolv'd never to bind my self to a Woman
for my whole Life, till I know whether I shall like her
Company for half an Hour—Suppose I marry'd a Woman
that wanted a Leg? Such a thing might be, unless I examin'd
the Goods before-hand; if People wou'd but try one another's
Constitutions before they engag'd, it wou'd prevent all these
250 Elopements, Divorces, and the Devil knows what.

Worthy. Nay, for that matter, the Town did not stick to say,
That—

Plume. I hate Country Towns for that Reason—If your
Town has a dishonourable Thought of *Silvia*, it deserves to be
burnt to the Ground—I love *Silvia*, I admire her frank,
generous Disposition; there's something in that Girl more
than Woman, her Sex is but a foil to her—The Ingratitude,
Dissimulation, Envy, Pride, Avarice, and Vanity of her Sister
Females, do but set off their Contraries in her—In short, were
I once a General, I wou'd marry her.   260

Worthy. Faith you have reason; for were you but a Corporal,
she wou'd marry you—But my *Melinda* coquets it with every
Fellow she sees—I lay fifty Pound she makes love to you.

Plume. I'll lay fifty Pound that I return it, if she does—
Lookye, *Worthy*, I'll win her, and give her to you afterwards.

Worthy. If you win her, you shall wear her, Faith; I wou'd
not give a Fig for the Conquest, without the Credit of the
Victory.

Enter Kite.

Kite. Captain, Captain, a word in your Ear.

Plume. You may speak out, here are none but Friends.   270

Kite. You know, Sir, that you sent me to comfort the good
Woman in the Straw, Mrs. *Molly*—My Wife, Mr. *Worthy*.

Worthy. Oho, very well—I wish you Joy, Mr. *Kite*.

Kite. Your Worship very well may,—for I have got both a
Wife and a Child in half an Hour,—but as I was a saying, you
sent me to comfort Mrs. *Molly*—My Wife, I mean. But what
d'ye think Sir? She was better comforted before I came.

Plume. As how?

Kite. Why, Sir, a Footman in a blue Livery had brought her
ten Guineas to buy her Baby Cloaths.   280

Plume. Who, in the Name of Wonder, cou'd send them?

Kite. Nay, Sir, I must whisper that—Mrs. *Silvia*. (*Whispers*
Plume.)

Plume. *Silvia*! Generous Creature.

Worthy. *Silvia*! Impossible.

Kite. Here be the Guinea's, Sir; I took the Gold as part of
my Wife's Portion: Nay farther, Sir, she sent word that the
Child shou'd be taken all imaginable Care of, and that she
intended to stand God-mother. The same Footman, as I was

coming to you with this News, call'd after me, and told me
290 that his Lady wou'd speak with me—I went; and upon
hearing that you were come to Town, she gave me half a
Guinea for the News, and order'd me to tell you, That Justice
Ballance her Father, who is just come out of the Country,
wou'd be glad to see you.

Plume. There's a Girl for you, *Worthy*—Is there any thing of
Woman in this? No, 'tis noble and generous, Manly Friendship,
show me another Woman that wou'd lose an Inch of her
Prerogative that way, without Tears, Fits, and Reproaches.
The common Jealousie of her Sex, which is nothing but their
300 Avarice of Pleasure, she despises; and can part with the Lover,
tho' she dies for the Man—Come *Worthy*— Where's the best
Wine? For there I'll quarter.

Worthy. *Horton* has a fresh Pipe of choice *Barcelona*, which I
wou'd not let him pierce before, because I reserv'd the
Maidenhead of it for your welcome to Town.

Plume. Let's away then—Mr. *Kite*, wait on the Lady with
my humble Service, and tell her, That I shall only refresh a
little, and wait on her.

Worthy. Hold, *Kite*—Have you seen the other Recruiting
310 Captain?

Kite. No. Sir.

Plume. Another, who is he?

Worthy. My Rival in the first place, and the most unaccountable Fellow—But I'll tell you more as we go.

Exeunt.

ACT I. Scene ii.

SCENE, *An Apartment*

Melinda *and* Silvia *Meeting.*

Melinda. Welcome to Town, Cosin *Silvia* (*Salute.*) I envy'd
you your Retreat in the Country; for *Shrewsbury*, methinks, and
all your Heads of Shires, are the most irregular Places for
living, here we have Smoak, Noise, Scandal, Affectation, and

Pretension; in short, every thing to give the Spleen, and
nothing to divert it—Then the Air is intolerable.

Silvia. Oh! Madam, I have heard the Town commended for
its Air.

Melinda. But you don't consider, *Silvia*, how long I have
liv'd in it; for I can assure you, that to a Lady the least nice in 10
her Constitution, no Air can be good above half a Year;
Change of Air I take to be the most agreeable of any Variety
in Life.

Silvia. As you say, Cosin *Melinda*, there are several sorts of
Airs, Airs in Conversation, Airs in Behaviour, Airs in Dress;
then we have our Quality Airs, our sickly Airs, our reserv'd
Airs, and sometimes our impudent Airs.

Melinda. Pshaw—I talk only of the Air we breath, or more
properly of that we taste—Have not you, *Silvia*, found a vast
Difference in the Taste of Airs?   20

Silvia. Pray Cosin, are not Vapours a sort of Air? Taste Air!
You may as well tell me I might feed upon Air; but prithee, my
dear *Melinda*, don't put on such Airs to me, your Education
and mine were just the same, and I remember the time when
we never troubled our Heads about Air, but when the sharp
Air from the *Welsh* Mountains made our Noses drop in a cold
Morning at the Boarding-School.

Melinda. Our Education, Cosin, was the same, but our
Temperaments had nothing alike; you have the Constitution
of a Horse—   30

Silvia. So far as to be troubled with neither Spleen, Cholick,
nor Vapours, I need no Salts for my Stomach, no Hart's-horn
for my Head, nor Wash for my Complexion; I can gallop all
the Morning after the Hunting Horn, and all the Evening
after a Fiddle: In short, I can do every thing with my Father
but drink and shoot flying; and I'm sure I can do every thing
my Mother cou'd, were I put to the Tryal.

Melinda. You are in a fair way of being put to't; for I'm told
your Captain is come to Town.

Silvia. Ay, *Melinda*, he is come, and I'll take care he shan't 40
go without a Companion.

I.ii. 15–17 Airs in Conversation . . . impudent Airs.] om. in Q2.
26 Noses drop] Q2 reads 'Fingers ake'   32 Salts] Q2; Salt   38 You are]
Q2; You're ~

Melinda. You're certainly mad, Cosin.

Silvia. And there's a Pleasure sure, in being mad,
Which none but Mad-men know.

Melinda. Thou poor Romantick *Quixote*, hast thou the Vanity to imagine that a young sprightly Officer that rambles over half the Globe in half a Year, can confine his Thoughts to the little Daughter of a Country Justice in an obscure corner of the World?

50 *Silvia.* Pshaw! What care I for his Thoughts? I shou'd not like a Man with confin'd Thoughts, it shows a Narrowness of Soul. Constancy is but a dull, sleepy Quality at best; they will hardly admit it among the Manly Vertues, nor do I think it deserves a Place with Bravery, Knowledge, Policy, Justice, and some other Qualities that are proper to that noble Sex. In short, *Melinda*, I think a Petticoat a mighty simple thing, and I'm heartily tir'd of my Sex.

Melinda. That is, you are tir'd of an Appendix to our Sex, that you can't so handsomly get rid of in Petticoats as if you
60 were in Breeches—O'my Conscience, *Silvia*, hadst thou been a Man, thou hadst been the greatest Rake in *Christendom*.

Silvia. I shou'd endeavour to know the World, which a Man can never do thoroughly without half a hundred Friendships, and as many Amours. But now I think on't, how stands your Affair with Mr. *Worthy*?

Melinda. He's my Aversion.

Silvia. Vapours.

Melinda. What do you say, Madam?

Silvia. I say, that you shou'd not use that honest Fellow so
70 inhumanely, he's a Gentleman of Parts and Fortune, and beside that he's my *Plume*'s Friend; and by all that's sacred, if you don't use him better, I shall expect Satisfaction.

Melinda. Satisfaction! You begin to fancy your self in Breeches in good earnest—But to be plain with you, I like *Worthy* the worse for being so intimate with your Captain; for I take him to be a loose, idle, unmannerly Coxcomb.

Silvia. Oh! Madam—You never saw him, perhaps, since you were Mistress of twenty thousand Pound; you only knew him when you were capitulating with *Worthy* for a Settlement,

48 corner] Q2 reads 'Part'

which perhaps might incourage him to be a little loose and 80
unmannerly with you.

Melinda. What do you mean, Madam?

Silvia. My Meaning needs no Interpretation, Madam.

Melinda. Better it had, Madam—for methinks you're too
plain.

Silvia. If you mean the Plainness of my Person, I think your
Ladyship as plain as me to the full.

Melinda. Were I assur'd of that, I shou'd be glad to take up
with a Rakely Officer as you do.

Silvia. Again! Look'e, Madam—You're in your own House. 90

Melinda. And if you had kept in yours, I shou'd have
excus'd you.

Silvia. Don't be troubl'd, Madam—I shan't desire to have
my Visit return'd.

Melinda. The sooner therefore you make an end of this, the
better.

Silvia. I'm easily advis'd to follow my Inclinations—So
Madam—Your humble Servant.   *Exit.*

Melinda. Saucy thing!

Enter Lucy.

Lucy. What's the matter, Madam?   100

Melinda. Did you not see the proud Nothing, how she swells
upon the Arrival of her Fellow?

Lucy. Her Fellow has not been long enough arriv'd to
occasion any great swelling, Madam—I don't believe she has
seen him yet.

Melinda. Nor shan't if I can help it; let me see—I have
it—Bring me Pen and Ink—Hold, I'll go write in my Closet.

Lucy. An Answer to this Letter, I hope, Madam—(*Presents a
Letter.*)

Melinda. Who sent it?

Lucy. Your Captain, Madam—   110

Melinda. He's a Fool, and I'm tir'd of him; send it back
unopen'd.

Lucy. The Messenger's gone, Madam—

Melinda. Then how shall I send an Answer? call him back
immediately, while I go write.

Exeunt severally.

97 advis'd] Q2 reads 'persuaded'

ACT II. Scene i.

SCENE, *An apartment.*

Enter Justice Ballance *and* Plume.

Ballance. Look'e, Captain, give us but Blood for our Money, and you shan't want Men; I remember, that for some Years of the last War, we had no Blood nor Wounds but in the Officers Mouths, nothing for our Millions but News Papers not worth a reading, our Armies did nothing but play at Prison Bars, and hide and seek with the Enemy, but now ye have brought us Colours, and Standards, and Prisoners; odsmylife, Captain, get us but another Mareschal of *France*, and I'll go my self for a Soldier.

10 *Plume.* Pray, Mr. *Ballance*, how does your fair Daughter?

Ballance. Ah! Captain, what is my Daughter to a Mareschal of *France*? We're upon a nobler Subject, I want to have a particular Description of the Battel of *Hochstet*.

Plume. The Battel, Sir, was a very pretty Battel as one shou'd desire to see, but we were all so intent upon Victory, that we never minded the Battel; all that I know of the matter is, our General commanded us to beat the *French*, and we did so, and if he pleases to say the word, we'll do't again—But pray, Sir, how does Mrs. *Silvia*?

20 *Ballance.* Still upon *Silvia*! For shame, Captain—You're engag'd already, wedded to the War, War is your Mistress, and it is below a Soldier to think of any other.

Plume. As a Mistress, I confess, but as a Friend, Mr. *Ballance.*

Ballance. Come, come, Captain, never mince the matter, wou'd not you debauch my Daughter if you cou'd?

Plume. How Sir! I hope she is not to be debauch'd.

Ballance. Faith but she is, Sir, and any Woman in *England* of her Age and Complexion, by a Man of your Youth and 30 Vigour. Look'e, Captain, once I was young, and once an Officer as you are; and I can guess at your Thoughts now by what mine were then, and I remember very well, that I wou'd

II.i 17 General] Q2; Generals   21 War is] Q2 reads 'Victory is' have given one of my Legs to have deluded the Daughter of an old plain Country Gentleman, as like me as I was then like you.

Plume. But, Sir, was that Country Gentleman your Friend and Benefactor?

Ballance. Not much of that.

Plume. There the Comparison breaks; the Favours, Sir, that— 40

Ballance. Pho! I hate Speeches; if I have done you any Service, Captain, 'twas to please my self, for I love thee; and if I cou'd part with my Girl, you shou'd have her as soon as any young Fellow I know; but I hope you have more Honour than to quit the Service, and she more Prudence than to follow the Camp: But she's at her own Disposal, she has fifteen hundred Pound in her Pocket, and so, *Silvia, Silvia.* (*Calls.*)

Enter Silvia.

Silvia. There are some Letters, Sir, come by the Post from *London*, I left them upon the Table in your Closet.

Ballance. And here is a Gentleman from *Germany* (*Presents* 50 Plume *to her.*) Captain, you'll excuse me, I'll go read my Letters and wait on you.

Exit.

Silvia. Sir, you're welcome to *England*.

Plume. You are indebted to me a Welcome, Madam, since the hopes of receiving it from this fair Hand, was the principal Cause of my seeing *England*.

Silvia. I have often heard that Soldiers were sincere, shall I venture to believe publick Report?

Plume. You may, when 'tis back'd by private Insurance; for I swear, Madam, by the Honour of my Profession, that 60 whatever Dangers I went upon, it was with the hope of making my self more worthy of your Esteem, and if I ever had thoughts of preserving my Life, 'twas for the Pleasure of dying

34 plain] om. in Q2   54–67 *Plume.* You are . . . beforehand] Q2:
   Plume. Blessings in Heaven we shou'd receive in a prostrate Posture, let me receive
my welcome thus. (*Kneels and kisses her Hand.*)
   Silvia. Pray rise, Sir, I'll give you fair Quarter.
   Plume. All Quarter I despite, the Height of Conquest is to die at your Feet. (*Kissing
her Hand again.*)
   Silvia. Well, well, you shall die at my Feet, or where you will; but first let me desire
you to make your Will, perhaps you'll leave me something.

at your Feet.

Silvia. Well, well, you shall dye at my Feet, or where you will; but you know, Sir, there is a certain Will and Testament to be made beforehand.

Plume. My Will, Madam, is made already, and there it is, (*Gives her a Parchment.*) and if you please to open that
70 Parchment, which was drawn the Evening before the Battel of *Blenheim*, you will find whom I left my Heir.

Silvia. (Silvia *opens the Will, and reads.*) Mrs. *Silvia Ballance*— Well, Captain, this is a handsome and a substantial Compliment, but I can assure you I am much better pleas'd with the bare Knowledge of your Intention, than I shou'd have been in the Possession of your Legacy; but methinks, Sir, you shou'd have left something to your little Boy at the *Castle*.

Plume. That's home; (*Aside.*) my little Boy! Lack-a-day, Madam, that alone may convince you 'twas none of mine;
80 why the Girl, Madam, is my Serjeant's Wife, and so the poor Creature gave out that I was Father, in hopes that my Friends might support her in case of Necessity, that was all Madam,— my Boy! No, no.

Enter Servant.

Servant. Madam, my Master has receiv'd some ill News from *London*, and desires to speak with you immediately, and he begs the Captain's Pardon that he can't wait on him as he promis'd.

Plume. Ill News! Heavens avert it; nothing cou'd touch me nearer than to see that generous worthy Gentleman afflicted;
90 I'll leave you to comfort him, and be assur'd that if my Life and Fortune can be any way serviceable to the Father of my *Silvia*, she shall freely command both.

Silvia. The Necessity must be very pressing, that wou'd engage me to do either.

Exeunt severally.

92 she] Q2 reads 'he'   94 do] Q2 reads 'endanger'

[ACT II. Scene ii.]

SCENE *changes to another Apartment.*

Enter Ballance *and* Silvia.

Silvia. Whilst there is Life there is hope, Sir; perhaps my Brother may recover.

Ballance. We have but little reason to expect it. Dr. *Kilman* acquaints me here, that before this comes to my hands, he fears I shall have no Son—Poor *Owen*! But the Decree is just, I was pleas'd with the Death of my Father, because he left me an Estate, and now I'm punish'd with the Loss of an Heir to inherit mine. I must now look upon you as the only Hopes of my Family, and I expect that the Augmentation of your Fortune will give you fresh Thoughts and new Prospects.   10

Silvia. My desire of being punctual in my Obedience, requires that you wou'd be plain in your Commands, Sir.

Ballance. The Death of your Brother makes you sole Heiress to my Estate, which three or four Years hence will amount to twelve hundred Pound *per Annum*; this Fortune gives you a fair Claim to Quality and a Title, you must set a just Value upon your self, and in plain Terms think no more of Captain *Plume*.

Silvia. You have often commended the Gentleman, Sir.

Ballance. And I do so still, he's a very pretty Fellow; but tho' I lik'd him well enough for a bare Son-in-Law, I don't 20 approve of him for an Heir to my Estate and Family, fifteen hundred Pound, indeed, I might trust in his hands, and it might do the young Fellow a Kindness, but odsmylife, twelve hundred Pound a Year wou'd ruine him, quite turn his Brain. A Captain of Foot worth twelve hundred Pound a Year! 'Tis a Prodigy in Nature: Besides this, I have five or six thousand Pounds in Woods upon my Estate; Oh! That wou'd make him stark mad, for you must know that all Captains have a mighty Aversion to Timber, they can't endure to see Trees standing; then I shou'd have some Rogue of a Builder by the help of his 30 damn'd Magick Art transform my noble Oaks and Elms into

II.ii. 14–15 three . . . *Annum*;] Q2 reads 'you know is about twelve hundred Pounds a Year:'

Cornishes, Portals, Sashes, Birds, Beasts, Gods and Devils, to
adorn some magotty, new-fashion'd Bauble upon the *Thames*;
and then you shou'd have a Dog of a Gardner bring a *Habeas
Corpus* for my *Terra Firma*, remove it to *Chelsea* or *Twitnam*, and
clap it into Grass-plats and Gravel-walks.

Enter a Servant.

Servant. Sir, here's one below with a Letter for your
Worship, but he will deliver it into no hands but your own.

Ballance. Come, show me the Messenger.

Exit with Servant.

40 *Silvia.* Make the Dispute between Love and Duty, and I am
Prince *Prettyman* exactly—If my Brother dies, Ah! poor
Brother; if he lives, Ah! poor Sister—'Tis bad both ways, I'll
try again, follow my own Inclinations and break my Father's
Heart, or obey his Commands and break my own, worse and
worse—Suppose I take thus—A moderate Fortune, a pretty
Fellow and a Pad,—or a fine Estate, a Coach and six, and an
Ass—That will never do neither.

Enter Ballance *and* Servant.

Ballance. Put four Horses into the Coach. (*To the* Servant *who
goes out.*) Silvia—

50 *Silvia.* Sir.

Ballance. How old were you when your Mother dy'd?

Silvia. So young that I don't remember I ever had one; and
you have been so careful, so indulgent to me since, that indeed
I never wanted one.

Ballance. Have I ever deny'd you any thing you ask'd of me?

Silvia. Never, that I remember.

Ballance. Then *Silvia*, I must beg that once in your Life you
wou'd grant me a Favour.

Silvia. Why shou'd you question it, Sir?

60 *Ballance.* I don't, but I wou'd rather counsel than command
—I don't propose this with the Authority of a Parent, but as
the Advice of your Friend, that you wou'd take the Coach this
Moment, and go into the Country.

Silvia. Does this Advice proceed from the Contents of the
Letter you receiv'd just now?

Ballance. No matter, I shall be with you in three or four

32 Gods] om. in Q2

days, and then give you my Reasons—But before you go, I
expect you will make me one solemn Promise.

Silvia. Propose the thing, Sir.

Ballance. That you will never dispose of your self to any 70
Man, without my Consent.

Silvia. I promise.

Ballance. Very well, and to be even with you, I promise,
That I will never dispose of you without your own Consent;
and so *Silvia*, the Coach is ready, farewel.

> *Leads her to the Door and returns.*

Now she's gone, I'll examine the Contents of this Letter a little
nearer. (*Reads.*)

SIR,

> *My Intimacy with Mr.* Worthy *has drawn a Secret from him,
> that he had from his Friend Captain* Plume, *and my Friendship* 80
> *and Relation to your Family oblige me to give you timely notice of
> it; the Captain has dishonourable Designs upon my
> Cosin* Silvia, *Evils of this Nature are more easily prevented than
> amended, and that you wou'd immediately send my Cosin into the
> Country is the Advice of,*

> SIR,
> Your humble Servant,
> *MELINDA.*

Why the Devil's in the young Fellows of this Age, they're ten
times worse than they were in my time; had he made my 90
Daughter a Whore, and forswore it like a Gentleman, I cou'd
have almost pardon'd it; but to tell Tales before-hand is
monstrous! Hang it, I can fetch down a Woodcock or Snipe,
and why not a Hat and Feather? I have a Case of good Pistols,
and have a good mind to try.

> *Enter* Worthy.

Ballance. Worthy, your Servant.

Worthy. I'm sorry, Sir, to be the Messenger of ill News.

Ballance. I apprehend it, Sir; you have heard that my Son
Owen is past Recovery.

Worthy. My Advices say he's dead, Sir.   100

Ballance. He's happy, and I am satisfy'd; the Strokes of

---

100 Advices] Q2 reads 'Letters'

Heaven I can bear, but Injuries from Men, Mr. *Worthy*, are
not so easily supported.

Worthy. I hope, Sir, you are under no Apprehension of
Wrong from any Body?

Ballance. You know I ought to be.

Worthy. You wrong my Honour, Sir, in believing I cou'd
know any thing to your Prejudice without resenting it as much
as you shou'd.

110   *Ballance*. This Letter, Sir, which I tear in pieces to conceal
the Person that sent it, informs me that *Plume* has a Design
upon *Silvia*, and that you are privy to't.

Worthy. Nay, then Sir, I must do my self Justice, and
endeavour to find out the Author. (*Takes up a piece of the Letter.*)
Sir, I know the Hand, and if you refuse to discover the
Contents, *Melinda* shall tell me. (*Going.*)

Ballance. Hold, Sir, the Contents I have told you already,
only with this Circumstance, that her Intimacy with
Mr. *Worthy* had drawn the Secret from him.

120   *Worthy*. Her Intimacy with me!—Dear Sir, let me pick up
the pieces of this Letter, 'twill give me such a hank upon her
Pride, to have her own an Intimacy under her hand, 'twas the
luckiest Accident. (*Gathering up the Letter.*) The Aspersion, Sir,
was nothing but Malice, the Effect of a little Quarrel between
her and Mrs. *Silvia*.

Ballance. Are you sure of that, Sir?

Worthy. Her Maid gave me the History of part of the Battel
just now, as she overheard it.

Ballance. 'Tis probable, I am satisfy'd.

130   *Worthy*. But I hope, Sir, your Daughter has suffer'd nothing
upon the Account?

Ballance. No, no—Poor Girl, she is so afflicted with the
News of her Brother's Death, that to avoid Company she
beg'd Leave to be gone into the Country.

Worthy. And is she gone?

Ballance. I cou'd not refuse her, she was so pressing, the
Coach went from the door the Minute before you came—

Worthy. So pressing to be gone, Sir—I find her Fortune will
give her the same Airs with *Melinda*, and then *Plume* and I may

---

laugh at one another.   140

Ballance. Like enough—Women are as subject to Pride as
we are, and why may'nt great Women as well as great Men
forget their old Acquaintance—But come—Where's this
young Fellow, I love him so well, it wou'd break the Heart of
me to think him a Rascal—I'm glad my Daughter's gone
fairly off tho' (*Aside.*) Where does the Captain quarter?

Worthy. At *Horton*'s I'm to meet him there two Hours hence,
and we shou'd be glad of your Company.

Ballance. Your pardon, dear *Worthy*, I must allow a Day or
two to the Death of my Son; the Decorum of Mourning is what   150
we owe the World, because they pay it to us. Afterwards, I'm
yours over a Bottle, or how you will.

Worthy. Sir, I'm your humble Servant.

                                                        Exeunt severally.

[ACT II. Scene iii.]

SCENE, *the Street.*

Enter Kite, *with one of the Mob in each hand, drunk.*

Kite. (*Sings.*)   *Our Prentice* Tom *may now refuse*
                    To wipe his scoundrel Master's Shoes;
                    For now he's free to sing and play,
                    Over the Hills and far away—*Over the Hills,* &c.
                    (*The Mob sing the Chorus.*)

                    We all shall lead more happy Lives,
                    By getting rid of Brats and Wives,
                    That scold and brawl both Night and Day;
                    Over the Hills and far away—*Over the Hills,* &c.

Kite. Hey Boys—Thus we Solders live, drink, sing, dance,
play; we live, as one shou'd say—We live—'Tis impossible to   10
tell how we live—We're all Princes—Why—Why you're a
King—You're an Emperour, and I'm a Prince—Now—an't
we—

---

151 us. Afterwards,] 1728; ~ ∧ afterwards.

Costar Pearmain. No, Serjeant—I'll be no Emperour.

Kite. No!

Costar Pearmain. No, I'll be a Justice of Peace.

Kite. A Justice of Peace, Man!

Costar Pearmain. Ay, wauns will I, for since this pressing Act they are greater than any Emperor under the Sun.

20 *Kite.* Done, you're a Justice of Peace, and you're a King, and I'm a Duke, and a Rum Duke, an't I?

Thomas Appletree. No, but I'll be no King.

Kite. What then?

Thomas Appletree. I'll be a Queen.

Kite. A Queen!

Thomas Appletree. Ay, Queen of *England*—That's greater than any King of 'em all.

Kite. Bravely said! Faith: Huzza for the Queen. (*All Huzza.*) But heark'e, you Mr. Justice, and you Mr. Queen, did 30 you ever see the Queen's Picture?

Costar Pearmain and Thomas Appletree. No, no.

Kite. I wonder at that, I have two of 'em set in Gold, and as like her Majesty, God bless the Mark. (*He takes two Broad Pieces out of his Pocket.*) See here, they're set in Gold. (*Gives one to each.*)

Costar Pearmain. (*Looking earnestly upon the Piece.*) The wonderful Works of Nature!

Costar Pearmain. What's this written about? Here's a Posy, I believe. *Ca-ro-lus*—What's that Serjeant?

Kite. O *Carolus*—Why *Carolus* is *Latin* for Queen *Ann*, that's 40 all.

Thomas Appletree. 'Tis a fine thing to be a Scollard, Serjeant, will you part with this? I'll buy it on you, if it come within the Compass of a Crawn.

Kite. A Crown! Never talk of buying—'Tis the same thing among Friends you know, I present them to you both, you shall give me as good a thing; put them up, and remember your old Friend, when I'm *over the Hills and far away.* (*Singing.*)
   They sing and put up the Money.

II.iii. 14 ff. *Costar Pearmain*] 1728 [*Cost.*]; 1st Mob. The speech prefixes for Costar Pearmain and Thomas Appletree are changed for clarification   22 ff. *Thomas Appletree*] 1728 [*Tho.*]; 2d. *Mob*   22 No] Q2 reads 'Ay'   30 ever] Q2 reads 'never'

Enter Plume *singing.*

Plume. *Over the Hills, and o're the Main,*
  To Flanders, Portugal, *or* Spain;
  The Queen commands, and we'll obey,   50
  Over the Hills and far away.

Come on my Men of Mirth, away with it, I'll make one among
ye; who are these hearty Lads?

Kite. Off with your Hats, Ouns, off with your Hats; this is
the Captain, the Captain.

Costar Pearmain. We have seen Captains afore now, mun.

Thomas Appletree. Ay, and Lieutenant Captains too; Flesh,
I'se keep on my Nab.

Costar Pearmain. And I'se scarcely d'off mine for any
Captain in *England*, my Vether's a Freeholder.   60

Plume. Who are these jolly Lads, Serjeant?

Kite. A couple of honest brave Fellows, that are willing to
serve the Queen; I have entertain'd them just now as
Volunteers under your Honour's Command.

Plume. And good Entertainment they shall have, Volunteers
are the Men I want, those are the Men fit to make Soldiers,
Captains, Generals.

Costar Pearmain. Wauns, *Tummas,* What's this? Are you
listed?

Thomas Appletree. Flesh, not I, are you, *Costar*?   70

Costar Pearmain. Wauns, not I.

Kite. What, not listed! Ha, ha, ha, a very good Jest, Faith.

Costar Pearmain. Come, *Tummas,* we'll go whome.

Thomas Appletree. Ay, ay, come.

Kite. Home! For shame, Gentlemen, behave your selves
better before your Captain—Dear *Tummas,* honest *Costar*—

Thomas Appletree. No, no, we'll be gone. (*Going.*)

Kite. Nay, then I command you to stay, I place you both
Centinels in this place for two Hours to watch the Motion of
St. *Mary*'s Clock you, and you the Motion of St. *Chad*s, and he   80
that dare stir from his Post till he be relieved, shall have my
Sword in his Guts the next Minute.

Plume. What's the matter, Serjeant—I'm afraid you're too
rough with these Gentlemen.

51 *Hills*] Q2; *Hill*

Kite. I'm too mild, Sir, they disobey Command, Sir, and one of them shou'd be shot for an Example to the other.

Costar Pearmain. Shot! *Tummas.*

Plume. Come, Gentlemen, what is the matter?

Costar Pearmain. We don't know, the noble Serjeant is
90 pleas'd to be in a Passion, Sir—But—

Kite. They disobey Command, they deny their being listed.

Thomas Appletree. Nay, Serjeant, we don't downright deny it neither, that we dare not do for fear of being shot; but we humbly conceive in a civil way, and begging your Worship's Pardon that we may go home.

Plume. That is easily known, have either of you receiv'd any of the Queen's Money.

Costar Pearmain. Not a brass Farthing, Sir.

Kite. Sir, they have each of them receiv'd three and twenty
100 Shillings and Six-pence, and 'tis now in their Pockets.

Costar Pearmain. Wauns! If I have a Penny in my Pocket, but a bent Six-pence, I'll be content to be listed, and shot into the Bargain.

Thomas Appletree. And I, look'e here, Sir.

Costar Pearmain. Ay, here's my Stock too, nothing but the Queen's Picture that the Serjeant gave me just now.

Kite. See there, a broad Piece, three and twenty Shillings and Six-pence, the t'other has the Fellow on't.

Plume. The Case is plain, Gentlemen, the Goods are found
110 upon you, those Pieces of Gold are worth three and twenty and Six-pence each.

Costar Pearmain. So it seems that *Carolus* is three and twenty Shillings and Six-pence in *Latin.*

Thomas Appletree. 'Tis the same thing in the *Greek*, for we are listed.

Costar Pearmain. Flesh, but we an't *Tummas*, I desire to be carry'd before the Mayar, Captain. (*While they talk,* Plume *and* Kite *whisper.*)

Plume. 'Twill never do, *Kite*; your damn'd Tricks will ruine me at last, I won't lose the Fellows tho', if I can help it—Well,
120 Gentlemen, there must be some Trick in this, my Serjeant offers here to take his Oath that you're fairly listed.

117–117.1 Plume *and* Kite] ed.; *the Captain and Serjeant*

Thomas Appletree. Why, Captain, we know that you Soldiers have more Liberty of Conscience than other Folks, but for me or Neighbour *Costar* here to take such an Oath, 'twou'd be downright Perjuration.

Plume. Look'e, you Rascal, you Villain, if I find that you have impos'd upon these two honest Fellows, I'll trample you to Death, you Dog; come, how was't?

Thomas Appletree. Nay, then we will speak, your Serjeant, as you say, is a Rogue, begging your Worship's Pardon—And— 130

Costar Pearmain. Nay, *Tummas*, let me speak, you know I can read; and so, Sir, he gave us those two pieces of Money for Pictures of the Queen by way of a Present.

Plume. How! By way of a Present! The Son of a Whore! I'll teach him to abuse honest Fellows like you; Scoundrel, Rogue, Villain, &c.

                    Beats Kite *off the Stage, and follows him out.*

Both Costar Pearmain and Thomas Appletree. O brave Noble Captain, huzza, a brave Captain, Faith.

Costar Pearmain. Now *Tummas*, *Corolus* is *Latin* for a beating: This is the bravest Captain I ever saw, Wauns, I have a 140 Month's mind to go with him.

                    Re-enter Plume.

Plume. A Dog! To abuse two such pretty Fellows as you; Look'e, Gentlemen, I love a pretty Fellow, I come among you here as an Officer to list Soldiers, not as a Kidnapper, to steal Slaves.

Costar Pearmain. Mind that, *Tummas*.

Plume. I desire no Man to go with me, but as I went my self, I went a Volunteer, as you or you may do, for a little time carry'd a Musket, and now I command a Company.

Thomas Appletree. Mind that, *Costar*, a sweet Gentleman.   150

Plume. 'Tis true, Gentlemen, I might take an advantage of you, the Queen's Money was in your Pockets; my Serjeant was ready to take his Oath that you were listed, but I scorn to do a base thing, you are both of you at your Liberty.

Costar Pearmain. Thank you, Noble Captain, I cod, I cannot find in my Heart to leave him, he talks so finely.

Thomas Appletree. Ay, *Costar*, wou'd he alway hold in this

122 *Thomas Appletree.*] 1728 [*Tho.*]; 1st *Mob*   136.1 Kite] ed.; *the Serjeant*
142 pretty] Q2 reads 'honest'   144 here] om. in Q2   147 do] Q2 reads 'go'

Mind.

Plume. Come, my Lads, one thing more I'll tell you, you're
160 both young tight Fellows, and the Army is the place to make
you Men for ever, every Man has his Lot, and you have yours;
What think you know of a Purse full of *French* Gold out of a
Monsieur's Pocket, after you have dash'd out his Brains with
the But of your Firelock, eh—

Costar Pearmain. Wauns, I'll have it, Captain, give me a
Shilling, I'll follow you to the end of the World.

Thomas Appletree. Nay, dear *Costar*, duna, be advis'd.

Plume. Here, my Heroe, here are two Guineas for thee, as
earnest of what I'll do farther for thee.

170 *Thomas Appletree.* Duna take it, duna, dear *Costar*. (*Cries and
pulls back his Arm.*)

Costar Pearmain. I wull, I wull, Wauns, my Mind gives me
that I shall be a Captain my self; I take your Money, Sir, and
now I'm a Gentleman.

Plume. Give me thy hand—And now you and I will travel
the World o're, and command wherever we tread—Bring your
Friend with you if you can. (*Aside.*)

Costar Pearmain. Well, *Tummas*, must we part—

Thomas Appletree. No, *Costar*, I cannot leave thee—Come,
Captain, (*Crying.*) I'll e'ne go along too; and if you have two
180 honester, simpler Lads in your Company than we twa
been—I'll say no more—

Plume. Here, my Lad (*Gives him Money.*) now your Name.

Thomas Appletree. *Thomas Appletree.*

Plume. And yours?

Costar Pearmain. *Costar Pearmain.*

Plume. Born where?

Costar Pearmain. Both in *Herefordshire.*

Plume. Very well; Courage, my Lads, now we will sing *Over
the Hills and far away.*

190   *Courage, Boys, 'tis one to ten,
          But we return all Gentlemen,*

162 full] om. in Q2   179 two] Q2; too   180 than] Q4; that
183 *Thomas Appletree*] 1728; 1st *Mob*   185 *Costar Pearmain*] 1728; 2d. *Mob*
187 *Costar Pearmain*] 1728; 1st *Mob*

While Conquering Colours we display,
Over the Hills and far away.

[*Exeunt.*]

[*The End of the Second Act.*]

ACT III. Scene i.

SCENE, *The Market-Place.*

Plume *and* Worthy.

Worthy. I can'nt forbear admiring the Equality of our two
Fortunes, we lov'd two Ladies; they met us half way, and just
as we were upon the point of leaping into their Arms, Fortune
drops into their Laps, Pride possesses their Hearts, a Maggot
fills their Heads, Madness takes 'em by the Tails, they snort,
kick up their Heels, and away they run.

Plume. And leave us here to mourn upon the Shore—a
couple of poor melancholy Monsters—What shall we do?

Worthy. I have a Trick for mine; the Letter you know, and
the Fortune-teller.   10

Plume. And I have a Trick for mine.

Worthy. What is't?

Plume. I'll never think of her again.

Worthy. No!

Plume. No; I think my self above administring to the Pride
of any Woman, were she worth twelve thousand a Year, and I
han't the Vanity to believe I shall ever gain a Lady worth
twelve hundred; the generous good-natur'd *Silvia* in her
Smock I admire, but the haughty scornful *Silvia*, with her
Fortune, I despise.   20

A SONG

I.

Come, fair one, be kind
You never shall find
A Fellow so fit for a Lover:

192–3 *While . . . away.*] 1728; [om.]

> *The World shall view*
> *My Passion for you,*
> *But never your Passion discover.*

2.

> *I still will complain*
> *Of Frowns and Disdain,*
> *Tho I revel thro' all your Charms:*
30 > *The World shall declare,*
> *I die with Despair,*
> *When only I die in your Arms,*

3.

> *I still will adore,*
> *Love more and more,*
> *But, by Jove, if you chance to prove cruel:*
> *I'll get me a Miss.*
> *That freely will kiss,*
> *Tho' after I drink Water-gruel.*

What! Sneak out o' Town, and not so much as a Word, a Line,
40 a Complement! 'Sdeath, how far off does she live? I'll go and
break her Windows.

Worthy. Ha, ha, ha; ay, and the Window Bars too to come
at her. Come, come Friend, no more of your rough Military
Airs.

Enter Kite.

Kite. Captain, Sir, look yonder, she's coming this way, 'tis
the prettiest cleanest little Tit—

Plume. Now, *Worthy,* to show you how much I'm in
Love—Here she comes, and what is that great Country Fellow
with her?

50 *Kite.* I can't tell, Sir.

Enter Rose *and her Brother* Bullock, Rose *with a Basket
on her Arm, crying Chickens.*

III.i. 28 [om.] *frowns*] Broadside; your ∼   Corrections in the Song are taken from
the engraved music. Farquhar probably originally wrote the words in Q1; when
Leveridge set the song, he had to revise slightly to fit the lyrics to the music
31 [om.] *I*] Broadside; *That* ∼   32 *only I*] Broadside; *I only*   34 [om.] *Love*]
Broadside; *And love*   38 *after I*] Broadside; *I afterwards*   40 I'll] Q2; I'd

Rose. Buy Chickens young and tender—young and tender Chickens.

Plume. Here, you Chickens—

Rose. Who calls?

Plume. Come hither, pretty Maid.

Rose. Will you please to buy, Sir?

Worthy. Yes, Child, we'll both buy.

Plume. Nay, *Worthy*, that's not fair, market for your self; come, my Child, I'll buy all you have.

Rose. Then all I have is at your Sarvice. (*Curtsies.*)   60

Worthy. Then I must shift for my self, I find.

                                                  Exit.

Plume. Let me see—Young and tender, you say? (*Chucks her under the Chin.*)

Rose. As ever you tasted in your Life, Sir. (*Curtsies.*)

Plume. Come, I must examine your Basket to the Bottom, my Dear.

Rose. Nay, for that matter, put in your hand, feel, Sir; I warrant my Ware as good as any in the Market.

Plume. And I'll buy it all, Child, were it ten times more.

Rose. Sir, I can furnish you.

Plume. Come then; we don't quarrel about the Price, 70 they're fine Birds; pray what's your Name, pretty Creature.

Rose. Rose, Sir, my Father is a Farmer within three short Mile o' th' Town; we keep this Market, I sell Chickens, Eggs, and Butter, and my Brother *Bullock* there sells Corn.

Bullock. Come, Sister, hast ye, we shall be liate a whome. (*All this while* Bullock *whistles about the Stage.*)

Plume. Kite! (*He tips the wink upon* Kite, *who returns it.*) Pretty Mrs. *Rose!* You have—Let me see—How many?

Rose. A Dozen, Sir—And they are richly worth a Crawn.

Bullock. Come *Ruose, Ruose,* I sold fifty Stracke o'Barley to Day in half this time; but you will higgle and higgle for a 80 Penny more than the Commodity is worth.

Rose. What's that to you, Oaf? I can make as much out of a Groat, as you can out of four-pence, I'm sure—The Gentleman bids fair, and when I meet with a Chapman, I know how to make the best on him—And so, Sir, I say, for a Crawn Piece the Bargain is yours.

Plume. Here's a Guinea, my Dear.

Rose. I con't change your Money, Sir.

Plume. Indeed, indeed but you can—My Lodging is hard
90 by, you shall bring home the Chickens, and we'll make
Change there.

Goes off, she follows him.

Kite. So, Sir, as I was telling you, I have seen one of these
Hussars eat up a Ravelin for his Breakfast, and afterwards pick
his Teeth with a Palisado.

Bullock. Ay, you Soldiers see very strange things—But pray
Sir, what is a Ravelin?

Kite. Why 'tis like a modern minc'd Pye, but the Crust is
confounded hard, and the Plumbs are somewhat hard of
Digestion!

100 *Bullock.* Then your Palisado, pray what may he be?—Come,
Ruose, pray ha' done.

Kite. Your Palisado is a pretty sort of Bodkin, about the
Thickness of my Leg.

Bullock. That's a Fib, I believe (*Aside.*)—Eh, where's *Ruose*,
Ruose, *Ruose*, 'sflesh, where's *Ruose* gone?

Kite. She's gone with the Captain.

Bullock. The Captain! Wauns, there's no pressing of Women,
sure.

Kite. But there is, Sir.

110 *Rose.* If the Captain shou'd press *Ruose*, I shou'd be ruin'd;
which way went she—O! The Devil take your Rablins and
Palisaders.

Exit.

Kite. You shall be better acquainted with them, honest
Bullock, or I shall miss of my Aim.

Enter Worthy.

Worthy. Why, thou'rt the most useful Fellow in Nature to
your Captain, admirable in your way, I find.

Kite. Yes, Sir, I understand my Business, I will say it; you
must know, Sir, I was born a Gypsie, and bred among that
Crew till I was ten Year old, there I learn'd Canting and
120 Lying; I was bought from my Mother *Cleopatra* by a certain
Nobleman for three Pistoles, who liking my Beauty made me

90 you shall bring home the] om. in Q2   121 Pistoles] Q2; Pistols

his Page, there I learn'd Impudence and Pimping; I was
turn'd off for wearing my Lord's Linen, and drinking my
Lady's Brandy, and then turn'd Bailiff's Follower, there I
learn'd Bullying and Swearing—I at last got into the Army,
and there I learn'd Whoring and Drinking—So that if your
Worship pleases to cast up the whole Sum, *viz.* Canting,
Lying, Impudence, Pimping, Bullying, Swearing, Whoring,
Drinking, and a Halbard, you will find the Sum Total will
amount to a Recruiting Serjeant.   130

Worthy. And pray, what induc'd you to turn Soldier?

Kite. Hunger and Ambition—The Fears of starving and
Hopes of a Truncheon, led me along to a Gentleman with a
fair Tongue and fair Perriwig, who loaded me with Promises;
but I gad 'twas the lightest Load that I ever felt in my
Life—He promis'd to advance me, and indeed he did so—To
a Garret in the *Savoy*—I ask'd him why he put me in Prsion, he
call'd me lying Dog, and said I was in Garrison, and indeed
'tis a Garison that may hold out till Doom's-day before I
shou'd desire to take it again; but here comes Justice *Ballance*. 140

Enter Ballance *and* Bullock.

Ballance. Here, you Serjeant, where's your Captain? Here's
a poor foolish Fellow comes clamouring to me with a
Complaint, that your Captain has press'd his Sister, do you
know any thing of this Matter, *Worthy*?

Worthy. Ha, ha, ha, I know his Sister is gone with *Plume* to
his Lodgings to sell him some Chickens.

Ballance. Is that all? The Fellow's a Fool.

Bullock. I know that, an't please you; but if your Worship
pleases to grant me a Warrant to bring her before you for fear
o'th' worst.   150

Ballance. Thou art a mad Fellow, thy Sister's safe enough.

Kite. I hope so too. (*Aside.*)

Worthy. Hast thou no more Sense, Fellow, than to believe
that the Captain can list Women?

Bullock. I know not whether they list them, or what they do
with them, but I'm sure they carry as many Women as Men
with them out of the Country.

---

124 Brandy] Q2 reads 'Ratafia'   151 Thou art a mad Fellow] Q2 reads
'Thou'rt mad, Fellow'

Ballance. But how came you not to go along with your Sister?

160 *Bullock*. Luord, Sir, I thought no more of her going than I do of the Day I shall die; but this Gentleman, here, not suspecting any Hurt neither, I believe—You thought no Harm, Friend, did ye?

Kite. Lack-a-day, Sir, not I—Only that I believe I shall marry her to Morrow. (*Aside*.)

Ballance. I begin to smell Powder—Well, Friend, but what did that Gentleman with you?

Bullock. Why, Sir, he entertain'd me with a fine Story of a great Fight between the *Hungarians*, I think it was, and the 170 *Irish*; and so, Sir, while we were in the heat of the Battel, the Captain carry'd off the Baggage.

Ballance. Serjeant, go along with this Fellow to your Captain, give him my humble Service, and I desire him to discharge the Wench, tho' he has listed her.

Bullock. Ay—And if he ben't free for that, he shall have another Man in her place.

Kite. Come, honest Friend—You shall go to my Quarters instead of the Captain's. (*Aside*.)

Exeunt Kite *and* Bullock.

Ballance. We must get this mad Captain his Compliment of 180 Men, and send him a packing, else he'll over-run the Country.

Worthy. You see, Sir, how little he values your Daughter's Disdain.

Ballance. I like him the better, I was just such another Fellow at his Age; I never set my Heart upon any Woman so much as to make me uneasie at the Disappointment, but what was very surprising both to my self and Friends, I chang'd o'th' sudden from the most fickle Lover to be the most constant Husband in the World; but how goes your Affair with *Melinda*?

190 *Worthy*. Very slowly, *Cupid* had formerly Wings, but I think in this Age he goes upon Crutches, or I fancy *Venus* had been dallying with her Cripple *Vulcan* when my Amour commenc'd, which has made it go on so lamely; my Mistress has got a Captain too, but such a Captain! As I live yonder he comes.

183 just] Q2; much   191 had] Q2; has

Ballance. Who? That bluff Fellow in the Sash. I don't know him.

Worthy. But I engage he knows you, and every Body at first sight, his Impudence were a Prodigy, were not his Ignorance proportionable; he has the most universal Acquaintance of any Man living, for he won't be alone, and no body will keep 200 him Company twice; then he's a *Cæsar* among the Women, *Veni, Vidi, Vici,* that's all. If he has but talk'd with the Maid, he swears he has lain with the Mistress; but the most surprizing part of his Character is his Memory, which is the most prodigious, and the most trifling in the World.

Ballance. I have met with such Men, and I take this good-for-nothing Memory to proceed from a certain Contexture of the Brain, which is purely adapted to Impertinencies, and there they lodge secure, the Owner having no Thoughts of his own to disturb them. I have known a Man as perfect as a 210 Chronologer as to the Day and Year of most important Transactions, but be altogether ignorant of the Causes, Springs, or Consequences of any one thing of moment; I have known another acquire so much by Travel, as to tell you the Names of most Places in *Europe*, with their Distances of Miles, Leagues or Hours, as punctually as a Post-boy; but for any thing else, as ignorant as the Horse that carries the Mail.

Worthy. This is your Man, Sir, add but the Traveller's Privilege of lying, and even that he abuses; this is the Picture, behold the Life!

220

Enter Brazen.

Brazen. Mr. *Worthy*, I'm your Servant, and so forth—Heark'e my Dear—

Worthy. Whispering, Sir, before Company is not Manners, and when no body's by, 'tis foolish.

Brazen. Company! *Mor't de ma vie,* I beg the Gentleman's Pardon, who is he?

Worthy. Ask him.

Brazen. So I will—My Dear, I'm your Servant, and so forth, your Name, my Dear?

Ballance. Very *Laconick*, Sir. 230

Brazen. Laconick, a very good Name truly; I have known several of the *Laconicks* abroad, poor *Jack Laconick*! He was kill'd at the Battel of *Landen.* I remember that he had a blew

Ribbond in his Hat that very Day, and after he fell, we found a piece of Neat's Tongue in his Pocket.

Ballance. Pray Sir, did the *French* attack us, or we them, at *Landen*?

Brazen. The *French* attack us! Oons, Sir, are you a *Jacobite*?

Ballance. Why that Question?

240 *Brazen.* Because none but a *Jacobite* cou'd think that the *French* durst attack us—No, Sir, we attack'd them on the—I have reason to remember the time, for I had two and twenty Horses kill'd under me that Day.

Worthy. Then, Sir, you rid mighty hard.

Ballance. Or perhaps, Sir, like my Countryman, you rid upon half a dozen Horses at once.

Brazen. What d'e mean, Gentlemen, I tell you they were kill'd; all torn to pieces by Cannon-shot, except six that I stak'd to Death upon the Enemies *Chevaux de Frise.*

250 *Ballance.* Noble Captain, may I crave your Name?

Brazen. Brazen, at your Service.

Ballance. Oh, *Brazen*! A very good Name, I have known several of the *Brazens* abroad.

Worthy. Do you know Captain *Plume*, Sir?

Brazen. Is he any thing related to *Frank Plume* in *Northamptonshire*—Honest *Frank*! Many, many a dry Bottle have we crack'd hand to fist; you must have known his Brother *Charles* that was concern'd in the *India* Company, he marry'd the Daughter of Old *Tongue-Pad* the Master in Chancery, a very

260 pretty Woman, only squinted a little; she dy'd in Child-bed of her first Child, but the Child surviv'd, 'twas a Daughter, but whether 'twas call'd *Margaret* or *Marjory*, upon my Soul I can't remember—But, Gentlemen (*Looking on his Watch.*) I must meet a Lady, a twenty thousand Pounder presently, upon the Walk by the Water—*Worthy*, your Servant, *Laconick*, yours.

Exit.

Ballance. If you can have so mean an Opinion of *Melinda*, as to be jealous of this Fellow, I think she ought to give you Cause to be so.

Worthy. I don't think she encourages him so much for

270 gaining her self a Lover, as to set me up a Rival; were there

<hr>

245 rid] Q2 reads 'must have rid'

The Recruiting Officer

any Credit to be given to his words, I shou'd believe *Melinda* had made him this Assignation; I must go see—Sir, you'll pardon me.

Ballance. Ay, ay, Sir, you're a Man of Business; but what have we got here?

Enter Rose *singing what she pleases.*

Rose. And I shall be a Lady, a Captain's Lady; and ride single upon a white Horse with a Star, upon a Velvet Side-saddle, and I shall go to *London* and see the Tombs and the Lions, and the Queen. Sir—an't please your Worship, I have often seen your Worship ride thro' our Grounds a hunting, 280 begging your Worship's Pardon—Pray what may this Lace be worth a Yard? (*Showing some Lace.*)

Ballance. Right *Mechelin*, by this Light! Where did you get this Lace, Child?

Rose. No matter for that, Sir, I come honestly by't.

Ballance. I question it much.

Rose. And see here, Sir, a fine *Turky*-shell Snuff-box, and fine *Mangeree*, see here; (*She takes Snuff affectedly.*) the Captain learnt me how to take it with an Air.

Ballance. Oho, the Captain! Now the Murder's out, and so 290 the Captain taught you to take it with an Air?

Rose. Yes, and give it with an Air, too—Will your Worship please to taste my Snuff. (*Offers the Box affectedly.*)

Ballance. You'r a very apt Scholar, pretty Maid, and pray what did you give the Captain for these fine things?

Rose. He's to have my Brother for a Soldier, and two or three Sweet-hearts that I have in the Country, they shall all go with the Captain; O he's the finest Man, and the humblest withal, wou'd you believe it, Sir? He carry'd me up with him to his own Chamber with as much Familiarity, as if I had 300 been the best Lady in the Land.

Ballance. O he's a mighty familiar Gentleman as can be.

Enter Plume *singing.*

302 be. [om.]] Q2: ~

Rose. But I must beg your Worship's Pardon, I must go seek out my Brother *Bullock.* (*Runs off singing.*)

Ballance. If all Officers took the same Method of Recruiting with this Gentleman, they might come in time to be Fathers as well as Captains of their Companies.

Rose's exit must be deleted because she has lines later in the scene. The omission of Ballance's line is explicable only in terms of salving the stage reformers.

Plume. But it is not so
  With those that go
  Thro' Frost and Snow
  Most apropo,
  My Maid with the Milking-pail. (Takes hold on Rose.)
How, the Justice! Then I'm arraign'd, condemn'd, and
executed. [*Aside.*]

310 *Ballance.* Oh, my Noble Captain.
  Rose. And my Noble Captain too, Sir.
  Plume. 'Sdeath, Child, are you mad?—Mr. *Ballance*, I am so
full of Business about my Recruits, that I ha'n't a Moment's
time to—I have just now three or four People to—
  Ballance. Nay, Captain, I must speak to you.
  Rose. And so must I too, Captain.
  Plume. Any other time, Sir; I cannot for my Life, Sir—
  Ballance. Pray, Sir.
  Plume. Twenty thousand things—I wou'd but—now, Sir,
320 pray—Devil take me—I cannot—I must—

Breaks away.

  Ballance. Nay, I'll follow you.

Exit.

  Rose. And I too.

Exit.

ACT III. Scene ii.

SCENE, *the Walk, by the* Severn *side.*

Enter Melinda *and her Maid* Lucy.

  Melinda. And pray, was it a Ring, or Buckle, or Pendants,
or Knots; or in what Shape was the Almighty Gold
transform'd that has brib'd you so much in his Favour?
  Lucy. Indeed, Madam, the last Bribe I had was from the
Captain, and that was only a small piece of *Flanders* edging for
Pinners.
  Melinda. Ay, *Flanders* Lace, is as constant a Present from
Officers to their Women, as something else is from their
Women to them. They every Year bring over a Cargo of Lace

to cheat the Queen of her Duty, and her Subjects of their 10
Honesty.

Lucy. They only barter one sort of prohibited Goods for
another, Madam.

Melinda. Has any of them been bartering with you,
Mrs. Pert, that you talk so like a Trader?

Lucy. Madam, you talk as peevishly to me as if it were my
Fault, the Crime is none of mine tho' I pretend to excuse it;
tho' he shou'd not see you this Week can I help it? But as I
was saying, Madam, his Friend Captain *Plume* has so taken
him up these two Days—   20

Melinda. Psha! wou'd his Friend, the Captain, were ty'd on
his Back; I warrant he has never been sober since that
confounded Captain came to Town: The Devil take all
Officers, I say, they do the Nation more harm by debauching
us at home, than they do good by defending us abroad: No
sooner a Captain comes to Town, but all the young Fellows
flock about him, and we can't keep a Man to our selves.

Lucy. One wou'd imagine, Madam, by your Concern for
Worthy's Absence, that you shou'd use him better when he's
with you.   30

Melinda. Who told you, pray, that I was concern'd for his
Absence? I'm only vex'd that I've had nothing said to me
these two Days: One may like the Love, and despise the
Lover, I hope; as one may love the Treason, and hate the
Traytor. Oh! here comes another Captain, and a Rogue that
has the Confidence to make Love to me; but indeed I don't
wonder at that, when he has the Assurance to fancy himself a
fine Gentleman.

Lucy. If he shou'd speak o'th' Assignation, I shou'd be
ruin'd. (*Aside.*)   40
                    Enter Brazen.

Brazen. True to the Touch, Faith. (*Aside.*) I'll draw up all
my Complements into one grand Platoon, and fire upon her at
once.

> *Thou peerless Princess of* Salopian *Plains,*
> *Envy'd by Nymphs, and worship'd by the Swains,*
> *Behold how humbly do's the* Severn *glide,*
> *To greet thee Princess of the* Severn *side.*

III.ii. 41–7 I'll draw . . . Severn *side.*] om. in Q2

Madam, I'm your humble Servant, and all that, Madam—A
fine River this same *Severn*, do you love Fishing, Madam?

50   *Melinda.* 'Tis a pretty melancholy Amusement for Lovers.

Brazen. I'll go buy Hooks and Lines presently; for you must
know, Madam, that I have serv'd in *Flanders* against the
French, in *Hungary* against the *Turks*, and in *Tangier* against the
Moors, and I was never so much in Love before; and split me,
Madam, in all the Campaigns I ever made I have not seen so
fine a Woman as your Ladyship.

Melinda. And from all the Men I ever saw I never had so
fine a Complement; but you Soldiers are the best bred Men,
that we must allow.

60   *Brazen.* Some of us, Madam, but there are Brutes among us
too, very sad Brutes; for my own part, I have always had the
good Luck to prove agreeable: I have had very considerable
Offers, Madam, I might have marry'd a *German* Princess
worth Fifty thousand Crowns a Year, but her Stove disgusted
me; the Daughter of a *Turkish Bashaw* fell in Love with me too
when I was Prisoner among the Infidels, she offer'd to rob her
Father of his Treasure, and make her Escape with me, but I
don't know how, my time was not come, Hanging and
Marriage, you know, go by Destiny; Fate has reserved me for

70   a *Shropshire* Lady with twenty thousand Pound—Do you know
any such Person, Madam?

Melinda. Extravagant Coxcomb! [*Aside.*] to be sure a great
many Ladies of that Fortune wou'd be proud of the Name of
Mrs. *Brazen.*

Brazen. Nay, for that matter, Madam, there are Women of
very good Quality of the Name of *Brazen.*

                    Enter Worthy.

Melinda. O! are you there, Gentleman?—Come, Captain,
we'll walk this way, give me your Hand.

Brazen. My Hand, Heart's Blood and Guts are at your

80   Service.—Mr. *Worthy*,—your Servant, my Dear.

                    Exit leading Melinda.

Worthy. Death and Fire! this is not to be born.

                    Enter Plume.

Plume. No more it is, Faith.

Worthy. What?

Plume. The *March* Beer at the *Raven*; I have been doubly

serving the Queen,—raising Men, and raising the Excise—
Recruiting and Elections are good Friends to the Excise.

Worthy. You an't drunk?

Plume. No, no, whimsical only; I cou'd be mighty foolish,
and fancy my self mighty witty; Reason still keeps its Throne,
but it nods a little, that's all.   90

Worthy. Then you're just fit for a Frolick?

Plume. As fit as close Pinners for a Punk in the Pit.

Worthy. There's your Play then, recover me that Vessel
from that *Tangerine.*

Plume. She's well rigg'd, but how is she mann'd?

Worthy. By Captain *Brazen* that I told you of to Day; the
Frigot is call'd the *Melinda,* a first Rate I can assure you; she
sheer'd off with him just now on purpose to affront me, but
according to your Advice I wou'd take no notice, because I
wou'd seem to be above a Concern for her Behaviour; but 100
have a care of a Quarrel.

Plume. No, no, I never quarrel with any thing in my Cups
but with an Oyster Wench or a Cook Maid, and if they ben't
civil, I knock 'em down: But heark'e my Friend, I will make
Love, and I must make Love—I tell'e what, I'll make Love
like a Platoon.

Worthy. A Platoon! how's that?

Plume. I'll kneel, stoop and stand, Faith; most Ladies are
gain'd by Platooning.

Worthy. Here they come; I must leave you.   110

                                         Exit.

Plume. Soh—Now I must look as sober and demure as a
Whore at a Christning.

             Enter Brazen *and* Melinda.

Brazen. Who's that, Madam?

Melinda. A Brother Officer of yours, I suppose.

Brazen. Ay!—My Dear. (*To* Plume.)

Plume. My Dear! (*They run and embrace.*)

Brazen. My dear Boy, how is't?—Your Name, my Dear, if I
be not mistaken, I have seen your Face.

Plume. I never see your's in my Life, my Dear—But there's
a Face well known as the Sun's, that shines on all, and is by all 120
ador'd.

Brazen. Have you any Pretensions, Sir?

Plume. Pretensions!

Brazen. That is, Sir, have you ever serv'd abroad?

Plume. I have serv'd at Home, Sir; For Ages serv'd this cruel Fair—And that will serve the turn, Sir.

Melinda. Soh—Between the Fool and the Rake, I shall bring a fine spot of Work upon my hands—I see *Worthy* yonder, I cou'd be content to be Friends with him wou'd he
130 come this way. (*Aside.*)

Brazen. Will you fight for the Lady, Sir?

Plume. No, Sir, but I'll have her notwithstanding.

> *Thou Peerless Princess of* Salopian *Plains,*
> *Envy'd by Nymphs, and worshipp'd by the Swains.*

Brazen. Oons, Sir, not fight for her!

Plume. Prithee be quiet, I shall be out.

> *Behold how humbly do's the* Severn *glide*
> *To greet thee, Princess of the* Severn *side.*

Brazen. Don't mind him, Madam, if he were not so well
140 drest I shou'd take him for a Poet; but I'll show the Difference presently—Come, Madam, we'll place you between us, and now the longest Sword carries her. (*Draws,* Melinda *shrieks.*)

Enter Worthy.

Melinda. Oh! Mr. *Worthy,* save me from these Madmen.

> *Runs off with* Worthy.

Plume. Ha, ha, ha, why don't you follow, Sir, and fight the bold Ravisher?

Brazen. No, Sir, you're my Man.

Plume. I don't like the Wages, and I won't be your Man.

Brazen. Then you're not worth my Sword.

Plume. No! Pray what did it cost?

150 *Brazen.* It cost me twenty Pistoles in *France,* and my Enemies thousands of Lives in *Flanders.*

Plume. Then they had a dear Bargain.

Enter Silvia *drest in Man's Apparel.*

Silvia. Save ye, save ye, Gentlemen.

Brazen. My Dear, I'm yours.

Plume. Do you know the Gentleman?

Brazen. No, but I will presently—Your Name, my Dear.

150–1 It cost . . . *Flanders.*] Q2; It cost my Enemies thousands of Lives, Sir.

Silvia. *Wilfull, Jack Wilfull*, at your Service.

Brazen. What! The *Kentish Wilfulls*, or those of *Staffordshire?*

Silvia. Both sir, both; I'm related to all the *Wilfulls* in *Europe*, and I'm Head of the Family at present.   160

Plume. Do you live in this Country, Sir?

Silvia. Yes, Sir, I live where I stand; I have neither Home, House, nor Habitation beyond this spot of Ground.

Brazen. What are you, Sir?

Silvia. A Rake.

Plume. In the Army I presume.

Silvia. No, but I intend to list immediately—Look'e, Gentlemen, he that bids me fairest shall have me.

Brazen. Sir, I'll prefer you, I'll make you a Corporal this Minute.   170

Plume. A Corporal! I'll make you my Companion, you shall eat with me.

Brazen. You shall drink with me.

Plume. You shall lie with me, you young Rogue. (*Kisses her.*)

Brazen. You shall receive your Pay, and do no Duty.

Silvia. Then you must make me a Field-Officer.

Plume. Pho, pho, I'll do more than all this, I'll make you a Corporal, and give you a Brevet for Serjeant.

Brazen. Can you read and write, Sir?

Silvia. Yes.   180

Brazen. Then your Business is done, I'll make you Chaplain to the Regiment.

Silvia. Your Promises are so equal, that I'm at a loss to chuse, there is one *Plume* that I hear much commended in Town, pray which of you is Captain *Plume?*

Plume. I'm Captain *Plume.*

Brazen. No, no, I am Captain *Plume.*

Silvia. Hey day!

Plume. Captain *Plume*, I'm your Servant, my Dear.

Brazen. Captain *Brazen*, I'm yours—The Fellow dare not 190 fight.

Enter Kite.

Kite. Sir, if you please—(*Goes to whisper* Plume.)

Plume. No, no, there's your Captain—Captain *Plume*, your

Serjeant here has got so drunk he mistakes me for you.

Brazen. He's an incorrigible Sot—Here, my *Hector* of *Holbourn*, forty Shillings for you.

Plume. I forbid the Banes—Look'e, Friend, you shall list with Captain *Brazen*.

Silvia. I will see Captain *Brazen* hang'd first, I will list with
200 Captain *Plume*; I'm a free born *Englishman*, and will be a Slave my own way—Look'e, Sir, will you stand by me? (*To* Brazen)

Brazen. I warrant you, my Lad.

Silvia. Then I will tell you, Captain *Brazen* (*To* Plume.) that you are an ignorant, pretending, impudent Coxcomb.

Brazen. Ay, ay, a sad Dog.

Silvia. A very sad Dog, give me the Money Noble Captain *Plume*.

Plume. Hold, hold, then you won't list with Captain *Brazen*?

Silvia. I won't.

210 *Brazen.* Never mind him, Child, I'll end the Dispute presently; heark'e, my Dear. (*Takes* Plume *to one side of the Stage, and entertains him in dumb Show*.)

Kite. Sir, he in the plain Coat is Captain *Plume*, I'm his Serjeant, and will take my Oath on't.

Silvia. What! Are you Serjeant *Kite*?

Kite. At your Service.

Silvia. Then I wou'd not take your Oath for a Farthing.

Kite. A very understanding Youth of his Age! Pray Sir, let me look you full in the Face.

Silvia. Well, Sir, what have you to say to my Face?

220 *Kite.* The very Image and Superscription of my Brother, two Bullets of the same Caliber were never so like; sure it must be *Charles*, *Charles*—

Silvia. What d'ye mean by *Charles*?

Kite. The Voice too, only a little Variation in C fa ut flat; my dear Brother, for I must call you so, if you shou'd have the Fortune to enter into the most Noble Society of the Sword, I bespeak you for a Comrade.

Silvia. No, Sir, I'll be your Captain's Comrade if any body's.

230 *Kite.* Ambition! There again, 'tis a noble Passion for a

208 Hold, hold,] om. in Q2   220 and Superscription] om. in Q2
224 C fa] Q2 reads 'Effa'

Soldier; by that I gain'd this glorious Halberd. Ambition! I
see a Commission in his Face already, pray noble Captain
give me leave to salute you. (*Offers to kiss her.*)

Silvia. What! Men kiss one another!

Kite. We Officers do, 'tis our way; we live together like Man
and Wife, always either kissing or fighting—But I see a Storm
a coming.

Silvia. Now, Serjeant, I shall see who is your Captain by
your knocking down the t'other.

Kite. My Captain scorns Assistance, Sir.   240

Brazen. How dare you contend for any thing, and not dare
to draw your Sword? But you're a young Fellow, and have not
been much abroad, I excuse that; but prithee resign the Man,
prithee do, you're a very honest Fellow.

Plume. You lye, and you're a Son of a Whore. (*Draws, and
makes up to* Brazen.)

Brazen. (*Retiring.*) Hold, hold, did not you refuse to fight for
the Lady?

Plume. I always do, but for a Man I'll fight Knee deep, so
you lye again.

> Plume *and* Brazen *fight a Traverse or two about the Stage;*
> Silvia *draws, and is held by* Kite, *who sounds to Arms
> with his Mouth, takes* Sylvia *in his Arms, and carries her
> off the Stage.*

Brazen. Hold—Where's the Man?   250

Plume. Gone.

Brazen. Then what do we fight for? (*Puts up.*) Now let's
embrace, my Dear.

Plume. With all my heart, my Dear, (*Puts up.*) I suppose *Kite*
has listed him by this time. (*They embrace.*)

Brazen. You're a brave Fellow, I always fight with a Man
before I make him my Friend; and if once I find he will fight, I
never quarrel with him afterwards—And now I'll tell you a
Secret, my dear Friend, that Lady that we frighted out o' the
Walk just now I found in Bed this Morning, so beautiful, so   260
inviting—I presently lock'd the Door—But I'm a Man of
Honour—But I believe I shall marry her nevertheless; her
twenty thousand Pound you know will be a pretty Convenience,
I had an Assignation with her here, but your coming spoil'd
my Sport, curse ye, my Dear,—But don't do so again.

Plume. No, no, my dear, Men are my Business at present.
                                                    Exeunt.

[*The End of the Third Act.*]

ACT IV. [Scene i.]

SCENE *of the Walk continues.*

Rose *and* Bullock *meeting.*

Rose. Where have you been, you great Booby, you're always out o'th' way in the time of Preferment?

Bullock. Preferment! who shou'd prefer me?

Rose. I wou'd prefer you, who shou'd prefer a Man but a Woman? Come throw away that great Club, hold up your Head, cock your Hat, and look big.

Bullock. Ah! *Ruose, Ruose,* I fear somebody will look big sooner than Folk think of; this genteel Breeding never comes into the Country without a Train of Followers.—Here has
10 been *Cartwheel* your Sweet-heart, what will become o' him?

Rose. Look'e, I'm a great Woman, and will provide for my Relations; I told the Captain how finely he could play upon the Tabor and Pipe, so he has set him down for a Drum-Major.

Bullock. Nay, Sister, why did not you keep that Place for me? You know I always lov'd to be a drumming, if it were but on a Table, or on a Quart Pot.

Enter Silvia.

Silvia. Had I but a Commission in my Pocket I fancy my Breeches wou'd become me as well as any ranting Fellow of 'um
20 all; for I take a bold Step, a rakish Toss, a smart Cock, and an impudent Air to be the principal Ingredients in the Composition of a Captain.—What's here, *Rose,* my Nurse's Daughter? I'll go and practice—Come, Child kiss me at once, (*Kisses* Rose.) And her Brother too! [*Aside.*]—Well, honest Dungfork, do you know the Difference between a Horse Cart, and a Cart Horse, eh?

Bullock. I presume that your Worship is a Captain by your Cloaths and your Courage.

Silvia. Suppose I were, wou'd you be contended to list, Friend?   30

Rose. No, no, tho' your Worship be a handsome Man, there be others as fine as you; my Brother is engag'd to Captain *Plume.*

Silvia. Plume! do you know Captain *Plume?*

Rose. Yes, I do, and he knows me.—He took the very Ribbands out of his Shirt Sleeves, and put them into my Shoes.—See there—I can assure you that I can do any thing with the Captain.

Bullock. That is, in a modest way, Sir.—Have a care what you say, *Ruose,* don't shame your Parentage.   40

Rose. Nay, for that matter I am not so simple as to say that I can do any thing with the Captain, but what I may do with any body else.

Silvia. Soh,!—and pray what do you expect from this Captain, Child?

Rose. I expect, Sir! I expect,—but he order'd me to tell no body—but suppose that he shou'd promise to marry me.

Silvia. You shou'd have a care, my Dear, Men will promise any thing before-hand.

Rose. I know that, but he promis'd to marry me afterwards. 50

Bullock. Wauns, *Ruose,* what have you said?

Silvia. Afterwards! after what?

Rose. After I had sold him my Chickens,—I hope there's no Harm in that, tho' there be an ugly Song of Chickens and Sparragus.

Enter Plume.

Plume. What! Mr. *Wilfull,* so close with my Market Woman!

Silvia. I'll try if he loves her. (*Aside.*) Close, Sir! ay, and closer yet, Sir—Come, my pretty Maid, you and I will withdraw a little—   60

Plume. No, no, Friend, I han't done with her yet.

Silvia. Nor have I begun with her, so I have as good a Right as you have.

Plume. Thou art a bloody impudent Fellow.

IV.i 37 you] Q2; [om.]   54–5 tho there be an ugly Song of Chickens and Sparragus] om. in Q2

Silvia. Sir, I wou'd qualifie my self for the Service.

Plume. Hast thou really a Mind to the Service?

Silvia. Yes, Sir: So let her go.

Rose. Pray, Gentlemen, don't be so violent.

Plume. Come, leave it to the Girl's own Choice.—Will you
70 belong to me or to that Gentleman?

Rose. Let me consider, you're both very handsom.

Plume. Now the natural Unconstancy of her Sex begins to
work.

Rose. Pray, Sir, what will you give me?

Bullock. Don't be angry, Sir, that my Sister shou'd be
Mercenary, for she's but young.

Silvia. Give thee, Child!—I'll set thee above Scandal; you
shall have a Coach with Six before and Six behind, an
Equipage to make Vice fashionable, and put Vertue out of
80 Countenance.

Plume. Pho, that's easily done, I'll do more for thee, Child,
I'll buy you a furbuloe Scarf, and give you a Ticket to see a
Play.

Bullock. A Play, Wauns *Ruose* take the Ticket, and let's see
the Show.

Silvia. Look'e, Captain, if you won't resign, I'll go list with
Captain *Brazen* this Minute.

Plume. Will you list with me if I give up my Title?

Silvia. I will.

90 *Plume.* Take her: I'll change a Woman for a Man at any
time.

Rose. But I hope, Captain, you won't part with me. (*Crys.*) I
have heard before indeed that you Captains use to sell your
Men.

65-90 *Silvia.* Sir, I wou'd . . . *Plume.* Take her:] Q1 reads:
    Plume. . . .—let her go, I say.
    Silvia. Do you let her go.
    Plume. Entendez vous Francois, mon petit Garson.
    Silvia. Ouy.
    Plume. Si voulez vous donc vous enroller dans ma Companie, la damoiselle sera a vous.
    Silvia. Avez vous couche aver elle.
    Plume. Non.
    Silvia. Assurement?
    Plume. Ma foi.
    Silvia. C'est assez—Je serai votre soldat.
    Plume. La prenez donc—
92 But I hope, Captain, you won't part with me. (*Crys.*)] om. in Q2

Bullock. (*Crying.*) Pray, Captain, don't send *Ruose* to the West-Indies.

Plume. Ha, ha, ha, *West-Indies*! no, no, my honest Lad, give me thy Hand, nor you, nor she shall move a step farther than I do.—This Gentleman is one of us, and will be kind to you, Mrs. *Rose.*   100

Rose. But will you be so kind to me, Sir, as the Captain wou'd?

Silvia. I can't be altogether so kind to you, my Circumstances are not so good as the Captain's—but I'll take care of you, upon my Word.

Plume. Ay, ay, we'll all take care of her,—She shall live like a Princess, and her Brother here shall be—what wou'd you be?

Bullock. Ah! Sir, if you had not promis'd the Place of Drum-Major.   110

Plume. Ay, that is promis'd—but what think ye of Barrack-Master? You're a Person of Understanding, and Barrack-Master you shall be.—But what's become of this same *Cartwheel* you told me of, my dear?

Rose. We'll go fetch him—Come, Brother Barrack-Master —We shall find you at home, noble Captain?

> *Exeunt* Rose *and* Bullock.

Plume. Yes, yes—and now, Sir, here are your forty Shillings.

Silvia. Captain *Plume*, I despise your Listing-money, if I do serve, 'tis purely for Love—of that Wench I mean; for you must know, that among my other Sallies, I have spent the best 120 part of my Fortune in search of a Maid, and cou'd never find one hitherto; so you may be assur'd that I won't sell my Freedom under a less Purchase than I did my Estate,—so before I list I must be certify'd that this Girl is a Virgin.

Plume. Mr. *Wilfull*, I can't tell how you can be certify'd in that point, till you try, but upon my Honour she may be a Vestal for ought that I know to the contrary.—I gain'd her Heart indeed by some trifling Presents and Promises, and knowing that the best Security for a Woman's Soul is her Body, I wou'd have made my self Master of that too, had not 130 the Jealousie of my impertinent Landlady interpos'd.

123 that I won't] Q2 reads 'I'd'

Silvia. So you only want an Opportunity for accomplishing your Designs upon her.

Plume. Not at all, I have already gain'd my Ends, which were only the drawing in one or two of her Followers; the Women, you know, are the Loadstones every where—gain the Wives, and you're caress'd by the Husbands; please the Mistresses, and you are valu'd by their Gallants; secure an Interest with the finest Women at Court, and you procure the
140 Favour of the greatest Men: So kiss the prettiest Country Wenches, and you are sure of listing the lustiest Fellows. Some People may call this Artifice, but I term it Stratagem, since it is so main a part of the Service—Besides, the Fatigue of Recruiting is so intollerable, that unless we cou'd make our selves some Pleasure amidst the Pain, no mortal Man wou'd be able to bear it.

Silvia. Well, Sir, I'm satisfy'd as to the Point in Debate— But now let me beg you to lay aside your Recruiting Airs, put on the Man of Honour, and tell me plainly what Usage I must
150 expect when I'm under your Command.

Plume. You must know in the first place then, that I hate to have Gentlemen in my Company, for they are always troublesome and expensive, sometimes dangerous; and 'tis a constant Maxim among us, That those who know the least, obey the best.—Notwithstanding all this, I find something so agreeable about you, that engages me to court your Company; and I can't tell how it is, but I shou'd be uneasy to see you under the Command of any body else.—Your Usage will chiefly depend upon your Behaviour, only this you must
160 expect, that if you commit a small Fault I will excuse it, if a great one, I'll discharge you, for something tells me I shall not be able to punish you.

Silvia. And something tells me, that if you do discharge me 'twill be the greatest Punishment you will inflict; for were we this moment to go upon the greatest Dangers in your Profession, they wou'd be less terrible to me, than to stay behind you.—And now your Hand,—this lists me—and now you are my Captain.

Plume. Your Friend—(*Kisses her.*) 'Sdeath! there's something
170 in this Fellow that charms me.

143 Fatigue] Q2; Fatigues

Silvia. One Favour I must beg—This Affair will make some Noise, and I have some Friends that wou'd censure my Conduct if I threw my self into the Circumstances of a private Centinel of my own Head, I must therefore take care to be impress'd by the Act of Parliament, you shall leave that to me—

Plume. What you please as to that—Will you lodge at my Quarters in the mean time? You shall have part of my Bed.

Silvia. O fie, lye with a Common Soldier!—wou'd not you rather lye with a common Woman? 180

Plume. No, Faith, I am not that Rake that the World imagines, I have got an Air of Freedom, which People mistake for Lewdness in me, as they mistake Formality in others for Religion; the World is all a Cheat, only I take mine which is undesign'd to be more excusable than theirs, which is hypocritical; I hurt no body but my self, and they abuse all Mankind—Will you lye with me?

Silvia. No, no, Captain, you forget *Rose*, she's to be my Bedfellow you know.

Plume. I had forgot, pray be kind to her. 190

Exeunt severally.

[ACT IV. Scene ii.]

Enter Melinda *and* Lucy.

Melinda. 'Tis the greatest Misfortune in Nature for a Woman to want a Confident, we are so weak that we can do nothing without Assistance, and then a Secret racks us worse than the Cholick; I'm at this Minute so sick of a Secret, that I'm ready to faint away—help me, *Lucy.*

Lucy. Bless me, Madam, what's the matter?

Melinda. Vapours only—I begin to recover—if *Silvia* were in Town, I cou'd heartily forgive her Faults for the Ease of discovering my own.

Lucy. You're thoughtful, Madam, am not I worthy to know 10 the Cause?

Melinda. You're a Servant, and a Secret wou'd make you saucy.

Lucy. Not unless you shou'd find fault without a Cause, Madam.

Melinda. Cause or not Cause, I must not lose the Pleasure of chiding when I please; Women must discharge their Vapours some where, and before we get Husbands, our Servants must expect to bear with 'um.

20 *Lucy.* Then, Madam, you had better raise me to a degree above a Servant, you know my Family, and that five hundred Pound wou'd set me upon the Foot of a Gentlewoman, and make me worthy the Confidence of any Lady in the Land; besides, Madam, 'twill extremely encourage me in the great Design that I now have in hand.

Melinda. I don't find that your Design can be of any great Advantage to you, 'twill please me indeed in the Humour I have of being reveng'd on the Fool for his Vanity of making Love to me, so I don't much care if I do promise you five

30 hundred Pound the Day of my Marriage.

Lucy. That is the way, Madam, to make me diligent in the Vocation of a Confident, which I think is generally to bring People together.

Melinda. O, *Lucy,* I can hold my Secret no longer—You must know that hearing of the famous Fortune-teller in Town, I went disguis'd to satisfie a Curiosity which has cost me dear; that Fellow is certainly the Devil, or one of his Bosom-favourites, he has told me the most surprising things of my past Life—

40 *Lucy.* Things past, Madam, can hardly be reckon'd surprising, because we know them already; did he tell you any thing surprising that was to come.

Melinda. One thing very surprizing, he said I shou'd die a Maid.

Lucy. Die a Maid—Come into the World for nothing! Dear Madam, if you shou'd believe him, it might come to pass; for the bare Thought on't might kill one in four and twenty Hours—And did you ask him any Questions about me?

Melinda. You! Why, I pass'd for you.

50 *Lucy.* So 'tis I that am to die a Maid—But the Devil was a Lyar from the beginning, he can't make me die a Maid—I have put it out of his Power already.

Melinda. I do but jest, I wou'd have pass'd for you, and

call'd my self *Lucy*, but he presently told me my Name, my
Quality, my Fortune, and gave me the whole History of my
Life; he told me of a Lover I had in this Country, and
describ'd *Worthy* exactly, but in nothing so well as in his
present Indifference—I fled to him for Refuge here to
day—He never so much as incourag'd me in my Fright, but
coldly told me that he was sorry for the Accident, because it 60
might give the Town cause to censure my Conduct; excus'd
his not waiting on me home, made me a careless Bow, and
walk'd off. 'Sdeath, I cou'd have stab'd him, or my self, 'twas
the same thing—Yonder he comes—I will so slave him.

Lucy. Don't exasperate him, consider what the Fortune-
teller told you, Men are scarce; and as Times go, it is not
impossible for a Woman to die a Maid.

Enter Worthy.

Melinda. No matter.

Worthy. I find she's warm'd, I must strike while the Iron is
hot,—You have a great deal of Courage, Madam, to venture 70
into the Walks where you were so late frighted.

Melinda. And you have a Quantity of Impudence to appear
before me, that you have so lately affronted.

Worthy. I had no design to affront you, nor appear before
you either, Madam; I left you here, because I had Business in
another Place, and came hither thinking to meet another
Person.

Melinda. Since you find your self disappointed, I hope
you'll withdraw to another part of the Walk.

Worthy. The Walk is as free for me as you, Madam, and 80
broad enough for us both. (*They walk one by another, he with his
Hat cockt, she fretting and tearing her Fan.*) Will you please to take
Snuff, Madam. (*He offers her his Box, she strikes it out of his hand,
while he is gathering it up, enter* Brazen *who takes* Melinda *about the
Middle, she cuffs him.*)

Brazen. What! Here before me! My Dear.

Melinda. What means this Insolence?

Lucy. (*Runs to* Brazen.) Are you mad? Don't you see Mr.
Worthy?

Brazen. No, no, I'm struck blind—*Worthy*! Adso, well

turn'd, my Mistress has Wit at her Fingers ends—Madam, I
90 ask your pardon, 'tis our way abroad—Mr. *Worthy*, you're the
happy Man.

   Worthy. I don't envy your Happiness very much, if the
Lady can afford no other sort of Favours but what she has
bestow'd upon you.

   Melinda. I'm sorry the Favour miscarry'd, for it was
design'd for you, Mr. *Worthy*; and be assur'd, 'tis the last and
only Favour you must expect at my hands—Captain, I ask
your Pardon—

                                          Exit with Lucy.

   Brazen. I grant it—You see, Mr. *Worthy*, 'twas only a
100 random shot, it might ha' taken off your Head as well as
mine—Courage, my Dear, 'tis the Fortune of War—But the
Enemy has thought fit to withdraw, I think.

   Worthy. Withdraw! Oons, Sir, what d'ye mean by withdraw?

   Brazen. I'll show you.

                                                   Exit.

   Worthy. She's lost, irrecoverably lost, and *Plume*'s Advice
has ruin'd me; 'sdeath, why shou'd I that knew her haughty
Spirit be rul'd by a Man that is a Stranger to her Pride.

                              Enter Plume.

   Plume. Ha, ha, ha, a Battel Royal; don't frown so, Man,
she's your own, I tell'e; I saw the Fury of her Love in the
110 Extremity of her Passion, the Wildness of her Anger is a
certain sign that she loves you to Madness; that Rogue, *Kite*,
began the Battel with abundance of Conduct, and will bring
you off victorious, my Life on't; he plays his Part admirably,
she's to be with him again presently.

   Worthy. But what cou'd be the meaning of *Brazen*'s Familiarity with her.

   Plume. You are no Logician if you pretend to draw
Consequences from the Actions of Fools, there's no arguing by
the Rule of Reason upon a Science without Principles, and
120 such is their Conduct; Whim, unaccountable Whim, hurries
them on, like a Man drunk with Brandy before ten a Clock in
the Morning—But we lose our sport, *Kite* has open'd above an
Hour ago, let's away.

                                                Exeunt.

[ACT IV. Scene iii.]

SCENE, *A Chamber, a Table with Books and Globes.*

Kite *disguis'd in a strange Habit, and sitting at the Table.*

Kite. (*Rising.*) By the Position of the Heavens, gain'd from my Observation upon these Celestial Globes, I find that *Luna* was a Tide-waiter, *Sol* a Surveyor, *Mercury* a Thief, *Venus* a Whore, *Saturn* an Alderman, *Jupiter* a Rake, and *Mars* a Serjeant of Granadeers—And this is the Sistem of *Kite* the Conjurer.

Enter Plume *and* Worthy.

Plume. Well, what Success?

Kite. I have sent away a Shoemaker and a Taylor already, one's to be a Captain of Marines, and the other a Major of Dragoons, I am to manage them at Night—Have you seen the 10 Lady Mr. *Worthy?*

Worthy. Ay, But it won't do—Have you show'd her her Name that I tore off from the bottom of the Letter?

Kite. No, Sir, I reserve that for the last stroak.

Plume. What Letter?

Worthy. One that I wou'd not let you see, for fear you shou'd break *Melinda's* Windows in good earnest. (*Knocking at the Door.*)

Kite. Officers to your Post—*Tycho*, mind the Door.

Exeunt Worthy *and* Plume.

Servant *opens the Door, and enter a* Smith.

Smith. Well, Master, are you the cunning Man?

Kite. I am the learn'd *Copernicus.*   20

Smith. Well, Master *Coppernose*, I'm but a poor Man, and I can't afford above a Shilling for my Fortune.

Kite. Perhaps, that is more than 'tis worth.

Smith. Look'e, Doctor, Let me have something that's good for my Shilling, or I'll have my Money again.

Kite. If there be Faith in the Stars, you shall have your Shilling forty fold. You're hand, Countryman—You are by Trade a Smith.

Smith. How the Devil shou'd you know that?

30 *Kite.* Because the Devil and you are Brother Tradesmen— You were born under *Forceps*.

Smith. *Forceps*! What's that?

Kite. One of the Signs; there's *Leo, Sagitarius, Forceps, Furns, Dixmude, Namur, Brussels, Charleroy*, and so forth—Twelve of 'em—Let me see—Did you ever make any Bombs or Cannon Bullets.

Smith. Not I.

Kite. You either have, or will—The Stars have decreed, that you shall be—I must have more Money, Sir, your 40 Fortune's great—

Smith. Faith, Doctor, I have no more.

Kite. O, Sir, I'll trust you, and take it out of your Arrears.

Smith. Arrears! What Arrears?

Kite. The five hundred Pound that's owing to you from the Government.

Smith. Owing me!

Kite. Owing you, Sir—Let me see your t'other hand—I beg your pardon, it will be owing to you; and the Rogue of an Agent will demand fifty *per Cent.* for a Fortnight's Advance.

50 *Smith.* I'm in the Clouds, Doctor, all this while.

Kite. So am I, Sir, among the Stars—In two Years, three Months, and two Hours, you will be made Captain of the Forges to the grand Train of Artillery, and will have ten Shillings a Day, and two Servants; 'tis the Decree of the Stars, and of the fix'd Stars, that are as immoveable as your Anvil—Strike, Sir, while the Iron is hot—Fly, Sir, be gone—

Smith. What, what wou'd you have me do, Doctor? I wish the Stars wou'd put me in a way for this fine Place.

Kite. The Stars do—Let me see—Ay, about an Hour hence 60 walk carelesly into the Market-place, and you'll see a tall slender Gentleman cheapning a Pen'worth of Apples, with a Cane hanging upon his Button—This Gentleman will ask you—What'sa Clock—He's your Man, and the Maker of your Fortune; follow him, follow him: And now go home, and take leave of your Wife and Children—An Hour hence exactly is your time—

35 Cannon] Q2; Cannons   51 So am I, Sir,] Q2 reads 'Sir, I am above' em,'

Smith. A tall slender Gentleman you say! With a Cane, pray what sort of a Head has the Cane?

Kite. An Amber Head, with a black Ribband.

Smith. But pray, of what Employment is the Gentleman?   70

Kite. Let me see—He's either a Collector of the Excise, a Plenipotentiary, or a Captain of Granadeers—I can't tell exactly which—But he'll call you honest—Your Name is—

Smith. Thomas.

Kite. Right, he'll call you honest *Tom*—

Smith. But how the Devil shou'd he know my Name?

Kite. O, there are several sorts of *Toms*—*Tom a Lincoln, Tom-tit, Tom Telltroth, Tom o' Bedlam, Tom Fool*—(*Knocking at the Door.*) Be gone—An Hour hence precisely—

Smith. You say he'll ask me what's a Clock?   80

Kite. Most certainly, and you'll answer—You don't know, and be sure you look at St. *Mary*'s Dial, for the Sun won't shine, and if it shou'd, you won't be able to tell the Figures.

Smith. I will, I will.   *Exit.*

Plume. (*Behind.*) Well done, Conjurer, go on and prosper.

Kite. As you were.

Enter a Butcher.

Kite. What! My old Friend *Pluck*, the Butcher—I offer'd the surly Bull-dog five Guineas this Morning, and he refus'd it. (*Aside.*)

Butcher. So, Master Conjurer—Here's half a Crown—And now you must understand—   90

Kite. Hold, Friend, I know your Business beforehand.

Butcher. You're devilish cunning then; for I don't well know it my self.

Kite. I know more than you, Friend—You have a foolish Saying, that such a one knows no more than the Man-in-the-Moon; I tell you the Man in the Moon knows more than all the Men under the Sun, don't the Moon see all the World?

Butcher. All the World see the Moon. I must confess.

Kite. Then she must see all the World, that's certain—Give me your hand—You are by Trade either a Butcher or a   100 Surgeon.

Butcher. True—I am a Butcher.

Kite. And a Surgeon you will be, the Employments differ only in the Name—He can cut up an Ox, may dissect a Man;

and the same Dexterity that cracks a Marrow-bone, will cut off a Leg or an Arm.

Butcher. What d'ye mean, Doctor, what d'ye mean?

Kite. Patience, Patience, Mr. Surgeon General, the Stars are great Bodies, and move slowly.

110 *Butcher.* But what d'ye mean by Surgeon General, Doctor?

Kite. Nay, Sir, if your Worship won't have Patience, I must beg the Favour of your Worship's absence.

Butcher. My Worship, my Worship! But why my Worship!

Kite. Nay, then I have done. (*Sits.*)

Butcher. Pray, Doctor.

Kite. Fire and Fury, Sir, (*Rises in a Passion.*) do you think the Stars will be hurry'd—Do the Stars owe you any Money, Sir, that you dare to dun their Lordships at this rate—Sir, I am Porter to the Stars, and I am order'd to let no Dun come near 120 their Doors.

Butcher. Dear Doctor, I never had any Dealings with the Stars, they don't owe me a Penny—But since you are their Porter, please to accept of this Half Crown to drink their Healths, and don't be angry.

Kite. Let me see your hand then, once more—Here has been Gold—Five Guineas, my Friend, in this very hand this Morning.

Butcher. Nay, then he is the Devil—Pray, Doctor, were you born of a Woman, or did you come into the World of your own 130 Head?

Kite. That's a Secret—This Gold was offer'd you by a proper handsome Man call'd *Hawk*, or *Buzzard*, or—

Butcher. *Kite* you mean.

Kite. Ay, ay, *Kite*.

Butcher. As errant a Rogue as ever carry'd a Halbard—the impudent Rascal wou'd have decoy'd me for a Soldier.

Kite. A Soldier! A Man of your Substance for a Soldier! Your Mother has a hundred Pound in hard Money lying at this Minute in the hands of a Mercer, not forty Yards from 140 this Place.

Butcher. Oons, and so she has; but very few know so much.

Kite. I know it, and that Rogue, what's his Name, *Kite*, knew it? And offer'd you five Guineas to list, because he knew

122 their] Q2; the

your poor Mother wou'd give the hundred for your Discharge—

Butcher. There's a Dog now—'Flesh, Doctor, I'll give you t'other half Crown, and tell me that this same *Kite* will be hang'd.

Kite. He's in as much Danger as any Man in the County of *Salop*.

Butcher. There's your Fee—But you have forgot the Surgeon 150 General all this while.

Kite. You put the Stars in a Passion (*Looks on his Books.*) But now they're pacify'd again—Let me see—Did you never cut off a Man's Leg?

Butcher. No.

Kite. Recollect, pray.

Butcher. I say no.

Kite. That's strange, wonderful strange; but nothing is strange to me, such wonderful Changes have I seen—The second, or third, ay, the third Campaign that you make in 160 *Flanders*, the Leg of a great Officer will be shatter'd by a great Shot; you will be there accidentally, and with your Cleaver chop off the Limb at a Blow: In short, the Operation will be perform'd with so much Dexterity, that with the general Applause you will be made Surgeon General of the whole Army.

Butcher. Nay, for the matter of cutting off a Limb—I'll do't—I'll do't with any Surgeon in *Europe*, but I have no Thoughts of making a Campaign.

Kite. You have no Thoughts! What matter for your 170 Thoughts? The Stars have decreed it, and you must go.

Butcher. The Stars decree it! Oons, Sir, the Justices can't press me.

Kite. Nay, Friend, 'tis none of my Business, I ha' done— Only mind this—You'll know more an Hour and a half hence—That's all—Farwel. (*Going.*)

Butcher. Hold, hold, Doctor, Surgeon General! Pray what is the Place worth, pray.

Kite. Five hundred Pound a Year, beside Guineas for Claps.
                                                                    180
Butcher. Five hundred Pound a Year!—An Hour and half hence you say?

150 your] Q2; you're   164 the general] om. in Q2

Kite. Prithee Friend be quiet, don't be so troublesome—
Here's such a Work to make a Booby Butcher accept of five
hundred Pound a Year [*Aside.*]—But if you must hear it—I
tell you in short, you'll be standing in your Stall an Hour and
half hence, and a Gentleman will come by with a Snuff-box in
his hand, and the tip of his Handkerchief hanging out of his
right Pocket—He'll ask you the Price of a Loyn of Veal, and at
190 the same time stroak your great Dog upon the Head, and call
him *Chopper.*

Butcher. Mercy upon us—*Chopper* is the Dog's Name.

Kite. Look'e there—What I say is true, things that are to
come must come to pass—Get you home, sell off your Stock,
don't mind the whining and the sniveling of your Mother and
your Sister, Women always hinder Preferment; make what
Money you can, and follow that Gentleman—His Name
begins with a *P*—Mind that—there will be the Barber's
Daughter too, that you promis'd Marriage to, she will be
200 pulling and haleing you to pieces.

Butcher. What! Know *Sally* too? He' the Devil, and he needs
must go that the Devil drives—(*Going.*) The tip of his
Handkerchief out of his left Pocket?

Kite. No, no, his right Pocket, if it be the left, 'tis none of the
Man.

Butcher. Well, well, I'll mind him.

                                                        Exit.

Plume. (*Behind with his Pocket-book.*) The right Pocket, you
say?

Kite. I hear the rustling of Silks, (*Knocking.*) Fly, Sir, 'tis
210 Madam *Melinda.*

                    Enter Melinda *and* Lucy.

Kite. Tycho, Chairs for the Ladies.

Melinda. Don't trouble your self, we shan't stay, Doctor.

Kite. Your Ladyship is to stay much longer than you
imagine.

Melinda. For what?

Kite. For a Husband—For your part, Madam, (*To* Lucy.)
you won't stay for a Husband.

Lucy. Pray, Doctor, do you converse with the Stars, or with
the Devil?

220 *Kite.* With both; when I have the Destinies of Men in

search, I consult the Stars, when the Affairs of Women come under my Hands, I advise with my t'other Friend.

Melinda. And have you rais'd the Devil upon my account?

Kite. Yes, Madam, and he's now under the Table.

Lucy. Oh! Heavens protect us—dear Madam, let us be gone.

Kite. If you be afraid of him, why do you come to consult him?

Melinda. Don't fear, Fool. Do you think, Sir, that because I'm a Woman I'm to be fool'd out of my Reason, or frighted 230 out of my Senses?—Come, show me this Devil.

Kite. He's a little busie at present, but when he has done he shall wait on you.

Melinda. What is he doing?

Kite. Writing your Name in his Pocket-book.

Melinda. Ha, ha, ha, my Name! pray what have you or he to do with my Name?

Kite. Look'e, fair Lady,—the Devil is a very modest Person, he seeks no body unless they seek him first; he's chain'd up like a Mastiff, and cannot stir unless he be let loose.—You 240 come to me to have your Fortune told—do you think, Madam, that I can answer you of my own Head? No, Madam, the Affairs of Women are so irregular, that nothing less than the Devil can give any account of 'em. Now to convince you of your Incredulity, I'll show you a Tryal of my Skill.—Here, you, *Cacodemon del fuego*, exert your Power,—draw me this Lady's Name, the word *Melinda* in the proper Letters and Character of her own hand writing.—Do it at three Motions, —one, two, three—'tis done—Now, Madam, will you please to send your Maid to fetch it. 250

Lucy. I fetch it! the Devil fetch me if I do.

Melinda. My Name in my own Hand-writing! that wou'd be convincing indeed.

Kite. Seeing's believing (*Goes to the Table, lifts up the Carpet.*) Here *Tre, Tre*, poor *Tre*, give me the Bone, Sirrah—Oh! oh! the Devil, the Devil in good earnest, my Hand, my Hand, the Devil, my Hand! (*He puts his Hand under the Table,* Plume *steals to the other side of the Table and catches him by the Hand.* Melinda

222 Hands] Q2; had   246 *fuego*] Q2 reads, convincingly, '*Plumo*'
255-65 —Oh! oh . . . the Blood comes—but] om. in Q2   248 Character] Q2
reads 'Characters'

and Lucy *shriek, and run to a Corner of the Stage.*—Kite *discovers* Plume, *and gets away his Hand.*) A plague o' your Pincers, he has fixt his Nails in my very Flesh. Oh! Madam, you put the
260 Demon into such a Passion with your Scruples, that it has almost cost me my Hand.

Melinda. It has cost us our Lives almost—but have you got the Name?

Kite. Got it! Ay, Madam, I have got it here—I'm sure the Blood comes—but there's your Name upon that square piece of Paper—behold—

Melinda. 'Tis wonderful—My very Letters to a tittle.

Lucy. 'Tis like your Hand, Madam, but not so like your Hand neither, and now I look nearer, 'tis not like your Hand
270 at all.

Kite. Here's a Chamber-maid now that will out-lie the Devil.

Lucy. Look'e, Madam, they shan't impose upon us, People can't remember their Hands no more than they can their Faces—Come, Madam, let us be certain, write your Name upon this Paper—(*Takes out Paper and folds it.*) then we'll compare the two Names.

Kite. Any thing for your Satisfaction, Madam,—here's Pen and Ink—(Melinda *writes, and* Lucy *holds the Paper.*)
280 *Lucy.* Let me see it, Madam, 'tis the same, the very same.—But I'll secure one Copy for my own Affairs. (*Aside.*)

Melinda. This is Demonstration.

Kite. 'Tis so, Madam, the word Demonstration comes from Demon the Father of Lies. [*Aside.*]

Melinda. Well, Doctor, I'm convinc'd; and now pray what account can you give me of my future Fortune?

Kite. Before the Sun has made one Course round this earthly Globe, your Fortune will be fixt for Happiness or Misery.
290 *Melinda.* What! so near the Crisis of my Fate!

Kite. Let me see—about the Hour of Ten to Morrow Morning you will be saluted by a Gentleman who will come to take his Leave of you, being design'd for Travel. His Intention of going abroad is sudden, and the Occasion a Woman. Your Fortune and his are like the Bullet and the Barrel, one runs plump into the t'other—in short, if the Gentleman travels he will die abroad; and if he does you will die before he comes home.

Melinda. What sort of Man is he?

Kite. Madam, he is a fine Gentleman, and a Lover—that is, a Man of very good Sense, and a very great Fool.

Melinda. How is that possible, Doctor?

Kite. Because, Madam,—because it is so: A Woman's Reason is the best for a Man's being a Fool.

Melinda. Ten a Clock you say.

Kite. Ten, about the Hour of Tea drinking throughout the Kingdom.

Melinda. Here, Doctor, (*Gives him Money.*) *Lucy*, have you any Questions to ask?

Lucy. O! Madam, a thousand.

Kite. I must beg your Patience till another time, for I expect more Company this Minute; besides, I must discharge the Gentleman under the Table.

Lucy. Pray, Sir, discharge us first.

Kite. *Tycho*, wait on the Ladies down Stairs.

Exeunt Melinda *and* Lucy.
Enter Plume *and* Worthy *laughing.*

Kite. Ay, you may well laugh, Gentlemen, not all the Cannon of the *French* Army cou'd have frighted me so much as that Gripe you gave me under the Table.

Plume. I think, Mr. Doctor, I out-conjur'd you that bout.

Kite. I was surpriz'd, for I shou'd not have taken a Captain for a Conjurer.

Plume. No more than I shou'd a Serjeant for a Wit.

Kite. Mr. *Worthy*, you were pleas'd to wish me Joy to Day, I hope to be able to return the Complement to Morrow.

Worthy. I'll make it the best Complement to you that ever I made in my Life, if you do; but I must be a Traveller you say?

Kite. No farther than the Chops of the Channel, I presume, Sir.

Plume. That we have concerted already. (*Knocking hard.*) Hey day! you don't profess Midwifry, Doctor?

Kite. Away to your Ambuscade.

Exeunt Plume *and* Worthy.

316–22 *Kite.* Ay, you may well . . . Serjeant for a Wit.] om. in Q2
325–6 ever I made in my] Q2; you ever made in your

Enter Brazen.

Brazen. Your Servant, Servant, my dear.

Kite. Stand off—I have my Familiar already.

Brazen. Are you bewitch'd, my dear?

Kite. Yes, my dear, but mine is a peaceable Spirit, and hates Gunpowder—thus I fortify my self, (*Draws a Circle round him.*) and now, Captain, have a care how you force my Lines.

Brazen. Lines! what dost talk of Lines? You have something like a Fishing Rod there, indeed; but I come to be acquainted
340 with you, Man—what's your Name, my dear?

Kite. Conundrum.

Brazen. Conundrum! rat me, I know a famous Doctor in *London* of your Name, where were you born?

Kite. I was born in *Algebra.*

Brazen. Algebra!—'Tis no Country in *Christendom* I'm sure, unless it be some pitiful Place in the Highlands of *Scotland.*

Kite. Right! I told you I was bewitch'd.

Brazen. So am I, my dear, I'm going to be marry'd.—I've had two Letters from a Lady of Fortune that Loves me to
350 Madness, Fits, Chollick, Spleen, and Vapours—Shall I marry her in four and twenty Hours, ay or no?

Kite. I must have the Year and Day o'th' Month when these Letters were dated.

Brazen. Why, you old Bitch, did you ever hear of Love Letters dated with the Year and Day o'th' Month, do you think *Billets Deux* are like Bank Bills?

Kite. They are not so good—but if they bear no Date, I must examine the Contents.

Brazen. Contents, that you shall, old Boy, here they be
360 both.

Kite. Only the last you receiv'd, if you please. (*Takes the Letter.*) Now Sir, if you please to let me consult my Books for a Minute, I'll send this Letter inclos'd to you with the Determination of the Stars upon it to your Lodgings.

Brazen. With all my Heart—I must give him—(*Puts his Hand in's Pocket.*) *Algebra!* I fancy, Doctor, 'tis hard to calculate the Place of your Nativity—Here—(*Gives him Money.*) and if I succeed, I'll build a Watch-Tower upon the top of the highest Mountain in *Wales* for the Study of Astrology, and the Benefit
370 of *Conundrums.*   *Exit.*

Enter Plume *and* Worthy.

Worthy. O! Doctor, that Letter's worth a Million, let me see it—and now I have it, I'm afraid to open it.

Plume. Pho, let me see it, (*Opening the Letter.*) if she be a Jilt—Damn her, she is one—there's her Name at the bottom on't.

Worthy. How!—then I will travel in good earnest—by all my hopes, 'tis *Lucy's* Hand.

Plume. Lucy's!

Worthy. Certainly, 'tis no more like *Melinda's* Character than black is to white.   380

Plume. Then 'tis certainly *Lucy's* Contrivance to draw in *Brazen* for a Husband—but are you sure 'tis not *Melinda's* Hand?

Worthy. You shall see, where's the bit of Paper I gave you just now that the Devil writ *Melinda* upon.

Kite. Here, Sir.

Plume. 'Tis plain, they're not the same; and is this the malicious Name that was subscrib'd to the Letter which made Mr. *Ballance* send his Daughter into the Country?

Worthy. The very same, the other Fragments I show'd you 390 just now, I once intended it for another use, but I think I have turn'd it now to better Advantage.

Plume. But 'twas barbarous to conceal this so long, and to continue me so many Hours in the pernicious Heresie of believing that angelick Creature cou'd change—poor *Silvia.*

Worthy. Rich *Silvia*, you mean, and poor Captain—ha, ha, ha; come, come, Friend, *Melinda* is true, and shall be mine; *Silvia* is constant, and may be yours.

Plume. No, she's above my Hopes—but for her sake I'll recant my Opinion of her Sex.   400

> *By some the Sex is blam'd without Design,*
> *Light harmless Censure, such as yours and mine,* ⎫
> *Sallies of Wit, and Vapours of our Wine.*   ⎬
>
> *Others the Justice of the Sex condemn,*
> *And wanting Merit to create Esteem,*   ⎫
> *Wou'd hide their own Defects by cens'ring them.*   ⎬

391–2 I once intended . . . Advantage] om. in Q2

But they secure in their all-conqu'ring Charms
Laugh at the vain Efforts of false Alarms,
He magnifies their Conquests who complains,
For none wou'd struggle were they not in Chains.

410

[*Exeunt.*]

[*The End of the Fourth Act.*]

ACT V. [Scene i.]

SCENE, *an Antichamber, with a Perrywig, Hat and Sword
upon the Table.*

Enter Silvia *in her Night Cap.*

Silvia. I have rested but indifferently, and I believe my
Bedfellow was as little pleas'd; poor *Rose!* here she comes—
Enter Rose.
Good morrow, my dear, how d'ye this Morning?

Rose. Just as I was last Night, neither better nor worse for
you.

Silvia. What's the matter? did you not like your Bedfellow?

Rose. I don't know whether I had a Bedfellow or not.

Silvia. Did not I lye with you?

Rose. No—I wonder you cou'd have the Conscience to
10 ruine a poor Girl for nothing.

Silvia. I have sav'd thee from Ruin, Child; don't be
melancholy, I can give you as many fine things as the Captain
can.

Rose. But you can't I'm sure. (*Knocking at the Door.*)

Silvia. Odso! my Accoutrements, (*Puts on her Perriwig, Hat
and Sword.*) Who's at the Door?

Without. Open the Door, or we'll break it down.

Silvia. Patience a little—(*Opens the Door.*)
Enter Constable *and Mob.*

Constable. We have 'um, we have 'um, the Duck and the
20 Mallard both in the Decoy.

Silvia. What means this Riot? Stand off. (*Draws.*) The Man

v.i. 1–41 (v.i) The entire scene om. in Q2

dies that comes within reach of my Point.

Constable. That is not the Point, Master, put up your Sword or I shall knock you down; and so I command the Queen's Peace.

Silvia. You are some Blockhead of a Constable.

Constable. I am so, and have a Warrant to apprehend the Bodies of you and your Whore there.

Rose. Whore! never was poor Woman so abus'd.

Enter Bullock *unbutton'd.*

Bullock. What's matter now?—O! Mr. *Bridewell*, what 30 brings you abroad so early?

Constable. This, Sir—(*Lays hold of* Bullock.) you're the Queen's Prisoner.

Bullock. Wauns, you lye, Sir, I'm the Queen's Soldier.

Constable. No matter for that, you shall go before Justice *Ballance.*

Silvia. *Ballance!* 'tis what I wanted—Here, Mr. *Constable*, I resign my Sword.

Rose. Can't you carry us before the Captain, Mr. *Bridewell.*

Constable. Captain! ha'n't you got your Belly full of Captains 40 yet? Come, come, make way there.

Exeunt.

[ACT V. Scene ii.]

SCENE, *Justice* Ballance's *House.*

Ballance *and* Scale.

Scale. I say 'tis not to be born Mr. *Ballance.*

Ballance. Look'e, Mr. *Scale*, for my own part I shall be very tender in what regards the Officers of the Army; they expose their Lives to so many Dangers for us Abroad, that we may give them some Grains of Allowance at Home.

Scale. Allowance! This poor Girl's Father is my Tenant, and if I mistake not, her Mother nurst a Child for you; shall they debauch our Daughters to our Faces?

Ballance. Consider, Mr. *Scale*, that were it not for the

10 Bravery of these Officers we shou'd have *French* Dragoons among us, that wou'd leave us neither Liberty, Property, Wife, nor Daughter.—Come, Mr. *Scale*, the Gentlemen are vigorous and warm, and may they continue so; the same Heat that stirs them up to Love, spurs them on to Battel: You never knew a great General in your Life that did not love a Whore—this I only speak in reference to Captain *Plume*,—for the other Spark I know nothing of.

Scale. Nor can I hear of any body that do's—O! here they come.

20 *Enter* Silvia, Bullock, Rose, *Prisoners*, Constable, *and Mob*.

Constable. May it please your Worships, we took them in the very Act, *re infecta*, Sir; the Gentleman indeed behav'd himself like a Gentleman, for he drew his Sword and swore, and afterwards laid it down and said nothing.

Ballance. Give the Gentleman his Sword again—wait you without.

Exeunt Constable, &c.

I'm sorry, Sir, (*To* Silvia.) to know a Gentleman upon such Terms, that the occasion of our meeting shou'd prevent the Satisfaction of an Acquaintance.

30 *Silvia*. Sir, you need make no Apology for your Warrant, no more than I shall do for my Behaviour.—My Innocence is upon an equal Foot with your Authority.

Scale. Innocence! have you not seduc'd that young Maid?

Silvia. No, Mr. Goose-Cap, she seduc'd me.

Bullock. So she did I'll swear,—for she propos'd Marriage first.

Ballance. What! then you're marry'd, Child? (*To* Rose.)

Rose. Yes, Sir, to my Sorrow.

Ballance. Who was Witness?

40 *Bullock*. That was I—I danc'd, threw the Stocking, and spoke Jokes by their Bed side I'm sure.

Ballance. Who was the Minister?

Bullock. Minister! we are Soldiers, and want no Ministers— they were marry'd by the Articles of War.

Ballance. Hold thy prating, Fool; your Appearance, Sir, promises some Understanding, pray, what does this Fellow mean?

Silvia. He means Marriage, I think,—but that, you know, is

so odd a thing, that hardly any two People under the Sun
agree in the Ceremony; some make it a Sacrament, others a 50
Convenience, and others make it a Jest; but among Soldiers
'tis most Sacred, our Sword, you know, is our Honour, that we
lay down, the Hero jumps over its first, and the *Amazon*
after—leap Rogue, follow Whore, the Drums beats a Ruff, and
so to Bed; that's all, the Ceremony is concise.

Bullock. And the prettiest Ceremony, so full of Pastime and
Prodigality—

Ballance. What! are you a Soldier?

Bullock. Ay, that I am—Will your Worship lend me your
Cane, and I'll show you how I can exercise.   60

Ballance. Take it (*Strike him over the Head.*) Pray, Sir, what
Commission may you bear? (*To* Silvia.)

Silvia. I'm call'd Captain, Sir, by all the Coffee-men,
Drawers, Whores and Groom Porters in *London,* for I wear a
red Coat, a Sword, a Hat *bien troussee,* a Martial Twist in my
Cravat, a fierce Knot in my Perriwig, a Cane upon my Button;
Picket in my Head, and Dice in my Pocket.

Scale. Your Name, pray Sir.

Silvia. Captain *Pinch*; I cock my Hat with a Pinch, I take
Snuff with a Pinch, pay my Whores with a Pinch; in short, I 70
can do any thing at a Pinch, but fight and fill my Belly.

Ballance. And pray, Sir, what brought you into *Shropshire?*

Silvia. A Pinch, Sir, I knew that you Country Gentlemen
want Wit, and you know that we Town Gentlemen want
Money, and so—

Ballance. I understand you, Sir; here, *Constable*—

Enter Constable.

Take this Gentleman into Custody till farther Orders.

Rose. Pray your Worship, don't be uncivil to him, for he did
me no Hurt, he's the most harmless Man in the World, for all
he talks so.   80

Scale. Come, come Child, I'll take care of you.

Silvia. What, Gentlemen, rob me of my Freedom and my
Wife at once! 'tis the first time they ever went together.

Ballance. Heark'e, *Constable*—(*Whispers the* Constable.)

Constable. It shall be done, Sir,—Come along, Sir.

Exeunt Constable, Bullock *and* Silvia.

v. ii. 65 Coat, a [om]]Q2; ~ a a

Ballance. Come, Mr. *Scale*, we'll manage the Spark presently.
                                    Exeunt Ballance *and* Scale.

[ACT V. Scene iii.]

SCENE *changes to* Melinda's *Apartment.*

Melinda *and* Worthy.

Melinda. So far the Prediction is right, 'tis ten exactly;
(*Aside.*) and pray, Sir, how long have you been in this
travelling Humour?

Worthy. 'Tis natural, Madam, for us to avoid what disturbs
our Quiet.

Melinda. Rather the Love of Change, which is more
natural, may be the Occasion of it.

Worthy. To be sure, Madam, there must be Charms in
Variety, else neither you nor I shou'd be so fond of it.

10 *Melinda.* You mistake, Mr. *Worthy*, I am not so fond of
Variety, as to travel for it; nor do I think it Prudence in you to
run your self into a certain Expence and Danger, in hopes of
precarious Pleasures, which at best never answer Expectation,
as 'tis evident from the Example of most Travellers, that long
more to return to their own Country than they did to go
abroad.

Worthy. What Pleasures I may receive abroad are indeed
uncertain; but this I am sure of, I shall meet with less Cruelty
among the most barbarous Nations, than I have found at
20 home.

Melinda. Come, Sir, you and I have been jangling a great
while—I fancy if we made up our Accounts, we shou'd the
sooner come to an Agreement.

Worthy. Sure, Madam, you won't dispute your being in my
Debt—My Fears, Sighs, Vows, Promises, Assiduities, Anxieties,
Jealousies, have run on for a whole Year, without any
Payment.

Melinda. A Year! O Mr. *Worthy*, what you owe to me is not
to be paid under a seven Years Servitude; how did you use me
30 the Year before, when taking the Advantage of my Innocence,

and Necessity, you wou'd have made me your Mistress, that is, your Slave—Remember the wicked Insinuations, artful Baits, deceitful Arguments, cunning Pretences; then your impudent Behaviour, loose Expressions, familiar Letters, rude Visits, remember those, those Mr. *Worthy*.

Worthy. I do remember, and am sorry I made no better use of 'em (*Aside*.) But you may remember, Madam—that—

Melinda. Sir, I'll remember nothing, 'tis your Interest that I shou'd forget; you have been barbarous to me, I have been cruel to you—Put that and that together, and let one balance 40 the other—Now if you will begin upon a new Score, lay aside your adventering Airs, and behave your self handsomly till *Lent* be over—Here's my hand, I'll use you as a Gentleman shou'd be.

Worthy. And if I don't use you as a Gentlewoman shou'd be, may this be my Poyson. (*Kissing her Hand*.)

Enter Servant.

Servant. Madam, the Coach is at the Door.

Melinda. I'm going to Mr. *Ballance*'s Country-house to see my Cosin *Silvia*, I have done her an Injury, and can't be easie till I have ask'd her Pardon. 50

Worthy. I dare not hope for the Honour of waiting on you.

Melinda. My Coach is full, but if you will be so Gallant as to mount your own Horses and follow us, we shall be glad to be overtaken; if you bring Captain *Plume* with you, we shan't have the worse Reception.

Worthy. I'll endeavour it.

Exit Worthy *leading* Melinda.

[ACT V. Scene iv.]

SCENE, *The Market-Place*.

Plume *and* Kite.

Plume. A Baker, a Taylor, a Smith, and a Butcher—I believe the first Colony planted at *Virginia* had not more Trades in their Company than I have in mine.

<hr>

v.iii. 43 Gentleman] Q2; Gentlemen

Kite. The Butcher, Sir, will have his hands full; for we have two Sheep-stealers among us—I hear of a Fellow too committed just now for stealing of Horses.

Plume. We'll dispose of him among the Dragoons—Have we never a Poulterer among us?

Kite. Yes, Sir, the King of the Gypsies is a very good one, he has an excellent hand at a Goose, or a Turkey; here's Captain *Brazen*—Sir, I must go look after the Men.

                                                                    Exit.

Enter Brazen, *reading a Letter.*

Brazen. Um, um, um, the Canonical Hour—Um, um, very well—My dear *Plume*! Give me a Buss.

Plume. Half a score, if you will, my Dear; what hast got in thy hand, Child?

Brazen. 'Tis a Project for laying out a thousand Pound.

Plume. Were it not requisite to project first how to get it in?

Brazen. You can't imagine, my Dear, that I want twenty thousand Pound; I have spent twenty times as much in the Service—Now, my Dear, pray advise me, my Head runs much upon Architecture; shall I build a Privateer or a Play-house?

Plume. An odd Question—A Privateer or a Play-house! 'Twill require some Consideration—Faith, I'm for a Privateer.

Brazen. I'm not of your Opinion, my Dear—For in the first place a Privateer may be ill built.

Plume. And so may a Play-house.

Brazen. But a Privateer may be ill mann'd.

Plume. And so may a Play-house.

Brazen. But a Privateer may run upon the Shallows.

Plume. Not so often as a Play-house.

Brazen. But, you know, a Privateer may spring a Leak.

Plume. And I know that a Play-house may spring a great many.

Brazen. But suppose the Privateer come home with a rich Booty, we shou'd never agree about our Shares.

Plume. 'Tis just so in a Play-house—So by my Advice, you shall fix upon the Privateer.

Brazen. Agreed—But if this twenty thousand shou'd not be in Specie—

Plume. What twenty thousand?

Brazen. Heark'e—(*Whispers.*)

Plume. Marry'd!

Brazen. Presently, we're to meet about half a Mile out of Town at the Water-side—And so forth—(*Reads.*) *For fear I shou'd be known by any of* Worthy*'s Friends, you must give me leave to wear my Mask till after the Ceremony, which will make me ever yours*—Look'e there, my dear Dog—(*Shows the bottom of the Letter to* Plume.)

Plume. Melinda! And by this Light, her own hand!—Once more, if you please, my Dear; her hand exactly!—Just now you say?

Brazen. This Minute I must be gone.

Plume. Have a little Patience, and I'll go with you.

Brazen. No, no, I see a Gentleman coming this way that may be inquisitive; 'tis *Worthy*, do you know him?

Plume. By sight only.

Brazen. Have a care, the very Eyes discover Secrets—

Exit.

Enter Worthy.

Worthy. To boot, and saddle, Captain, you must mount.

Plume. Whip and spur, *Worthy*, or you won't mount.

Worthy. But I shall, *Melinda* and I are agreed, she is gone to visit *Silvia*; we are to mount and follow, and cou'd we carry a Parson with us, who knows what might be done for us both?

Plume. Don't trouble your Head, *Melinda* has secur'd a Parson already.

Worthy. Already! Do you know more than I?

Plume. Yes, I saw it under her hand—*Brazen* and she are to meet half a Mile hence at the Water-side, there to take Boat, I suppose to be ferry'd over to the *Elisian* Fields, if there be any such thing in Matrimony.

Worthy. I parted with *Melinda* just now, she assur'd me she hated *Brazen*, and that she resolv'd to discard *Lucy* for daring to write Letters to him in her Name.

Plume. Nay, nay, there's nothing of *Lucy* in this—I tell ye I saw *Melinda*'s hand as surely as this is mine.

Worthy. But I tell you, she's gone this Minute to Justice *Ballance*'s Country House.

Plume. But I tell you, she's gone this Minute to the Water-side.

Enter a Servant.

50

60

70

Servant. (*To* Worthy.) Madam *Melinda* has sent word that
you need not trouble your self to follow her; because her
80 Journey to Justice *Ballance*'s is put off, and she's gone to take
the Air another way.

Worthy. How! Her Journey put off?

Plume. That is, her Journey was a put-off to you.

Worthy. 'Tis plain, plain—But how, where, when is she to
meet *Brazen?*

Plume. Just now, I tell you, half a Mile hence at the Water
side.

Worthy. Up, or down the Water?

Plume. That I don't know.

90 *Worthy.* I'm glad my Horses are ready—*Jack*, get 'em out.

Plume. Shall I go with you?

Worthy. Not an Inch—I shall return presently.

Exit.

Plume. You'll find me at the Hall, the Justices are sitting by
this time, and I must attend them.

Exit.

[ACT V. Scene v.]

SCENE, *a Court of Justice*, Ballance, Scale, Scruple,
upon the Bench.

Constable, Kite, Mob.
Kite *and* Constable *advance to the Front of the Stage.*

Kite. Pray, who are those honourable Gentlemen upon the
Bench?

Constable. He in the middle is Justice *Ballance*, he on the
Right is Justice *Scale*, and he on the Left is Justice *Scruple*, and
I am Mr. *Contable*, four very honest Gentlemen.

Kite. O dear Sir, I'm your most obedient Servant, (*Saluting
the* Constable.) I fancy, Sir, that your Employment and mine
are much the same, for my Business is to keep People in order,
and if they disobey, to knock 'em down; and then we're both
10 Staff-Officers.

Constable. Nay, I'm a Serjeant my self—Of the Militia—

v.iv. 78 *Servant.*] Q2 [*Serv.*]; Sir,

Come, Brother, you shall see me exercise—Suppose this is a
Musquet now, (*He puts his Staff on his Right Shoulder.*) Now I'm
shoulder'd.

Kite. Ay, you're shoulder'd pretty well for a Constable's
Staff, but for a Musquet you must put it on t'other Shoulder,
my Dear.

Constable. Adso, that's true,—Come, now give the Word
o'Command.

Kite. Silence.   20

Constable. Ay, ay, so we will,—We will be silent.

Kite. Silence, you Dog, Silence—(*Strikes him over the Head
with his Halberd.*)

Constable. That's the way to silence a Man with a witness—
What d'ye mean, Friend?

Kite. Only to exercise you, Sir.

Constable. Your Exercise differs so from ours, that we shall
ne'er agree about it; if my own Captain had given me such a
Rap I had taken the Law of him.

                    Enter Plume.

Ballance. Captain, you're welcome.

Plume. Gentlemen, I thank'e.   30

Scruple. Come, honest Captain, sit by me, (*Plume ascends,
and sits upon the Bench.*) Now produce your Prisoners—Here,
that Fellow there,—Set him up—Mr. *Constable*, what have you
to say against this Man?

Constable. I have nothing to say against him, an't please ye.

Ballance. No! What made you bring him hither?

Constable. I don't know, an't please your Worship.

Scruple. Did not the Contents of your Warrant direct you
what sort of Men to take up?

Constable. I can't tell, an't please ye, I can't read.   40

Scruple. A very pretty *Constable* truly! I find we have no
Business here.

Kite. May it please the Worship Bench, I desire to be heard
in this Case, as being Counsel for the Queen.

Ballance. Come, Serjeant, you shall be heard, since no body
else will speak; we won't come here for nothing—

Kite. This Man is but one Man, the Country may spare
him, and the Army wants him, besides he's cut out by Nature
for a Granadeer, he's five Foot ten Inches high, he shall Box,

50 Wrestle, or dance the *Cheshire* Round with any Man in the County, he gets drunk every Sabbath-Day, and he beats his Wife.

Wife. You lie, Sirrah, you lie an't please your Worship, he's the best natur'd pains-taking Man in the Parish, witness my five poor Children.

Scruple. A Wife and five Children! you *Constable*, you Rogue, how durst you Impress a Man that has a Wife and five Children?

Scale. Discharge him, discharge him.

60 *Ballance.* Hold, Gentlemen—Hark'e, Friend, how do you maintain your Wife and Children?

Plume. They live upon Wild Fowl and Venison, Sir, the Husband keeps a Gun, and kills all the Hares and Partridges within five Miles round.

Ballance. A Gun! Nay, if he be so good at Gunning he shall have enough on't—He may be of use against the *French*, for he shoots flying to be sure.

Scruple. But his Wife and Children, Mr. *Ballance.*

Wife. Ay, ay, that's the Reason you wou'd send him
70 away—You know I have a Child every Year, and you're afraid they should come upon the Parish at last.

Plume. Look'e there, Gentlemen, the honest Woman has spoke it at once, the Parish had better maintain five Children this Year than six or seven the next; that Fellow upon his high feeding may get you two or three Beggars at a Birth.

Wife. Look'e, Mr. Captain, the Parish shall get nothing by sending him away, for I won't loose my Teeming-Time if there be a Man left in the Parish.

Ballance. Send that Woman to the House of Correction—
80 and the Man—

Kite. I'll take care o' him, if you please. (*Takes the Man down.*)

Scale. Here, you *Constable*, the next—Set up that black-fac'd Fellow, he has a Gun-powder Look, what can you say against this Man, *Constable*?

Constable. Nothing, but that he's a very honest Man.

Plume. Pray, Gentlemen, let me have one honest Man in my Company for the Novelty's sake.

Ballance. What are you, Friend?

Mob. A Collier, I work in the Colepits.

Scruple. Look'e Gentlemen, this Fellow has a Trade, and 90
the Act of Parliament here expresses, that we are to impress
no Man that has any visible means of a Livelihood.

Kite. May it please your Worships, this Man has no visible
means of a Livelihood, for he works under-ground.

Plume. Well said *Kite*—Besides, the Army wants Miners.

Ballance. Right! and had we an Order of Government for't,
we cou'd raise you in this and the neighbouring County of
Stafford five hundred Colliers that wou'd run you under-
ground like Moles, and do more Service in a Siege than all the
Miners in the Army.   100

Scruple. Well, Friend, what have you to say for your self?

Mob. I'm Marry'd.

Kite. Lack-a-day, so am I.

Mob. Here's my Wife, poor Woman.

Ballance. Are you marry'd, good Woman?

Woman. I'm marry'd in Conscience.

Kite. May it please your Worship, she's with Child in
Conscience.

Scale. Who marry'd you, Mistress?

Woman. My Husband—We agreed that I shou'd call him 110
Husband to avoid passing for a Whore, and that he shou'd
call me Wife to shun going for a Soldier.

Scruple. A very pretty Couple—Pray, Captain, will you take
'em both—

Plume. What say you, Mr. *Kite*—Will you take care of the
Woman?

Kite. Yes, Sir, she shall go with us to the Sea side, and there
if she has a mind to drown her self, we'll take care that no
Body shall hinder her.

Ballance. Here, *Constable*, bring in my Man (*Exit* Constable.) 120
Now Captain, I'll fit you with a Man, such as you ne'er listed
in your Life.

            Enter Constable *and* Silvia.

O my Friend *Pinch*—I'm very glad to see you.

Silvia. Well Sir, and what then?

Scale. What then! Is that your Respect to the Bench?

---

v.v 123 *Pinch*] Plume knows Silvia as Jack Wilfull, not Pinch. The inconsistency
was never corrected.

Silvia. Sir, I don't care a Farthing for you nor your Bench neither.

Scruple. Look'e, Gentlemen, that's enough, he's a very impudent Fellow, and fit for a Soldier.

130   *Scale.* A notorious Rogue, I say, and very fit for a Soldier.

Constable. A Whoremaster, I say, and therefore fit to go.

Ballance. What think you, Captain?

Plume. I think he's very pretty Fellow, and therefore fit to serve.

Silvia. Me for a Soldier! Send your own lazy lubberly Sons at home, Fellows that hazard their Necks every day in pursuit of a Fox, yet dare not peep abroad to look an Enemy in the Face.

Constable. May it please your Worships, I have a Woman at

140   the Door to swear a Rape against this Rogue.

Silvia. Is it your Wife or Daughter, Booby? I ravish'd 'em both yesterday.

Ballance. Pray, Captain, read the Articles of War, we'll see him listed immediately. (Plume *reads Articles of War against Mutiny and Desertion.*)

Silvia. Hold, Sir—Once more, Gentlemen, have a care what you do, for you shall severely smart for any Violence you offer to me, and you, Mr. *Ballance*, I speak to you particularly, you shall heartily repent it.

Plume. Look'ee, young Spark, say but one Word more and

150   I'll build a Horse for you as high as the Ceiling, and make you ride the most tiresom Journey that ever you made in your Life.

Silvia. You have made a fine Speech, good Captain *Huffcap*—But you had better be quiet, I shall find a way to cool your Courage.

Plume. Pray, Gentlemen, don't mind him, he's distracted.

Silvia. 'Tis false—I'm descended of as good a Family as any in your County, my Father is as good a Man as any upon your Bench, and I am Heir to twelve hundred Pound a Year.

Ballance. He's certainly mad,—Pray, Captain, read the

160   Articles of War.

Silvia. Hold, once more,—Pray, Mr. *Ballance*, to you I speak, suppose I were your Child, wou'd you use me at this rate?

Ballance. No Faith, were you mine, I would send you to

Bedlam first, and into the Army afterwards.

Silvia. But consider, my Father, Sir, he's as good, as generous, as brave, as just a Man as ever serv'd his Country; I'm his only Child, perhaps the loss of me may break his Heart.

Ballance. He's a very great Fool if it does. Captain, if you 170 don't list him this Minute, I'll leave the Court.

Plume. Kite, do you distribute the Levy Money to the Men whilst I read.

Kite. Ay, Sir,—Silence Gentlemen. (Plume *reads the Articles of War.*)

Ballance. Very well; now, Captain, let me beg the Favour of you not to discharge this Fellow upon any account whatsoever. —Bring in the rest.

Constable. There are no more, an't please your Worship.

Ballance. No more! there were five two Hours ago.

Silvia. 'Tis true, Sir, but this Rogue of a *Constable* let the rest 180 escape for a Bribe of eleven Shillings a Man, because he said that the Act allows him but ten, so the odd Shilling was clear Gains.

All Justices. How!

Silvia. Gentlemen, he offer'd to let me get away for two Guineas, but I had not so much about me.—This is Truth, and I'm ready to swear it.

Kite. And I'll swear it, give me the Book, 'tis for the good of the Service.

Mob. May it please your Worship, I gave him half a Crown 190 to say that I was an honest Man,—and now that your Worships have made me a Rogue, I hope I shall have my Money again.

Ballance. 'Tis my Opinion that this *Constable* be put into the Captain's Hands, and if his Friends don't bring four good Men for his Ransom by to Morrow Night,—Captain, you shall carry him to *Flanders.*

Scale, Scruple. Agreed, agreed.

Plume. Mr. *Kite*, take the *Constable* into Custody.

Kite. Ay, ay; Sir,—(*To the* Constable.) will you please to 200 have your Office taken from you, or will you handsomely lay down your Staff as your Betters have done before you. (*The* Constable *drops his Staff.*)

Ballance. Come, Gentlemen, there needs no great Ceremony in adjourning this Court;—Captain you shall dine with me.

Kite. Come Mr. Militia Serjeant, I shall silence you now I believe, without your taking the Law of me.

Exeunt Omnes.

[ACT V. Scene vi.]

SCENE *changes to the Fields,*

Brazen *leading in* Lucy *mask'd.*

Brazen. The Boat is just below here.
Enter Worthy *with a Case of Pistols under his Arm, parts* Brazen *and* Lucy.
Worthy. Here, Sir, take your Choice. (*Offering the Pistols.*)
Brazen. What! Pistols! are they charg'd, my dear?
Worthy. With a brace of Bullets each.
Brazen. But I'm a Foot Officer, my dear, and never use Pistols, the Sword is my way, and I won't be put out of my Road to please any Man.
Worthy. Nor I neither, so have at you. (*Cock one Pistol.*)
Brazen. Look'e, my dear, I do not care for Pistols;—pray 10 oblige me and let us have a bout at Sharps, dam't there's no parrying these Bullets.
Worthy. Sir, if you han't your Belly full of these, the Swords shall come in for Second Course.
Brazen. Why then Fire and Fury! I have eaten Smoak from the Mouth of a Cannon; Sir, don't think I fear Powder, for I live upon't; let me see, (*Takes a Pistol.*) and now, Sir, how many paces distant shall we fire?
Worthy. Fire you when you please, I'll reserve my shot till I be sure of you.
20 *Brazen.* Come, where's your Cloak?
Worthy. Cloak! what d'ye mean?
Brazen. To fight upon, I always fight upon a Cloak, 'tis our way abroad.
Lucy. Come, Gentlemen, I'll end the Strife. (*Pulls off her Mask.*)

v.vi. 24, 29, 36, 40 *Lucy.*] cd.; *Lucia,*

Worthy. *Lucy*! take her.

Brazen. The Devil take me if I do—Huzza, (*Fires his Pistol.*) d'ye hear, d'ye hear, you plaguy Harrydan, how those Bullets whistle, suppose they had been lodg'd in my Gizzard now?—

Lucy. Pray, Sir, pardon me.

Brazen. I can't tell, Child, till I know whether my Money be 30 safe; (*Searching his Pockets.*) Yes, yes, I do pardon you,—but if I had you in the *Rose* Tavern, *Covent Garden*, with three or four hearty Rakes, and three or four smart Napkins, I would tell you another Story, my dear.

Exit.

Worthy. And was *Melinda* privy to this?

Lucy. No, Sir, she wrote her Name upon a piece of Paper at the Fortune-tellers last Night, which I put in my Pocket, and so writ above it to the Captain.

Worthy. And how came *Melinda*'s Journey put off?

Lucy. At the Towns end she met Mr. *Ballance*'s Steward, 40 who told her that Mrs. *Silvia* was gone from her Father's, and no body could tell whither.

Worthy. *Silvia* gone from her Fathers! this will be News to *Plume.* Go home, and tell your Lady how near I was being shot for her.

Exeunt.

[ACT V. Scene vii.]

[SCENE, Ballance's *House.*]

Enter Ballance *with a Napkin in his Hand as risen from Dinner, talking with his* Steward.

Steward. We did not miss her till the Evening, Sir, and then searching for her in the Chamber that was my young Master's, we found her Cloaths there, but the Suit that your Son left in the Press when he went to *London*, was gone.

Ballance. The white, trimm'd with Silver!

Steward. The same.

Ballance. You han't told that Circumstance to any body.

Steward. To none but your Worship.

Ballance. And be sure you don't. Go into the Dining-

10 Room, and tell Captain *Plume* that I beg to speak with him.

    Steward. I shall.

Exit.

    Ballance. Was ever man so impos'd upon? I had her Promise indeed that she shou'd never dispose of herself without my Consent.—I have consented with a Witness, given her away as my Act and Deed; and this, I warrant, the Captain thinks will pass; no, I shall never pardon him the Villany, first of robbing me of my Daughter, and then the mean Opinion he must have of me to think that I cou'd be so wretchedly imposed upon; her extravagant Passion might
20 encourage her in the Attempt, but the Contrivance must be his—I'll know the Truth presently.

Enter Plume.

Pray, Captain, what have you done with your young Gentleman Souldier?

    Plume. He's at my Quarters, I suppose, with the rest of my Men.

    Ballance. Does he keep Company with the Common Souldiers?

    Plume. No, he's generally with me.

    Ballance. He lies with you, I presume.

30   *Plume.* No, Faith,—I offer'd him part of my Bed, but the young Rogue fell in love with *Rose*, and has layn with her, I think, since he came to Town.

    Ballance. So that between you both, *Rose* has been finely manag'd.

    Plume. Upon my Honour, Sir, she had no harm from me.

    Ballance. All's safe, I find [*Aside.*]—Now Captain, you must know that the young Fellow's Impudence in Court was well grounded; he said that I should heartily repent his being listed, and I do from my Soul.

40   *Plume.* Ay! for what reason?

    Ballance. Because he is no less than what he said he was, born of as good a Family as any in this County, and is Heir to twelve hundred pound a Year.

    Plume. I'm very glad to hear it, for I wanted but a Man of that Quality to make my Company a perfect Representative of the whole Commons of *England*.

    Ballance. Won't you discharge him?

Plume. Not under a hundred Pound Sterling.

Ballance. You shall have it, for his Father is my intimate
Friend.

Plume. Then you shall have him for nothing.   50

Ballance. Nay, Sir, you shall have your Price.

Plume. Not a Penny, Sir, I value an Obligation to you much
above a hundred Pound.

Ballance. Perhaps, Sir, you shan't repent your Generosity.
—Will you please to write his Discharge in my Pocket Book,
(*Gives his Book.*) In the mean time we'll send for the
Gentleman. Who waits there?

Enter Servant.

Go to the Captain's Lodgings, and inquire for Mr. *Wilfull*, tell
him his Captain wants him here immediately.   60

Servant. Sir, the Gentleman's below at the Door enquiring
for the Captain.

Plume. Bid him come up—here's the Discharge, Sir.—

Ballance. Sir, I thank you—'tis plain he had no hand in't.
(*Aside.*)

Enter Silvia.

Silvia. I think, Captain, you might have us'd me better,
than to leave me yonder among your swearing, drunken Crew;
and you, Mr. Justice, might have been so civil as to have
invited me to Dinner, for I have eaten with as good a Man as
your Worship.

Plume. Sir, you must charge our want of Respect upon our   70
Ignorance of your Quality—but now you're at Liberty—I
have discharged you.

Silvia. Discharg'd me!

Ballance. Yes, Sir, and you must once more go home to your
Father.

Silvia. My Father! then I'm discovered—O, Sir, (*Kneeling.*)
I expect no Pardon.

Ballance. Pardon! no, no, Child; your Crime shall be your
Punishment; here, Captain, I deliver her over to the conjugal
Power for her Chastisement; since she will be a Wife, be you a   80
Husband, a very Husband: when she tells you of her Love,
upbraid her with her Folly, be modishly ungrateful, because
she has been unfashionably kind; and use her worse than you
wou'd any Body else, because you can't use her so well as she
deserves.

Plume. And are you *Silvia* in good earnest?

Silvia. Earnest! I have gone too far to make it a Jest, Sir.

Plume. And do you give her to me in good earnest?

*Ballance.*If you please to take her, Sir.

90 *Plume.* Why then I have sav'd my Legs and Arms, and lost my Liberty, secure from Wounds I'm prepar'd for the Gout, farewel Subsistence, and welcome Taxes.—Sir, my Liberty and hopes of being a General are much dearer to me than your twelve hundred Pound a Year, but to your Love, Madam, I resign my Freedom, and to your Beauty, my Ambition; greater in obeying at your Feet, than Commanding at the Head of an Army.

Enter Worthy.

Worthy. I'm sorry to hear, Mr. *Ballance*, that your Daughter is lost.

100 *Ballance.* So am not I, Sir, since an honest Gentleman has found her.

Enter Melinda.

Melinda. Pray, Mr. *Ballance*, what's become of my Cousin *Silvia*?

Ballance. Your Cousin *Silvia* is talking yonder with your Cousin *Plume*.

Melinda and Worthy. How!

Silvia. Do you think it strange, Cousin, that a Woman should change? But, I hope, you'll excuse a Change that has proceeded from Constancy, I alter'd my Outside, because I 110 was the same within, and only laid by the Woman to make sure of my Man, that's my History.

Melinda. Your History is a little romantick, Cousin, but since Success has crown'd your Adventures you will have the World o'your side, and I shall be willing to go with the Tide, provided you pardon an Injury I offer'd you in the Letter to your Father.

Plume. That Injury, Madam, was done to me, and the Reparation I expect shall be made to my Friend, make Mr. *Worthy* happy, and I shall be satisfy'd.

120 *Melinda.* A good Example, Sir, will go a great way—when my Cousin is pleas'd to surrender, 'tis probable, I shan't hold out much longer.

Enter Brazen.

Brazen. Gentlemen, I am yours, Madam, I am not yours.

Melinda. I'm glad on't, Sir.

Brazen. So am I—you have got a pretty House here, Mr. *Laconick.*

Ballance. 'Tis time to right all Mistakes—my Name, Sir, is *Ballance.*

Brazen. *Ballance!* Sir, I'm your most obedient.—I know your whole Generation,—had not you an Unkle that was Governour 130 of the *Leeward* Islands some Years ago?

Ballance. Did you know him?

Brazen. Intimately, Sir, he play'd at Billiards to a miracle; you had a Brother too, that was Captain of a Fireship—poor *Dick*, he had the most engaging way with him—of making Punch,—and then his Cabbin was so neat—but his Boy *Jack* was the most comical Bastard, ha, ha, ha, a pickled Dog, I shall never forget him.

Plume. Well, Captain, are you fix'd in your Project yet, are you still for the Privateer?   ·140

Brazen. No, no, I had enough of a Privateer just now, I had like to have been pick'd up by a Cruiser under false Colours, and a *French* Pickaroon for ought I know.

Plume. But have you got your Recruits, my Dear?

Brazen. Not a Stick, my Dear.

Plume. Probably I shall furnish you.

Enter Rose and Bullock.

Rose. Captain, Captain, I have got loose once more, and have persuaded my Sweetheart *Cartwheel*, to go with us, but you must promise not to part with me again.

Silvia. I find Mrs. *Rose* has not been pleas'd with her 150 Bedfellow.

Rose. Bedfellow! I don't know whether I had a Bedfellow or not.

Silvia. Don't be in a Passion, Child, I was as little pleas'd with your Company as you cou'd be with mine.

Bullock. Pray, Sir, dunna be offended at my Sister, she's something underbred—but if you please I'll lye with you in her stead.

Plume. I have promis'd, Madam, to provide for this Girl; now will you be pleas'd to let her wait upon you, or shall I 160 take care of her.

Silvia. She shall be my Charge, Sir, you may find it Business enough to take care of me.

Bullock. Ay, and of me, Captain, for wauns if ever you lift your Hand against me, I'll desert.

Plume. Captain *Brazen* shall take care o'that—My Dear, instead of the twenty thousand Pound you talk'd of, you shall have the twenty brave Recruits that I have rais'd, at the rate they cost me—my Commission I lay down to be taken up by
170 some braver Fellow, that has more Merit, and less good Fortune, whilst I endeavour by the Example of this worthy Gentleman to serve my Queen and country at home.

> *With some Regret I quit the active Field,*
> *Where Glory full reward for Life does yield;*
> *But the Recruiting Trade with all its train,*
> *Of lasting Plague, Fatigue, and endless Pain,*
> *I gladly quit, with my fair Spouse to stay,*
> *And raise Recruits the Matrimonial Way.*

[*Exeunt.*]

[FINIS.]

EPILOGUE.

All Ladies and Gentlemen, that are willing to see the Comedy call'd the *Recruiting Officer*, let them repair to morrow Night by six a Clock to the Sign of the *Theatre Royal* in *Drury Lane*, and they shall be kindly entertain'd—

> *We scorn the vulgar Ways to bid you come,*
> *Whole* Europe *now obeys the Call of Drum.*
> *The Soldier, not the Poet, here appears,*
> *And beats up for a* Corp's *of Volunteers:*
> *He finds that Musick chiefly do's delight ye,*
> *And therefore chuses Musick to invite ye.*   10

Beat the Granadeer March—Row, row, tow—Gentlemen, this Piece of Musick, call'd an *Overture to a Battel*, was compos'd by a famous *Italian* Master, and was perform'd with wonderful Success, at the great *Opera*'s of *Vigo, Schellenberg*, and *Blenheim*; it came off with the Applause of all *Europe*, excepting *France*; the *French* found it a little too rough for their *Delicatesse*.

> *Some that have acted on those glorious Stages,* ⎫
> *Are here to witness to succeeding Ages,* ⎬
> *That no Musick like the Granadeer's engages.* ⎭

Ladies, we must own that this Musick of ours is not 20 altogether so soft as *Bonancini*'s, yet we dare affirm, that it has laid more People asleep than all the *Camilla*'s in the World; and you'll condescend to own, that it keeps one awake, better than any *Opera* that ever was acted.

The Granadeer March seems to be a Composure excellently adapted to the Genius of the *English*; for no Musick was ever follow'd so far by us, nor with so much Alacrity; and with all Defference to the present Subscription, we must say that the Granadeer March has been subscrib'd for by the whole Grand Alliance; and we presume to inform the Ladies, that it always 30 has the Pre-eminence abroad, and is constantly heard by the tallest, handsomest Men in the whole Army. In short, to gratifie the present Taste, our Author is now adapting some Words to the Granadeer March, which he intends to have perform'd to Morrow, if the Lady who is to sing it shou'd not happen to be sick.

> *This he concludes to be the surest way*
> *To draw you hither, for you'll all obey*
> *Soft Musick's Call, tho' you shou'd damn his Play.*

APPENDIX

SONG

I.

Ye Nymphs and *Sylvan* Gods,
That Love Green Fields and Woods,
   When Spring newly born,
   Her self does adorn,
With Flowers and Blooming Buds;
   Come Sing in the praise,
   Whilst Flocks do graze
In yonder pleasant Vale,
   Of those that choose
   That sleeps to lose,
   And in cold Dews,
   With clouted Shooes,
Do carry the Milking Pail.

II.

The Goddess of the Morn,
With blushes they adorn,
   And take the fresh Air;
   Whilst Linnets prepare
A Consort on each green Thorn,
   The Ousle and Thrush,
   On every Bush;
And the Charming Nightingal;
   In merry Vain,
   Their Throats do strain,
   To entertain
   The Jolly train
That carry the Milking Pail.

III.

When cold bleak Winds do Roar,
And Flow'rs can spring no more,
 The Fields that were seen,
 So pleasant and green,
By winter all Candy'd o're,
 Oh! how the Town Lass,
Looks with her white Face,
And her Lips of Deadly Pale:
 But it is not so,
 With those that go,
 Through Frost and Snow,
 With Cheeks that glow,
And carry the Milking Pail.

IV.

The Miss of Courtly mould,
Adorn'd with Pearl and Gold,
 With washes and Paint,
 Her Skin does so Taint,
She's wither'd before She's old,
 Whilst She in Commode,
 Puts on a Cart-load;
And with Cushions plumps her Tayl;
 What Joys are found,
 In Russet Gown,
 Young, Plump and Round,
 And sweet and sound,
That carry the Milking Pail.

V.

The Girls of *Venus* game,
That venture Health and Fame,
 In practising Feats,
With Colds and with Heats,
Make Lovers grow Blind and Lame;
 If Men were so Wise,
 To value the prize,
Of the Wares most fit for sale,

What store of Beaus,
Wou'd dawb their Cloaths,
To save a Nose,
By following those
That carry the Milking Pail.

(From Thomas D'Urfey, *The Comical History of Don Quixote*
[London, 1694], pp. 22–3.)

The Recruiting Officer; *Or the Merrie Voluntiers.*
Being an Excellent New Copy *of Verses upon Raising*
Recruits.

Hark! now the Drums beat up agen,
For all true Soldiers Gentlmen;
Then let us list and March I say,
Over the the Hills and far away,
Over the Hills and o're the Main,
To *Flanders, Portugal* and *Spain*,
Queen *Ann* Commands and we'll obey,
Over the Hills and far away.

All Gentlemen that have a Mind,
To serve the Queen that's good and kind,   10
Come list and enter into Pay,
Then o're the Hills and far away;
Over the Hills and o're the Main,
To *Flanders, Portugal* and *Spain*,
Queen *Ann*, &c.

Here's Forty Shillings on the Drum,
For those that Voluntiers do come,
With Shirts and Cloaths and present Pay,
When o're the Hill and far away;
Over the Hills, &c.   20

Hear that brave Boys and let us go,
Or else we shall be Prest you know,
Then List and enter into Pay,
And o're the Hills and far away;
O're the Hills, &c.

The Constables they search about,
To find such brisk young Fellows out,
Then let's be Voluntiers I say,
Over the Hills and far away;
Over the hills, &c.

Since now the French so low are brought,
And wealth and honours to be got,
Who then behind wou'd sneaking stay,
When o're the Hills and far away;
Over, &c.

No more from sound of Drum retreat,
While *Marlborough* and *Gallaway* beat,
The French and Spaniards every day,
When over the hills and far away; &c.

He that is forc'd to go and Fight,
Will never get true honour by't,
While Voluntiers shall win the Day,
When o're the Hill and far away;
Over, &c.

What tho our Friends our absence mourn,
We all with honour shall return,
And then we'll sing both Night and day,
Over the Hills and far away;
Over, &c.

The Prentice *Tom* he may refuse,
To wipe his angry Master's Shooes;
For then he's free to Sing and play,
Over the Hills and far away, &c.

Over Rivers, Bogs and Springs,
We all shall live as great as Kings,
And Plunder get both Night and day,
When over the Hills and far away, &c.

We then shall lead more happy Lives,
By getting rid of brats and Wives,
That scold on both Night and Day,
When o're the Hills and far away, &c.

Come on then Boys and You shall see.
We every one shall Captans be,
To Whore and Rant as well as they,
When o're the Hills and far away, &c.

For it we go 'tis one to ten,
But we return all Gentlemen,
All Gentlemen as well as they,
When o're the Hills and far away, &c.

(From Thomas D'Urfey, *Wit and Mirth: or Pills to
Purge Melancholy* [London, 1706] iv. 102–4.)

THE BEAUX STRATAGEM

INTRODUCTION

SOURCES AND COMPOSITION

ON 27 January 1707 Bernard Lintott paid George Farquhar £30 for the rights to *The Beaux Stratagem*.[1] The January number of the *Muses Mercury*, which did not actually appear until mid February, announced that Farquhar had a new comedy ready for representation.[2] On 7 February a notice appeared in the *Daily Courant*:

There will speedily be acted at the Queen's Theatre in the Hay-Market, a new Comedy, call'd The Broken Beaux. Written by Mr. Farquhar, Author of the Recruiting Officer. This Comedy, when Acted, will be printed for Bernard Lintott at Nando's Coffee-House, Temple Bar.[3]

The play opened on 8 March at the Queen's Theatre in the Haymarket.

The dates of the transactions with Lintott and the pre-opening volleys do not disprove the traditional story of composition:

His last Comedy, the *Stratagem*, he began and ended in six Weeks with a settled Sickness upon him all the time; nay, he even perceiv'd the Approaches of Death, e'er he had finish'd the second Act, and (as he had often foretold) dy'd before the Run of this Play was over.[4]

The basic outlines are embellished by most biographers. One of the most florid accounts was provided by Thomas Wilkes, who claimed he had got it from Colley Cibber:

Mr. Farquhar was a constant attendant on the Theatre; but Mr. Wilkes having missed him there, for upwards of two months, went to the house where he lodged in York-buildings to enquire for him; and was informed that he had left it, but could not learn where he lived; Mr. Wilkes a few days after, received a letter from Farquhar, desiring to see him at his lodgings in St. Martin's lane; Wilkes went there and found him in a most miserable situation, lodged in a back garret, and under the greatest agitation of mind; Wilkes enquired the reason of his distress, and Farquhar acquainted him with the whole affair; and that what gave him the greatest concern was the fear of losing the Earl of Orrery's favour by selling his commission. Wilkes advised him to write a Play and that it should be brought on the Stage with all expedition; 'Write, says Farquhar! it is impossible that a man can write common sense who is heartless, and has not a shilling in his pocket.' 'Come George, replied Wilkes, banish melancholy, draw your Drama, and I will call on you this day week to see it, but as an empty pocket may cramp your genius, I desire you will accept of my mite,' and gave him twenty guineas. Mr. Farquhar immediately drew up the Drama of the Beaux-Stratagem; which he delivered to Mr. Wilkes, and it was approved of by him and the Managers, and finished in six weeks. Mr. Farquhar during his writing this Play had a settled sickness on him, and most of it he wrote in his bed, and before he had finished the second Act, he perceived the approaches of death. The first night that it was performed, his good friend Mr. Wilkes came to give him an account of its great success, but remarked to him that Mrs. Oldfield (who performed the character of Mrs. Sullen) thought he had dealt too freely with her character in the Play, by giving her to Archer without a proper divorce, which was not a security for her husband; 'to salve this, replied our author, I'll get a real divorce, marry her myself, and give her my bond she shall be a real Widow in less than a fortnight.' On the third night of it's being performed, which was for his Benefit, he died, which was the last week in April 1707.[5]

The tales have been at the least somewhat romanticized. Farquhar did not, for example, die during the third night, for he was not buried until 23 May.[6] But one can safely assume that he was terminally ill and writing for money. Before *The Recruiting Officer* opened, he had resigned his commission in the army; recruiting proved an expensive venture, and he may have needed to sell the lieutenancy to pay debts. His replacement had been named by 1 March 1706.[7] *The Recruiting Officer* had supported him and his family for a while, and he had probably attempted unsuccessfully to regain his commission.[8] He wrote a prologue for Wilks to speak at the opening of the theatre on 15 October 1706 and one for Susanna Centlivre's *The Platonick Lady*, at the same theatre on 25 November.[9] The fact that he was once again writing prologues, after a lapse of almost four years, shows that he was back in London, back in close contact with a theatrical company, now at the Queen's Theatre, to which Wilks had transferred. He was probably also working on a new play.

The pathetic tale of the 29-year-old playwright on his death-bed, writing his joyous comedy even as his health wasted away, has been perpetuated; it may well have been accurate. Farquhar, after all, had interspersed his theatrical career with illnesses: he probably spent a month ill at Coventry before his first play was written, since such an illness is mentioned—irrelevantly—by the protagonist; he was ill again, as he mentioned in *Love and Business*, around 1700. Whether the disease which finally consumed him had bedevilled him for a decade or whether he was merely prone to fevers, he must have had prior experience at writing from his sick-bed. This time he did not recover.

Once again he moulded from the traditions of English comedy a play that was sparklingly original. Rothstein speaks of his creation of an intellectual and formal structure that is 'openly novel'.[10] Those that had spitefully condemned Farquhar for plagiarism could not begin to accuse him of imitating his superiors in this play. In fact, there have been few suggestions of sources or analogues. Stonehill cites *The Provok'd Wife*, *The Relapse*, and Shadwell's *Epsom Wells*.[11] Richard Hindry Barker claims that Farquhar used a scene from Cibber's *She Wou'd and She Wou'd Not* 'with a few changes and improvements'[12] in the scene in which Archer and Aimwell inquire about supper at the inn. Curt A. Zimansky mentions that Aimwell resembles Fashion in *The Relapse* in going into the country under his brother's title to marry a fortune, but Zimansky rightly does not consider this a debt to Vanbrugh.[13] A closer relationship is the one to Steele's *The Lying Lover* (1703) in which Bookwit and Latine pose as master and servant, and Latine, as the servant, enchants Penelope and Victoria with his hyperbolic and allusive praise.[14]

Lawrence and Kavanagh made fanciful attempts to associate the characters with living models. Lawrence claimed that Foigard was based on an Irish priest named Father Fogourdy mentioned by Pepys on 6 February 1663/4,[15] long before Farquhar's birth. Kavanagh opined that the characters were founded on people Farquhar had met in Lichfield during his recruiting tour. Perhaps his attribution was based on Thomas Wilkes's assertion that Bonniface was drawn from a landlord of an inn at Lichfield 'whose picture is now to be seen there' and Scrub 'was well known at that time, he died at Salisbury in the year 1744'.[16]

Cherry's catechism scene (II.ii) was based on a mode of witty catechisms that had become popular during the first decade of the eighteenth century. Farquhar himself had written a scene in *Love and a Bottle*, IV.iii, in which Lovewell catechizes Lyric about being a poet. A series of single-sheet pamphlets, such as *The Beaux Catechism* (1703), *The Ladies Catechism* (1703), *The Players Catechism* (1704), and *The Atheists Catechism* (1704) were marketed, and the dialogue between Archer and Cherry was in fact the basis of *Love's Catechism* (copies in the Bodleian, British Library).

Farquhar draws heavily on Milton's *Doctrine and Discipline of Divorce* for the discussion of divorce.[17] As Martin A. Larson accurately states, the play 'is shot through with ideas, phrases, and sentences borrowed from Milton's tract'. Literary scholars have generally assumed that Farquhar's interest in divorce derived from his own miserable marriage, although there have certainly been no proofs that his marriage was an unhappy one. His interest might have been fostered, in fact, by his friendship and admiration for Henry Brett, to whom he had dedicated *The Twin-Rivals*. Brett, who joined the management at Drury Lane in 1707, had married the divorced wife of the Earl of Macclesfield. The sensationalism of the divorce trial must have affected Brett and his wife adversely, even in 1707, eight years after the divorce proceedings ended and seven years after their marriage. Farquhar may well have been drawn to the subject of divorce by Brett's situation as well as the contemporary theatrical interest in flawed marriages. The dissolution of the Sullens' marriage actually derived not from English law, but from Milton's conviction that mutual consent should be a fully sufficient cause for divorce. By using divorce by mutual consent in the denouement, Farquhar found an easy way out of his plot dilemma, perhaps expressed a personal conviction, and provided critics for generations a topic for discussion and condemnation.

If Farquhar was, in fact, in his sickbed, sinking to his death, and if he wrote his scenes *seriatim*, weakness may excuse the improbability of his solution. He dispatched Aimwell's older brother without any proper preparation to clear the way for one marriage, but he could not very well kill off Sullen in the same comedy, even had he not wanted to treat the divorce issue seriously. The Sullens' mutual consent, albeit intellectually satisfying, was dramatically inept. For the first time in his entire career, Farquhar used a dance to cover the confusions of a sloppy conclusion, a device other playwrights often stooped to use.

STAGE HISTORY

Some time between 7 February, when the *Daily Courant* noted that Farquhar had 'The Broken Beaux' in rehearsal and 8 March when the *première* took place, the title of the comedy had evolved to *The Stratagem*. For most of the century the stage title remained the same, although the play was always printed as *The Beaux Stratagem*.

Farquhar, on his death-bed, had little to do with theatrical preparations for his final play. He did write his final prologue for Wilks. An epilogue 'Design'd to be spoke in the Beaux Stratagem' was published in the first edition, nineteen days after the *première*; the phrase 'Design'd to be spoke' suggests that the epilogue was not actually used. Later editions identified the author as Edmund Smith, the author of *Phaedra and Hippolytus*, a play that opened at the Queen's on 21 April 1707 and was published by Lintott. Whether the epilogue, with its lachrymose lines on the 'expiring Author', was spoken on the first night cannot be ascertained.

The play called for stock sets, the inn and rooms in Lady Bountiful's house. The props and costumes were also standard. Even the cast offered no surprises: Wilks and Mills took Archer and Aimwell, cast as usual as the airy hero and his upright friend; Anne Oldfield played Mrs Sullen, and Lucretia Bradshaw, who had become a regular performer at the Queen's Theatre that season, played Dorinda. The comedian Bullock predictably played Bonniface. Scrub, obviously created and named for the diminutive Norris, fell naturally to him. Cibber played Gibbet, Verbruggen took

Sullen, Bowen Foigard, and Keen Freeman. Mrs Powell played Lady Bountiful, and Mrs Bicknell, who had played Rose in *The Recruiting Officer* at the Queen's in 1706, took Cherry.

Jean-Claude Gillier wrote the act music for *The Stratagem*, an overture, trumpet tune, allemande, two airs, saraband, gavotte, and two jigs.[18] Wilks sang the only two songs, 'But you look so bright' in Act I and Farquhar's 'Song of a Trifle' in III.iii. In V.iv Archer and Mrs. Sullen lead the country dance to 'The Trifle'. The *Dancing Master* for 1718 includes a dance called 'The Beaus Stratagem', possibly the one which ended the play.[19]

The public relations efforts, begun on 7 February with the *Daily Courant* item on 'The Broken Beaux' and the item in the *Muses Mercury*, continued on Wednesday, 5 March, when the *Daily Courant* advertised for the following Saturday 'a new Comedy (never Acted before) call'd The Stratagem and Written by the Author of the Recruiting Officer'. The advertisement was repeated on 6 and 7 March (revised to read 'Tomorrow'). The *première* was advertised on Saturday, 8 March, with the additional information that because the theatre was obliged to act *The Careless Husband* on Monday for Cibber's benefit, *The Stratagem* would be acted again on Tuesday. Monday's advertisement contained a reminder of the Tuesday performance, and on each subsequent day up to 20 March a notice was inserted for the next performance, whether it was the same night or the night following. On Monday, 17 March, the *Daily Courant* noted the evening's performance and added an explanation that the theatre was obliged to act *The Spanish Friar* for Betterton's benefit on Tuesday so that the next performance of *The Stratagem* would be Thursday (the house was dark on Wednesday). All in all, twenty-nine advertisements publicized the twelve performances that season, a remarkably strong advertising campaign for the period. The notices regularly reminded prospective members of the audience that *The Stratagem* was written by the author of *The Recruiting Officer*.

March 1707 seemed to be Farquhar Month; of thirty-three performances, thirteen were comedies by Farquhar. Drury Lane, as though inadvertently heralding the new play, ran *The*

Recruiting Officer 3 and 6 March. *The Stratagem* opened 8 March at the Queen's and ran eight times during the month. Drury Lane countered with two more productions of *The Recruiting Officer*, one which played against *The Stratagem* on 17 March and the other against *The Constant Couple* on 27 March. Perhaps Farquhar's settled illness heightened the piquancy of the performances; more likely, financial self-interest encouraged the frequent productions of his plays.

The first run of Farquhar's final play was predictably successful, although Colley Cibber claimed that it, as well as other plays, suffered acoustically from the 'immoderate Wideness' of the theatre:

. . . the Difficulty of Hearing, may be said to have bury'd half the Auditors Entertainment. This Defect seem'd evident, from the much better Reception several new Plays (first acted there) met with when they afterwards came to be play'd by the same Actors, in *Drury-Lane*: Of this Number were the *Stratagem*. . .[20]

Although the audience may well have heard the lines better in subsequent seasons, one cannot argue lack of success at the Queen's Theatre, for the comedy had run twelve times by 5 June. The third, sixth, and eleventh performances were benefits for Farquhar; there is no explanation for the delay of the third benefit to the eleventh night, particularly for a man desperately ill and impoverished. Instead, Bullock's benefit fell on the ninth night, 31 March. It was advertised with Bonniface's catch-phrase, indicating the popularity and immediate familiarity of the portrayal: 'For the Benefit of Will Bullock, as the Saying is'. The performance on 5 June benefited Norris. But by the time the little man who created Farquhar's Jubilee Dicky, Petit, and Costar Pearmain profited at his benefit performance as Scrub, Farquhar, not yet thirty years old, lay in his grave.

Twelve nights' run, interrupted by necessity by previous commitments for benefit performances, demonstrates the immediate success of the play. The inordinate number of advertisements does too. There were other indications as well that *The Stratagem* became the sensation that the advertising campaign was designed to create. Perhaps one of the most telling lay in the Drury Lane advertisement of *The Recruiting*

Officer on 17 April, which for the first time reversed the formula to read 'Written by the Author of the Beaux Stratagem'. In the context of the frequency and popularity of Farquhar's comedies on stage in 1706 and 1707, one can well understand the opinion expressed in the *Muses Mercury* in September: 'As for *Comedies*, there's no great Expectation of any thing of that kind, since Mr. *Farquhar*'s Death.'

The following decades bore out the doleful prediction. The dearth of rich new comic materials provided a repertory gulf that the plays of Farquhar and his contemporaries filled. Of all Farquhar's plays, of all the comedies of his era, none fared better than *The Stratagem*. In all, it ran 632 times in London in the eighteenth century, an average of almost seven times per year. A tabulation by decade demonstrates once again the curve of popularity that marked the writers of humane comedy:

Decades	Performance count
1707–10	26 performances
1710–20	40 performances
1720–30	94 performances
1730–40	106 performances
1740–50	114 performances
1750–60	69 performances
1760–70	66 performances
1770–80	59 performances
1780–90	38 performances
1790–1800	20 performances

Statistics for the two most fertile seven-year spans are even more impressive: the play ran ninety-eight times in the 1729–36 seasons, and ninety times in 1740–7. Perhaps even more incredibly, during the entire eighteenth century, *The Stratagem* was performed in London every season but one, 1795–6.

Like *The Recruiting Officer*, *The Stratagem* proved a great favourite for benefit nights: 194 of the 632 eighteenth-century performances, more than 30 per cent, were benefits.[21] More than 60 per cent were for performers, albeit often singers, dancers, or others who did not perform in the main piece. Twenty-four per cent benefited other house officers, and more than 10 per cent were charity benefits, including two, on 14 May 1737 and 19 December 1750, for Farquhar's daughters. Three benefited Farquhar, and four were for authors of materials added to the programme, either after-pieces or prologues. Actors preferred *The Stratagem* even over *The Recruiting Officer* for their benefits—Norris, Bullock, Pinkethman, Oldfield, and generations of later actors, Woffington included, found the main roles an ideal choice for a benefit performance.

The comedy was often played by royal command. Between 1714 and 1775 twenty-eight performances were commanded by various members of the royal family; half of those fell within the decade 1736–46. On 23 September 1734 the comedy played at Covent Garden 'For the Entertainment of Tomo Chachi, Micho or King of the Yamicraw, Senauki his Wife, and the rest of the Indians'.[22] History has not recorded the reactions of Tomo Chachi or Senauki to such scenes as the near-seduction of Mrs Sullen or the divorce discussions.

The quirks of theatrical management which had affected *The Recruiting Officer*, making it a repertory piece at both houses after its first season, did not similarly affect *The Stratagem*. In January 1708 an agreement was struck between Drury Lane and the Queen's to offer plays at Drury Lane, opera at the Queen's because of the acoustics. The two theatres, therefore, did not compete for actors or plays, as they had with *The Recruiting Officer*. Performances took place at both houses in the first five seasons, but the same core group of actors performed at either location. In fact, the Drury Lane company all but monopolized the play, as was usual in the period, until the 1721–2 season, when Lincoln's Inn Fields mounted its first production. The only other previous productions outside the Queen's–Drury Lane run had been one at which the same cast performed elsewhere, one at Hampton Court, and a performance at St Martin's Lane mounted by the children of actors, including Young Norris as Scrub, Bullock's youngest son as Bonniface, Young Bowman as Aimwell, and other budding thespians. Both Drury Lane and Lincoln's Inn Fields regularly ran the play at least three and often more times for the next eight seasons, and the Haymarket occasionally gave a performance. When Goodman's Fields opened in October 1729, the new contenders immediately gave stiff competition with multiple performances each of the next seven seasons.

The revitalized Haymarket, invigorated by the successes of Fielding's plays, ran *The Stratagem* annually until the fateful 1736–7 season. The Lincoln's Inn Fields troupe moved to Covent Garden in 1732–3. The competition between Covent Garden and Drury Lane remained active throughout the century. During the century almost half of the performances were given at Drury Lane, but other theatres were also active:[23]

Theatre	Performance count	Percentage of total
Drury Lane	282	45 per cent
Queen's	19	3 per cent
Lincoln's Inn Fields	65	10 per cent
Covent Garden	156	25 per cent
Goodman's Fields	46	7 per cent
Southwark	5	1 per cent
Haymarket	41	6 per cent
Other	18	3 per cent[24]

The century's best actors and actresses embodied Farquhar's characters. Archer was the last airy spark that Farquhar created for his friend Wilks, and perhaps the best, for the combination of good humour and good sense which marked Sir Harry had now a kind of mellowness perhaps born of Farquhar's own seasoning in life. Wilks seemed to be sole proprietor of the role (with the exception of Young Pervil at the Lilliputian performance at St Martin's Lane and an unknown performer at the Haymarket, 14 July 1717) until challenged at Lincoln's Inn Fields by Ryan, who first played Archer on 18 November 1721 and regularly took the role thereafter; the two competed in the role, almost without other challengers, until Giffard entered the lists at Goodman's Fields in 1729. Wilks continued to play Archer throughout his career, his last performance occurring on 26 April 1732. Other Archers included Orfeur, Bridgwater, Lacy, Hewson, Chapman, Hind, Walker, Selwin 'the first time of his appearing on any stage', Wilks's nephew, Stoppelaer, Oates, Mills, Ryan, Garrick, Townly, Mrs Charke, Cushing, Dyer, Murphy, Griffith 'first appearance that stage', Smith, O'Brien, King, Kennedy, Palmer, 'a Gentleman, first time on the stage', Lee, Aickin, Ross, Death 'from the Theatre in

Norwich', Whitfield, Lewis, Wroughton, Gardner, Sterne, Bernard from the Theatre Royal in Bath, and Barrymore. Many of the Archers acted Plume and other Farquharian blades as well.

Garrick, who first played Archer on 22 December 1742, continued in the role as long as he acted, his last performance on 7 May 1776. On 30 March 1745 Peg Woffington, who often played Mrs Sullen, played Cherry to Garrick's Archer. Garrick excelled in the role; Genest describes his performance as capital, particularly in the scenes with Cherry.[25] But he had his difficult moments; there was the night of 21 November 1755, when he had to quieten the clapping and hissing of a rowdy audience before he could continue and perhaps an even worse moment on 1 December 1775, described in the Hopkins Diary:

In Saluting Cherry. She tumbled down upon the Stage—and Miss Jaratt being in certain condition Mr. G. could not very easily raise her.[26]

Perennially applauded as Archer, Garrick also switched roles in the play: as he had tried Kite on occasion, he chose Scrub on 10 April 1761 and several times thereafter.

The Mrs Sullens, Scrubs, and Bonnifaces of the century were also bountifully numerous. They reflected, as did the Archers, the fullness and variety of staging practices in the period. Some inspirations fizzled: Mrs Abington's appearance as Scrub, for example, for her benefit on 10 February 1786, although financially overwhelmingly rewarding, may have proved an embarrassment. The critic in the *Public Advertiser* found her portrayal well conceived and sprightly, but the *Morning Post* found her 'inattentive and torpid', and Henry Angelo in his *Reminiscences* felt she entirely failed, that her physical appearance was preposterous and her gestures ineffective, the whole, in fact, 'disgusting and absurd'.[27] But by and large the roles proved reliably workable ones. Few plays of the period, or in fact of any period, contain as many choice parts as *The Stratagem*—perhaps the richness of the roles explains in part its popularity as a benefit piece.

When his earlier plays opened, Farquhar was a close associate of the theatre. He was a devoted friend of the chief actor Wilks, he wrote prologues and epilogues for Wilks's company; he supposedly discovered Anne Oldfield and almost certainly had an affair with her not to mention assorted other actresses and female playwrights that he courted; he drank at the Rose Tavern; and he saw plays. He was around the theatre if scenes needed revision or prologues needed to be written for special occasions. We know that he revised *The Constant Couple* and *The Recruiting Officer*; we cannot know whether he introduced major or minor revisions to other plays, because if he did they never reached the print shop. But for *The Stratagem* Farquhar clearly could not have been greatly involved in revisions at least for any length of time because of his failing health. Yet playhouse revisions clearly occurred.

The manuscript that Lintott published included the part of Count Bellair, played in the original run by Boman, according to the Dramatis Personae. In editions of 1728, 1730, 1733, and later, the following note occurs at the point at which Count Bellair enters in III.iii:

This Scene printed in *Italick*, with the entire Part of the *Count*, was cut out by the Author, after the first Night's Representation; and where he shou'd enter in the last Scene of the fifth Act, it is added to the Part of *Foigard*.

The 1728 edition also revises one of Archer's lines and the 1730 edition identifies Smith as the author of the Epilogue. Although the cast list does not appear in advertisements for the first season, for the second season on no mention is made of Count Bellair. Other minor characters are often also omitted from cast-lists, including Gypsey, Hounslow, and Bagshot in *The Stratagem*, but the possibility of deletion of the character certainly exists. Boman, who played the Count, had, in fact, left the company by the following season. Archer's change of line from the statement that he will pay the ten thousand pounds to 'I'll pay it: my Lord, I thank him, has enabled me, and if the Lady pleases, she shall go home with me' occurs at the point that Mrs Sullen is paired with Archer despite the lack of a proper divorce; the revision does not, however, seem to improve matters.

On 26 August 1735 a production at the Haymarket advertised *The Stratagem* as 'Newly Revis'd and Alter'd'. The reviser observed his reasons for amending the play:

> . . . tho' he thinks the Chief Characters in this Play, are drawn with
> a great deal of Life and Spirit; Yet that even in this very sprightly
> Play there are several very obvious Faults. That as the Character of
> the French Count, and that of the Irish Priest, are in no sort
> conducive to the Plot of the Play; they may therefore be look'd upon
> as superfluous: That the Parting of Sullen and his Wife is extreamly
> unnatural; and that the Ending of the Play (with respect to Archer)
> is abrupt to a Degree. . . .[28]

If, in fact, *The Stratagem* had played at Drury Lane and
perhaps other theatres since the beginning without Count
Bellair, the reviser was unaware of it. Yet had he revised from
a copy printed after 1728 he should have known of the absence
of Bellair.

On 26 January 1789 Drury Lane opened *The Impostors*, a
play by Richard Cumberland based on *The Stratagem*. The
play ran six nights, but never challenged the original. Not
until the end of the century did *The Beaux Stratagem* become the
title used in the theatre, first at a performance at Crown Inn
Islington and then at Covent Garden. By 21 November 1789
even Drury Lane advertised *The Beaux Stratagem*.

The success of the play of course was confined by neither
chronology nor geography to London in the eighteenth
century. It was one of the most popular plays to travel across
England, Wales, and Scotland, and played frequently in both
Dublin and the Irish towns of Belfast, Tralee, Kilkenny,
Fethard, Cork, Waterford, and Londonderry. It crossed the
ocean to colonial America. It continued to play in the
nineteenth century. Of the few early eighteenth-century plays
staged in the twentieth century, *The Beaux Stratagem* is one of
the most frequent.

REPUTATION AND INFLUENCE

Farquhar's reputation in the twentieth century seems to be
based on *The Recruiting Officer* and *The Beaux Stratagem*; in his
own century, popularity extended well beyond these plays,
but they were considered his finest works. Perhaps because of
Farquhar's death, perhaps because new comedies had become

a less important element in the theatrical repertory, the success of *The Beaux Stratagem* did not kindle fires of critical animosity as *The Constant Couple* had. The play was immediately accepted and long continued as one of the most familiar plays. The writers of the eighteenth century were familiar with it. Boswell, Goldsmith, and Johnson knew it, among other reasons for the popularity of their friend Garrick as Archer and Scrub. Lady Mary Wortley Montagu and Mrs Thrale refer to it casually in their letters.[29] Fielding was also familiar with the play, not only from the playhouse but from his own library. The play's popularity would have made it almost inescapable to anyone who read books or saw plays.

It won accolades from early playgoers, and it remained popular with later critics. Generally it has been deemed Farquhar's best play as well as his most popular. Hazlitt, for example, found it 'infinitely lively, bustling, and full of point and interest'. He singled out the character of Scrub as 'an indispensable appendage to a country gentleman's kitchen, and an exquisite confidant for the secrets of young ladies'.[30] Leigh Hunt found its plot 'new, simple, and interesting; the characters various, without confusing it; the dialogue sprightly and characteristic; the moral bold, healthy, admirable, and doubly needed in those times, when sottishness was a fashion'. He admires the characterizations:

Archer and *Aimwell*, who set out as mere intriguers, prove in the end true gentlemen, candid, conscientious, and generous. *Scrub* and *Boniface*, though but a servant and an innkeeper, are quotable fellows both, and have made themselves prominent in theatrical recollection,—the former especially, for his quaint ignorance and sordid cunning. And *Mrs. Sullen* is the more touching in her distress, from the cheerfulness with which she wipes away her tears.[31]

Hunt, like earlier critics, felt the conclusion was flawed because the law did not provide the 'sanction' for it. Ever since Mrs Oldfield supposedly complained that Farquhar had dealt too freely with her character by giving Mrs Sullen to Archer without benefit of a proper divorce, the improbability of the final scene has caused comment. But it has never destroyed the critics' appreciation of the rest of the play.

The admiration continues in the twentieth century. *The*

Stratagem is perceived as the finest of his plays in terms of plot and character development. Hume says Farquhar's last two plays represent humane comedy at its finest,[32] a view with which few contemporary critics would, I believe, disagree.

Reputation is one thing; influence quite another. I have argued that *The Recruiting Officer* had little provable direct influence on later plays. The same can be said of *The Beaux Stratagem*, although one could point directly to Cumberland's *The Imposters*. Stonehill also points to Robert Dodsley's *The Toy-Shop*, a dramatic satire published in 1777, which was inspired by the Song of the Trifle. In it, the Master says:

. . . as it is a trifling age, so nothing but trifles are valued in it. Men read none but trifling authors, pursue none but trifling amusements, and contend for none but trifling opinions. A trifling fellow is preferr'd; a trifling woman admir'd. Nay, as if there were not real trifles enow, they now make trifles of the most serious and valuable things. Their time, their health, their money, their reputation, are trifled away. Honesty is become a trifle, conscience a trifle, honour a mere trifle, and religion the greatest trifle of all.

Presumably the play had its influence on the Germans; Robertson claims that it influenced Lessing's *Minna von Barnheim* more than *The Constant Couple* did.[33]

Steele imitated the scene in which Aimwell feigns illness, holds one hand limp for Lady Bountiful, and squeezes Dorinda's fingers with the other; in *The Conscious Lovers* Myrtle uses the same trick. Goldsmith certainly demonstrates familiarity with the play in two scenes in *She Stoops to Conquer*. Hastings's and Marlow's contempt for the menu in II.i is reminiscent of the discussion of Bonniface's menu by Archer and Aimwell in Act I. In III.i, Kate dons her housewife's dress, saying 'Don't you think I look something like Cherry in *The Beaux Stratagem*?' and then parries with Marlow in a scene in which she clearly imitates Cherry's character and situation but not her specific lines.

In fact the kind of influence Farquhar had on later authors cannot be measured in terms of direct imitations. Instead, one must consider *The Beaux Stratagem* and with it Farquhar's entire canon in terms of more genial and general influences on later writers, those basic changes in tone, in plot development, in characterization, in stage business, that marked him as a writer of humane comedy.

Most notable of his contributions, perhaps, was his new treatment of comic characters, not as butts of satire to be derided but as lovable eccentrics to be enjoyed with some gentleness and good nature. Lady Bountiful, for example, a far cry from the Wishforts and Loveits of Restoration comedy, is both likable and laughable, likable for her good works among the poor, laughable because she is so busy with her possets and caudles that she cannot see that her daughter is being courted under her nose. The young heroes, as bent on adventure as the Restoration rakes, have more good nature and human kindness, less dominant self-interest than their forebears. Cherry, a sister to Rose who has blossomed into full glory, is surely more complex and winsome than any barmaid that preceded her; in her plight, born to the wrong father, she borders on pathos, but always below a cheerful surface. No wonder Kate Hardcastle would choose to play her. So does Mrs Sullen, whose plight is worse—married to a drunken, brutish nincompoop with no saving social or intellectual graces. Even Bonniface, with his ever-present tag, prefigures techniques of characterization not only in later plays but in the comic novel that was to develop as a genre from mid-century.

Moreover, the seriousness underlying the uproarious plots of good-natured plays and novels was prefigured in Farquhar and some of his contemporaries. Restoration plays satirize bad marriages; their plots also prepare the way for heroes and heroines to wed on the basis of parrying well in the witty battle of the sexes. But they do not really focus on the grave reality of inescapable unhappy marriages. Farquhar does, most strikingly in *The Beaux Stratagem*, but in earlier plays as well. He allows glimpses at the true cruelties of the battle of the sexes, through Sir Harry's desertion of Angelica, through Mirabel's irresponsibility toward Oriana, and through Sullen's despicable sottishness. Even in the least realistic plots of trickery and disguise there is an air of verisimilitude created by the way the characters are developed and by the implications of threats below the calm surface of British social behaviour; Farquhar's world seems very real.

The highly energetic action also became a part of British tradition in the theatre and in the novel, and Farquhar excelled all his previous efforts in the tightness of the structure and the neatness of the plot development in *The Beaux Stratagem*. The coalescence of the two love plots and the robbery threat in the final act brings together the strands of a comedy as neatly as any in the period. The hilarity of the action and the breath of danger in the midst of frivolous romancing perfectly balance the serious undercurrent of the far greater dangers of ordinary married life.

Farquhar's contributions, in *The Beaux Stratagem* and cumulatively in all his plays, cannot be proved by direct quotation of later works. But the view of life that informed his plays (and reached full fruition in his last) and the dramatic techniques that made him extraordinarily successful in the theatre became part of the intellectual milieu of British writers.

THE TEXT

The printing history of *The Beaux Stratagem* is relatively as full and complex as the stage history. At least fifty editions appeared during the eighteenth century in England, Scotland, and Ireland, bespeaking a large and continuing market.

Lintott had purchased the rights on 27 January 1707, forty-one days before the *première*. He almost doubled the price he paid for *The Recruiting Officer* the year before, this time offering the destitute Farquhar £30. The *Daily Courant* item announcing that Farquhar's new play would 'speedily be acted' indicates that by 7 February the play had reached the playhouse and was probably in rehearsal or soon to be. Lintott, who had issued three editions of *The Recruiting Officer* before striking the deal for *The Beaux Stratagem*, was eager to profit from Farquhar's success the previous season; otherwise, he would never have advertised the new play so far ahead of time.

Although the formulaic advertisements by Knapton and Lintott ran with the daily announcements of performances of *The Beaux Stratagem* as well as other plays, the *Daily Courant* of 27 March announced 'This Day is publish'd, The Beaux Stratagem, A Comedy, written by Mr. Farquhar, Author of the Recruiting Officer . . .' and the issue of 28 March advertised the book as 'Just publish'd'.³⁴ Two points should be noted about the advertisement on the day of publication: first, the book was called *The Beaux Stratagem* rather than *The Stratagem* even to the public that knew the play under its performance title, and second, *The Recruiting Officer* was invoked to sell copies as it had been to sell seats in the theatre.

That Farquhar was too ill to prepare proper copy for Lintott is clear from his apology in the Advertisement of the quarto, 'The Reader may find some Faults in this Play, which my Illness prevented the amending of'. One of the early memoirs published with his *Works* claimed that he designed to dedicate the play to Lord Cadogan, who evaded the dedication but made him a handsome gift and promises of future favours. Whether the story is true or apocryphal, no dedication accompanied the play, despite Farquhar's reputed desperation for funds.

Farquhar's apologies for the state of the text were unnecessary; the first edition is clean and readable. Lintott, obviously surprised by the unexpected demand for copies of *The Recruiting Officer* the previous year, prepared what must have been a larger printing of the new play. The undated title-page bears the byline *'Written by Mr.* Farquhar, *Author of the* Recruiting-Officer'.

The first quarto has the collational formula [A]¹ B–K⁴. [A]1ʳ bears the half-title and [A]2ʳ the title-page. The Advertisement is printed on [A]3ʳ, backed by the Prologue, and the Epilogue appears on [A]4ʳ, backed by the Dramatis Personae (copies in the Bodleian, British Library, Huntington, Harvard, Clark, Princeton, University of Pennsylvania, University of Texas). Two other states of the prelims exist, however: sheet [A] of one Bodleian copy, shelfmarked Malone 138, was folded inside out, that is, the inner forme became the outer forme by virtue of incorrect folding. As a result the order of the leaves appears to be [A]1ʳ title-page, [A]2ʳ half-title, [A]3ʳ Epilogue, [A]3ᵛ Dramatis Personae, [A]4ʳ Advertisement, [A]4ᵛ Prologue. Yet another state (copies at the Huntington, University of Texas shelfmarked Ak F239 707bb) contains a two-leaf [A] gathering with the title-page on [A]1ʳ and the Dramatis Personae on [A]2ʳ, both versos blank. Such a combination could not have resulted from the normal printing of sheet [A] since it involves two pages ordinarily imposed on opposite quarters of the inner forme. An asterisk appears at the signature location on [A]3^r, the page on which the Advertisement appears in the copies containing the entire [A] gathering (including Malone 138). Some copies of the four-leaf prelims contain the incorrect spelling 'Gentlewo-/woman' in the Dramatis Personae (copies at Harvard, Huntington, Folger, Library of Congress); most copies have the corrected spelling Gentlewo-/man'. Since the two-leaf [A] gathering has the corrected spelling, it must have been printed last, perhaps when a shortage of the sheet necessitated the quick addition of a title-page for the play.

The text of the play appears in B–K^4, pp. *1–72*. The composition is relatively neat and free of errors in comparison to many first editions of the period. Evidence suggests that a single compositor set the entire text *seriatim*.

The second quarto is a page-by-page reprint of the first except that an extra line is added on p. 45; p. 46 also carries an additional line; and p. 47, short by one line, returns to the pagination of the earlier edition.

No additional quartos were printed, although the *Cambridge Bibliography of English Literature* mistakenly lists a total of nine editions in 1707. The next printing was the octavo included in the first edition of the *Comedies*, published by Lintott on 27 March 1708.[35] Then followed many editions, more than fifty in all in the eighteenth century. Lintott was involved in more than twenty of them, sometimes alone, sometimes with other booksellers. T. Johnson imported copies printed at The Hague in 1710 and again in 1720. A 1739 edition was printed for the 'Booksellers in Town and Country'. Leading booksellers like the Knaptons, Strahan, Clark, and Henry Lintott were listed in the imprints of the 1730s, 1740s, and 1750s, and in the 1760s, the Rivingtons, Fletcher, Crowder, Caslon, Lowndes, Woodgate, and Brooks were.[36] Late in the century editions by Bell, Butters, Wenman, Cawthorn, and Cumberland appeared. Editions were also published in Dublin, Edinburgh, and Belfast.

The bibliography is complex because on a number of occasions editions that appear the same, perhaps even share a title-page, are actually different settings of type. A 1733 edition by the same meticulous pirate that printed *The Recruiting Officer* that year looks so much like the authoritative edition printed for Lintott and sold by Feales that it is almost indistinguishable.[37] But the complexities of the printing history, of great value in studying the book trade in the eighteenth century, offer little insight into the textual cruces of *The Beaux Stratagem.*

The most notable exception is the 1728 edition with Lintott's imprint, which appeared in the second volume of *The Works of the late Ingenious Mr. George Farquhar . . . The Sixth Edition. Corrected from the Errors of former Impressions. To which are added some Memoirs of the Author, never before Publish'd.*[38] This edition, published twenty-one years after Farquhar's death, contains revisions of *The Twin-Rivals* and *The Recruiting Officer* that had not appeared earlier and that seem to bear some theatrical authority.[39] The 1728 *Works* contains some even more remarkable additions to *The Beaux Stratagem.* First of all, the words to both songs are printed, 'But you look so bright' within the text of Act I and the 'Song of the Trifle' on two pages following the epilogue. In Act III Count Bellair's scene is printed in italic with the note that the scene and the entire part of the Count were cut by the author after the first night 'and where he shou'd enter in the last Scene of the fifth Act, it is added to the Part of *Foigard*'. In v.iv the Count's lines are not only given to Foigard but recast to turn the Count's Frenchified language into Irish phrasing. Archer's line on paying Mrs Sullen's portion is expanded. In Lintott's 1730 edition, for the first time, the Epilogue contains the byline, 'By Mr. Smith, the Author of *Phaedra and Hypolitus*'.[40]

Once again the theatre seems the most likely source for the revisions. Once again the revisions show convincing awareness of how the play would have worked on stage.

'Mr Gilliers Musick in the Play call'd the Stratagem' was first advertised on 18–20 November 1707.[41] I have found no engraved music for the Song 'But you look so bright', and since 'The Trifle' was written to the old tune of 'Sir Simon the King', which had long been familiar, there was no need to print the music. An early form of the tune had been published as long ago as 1652, and versions continued to be published as the tune was used for different sets of lyrics.[42] The words to the song, however, were frequently reprinted in editions of *The Stage-Coach* and the *Works*. They also appeared as '*Never Before Printed*' in a collection of 'Poems on Several Occasions' printed with Giles Jacob's *Rape of a Smock* in 1717 (copy in the Clark Library).

For the present edition I have used the first quarto as copy-text. I have, however, introduced the full texts of the songs from the 1728 edition. Even though the Jacob volume printed 'The Trifle' earlier, I have chosen the 1728 version because of the theatrical relationship; there is no reason to assume that the 1717 edition, printed a decade after Farquhar's death, has any particular authorial connection.[43] I have not deleted the Count's role, although I have noted the scene italicized in 1728 and the revision of the Count's lines in v.iv for Foigard, as well as other revisions. I have also accepted and reprinted the attribution of the Epilogue to Smith from the 1730 duodecimo.

I have collated the following copies: first edition, Bodleian (two copies), British Library, Huntington (two copies), Clark, Harvard, University of Texas (two copies), Princeton, University of Pennsylvania; second edition, Folger, Johns Hopkins; *Comedies*, first edition, Clark; second edition, Library of Congress, personal copy; third edition, Library of Congress; 1728, Library of Congress; 1733, Folger, personal copies; 1736, Folger. I have also examined all other editions down to mid-century and all editions by the 'authorized' booksellers, but since they do not affect the text, they need not be recorded here.

NOTES

1. Nichols, viii. 296.
2. Quoted in George A. Aitken, *The Life of Richard Steele* (2 vols., London, 1889), i. 151.
3. Verlyn Flieger, 'Notes on the Titling of George Farquhar's "The Beaux Stratagem"', *N&Q* NS 26 (1979), 21–3.
4. 'Some Memoirs of Mr. George Farquhar', in *The Stage-Coach* (1735), p. ix.
5. Wilkes, i, pp. xi–xiii.
6. Rothstein, p. 29, W. J. Lawrence, 'George Farquhar: Thomas Wilkes', *TLS*, 26 June 1930, p. 534.
7. Jordan, p. 262.

8. For the account of his attempts, see Jordan, pp. 251–2, 262–3.
9. Kenny, 'George Farquhar and the "Bus'ness of a Prologue"', p. 153.
10. Rothstein, p. 142.
11. Stonehill, ii. 117.
12. Richard Hindry Barker, *Mr. Cibber of Drury Lane* (New York, 1939), p. 46.
13. *The Relapse*, ed. Curt A. Zimansky, Regents Restoration Drama Series (Lincoln, Neb., 1970), p. xix.
14. *Steele*, pp. 119–23, 162–5.
15. W. J. Lawrence, 'Foigard in "The Beaux' Stratagem"', *N&Q*, 9th ser. 11 (1903), 46–7.
16. Kavanagh, p. 227. Wilkes, i, pp. xiii.
17. For a full discussion, see Martin A. Larson, 'The Influence of Milton's Divorce Tracts on Farquhar's, *Beaux' Stratagem*', *PMLA*, 39 (1924), 174–8.
18. Price, p. 150.
19. *Dancing Master* (1718), p. 169, cited in Price, p. 150.
20. Cibber, *Apology*, p. 182.
21. The total of 194 should be considered somewhat approximate since data on benefits are sometimes unreliable. Some were advertised but not given, others given but not advertised. Sometimes the tickets of minor functionaries were accepted for plays not originally planned for their benefit. The figure 194 represents as accurate a figure as can be reached from the data in the *London Stage*.
22. *London Stage*, Part 3, i. 416.
23. The performance count refers to theatrical locations, not companies. The performances at the Queen's Theatre and the early Drury Lane performances, for example, involved the same actors, and the Lincoln's Inn Fields company under the management of John Rich moved to Covent Garden on 7 Dec. 1732. Some summer performances at alternate locations also occur.
24. This category includes Two Golden Balls, St Martin's Lane; Hampton Court; Richmond; Front Long Room; York Buildings; Hampstead; James Street; May Fair; New Wells, Mayfair; New Wells, Shepherd's Market; New Theatre, Mr Bradley's Distiller in Wapping; New Wells, London Spa, Clerkenwell; Kingston; Crown Inn, Islington; and Red-Lion Inn, Stoke Newington.
25. Genest, iv. 33.
26. *London Stage*, Part 4, ii. 510; iii., 1934.
27. *Ibid.*, Part 5, iii. 861.
28. *Ibid.*, Part 3, i. 505.
29. *Boswell's London Journal*, p. 47. *Boswell's Life of Johnson*, v. 133 n. 1; iv. 52, 70; ii. 461; iii. 89 n. 2. *The Complete Letters of Lady Mary Wortley Montagu*, ed. Robert Halsband (Oxford, 1966, ii. 123. *Horace Walpole's Correspondence*, ed. W. S. Lewis (New Haven, Conn., 1937–), xi. 101.
30. Hazlitt, pp. 88–9.
31. Hunt, pp. lxxiv–lxxv.
32. Hume, p. 467.
33. Robertson, p. 57.
34. See also *The Generous Advertiser*, 25–8 Mar. 1707.
35. Advertisement, *Daily Courant*, 27 Mar. 1708, 'This Day is publish'd'.
36. For a discussion of Lowndes's acquisition of Farquhar rights, see Kenny, 'The Publication of Plays', pp. 330–1.
37. See Kenny, 'Piracies of Two Plays by Farquhar', pp. 297–305.
38. Volume II in the Bodleian and British Library copies is labelled as the fifth edition rather than the sixth, but carries the date 1728.
39. The third version of *The Stage-Coach*, which also was connected to the theatre, was not printed until the *Dramatick Works* of 1736. The Memoirs printed in the 1728

Works say that Farquhar 'assisted Mr. *Motteux* in *The Stage-Coach*'; like all earlier editions of the *Comedies* and the *Works*, the 1728 *Works* omits the farce. It seems fairly certain, however, that the source of *The Stage-Coach* of 1736 as well as *The Recruiting Officer* of 1728 was the Drury Lane promptbook.

40. Smith himself had died in 1710, so he could not have been the source of the information.

41. Price, p. 243.

42. Claude M. Simpson, *The British Broadside Ballad and Its Music* (New Brunswick, N.J., 1966), pp. 545–51.

43. Three substantive variants occur: the Jacob text uses 'them' for ''em' in the 1728 text in l. 187, omits 'of' in l. 191, and uses 'by *Gad*' for 'egad' in l. 207.

The ladies revive Aimwell, Act IV, Scene i. Frontispiece, *The Beaux Stratagem*, printed for Lintott and sold by Feales, 1733. By permission of the Folger Shakespeare Library.

THE
BEAUX STRATAGEM.
A COMEDY.

ABBREVIATIONS USED IN THE NOTES

Q1   First edition. London: Lintott, [1707].
Q2   Second edition. London: Lintott, [1707].
O1   *Comedies.* London: Knapton, Smith, Strahan, and Lintott, [1708].
O2   *Comedies.* Second edition. London: Knapton, Smith, Strahan, and Lintott, [1711].
1728 *Works.* Sixth edition (Vol. II labelled fifth edition). London: J. and J. Knapton, Lintott, Strahan, and Clark. 1728.
1730 Seventh edition. London: Lintott, 1730.
1733 Eighth edition. London: Lintott and Feales, 1733.

ADVERTISEMENT.

The Reader may find some Faults in
this Play, which my Illness prevented
the amending of, but there is great Amends
made in the Representation, which cannot be
match'd, no more than the friendly and indefatigable Care of Mr. *Wilks*, to whom I
chiefly owe the Success of the Play.

GEORGE FARQUHAR.

PROLOGUE

Spoken by Mr. *Wilks.*

When Strife disturbs or Sloth Corrupts an Age,
Keen Satyr is the Business of the Stage.
When the Plain-Dealer *writ, he lash'd those Crimes*
Which then infested most—The Modish Times:
But now, when Faction sleeps and Sloth is fled,
And all our Youth in Active Fields are bred;
When thro' GREAT BRITAIN*'s fair extensive Round,*
The Trumps of Fame the Notes of UNION *sound;*
When ANNA*'s Scepter points the Laws their Course,*
And Her Example gives her Precepts Force:
There scarce is room for Satyr, all our Lays
Must be, or Songs of Triumph, or of Praise:
But as in Grounds best cultivated, Tares
And Poppies rise among the Golden Ears;
Our Products so, fit for the Field or School,
Must mix with Nature's Favourite Plant—A Fool:
A Weed that has to twenty Summer's ran,
Shoots up in Stalk, and Vegetates to Man.
Simpling our Author goes from Field to Field,
And culls such Fools, as may Diversion yield;
And, Thanks to Nature, there's no want to those,
For Rain, or Shine, the thriving Coxcomb grows.
Follies, to Night we shew, ne'er lash'd before,
Yet, such as Nature shews you ever Hour;
Nor can the Picture's give a Just Offence,
For Fools are made for Jests to Men of Sense.

Dramatis Personæ.

MEN.

Aimwell,	Two Gentlemen of broken Fortunes, the first as Master,	Mr. *Mills.*
Archer,	and the second as Servant.	Mr. *Wilks.*
Count Bellair,	A *French* Officer, Prisoner at *Litchfield.*	Mr. *Bowman.*
Sullen,	A Country Blockhead, brutal to his Wife.	Mr: *Verbruggen.*
Freeman,	A Gentleman from *London.*	Mr. *Keen.*
Foigard,	A Priest, Chaplain to the *French* Officers.	Mr. *Bowen.*
Gibbet,	A High-way-man.	Mr. *Cibber.*
Hounslow, Bagshot,	His Companions.	
Bonniface,	Landlord of the Inn.	Mr. *Bullock.*
Scrub,	Servant to Mr. *Sullen.*	Mr. *Norris.*

10

WOMEN.

Lady Bountiful,	An old civil Country Gentlewoman, that cures all her Neighbours of all Distempers, and foolishly fond of her Son *Sullen,*	Mrs. *Powel.*
Dorinda,	Lady *Bountiful*'s Daughter.	Mrs. *Bradshaw.*
Mrs. Sullen,	Her Daughter-in-law.	Mrs. *Oldfield.*
Gipsey,	Maid to the Ladies.	Mrs. *Mills.*
Cherry,	The Landlord's Daughter in the Inn.	Mrs. *Bignal.*

20

[*Fellow, Servants.*]

SCENE, *Litchfield.*

THE

Beaux Stratagem.

ACT I.

SCENE, *an Inn.*

Enter Bonniface *running.*

Bonniface. Chamberlain, Maid, *Cherry*, Daughter *Cherry*, all asleep, all dead?

Enter Cherry *running.*

Cherry. Here, here, Why d'ye baul so, Father? dy'e think we have no Ears?

Bonniface. You deserve to have none, you young Minx;— The Company of the *Warrington* Coach has stood in the Hall this Hour, and no Body to shew them to their Chambers.

Cherry. And let 'em wait farther; there's neither Red-Coat in the Coach, nor Footman behind it.

10 *Bonniface.* But they threaten to go to another Inn to Night.

Cherry. That they dare not, for fear the Coachman should overturn them to Morrow—Coming, coming: Here's the *London* Coach arriv'd.

Enter several People with Trunks, Band-boxes, and other Luggage, and cross the Stage.

Bonniface. Welcome, Ladies.

Cherry. Very welcome, Gentlemen—Chamberlain, shew the *Lyon* and the *Rose.*

Exit with the Company.

Enter Aimwell *in riding Habit,* Archer *as Footman carrying a Portmantle.*

Bonniface. This way, this way, Gentlemen.

Aimwell. Set down the things, go to the Stable, and see my Horses well rubb'd.

20 *Archer.* I shall, Sir.

Exit.

Aimwell. You're my Landlord, I suppose?

Bonniface. Yes, Sir, I'm old *Will. Bonniface*, pretty well known upon this Road, as the saying is.

Aimwell. O Mr. *Bonniface*, your Servant.

Bonniface. O Sir—What will your Honour please to drink, as the saying is?

Aimwell. I have heard your Town of *Litchfield* much fam'd for Ale, I think I'll taste that.

Bonniface. Sir, I have now in my Cellar Ten Tun of the best Ale in *Staffordshire*; 'tis smooth as Oil, sweet as Milk, clear as Amber, and strong as Brandy; and will be just Fourteen Year old the Fifth Day of next *March* old Stile.

Aimwell. You're very exact, I find, in the Age of your Ale.

Bonniface. As punctual, Sir, as I am in the Age of my Children: I'll shew you such Ale—Here, Tapster, broach Number 1706, as the saying is;—Sir, you shall taste my *Anno Domini*;—I have liv'd in *Litchfield* Man and Boy above Eight and fifty Years, and I believe have not consum'd Eight and fifty Ounces of Meat.

Aimwell. At a Meal, you mean, if one may guess your Sense by your Bulk.

Bonniface. Not in my Life, Sir, I have fed purely upon Ale; I have eat my Ale, drank my Ale, and I always sleep upon Ale.

Enter Tapster with a Bottle and Glass.

Now, Sir, you shall see (*Filling it out.*) your Worship's Health; ha! delicious, delicious,—fancy it *Burgundy*, only fancy it, and 'tis worth Ten Shillings a Quart.

Aimwell. (*Drinks.*) 'Tis confounded strong.

Bonniface. Strong! It must be so, or how should we be strong that drink it?

Aimwell. And have you liv'd so long upon this Ale, Landlord?

Bonniface. Eight and fifty Years, upon my Credit, Sir; but it kill'd my Wife, poor Woman, as the saying is.

Aimwell. How came that to pass?

Bonniface. I don't know how, Sir; she would not let the Ale take its natural Course, Sir, she was for qualifying it every now and then with a Dram, as the saying is; and an honest Gentleman that came this way from *Ireland*, made her a Present of a dozen Bottles of Usquebaugh—But the poor

60 Woman was never well after: But howe're, I was obliged to
the Gentleman, you know.

Aimwell. Why, was it the Usquebaugh that kill'd her?

Bonniface. My *Lady Bountiful* said so,—She, good Lady, did
what could be done, she cured her of Three Tympanies, but
the Fourth carry'd her off; but she's happy, and I'm
contented, as the saying is.

Aimwell. Who's that *Lady Bountiful*, you mention'd?

Bonniface. Ods my Life, Sir, we'll drink her Health.
(*Drinks.*) My Lady *Bountiful* is one of the best of Women: Her
70 last Husband Sir *Charles Bountiful* left her worth a Thousand
Pound a Year; and I believe she lays out one half on't in
charitable Uses for the Good of her Neighbours; she cures
Rheumatisms, Ruptures, and broken Shins in Men, Green
Sickness, Obstructions, and Fits of the Mother in Women;—
The Kings-Evil, Chin-Cough, and Chilblains in Children; in
short, she has cured more People in and about *Litchfield* within
Ten Years than the Doctors have kill'd in Twenty; and that's
a bold Word.

Aimwell. Has the Lady been any other way useful in her
80 Generation?

Bonniface. Yes, Sir, She has a Daughter by Sir *Charles*, the
finest Woman in all our Country, and the greatest Fortune.
She has a Son too by her first Husband Squire *Sullen*, who
marry'd a fine Lady from *London* t'other Day; if you please,
Sir, we'll drink his Health?

Aimwell. What sort of a Man is he?

Bonniface. Why, Sir, the Man's well enough; says little,
thinks less, and does—nothing at all, Faith: But he's a Man of
a great Estate, and values no Body.

90 *Aimwell.* A Sportsman, I suppose.

Bonniface. Yes, Sir, he's a Man of Pleasure, he plays at
Whisk, and smoaks his Pipe Eight and forty Hours together
sometimes.

Aimwell. And marry'd, you say?

Bonniface. Ay, and to a curious Woman, Sir,—But he's
a—He wants it, here, Sir. (*Pointing to his Forehead.*)

Aimwell. He has it there, you mean.

Bonniface. That's none of my Business, he's my Landlord,
and so a Man you know, wou'd not,—But—I cod, he's no

better than—Sir, my humble Service to you. (*Drinks.*) Tho' I 100
value not a Farthing what he can do to me; I pay him his Rent
at Quarter day, I have a good running Trade, I have but one
Daughter, and I can give her—But no matter for that.

Aimwell. You're very happy, Mr. *Bonniface*, pray what other
Company have you in Town?

Bonniface. A power of fine Ladies, and then we have the
French Officers.

Aimwell. O that's right, you have a good many of those
Gentlemen: Pray how do you like their Company?

Bonniface. So well, as the saying is, that I cou'd wish we had 110
as many more of 'em, they're full of Money, and pay double
for every thing they have; they know, Sir, that we pay'd good
round Taxes for the taking of 'em, and so they are willing to
reimburse us a little; one of 'em lodges in my House.

Enter Archer.

Archer. Landlord, there are some *French* Gentlemen below
that ask for you.

Bonniface. I'll wait on 'em;—Does your Master stay long in
Town, as the saying is? (*To* Archer.)

Archer. I can't tell, as the saying is.

Bonniface. Come from *London*?
                                                            120
Archer. No.

Bonniface. Going to *London*, may hap?

Archer. No.

Bonniface. An odd Fellow this. [*Aside.*] I beg your Worship's
Pardon, I'll wait on you in half a Minute.

Exit.

Aimwell. The Coast's clear, I see,—Now my dear *Archer*,
welcome to *Litchfield*.

Archer. I thank thee, my dear Brother in Iniquity.

Aimwell. Iniquity! prithee leave Canting, you need not
change your Stile with your Dress.   130

Archer. Don't mistake me, *Aimwell*, for 'tis still my Maxim,
that there is no Scandal like Rags, nor any Crime so shameful
as Poverty.

Aimwell. The World confesses it every Day in its Practice,
tho' Men won't own it for their Opinion: Who did that worthy
Lord, my Brother, single out of the Side-box to sup with him
t'other Night?

Archer. Jack Handycraft, a handsom, well dress'd, mannerly, sharping Rogue, who keeps the best Company in Town.

140 *Aimwell.* Right, and pray who marry'd my Lady *Manslaughter* t'other Day, the great Fortune?

Archer. Why, *Nick Marrabone*, a profess'd Pick-pocket, and a good Bowler; but he makes a handsom Figure, and rides in his Coach, that he formerly used to ride behind.

Aimwell. But did you observe poor *Jack Generous* in the Park last Week?

Archer. Yes, with his Autumnal Perriwig, shading his melancholly Face, his Coat older than any thing but its Fashion, with one Hand idle in his Pocket, and with the other
150 picking his useless Teeth; and tho' the Mall was crowded with Company, yet was poor *Jack* as single and solitary as a Lyon in a Desart.

Aimwell. And as much avoided, for no Crime upon Earth but the want of Money.

Archer. And that's enough; Men must not be poor, Idleness is the Root of all Evil; the World's wide enough, let 'em bustle; Fortune has taken the weak under her Protection, but Men of Sense are left to their Industry.

Aimwell. Upon which Topick we proceed, and I think
160 luckily hitherto: Wou'd not any Man swear now that I am a Man of Quality, and you my Servant, when if our intrinsick Value were known—

Archer. Come, come, we are the Men of intrinsick Value, who can strike our Fortunes out of our selves, whose worth is independent of Accidents in Life, or Revolutions in Government; we have Heads to get Money, and Hearts to spend it.

Aimwell. As to our Hearts, I grant'ye, they are as willing Tits as any within Twenty Degrees; but I can have no great opinion of our Heads from the Service they have done us
170 hitherto, unless it be that they have brought us from *London* hither to *Litchfield*, made me a Lord, and you my Servant.

Archer. That's more than you cou'd expect already. But what Money have we left?

Aimwell. But Two hundred Pound.

Archer. And our Horses, Cloaths, Rings, &c. why we have very good Fortunes now for moderate People; and let me tell you, besides Thousand, that this Two hundred Pound, with

the experience that we are now Masters of, is a better Estate
than the Ten we have spent.—Our Friends indeed began to
suspect that our Pockets were low; but we came off with flying 180
Colours, shew'd no signs of want either in Word or Deed.

Aimwell. Ay, and our going to *Brussels* was a good Pretence
enough for our sudden disappearing; and I warrant you, our
Friends imagine that we are gone a volunteering.

Archer. Why Faith, if this Prospect fails, it must e'en come
to that, I am for venturing one of the Hundreds if you will
upon this Knight-Errantry; but in case it should fail, we'll
reserve the t'other to carry us to some Counterscarp, where we
may die as we liv'd in a Blaze.

Aimwell. With all my Heart; and we have liv'd justly, 190
Archer, we can't say that we have spent our Fortunes, but that
we have enjoy'd 'em.

Archer. Right, so much Pleasure for so much Money, we
have had our Penyworths, and had I Millions, I wou'd go to
the same Market again. O *London, London!* well, we have had
our share, and let us be thankful; Past Pleasures, for ought I
know are best, such as we are sure of, those to come may
disappoint us.

Aimwell. It has often griev'd the Heart of me, to see how
some inhumane Wretches murther their kind Fortunes; those 200
that by sacrificing all to one Appetite, shall starve all the
rest.—You shall have some that live only in their Palates, and
in their sense of tasting shall drown the other Four: Others are
only Epicures in Appearances, such who shall starve their
Nights to make a Figure a Days, and famish their own to feed
the Eyes of others: A contrary Sort confine their Pleasures to
the dark, and contract their spacious Acres to the Circuit of a
Muff-string.

Archer. Right; but they find the *Indies* in that Spot where
they consume 'em, and I think your kind Keepers have much 210
the best on't; for they indulge the most Senses by one
Expence, there's the Seeing, Hearing, and Feeling amply
gratify'd; and some Philosophers will tell you, that from such
a Commerce there arises a sixth Sense that gives infinitely
more Pleasure than the other five put together.

Aimwell. And to pass to the other Extremity, of all Keepers,
I think those the worst that keep their Money.

Archer. Those are the most miserable Wights in being, they destroy the Rights of Nature, and disappoint the Blessings of 220 Providence: Give me a Man that keeps his Five Senses keen and bright as his Sword, that has 'em always drawn out in their just order and strength, with his Reason as Commander at the Head of 'em, that detaches 'em by turns upon whatever Party of Pleasure agreeably offers, and commands 'em to retreat upon the least Appearance of Disadvantage or Danger:—For my part I can stick to my Bottle, while my Wine, my Company, and my Reason holds good; I can be charm'd with *Sappho*'s singing without falling in Love with her Face; I love Hunting, but wou'd not, like *Acteon*, be eaten up 230 by my own Dogs; I love a fine House, but let another keep it; and just so I love a fine Woman.

Aimwell. In that last particular you have the better of me.

Archer. Ay, you're such an amorous Puppy, that I'm afraid you'll spoil our Sport; you can't counterfeit the Passion without feeling it.

Aimwell. Tho' the whining part be out of doors in Town, 'tis still in force with the Country Ladies;—And let me tell you *Frank*, the Fool in that Passion shall outdoe the Knave at any time.

240 *Archer.* Well, I won't dispute it now, you Command for the Day, and so I submit;—At *Nottingham* you know I am to be Master.

Aimwell. And at *Lincoln* I again.

Archer. Then at *Norwich* I mount, which, I think, shall be our last Stage; for if we fail there, we'll imbark for *Holland*, bid adieu to *Venus*, and welcome *Mars*.

Aimwell. A Match! (*Enter* Bonniface.) Mum.

Bonniface. What will your Worship please to have for Supper?

250 *Aimwell.* What have you got?

Bonniface. Sir, we have a delicate piece of Beef in the Pot, and a Pig at the Fire.

Aimwell. Good Supper-meat, I must confess,—I can't eat Beef, Landlord.

Archer. And I hate Pig.

Aimwell. Hold your prating, Sirrah, do you know who you are?

Bonniface. Please to bespeak something else, I have every thing in the House.

Aimwell. Have you any Veal?   260

Bonniface. Veal! Sir, we had a delicate Loin of Veal on *Wednesday* last.

Aimwell. Have you got any Fish or Wildfowl?

Bonniface. As for Fish, truly Sir, we are an inland Town, and indifferently provided with Fish, that's the Truth ont, and then for Wildfowl,—We have a delicate Couple of Rabbets.

Aimwell. Get me the Rabbets fricasy'd.

Bonniface. Fricasy'd! Lard, Sir, they'll eat much better smother'd with Onions.

Archer. Pshaw! damn your Onions.   270

Aimwell. Again, Sirrah!—Well, Landlord, what you please; but hold, I have a small Charge of Money, and your House is so full of Strangers, that I believe it may be safer in your Custody than mine; for when this Fellow of mine gets drunk, he minds nothing.—Here, Sirrah, reach me the strong Box.

Archer. Yes, Sir,—This will give us a Reputation. (*Aside.*)
                    (*Brings the Box.*)

Aimwell. Here, Landlord, the Locks are sealed down both for your Security and mine; it holds somewhat above Two hundred Pound; if you doubt it, I'll count it to you after Supper; but be sure you lay it where I may have it at a 280 Minute's warning; for my Affairs are a little dubious at present, perhaps I may be gone in half an Hour, perhaps I may be your Guest till the best part of that be spent; and pray order your Ostler to keep my Horses always sadled; but one thing above the rest I must beg, that you would let this Fellow have none of your *Anno Domini*, as you call it;—For he's the most insufferable Sot—Here, Sirrah, light me to my Chamber.

                              Exit lighted by Archer.

Bonniface. Cherry, Daughter *Cherry*?
                    Enter Cherry.

Cherry. D'ye call, Father?

Bonniface. Ay, Child, you must lay by this Box for the 290 Gentleman, 'tis full of Money.

Cherry. Money! all that Money! why, sure Father the Gentleman comes to be chosen Parliament-man. Who is he?

Bonniface. I don't know what to make of him, he talks of

keeping his Horses ready sadled, and of going perhaps at a minute's warning, or of staying perhaps till the best part of this be spent.

Cherry. Ay, ten to one, Father, he's a High-way-man.

Bonniface. A High-way-man! upon my Life, Girl, you have 300 hit it, and this Box is some new purchased Booty.—Now cou'd we find him out, the Money were ours.

Cherry. He don't belong to our Gang?

Bonniface. What Horses have they?

Cherry. The Master rides upon a Black.

Bonniface. A Black! ten to one the Man upon the black Mare; and since he don't belong to our Fraternity, we may betray him with a safe Conscience; I don't think it lawful to harbour any Rogues but my own.—Look'ye, Child, as the saying is, we must go cunningly to work, Proofs we must have, 310 the Gentleman's Servant loves Drink, I'll ply him that way, and ten to one loves a Wench; you must work him t'other way.

Cherry. Father, wou'd you have me give my Secret for his?

Bonniface. Consider, Child, there's Two hundred Pound to Boot. (*Ringing without.*) Coming, coming.—Child, mind your Business.

Cherry. What a Rogue is my Father! my Father! I deny it.—My Mother was a good, generous, free-hearted Woman, and I can't tell how far her good Nature might have extended for the good of her Children. This Landlord of mine, for I 320 think I can call him no more, would betray his Guest, and debauch his Daughter into the bargain,—By a Footman too!

Enter Archer.

Archer. What Footman, pray, Mistress, is so happy as to be the Subject of your Contemplation?

Cherry. Whoever he is, Friend, he'll be but little the better for't.

Archer. I hope so, for I'm sure you did not think of me.

Cherry. Suppose I had?

Archer. Why then you're but even with me; for the Minute I came in, I was a considering in what manner I should make 330 love to you.

Cherry. Love to me, Friend!

Archer. Yes, Child.

Cherry. Child! Manners; if you kept a little more distance,

Friend, it would become you much better.

Archer. Distance! good night, Sauce-box. (*Going.*)

Cherry. A pretty Fellow! A like his Pride, [*Aside.*]—Sir, pray, Sir, you see, Sir, (Archer *returns.*) I have the Credit to be intrusted with your Master's Fortune here, which sets me a Degree above his Footman; I hope, Sir, you an't affronted.

Archer. Let me look you full in the Face, and I'll tell you 340 whether you can affront me or no.—S'death, Child, you have a pair of delicate Eyes, and you don't know what to do with 'em.

Cherry. Why, Sir, don't I see every body?

Archer. Ay, but if some Women had 'em, they wou'd kill every body.—Prithee, instruct me, I wou'd fain make Love to you, but I don't know what to say.

Cherry. Why, did you never make Love to any body before?

Archer. Never to a Person of your Figure, I can assure you, Madam, my Addresses have been always confin'd to People 350 within my own Sphere, I never aspir'd so high before. [*Sings.*]

A SONG

> *But you look so bright,*
> *And are dress'd so tight,*
> *That a Man wou'd swear you're Right,*
> *As Arm was e'er laid over.*
> *Such an Air*
> *You freely wear*
> *To ensnare*
> *As makes each Guest a Lover.*

> *Since then, my Dear, I'm your Guest,*   360
> *Prithee give me of the Best*
> *Of what is ready Drest:*
> *Since then, my Dear,* &c.

Cherry. What can I think of this Man? (*Aside.*) Will you give me that Song, Sir?

Archer. Ay, my Dear, take it while 'tis warm. (*Kisses her.*) Death and Fire! her Lips are Honey-combs.

Cherry. And I wish there had been Bees too, to have stung you for your Impudence.

l. 352–63 [SONG] 1728; [om. except first two lines].

370   *Archer.* There's a swarm of *Cupids*, my little *Venus*, that has
done the Business much better.
        Cherry. This Fellow is misbegotten as well as I. (*Aside.*)
What's your Name, Sir?
        Archer. Name! I gad, I have forgot it. (*Aside.*) Oh! *Martin.*
        Cherry. Where were you born?
        Archer. In St. *Martin*'s Parish.
        Cherry. What was your Father?
        Archer. St. *Martin*'s Parish.
        Cherry. Then, Friend, good night.
380   *Archer.* I hope not.
        Cherry. You may depend upon't.
        Archer. Upon what?
        Cherry. That you're very impudent.
        Archer. That you're very handsome.
        Cherry. That you're a Footman.
        Archer. That you're an Angel.
        Cherry. I shall be rude.
        Archer. So shall I.
        Cherry. Let go my Hand.
390   *Archer.* Give me a Kiss. (*Kisses her.*)
        Call without. Cherry, Cherry.
        Cherry. I'mm—My Father calls; you plaguy Devil, how
durst you stop my Breath so?—Offer to follow me one step, if
you dare.

                                              [*Exit.*]

        Archer. A fair Challenge by this Light; this is a pretty fair
opening of an Adventure; but we are Knight-Errants, and so
Fortune be our Guide.

                                              Exit.

                The End of the First Act.

                    ACT II. [Scene i.]

        SCENE, *A Gallery in* Lady Bountiful*'s House.*

            Mrs. Sullen *and* Dorinda *meeting.*

        Dorinda. Morrow, my dear Sister; are you for Church this
Morning?

Mrs. Sullen. Any where to Pray; for Heaven alone can help me: But, I think, *Dorinda*, there's no Form of Prayer in the Liturgy against bad Husbands.

Dorinda. But there's a Form of Law in *Doctors-Commons*; and I swear, Sister *Sullen*, rather than see you thus continually discontented, I would advise you to apply to that: For besides the part that I bear in your vexatious Broils, as being Sister to the Husband, and Friend to the Wife; your Example gives me such an Impression of Matrimony, that I shall be apt to condemn my Person to a long Vacation all its Life.—But supposing, Madam, that you brought it to a Case of Separation, what can you urge against your Husband? My Brother is, first, the most constant Man alive.

Mrs. Sullen. The most constant Husband, I grant'ye.

Dorinda. He never sleeps from you.

Mrs. Sullen. No, he always sleeps with me.

Dorinda. He allows you a Maintenance suitable to your Quality.

Mrs. Sullen. A Maintenance! do you take me, Madam, for an hospital Child, that I must sit down, and bless my Benefactors for Meat, Drinks and Clothes? As I take it, Madam, I brought your Brother Ten thousand Pounds, out of which, I might expect some pretty things, call'd Pleasures.

Dorinda. You share in all the Pleasures that the Country affords.

Mrs. Sullen. Country Pleasures! Racks and Torments! dost think, Child, that my Limbs were made for leaping of Ditches, and clambring over Stiles; or that my Parents wisely foreseeing my future Happiness in Country-pleasures, had early instructed me in the rural Accomplishments of drinking fat Ale, playing at Whisk, and smoaking Tobacco with my Husband; or of spreading of Plaisters, brewing of Diet-drinks, and stilling Rosemary-Water with the good old Gentlewoman, my Mother-in-Law.

Dorinda. I'm sorry, Madam, that it is not more in our power to divert you; I cou'd wish indeed that our Entertainments were a little more polite, or your Taste a little less refin'd: But, pray, Madam, how came the Poets and Philosophers that labour'd so much in hunting after Pleasure, to place it at last in a Country Life?

Mrs. Sullen. Because they wanted Money, Child, to find out the Pleasures of the Town: Did you ever see a Poet or Philosopher worth Ten thousand Pound; if you can shew me such a Man, I'll lay you Fifty Pound you'll find him somewhere within the weekly Bills.—Not that I disapprove rural Pleasures, as the Poets have painted them; in their Landschape every *Phillis* has her *Coridon*, every murmuring
50 Stream, and every flowry Mead gives fresh Alarms to Love.—Besides, you'll find, that their Couples were never marry'd:—But yonder I see my *Coridon*, and a sweet Swain it is, Heaven knows.—Come, *Dorinda*, don't be angry, he's my Husband, and your Brother; and between both is he not a sad Brute?

Dorinda. I have nothing to say to your part of him, you're the best Judge.

Mrs. Sullen. O Sister, Sister! if ever you marry, beware of a sullen, silent Sot, one that's always musing, but never
60 thinks:—There's some Diversion in a talking Blockhead; and since a Woman must wear Chains, I wou'd have the Pleasure of hearing 'em rattle a little.—Now you shall see, but take this by the way;—He came home this Morning at his usual Hour of Four, waken'd me out of a sweet Dream of something else, by tumbling over the Tea-table, which he broke all to pieces, after his Man and he had rowl'd about the Room like sick Passengers in a Storm, he comes flounce into Bed, dead as a Salmon into a Fishmonger's Basket; his Feet cold as Ice, his Breath hot as a Furnace, and his Hands and his Face as
70 greasy as his Flanel Night-cap.—Oh Matrimony!—He tosses up the Clothes with a barbarous swing over his Shoulders, disorders the whole Oeconomy of my Bed, leaves me half naked, and my whole Night's Comfort is the tuneable Serenade of that wakeful Nightingale, his Nose.—O the Pleasure of counting the melancholly Clock by a snoring Husband!—But now, Sister, you shall see how handsomely, being a well-bred Man, he will beg my Pardon.

Enter Sullen.

Sullen. My Head akes consumedly.

Mrs. Sullen. Will you be pleased, my Dear, to drink Tea
80 with us this Morning? it may do your Head good.

Sullen. No.

Dorinda. Coffee? Brother.

Sullen. Pshaw.

Mrs. Sullen. Will you please to dress and go to Church with me, the Air may help you.

Sullen. Scrub.

Enter Scrub.

Scrub. Sir.

Sullen. What Day o'th Week is this?

Scrub. Sunday, an't please your Worship.

Sullen. Sunday! bring me a Dram, and d'ye hear, set out the 90 Venison-Pasty, and a Tankard of strong Beer upon the Hall-Table, I'll go to breakfast. (*Going.*)

Dorinda. Stay, stay, Brother, you shan't get off so; you were very naught last Night, and must make your Wife Reparation; come, come, Brother, won't you ask Pardon?

Sullen. For what?

Dorinda. For being drunk last Night.

Sullen. I can afford it, can't I?

Mrs. Sullen. But I can't, Sir.

Sullen. Then you may let it alone. 100

Mrs. Sullen. But I must tell you, Sir, that is not to be born.

Sullen. I'm glad on't.

Mrs. Sullen. What is the Reason, Sir, that you use me thus inhumanely?

Sullen. Scrub?

Scrub. Sir.

Sullen. Get things ready to shave my Head.

Exeunt.

Mrs. Sullen. Have a care of coming near his Temples, *Scrub*, for fear you meet something there that may turn the Edge of your Razor.—Inveterate Stupidity! did you ever know so 110 hard, so obstinate a Spleen as his? O Sister, Sister! I shall never ha' Good of the Beast till I get him to Town; *London*, dear *London* is the Place for managing and breaking a Husband.

Dorinda. And has not a Husband the same Opportunities there for humbling a Wife?

Mrs. Sullen. No, no, Child, 'tis a standing Maxim in

conjugal Discipline, that when a Man wou'd enslave his Wife, he hurries her into the Country; and when a Lady would be
120 arbitrary with her Husband, she wheedles her Booby up to Town.—A Man dare not play the Tyrant in *London*, because there are so many Examples to encourage the Subject to rebel. O *Dorinda, Dorinda*! a fine Woman may do any thing in *London*: O'my Conscience, she may raise an Army of Forty thousand Men.

Dorinda. I fancy, Sister, you have a mind to be trying your Power that way here in *Litchfield*; you have drawn the *French* Count to your Colours already.

Mrs. Sullen. The *French* are a People that can't live without
130 their Gallantries.

Dorinda. And some *English* that I know, Sister, are not averse to such Amusements.

Mrs. Sullen. Well, Sister, since the Truth must out, it may do as well now as hereafter; I think one way to rouse my Lethargick sotish Husband, is, to give him a Rival; Security begets Negligence in all People, and Men must be alarm'd to make 'em alert in their Duty: Women are like Pictures of no Value in the Hands of a Fool, till he hears Men of Sense bid high for the Purchase.

140 *Dorinda.* This might do, Sister, if my Brother's Understanding were to be convinc'd into a Passion for you; but I fancy there's a natural Aversion of his side; and I fancy, Sister, that you don't come much behind him, if you dealt fairly.

Mrs. Sullen. I own it, we are united Contradictions, Fire and Water: But I cou'd be contented, with a great many other Wives, to humour the censorious Mob, and give the World an Appearance of living well with my Husband, cou'd I bring him but to dissemble a little Kindness to keep me in Countenance.

150 *Dorinda.* But how do you know, Sister, but that instead of rousing your Husband by this Artifice to a counterfeit Kindness, he should awake in a real Fury.

Mrs. Sullen. Let him:—If I can't entice him to the one, I wou'd provoke him to the other.

Dorinda. But how much I behave my self between ye.

Mrs. Sullen. You must assist me.

Dorinda. What, against my own Brother!

Mrs. Sullen. He's but half a Brother, and I'm your entire
Friend: If I go a step beyond the Bounds of Honour, leave me;
till then I expect you should go along with me in every thing, 160
while I trust my Honour in your Hands, you may trust your
Brother's in mine.—The *Count* is to dine here to Day.

Dorinda. 'Tis a strange thing, Sister, that I can't like that
Man.

Mrs. Sullen. You like nothing, your time is not come; Love
and Death have their Fatalities, and strike home one time or
other:—You'll pay for all one Day, I warrant'ye.—But, come,
my Lady's Tea is ready, and 'tis almost Church-time.

Exeunt.

[ACT II. Scene ii.]

SCENE, *The Inn.*

Enter Aimwell *dress'd, and* Archer.

Aimwell. And was she the Daughter of the House?

Archer. The Landlord is so blind as to think so; but I dare
swear she has better Blood in her Veins.

Aimwell. Why dost think so?

Archer. Because the Baggage has a pert *Je ne scai quoi*, she
reads Plays, keeps a Monkey, and is troubled with Vapours.

Aimwell. By which Discoveries I guess that you know more
of her.

Archer. Not yet, Faith, the Lady gives her self Airs, forsooth,
nothing under a Gentleman.   10

Aimwell. Let me take her in hand.

Archer. Say one Word more o'that, and I'll declare my self,
spoil your Sport there, and every where else; look'ye, *Aimwell*,
every Man in his own Sphere.

Aimwell. Right; and therefore you must pimp for your
Master.

Archer. In the usual Forms, good Sir, after I have serv'd my
self.—But to our Business:—You are so well dress'd, *Tom*, and
make so handsome a Figure, that I fancy you may do
Execution in a Country Church; the exteriour part strikes 20

first, and you're in the right to make that Impression favourable.

Aimwell. There's something in that which may turn to Advantage: The Appearance of a Stranger in a Country Church draws as many Gazers as a blazing Star; no sooner he comes into the Cathedral, but a Train of Whispers runs buzzing round the Congregation in a moment;—Who is he? whence comes he? do you know him?—Then I, Sir, tips me the Verger with half a Crown; he pockets the Simony, and
30 Inducts me into the best Pue in the Church, I pull out my Snuff-box, turn my self round, bow to the Bishop, or the Dean, if he be the commanding Officer; single out a Beauty, rivet both my Eyes to hers, set my Nose a bleeding by the Strength of Imagination, and shew the whole Church my concern by my endeavouring to hide it; after the Sermon, the whole Town gives me to her for a Lover, and by perswading the Lady that I am a dying for her, the Tables are turn'd, and she in good earnest falls in Love with me?

Archer. There's nothing in this, *Tom*, without a Precedent;
40 but instead of riveting your Eyes to a Beauty, try to fix 'em upon a Fortune, that's our Business at present.

Aimwell. Pshaw, no Woman can be a Beauty without a Fortune.—Let me alone, for I am a Mark'sman.

Archer. *Tom*.

Aimwell. Ay.

Archer. When were you at Church before, pray?

Aimwell. Um—I was there at the Coronation.

Archer. And how can you expect a Blessing by going to Church now?

50 *Aimwell*. Blessing! nay, *Frank*, I ask but for a Wife.

Exit.

Archer. Truly the Man is not very unreasonable in his Demands.

Exit at the opposite Door.
Enter Bonniface *and* Cherry.

Bonniface. Well Daughter, as the saying is, have you brought *Martin* to confess?

Cherry. Pray, Father, don't put me upon getting any thing out of a Man; I'm but young you know, Father, and I don't understand Wheedling.

Bonniface. Young! why you Jade, as the saying is, can any Woman wheedle that is not young, you'r Mother was useless at five and twenty; not wheedle! would you make your Mother 60 a Whore and me a Cuckold, as the saying is? I tell you his Silence confesses it, and his Master spends his Money so freely, and is so much a Gentleman every manner of way that he must be a Highwayman.

　　　　　Enter Gibbet *in a Cloak.*

Gibbet. Landlord, Landlord, is the Coast clear?

Bonniface. O, Mr. *Gibbet*, what's the News?

Gibbet. No matter, ask no Questions, all fair and honourable, here, my dear *Cherry* (*Gives her a Bag.*) Two hundred Sterling Pounds as good as any that ever hang'd or sav'd a Rogue; lay 'em by with the rest, and here—Three wedding or mourning 70 Rings, 'tis much the same you know—Here, two Silver-hilted Swords; I took those from Fellows that never shew any part of their Swords but the Hilts: Here is a Diamond Necklace which the Lady hid in the privatest place in the Coach, but I found it out: This Gold Watch I took from a Pawn-broker's Wife; it was left in her Hands by a Person of Quality, there's the Arms upon the Case.

Cherry. But who had you the Money from?

Gibbet. Ah! poor Woman! I pitied her;—From a poor Lady just elop'd from her Husband, she had made up her Cargo, 80 and was bound for *Ireland*, as hard as she cou'd drive; she told me of her Husband's barbarous Usage, and so I left her half a Crown: But I had almost forgot, my dear *Cherry*, I have a Present for you.

Cherry. What is't?

Gibbet. A Pot of Cereuse, my Child, that I took out of a Lady's under Pocket.

Cherry. What, Mr. *Gibbet*, do you think that I paint?

Gibbet. Why, you Jade, your Betters do; I'm sure the Lady that I took it from had a Coronet upon her Handkerchief.— 90 Here, take my Cloak, and go, secure the Premises.

Cherry. I will secure 'em.

　　　　　　　　　　　　　　　　　　　　Exit.

Bonniface. But, heark'ye, where's *Hounslow* and *Bagshot*?

Gibbet. They'll be here to Night.

Bonniface. D'ye know of any other Gentlemen o'the Pad on

this Road?

Gibbet. No.

Bonniface. I fancy that I have two that lodge in the House just now.

100   *Gibbet.* The Devil! how d'ye smoak 'em?

Bonniface. Why, the one is gone to Church.

Gibbet. That's suspitious, I must confess.

Bonniface. And the other is now in his Master's Chamber; he pretends to be Servant to the other, we'll call him out, and pump him a little.

Gibbet. With all my Heart.

Bonniface. Mr. *Martin*, Mr. *Martin*?

      Enter Archer *combing a Perrywig, and singing.*

Gibbet. The Roads are consumed deep; I'm as dirty as old *Brentford* at *Christmas.*—A good pretty Fellow that; who's
110 Servant are you, Friend?

Archer. My Master's.

Gibbet. Really?

Archer. Really.

Gibbet. That's much.—The Fellow has been at the Bar by his Evasions:—But, pray, Sir, what is your Master's Name?

Archer. Tall, all dall; (*Sings and combs the Perrywig.*) This is the most obstinate Curl—

Gibbet. I ask you his Name?

Archer. Name, Sir,—*Tall, all dal*—I never ask'd him his
120 Name in my Life. *Tall, all dall.*

Bonniface. What think you now?

Gibbet. Plain, plain, he talks now as if he were before a Judge: But, pray, Friend, which way does your Master travel?

Archer. A Horseback.

Gibbet. Very well again, an old Offender, right;—But, I mean does he go upwards or downwards?

Archer. Downwards, I fear, Sir: *Tall, all.*

Gibbet. I'm afraid my Fate will be a contrary way.

Bonniface. Ha, ha, ha! Mr. *Martin* you're very arch.—This
130 Gentleman is only travelling towards *Chester*, and wou'd be glad of your Company, that's all.—Come, Captain. you'll stay to Night, I suppose; I'll shew you a Chamber—Come, Captain.

        II.ii. 107.1 Archer] 1728; Martin

Gibbet. Farwel, Friend—

Exeunt.

Archer. Captain, your Servant.—Captain! a pretty Fellow; s'death, I wonder that the Officers of the Army don't conspire to beat all Scoundrels in Red, but their own.

Enter Cherry.

Cherry. Gone! and *Martin* here! I hope he did not listen; I wou'd have the Merit of the discovery all my own, because I wou'd oblige him to love me. (*Aside.*) Mr. *Martin*, who was 140 that Man with my Father?

Archer. Some Recruiting Serjeant, or whip'd out Trooper, I suppose.

Cherry. All's safe, I find. [*Aside.*]

Archer. Come, my Dear, have you con'd over the Catechise I taught you last Night?

Cherry. Come, question me.

Archer. What is Love?

Cherry. Love is I know not what, it comes I know not how, and goes I know not when. 150

Archer. Very well, an apt Scholar. (*Chucks her under the Chin.*) Where does Love enter?

Cherry. Into the Eyes.

Archer. And where go out?

Cherry. I won't tell'ye.

Archer. What are Objects of that Passion?

Cherry. Youth, Beauty, and clean Linen.

Archer. The Reason?

Cherry. The two first are fashionable in Nature, and the third at Court. 160

Archer. That's my Dear: What are the Signs and Tokens of that Passion?

Cherry. A stealing Look, a stammering Tongue, Words improbable, Designs impossible, and Actions impracticable.

Archer. That's my good Child, kiss me.—What must a Lover do to obtain his Mistress.

Cherry. He must adore the Person that disdains him, he must bribe the Chambermaid that betrays him, and court the Footman that laughs at him;—He must, he must—

Archer. Nay, Child, I must whip you if you don't mind your 170

Lesson; he must treat his—

Cherry. O, ay, he must treat his Enemies with Respect, his Friends with Indifference, and all the World with Contempt; he must suffer much, and fear more; he must desire much, and hope little; in short, he must embrace his Ruine, and throw himself away.

Archer. Had ever Man so hopeful a Pupil as mine? come, my Dear, why is Love call'd a Riddle?

Cherry. Because being blind, he leads those that see, and 180 tho' a Child, he governs a Man.

Archer. Mighty well.—And why is Love pictur'd blind?

Cherry. Because the Painters out of the weakness or privilege of their Art chose to hide those Eyes that they cou'd not draw.

Archer. That's my dear little Scholar, kiss me again.—And why shou'd Love, that's a Child, govern a Man?

Cherry. Because that a Child is the end of Love.

Archer. And so ends Love's Catechism.—And now, my Dear, we'll go in, and make my Master's Bed.

190 *Cherry.* Hold, hold, Mr. *Martin*,—You have taken a great deal of Pains to instruct me, and what d'ye think I have learn't by it?

Archer. What?

Cherry. That your Discourse and your Habit are Contradictions, and it wou'd be nonsense in me to believe you a Footman any longer.

Archer. 'Oons, what a Witch it is!

Cherry. Depend upon this, Sir, nothing in this Garb shall ever tempt me; for tho' I was born to Servitude, I hate 200 it:—Own your Condition, swear you love me, and then—

Archer. And then we shall go make the Bed.

Cherry. Yes.

Archer. You must know then, that I am born a Gentleman, my Education was liberal; but I went to *London* a younger Brother, fell into the Hands of Sharpers, who stript me of my Money, my Friends disown'd me, and now my Necessity brings me to what you see.

Cherry. Then take my Hand—promise to marry me before you sleep, and I'll make you Master of two thousand Pound.

210 *Archer.* How!

Cherry. Two thousand Pound that I have this Minute in my own Custody; so throw off your Livery this Instant, and I'll go find a Parson.

Archer. What said you? A Parson!

Cherry. What! do you scruple?

Archer. Scruple! no, no, but—two thousand Pound you say?

Cherry. And better.

Archer. S'death, what shall I do—but heark'e, Child, what need you make me Master of your self and Money, when you may have the same Pleasure out of me, and still keep your 220 Fortune in your Hands.

Cherry. Then you won't marry me?

Archer. I wou'd marry you, but—

Cherry. O sweet, Sir, I'm your humble Servant, you're fairly caught, wou'd you perswade me that any Gentleman who cou'd bear the Scandal of wearing a Livery, wou'd refuse two thousand Pound let the Condition be what it wou'd—no, no, Sir,—but I hope you'll Pardon the Freedom I have taken, since it was only to inform my self of the Respect that I ought to pay you. (*Going.*) 230

Archer. Fairly bit, by *Jupiter*—hold, hold, and have you actually two thousand Pound.

Cherry. Sir, I have my Secrets as well as you—when you please to be more open, I shall be more free, and be assur'd that I have Discoveries that will match yours, be what they will—in the mean while be satisfy'd that no Discovery I make shall ever hurt you, but beware of my Father.—

            [*Exit.*]

Archer. So—we're like to have as many Adventures in our Inn, as *Don Quixote* had in his—let me see,—two thousand Pound! If the Wench wou'd promise to dye when the Money 240 were spent, I gad, one wou'd marry her, but the Fortune may go off in a Year or two, and the Wife may live—Lord knows how long? then an Innkeeper's Daughter; ay that's the Devil—there my Pride brings me off.

  For whatsoe'er the Sages charge on Pride
  The Angels fall, and twenty Faults beside,
  On Earth I'm sure, 'mong us of mortal Calling,
  Pride saves Man oft, and Woman too from falling.

               Exit.

  [*The*] *End of the Second Act.*

ACT III. [Scene i.]

SCENE, Lady Bountiful*'s House*

Enter Mrs. Sullen, Dorinda.

Mrs. Sullen. Ha, ha, ha, my dear Sister, let me embrace thee, now we are Friends indeed! for I shall have a Secret of yours, as a Pledge for mine—now you'll be good for something, I shall have you conversable in the Subjects of the Sex.

Dorinda. But do you think that I am so weak as to fall in Love with a Fellow at first sight?

Mrs. Sullen. Pshaw! now you spoil all, why shou'd not we be as free in our Friendships as the Men? I warrant you the
10 Gentleman has got to his Confident already, has avow'd his Passion, toasted your Health, call'd you ten thousand Angels, has run over your Lips, Eyes, Neck, Shape, Air and every thing, in a Description that warms their Mirth to a second Enjoyment.

Dorinda. Your Hand, Sister, I an't well.

Mrs. Sullen. So,—she's breeding already—come Child up with it—hem a little—so—now tell me, don't you like the Gentleman that we saw at Church just now?

Dorinda. The Man's well enough.
20 *Mrs. Sullen.* Well enough! is he not a Demigod, a *Narcissus*, a Star, the Man i'the Moon?

Dorinda. O Sister, I'm extreamly ill.

Mrs. Sullen. Shall I send to your Mother, Child, for a little of her Cephalick Plaister to put to the Soals of your Feet, or shall I send to the Gentleman for something for you?—Come, unlace your Steas, unbosome your self—the Man is perfectly a pretty Fellow, I saw him when he first came into Church.

Dorinda. I saw him too, Sister, and with an Air that shone, methought like Rays about his Person.
30 *Mrs. Sullen.* Well said, up with it.

Dorinda. No forward Coquett Behaviour, no Airs to set him off, no study'd Looks nor artful Posture,—but Nature did it all—.

III.i.0.2, Lady Bountiful*'s House*] 1728; *continues*

Mrs. Sullen. Better and better—one Touch more—come.—

Dorinda. But then his Looks—did you observe his Eyes?

Mrs. Sullen. Yes, yes, I did—his Eyes, well, what of his Eyes?

Dorinda. Sprightly, but not wandring; they seem'd to view, but never gaz'd on any thing but me—and then his Looks so humble were, and yet so noble, that they aim'd to tell me that 40 he cou'd with Pride dye at my Feet, tho' he scorn'd Slavery any where else.

Mrs. Sullen. The Physick works purely—How d'ye find your self now, my Dear?

Dorinda. Hem! much better, my Dear—O here comes our Mercury!

Enter Scrub.

Well *Scrub*, what News of the Gentleman?

Scrub. Madam, I have brought you a Packet of News.

Dorinda. Open it quickly, come.

Scrub. In the first place I enquir'd who the Gentleman 50 was? they told me he was a Stranger, Secondly, I ask'd what the Gentleman was, they answer'd and said, that they never saw him before. Thirdly, I enquir'd what Countryman he was, they reply'd 'twas more than they knew. Fourthly, I demanded whence he came, their Answer was, they cou'd not tell. And Fifthly, I ask'd whither he went, and they reply'd they knew nothing of the matter,—and this is all I cou'd learn.

Mrs. Sullen. But what do the People say, can't they guess?

Scrub. Why some think he's a Spy, some guess he's a Mountebank, some say one thing, some another; but for my 60 own part, I believe he's a Jesuit.

Dorinda. A Jesuit! why a Jesuit?

Scrub. Because he keeps his Horses always ready sadled, and his Footman talks *French*.

Mrs. Sullen. His Footman!

Scrub. Ay, he and the Count's Footman were Gabbering *French* like two intreaguing Ducks in a Mill-Pond, and I believe they talk'd of me, for they laugh'd consumedly.

Dorinda. What sort of Livery has the Footman?

Scrub. Livery! Lord, Madam, I took him for a Captain, he's 70 so bedizen'd with Lace, and then he has Tops to his Shoes, up to his mid Leg, a silver headed Cane dangling at his

Nuckles,—he carries his Hands in his Pockets just so—(*Walks
in the* French *Air.*) and has a fine long Perriwig ty'd up in a
Bag—Lord, Madam, he's clear another sort of Man than I.

Mrs. Sullen. That may easily be—but what shall we do now,
Sister?

Dorinda. I have it—This Fellow has a world of Simplicity,
and some Cunning, the first hides the latter by abundance—
80 *Scrub.*

Scrub. Madam.

Dorinda. We have a great mind to know who this Gentleman
is, only for our Satisfaction.

Scrub. Yes, Madam, it would be a Satisfaction, no doubt.

Dorinda. You must go and get acquainted with his Footman,
and invite him hither to drink a Bottle of your Ale, because
you're Butler to Day.

Scrub. Yes, Madam, I am Butler every Sunday.

Mrs. Sullen. O brave, Sister, O my Conscience, you
90 understand the Mathematicks already—'tis the best Plot in
the World, your Mother, you know, will be gone to Church,
my Spouse be got to the Ale-house with his Scoundrels, and
the House will be our own—so we drop in by Accident and
ask the Fellow some Questions our selves. In the Countrey
you know any Stranger is Company, and we're glad to take up
with the Butler in a Country Dance, and happy if he'll do us
the Favour.

Scrub. Oh! Madam, you wrong me, I never refus'd your
Ladyship the Favour in my Life.

Enter Gipsey.

100 *Gipsey.* Ladies, Dinner's upon Table.

Dorinda. Scrub, We'll excuse your waiting—Go where we
order'd you.

Scrub. I shall.

Exeunt.

[ACT III. Scene ii.]

SCENE *changes to the Inn.*

Enter Aimwell *and* Archer.

Archer. Well, *Tom,* I find you're a Marksman.

Aimwell. A Marksman! who so blind cou'd be, as not
discern a Swan among the Ravens.

Archer. Well, but heark'ee, *Aimwell.*

Aimwell. Aimwell! call me *Oroondates, Cesario, Amadis,* all that
Romance can in a Lover paint, and then I'll answer. O *Archer,*
I read her thousands in her Looks, she look'd like *Ceres* in her
Harvest, Corn, Wine and Oil, Milk and Honey, Gardens,
Groves and Purling Streams play'd on her plenteous Face.

Archer. Her Face! her Pocket, you mean; the Corn, Wine 10
and Oil lies there. In short, she has ten thousand Pound,
that's the *English* on't.

Aimwell. Her Eyes—

Archer. Are Demi-Cannons to be sure, so I won't stand their
Battery. (*Going.*)

Aimwell. Pray excuse me, my Passion must have vent.

Archer. Passion! what a plague, d'ee think these Romantick
Airs will do our Business? Were my Temper as extravagant as
yours, my Adventures have something more Romantick by
half.   20

Aimwell. Your Adventures!

Archer. Yes, *The Nymph that with her twice ten hundred Pounds*
        With brazen Engine hot, and Quoif clear starch'd
        Can fire the Guest in warming of the Bed—
There's a Touch of Sublime *Milton* for you, and the Subject
but an Inn-keeper's Daughter; I can play with a Girl as an
Angler do's with his Fish; he keeps it at the end of his Line,
runs it up the Stream, and down the Stream, till at last, he
brings it to hand, tickles the Trout, and so whips it into his
Basket.   30

Enter Bonniface.

Bonniface. Mr. *Martin,* as the saying is—yonder's an honest
Fellow below, my *Lady Bountiful's* Butler, who begs the

Honour that you wou'd go Home with him and see his Cellar.

Archer. Do my *Baisemains* to the Gentleman, and tell him I will do my self the Honour to wait on him immediately.

Exit Bonniface.

Aimwell. What do I hear? soft *Orpheus* Play, and fair *Toftida* sing?

Archer. Pshaw! damn your Raptures, I tell you here's a Pump going to be put into the Vessel, and the Ship will get
40 into Harbour, my Life on't. You say there's another Lady very handsome there.

Aimwell. Yes, faith.

Archer. I'am in love with her already.

Aimwell. Can't you give me a Bill upon *Cherry* in the mean time.

Archer. No, no, Friend, all her Corn, Wine and Oil is ingross'd to my Market.—And once more I warn you to keep your Anchorage clear of mine, for if you fall foul of me, by this Light you shall go to the Bottom.—What! make Prize of my
50 little Frigat, which I am upon the Cruise for you.

Exit.

Enter Bonniface.

Aimwell. Well, well, I won't—Landlord, have you any tolerable Company in the House, I don't care for dining alone.

Bonniface. Yes, Sir, there's a Captain below; as the saying is, that arrived about an Hour ago.

Aimwell. Gentlemen of his Coat are welcome every where; will you make him a Complement from me, and tell him I should be glad of his Company.

Bonniface. Who shall I tell him, Sir, wou'd.—

Aimwell. Ha! that Stroak was well thrown in [*Aside.*]—I'm
60 only a Traveller like himself, and wou'd be glad of his Company, that's all.

Bonniface. I obey your Commands, as the saying is.

Exit.

Enter Archer.

Archer. S'Death! I had forgot, what Title will you give your self?

Aimwell. My Brother's to be sure, he wou'd never give me any thing else, so I'll make bold with his Honour this bout—you know the rest of your Cue.

Archer. Ay, ay.

Enter Gibbet.

Gibbet. Sir, I'm yours.

Aimwell. 'Tis more than I deserve, Sir, for I don't know 70
you.

Gibbet. I don't wonder at that, Sir, for you never saw me
before, I hope. (*Aside.*)

Aimwell. And pray, Sir, how came I by the Honour of
seeing you now?

Gibbet. Sir, I scorn to intrude upon any Gentleman—but
my Landlord—

Aimwell. O, Sir, I ask your Pardon, you're the Captain he
told me of.

Gibbet. At your Service, Sir.   80

Aimwell. What Regiment, may I be so bold?

Gibbet. A marching Regiment, Sir, an old Corps.

Aimwell. Very old, if your Coat be Regimental, (*Aside.*) You
have serv'd abroad, Sir?

Gibbet. Yes, Sir, in the Plantations, 'twas my Lot to be sent
into the worst Service, I wou'd have quitted it indeed, but a
Man of Honour, you know—Besides 'twas for the good of my
Country that I shou'd be abroad—Any thing for the good of
one's Country—I'm a *Roman* for that.

Aimwell. One of the first, I'll lay my Life (*Aside.*) You found 90
the *West Indies* very hot, Sir?

Gibbet. Ay, Sir, too hot for me.

Aimwell. Pray, Sir, han't I seen your Face at *Will*'s Coffee-
house?

Gibbet. Yes, Sir, and at *White*'s too.

Aimwell. And where is your Company now, Captain?

Gibbet. They an't come yet.

Aimwell. Why, d'ye expect 'em here?

Gibbet. They'll be here to Night, Sir.

Aimwell. Which way do they march?   100

Gibbet. Across the Country—the Devil's in't, if I han't said
enough to encourage him to declare—but I'm afraid he's not
right, I must tack about. [*Aside.*]

Aimwell. Is your Company to quarter in *Litchfield*?

III.ii. 68.1 [om.] || Q2; *Exit.* Bon.

Gibbet. In this House, Sir.

Aimwell. What! all?

Gibbet. My Company's but thin, ha, ha, ha, we are but three, ha, ha, ha.

Aimwell. You're merry, Sir.

110   *Gibbet.* Ay, Sir, you must excuse me, Sir, I understand the World, espccially the Art of Travelling; I don't care, Sir, for answering Questions directly upon the Road—for I generally ride with a Charge about me.

Aimwell. Three or four, I believe. (*Aside.*)

Gibbet. I am credibly inform'd that there are Highway-men upon this Quarter, not, Sir, that I cou'd suspect a Gentleman of your Figure—But truly, Sir, I have got such a way of Evasion upon the Road, that I don't care for speaking Truth to any Man.

120   *Aimwell.* Your Caution may be necessary—Then I presume you're no Captain?

Gibbet. Not I, Sir, Captain is a good travelling Name, and so I take it; it stops a great many foolish Inquiries that are generally made about Gentlemen that travel, it gives a Man an Air of something, and makes the Drawers obedient—And thus far I am a Captain, and no farther.

Aimwell. And pray, Sir, what is your true Profession?

Gibbet. O, Sir, you must excuse me—upon my Word, Sir, I don't think it safe to tell you.

130   *Aimwell.* Ha, ha, ha, upon my word I commend you.

Enter Bonniface.

Well, Mr. *Bonniface*, what's the News?

Bonniface. There's another Gentleman below, as the saying is, that hearing you were but two, wou'd be glad to make the third Man if you wou'd give him leave.

Aimwell. What is he?

Bonniface. A Clergyman, as the saying is.

Aimwell. A Clergyman! is he really a Clergyman? or is it only his travelling Name, as my Friend the Captain has it.

Bonniface. O, Sir, he's a Priest and Chaplain to the *French*
140 Officers in Town.

Aimwell. Is he a *French*-man?

Bonniface. Yes, Sir, born at *Brussels*.

Gibbet. A *French*-man, and a Priest! I won't be seen in his

Company, Sir; I have a Value for my Reputation, Sir.

Aimwell. Nay, but Captain, since we are by our selves—Can he speak *English*, Landlord.

Bonniface. Very well, Sir, you may know him, as the saying is, to be a Foreigner by his Accent, and that's all.

Aimwell. Then he has been in *England* before?

Bonniface. Never, Sir, but he's a Master of Languages, as 150 the saying is, he talks *Latin*, it do's me good to hear him talk *Latin*.

Aimwell. Then you understand *Latin*, Mr. *Bonniface*?

Bonniface. Not I, Sir, as the saying is, but he talks it so very fast that I'm sure it must be good.

Aimwell. Pray desire him to walk up.

Bonniface. Here he is, as the saying is.

Enter Foigard.

Foigard. Save you, Gentlemen's, both.

Aimwell. A *French*-man! Sir, your most humble Servant.

Foigard. Och, dear Joy, I am your most faithful Shervant, 160 and yours alsho.

Gibbet. Doctor, you talk very good *English*, but you have a mighty Twang of the Foreigner.

Foigard. My *English* is very vel for the vords, but we Foreigners you know cannot bring our Tongues about the Pronunciation so soon.

Foigard. A Foreigner! a down-right *Teague* by this Light. (*Aside*.) Were you born in *France*, Doctor.

Foigard. I was educated in *France*, but I was borned at *Brussels*, I am a Subject of the King of *Spain*, Joy.   170

Gibbet. What King of *Spain*, Sir, speak.

Foigard. Upon my Shoul Joy, I cannot tell you as yet.

Aimwell. Nay, Captain, that was too hard upon the Doctor, he's a Stranger.

Foigard. O let him alone, dear Joy, I am of a Nation that is not easily put out of Countenance.

Aimwell. Come, Gentlemen, I'll end the Dispute.—Here, Landlord, is Dinner ready?

Bonniface. Upon the Table, as the saying is.

Aimwell. Gentlemen—pray—that Door—   180

Foigard. No, no fait, the Captain must lead.

Aimwell. No, Doctor, the Church is our Guide.

Gibbet. Ay, ay, so it is.—

Exit foremost, they follow.

[ACT III. Scene iii.]

SCENE *Changes to a Gallery in* Lady Bountiful's
House.

Enter Archer *and* Scrub *singing, and hugging one another,* Scrub
with a Tankard in his Hand, Gipsey *listning at a distance.*

Scrub. Tall, all dall—Come, my dear Boy—Let's have that
Song once more.

Archer. No, no, we shall disturb the Family;—But will you
be sure to keep the Secrets?

Scrub. Pho! upon my Honour, as I'm a Gentleman.

Archer. 'Tis enough.—You must know then that my Master
is the Lord Viscount *Aimwell*; he fought a Duel t'other day in
London, wounded his Man so dangerously, that he thinks fit to
withdraw till he hears whether the Gentleman's Wounds be
10 mortal or not: He never was in this part of *England* before, so
he chose to retire to this Place, that's all.

Gipsey. And that's enough for me.

Exit.

Scrub. And where were you when your Master fought?

Archer. We never know of our Masters Quarrels.

Scrub. No! if our Masters in the Country here receive a
Challenge, the first thing they do is to tell their Wives; the
Wife tells the Servants, the Servants alarm the Tenants, and
in half an Hour you shall have the whole County in Arms.

Archer. To hinder two Men from doing what they have no
20 mind for:—But if you should chance to talk now of my
Business?

Scrub. Talk! ay, Sir, had I not learn't the knack of holding
my Tongue, I had never liv'd so long in a great Family.

Archer. Ay, ay, to be sure there are Secrets in all Families.

Scrub. Secrets, ay;—But I'll say no more.—Come, sit down,
we'll make an end of our Tankard: Here—

Archer. With all my Heart; who knows but you and I may

come to be better acquainted, eh—Here's your Ladies Healths; you have three, I think, and to be sure there must be Secrets among 'em.

Archer. Secrets! Ay, Friend; I wish I had a Friend— 30

Archer. Am not I your Friend? come, you and I will be sworn Brothers.

Scrub. Shall we?

Archer. From this Minute.—Give me a kiss—And now Brother *Scrub*—

Scrub. And now, Brother *Martin*, I will tell you a Secret that will make your Hair stand on end:—You must know, that I am consumedly in Love.

Archer. That's a terrible Secret, that's the Truth on't. 40

Scrub. That Jade, *Gipsey*, that was with us just now in the Cellar, is the arrantest Whore that ever wore a Petticoat; and I'm dying for love of her.

Archer. Ha, ha, ha—Are you in love with her Person, or her Vertue, Brother *Scrub*?

Archer. I should like Vertue best, because it is more durable than Beauty; for Vertue holds good with some Women long, and many a Day after they have lost it.

Archer. In the Country, I grant ye, where no Woman's Vertue is lost, till a Bastard be found. 50

Scrub. Ay, cou'd I bring her to a Bastard, I shou'd have her all to my self; but I dare not put it upon that Lay, for fear of being sent for a Soldier.—Pray, Brother, how do you Gentlemen in *London* like that same Pressing Act?

Archer. Very ill, Brother *Scrub*;—'Tis the worst that ever was made for us: Formerly I remember the good Days, when we cou'd dun our Masters for our Wages, and if they refused to pay us, we cou'd have a Warrant to carry 'em before a Justice; but now if we talk of eating, they have a Warrant for us, and carry us before three Justices. 60

Scrub. And to be sure we go, if we talk of eating; for the Justices won't give their own Servants a bad Example. Now this is my Misfortune—I dare not speak in the House, while that Jade *Gipsey* dings about like a Fury—Once I had the better end of the Staff.

Archer. And how comes the Change now?

Scrub. Why, the Mother of all this Mischief is a Priest.

Archer. A Priest!

Scrub. Ay, a damn'd Son of a Whore of *Babylon*, that came
70 over hither to say Grace to the *French* Officers, and eat up our
Provisions—There's not a Day goes over his Head without
Dinner or Supper in this House.

Archer. How came he so familiar in the Family?

Scrub. Because he speaks *English* as if he had liv'd here all
his Life; and tells Lies as if he had been a Traveller from his
Cradle.

Archer. And this Priest, I'm afraid has converted the
Affections of your *Gipsey*.

Scrub. Converted! ay, and perverted, my dear Friend:—For
80 I'm afraid he has made her a Whore and a *Papist*.—But this is
not all; there's the *French* Count and Mrs. *Sullen*, they're in the
Confederacy, and for some private Ends of their own to be
sure.

Archer. A very hopeful Family yours, Brother *Scrub*; I
suppose the Maiden Lady has her Lover too.

Scrub. Not that I know;—She's the best on 'em, that's the
Truth on't: But they take care to prevent my Curiosity, by
giving me so much Business, that I'm a perfect Slave.—What
d'ye think is my Place in this Family?

90 *Archer.* Butler, I suppose.

Scrub. Ah, Lord help you—I'll tell you—Of a *Monday*, I
drive the Coach; of a *Tuesday*, I drive the Plough; on *Wednesday*,
I follow the Hounds; a *Thurdsay*, I dun the Tenants; on *Fryday*,
I go to Market; on *Saturday*, I draw Warrants; and a *Sunday*, I
draw Beer.

Archer. Ha, ha, ha! if variety be a Pleasure in Life, you have
enough on't, my dear Brother—But what Ladies are those?

Scrub. Ours, ours; that upon the right Hand is Mrs. *Sullen*,
and the other is Mrs. *Dorinda*.—Don't mind 'em, sit still,
100 Man—

Enter Mrs. Sullen, *and* Dorinda.

Mrs. Sullen. I have heard my Brother talk of my Lord
Aimwell, but they say that his Brother is the finer Gentleman.

Dorinda. That's impossible, Sister.

Mrs. Sullen. He's vastly rich, but very close, they say.

Dorinda. No matter for that; if I can creep into his Heart, I'll open his Breast, I warrant him: I have heard say, that People may be guess'd at by the Behaviour of their Servants; I cou'd wish we might talk to that Fellow.

Mrs. Sullen. So do I; for, I think he's a very pretty Fellow: Come this way, I'll throw out a Lure for him presently.   110

They walk a turn towards the opposite side of the Stage,
Mrs. Sullen *drops her Glove,* Archer *runs, takes it up, and
gives it to her.*

Archer. Corn, Wine, and Oil, indeed—But, I think, the Wife has the greatest plenty of Flesh and Blood; she should be my Choice [*Aside.*]—Ah, a, say you so—Madam—Your Ladyship's Glove.

Mrs. Sullen. O, Sir, I thank you—what a handsom Bow the Fellow has?

Dorinda. Bow! why I have known several Footmen come down from *London* set up here for Dancing-Masters, and carry off the best Fortune in the Country.

Archer. That Project, for ought I know, had been better 120 than ours, (*Aside.*) Brother *Scrub*—Why don't you introduce me.

Scrub. Ladies, this is the strange Gentleman's Servant that you see at Church to Day; I understood he came from *London*, and so I invited him to the Cellar, that he might show me the newest Flourish in whetting my Knives.

Dorinda. And I hope you have made much of him?

Archer. O yes, Madam, but the Strength of your Ladyship's Liquour is a little too potent for the Constitution of your humble Servant.   130

Mrs. Sullen. What, then you don't usually drink Ale?

Archer. No, Madam, my constant Drink is Tea, or a little Wine and Water; 'tis prescrib'd me by the Physician for a Remedy against the Spleen.

Scrub. O la, O la!—a Footman have the Spleen.—

Mrs. Sullen. I thought that Distemper had been only proper to People of Quality.

Archer. Madam, like all other Fashions it wears out, and so descends to their Servants; tho' in a great many of us, I believe it proceeds from some melancholly Particles in the Blood, 140 occasion'd by the Stagnation of Wages.

Dorinda. How affectedly the Fellow talks—How long, pray, have you serv'd your present Master?

Archer. Not long; my Life has been mostly spent in the Service of the Ladies.

Mrs. Sullen. And pray, which Service do you like best?

Archer. Madam, the Ladies pay best; the Honour of serving them is sufficient Wages; there is a Charm in their looks that delivers a Pleasure with their Commands, and gives our Duty
150 the Wings of Inclination.

Mrs. Sullen. That Flight was above the pitch of a Livery; and, Sir, wou'd not you be satisfied to serve a Lady again?

Archer. As a Groom of the Chamber, Madam, but not as a Footman.

Mrs. Sullen. I suppose you serv'd as a Footman before.

Archer. For that Reason I wou'd not serve in that Post again; for my Memory is too weak for the load of Messages that the Ladies lay upon their Servants in *London*; my Lady *Howd'ye*, the last Mistress I serv'd call'd me up one Morning,
160 and told me, *Martin*, go to my Lady *Allnight* with my humble Service; tell her I was to wait on her Ladyship yesterday, and left word with Mrs. *Rebecca*, that the Preliminaries of the Affair she knows of, are stopt till we know the concurrence of the Person that I know of, for which there are Circumstances wanting which we shall accommodate at the old Place; but that in the mean time there is a Person about her Ladyship, that from several Hints and Surmises, was accessary at a certain time to the disappointments that naturally attend things, that to her knowledge are of more Importance.

170 *Mrs. Sullen.* }
   Dorinda. } Ha, ha, ha! where are you going, Sir?

Archer. Why, I han't half done.—The whole Howd'ye was about half an Hour long; so I hapned to misplace two Syllables, and was turn'd off, and render'd incapable—

Dorinda. The pleasantest Fellow, Sister, I ever saw.—But, Friend, if your Master be marry'd,—I presume you still serve a Lady.

Archer. No, Madam, I take care never to come into a marry'd Family; the Commands of the Master and Mistress are always so contrary, that 'tis impossible to please both.

Dorinda. There's a main point gain'd.—My Lord is not 180
marry'd, I find. (*Aside.*)

Mrs. Sullen. But, I wonder, Friend, that in so many good
Services, you had not a better Provision made for you.

Archer. I don't know how, Madam.—I had a Lieutenancy
offer'd me three or four Times; but that is not Bread,
Madam—I live much better as I do.

Scrub. Madam, he sings rarely.—I was thought to do pretty
well here in the Country till he came; but alack a day, I'm
nothing to my Brother *Martin.*

Dorinda. Does he? Pray, Sir, will you oblige us with a Song? 190

Archer. Are you for Passion, or Humour?

Scrub. O la! he has the purest Ballad about a Trifle—

Mrs. Sullen. A Trifle! pray, Sir, let's have it.

Archer. I'm asham'd to offer you a Trifle, Madam: But since
you command me—(*Sings to the Tune of Sir* Simon *the King.*)

SONG OF A TRIFLE.

A trifling Song you shall hear,
Begun with a Trifle and ended:
All Trifling People draw near,
And I shall be Nobly attended.

Were it not for Trifles, a few,   200
That lately have come into Play;
The Men would want something to do,
And the Women want something to say.

What makes Men trifle in Dressing?
Because the Ladies (they know)
Admire, by often Possessing,
That eminent Trifle a Beau.

When the Lover his Moments has trifled,
The Trifle of Trifles to gain:
No sooner the Virgin is Rifled,   210
But a Trifle shall part 'em again.

---

192 la] 1728; le   196 [SONG OF A TRIFLE] 1728; [om. except first two
lines.] The entire song, as printed following the Epilogue in 1728, is printed here.
Probably fewer verses were sung on stage.

What mortal Man wou'd be able,
At White's half an Hour to sit?
Or who cou'd bear a Tea-Table,
Without talking of Trifles for Wit?

The Court is from Trifles secure,
Gold Keys are no Trifles, we see:
White Rods are no Trifles, I'm sure,
Whatever their Bearer may be.

220   But if you will go to the Place,
Where Trifles abundantly breed,
The Levee will show you his Grace
Makes Promises Trifles indeed.

A Coach with six Footmen behind,
I count neither Trifle nor Sin:
But, ye Gods! how oft do we find,
A scandalous Trifle within?

A Flask of Champaign, People think it
A Trifle, or something as bad:
230   But if you'll contrive how to drink it,
You'll find it no Trifle egad.

A Parson's a Trifle at Sea,
A Widow's a Trifle in Sorrow:
A Peace is a Trifle to-day,
Who knows what may happen to-morrow.

A Black Coat a Trifle may cloak,
Or to hide it, the Red may endeavour:
But if once the Army is broke,
We shall have more Trifles than ever.

240   The Stage is a Trifle, they say,
The Reason, pray carry along,
Because at ev'ry new Play,
The House they will Trifles so throng.

But with People's Malice to Trifle,
And to set us all on a Foot:
The Author of this is a Trifle,
And his Song is a Trifle to boot.

Mrs. Sullen. Very well, Sir, we're obliged to you.—Something for a pair of Gloves. (*Offering him Money.*)

Archer. I humbly beg leave to be excused: My Master, 250 Madam, pays me; nor dare I take Money from any other Hand without injuring his Honour, and disobeying his Commands.

                                                                    Exit.

Dorinda. This is surprising: Did you ever see so pretty a well bred Fellow?

Mrs. Sullen. The Devil take him for wearing that Livery.

Dorinda. I fancy, Sister, he may be some Gentleman, a Friend of my Lords, that his Lordship has pitch'd upon for his Courage, Fidelity, and Discretion to bear him Company in this Dress, and who, ten to one was his Second too.   260

Mrs. Sullen. It is so, it must be so, and it shall be so:—For I like him.

Dorinda. What! better than the *Count?*

Mrs. Sullen. The *Count* happen'd to be the most agreeable Man upon the Place; and so I chose him to serve me in my Design upon my Husband.—But I shou'd like this Fellow better in a Design upon my self.

Dorinda. But now, Sister, for an Interview with this Lord, and this Gentleman; how shall we bring that about?

Mrs. Sullen. Patience! you Country Ladies give no Quarter, 270 if once you be enter'd.—Wou'd you prevent their Desires, and give the Fellows no wishing-time.—Look'ye, *Dorinda*, if my Lord *Aimwell* loves you or deserves you, he'll find a way to see you, and there we must leave it.—My Business comes now upon the Tapis—Have you prepar'd your Brother?

Dorinda. Yes, yes.

Mrs. Sullen. And how did he relish it?

Dorinda. He said little, mumbled something to himself, promis'd to be guided by me: But here he comes—

                              Enter Sullen.

Sullen. What singing was that I heard just now?   280

Mrs. Sullen. The singing in you're Head, my Dear, you complain'd of it all Day.

Sullen. You're impertinent.

257 Gentleman] Q2; Gentlemen

Mrs. Sullen. I was ever so, since I became one Flesh with you.

Sullen. One Flesh! rather two Carcasses join'd unnaturally together.

Mrs. Sullen. Or rather a living Soul coupled to a dead Body.

Dorinda. So, this is fine Encouragement for me.

290 *Sullen.* Yes, my Wife shews you what you must do.

Mrs. Sullen. And my Husband shews you want you must suffer.

Sullen. S'death, why can't you be silent?

Mrs. Sullen. S'death, why can't you talk?

Sullen. Do you talk to any purpose?

Mrs. Sullen. Do you think to any purpose?

Sullen. Sister, heark'ye; (*Whispers.*) I shan't be home till it be late.

Exit.

Mrs. Sullen. What did he whisper to ye?

300 *Dorinda.* That he wou'd go round the back way, come into the Closet, and listen as I directed him.—But let me beg you once more, dear Sister, to drop this Project; for, as I told you before, instead of awaking him to Kindness, you may provoke him to a Rage; and then who knows how far his Brutality may carry him?

Mrs. Sullen. I'm provided to receive him, I warrant you: But here comes the *Count*, vanish.

Exit Dorinda.

Enter Count Bellair.

Don't you wonder, *Monsieur le Count*, that I was not at Church this Afternoon?

310 *Count.* I more wonder, Madam, that you go dere at all, or how you dare to lift those Eyes to Heaven that are guilty of so much killing.

Mrs. Sullen. If Heaven, Sir, has given to my Eyes with the Power of killing, the Virtue of making a Cure, I hope the one may atone for the other.

Count. O largely, Madam; wou'd your Ladyship be as ready to apply the Remedy as to give the Wound?—Consider,

---

307.2–451 [Scene with Count Bellair] This entire scene was printed in italics in 1728 and later editions, with a note explaining that the scene was 'cut out by the Author, after the first Night's Representation'.

Madam, I am doubly a Prisoner; first to the Arms of your
General, then to your more conquering Eyes; my first Chains
are easy, there a Ransom may redeem me, but from your 320
Fetters I never shall get free.

Mrs. Sullen. Alass, Sir, why shou'd you complain to me of
your Captivity, who am in Chains my self? you know, Sir, that
I am bound, nay, must be tied up in that particular that might
give you ease: I am like you, a Prisoner of War—Of War
indeed:—I have given my Parole of Honour; wou'd you break
yours to gain your Liberty?

Count. Most certainly I wou'd, were I a Prisoner among the
Turks; dis is your Case; you're a Slave, Madam, Slave to the
worst of *Turks*, a Husband.   330

Mrs. Sullen. There lies my Foible, I confess; no Fortifications,
no Courage, Conduct, nor Vigilancy can pretend to defend a
Place, where the Cruelty of the Governour forces the Garrison
to Mutiny.

Count. And where de Besieger is resolv'd to die before de
Place—Here will I fix; (*Kneels.*) With Tears, Vows, and
Prayers assault your Heart, and never rise till you surrender;
or if I must storm—Love and St. *Michael*—And so I begin the
Attack—

Mrs. Sullen. Stand off—Sure he hears me not—And I cou'd 340
almost wish me—did not.—The Fellow makes love very
prettily. (*Aside.*) But, Sir, why shou'd you put such a Value
upon my Person, when you see it despis'd by one that knows it
so much better.

Count. He knows it not, tho' he possesses it; if he but knew
the Value of the Jewel he is Master of, he wou'd always wear it
next his Heart, and sleep with it in his Arms.

Mrs. Sullen. But since he throws me unregarded from him.

Count. And one that knows your Value well, comes by, and
takes you up, is it not Justice. (*Goes to lay hold on her.*) 350
        Enter Sullen *with his Sword drawn.*

Sullen. Hold, Villain, hold.

Mrs. Sullen. (*Presenting a Pistol.*) Do you hold.

Sullen. What! Murther your Husband, to defend your
Bully.

324 must] Q2; most

Mrs. Sullen. Bully! for shame, Mr. *Sullen*; Bullies wear long Swords, the Gentleman has none, he's a Prisoner you know—I was aware of your Outrage, and prepar'd this to receive your Violence, and, if Occasion were, to preserve my self against the Force of this other Gentleman.

360   *Count.* O Madam, your Eyes be bettre Fire Arms than your Pistol, they nevre miss.

Sullen. What! court my Wife to my Face!

Mrs. Sullen. Pray, Mr. *Sullen*, put up, suspend your Fury for a Minute.

Sullen. To give you time to invent an Excuse.

Mrs. Sullen. I need none.

Sullen. No, for I heard every Sillable of your Discourse.

Count. Ay! and begar, I tink de Dialogue was vera pretty.

Mrs. Sullen. Then I suppose, Sir, you heard something of
370   your own Barbarity.

Sullen. Barbarity! oons what does the Woman call Barbarity? do I ever meddle with you?

Mrs. Sullen. No.

Sullen. As for you, Sir, I shall take another time.

Count. Ah, begar, and so must I.

Sullen. Look'e, Madam, don't think that my Anger proceeds from any Concern I have for your Honour, but for my own, and if you can contrive any way of being a Whore without making me a Cuckold, do it and welcome.

380   *Mrs. Sullen.* Sir, I thank you kindly, you wou'd allow me the Sin but rob me of the Pleasure—No, no, I'm resolv'd never to venture upon the Crime without the Satisfaction of seeing you punish'd for't.

Sullen. Then will you grant me this, my Dear? let any Body else do you the Favour but that *French*-man, for I mortally hate his whole Generation.

Exit.

Count. Ah, Sir, that be ungrateful, for begar, I love some of your's, Madam.—(*Approaching her.*)

Mrs. Sullen. No, Sir.—

390   *Count.* No, Sir,—Garzoon, Madam, I am not your Husband.

Mrs. Sullen. 'Tis time to undeceive you, Sir,—I believ'd

371 Woman] Q2; Women

your Addresses to me were no more than an Amusement, and
I hope you will think the same of my Complaisance, and to
convince you that you ought, you must know, that I brought
you hither only to make you instrumental in setting me right
with my Husband, for he was planted to listen by my
Appointment.

Count. By your Appointment?

Mrs. Sullen. Certainly.

Count. And so, Madam, while I was telling twenty Stories 400
to part you from your Husband, begar, I was bringing you
together all the while.

Mrs. Sullen. I ask your Pardon, Sir, but I hope this will give
you a Taste of the Vertue of the *English* Ladies.

Count. Begar, Madam, your Vertue be vera Great, but
Garzoon your Honeste be vera little.

Enter Dorinda.

Mrs. Sullen. Nay, now you're angry, Sir.

Count. Angry! fair *Dorinda* (*Sings* Dorinda *the Opera Tune, and
addresses to* Dorinda.) Madam, when your Ladyship want a
Fool, send for me, fair *Dorinda, Revenge, &c.* 410

Exit.

Mrs. Sullen. There goes the true Humour of his Nation,
Resentment with good Manners, and the height of Anger in a
Song,—Well Sister, you must be Judge, for you have heard
the Trial.

Dorinda. And I bring in my Brother Guilty.

Mrs. Sullen. But I must bear the Punishment,—'Tis hard
Sister.

Dorinda. I own it—but you must have Patience.

Mrs. Sullen. Patience! the Cant of Custom—Providence
sends no Evil without a Remedy—shou'd I lie groaning under 420
a Yoke I can shake off, I were accessary to my Ruin, and my
Patience were no better than self-Murder.

Dorinda. But how can you shake off the Yoke—Your
Divisions don't come within the Reach of the Law for a
Divorce.

Mrs. Sullen. Law! what Law can search into the remote
Abyss of Nature, what Evidence can prove the unaccountable,

Disaffections of Wedlock—can a Jury sum up the endless
Aversions that are rooted in our Souls, or can a Bench give
430 Judgment upon Antipathies.

    Dorinda. They never pretended Sister, they never meddle
but in case of Uncleanness.

    Mrs. Sullen. Uncleanness! O Sister, casual Violation is a
transient Injury, and may possibly be repair'd, but can
radical Hatreds be ever reconcil'd—No, no, Sister, Nature is
the first Lawgiver, and when she has set Tempers opposite,
not all the golden Links of Wedlock, nor Iron Manacles of
Law can keep 'um fast.

      Wedlock we own ordain'd by Heaven's Decree,
440   *But such as Heaven ordain'd it first to be,*
      Concurring Tempers in the Man and Wife
      As mutual Helps to draw the Load of Life.
      View all the Works of Providence above,
      The Stars with Harmony and Concord move;
      View all the Works of Providence below, ⎫
      The Fire the Water, Earth, and Air, we know ⎬
      All in one Plant agree to make it grow. ⎭
      Must Man the chiefest Work of Art Divine,
      Be doom'd in endless Discord to repine.
450   *No, we shou'd injure Heaven by that surmise*
      Omnipotence is just, were Man but wise.

               [*The*] End of the Third Act.

ACT IV. [Scene i.]

SCENE *continues.*

Enter Mrs. Sullen.

    Mrs. Sullen. Were I born an humble *Turk*, where Women
have no Soul nor Property there I must sit contented—But in
England, a Country whose Women are it's Glory, must
Women be abus'd, where Women rule, must Women be
enslav'd? nay, cheated into Slavery, mock'd by a Promise of
comfortable Society into a Wilderness of Solitude—I dare not

keep the Thought about me—O, here comes something to divert me—

Enter a Country Woman.

Woman. I come an't please your Ladyship, you're my *Lady Bountiful.* an't ye?

Mrs. Sullen. Well, good Woman go on.   10

Woman. I come seventeen long Mail to have a Cure for my Husband's sore Leg.

Mrs. Sullen. Your Husband! what Woman, cure your Husband!

Woman. Ay, poor Man, for his Sore Leg won't let him stir from Home.

Mrs. Sullen. There, I confess, you have given me a Reason. Well good Woman, I'll tell you what you must do—You must lay your Husband Leg upon a Table, and with a Choping- 20 knife, you must lay it open as broad as you can, then you must take out the Bone, and beat the Flesh soundly with a rowling-pin, then take Salt, Pepper, Cloves, Mace and Ginger, some sweet Herbs, and season it very well, then rowl it up like Brawn, and put it into the Oven for two Hours.

Woman. Heavens reward your Ladyship—I have two little Babies too that are pitious bad with the Graips, an't please ye.

Mrs. Sullen. Put a little Pepper and Salt in their Bellies, good Woman.

Enter Lady Bountiful.

I beg your Ladyship's Pardon for taking your Business out of 30 your Hands, I have been a tampering here a little with one of your Patients.

Lady Bountiful. Come, good Woman, don't mind this mad Creature, I am the Person that you want, I suppose—What wou'd you have, Woman?

Mrs. Sullen. She wants something for her Husband's sore Leg.

Lady Bountiful. What's the matter with his Leg, Goody?

Woman. It come first as one might say with a sort of Dizziness in his Foot, then he had a kind of a Laziness in his 40 Joints, and then his Leg broke out, and then it swell'd, and then it clos'd again, and then it broke out again, and then it

IV.i. 9 Ladyship] Q2; Ladyships

fester'd, and then it grew better, and then it grew worse again.

Mrs. Sullen. Ha, ha, ha.

Lady Bountiful. How can you be merry with the Misfortunes of other People?

Mrs. Sullen. Because my own make me sad, Madam.

Lady Bountiful. The worst Reason in the World, Daughter, your own Misfortunes shou'd teach you to pitty others.

50 *Mrs. Sullen.* But the Woman's Misfortunes and mine are nothing alike, her Husband is sick, and mine, alas, is in Health.

Lady Bountiful. What! wou'd you wish your Husband sick?

Mrs. Sullen. Not of a sore Leg, of all things.

Lady Bountiful. Well, good Woman, go to the Pantrey, get your Belly-full of Victuals, then I'll give you a Receipt of Diet-drink for your Husband—But d'ye hear Goody, you must not let your Husband move too much.

Woman. No, no, Madam, the poor Man's inclinable enough
60 to lye still.

Exit.

Lady Bountiful. Well, Daughter *Sullen*, tho' you laugh, I have done Miracles about the Country here with my Receipts.

Mrs. Sullen. Miracles, indeed, if they have cur'd any Body, but, I believe, Madam, the Patient's Faith goes farther toward the Miracle than your Prescription.

Lady Bountiful. Fancy helps in some Cases, but there's your Husband who has as little Fancy as any Body, I brought him from Death's-door.

Mrs. Sullen. I suppose, Madam, you made him drink
70 plentifully of Asse's Milk.

Enter Dorinda, *runs to* Mrs. Sullen.

Dorinda. News, dear Sister, news, news,

Enter Archer *running.*

Archer. Where, where is my *Lady Bountiful*—Pray which is the old Lady of you three?

Lady Bountiful. I am.

Archer. O, Madam, the Fame of your Ladyship's Charity, Goodness, Benevolence, Skill and Ability have drawn me hither to implore your Ladyship's Help in behalf of my unfortunate Master, who is this Moment breathing his last.

Lady Bountiful. Your Master! where is he?

Archer. At your Gate, Madam, drawn by the Appearance of 80
your handsome House to view it nearer, and walking up the
Avenue within five Paces of the Court-Yard, he was taken ill
of a sudden with a sort of I know not what, but down he fell,
and there he lies.

Lady Bountiful. Here, *Scrub, Gipsey,* all run, get my easie
Chair down Stairs, put the Gentleman in it, and bring him in
quickly, quickly.

Archer. Heaven will reward your Ladyship for this charitable
Act.

Lady Bountiful. Is your Master us'd to these Fits?   90

Archer. O yes, Madam, frequently—I have known him have
five or six of a Night.

Lady Bountiful. What's his Name?

Archer. Lord, Madam, he's a dying, a Minute's Care or
Neglect may save or destroy his Life.

Lady Bountiful. Ah, poor Gentleman! come Friend, show me
the way, I'll see him brought in my self.

Exit with Archer.

Dorinda. O Sister my Heart flutters about strangely, I can
hardly forbear running to his Assistance.

Mrs. Sullen. And I'll lay my Life, he deserves your 100
Assistance more than he wants it; did not I tell you that my
Lord wou'd find a way to come at you. Love's his Distemper,
and you must be the Physitian; put on all your Charms,
summon all your Fire into your Eyes, plant the whole Artillery
of your Looks against his Breast, and down with him.

Dorinda. O Sister, I'm but a young Gunner, I shall be
afraid to shoot, for fear the Piece shou'd recoil and hurt my
self.

Mrs. Sullen. Never fear, you shall see me shoot before you, if
you will.

110

Dorinda. No, no, dear Sister, you have miss'd your Mark so
unfortunately, that I shan't care for being instructed by you.

Enter Aimwell *in a Chair, carry'd by* Archer *and* Scrub,
Lady Bountiful, Gipsey. Aimwell *counterfeiting a
Swoon.*

Lady Bountiful. Here, here, let's see the Hartshorn-drops—
Gipsey a Glass of fair Water, his Fit's very strong—Bless me,
how his Hands are clinch'd.

Archer. For shame, Ladies, what d'ye do? why don't you help us—Pray, Madam, (*To* Dorinda.) Take his Hand and open it if you can, whilst I hold his Head. (Dorinda *takes his Hand.*)

Dorinda. Poor, Gentleman,—Oh—he has got my Hand
120 within his, and squeezes it unmercifully—

Lady Bountiful. 'Tis the Violence of his Convulsion, Child.

Archer. O, Madam, he's perfectly possess'd in these Cases —he'll bite if you don't have a care.

Dorinda. Oh, my Hand, my Hand.

Lady Bountiful. What's the matter with the foolish Girl? I have got his Hand open, you see, with a great deal of Ease.

Archer. Ay, but, Madam, your Daughter's Hand is some-what warmer than your Ladyship's, and the Heat of it draws the Force of the Spirits that way.

130 *Mrs. Sullen.* I find, Friend, you're very learned in these sorts of Fits.

Archer. 'Tis no wonder, Madam, for I'm often troubled with them my self, I find my self extreamly ill at this Minute. (*Looking hard at* Mrs. Sullen.)

Mrs. Sullen. I fancy I cou'd find a way to cure you. (*Aside.*)

Lady Bountiful. His Fit holds him very long.

Archer. Longer than usual, Madam,—Pray, young Lady, open his Breast, and give him Air.

Lady Bountiful. Where did his Illness take him first, pray?

Archer. To Day at Church, Madam.

140 *Lady Bountiful.* In what manner was he taken?

Archer. Very strangely, my Lady. He was of a sudden touch'd with something in his Eyes, which at the first he only felt, but cou'd not tell whether 'twas Pain or Pleasure.

Lady Bountiful. Wind, nothing but Wind.

Archer. By soft Degrees it grew and mounted to his Brain, there his Fancy caught it; there form'd it so beautiful, and dress'd it up in such gay pleasing Colours, that his transported Appetite seiz'd the fair Idea, and straight convey'd it to his Heart. That hospitable Seat of Life sent all its sanguine Spirits
150 forth to meet, and open'd all its sluicy Gates to take the Stranger in.

Lady Bountiful. Your Master shou'd never go without a Bottle to smell to—Oh!—He recovers—The Lavender Water

—Some Feathers to burn under his Nose—*Hungary*-water to
rub his Temples—O, he comes to himself. Hem a little, Sir,
hem—*Gipsey*, bring the Cordial-water. (Aimwell *seems to awake
in amaze.*)

Dorinda. How d'ye, Sir?

Aimwell. Where am I? (*Rising.*)

Sure I have pass'd the Gulph of silent Death,
And now I land on the Elisian *Shore*—   160
Behold the Goddess of those happy Plains
Fair Proserpine—*Let me adore thy bright Divinity.* (*Kneels*
to Dorinda *and kisses her Hand.*)

Mrs. Sullen. So, so, so, I knew where the Fit wou'd end.

Aimwell. Euridice *perhaps—How cou'd thy* Orpheus *keep his*
          word,
          And not look back upon thee;
          No Treasure but thy self cou'd sure have brib'd him
          To look one Minute off thee.

Lady Bountiful. Delirious, poor Gentleman.

Archer. Very Delirious, Madam, very Delirious.   170

Aimwell. Martin's Voice, I think.

Archer. Yes, my Lord—How do's your Lordship?

Lady Bountiful. Lord! did you mind that, Girls.

Aimwell. Where am I?

Archer. In very good Hands, Sir,—You were taken just now
with one of your old Fits under the Trees just by this good
Lady's House, her Ladyship had you taken in, and has
miraculously brought you to your self, as you see—

Aimwell. I am so confounded with Shame, Madam, that I
can now only beg Pardon—And refer my Acknowledgements 180
for your Ladyship's Care, till an Opportunity offers of making
some Amends—I dare be no longer troublesome—*Martin*, give
two Guineas to the Servants. (*Going.*)

Dorinda. Sir, you may catch cold by going so soon into the
Air, you don't look, Sir, as if you were perfectly recover'd.

Here Archer *talks to* Lady Bountiful *in dumb shew.*

Aimwell. That I shall never be, Madam, my present Illness
is so rooted, that I must expect to carry it to my Grave.

Mrs. Sullen. Don't despair, Sir, I have known several in
your Distemper shake it off, with a Fortnight's Physick.

Lady Bountiful. Come, Sir, your Servant has been telling me 190 that you're apt to relapse if you go into Air—Your good Manners shan't get the better of ours—You shall sit down again, Sir,—Come, Sir, we don't mind Ceremonies in the Country—Here, Sir, my Service t'ye—You shall taste my Water; 'tis a Cordial I can assure you, and of my own making—drink it off, Sir, (Aimwell *drinks*.) And how d'ye find your self now, Sir.

Aimwell. Somewhat better—Tho' very faint still.

Lady Bountiful. Ay, ay, People are always faint after these
200 Fits—Come Girls, you shall show the Gentleman the House, 'tis but an old Family Building, Sir, but you had better walk about and cool by Degrees than venture immediately into the Air—You'll find some tolerable Pictures—*Dorinda*, show the Gentleman the way. I must go to the poor Woman below.

Exit.

Dorinda. This way, Sir.

Aimwell. Ladies shall I beg leave for my Servant to wait on you, for he understands Pictures very well.

Mrs. Sullen. Sir, we understand Originals, as well as he do's Pictures, so he may come along.

Exeunt Dorinda, Mrs. Sullen, Aimwell, Archer,
Aimwell *leads* Dorinda.

Enter Foigard *and* Scrub, *meeting.*

210 *Foigard.* Save you, Master *Scrub*.

Scrub. Sir, I won't be sav'd your way—I hate a Priest, I abhor the *French*, and I defie the Devil—Sir, I'm a bold *Briton*, and will spill the last drop of my Blood to keep out Popery and Slavery.

Foigard. Master *Scrub*, you wou'd put me down in Politicks, and so I wou'd be speaking with Mrs. *Shipsey*.

Scrub. Good Mr. Priest, you can't speak with her, she's sick, Sir, she's gone abroad, Sir, she's—dead two Months ago, Sir.

Enter Gipsey.

Gipsey. How now, Impudence; how dare you talk so saucily
220 to the Doctor? Pray, Sir, dont take it ill; for the Common-people of *England* are not so civil to Strangers, as—

Scrub. You lie, you lie—'Tis the Common People that are civilest to Strangers.

Gipsey. Sirrah, I have a good mind to—Get you out, I say.

Scrub. I won't.

Gipsey. You won't, Sauce-box—Pray, Doctor, what is the Captain's Name that came to your Inn last Night?

Scrub. The Captain! Ah, the Devil, there she hampers me again;—The Captain has me on one side, and the Priest on t'other:—So between the Gown and the Sword, I have a fine 230 time on't.—But, *Cedunt Arma togae.* (*Going.*)

Gipsey. What, Sirrah, won't you march?

Scrub. No, my Dear, I won't march—But I'll walk—And I'll make bold to listen a little too. [*Aside.*]

                   Goes behind the side-Scene, and listens.

Gipsey. Indeed, Doctor, the Count has been barbarously treated, that's the Truth on't.

Foigard. Ah, Mrs. *Gipsey*, upon my shoul, now, *Gra*, his Complainings wou'd mollifie the Marrow in your Bones, and move the Bowels of your Commiseration; he veeps, and he dances, and he fistles, and he swears, and he laughs, and he 240 stamps, and he sings: In Conclusion, Joy, he's afflicted, *a la Francois*, and a Stranger wou'd not know whider to cry, or to laugh with him.

Gipsey. What wou'd you have me do, Doctor?

Foigard. Noting, Joy, but only hide the Count in *Mrs. Sullen*'s Closet when it is dark.

Gipsey. Nothing! Is that nothing? it wou'd be both a Sin and a shame, Doctor.

Foigard. Here is twenty *Lewidores*, Joy, for your shame; and I will give you an Absolution for the Shin.   250

Gipsey. But won't that Money look like a Bribe?

Foigard. Dat is according as you shall tauk it.—If you receive the Money beforehand, 'twill be *Logicè* a Bribe; but if you stay till afterwards, 'twill be only a Gratification.

Gipsey. Well, Doctor, I'll take it *Logicè*.—But what must I do with my Conscience, Sir?

Foigard. Leave dat wid me, Joy; I am your Priest, *Gra*; and your Conscience is under my Hands.

Gipsey. But shou'd I put the Count into the Closet—

Foigard. Vel, is dere any Shin for a Man's being in a 260 Closhet; one may go to Prayers in a Closhet.

Gipsey. But if the Lady shou'd come into her Chamber, and go to Bed?

Foigard. Vel, and is dere any Shin in going to Bed, Joy?

Gipsey. Ay, but if the Parties shou'd meet, Doctor?

Foigard. Vel den—The Parties must be responsible.—Do you be after putting the Count in the Closet; and leave the Shins wid themselves.—I will come with the Count to instruct you in your Chamber.

270 *Gipsey.* Well, Doctor, your Religion is so pure—Methinks I'm so easie after an Absolution, and can sin afresh with so much security, that I'm resolv'd to die a Martyr to't.—Here's the Key of the Garden-door, in the back way when 'tis late,—I'll be ready to receive you; but don't so much as whisper, only take hold of my Hand, I'll lead you, and do you lead the Count, and follow me.

Exeunt.

Enter Scrub.

Scrub. What Witchcraft now have these two Imps of the Devil been a hatching here?—There's twenty *Lewidores*, I heard that, and saw the Purse: But I must give room to my
280 Betters.

Enter Aimwell *leading* Dorinda, *and making Love in
dumb Show*—Mrs. Sullen *and* Archer.

Mrs. Sullen. Pray, Sir, (*To* Archer.) how d'ye like that Piece?

Archer. O, 'tis *Leda.*—You find, Madam, how *Jupiter* comes disguis'd to make Love—

Mrs. Sullen. But what think you there of *Alexander*'s Battles?

Archer. We want only a *Le Brun*, Madam, to draw greater Battles, and a greater General of our own.—The *Danube*, Madam, wou'd make a greater Figure in a Picture than the *Granicus*; and we have our *Ramelies* to match their *Arbela*.

Mrs. Sullen. Pray, Sir, what Head is that in the Corner
290 there?

Archer. O, Madam, 'tis poor *Ovid* in his Exile.

Mrs. Sullen. What was he banish'd for?

Archer. His amibitious Love, Madam. (*Bowing.*) His Misfortune touches me.

Mrs. Sullen. Was he successful in his Amours?

Archer. There he has left us in the dark.—He was too much a Gentleman to tell.

Mrs. Sullen. If he were secret, I pity him.

Archer. And if he were successful, I envy him.

300 *Mrs. Sullen.* How d'ye like that *Venus* over the Chimney?

Archer. Venus! I protest, Madam, I took it for your Picture; but now I look again, 'tis not handsome enough.

Mrs. Sullen. Oh, what a Charm is Flattery! if you wou'd see my Picture, there it is, over that Cabinet;—How d'ye like it?

Archer. I must admire any thing, Madam, that has the least Resemblance of you—But, methinks, Madam—(*He looks at the Picture and* Mrs. Sullen *three or four times, by turns.*) Pray, Madam, who drew it?

Mrs. Sullen. A famous Hand, Sir.

Here Aimwell *and* Dorinda *go off.*

Archer. A famous Hand, Madam—Your Eyes, indeed, are 310 featur'd there; but where's the sparkling Moisture shining fluid, in which they swim. The Picture indeed has your Dimples; but where's the Swarm of killing *Cupids* that shou'd ambush there? the Lips too are figur'd out; but where's the Carnation Dew, the pouting Ripeness that tempts the Taste in the Original?

Mrs. Sullen. Had it been my Lot to have match'd with such a Man! [*Aside.*]

Archer. Your Breasts too, presumptuous Man! what! paint Heaven! *Apropo*, Madam, in the very next Picture is *Salmoneus*, 320 that was struck dead with Lightning, for offering to imitate *Jove's* Thunder; I hope you serv'd the Painter so, Madam?

Mrs. Sullen. Had my Eyes the power of Thunder, they shou'd employ their Lightning better.

Archer. There's the finest Bed in that Room, Madam, I suppose 'tis your Ladyship's Bed-Chamber.

Mrs. Sullen. And what then, Sir?

Archer. I think the Quilt is the richest that ever I saw:—I can't at this Distance, Madam, distinguish the Figures of the Embroidery; will you give me leave, Madam—   330

Mrs. Sullen. The Devil take his Impudence.—Sure if I gave him an opportunity, he durst not offer it.—I have a great mind to try.—(*Going.*) (*Returns.*) S'death, what am I doing?— And alone too! [*Aside.*]—Sister, Sister?

Runs out.

Archer. I'll follow her close—

For where a French-*man durst attempt to storm,*
A Briton *sure may well the Work perform.* (*Going.*)
Enter Scrub.

Scrub. Martin, Brother *Martin*.

Archer. O, Brother *Scrub*, I beg your Pardon, I was not a
340 going; here's a Guinea, my Master order'd you.

Scrub. A Guinea, hi, hi, hi, a Guinea! eh—by this Light it is
a Guinea; but I suppose you expect One and twenty Shillings
in change.

Archer. Not at all; I have another for *Gipsey*.

Scrub. A Guinea for her! Faggot and Fire for the Witch.—Sir,
give me that Guinea, and I'll discover a Plot.

Archer. A Plot!

Scrub. Ay, Sir, a Plot, and a horrid Plot.—First, it must be
a Plot because there's a Woman in't; secondly, it must be a
350 Plot because there's a Priest in't; thirdly, it must be a Plot
because there's *French* Gold in't; and fourthly, it must be a
Plot, because I don't know what to make on't.

Archer. Nor any body else, I'm afraid, Brother *Scrub*.

Scrub. Truly I'm afraid so too; for where there's a Priest and
a Woman, there's always a Mystery and a Riddle.—This I
know, that here has been the Doctor with a Temptation in one
Hand, and an Absolution in the other; and *Gipsey* has sold
her self to the Devil; I saw the Price paid down, my Eyes shall
take their Oath on't.

360 *Archer.* And is all this bustle about *Gipsey*.

Scrub. That's not all; I cou'd hear but a Word here and
there; but I remember they mention'd a Count, a Closet, a
back Door, and a Key.

Archer. The Count! did you hear nothing of *Mrs. Sullen*?

Scrub. I did hear some word that sounded that way; but
whether it was *Sullen* or *Dorinda*, I cou'd not distinguish.

Archer. You have told this matter to no Body, Brother?

Scrub. Told! No, Sir, I thank you for that; I'm resolv'd
never to speak one word *pro* nor *con*, till we have a Peace.

370 *Archer.* You're i'th right, Brother *Scrub*; here's a Treaty a
foot between the Count and the Lady.—The Priest and the
Chamber-maid are the Plenipotentiaries.—It shall go hard
but I find a way to be included in the Treaty.—Where's the
Doctor now?

Scrub. He and *Gipsey* are this moment devouring my Lady's
Marmalade in the Closet.

Aimwell. (*From without.*) Martin, Martin.

Archer. I come, Sir, I come.

Scrub. But you forget the other Guinea, Brother *Martin*.

Archer. Here, I give it with all my Heart.   380

Scrub. And I take it with all my Soul.

           Exit Archer.

I'cod I'll spoil your Plotting, Mrs. *Gipsey*; and if you shou'd set the Captain upon me, these two Guineas will buy me off.

             Exit.

   Enter Mrs Sullen *and* Dorinda *meeting*.

Mrs. Sullen. Well, Sister.

Dorinda. And well, Sister.

Mrs. Sullen. What's become of my Lord?

Dorinda. What's become of his Servant?

Mrs. Sullen. Servant! he's a prettier Fellow, and a finer Gentleman by fifty Degrees than his Master.

Dorinda. O'my Conscience, I fancy you cou'd beg that 390 Fellow at the Gallows-foot.

Mrs. Sullen. O'my Conscience, I cou'd, provided I cou'd put a Friend of yours in his Room.

Dorinda. You desir'd me, Sister to leave you, when you transgress'd the Bounds of Honour.

Mrs. Sullen. Thou dear censorious Country-Girl—What dost mean? you can't think of the Man without the Bedfellow, I find.

Dorinda. I don't find any thing unnatural in that thought, while the Mind is conversant with Flesh and Blood, it must 400 conform to the Humours of the Company.

Mrs. Sullen. How a little Love and good Company improves a Woman; why, Child, you begin to live—you never spoke before.

Dorinda. Because I was never spoke to.—My Lord has told me that I have more Wit and Beauty than any of my Sex; and truly I begin to think the Man is sincere.

Mrs. Sullen. You're in the right, *Dorinda*, Pride is the Life of the Woman, and Flattery is our daily Bread; and she's a Fool that won't believe a Man there, as much as she that believes 410 him in any thing else—But I'll lay you a Guinea, that I had finer things said to me than you had.

381.1 *Exit* Archer] ed.; *Exeunt severally*.

Dorinda. Done—What did your Fellow say to'ye?

Mrs. Sullen. My Fellow took the Picture of *Venus* for mine.

Dorinda. But my Lover took me for *Venus* her self.

Mrs. Sullen. Common Cant! had my Spark call'd me a *Venus* directly, I shou'd have believ'd him a Footman in good earnest.

Dorinda. But my Lover was upon his Knees to me.

420 *Mrs. Sullen.* And mine was upon his Tiptoes to me.

Dorinda. Mine vow'd to die for me.

Mrs. Sullen. Mine swore to die with me.

Dorinda. Mine spoke the softest moving things.

Mrs. Sullen. Mine had his moving things too.

Dorinda. Mine kiss'd my Hand Ten Thousand times.

Mrs. Sullen. Mine has all that Pleasure to come.

Dorinda. Mine offer'd Marriage.

Mrs. Sullen. O lard! D'ye call that a moving thing?

Dorinda. The sharpest Arrow in his Quiver, my dear 430 Sister,—Why, my Ten thousand Pounds may lie brooding here this seven Years, and hatch nothing at last but some ill natur'd Clown like yours:—Whereas, If I marry my Lord *Aimwell*, there will be Title, Place and Precedence, the Park, the Play, and the drawing-Room, Splendor, Equipage, Noise and Flambeaux—Hey, my Lady *Aimwell's* Servants there— Lights, Lights to the Stairs—My Lady *Aimwell's* Coach put forward—Stand by, make room for her Ladyship—Are not these things moving?—What! melancholly of a sudden?

Mrs. Sullen. Happy, happy Sister! your Angel has been 440 watchful for your Happiness, whilst mine has slept regardless of his Charge.—Long smiling Years of circling Joys for you, but not one Hour for me! (*Weeps.*)

Dorinda. Come, my Dear, we'll talk of something else.

Mrs. Sullen. O *Dorinda*, I own my self a Woman, full of my Sex, a gentle, generous Soul,—easie and yielding to soft Desires; a spacious Heart, where Love and all his Train might lodge. And must the fair Apartment of my Breast be made a Stable for a Brute to lie in?

Dorinda. Meaning your Husband, I suppose.

450 *Mrs. Sullen.* Husband! no,—Even Husband is too soft a Name for him.—But, come, I expect my Brother here to Night or to Morrow; he was abroad when my Father marry'd me;

perhaps he'll find a way to make me easy.

Dorinda. Will you promise not to make your self easy in the mean time with my Lord's Friend?

Mrs. Sullen. You mistake me, Sister—It happens with us, as among the Men, the greatest Talkers are the greatest Cowards; and there's a Reason for it; those Spirits evaporate in prattle, which might do more Mischief if they took another Course;—Tho' to confess the Truth, I do love that Fellow;— 460 And if I met him drest as he shou'd be, and I undrest as I shou'd be—Look'ye, Sister, I have no supernatural Gifts;—I can't swear I cou'd resist the Temptation,—tho' I can safely promise to avoid it; and that's as much as the best of us can do.

Exeunt Mrs. Sullen *and* Dorinda.

[ACT IV. Scene ii.]

[SCENE *changes to the Inn.*]

Enter Aimwell *and* Archer *laughing.*

Archer. And the awkward Kindness of the good motherly old Gentlewoman—

Aimwell. And the coming Easiness of the young one— S'death, 'tis pity to deceive her.

Archer. Nay, if you adhere to those Principles, stop where you are.

Aimwell. I can't stop; for I love her to distraction.

Archer. S'death, if you love her a hair's breadth beyond discretion, you must go no farther.

Aimwell. Well, well, any thing to deliver us from sauntering 10 away our idle Evenings at *White*'s, *Tom*'s or *Will*'s, and be stinted to bear looking at our old Acquaintance, the Cards; because our important Pockets can't afford us a Guinea for the mercenary Drabs.

Archer. Or be oblig'd to some Purse-proud Coxcomb for a scandalous Bottle, where we must not pretend to our share of the Discourse, because we can't pay our Club o'th Reckoning; —dam it, I had rather spunge upon *Morris*, and sup upon a Dish of *Bohee* scor'd behind the Door.

20   *Aimwell.* And there expose our want of Sense by talking Criticisms, as we shou'd our want of Money by railing at the Government.

  Archer. Or be oblig'd to sneak into the side-Box, and between both Houses steal two Acts of a Play, and because we han't Money to see the other three, we come away discontented, and damn the whole five.

  Aimwell. And Ten thousand such rascally Tricks,—had we outliv'd our Fortunes among our Acquaintance.—But now—

  Archer. Ay, now is the time to prevent all this.—Strike while 30 the Iron is hot.—This Priest is the luckiest part of our Adventure;—He shall marry you, and pimp for me.

  Aimwell. But I shou'd not like a Woman that can be so fond of a *Frenchman.*

  Archer. Alas, Sir, Necessity has no Law; the Lady may be in Distress; perhaps she has a confounded Husband, and her Revenge may carry her farther than her Love.—I gad, I have so good an Opinion of her, and of my self, that I begin to fancy strange things; and we must say this for the Honour of our Women, and indeed of our selves, that they do stick to their 40 Men, as they do to their *Magna Charta.*—If the Plot lies as I suspect,—I must put on the Gentleman.—But here comes the Doctor.—I shall be ready.

                                 Exit.

              Enter Foigard.

  Foigard. Sauve you, noble Friend.

  Aimwell. O Sir, your Servant; pray Doctor, may I crave your Name?

  Foigard. Fat Naam is upon me? my Naam is *Foigard,* Joy.

  Aimwell. Foigard, a very good Name for a Clergyman: Pray, Doctor *Foigard,* were you ever in *Ireland?*

  Foigard. Ireland! No Joy.—Fat sort of Plaace is dat saam 50 *Ireland?* dey say de People are catcht dere when dey are young.

  Aimwell. And some of 'em when they're old;—as for Example. (*Takes* Foigard *by the Shoulder.*) Sir, I arrest you as a Traytor against the Government; you're a Subject of *England,* and this Morning shew'd me a Commission, by which you serv'd as Chaplain in the *French* Army: This is Death by our Law, and your Reverence must hang for't.

  Foigard. Upon my Shoul, Noble Friend, dis is strange News

you tell me, Fader *Foigard* a Subject of *England*, de Son of a
Burgomaster of *Brussels*, a Subject of *England*! Ubooboo—

Aimwell. The Son of a Bogtrotter in *Ireland*; Sir, your 60
Tongue will condemn you before any Bench in the Kingdom.

Foigard. And is my Tongue all your Evidensh, Joy?

Aimwell. That's enough.

Foigard. No, no, Joy, for I vill never spake *English* no more.

Aimwell. Sir, I have other Evidence—Here, *Martin*, you
know this Fellow.

Enter Archer.

Archer. (*In a Brogue.*) Saave you, my dear Cussen, how do's
your Health?

Foigard. Ah! upon my Shoul dere is my Countryman, and
his Brogue will hang mine. (*Aside.*) *Mynheer, Ick wet neat watt hey* 70
zacht, Ick universton ewe neat, sacramant.

Aimwell. Altering your Language won't do, Sir, this Fellow
knows your Person, and will swear to your Face.

Foigard. Faace! fey, is dear a Brogue upon my Faash, too?

Archer. Upon my Soulvation dere ish Joy—But Cussen
Mack-shane vil you not put a remembrance upon me.

Foigard. *Mack-shane*! by St. *Paatrick*, dat is Naame, shure
enough. (*Aside.*)

Aimwell. I fancy *Archer*, you have it.

Foigard. The Devil hang you, Joy—By fat Acquaintance are 80
you my Cussen.

Archer. O, de Devil hang your shelf, Joy, you know we were
little Boys togeder upon de School, and your foster Moder's
Son was marry'd upon my Nurse's Chister, Joy, and so we are
Irish Cussens.

Foigard. De Devil taak the Relation! vel, Joy, and fat School
was it?

Archer. I tinks it vas—Aay—'Twas *Tipperary*.

Foigard. No, no, Joy, it was *Kilkenny*.

Aimwell. That's enough for us—Self-Confession—Come, 90
Sir, we must deliver you into the Hands of the next
Magistrate.

Archer. He sends you to Gaol, you're try'd next Assizes, and
away you go swing into Purgatory.

Foigard. And is it so wid you, Cussen?

IV.ii. 88 it] O1; is

Archer. It vil be sho wid you, Cussen, if you don't immediately confess the Secret between you and Mrs. *Gipsey*—Look'e, Sir, the Gallows or the Secret, take your Choice.

100   *Foigard.* The Gallows! upon my Shoul I hate that saam Gallow, for it is a Diseash dat is fatal to our Family—Vel den, dere is nothing, Shentlemens, but *Mrs. Shullen* wou'd spaak wid the *Count* in her Chamber at Midnight, and dere is no Haarm, Joy, for I am to conduct the *Count* to the Plash, my shelf.

Archer. As I guess'd—Have you communicated the matter to the *Count?*

Foigard. I have not sheen him since.

Archer. Right agen; why then, Doctor,—you shall conduct
110 me to the Lady instead of the *Count.*

Foigard. Fat my Cussen to the Lady! upon my Shoul, gra, dat is too much upon the Brogue.

Archer. Come, come, Doctor, consider we have got a Rope about your Neck, and if you offer to squeek, we'll stop your Wind-pipe, most certainly, we shall have another Job for you in a Day or two, I hope.

Aimwell. Here's Company coming this way, let's into my Chamber, and there concert our Affair farther.

Archer. Come, my dear Cussen, come along.

Exeunt.

Enter Bonniface, Hounslow *and* Bagshot *at one Door,*
Gibbet *at the opposite.*

120   *Gibbet.* Well, Gentlemen, 'tis a fine Night for our Enterprise.

Hounslow. Dark as Hell.

Bagshot. And blows like the Devil; our Landlord here has show'd us the Window where we must break in, and tells us the Plate stands in the Wainscoat Cupboard in the Parlour.

Bonniface. Ay, ay, Mr. *Bagshot*, as the saying is, Knives and Forks, and Cups, and Canns, and Tumblers, and Tankards—There's one Tankard, as the saying is, that's near upon as big as me, it was a Present to the Squire from his Godmother, and smells of Nutmeg and Toast like an *East India* Ship.

130   *Hounslow.* Then you say we must divide at the Stair-head?

Bonniface. Yes, Mr. *Hounslow*, as the saying is—At one end of that Gallery lies my *Lady Bountiful* and her Daughter, and at the other *Mrs. Sullen*—As for the Squire—

Gibbet. He's safe enough, I have fairly enter'd him, and he's more than half seas over already—But such a Parcel of Scoundrels are got about him now, that I gad I was asham'd to be seen in their Company.

Bonniface. 'Tis now Twelve, as the saying is—Gentlemen, you must set out at One.

Gibbet. Hounslow, do you and *Bagshot* see our Arms fix'd, 140 and I'll come to you presently.

Hounslow.⎫
Bagshot. ⎬ We will.

                                           Exeunt.

Gibbet. Well, my dear *Bonny*, you assure me that *Scrub* is a Coward.

Bonniface. A Chicken, as the saying is—You'll have no Creature to deal with but the Ladies.

Gibbet. And I can assure you, Friend, there's a great deal of Address and good Manners in robbing a Lady, I am the most a Gentleman that way that ever travell'd the Road—But, my dear *Bonny*, this Prize will be a Galleon, a *Vigo* Business—I 150 warrant you we shall bring off three or four thousand Pound.

Bonniface. In Plate, Jewels and Money, as the saying is, you may.

Gibbet. Why then, *Tyburn*, I defie thee, I'll get up to Town, sell off my Horse and Arms, buy my self some pretty Employment in the Household, and be as snug, and as honest as any Courtier of 'um all.

Bonniface. And what think you then of my Daughter *Cherry* for a Wife?

Gibbet. Look'ee, my dear *Bonny*—Cherry *is the Goddess I* 160 *adore*, as the Song goes; but it is a Maxim that Man and Wife shou'd never have it in their Power to hang one another, for if they should, the Lord have Mercy on'um both.

                                           Exeunt.

[*The*] *End of the Fourth Act.*

ACT V. [Scene i.]

SCENE continues. *Knocking without.*

Enter Bonniface.

Bonniface. Coming, coming—A Coach and six foaming Horses at this time o'Night! Some great Man, as the saying is, for he scorns to travel with other People.

Enter Sir Charles Freeman.

Sir Charles. What, Fellow! a Publick-house, and a Bed when other People Sleep.

Bonniface. Sir, I an't a Bed, as the saying is.

Sir Charles. Is Mr. *Sullen*'s Family a Bed, think'e?

Bonniface. All but the Squire himself, Sir, as the saying is, he's in the House.

10 *Sir Charles.* What Company has he?

Bonniface. Why, Sir, there's the Constable, Mr. *Gage* the Exciseman, the Hunchback'd-barber, and two or three other Gentlemen.

Sir Charles. I find my Sister's Letters gave me the true Picture of her Spouse.

Enter Sullen *Drunk.*

Bonniface. Sir, here's the Squire.

Sullen. The Puppies left me asleep—Sir.

Sir Charles. Well, Sir.

Sullen. Sir, I'm an unfortunate Man—I have three thousand 20 Pound a Year, and I can't get a Man to drink a Cup of Ale with me.

Sir Charles. That's very hard.

Sullen. Ay, Sir—And unless you have pitty upon me, and smoke one Pipe with me, I must e'en go home to my Wife, and I had rather go to the Devil by half.

Sir Charles. But, I presume, Sir, you won't see your Wife to Night, she'll be gone to Bed—you don't use to lye with your Wife in that Pickle?

Sullen. What! not lye with my Wife! why, Sir, do you take 30 me for an Atheist or a Rake.

v.i. 25 to] Q2; [om.]

Sir Charles. If you hate her, Sir, I think you had better lye from her.

Sullen. I think so too, Friend—But I'm a Justice of Peace, and must do nothing against the Law.

Sir Charles. Law! as I take it, Mr. Justice, no Body observes Law for Law's Sake, only for the good of those for whom it was made.

Sullen. But if the Law orders me to send you to Gaol, you must ly there, my Friend.

Sir Charles. Not unless I commit a Crime to deserve it.   40

Sullen. A Crime! Oons an't I marry'd?

Sir Charles. Nay, Sir, if you call Marriage a Crime, you must disown it for a Law.

Sullen. Eh!—I must be acquainted with you, Sir—But, Sir, I shou'd be very glad to know the Truth of this Matter.

Sir Charles. Truth, Sir, is a profound Sea, and few there be that dare wade deep enough to find out the bottom on't. Besides, Sir, I'm afraid the Line of your Understanding mayn't be long enough.

Sullen. Look'e, Sir, I have nothing to say to your Sea of 50 Truth, but if a good Parcel of Land can intitle a Man to a little Truth, I have as much as any He in the Country.

Bonniface. I never heard your Worship, as the saying is, talk so much before.

Sullen. Because I never met with a Man that I lik'd before—

Bonniface. Pray, Sir, as the saying is, let me ask you one Question, are not Man and Wife one Flesh?

Sir Charles. You and your Wife, Mr. Guts, may be one Flesh, because ye are nothing else—but rational Creatures 60 have minds that must be united.

Sullen. Minds.

Sir Charles. Ay, Minds, Sir, don't you think that the Mind takes place of the Body?

Sullen. In some People.

Sir Charles. Then the Interest of the Master must be consulted before that of his Servant.

Sullen. Sir, you shall dine with me to Morrow.—Oons I

38 Gaol] O2; Goal

always thought that we were naturally one.

70 *Sir Charles.* Sir, I know that my two Hands are naturally one, because they love one another, kiss one another, help one another in all the Actions of Life, but I cou'd not say so much, if they were always at Cuffs.

Sullen. Then 'tis plain that we are two.

Sir Charles. Why don't you part with her, Sir?

Sullen. Will you take her, Sir?

Sir Charles. With all my Heart.

Sullen. You shall have her to Morrow Morning, and a Venison-pasty into the Bargain.

80 *Sir Charles.* You'll let me have her Fortune too?

Sullen. Fortune! why, Sir, I have no Quarrel at her Fortune—I only hate the Woman, Sir, and none but the Woman shall go.

Sir Charles. But her Fortune, Sir—

Sullen. Can you play at Whisk, Sir?

Sir Charles. No, truly, Sir.

Sullen. Nor at All-fours.

Sir Charles. Neither!

Sullen. Oons! where was this Man bred. (*Aside.*) Burn me, 90 Sir, I can't go home, 'tis but two a Clock.

Sir Charles. For half an Hour, Sir, if you please—But you must consider 'tis late.

Sullen. Late! that's the Reason I can't go to Bed—Come, Sir.—

Exeunt.

Enter Cherry, *runs across the Stage and knocks at* Aimwell's *Chamber-door.*
Enter Aimwell *in his Night-cap and Gown.*

Aimwell. What's the matter, you tremble, Child, you're frighted.

Cherry. No wonder, Sir—But in short, Sir, this very Minute a Gang of Rogues are gone to rob my *Lady Bountiful*'s House.

Aimwell. How!

100 *Cherry.* I dogg'd 'em to the very Door, and left 'em breaking in.

Aimwell. Have you alarm'd any Body else with the News.

Cherry. No, no, Sir, I wanted to have discover'd the whole Plot, and twenty other things to your Man *Martin*; but I have search'd the whole House and can't find him; where is he?

Aimwell. No matter, Child, will you guide me immediately to the House?

Cherry. With all my Heart, Sir, my *Lady Bountiful* is my Godmother; and I love Mrs. *Dorinda* so well.—

Aimwell. Dorinda! The Name inspires me, the Glory and the 110 Danger shall be all my own—Come, my Life, let me but get my Sword.

Exeunt.

[ACT V. Scene ii.]

SCENE, *Changes to a Bed-chamber in* Lady Bountiful's *House.*

Enter Mrs. Sullen, Dorinda *undress'd, a Table and Lights.*

Dorinda. 'Tis very late, Sister, no News of your Spouse yet?

Mrs. Sullen. No, I'm condemn'd to be alone till towards four, and then perhaps I may be executed with his Company.

Dorinda. Well, my Dear, I'll leave you to your rest; you'll go directly to Bed, I suppose.

Mrs. Sullen. I don't know what to do? hey-hoe.

Dorinda. That's a desiring Sigh, Sister.

Mrs. Sullen. This is a languishing Hour, Sister.

Dorinda. And might prove a Critical Minute, if the pretty Fellow were here.   10

Mrs. Sullen. Here! what, in my Bed-chamber, at two a Clock o'th' Morning, I undress'd, the Family asleep, my hated Husband abroad, and my lovely Fellow at my Feet—O gad, Sister!

Dorinda. Thoughts are free, Sister, and them I allow you—So, my Dear, good Night.

[Exit.]

Mrs. Sullen. A good Rest to my dear *Dorinda*—Thoughts free! are they so? why then suppose him here, dress'd like a youthful, gay and burning Bridegroom, (*Here* Archer *steals out of the Closet.*) with Tongue enchanting, Eyes bewitching, 20 Knees imploring. (*Turns a little o' one side, and sees* Archer *in the Posture she describes.*) Ah! (*Shreeks, and runs to the other Side of the*

Stage.) Have my Thoughts rais'd a Spirit?—What are you, Sir, a Man or a Devil?

Archer. A Man, a Man, Madam. (*Rising*.)

Mrs. Sullen. How shall I be sure of it?

Archer. Madam, I'll give you Demonstration this Minute. (*Takes her Hand*.)

Mrs. Sullen. What, Sir! do you intend to be rude?

Archer. Yes, Madam, if you please.

30 *Mrs. Sullen.* In the Name of Wonder, Whence came ye?

Archer. From the Skies, Madam—I'm a *Jupiter* in Love, and you shall be my *Alcmena*.

Mrs. Sullen. How came you in?

Archer. I flew in at the Window, Madam, your Cozen *Cupid* lent me his Wings, and your Sister *Venus* open'd the Casement.

Mrs. Sullen. I'm struck dumb with Admiration.

Archer. And I with wonder. (*Looks passionately at her*.)

Mrs. Sullen. What will become of me?

Archer. How beautiful she looks—The teeming Jolly Spring
40 Smiles in her blooming Face, and when she was conceiv'd, her Mother smelt to Roses, look'd on Lillies—

Lillies unfold their white, their fragrant Charms,

When the warm Sun thus Darts into their Arms. (*Runs to her*.)

Mrs. Sullen. Ah! (*Shreeks*.)

Archer. Oons, Madam, what d'ye mean? you'll raise the House.

Mrs. Sullen. Sir, I'll wake the Dead before I bear this— What! approach me with the Freedom of a Keeper; I'm glad on't, your Impudence has cur'd me.

50 *Archer.* If this be Impudence (*Kneels.*) I leave to your partial self; no panting Pilgrim after a tedious, painful Voyage, e'er bow'd before his Saint with more Devotion.

Mrs. Sullen. Now, now, I'm ruin'd, if he kneels! (*Aside.*) rise thou prostrate Ingineer, not all thy undermining Skill shall reach my Heart—Rise, and know, I am a Woman without my Sex, I can love to all the Tenderness of Wishes, Sighs and Tears—But go no farther—Still to convince you that I'm more than Woman, I can speak my Frailty, confess my Weakness even for you—But—

60 *Archer.* For me! (*Going to lay hold on her*.)

Mrs. Sullen. Hold, Sir, build not upon that—For my most mortal hatred follows if you disobey what I command you now—leave me this Minute—If he denies, I'm lost. (*Aside*.)

Archer. Then you'll promise—

Mrs. Sullen. Any thing another time.

Archer. When shall I come?

Mrs. Sullen. To Morrow when you will.

Archer. Your Lips must seal the Promise.

Mrs. Sullen. Pshaw!

Archer. They must, they must (*Kisses her*.) Raptures and 70 Paradice! and why not now, my Angel? the Time, the Place, Silence and Secresy, all conspire—And the now conscious Stars have preordain'd this Moment for my Happiness. (*Takes her in his Arms*.)

Mrs. Sullen. You will not, cannot sure.

Archer. If the Sun rides fast, and disappoints not Mortals of to Morrow's Dawn, this Night shall crown my Joys.

Mrs. Sullen. My Sex's Pride assist me.

Archer. My Sex's Strength help me.

Mrs. Sullen. You shall kill me first.

Archer. I'll dye with you. (*Carrying her off*.)   80

Mrs. Sullen. Thieves, Thieves, Murther—

Enter Scrub *in his Breeches, and one Shoe*.

Scrub. Thieves, Thieves, Murther, Popery.

Archer. Ha! the very timorous Stag will kill in rutting time. (*Draws and offers to Stab* Scrub.)

Scrub. (*Kneeling*.) O, Pray, Sir, spare all I have and take my Life.

Mrs. Sullen. (*Holding* Archer's *Hand*.) What do's the Fellow mean?

Scrub. O, Madam, down upon your Knees, your Marrow-bones—He's one of 'um.

Archer. Of whom?   90

Scrub. One of the Rogues—I beg your Pardon, Sir, one of the honest Gentlemen that just now are broke into the House.

Archer. How!

Mrs. Sullen. I hope, you did not come to rob me?

Archer. Indeed I did, Madam, but I wou'd have taken nothing but what you might ha' spar'd, but your crying Thieves has wak'd this dreaming Fool, and so he takes 'em for granted.

v.ii. 73.1 *his*] O1; *her*

Scrub. Granted! 'tis granted, Sir, take all we have.

100 *Mrs. Sullen.* The Fellow looks as if he were broke out of Bedlam.

Scrub. Oons, Madam, they're broke in to the House with Fire and Sword, I saw them, heard them, they'll be here this Minute.

Archer. What, Thieves!

Scrub. Under Favour, Sir, I think so.

Mrs. Sullen. What shall we do, Sir?

Archer. Madam, I wish your Ladyship a good Night.

Mrs. Sullen. Will you leave me?

110 *Archer.* Leave you! Lord, Madam, did not you command me to be gone just now upon pain of your immortal Hatred.

Mrs. Sullen. Nay, but pray, Sir—(*Takes hold of him.*)

Archer. Ha, ha, ha, now comes my turn to be ravish'd.—You see now, Madam, you must use Men one way or other; but take this by the way, good Madam, that none but a Fool will give you the benefit of his Courage, unless you'll take his Love along with it.—How are they arm'd, Friend?

Scrub. With Sword and Pistol, Sir.

Archer. Hush—I see a dark Lanthorn coming thro' the 120 Gallery.—Madam, be assur'd I will protect you, or lose my Life.

Mrs. Sullen. Your Life! no, Sir, they can rob me of nothing that I value half so much; therefore, now, Sir, let me intreat you to be gone.

Archer. No, Madam, I'll consult my own Safety for the sake of yours, I'll work by Stratagem: Have you Courage enough to stand the appearance of 'em.

Mrs. Sullen. Yes, yes, since I have scap'd your Hands, I can face any thing.

130 *Archer.* Come hither, Brother *Scrub*, don't you know me?

Scrub. Eh! my dear Brother, let me kiss thee. (*Kisses* Archer.)

Archer. This way—Here—(Archer *and* Scrub *hide behind the* Bed.)

Enter Gibbet *with a dark Lanthorn in one Hand and a Pistol in t'other.*

Gibbet. Ay, ay, this is the Chamber, and the Lady alone.

Mrs Sullen. Who are you, Sir? what wou'd you have? d'ye come to rob me?

Gibbet. Rob you! alack a day, Madam, I'm only a younger Brother, Madam; and so, Madam, if you make a Noise, I'll shoot you thro' the Head; but don't be afraid, Madam. (*Laying his Lanthorn and Pistol upon the Table.*) These Rings, Madam, don't be concern'd, Madam, I have a profound Respect for 140 you, Madam; your Keys, Madam, don't be frighted, Madam, I'm the most of a Gentleman. (*Searching her Pockets.*) This Necklace, Madam, I never was rude to a Lady;—I have a Veneration—for this Necklace—

> Here Archer *having come round and seiz'd the Pistol, takes*
> Gibbet *by the Collar, trips up his Heels, and claps the*
> *Pistol to his Breast.*

Archer. Hold, profane Villain, and take the Reward of thy Sacrilege.

Gibbet. Oh! Pray, Sir, don't kill me; I an't prepar'd.

Archer. How many is there of 'em, *Scrub?*

Scrub. Five and Forty, Sir.

Archer. Then I must kill the Villain to have him out of the 150 way.

Gibbet. Hold, hold, Sir, we are but three upon my Honour.

Archer. *Scrub,* will you undertake to secure him?

Scrub. Not I, Sir; kill him, kill him.

Archer. Run to *Gipsey's* Chamber, there you'll find the Doctor; bring him hither presently.

> *Exit* Scrub *running.*

Come, Rogue, if you have a short Prayer, say it.

Gibbet. Sir, I have no Prayer at all; the Government has provided a Chaplain to say Prayers for us on these Occasions.

Mrs. Sullen. Pray, Sir, don't kill him;—You fright me as 160 much as him.

Archer. The Dog shall die, Madam, for being the Occasion of my disappointment.—Sirrah, this Moment is your last.

Gibbet. Sir, I'll give you Two hundred Pound to spare my Life.

Archer. Have you no more Rascal?

Gibbet. Yes, Sir, I can command Four hundred; but I must reserve Two of 'em to save my Life at the Sessions.

> *Enter* Scrub *and* Foigard.

Archer. Here, Doctor, I suppose *Scrub* and you between you may manage him.—Lay hold of him, Doctor. (Foigard *lays* 170

144.1 *Pistol*] 1728; *Pistols*   158 *Gibbet*] Q2 [*Gib.*]; *Gip.*

hold of Gibbet.)

  Gibbet. What! turn'd over to the Priest already.—Look'ye, Doctor, you come before your time; I'ant condemn'd yet, I thank'ye.

  Foigard. Come, my dear Joy, I vill secure your Body and your Shoul too; I vill make you a good *Catholick*, and give you an Absolution.

  Gibbet. Absolution! can you procure me a Pardon, Doctor?

  Foigard. No, Joy.—

  Gibbet. Then you and your Absolution may go to the Devil.

180 *Archer.* Convey him into the Cellar, there bind him:—Take the Pistol, and if he offers to resist, shoot him thro' the Head,—and come back to us with all the speed you can.

  Scrub. Ay, ay, come, Doctor, do you hold him fast, and I'll guard him. [*Takes the pistol.*]

  Mrs. Sullen. But how came the Doctor?

  Archer. In short, Madam—(*Shreeking without.*) S'death! the Rogues are at work with the other Ladies.—I'm vex'd I parted with the Pistol; but I must fly to their Assistance.—Will you stay here, Madam, or venture your self with me.

190 *Mrs. Sullen.* O, with you, dear Sir, with you.

               Takes him by the Arm and Exeunt.

[ACT V. Scene iii.]

SCENE, *Changes to another Apartment in the same House.*

Enter Bagshot *dragging in Lady* Bountiful, *and*
Hounslow *halling in* Dorinda; *the Rogues with Swords drawn.*

  Hounslow. Come, come, your Jewels, Mistriss.

  Bagshot. Your Keys, your Keys, old Gentlewoman.

        Enter Aimwell *and* Cherry.

  Aimwell. Turn this way, Villains; I durst engage an Army in such a Cause. (*He engages 'em both.*)

---

v.III. 0.3 Bagshot] ed.; Hounslow The dialogue in ll. 1–2 indicates that Bagshot drags in Lady Bountiful and Hounslow drags in Dorinda.   0.3 Hounslow] ed.; Bagshot

Dorinda. O, Madam, had I but a Sword to help the brave Man?

Lady Bountiful. There's three or four hanging up in the Hall; but they won't draw. I'll go fetch one however.

Exit.

Enter Archer *and* Mrs. Sullen.

Archer. Hold, hold, my Lord, every Man his Bird, pray.

They engage Man to Man, the Rogues are thrown and disarm'd.

Cherry. What! the Rogues taken! then they'll impeach my Father; I must give him timely Notice.

Runs out.

Archer. Shall we kill the Rogues?

Aimwell. No, no we'll bind them.

Archer. Ay, ay; here, Madam, lend me your Garter? (*To* Mrs. Sullen *who stands by him.*)

Mrs. Sullen. The Devil's in this Fellow; he fights, loves, and banters, all in a Breath. [*Aside.*]—Here's a Cord that the Rogues brought with 'em, I suppose.

Archer. Right, right, the Rogue's Destiny, a Rope to hang himself.—Come, my Lord,—This is but a scandalous sort of an Office, (*Binding the Rogues together.*) if our Adventures shou'd end in this sort of Hangman-work; but I hope there is something in prospect that—

Enter Scrub.

Well, *Scrub,* have you secur'd your *Tartar?*

Scrub. Yes, Sir, I left the Priest and him disputing about Religion.

Aimwell. And pray carry these Gentlemen to reap the Benefit of the Controversy.

Delivers the Prisoners to Scrub, *who leads 'em out.*

Mrs. Sullen. Pray, Sister, how came my Lord here?

Dorinda. And pray, how came the Gentleman here?

Mrs. Sullen. I'll tell you the great piece of Villainy (*They talk in dumb show.*)

Aimwell. I fancy, *Archer,* you have been more successful in your Adventures than the House-breakers.

Archer. No matter for my Adventure, yours is the principal. —Press her this Minute to marry you,—now while she's hurry'd between the Palpitation of her Fear, and the Joy of her Deliverance, now while the Tide of her Spirits are at High-

flood—Throw your self at her Feet; speak some *Romantick*
Nonsense or other;—Address her like *Alexander* in the height of
his Victory, confound her Senses, bear down her Reason, and
40 away with her—The Priest is now in the Cellar, and dare not
refuse to do the work.

Enter Lady Bountiful.

Aimwell. But how shall I get off without being observ'd?

Archer. You a Lover! and not find a way to get off—Let me
see.

Aimwell. You bleed, *Archer.*

Archer. S'death, I'm glad on't; this Wound will do the
Business—I'll amuse the old Lady and Mrs. *Sullen* about
dressing my Wound, while you carry off *Dorinda.*

Lady Bountiful. Gentlemen, cou'd we understand how you
50 wou'd be gratified for the Services—

Archer. Come, come, my Lady, this is no time for Complements, I'm wounded, Madam.

Lady Bountiful.⎱
Mrs. Sullen.   ⎰ How! wounded!

Dorinda. I hope, Sir, you have receiv'd no Hurt?

Aimwell. None but what you may cure.—(*Makes Love in
dumb show.*)

Lady Bountiful. Let me see your Arm, Sir.—I must have
some Powder-sugar to stop the Blood—O me! an ugly Gash
upon my Word, Sir, you must go into Bed.

Archer. Ay, my Lady a Bed wou'd do very well.—Madam,
60 (*To* Mrs. Sullen.) Will you do me the Favour to conduct me to
a Chamber?

Lady Bountiful. Do, do, Daughter—while I get the Lint and
the Probe and the Plaister ready.

Runs out one way, Aimwell *carries off* Dorinda *another.*

Archer. Come, Madam, why don't you obey your Mother's
Commands.

Mrs. Sullen. How can you, after what is past, have the
Confidence to ask me?

Archer. And if you go to that, how can you after what is
past, have the Confidence to deny me?—Was not this Blood
70 shed in your Defence, and my Life expos'd for your
Protection.—Look'ye, Madam, I'm none of your *Romantick*
Fools, that fight Gyants and Monsters for nothing; my Valour

is down right *Swiss*; I'm a Soldier of Fortune and must be paid.

Mrs. Sullen. 'Tis ungenerous in you, Sir, to upbraid me with your Services.

Archer. 'Tis ungenerous in you, Madam, not to reward 'em.

Mrs. Sullen. How! at the Expence of my Honour.

Archer. Honour! can Honour consist with Ingratitude? if you wou'd deal like a Woman of Honour, do like a Man of 80 Honour, d'ye think I wou'd deny you in such a Case?

Enter a Servant.

Servant. Madam, my Lady order'd me to tell you that your Brother is below at the Gate?

Mrs. Sullen. My Brother? Heavens be prais'd.—Sir, he shall thank you for your Services, he has it in his Power.

Archer. Who is your Brother, Madam?

Mrs. Sullen. Sir Charles Freeman.—You'll excuse me, Sir; I must go and receive him.

[*Exit.*]

Archer. Sir Charles Freeman! S'death and Hell!—My old Acquaintance. Now unless *Aimwell* has made good use of his 90 time, all our fair Machine goes souse into the Sea like the *Edistone.*

Exit.

[ACT V. Scene iv.]

SCENE, *Changes to the Gallery in the same House.*

Enter Aimwell *and* Dorinda.

Dorinda. Well, well, my Lord, you have conquer'd; your late generous Action will I hope, plead for my easie yielding, tho' I must own your Lordship had a Friend in the Fort before.

Aimwell. The Sweets of *Hybla* dwell upon her Tongue.—

Enter Foigard *with a Book.*

Here, Doctor—

Foigard. Are you prepar'd boat?

Dorinda. I'm ready: But, first, my Lord one Word;—I have

a frightful Example of a hasty Marriage in my own Family;
when I reflect upon't, it shocks me. Pray, my Lord, consider a
little—

Aimwell. Consider! Do you doubt my Honour or my Love?

Dorinda. Neither: I do believe you equally Just as Brave.—
And were your whole Sex drawn out for me to chuse, I shou'd
not cast a look upon the Multitude if you were absent.—But
my Lord, I'm a Woman; Colours, Concealments may hide a
thousand Faults in me;—Therefore know me better first; I
hardly dare affirm I know my self in any thing except my Love.

Aimwell. Such Goodness who cou'd injure; I find my self
unequal to the Task of Villain; she has gain'd my Soul, and
made it honest like her own;—I cannot, cannot hurt her.
(*Aside.*) Doctor, retire.

Exit Foigard.

Madam, behold your Lover and your Proselite, and judge of
my Passion by my Conversion.—I'm all a Lie, nor dare I give
a Fiction to your Arms; I'm all Counterfeit except my Passion.

Dorinda. Forbid it Heaven! a Counterfeit!

Aimwell. I am no Lord, but a poor needy Man, come with a
mean, a scandalous Design to prey upon your Fortune:—But
the Beauties of your Mind and Person have so won me from
my self, that like a trusty Servant, I prefer the Interest of my
Mistress to my own.

Dorinda. Sure I have had the Dream of some poor Mariner,
a sleepy image of a welcome Port, and wake involv'd in
Storms. Pray, Sir, who are you?

Aimwell. Brother to the Man whose Title I usurp'd, but
Stranger to his Honour or his Fortune.

Dorinda. Matchless Honesty—Once I was proud, Sir, of
your Wealth and Title, but now am prouder that you want it:
Now I can shew my Love was justly levell'd, and had no Aim
but Love. Doctor, come in.

Enter Foigard *at one Door*, Gipsey *at another, who
whispers* Dorinda.

Your Pardon, Sir, we shannot want you now, Sir? you must

v.iv. 41 want] Q2; won't

excuse me,—I'll wait on you presently.

Exit with Gipsey.

Foigard. Upon my Shoul, now, dis is foolish.

Exit.

Aimwell. Gone! and bid the Priest depart.—It has an ominous Look.

Enter Archer.

Archer. Courage, *Tom*—Shall I wish you Joy?

Aimwell. No.

Archer. Oons, Man, what ha' you been doing?

Aimwell. O, *Archer*, my Honesty, I fear has ruin'd me.

Archer. How!   50

Aimwell. I have discover'd my self.

Archer. Discover'd! and without my Consent? what! have I embark'd my small Remains in the same bottom with yours, and you dispose of all without my Partnership?

Aimwell. O, *Archer*, I own my Fault.

Archer. After Conviction—'Tis then too late for Pardon.— You may remember, Mr. *Aimwell*, that you propos'd this Folly—As you begun, so end it.—Henceforth I'll hunt my Fortune single.—So farwel.

Aimwell. Stay, my dear *Archer*, but a Minute.   60

Archer. Stay! what to be despis'd, expos'd and laugh'd at—No, I wou'd sooner change Conditions with the worst of the Rogues we just now bound, than bear one scornful Smile from the proud Knight that once I treated as my equal.

Aimwell. What Knight?

Archer. *Sir Charles Freeman*, Brother to the Lady that I had almost—But no matter for that, 'tis a cursed Night's Work, and so I leave you to make your best on't. (*Going.*)

Aimwell. Freeman!—One Word, *Archer*. Still I have Hopes; methought she receiv'd my Confession with Pleasure.   70

Archer. S'death! who doubts it?

Aimwell. She consented after to the Match; and still I dare believe she will be just.

Archer. To her self, I warrant her, as you shou'd have been.

Aimwell. By all my Hopes, she comes, and smiling comes.

Enter Dorinda *mighty gay*.

Dorinda. Come, my dear Lord,—I fly with Impatience to your Arms.—The Minutes of my Absence was a tedious Year.

Where's this tedious Priest?
                    Enter Foigard.
    Archer. Oons, a brave Girl.
80   *Dorinda.* I suppose, my Lord, this Gentleman is privy to our
Affairs?
    Archer. Yes, yes, Madam, I'm to be your Father.
    Dorinda. Come, Priest, do your Office.
    Archer. Make hast, make hast, couple 'em any way. (*Takes*
Aimwell*'s Hand.*) Come, Madam, I'm to give you—
    Dorinda. My Mind's alter'd, I won't.
    Archer. Eh—
    Aimwell. I'm confounded.
    Foigard. Upon my Shoul, and sho is my shelf.
90   *Archer.* What's the matter now, Madam?
    Dorinda. Look'ye, Sir, one generous Action deserves another
—This Gentleman's Honour oblig'd him to hide nothing from
me; my Justice engages me to conceal nothing from him: In
short, Sir, you are the Person that you thought you counter-
feited; you are the true Lord Viscount *Aimwell*; and I wish
your Lordship Joy. Now, Priest, you may be gone; if my Lord
is pleas'd now with the Match, let his Lordship marry me in
the face of the World.
    Aimwell. Archer. What do's she mean?
100 *Dorinda.* Here's a Witness for my Truth.
                Enter Sir Charles *and* Mrs. Sullen.
    Sir Charles. My dear Lord *Aimwell*, I wish you Joy.
    Aimwell. Of what?
    Sir Charles. Of your Honour and Estate: Your Brother died
the Day before I left *London*; and all your Friends have writ
after you to *Brussels*; among the rest I did my self the Honour.
    Archer. Hark'ye, Sir Knight, don't you banter now?
    Sir Charles. 'Tis Truth upon my Honour.
    Aimwell. Thanks to the pregnant Stars that form'd this
Accident.
110 *Archer.* Thanks to the Womb of Time that brought it forth;
away with it.
    Aimwell. Thanks to my Guardian Angel that led me to the
Prize—(*Taking* Dorinda*'s Hand.*)
    Archer. And double Thanks to the noble *Sir Charles Freeman.*
My Lord, I wish you Joy. My Lady I wish you Joy.—I Gad,

Sir Charles, you're the honestest Fellow living.—S'death, I'm grown strange airy upon this matter—My Lord, how d'ye?—a word, my Lord; don't you remember something of a previous Agreement, that entitles me to the Moyety of this Lady's Fortune, which, I think will amount to Five thousand Pound. 120

Aimwell. Not a Penny, *Archer*; You wou'd ha' cut my Throat just now, because I wou'd not deceive this Lady.

Archer. Ay, and I'll cut your Throat again, if you shou'd deceive her now.

Aimwell. That's what I expected; and to end the Dispute, the Lady's Fortune is Ten thousand Pound; we'll divide Stakes; take the Ten thousand Pound, or the Lady.

Dorinda. How! is your Lordship so indifferent?

Archer. No, no, no, Madam, his Lordship knows very well, that I'll take the Money; I leave you to his Lordship, and so 130 we're both provided for.

Enter Count Bellair.

Count. Mesdames, & *Massieurs*, I am your Servant trice humble: I hear you be rob, here.

Aimwell. The Ladies have been in some danger, Sir.

Count. And Begar, our Inn be rob too.

Aimwell. Our Inn? by whom?

Count. By the Landlord, begar—Garzoon he has rob himself and run away.

Archer. Rob'd himself!

Count. Ay, begar, and me too of a hundre Pound.   140

Archer. A hundred Pound.

Count. Yes, that I ow'd him.

Aimwell. Our Money's, gone, *Frank*.

---

116 *Charles*] ed.; *Freeman* This obvious correction was made in none of the early editions.

131–142 [Count's scene] The 1728 version reads:

Enter Foigard.

Foig. Arra fait, de People do say you be all rob'd, Joy.

Aim. The Ladies have been in some Danger, Sir, as you saw.

Foig. Upon my Shoul our Inn be rob too.

Aim. Our Inn! By whom?

Foig. Upon my Shalwation, our Landlord has rob'd himself, and run away wid da Money.

Arch. Rob'd himself!

Foig. Ay fait! and me too of a hundred Pounds.

Arch. Rob'd you of a hundred Pound!

Foig. Yes fait Honny, that I did owe to him.

Archer. Rot the Money, my Wench is gone—*Scavez vous quelque chose de Madamoiselle* Cherry?

          Enter a Fellow *with a strong Box and a Letter.*

Fellow. Is there one *Martin* here?

Archer. Ay, ay,—who wants him?

Fellow. I have a Box here and Letter for him.

   Archer. (*Taking the Box.*) Ha, ha, ha, what's here? *Legerdemain!*
150 by this Light, my Lord, our Money again; but this unfolds the
Riddle. (*Opening the Letter, reads.*) Hum, hum, hum—O, 'tis for
the Publick good, and must be communicated to the
Company.

    Mr. MARTIN,

    My Father being afraid of an Impeachment by the Rogues that are
    taken to Night is gone off, but if you can procure him a Pardon he
    will make great Discoveries that may be useful to the Country;
    cou'd I have met you instead of your Master to Night, I wou'd
    have deliver'd my self into your Hands with a Sum that much
160   *exceeds that in your strong Box, which I have sent you, with an*
    Assurance to my dear Martin, *that I shall ever be his most*
    faithful Friend till Death.

                        CHERRY BONNIFACE.

there's a *Billet-doux* for you—As for the Father I think he ought
to be encouraged, and for the Daughter,—Pray, my Lord,
persuade your Bride to take her into her Service instead of
Gipsey.

   Aimwell. I can assure you, Madam, your Deliverance was
owing to her Discovery.

170   *Dorinda.* Your Command, my Lord, will do without the
Obligation. I'll take care of her.

   Sir Charles. This good Company meets oportunely in favour
of a Design I have in behalf of my unfortunate Sister, I intend
to part her from her Husband—Gentlemen will you assist me?

   Archer. Assist you! S'Death who wou'd not.

   Count. Assist! Garzoon, we all assest.

                Enter Sullen.

   Sullen. What's all this?—They tell me Spouse that you had
like to have been rob'd.

---

176 *Count* . . . assest.] 1728 reads '*Foig.* Ay, upon my Shoul, we'll all asshist.'

Mrs. Sullen. Truly, Spouse, I was pretty near it—Had not these two Gentlemen interpos'd.   180

Sullen. How came these Gentlemen here?

Mrs. Sullen. That's his way of returning Thanks you must know.

Count. Garzoon, the Question be *a propo* for all dat.

Sir Charles. You promis'd last Night, Sir, that you wou'd deliver your Lady to me this Morning.

Sullen. Humph.

Archer. Humph. What do you mean by humph—Sir, you shall deliver her—In short, Sir, we have sav'd you and your Family, and if you are not civil we'll unbind the Rogues, join   190 with 'um and set fire to your House—What do's the Man mean? not part with his Wife!

Count. Ay, Garzoon de Man no understan Common Justice.

Mrs. Sullen. Hold, Gentlemen, all things here must move by consent, Compulsion wou'd Spoil us, let my Dear and I talk the matter over, and you shall judge it between us.

Sullen. Let me know first who are to be our Judges—Pray, Sir, who are you?

Sir Chalres. I am *Sir Charles Freeman*, to come to take away your Wife.   200

Sullen. And you, good Sir?

Aimwell. Charles Viscount Aimwell, come to take away your Sister.

Sullen. And you pray, Sir?

Archer. Francis Archer, Esq; come—

Sullen. To take away my Mother, I hope—Gentlemen, you're heartily welcome, I never met with three more obliging People since I was born—And now, my Dear, if you please, you shall have the first word.

Archer. And the last for five Pound.   210

Mrs. Sullen. Spouse.

Sullen. Ribb.

Mrs. Sullen. How long have we been marry'd?

Sullen. By the Almanak fourteen Months—But by my Account fourteen Years.

184 *Count* . . . dat.] 1728 reads '*Foig*. Ay, but upon my Conshience de question be apropro, for all dat.'   193 *Count* . . . Justice.] 1728 reads '*Foig*. Arra, not part wid your Wife! Upon my Shoul de Man dosh not understand common Shivility.'

Mrs. Sullen. 'Tis thereabout by my reckoning.

Count. Garzoon, their Account will agree.

Mrs. Sullen. Pray, Spouse, what did you marry for?

Sullen. To get an Heir to my Estate.

220   *Sir Charles.* And have you succeeded?

Sullen. No.

Archer. The Condition fails of his side—Pray, Madam, what did you marry for?

Mrs. Sullen. To support the Weakness of my Sex by the Strength of his, and to enjoy the Pleasures of an agreeable Society.

Sir Charles. Are your Expectations answer'd?

Mrs. Sullen. No.

Count. A clear Case, a clear Case.

230   *Sir Charles.* What are the Bars to your mutual Contentment.

Mrs. Sullen. In the first Place I can't drink Ale with him.

Sullen. Nor can I drink Tea with her.

Mrs. Sullen. I can't hunt with you.

Sullen. Nor can I dance with you.

Mrs. Sullen. I hate Cocking and Racing.

Sullen. And I abhor Ombre and Piquet.

Mrs. Sullen. Your Silence is intollerable.

Sullen. Your Prating is worse.

Mrs. Sullen. Have we not been a perpetual Offence to each
240 other—A gnawing Vulture at the Heart.

Sullen. A frightful Goblin to the Sight.

Mrs. Sullen. A Porcupine to the Feeling.

Sullen. Perpetual Wormwood to the Taste.

Mrs. Sullen. Is there on Earth a thing we cou'd agree in?

Sullen. Yes—To part.

Mrs. Sullen. With all my Heart.

Sullen. Your Hand.

Mrs. Sullen. Here.

Sullen. These Hands join'd us, these shall part us—away—
250   *Mrs. Sullen.* North.

Sullen. South.

Mrs. Sullen. East.

---

217 *Count . . .* agree.] 1728 reads '*Foig.* Upon my Conshience dere Accounts vil agree.'   229 *Count . . .* Case.] 1728 reads '*Foig.* Arra Honeys, a clear Caase, a clear Caase!

Sullen. West—far as the Poles asunder.

Count. Begar the Ceremony be vera pretty.

Sir Charles. Now, Mr. *Sullen*, there wants only my Sister's Fortune to make us easie.

Sullen. Sir *Charles*, you love your Sister, and I love her Fortune; every one to his Fancy.

Archer. Then you won't refund?

Sullen. Not a Stiver.   260

Archer. Then I find, Madam, you must e'en go to your Prison again.

Count. What is the Portion.

Sir Charles. Ten thousand Pound, Sir.

Count. Garzoon, I'll pay it, and she shall go home wid me.

Archer. Ha, ha, ha, *French* all over—Do you know, Sir, what ten thousand Pound *English* is?

Count. No, begar, not *justement*.

Archer. Why, Sir, 'tis a hundred thousand *Livres*.

Count. A hundred tousand *Livres*—A Garzoon, me canno'   270 do't, your Beauties and their Fortunes are both too much for me.

Archer. Then I will—This Nights Adventure has prov'd strangely lucky to us all—For Captain *Gibbet* in his Walk had made bold, Mr. *Sullen*, with your Study and Escritore, and had taken out all the Writings of your Estate, all the Articles of Marriage with your Lady, Bills, Bonds, Leases, Receipts to an infinite Value, I took 'em from him, and I deliver them to *Sir Charles.* (*Gives him a Parcel of Papers and Parchments.*)

Sullen. How, my Writings! my Head akes consumedly—   280 Well, Gentlemen, you shall have her Fortune, but I can't talk. If you have a mind, Sir *Charles*, to be merry, and celebrate my Sister's Wedding, and my Divorce, you may command my House—but my Head akes consumedly—*Scrub*, bring me a Dram.

Archer. Madam, (*To* Mrs. Sullen.) there's a Country Dance

261–73 *Archer.* Then ... I will—] 1728 reads:

Arch. What is her Portion?

Sir *Ch.* Ten thousand Pound, Sir.

Arch. I'll pay it: my Lord, I thank him, has enabled me, and if the Lady pleases, she shall go home with me.

277 your Lady] O2; his

to the Trifle that I sung to Day; your Hand, and we'll lead it up.

Here a Dance.

Archer. 'Twould be hard to guess which of these Parties
290 is the better pleas'd, the Couple Join'd, or the Couple Parted?
the one rejoycing in hopes of an untasted Happiness, and the
other in their Deliverance from an experienc'd Misery.

Both happy in their several States we find,
Those parted by consent, and those conjoin'd.
Consent, if mutual, saves the Lawyer's Fee,
Consent is Law enough to set you free.

FINIS.

AN
EPILOGUE,

Design'd to be spoke in the *Beaux Stratagem*.
By Mr. *Smith*, the Author of *Phaedra and Hypolitus*.

If to our Play Your Judgment can't be kind,
Let its expiring Author Pity find.
Survey his mournful Case with melting Eyes,
Nor let the Bard be dam'd before he dies.
Forbear you Fair on his last Scene to frown,
But his true Exit with a Plaudit Crown;
Then shall the dying Poet cease to Fear,
The dreadful Knell, while your Applause he hears.
At Leuctra *so, the Conqu'ring* Theban *dy'd,*
Claim'd his Friend's Praises, but their Tears deny'd: 10
Pleas'd in the Pangs of Death he greatly Thought
Conquest with loss of Life but cheaply bought.
The Difference this, the Greek *was one wou'd fight*
As brave, tho' not so gay as Serjeant Kite;
Ye Sons of Will's *what's that to those who write?*
To Thebes *alone the* Grecian *ow'd his Bays,* ⎫
You may the Bard above the Hero raise, ⎬
Since yours is greater than Athenian *Praise.* ⎭

0.4 By Mr. *Smith*, . . . *Hypolitus*.] 1730; [om.]

THE NON-DRAMATIC WORKS

THE ADVENTURES OF
COVENT-GARDEN

INTRODUCTION

SOURCES AND COMPOSITION

The Adventures of Covent-Garden, which appeared between the *première* and publication of *Love and a Bottle*, may well have been Farquhar's first essay into authorship for publication. He hints that possibility in the preface:

. . . perhaps I was very Young when I writ it, or Recovering from a fit of Sickness; perhaps I was very Old and near my great Climacterick; perhaps I write it in haste, or perhaps 'tis my first Essay.

The possibility of his being very old can be ruled out since he was twenty-one when it was published. But the other clues can be accepted as accurate: Farquhar was young; he had suffered a debilitating illness on his way from Dublin to London;[1] he had written, as he always did, in great haste; and very possibly this was his 'first Essay', as the chronology of publication suggests.

His source was supposedly Antoine Furetière's *Le Roman bourgeois*, published in 1666 and translated into English as *Scarron's City Romance, Made English* in 1671.

Whether in fact Farquhar had begun the novel before coming to London cannot be ascertained, although discussion of Collierism and theatrical criticism in ll. 393–464 must have been written after his arrival in London. In the preface to the reader, clearly written after he arrived in London, he refers to the new Lord Mayor, who was elected on 29 September 1698 and inaugurated on 29 October. Moreover, the satirical dedication to his 'Ingenious Acquaintance at *Will's Coffee-house*' doubtless stemmed from events after his arrival, as did the reference to contemporary pamphlet controversies in the preface. If Farquhar had got the hint for his novel from Furetière, he had certainly fleshed it out with full knowledge of contemporary disputes and social habits in London.

AUTHORSHIP

The Adventures of Covent-Garden was published anonymously, and none of Farquhar's early biographers attributed the work to him. Isaac Reed happened to acquire a copy of the novel, and with some considerable indignation condemned Farquhar for his reliance on it for incidents in *The Constant Couple*:

In . . . . 1699 was published a small volume, entitled *The Adventures of Covent Garden, in Imitation of Scarron's City Romance*, 12mo, a piece without the slightest degree of merit; yet from thence our author took the characters of Lady Lurewell and Colonel Standard, and the incidents of Beau Clincher and Tom Errand's change of clothes, with other circumstances . . . Perhaps his only fault may have been in not acknowledging the writer, contemptible as he is, to whom he had been obliged.[2]

In his own copy of the *Adventures* Isaac Reed in 1795 wrote 'From this piece it is evident Farquhar the next year borrowed a good deal of his Constant Couple'. Not until Leigh Hunt edited Farquhar's works in 1840 was Farquhar's hand publicly recognized. Hunt, who had acquired Reed's copy of the novel, recognized Farquhar's authorship and acknowledged it in the volume, now in the collection of the University of Iowa, adding to Reed's annotation 'This book was evidently written by Farquhar himself. /L.H.' and inserting on the title-page '(By Farquhar.)' In his edition of *The Dramatic Works of Wycherley, Congreve, Vanbrugh, and Farquhar*, Hunt argues both gleefully and convincingly for Farquhar's authorship:

Now on reading this book "without the slightest degree of merit," it is clear enough that the author, "contemptible as he is", was Farquhar himself! The "character" of Lady Lurewell, properly speaking, is not in the book, though some of her conduct is; neither is the production by any means "without the slightest degree of merit," for it possesses some good, hearty, criticism, in vindication of genius against rules; and what marks the production as Farquhar's, is not only this criticism (which he afterwards enlarged upon in his "Discourse upon Comedy"), and his mention of the author as "a young gentleman somewhat addicted to poetry and the diversions of the stage." to say nothing of his use of the "change of clothes," &c., but in this little prose work the poem first appears, which, with the addition of six lines, he afterwards published in his Miscellanies under the title of the "Lover's Night." . . . We are far from wishing

to undervalue the industry of Isaac Reed, or the utility of his
researches; and mistakes are common to everybody: but we here see
what was the amount of his criticism, when taken unawares. Scorn,
which is perilous to the pretensions of the greatest men, is ruinous to
those of the less.[3]

Farquhar's borrowings from the *Adventures* are, in fact,
altogether in keeping with his tendency to reuse materials,
particularly poetry, which apparently did not come as
effortlessly to him as did prose.

Farquhar's novel, then, perhaps his initial effort at authorship, although published anonymously, provided resources
which he often tapped during his few years as a struggling
writer in London. It provided lines used in *Love and a Bottle*,
plot and character devices used in *The Constant Couple*, a poem
expanded by six lines in *Love and Business*, and the ideas if not
the words developed in *A Discourse Upon Comedy*. Perhaps
Farquhar performed essential economies, but probably he had
simply not yet realized the fertility of his imagination—his
need to husband and reuse his materials lessened as his skills
were honed.

THE TEXT

The small octavo novel was printed by Henry Hills for
Richard Standfast and published with the date 1699. The
Reed-Leigh copy, however, has the date corrected in a third
hand seemingly contemporaneous with publication, '1698.
15. Decemb.' That date establishes publication as occurring
after the *première* of *Love and a Bottle* and before its publication
by Standfast and Francis Coggan on 29 December. The title-
page of *Love and a Bottle*, in fact, advertised 'There is lately
published, the Adventures of *Covent-Garden*, in imitation of
Scarrons City Romance: Printed for *Richard Standfast*. 1699.'
Perhaps Farquhar made a double contract with Standfast; at
any rate the bookseller issued the two volumes in very rapid
succession, the *Adventures* clearly preceding the printing of the
preliminary gathering of *Love and a Bottle*. The date
15 December, then, is altogether believable.

Whether Farquhar chose anonymity or was simply accorded
it by the printer or bookseller who saw the name as irrelevant

to the sale of copies cannot be ascertained. The genre of popular comical romances was a popular one; Congreve's *Incognita*, for example, had appeared in duodecimo in 1691. The short fiction provided a far easier possibility of publication than the machinations involved in getting a play accepted by the theatre for production.

The unusually small octavo has the collational formula A^6 B–D^8 E^6 ($4 signed; A2–3 missigned A3–4, and E3–4 unsigned). The pages of the novel are numbered 1–58. I have collated the following copies: Bodleian, Clark Library, Harvard, University of Iowa. The only variants occur on p. 29 l. 24, in which the Bodleian and Clark Library copies read 'Poets,' and the Harvard and Iowa copies 'Poets;'. In the same line, the Bodleian and Clark copies clearly read 'wit;' but the Iowa copy has lost the semi-colon and only shows an upright bar.

No later editions of the text appeared until Stonehill reprinted it in the *Complete Works* in 1930.

NOTES

1. See Introduction, *Love and a Bottle*, vol. i, p. 7.
2. *Biographia Dramatica*, ii. 123–4.
3. Hunt, pp. lxiv–lxv.

THE

Adventures
OF
COVENT-GARDEN,

In Imitation of *Scarron*'s *City Romance.*

Et quorum pars Magna fui.

THE
DEDICATION

To all my Ingenious Acquaintance at *Will's Coffee-House.*

Gentlemen,

I am,

> *Yours most Devoted,*
> *most Obedient, and*
> *most Faithful hum-*
> *ble Servant.*

TO THE
READER.

My Dedication looks very Blank upon the Matter, and 'tis no Wonder, since I expect no Present for it. But I may venture to say, that no Dedication was ever less Fulsom and Tedious, tho none can deny that I have given my Patrons a very fair Character. The Severe and Judicious may quarrel at me for Innovation in this Affair; but since the greatest Critick of our Age has Published a Dedication without denominating his Patron, so the least has ventured to ascribe his Patrons, and leave out the Dedication.

I have some few things to say in Relation to the Author, and touching the Book; the Author is a Person admired by the Ladies for his Discretion and Secrecy, as you may easily imagine by these Means he has chosen to confirm their good Opinion of him; and to make the Secret yet closer, he has let it loose among the Wits, who will so Chase it about *Covent-Garden*; but I question whether they ever Hunt it into the right Burrough. If ye are so good Philosophers as to find out the Author by a *Negative Definition* take it; he's neither *Collierist* nor *Poet*, neither *Æsop of Tunbridge*, nor *Æsop of Bath*, nor the *Dragon of Bow*, nor the *Grashopper at the Exchange*; and for an *Englishman* not to belong to any of these Factions, is somewhat strange.

As to the Book, 'tis for the most part, matter of Fact, and all Transacted within these Three Months. The Criticks may perhaps quarrel with me for breaking Unity of Time; for (say they) if an Heroick Poem must be limited to the space of Twelve Months, a Novel by the rule of Proportion should be confined to One. But I can urge enough in my defence; perhaps I was very Young when I writ it, or Recovering from a fit of Sickness; perhaps I was very Old and near my great Climacterick; perhaps I write it in haste, or perhaps 'tis my first Essay.

Now, Gentlemen, I have given you *Pick and Choise* of the most Fashionable Excuses, and if you are not satisfied, I think unreasonable.

Some may ask what I had to do with the *Church* and *Stage* in my Novel? Truly I have as little to do with either of them as any Wit among Ye, let them fight Dog, fight Bear, for me. But because I would make my Book *Beau*, I thought it convenient
40 to Equip him with an Air of the Times, and make him Chat on the most Modish Subject. As another Addition to his Finery, I have given him a *Description of Night*. This was altogether worn about Ten years ago, and may do well enough still for a Change. I build this Allegory of Foppery upon the Authority of a famous Modern, who certainly design'd his *Description of Night* for a *Beau-Wig* to his Piece, as may appear by this Line,

And Nights Black-Locks all Powder'd o're with Stars.

Some may accuse me for servile imitation of my Neighbours in this Description. Faith, I have a great mind to imitate
50 Them very closely now by Valuing my self upon it however.

You must not in this Piece expect any Wit, for that is grown too Dangerous and Scandalous since the Act against *Immorality and Profaneness*; besides, being within the City Liberties, I must not venture to be Facetious, till I know whether the New Lord M—r is *Dragon*, *Grashopper*, or what other Animal.

As for my imitating *Scarron*, I confess 'tis not *Copia vera*, as many draw their Imitations, but there is something as Odd in this Gentlemans Writings, as there was in Person, which may puzzle an Author as much as a Painter to delineate him.
60 There are some turns of Plot in the following Adventures that may seem incredible, but this very strangeness to any considerate Person will appear the most convincing Proof of their Truth; for unless they had really passed, I could never have thought of 'em.

One word to *Emilia*, and then—She only knows the Author, whom if she discovers, he certainly discovers her; there's a *Rowland for her Oliver*: her Character is drawn by so favourable a Hand, that it will make her Cunning more admired than her Falshood hated. My Love has still added a pleasing gloss
70 to her worst Designs, and amidst my severest Reflections on her Deceit, I have never forgot the Respect due to her as a fair Lady: Yet if she will be Angry, let her take what follows.

THE
ADVENTURES
OF
COVENT-GARDEN.

A Young Gentleman somewhat addicted to Poetry and the Diversions of the Stage, standing one Evening behind the Scenes in *Drury-lane* Playhouse, was accosted with a Message by the Door-keeper, that a Lady in the Entrance desir'd to speak with him; he readily obey'd the Charge, but was strangly surpris'd to be saluted by a Voice well known to him, and a Person whom he imagin'd in another Kingdom (one whom he passionately lov'd) and whose absence he much regretted; their Joys were mutual at the Interview, but his the greater, because heighth'd by surprise and unexpectancy; *for* 10 *Heavens sake, Madam (said the Spark in a transport) is your Husband dead? and may I hope at last that you are mine;* The Lady answer'd only by a deep Sigh, and conducting him to the Coach which waited for her, she gave him the following account. *You may remember, my dear* Peregrine, *(said she) that constrain'd by the Rigour of covetous Parents, who consulted my Fortune, not Inclinations, I broke my Vows and Protestations to you and married* Richly. *Revive not the fatal remembrance (answer'd* Peregrine*) which occasion'd me so much misery, forcing me thro grief to leave the Kingdom, and come hither for* London, *but rather declare* 20 *the cause which so happily has Blest me now with your Presence so far beyond my hopes. Alas Sir, reply'd* Emilia, *why shou'd you doubt the occasion, knowing your self and knowing me? how could I rest in the Embraces of Another, whilst nothing but a narrow Sea parted me from my dear* Peregrine. *I gave my friends the satisfaction to see me married to* Richly, *but did my self the Justice to live with none but my Dearest*—with which words pressing his Hand, and letting her Head fall with a Sigh in his Bosom, she murmur'd out the rest in a Language which Lovers only understand. The Coach stopt in *Bow-street Covent-Garden,* where the Lady had taken 30 Lodgings. *Peregrine* was a little startl'd to find himself exactly opposite to a House wherein dwelt a Lady whom he Courted; for being advis'd, that the only cure for the loss of an old Mistress is a new one, and his Fortune being very much weakn'd by expence of Travel, he had pitch'd on the aforesaid Lady of a considerable Fortune and good Family, to relieve his decay'd Estate by marrying her; He had won pretty far on the Ladies Inclinations, and Acted the Lover so well and so frequently, that he had almost made it habitual to him, and 40 through pure strength of imagination did almost believe her as captivating as his former Mistress; but it was only a fancy, for he soon forgot all his Passion at the first sight of *Emilia*; and his wavering Affection, like a lesser Light, was soon swallow'd in the appearance of a greater; he conducted *Emilia* to her Chamber, where they spent an Hour or Two, pleasantly repeating the Adventures of their past Courtship, and now and then making protestations to improve the future. How strangely ridiculous are Lovers! this Lady had been the greatest cause of many misfortunes to him, and he had 50 substantial reasons to believe, the rigour of her Parents was only urg'd as an excuse to break with him; a reasonable Person would have consider'd her as a Renegado from her lawful Husband, and might have had some regard to the Protestations made to the vertuous Lady, and the improvement of his Fortune; I doubt not but the Gentleman's reason, which was of the ripest growth, suggested all these considerations to him; but alas, that Ingenuity which shew'd him his errour, plung'd him the deeper in it; the Charms of his *Emilia* were so heightn'd by his creative fancy, his Wit looking 60 through the Perspective of his Love, shew'd all things so Charming that nothing but Passion could predominate; and certainly the most ingenious Men are the most liable to the Snares of the Fair; whether it be that their Intellects are more fine, and therefore more adapted for the reception of the subtile Passion, or being more subject to Vanity, may easily through a sense of their merit be drawn into a belief of their being belov'd, and consequently the more easily cheated.

However it was, *Peregrine* went away the most pleas'd Man alive, and coming to his Club at the *Rose*, surpris'd the

53 have] [om.]

Company with the Extravagancy of his Mirth; no less than 70
Bumpers wou'd go down, and all to his Mistresses health;
there was none of the company dispo'd to comply with his
humour, but a Captain, who swearing a bloudy Oath that put
his Scarlet out of countenance, declar'd he would Drink for his
Mistress such as *Peregrine* shou'd for his Guts, *and* Damme
*(continu'd he) I have got the prettiest, kindest creature, and she is newly
come to Town; but what is yet stranger, I have not yet enjoy'd her, tho I
have seen her twice. I shou'd think it more strange (said* Peregrine*) if
you ever enjoy her, if she be one that values her Reputation.* Zoons
(cry'd the Captain) you look like an honest Fellow, and I'll tell you a 80
secret; My Mistress is the prettiest Lady in England, *and she Lodges
hard by in* Bow-street. The whole Company, who knew that
Peregrine Courted a Lady in *Bow-street*, burst out a Laughing,
and one of them ask'd the Captain where about his Mistress
liv'd? *About the middle of the Street, (reply'd he)* which increas'd
the Laughter all about the Table. Here appear'd another
Caprice in the humour of our Lover: *Peregrine*, who just now
had forgot and laid by all thoughts of his former Mistress, had
his passion renew'd by the apprehension of a Rival, and his
Flame like other Fire, meeting with opposition, began to rage 90
more furiously; he ask'd the Captain what incouragment he
had receiv'd, to authorise him to call that Lady Mistress? *Only
this (said the Captain) that I am belov'd by her above all Men in the
World, for which I have her own Declaration.* Peregrine *being*
sensible how far a Lac'd Coat and Feathers usually work upon
the Female Sex, was very uneasy, and calling a Reckoning left
the Company.

Next Morning he went to *Emilia*'s Lodgings, but 'twas
answer'd by the House that she was gone abroad; he repeated
his Visit in the Afternoon with no better success; three or four 100
Days he continu'd to wait upon her thus, but could never find
her at home: The Lady over the way had perceiv'd him to go
frequently thither, and hearing that a strange Lady lodg'd
there, began to entertain some Jealous thoughts of him, she
therefore order'd a Footman to watch him at his next coming,
and to tell him that she desir'd to speak with him; the Message
was deliver'd accordingly, and he waited on *Selinda*. *Sir (said
she) I was afraid that you had mistaken my Lodgings, by your freequent
calling at another House so near me, and therefore I sent my Servant to*

110 *set you right.* He was waken'd from his sweet Dream of *Emilia*
by so just a charge; but the words of the Captain coming in his
Head, *Madam (said he) I saw the Sign of a Lac'd Coat hung out at
your House, which occasion'd my mistaking it.* The Lady desiring
him to explain his Expression, he plainly told her what the
Captain said; she assur'd him by very convincing reasons,
that she knew no such Person, and implicitly hinted to him,
that if he were the Lover he pretended, it lay upon him to
make the Blockhead beg her Pardon. *Peregrine* needed no such
instigation, for by this it appear'd to him that the Captains
120 words were out of a dull design of affronting him, and vowing
Revenge wou'd have immediately gone to have put it in
Execution. The Lady dreading the blustring title of Captain,
and fearing to Expose *Peregrine*, whom she really Lov'd,
detain'd him, by a pretence of his Accompanying her to
Bartholomew-Fair, whether she design'd to go that Evening to
Raffle; he could not decline waiting on her, and suspended
therefore his intended resentments. The Lady's Coach was got
ready, and they went to the *Cloysters*, where they Joyn'd in with
some very good Company to Raffle, among which was my
130 Lord *C*— who had a Lady Mask'd with him, and whom he
entertain'd with some Respect, yet mix'd with a little
Familiarity: The first Piece of small value my Lord won, and
presented to his Mask'd Lady; the second, worth Ten pound,
Peregrine carried; not so glad for his Success, as Proud to make
such a Present to his Mistress; he was turning towards her to
Present it, when the Mask'd Lady with a careless motion, as if
by accident, pull'd off her *Vizor*, and shew'd him the
Charming Face of his dear *Emilia*; she imagin'd, obliging him
to know her was Claim sufficient to the *China*. Gods! how great
140 was *Peregrine*'s surprise! What a strange Dilemma was he
brought to! all the rules of civility and good Manners, nay
even gratitude, oblig'd him to give the Present to *Selinda* whom
he had waited on to the Fair, nay, the Company had already
begun to congratulate her success in that of the Gentleman;
But *Emilia*, the charming *Emilia*, that held his Heart, detain'd
his Hand; he had long since made her a Present of his Soul,
and who now cou'd stand in competition with her for any
thing else: He never had such occasion for his Wits to bring
him off, but finding no Expedient readier, he pretending a Slip

let the *China* fall, and broke it, and feigning a dissatisfaction 150
for the Loss, wou'd throw no more: Both the Ladies were well
enough pleas'd, each imagining that he was vex'd upon her
score, supposing he intended it for her, which he purposely
broke, lest he shou'd oblige either by the displeasure of the
other.

But *Peregrine*'s trouble was not here at an end, he saw his
Emilia, who so lately and so lovingly caressed him, entertain'd
by a Nobleman, and one of the greatest Gallants in *England*;
but what wou'd have destroy'd anothers affection, only
increased his; he took a secret Pride in Rivalling so great a 160
Man, and it confirmed his great opinion of *Emilia*'s beauty, to
see her Admir'd by so accomplish't a Person and absolute
Courtier as my Lord *C*— These considerations augumenting
his Love, increased his Jealousy also, and every little
Familiarity that my Lord us'd, heightned his Love to her, and
hatred to his Lordship; he Lov'd her for being Admir'd by my
Lord, yet hated my Lord for Loving her. He was oblig'd
however to wait on *Selinda* home; besides he receiv'd no great
encouragement from *Emilia* to prompt him to offer his Service,
for she had not regarded him one Jot after he broke the *China*; 170
he went Home strangely distracted, which *Selinda* imagining it
to proceed from his resentment against the Captain, minded
no further than by advising him to desist, telling him that the
aspersions of a Fool are never minded, unless the Person
aspersed takes notice of them. He went Home never the more
satisfied, and resolving to quit himself of one trouble
imediatly, he writ the following Note.

SIR,

Your words at the Tavern the other night seem purely
design'd to affront me, since I am now satisfied they cou'd be 180
grounded on no other Foundation; if you dare repeat them,
meet me behind *Montague* House to morrow Morning at Six,
where only I can give you a proper answer,

Yours,

Peregrine.

This Letter he gave to a Porter, with orders to deliver it to

Captain — at his Lodgings, or if he were abroad to find him out, and to deliver it into his own Hand.

Peregrine rose early next Morning and came to the place
190 appointed, and walked about full of serious thoughts upon his Adventure, reflecting on the many inconveniences contracted by Womens conversation; he remembred that the greatest disquiets of his Life had proceeded from Female causes, and found himself that very Moment at the very brink of Destruction, involv'd in an unavoidable Dilemma of falling by the Sword, or dying by the Law, and all upon a Womans score; he found, that had he never Lov'd Woman, he had never hated Man, and had he never owned a Mistress, he had never feared an Enemy. The apprehensions of so many
200 dangers past and to come, occasioned chiefly by his fatal *Emilia*, began somewhat to alienate his affection, which backed by his supicion of her falshood, confirmed him in a resolution of weaning himself for the future from so childish a Passion. He walked thus ruminating above two hours, but no news of the Captain, and he was pretty well pleas'd not to meet his Adversary, being now convicted of the unreasonable grounds of his quarrel: Being upon serious reflections convinc'd, that the Captains words might have intended some other besides his Mistress, since he did not name *Selinda*, and that
210 she had assur'd him, she knew no such Man. He left the Field, establish'd in these Three calm Resolutions, First, for ever to avoid *Emilia*'s company which had been so fatal; Secondly, to beg the Captains pardon, when he first met him; and Lastly, to promote his Marriage with *Selinda* as speedily as he could. But here behold the strange weakness of a Lover, his Inclinations must lead him by *Emilia*'s Lodgings as he past homewards, and he gave this excuse to his reason, that he wou'd by that means try the firmness of his resolve, in passing by her Lodgings without looking once at her Window;
220 Walking therefore down *Bow-street*, when he was just opposite to the House, his foolish wavering fancy suggested, that there cou'd be no harm in looking up to her Window, since he believ'd she stood not there; yet to what end shou'd any reasonable Man but a Glasier look at a Window, when he expected no body at it. He never the less cast up his Eye, and behold how he was paid for his peeping.

Instead of the dear Casement which he only hoped to see, he discover'd Monsieur the Captain with his formidable Lac'd Coat standing out of the Window, and his belov'd *Emilia* standing familarly by him.

Now for our Sparks Resolutions, reason would have oblig'd him to continue them now stronger, for he had a new instance of *Emilia*'s falshood, and of the truth of the Captains words, but the sight wrought a clear contrary effect; he found himself now touch'd in the tenderest part, and the Captains Expressions which he could bear when the Company suppos'd them Apply'd to *Selinda*, he could not suffer now he found them meant of *Emilia*, *Gods (cry'd he out) shall I be outrivall'd by a Fool in the affection of one as Admirable for her sense as for her Beauty; tho the Coward durst not meet me at the place appointed, he will* 240 *certainly resent an affront in his Mistresses presence, which may afford me revenge of both.* Hereupon he comes to the Door, and opening it without any Ceremony, comes madly up, but was met upon the Stairs by *Emilia*; who running to him, caught him in her tender Arms, saying, *My dear* Peregrine, *how have I long'd to see You? and what have I done to Merit this strangeness of Yours?* She went to Kiss him, but he hearing a Person pass down Stairs by him, look'd about, and saw it was only a Porter. *O my dearest (concluded she) I am overjoy'd that you're come so oportunely for my relief; for I have been pester'd these Five or six Days incessantly by my* 250 *Lord C— who has sent just now to know if I am at leasure to receive a visit. I suppose Madam (answer'd* Peregrine*) that you are not at leasure, for you have Company above Stairs. None that shall detain me from entertaining you (replyed she.) Madam, (answered* Peregrine,*) you shall not prevent me from entertaining him by all your Artifices; for by Heavens I'll pull of his* Lions Skin, *and show the* Ass *in his own Colours. Who do you mean pray Sir (said she) a Coward in the King's Livery? Madam, your Captain above. A Captain! (replied* Emilia,*) ha, ha, ha, I'll be hang'd if you have not mistaken my Lord's Footman for an Officer, ha, ha, ha, a very good Jest, poor* Peregrine, *you have not* 260 *rub'd the Sleep out of your Eyes this Morning. Truly Madam (said* Peregrine*) your behaviour makes me doubt that I am Awake. No, no, (replyed she) you are Dreaming, as I shall convince you*; and leading him up into her Chamber, *Is this your Captain?* Peregrine was

259 *be hang'd*] *behang'd*

strangely amazed to find a very Sheepish Fellow leaning on the Window with a Lac'd Coat on, which he imagin'd the Captains. The occasion of which Metamorphosis was this.

The Porter which *Peregrine* employed the Night before to carry the Challenge to the Captain, heard at his Lodgings that the Captain would not be at home till it was late, and the poor Fellow being tir'd with trudging about all Day, and supposing it sufficient to deliver it in the Morning, went home to his Rest, and came accordingly in the Morning, where he was told by the Captains Servant, that his Master lay abroad all Night, but that he had appointed to meet him about two Hours hence at the Black-posts next door to the — in *Bow-street*. The Porter accordingly went thither, and found the Captain in *Emilia*'s Chamber, and had deliver'd him the Note just as *Peregrine* had look'd up at the Window. At the same instant *Emilia* spy'd him, and with great surprise cryed out, *O Lord; Sir, I am Ruin'd.* The Captain asked what was the matter? *O (said she) dear Sir, yonder's my Husband, who has seen you, and if we find not a device to impose upon him, he will Murder me. What shall we do (said the Captain) not all the Stratagems in the Art Military can save us. But I have one Stratagem in the Art of Love shall do, (said she;) Strip, strip, Sir, imediately, change Cloaths with the Porter.* The Captain very willing to oblige the Lady, obeyed her Commands, and equipp'd the Porter immediately, and puting on the Porters Coat, Frock, and Apron, slunk down Stairs by *Peregrine* undiscover'd, leaving the gawdy Porter in *Emilia*'s Chamber; which so much occasioned *Peregrine*'s wonder. He had the demonstration of his Eyes that it was the Captain but some Minutes before, and now by the same Evidence it appears that it is not he. *This is all Illusion (said* Peregrine *in a Consternation.) Illusion! (replyed* Emilia*) I little thought that* Peregrine *could have such ill thoughts of Me, as to believe I would entertain an Officer at this Hour in my Chamber. Truly Madam (answered* Peregrine*) tho Love be blind, I don't think Jealousy is so, and tho Women's Beauty depends on our fancy, their Vertue does not; we rightly can Judge of that, tho not of tother. Sir (said* Emilia*) you have never received any proofs of my immodesty, tho many of my Love, and I therefore think it both ingratitude and injustice in you to tax my Vertue, which you ought to defend, since you are sensible it has held out even against you whom I so dearly lov'd, and who (I thought) lov'd me, but I*

find now too late that I have been mistaken; upon which she burst
out in Tears. *Go back Sir (said she to the Porter) and tell your Lord
than I begin to suspect his designs upon me for vicious; alas, I am
unacquainted with the Tricks of this City, and did not imagine that a
Nobleman could have any base designs upon a Poor Womans Honour; go
quickly to him, I say, and bid him never trouble me again, for he has* 310
made me already an unfortunate Woman. With which words she
Wept most bitterly. O the bewitching Charms of Womankind,
that even their weaknesses should conquer our strongest
Resolves! how easily is vain Man drawn into a belief of his
being belov'd! We take forty Declarations of their indifference
or hatred for effects only of their Modesty, but the first
confession of their Love we presently Credit; when, alas, their
profession of the Latter is often as false, as of Former: But
what can't moving Tears of weeping Beauty melt. Love in
gaiety may take, but Love in Mourning only truly wounds. 320
The poor relenting *Peregrine* fell at her Feet, weeping as fast as
She.

> The fervent Lover Sigh'd, and Wept, and Swore,
> That he wou'd ne're distrust her Vertue more.
> About her Knees he Cling'd with amorous Bands,
> And prest his Vows upon her Lips and Hands.
> She often did her *Damon*, Faithless call,
> At last with sullen Cooing pardon'd all.
> He ravish'd rose, and Claspt the yielding Fair;
> His bounding Joy sprung higher from Despair. 330
> He Seal'd his Pardon with an endless Kiss,
> If there be Extasy in Love, 'tis this.

Behold how suddenly the Scheme is turn'd, the poor
deluded *Peregrine* imagins his Mistress a *Lucretia*; all his former
resolutions are melted in her Bosom, whilst she, innocent
creature, murmurs at his unkindness, checking and caressing
him at the same time, to shew how easily her Love conquered
her resentments. He at last left her, and passing out of the
Door, espied the Captain in the Porters Habit standing at the
entrance; he had stay'd there waiting *Peregrine*'s departure, 340
resolving upon that to return to *Emilia*, and with her to Laugh
at the Cuckold, as he imagined him; who had most occasion to
Laugh, we shall find presently. *Peregrine* immediately knew the

Frock and Porters Cloaths, and the Captain being of
somewhat a Porterly shape, he made no doubt but it was the
same Fellow he had imployed last Night to carry the
Challenge to the Captain, and immediately asked how he had
delivered his Message. The Captain ignorant of the matter,
could make no direct answer; which incensing *Peregrine*, *Sirrah*
350 *(said he) resolve me instantly or I'll break your Head, Rascal*. The
Officer unused to such words, began to mumble something
sawcily. Upon which, without any further ceremony, he raps
the poor Captain over the Head and Shoulders very smartly
with his Cane. The Captain roar'd out, *Bloud and Wounds*
immediately. Upon which *Peregrine* redoubled his stroaks and
liquor'd his Buff most abundantly, till some Gentlemen of
Peregrine's acquaintance took him off, an carried him to *Wills*
Coffeehouse. The poor Captain miserably beaten, was clear
off the Laughing pin; and coming up stairs to *Emilia*, inquir'd
360 for his Cloaths immediately. She answered, she had sent the
Porter down stairs to him; but the Porter was no such Fool, for
finding himself so richly Rigged, he slipt out of the back Door,
and was never heard of after. The poor Captain foam'd and
chafed outragiously at these abuses, and went to sculk home
as speedily as he might, to equip himself in another Suit; he
went through all the blind Alleys and Lanes that he could, for
fear of meeting any of his acquaintance; but when he got
pretty near his Lodgings, it was his bad fortune in one of these
by-places to pass by the House where the Porter lived; his
370 Wife accidentally stood at the Door, who knowing her
Husbands Cloaths, presently laid hold of him, crying out, that
the Villain had Murdered her Husband and stript him of his
Cloaths; her noise presently raised the Mobb, who flocking
about the unfortunate Captain, began to lug and hale him
most unsufferably; he cryed out with a Voice loud enough to
give the Word of Command, *that he was an Officer, a Captain &c.*
A mighty Butcher with a swell'd Face of Authority advances,
and desires to see his Commission; but that was gone in the
Pocket of his embroidered Wastcoat. *Some disbanded Rogue (cryes*
380 *the Butcher) that's now forced to live by cutting Throats; away with*
him, away with him before a Magistrate. The poor Captain ran the

363 of] off

Gauntlet most wretchedly till he came to the House of Justice
M— in *Drury-lane*, who upon the Oath of the Porters Wife, and
some of her creditable Neighbours, drew his Mittimus in
order for *Newgate*. Worse and worse! what must poor Buff do?
he must now discover himself to his Friends for Bail, and so be
made the Jest of the whole Town; he call'd the Justice aside,
and told him the whole story. The Magistrate answered,
unless the Porter could be found, that the Law would oblige
him to his Tryal at the *Old-Bayly*, and that he must be bound 390
over to answer at the next Sessions, and accordingly he was
so.

Peregrine losing a very good Jest by his ignorance in this
affair, goes next Evening to the Play; where meeting some of
his ingenious acquaintance, *viz.* Mr. *W—* Mr *H—* Mr. *M—*
with others of that Club, there arose a discourse concerning
the Battel between the Church and the Stage, with relation to
the Champions that mantained the parties; the result upon
the matter was this, that Mr. *Collier* showed to much Malice
and rancour for a Church-man, and his Adversaries too little 400
wit, for the Character of Poets; that their faults transversed
would show much better; Dulness being more familiar with
those of Mr. *Collier*'s Function, as Malice and ill nature is
more adapted to the Professors of wit. That the best way of
answering Mr. *Collier*, was not to have replyed at all; for there
was so much Fire in his Book, had not his Adversaries thrown
in Fuel, it would have fed upon it self, and so have gone out in
a Blaze. As to his respondents, that Captain *Va—* wrote too
like a Gentleman to be esteemed a good Casuist; that Mr.
C—'s passion in this business had blinded his reason, which 410
had shone so fair in his other Writings; that Mr. *S—le* wanted
the wit of Captain *Va—* as much as he did Mr. *Settle*'s gravity;
That the two Answers to Mr. *C—* have done his Book too
much honour, but themselves too great an Injury: In short,
upon the whole matter, that whoever gained the Victory, the
Stage must lose by it, being so long the seat of the War; And
unless Mr. *Dryden*, or Mr. *Wicherly* remove the combustion into
the Enemies Country, the *Theatre* must down. And the end of
this War will be attended by cashiering the Poets, as the last
Peace was by disbanding the Army. 420
Their discourse continued till the Play began, when

Peregrine spying his Mistress *Selinda* in a front Box, was obliged to leave his Friends to entertain her. This Lady had a great share of Sense, and was mightily pleased with what the Fair Sex call fine things, which, that Play, being the *Indian Emperour*, was plentifully stored with. *Peregrine* was so much a Courtier as to Joyn with her in the Applause, but being of a critical humour, he could not forbear making some severe remarks on the *Dramma*, and inconsistencies of Plots. *You*
430 *Criticks (said* Selinda*) make a mighty sputter about exactness of Plot, unity of time, place, and I know not what, which I can never find do any Play the least good.* (Peregrine *smild at her Female ignorance.) But (she continued,) I have one thing to offer in this dispute, which I think sufficient to convince you; I suppose the chief design of Plays is to please the People, and get the Play-House and Poet a Livelyhood. You must pardon me Madam, (replyed* Peregrine*) Instruction is the business of Plays. Sir (said the Lady) make it the business of the Audience First to be pleas'd with Instruction, and then I shall allow you it to be the chief end of Plays. But suppose Madam (said he) that I grant what you lay*
440 *down. Then Sir (answered she) you must allow that what ever Plays most exactly Answer this aforesaid end, are the most exact Plays. Now I can instance you many Plays, as all those by* Shakespear *and* Johnson, *and the most of Mr.* Dryden's, *which you Criticks quarrel at as irregular, which nevertheless still continue to please the Audience, and are a continual support to the* Theatre; *there's very little of your Unity of time or place in any of them, yet they never fail to Answer the proposed end very successfully. Besides Sir, I have heard your self say, that Poetry is purely an imitation of Nature; what business then can Art pretend in the affair?* O Madam, (Answered Peregrine*) this Art is*
450 *only the improvement or perfection of Nature, and is us'd in Poetry, as Geometrical Lines in Painting do delineate the peice to an exact Model or Form. Then certainly (replyed the Lady) these rules are ill understood, or our Nature has changed since they were made; for we find they have no such effects now as they had formerly. For Instance, I am told the* (Double Dealer) *and,* (Plot and no Plot) *are two very exact Plays, as you call them, yet all their Unity of Time, Place, and Action, neither pleased the Audience, nor got the Poets Money. A late Play too call'd* (Beauty in Distress) *in which the Author, no doubt, sweat as much in confining the whole Play to one Scene, as the Scene-Drawers*
460 *should were it to be changed a hundred times; this Play had indeed a commendatory Copy from Mr.* Dryden, *but I think he had better*

have altered the Scene, and pleased the Audience; in short had these Plays been a little more exact, as you call it, they had all been exactly Damn'd. Peregrine would have answered, but a pluck by the Sleeve obliged him to turn from *Selinda* to entertain a Lady Mask'd, who had given him the Nudg; he presently knew her to be *Emilia*, who whisperd him in the Ear, *I find Sir, what* Guyomar *said just now is very true,*

> *That Love which first took Root will first Decay,*
> *That of a fresher date, will longer stay.* 470

Peregrine, tho surprised, was pleased with her pretty Reprimand, being delivered without any Anger, but in murmuring complaining Accents, which never fail to move; insomuch that he could not forbear demonstrating his satisfaction in such Terms and Behaviour, as rendered him remarkable to all about him; he quite forgot *Selinda*, and his Argument. And she endeavour'd to forget him by remembring this Action of his; and tho many slips occasioned by Passion are pardonable, yet when Love causes Offences against it self in default of good Manners towards the Fair, 'tis unexcusable. 480 Had he used *Emilia* with that freedom and carelessness which Masks generally meet with in the Pit, *Selinda* would have imagined her familiarity with *Peregrine* to have only proceeded from a Pert and Impudent Behaviour, which such Creatures use with all Gentlemen; but he used something of a Fawning and Amorous respect to her, which raised *Selinda*'s Jealousy to the highest pitch. But this was not all the Mischief occasioned by the Interview, for my Lord *C—* had that very Evening made an Assignation with *Emilia* at the Play, whether she came early; she beheld *Peregrine* with Indifference whilst he 490 taulked among his Friends, nor had she the least Motion to discover her self to him; but spying him addressing a fine Lady in the Box, whom she perceived to entertain him with more than ordinary Civility, she felt a violent Inclination to interrupt him; She found by the Ladies freedom and gayety in Discourse, that she was fond of *Peregrine*'s conversation, and out of a pure malicious design would deprive her of it; She accomplish'd her design, *Peregrine* paid her an extraordinary respect, and she returned it with as much civility, purely to raise *Selinda*'s Jealously, whom she had now remembred to 500

have seen twice with *Peregrine*; but the Poor Lady was caught in her own Net; for at the Instant of her greatest freedom with *Peregrine*, my Lord discover'd her. He is the most Jealous Amourist in *England*, and to one of his temper, he saw enough to raise a distrust of his Mistresses discretion: Coming close up to her, he Whisperd her, *Madam, I am as good as my Appointment, but finding you better employed, I shan't be so rude as to interrupt you.* Upon which she presently turn'd from *Peregrine* to my Lord. Hey, pass, the Tides turned, and poor *Peregrine*'s left
510 upon the Sand; nay the Wind's turn'd too, for looking at *Selinda* he could see nothing but Storm and Tempest in her Brow. But he alone was not Shipwrackt, for poor *Emilia* ran the same fate; for she entertained my Lord with that earnestness, that it appeared how familiar she was still with his Lordship, which gave *Peregrine* a new proof of her falshood, but was not sufficient to convince my Lord of her Integrity, so that the result upon the transactions of this Evening, was, that *Selinda* through Jealousy of the Mask'd Lady had discarded *Peregrine*; He Jealous of my Lord *C*— had forsaken *Emilia*; and
520 she by her familiarity with *Peregrine* is deserted by his Lordship.

But above all, *Peregrine*'s trouble was much the greatest; he had lost the hopes of amending his Fortune by Marrying a vertuous Lady, and one whom he might reasonably suppose Lov'd him, and all through the means of a Person who ungratefully had abused his passion. A reflection on the Weakness of his temper in not sticking to his resolutions, was no small affliction; but above all, the falshood of his *Emilia* occasioned his distraction; he went to bed, hoping there to find
530 that rest which his waking thoughts denied.

> The Nights black Curtain o're the World was spread,
> And all Mankind lay Emblems of the Dead.
> A deep and awful silence, void of Light,
> With dusky Wings sat brooding o're the Night.
> The rowling Orbs mov'd slow from East to West,
> With harmony that lull'd the World to rest.
> The Moon withdrawn, the oozy Flouds lay dead,
> The very Influence of the Moon was fled.

526 reflection] re- The catchword 'flection' follows 're-', the last syllable of p. 38 in the first edition.

Some twinkling Stars that through the Clouds did peep,
Seeming to Wink as if they wanted sleep.   540
All Nature hush'd, as when dissolv'd, and laid
In silence *Chaos* e're the World was made.
Only the Beating of the Lovers Breast,
Made noise enough to keep his Eyes from Rest.
His little World, not like the greater, lay,
In loudest Tumults of disorder'd Day.
His Sun of beauty shone, to light his Breast,
With all its various Toyls and Labours prest.
The Sea of passion in his working Soul,
Rais'd by the Tempest of his sighs did rowl,   550
In towring Floods to overwhelm the whole.
Those Tyrants of the Mind, vain hope and fear,
That still by turns usurp an Empire there,
Now raising Man on high, then plunging in despair.
Thus *Damon* lies, his grief no rest affords,
Till swelling high, it thus burst out in Words.
Oh! I cou'd Curse all Womankind but one,
And yet my Griefs proceed from her alone.
Hell's greatest Curse a Woman, if unkind,
Yet Heavens great Blessing, if she Loves, we find.   560
Thus our chief Joys with most allays are Curst,
And our best things when once corrupted, worst.
But Heaven is just, our selves the Idols fram'd,
And are for such vain worship Justly damn'd.
Thus the poor Lover argu'd with his fate,
Emilia's charms now did his Love create,
That Love repuls'd now prompted him to hate.
Sometimes his Arms wou'd cross his Bosom rest,
Hugging her lovely Image printed in his Breast.
Where flattering Painter fancy show'd his art,   570
In charming draughts, his Pencil Cupid's Dart.
The shadow drawn so Lively did appear,
As made him think the real substance there.
He thought her Naked, soft, and yielding Waste,
Within his pressing Arms was folded fast,
Nay, in her Charms she really there was plac'd.

567 repuls'd] replus'd

Else, how cou'd Pleasure to such Raptures flow,
The effect was real, then the Cause was so.
What more can most substantial pleasure boast,
580   Than Joy when present, Memory when past?
Then bliss is real which the fancy frames,
Or those call'd real Joys are only Dreams.

Peregrine once more put on firm resolutions, not only of avoiding *Emilia*, but the whole Sex; but alas, such designs had been so often broken and patch'd up, that he could not expect they should last long; he rose fully resolved for the Country that Morning, hoping, that diversity of Company might wear off his trouble occasioned by the City conversation. He was just sending to take up a place in the *Tunbridge*-Coach, when a
590   Messenger brought him a Letter; which he opening, was surprised to find come from *Emilia*; he expected to find it full of Recantations and Excuses for her Familiarity with my Lord *C*— and slighting him the Night before at the Play; but before he would venture to read the Charm, he thought it convenient to say his Prayers in the following Words:

From Wit couch'd in Nonsense, which blinds all that Read,
From conjuring Scrawls which like Magick invade,
From words spelt as False as the Authors are made,
                              Libera nos, &c.

600   Then fully resolved to account all the contents as the Voice of a *Syren* that would destroy him, he Read with great amazement the following Words.

Dear Peregrine,
Being altogether a Stranger in Town, and destitute of Friends, I am compell'd to be troublesom to you, whom I have no reason to believe will desert me in my Necessity; I have urgent occasion for Twenty or Thirty Guineas, which I beg you to send me by the Bearer, and you will infinitely oblige,
610   *Yours*
                              Emilio
Thursday Morning

---

612 *Thursday* Morning] Farquhar ordinarily dated his letters before the text, but

A very odd turn of affairs, I must confess! and wrought as strange a turn in the humour of our Lover. He quite forgot all thoughts of her Falshood to deplore her Necessity, and the Scantiness of his own Fortune that confin'd him from relieving her. A foolish nicety of Honour suggested to him, that if he now forsook her, she would attribute his unkindness not to any fault of Hers, but reckon it a poor pretence for evading her Request. Here was an Instance of Female policy, here was 620 a Stratagem to recover a lost Lover, that (I believe) the most intreagueing Devil could never suggest to contriving Woman before. She was afraid that his Love was so shocked by her behaviour, that she could not build a Reconciliation upon that; and therefore resolv'd to draw his Honour in, to make up the breach, being conscious that Ingenious Men are as fruitful in discovering Niceties in that, as Beauties in their Mistress, and sometimes as much to their Prejudice. But the depth of her Contrivance went yet further, as shall hereafter appear.

Peregrine dismist the Messenger with this Answer, That he 630 would wait on the Lady imediately; and presently after, in his Riding suit, he went to her Lodgings, positively resolved to give her what Money he could spare, then upbraid her for her Falshood, and so take his last farewell. He found her in an Undress sitting on her Beds-feet in a very Melancholy posture; her Nightgown carelesly loose discovered her Snowy Breasts, which Agitated by the violence of her Sighs, heaved and fell with a most Languishing motion; her Eyes were fixt on the Ground, and without regarding *Peregrine*, she raised her Voice in a Mournful and moving sweetness, 640 singing, *Fool, Fool, that considered not when I was well*, concluding which with a deep Sigh, she cast a complaining Look on *Peregrine*, intimating that he alone had occasioned her Sorrows. He beheld those enticing Beauties, that too well knew the way to his Heart; He beheld the moving Charms of Female Sorrow, artfully express'd in a careless Melancholy; and to all this, he heard that tuneful start of Grief which made his ravished Soul strike Unison with the complaining Harmony. Let those who have ever felt the pleasing follies of Love, now guess at our Lovers thoughts. Such will Pardon his weakness, 650

in the text 'Thursday Morning' is printed a line above *Emilia*, probably due to compositorial error.

being conscious of the force of so many united Charms. He begged to know the Cause of her great Grief, making all protestations (that Passion could suggest) of using his utmost endeavours in relieving her. *Alas* Peregrine *(answered she) my Misfortunes are many, and all proceeding from so Dear an occasion, that I could wish them to continue, rather than think the Cause should cease. In short, (continued she Weeping) my Passion for you has drawn me into a necessity of being troublesom to one whose kindness will perhaps flow from a Principle of Charity, not Love. But Sir, I scorn to* 660 *be pitied; and if I can't merit your Esteem, I disdain to be an Object of your Compassion. Madam (replied he) my Charity may extend to share Superfluities, but no less motive then Love could engage me thus to distribute my necessaries.* Upon which he gave her Ten *Guineas,* leaving himself but One. *Well, my dear* Peregrine *(says she) I am too sensible of the unhappiness of your Circumstances, and will therefore Trespass no further upon them: You shall only spare me some of your Love to lay out upon Another, and that shall pay the Ransom for your Money.* Peregrine was strangely surprised at her Discourse! *Be not startled, Sir, (said she) for a Proof of your Affection it must be so: I* 670 *have long been Solicited by my Lord C— and have received some Presents from Him, and was in a fair way of Commanding what I pleased, had not my unlucky kindness to you at the Play last Night raised his Jealosy to that Degree, that he has forsaken me. Now, Sir, since your circumstances debar you from recompencing the loss, I think you are obliged to be Instrumental to Me in recovering his Affection; but do not think (my Dearest) that he can ever destroy your Interest in my Heart, but rather heighten it, being a means to support that Love which the scantiness of your Fortune would Starve.* Very reasonable Arguments to make *Peregrine* a downright Pimp! He was strangely Netled, 680 but being resolv'd to see the Utmost, *How Madam (said he) can I be Instrumental in your Reconciliation with his Lordship? Only thus (Replied she) you must know he is wonderfully Charmed with Wit and Writing fine, in a Woman; now I am sensible you have an Excellent Talent in Epistolary Stile, (which I must still remember since first your Charming Letters conquered me;) you must therefore write an Ingenious Letter for me, which I will Transcribe, and send to his Lordship, which will Infallibly reclaim him. But suppose Madam (said* Peregrine*) that my Lord discovers the difference of Stile if you Write to him*

653 protestations] potestations

again? No, no *(said she) you shall Answer all my Lords Letters for me.*
Peregrine immediately conceiving, that by this means he should 690
see my Lord *C*—'s Letters, and thereby discover if the
Intreague went any further then he would have it, undertook
the Task, and wrote a Letter which wrought the desired effect.

My Lord was already captivated by *Emilia*'s Beauty, but
was not Lover enough to think the Nonsense of a Mistress,
Wit; but this Letter, full of Passion and Ingenuity, fir'd him,
he found what he so admired in a Lady, there expressed in a
great degree, and immediately came to wait upon her.

By this time *Peregrine*, much confused by the Odness of this
Adventure, had departed; and *Emilia* Received his Lordship 700
in a contrary Humour to what she had shown to *Peregrine*,
entertaining him with all the gayety and briskness imaginable.
My Lord not abating of his Jealous Humour, desired to know
whom she entertained so freely at the Play. *'Tis a Creature, my*
Lord, (replyed she) called a necessary Lover. I have often heard (said he)
of a necessary Animal called a Husband, but never of a necessary Lover
before. Such, my Lord, (said she) are of the same use to us, as a
Husband to a Wife, to cover all our Faults. They defend our Honours in
all Company, being possessed of a good Opinion of our Vertue; which
Opinion once Established, we take all care to Improve. Methinks 710
(answered he) your freedom with that Gentleman were enough to destroy
that good Opinion, if he entertained any such before. No, my Lord (said
she) these are the Arts by which we secure them; for granting them all
innocent Freedoms and Incouragment without the least Favour, makes
them set a favourable construction upon such our Behaviour with others,
and induces them to believe all Stories prejudicial to our Reputation,
rather the effects of Mens Vanity, than our kindness: Besides, being once
drawn into a beliefe of their being beloved by us, their Vanity suggests,
that since we are Vertuous in respect of them, we must certainly be so in
regard of those that are more indifferent to us. But that Gentleman, 720
(Answered my Lord) if I am not Misinformed in his Charracter, has too
much Sense to be made such a Tool of. Only Ingenious Men (answered
she) are fit for our purpose, because such Persons are only able to Nourish
a Passion without Enjoyment; Secondly, *being conscious of their*
Merit, they imagine our Love very real because of the worthiness of the
Object; And Lastly, *being the Oracles of the Age, their words are*
taken among their Friends, and our Reputation thus Establish'd. My
Lord *C*— was Amazed at this open Confession of cunning,

which he had never discovered in the Sex before; and lest she
730 should make the same Fool of him, he pressed hard for a Proof
of the contrary, which I believe she granted, for he continued
his Visits with great Assiduity.

Peregrine all this while continued to Serve her with his Pen,
and was very fond of Answering my Lords Letters, because he
found them very Witty and Passionate; and having a good
memory at retaining what pleased him, he generally by once
or twice perusing, cou'd remember them, *verbatim*; and
constantly when he left *Emilia*, would write them down,
together with the Answers very distinctly, with which he used
740 to divert himself very often; for he found so much respect in all
my Lords Letters, that he could not suppose his Lordship had
made any Advances beyond him. But *Emilia* had forewarned
my Lord of making the least mention of any her Favours, lest
the Letter might Miscarry, and fall into Hands that might
Publish her shame. By which Artifice secur'd, she continued
her ingenious Correspondence with my Lord, which more and
more engaged his Affections, without giving *Peregrine* any
resonable grounds of Jealosy. He often pressed for a
Consummation of his Happiness; but she sticking to her
750 Principles, tantalized him with Caresses and Protestations of
her Love, and never wanted a Pretence for delay, until
unfortunately she lost Him and her Self on the following
Occasion.

One Morning three or four Gentlemen of the Law,
Peregrine's Acquaintance, came running into his Chamber,
and asked him to accompany them to the *Old-Baily* to hear the
Tryal. *What Tryal (answered he?) Why, the famous Tryal of
Captain* — *who is Arraigned for Murthering a Porter.* This was News
to him, and he went with them. The Indictment was Read,
760 and the Tryal come on before they reach'd the Court; *Peregrine*
was strangely surpris'd to hear *Emilia*'s Voice at the Bar, and
distrusting the truth of his Ears, cou'd not be satisfied till he
saw her; She was Summon'd as a Witness for the Captain,
where upon her Oath she was forced to declare how she made
the Captain change Cloaths with the Porter in her Chamber,
how she sent him down Stairs in the Porters Habit, and how
the Porter had gone off with His; in short, the whole Story,
with all the Circumstances of the Intreague, was discovered

before the whole Court, and in *Peregrine*'s hearing; who now fully Convicted of the Treachery of his Mistress by her own Oath, has once more put on firm Resolutions of ever forsaking her; and that he may draw my Lord *C—* out of the same Errour, he has given a Copy of all my Lords Letter's and their Answers to a Friend of his, who immediately designs to publish a Collection of Letters, where his Lordship may read his own Wit, and the Falshood of *Emilia*.

FINIS.

LOVE AND BUSINESS

INTRODUCTION

SOURCES AND COMPOSITION

ALTHOUGH Farquhar's primary interest was the drama, he toyed with most other genres—the novella, long and short poems, songs, and letters. His talents clearly lay with comedy, but his dabbling produced some ready money for a young man trying to make his way in London.

The vogue for miscellanies published in London at the turn of the century produced a number of volumes, some in translation, some original contributions of hack-writers, some the work of artists. Men of little fame or talent could make a few shillings by contributing to them; the informal collections of more esteemed writers promised some modest financial success. Farquhar, whose first three comedies had rendered him famous, might well profit from publishing a miscellany; Bernard Lintott must have realized the potential profit when, on 3 July 1701, he paid Farquhar £3 4s. 6d. for the rights to publish his 'Letters and Poems'.[1]

Farquhar had contributed to several other miscellanies previously. Some of his contributions will probably never be incontrovertibly identified. However, his propensity to reuse lines makes identification of some of them possible. Portions of letters published in *Familiar and Courtly Letters, Written by Monsieur Voiture* (1700 and 1701) and Cardinal Bentivoglio's *Letters of Wit, Politicks and Morality* (1701) reappeared with only slight alterations in *Love and Business*.

The contents of *Love and Business* are truly miscellaneous; one suspects that Farquhar swept together bits and pieces accrued over the previous several years. The Pindaric 'On the Death of General *Schomberg*', which opens the collection, is the only attempt at exalted verse; the other poems are largely light-hearted bits of frippery, primarily courtship poems. Two travel letters accompany the courtship letters. Farquhar's critical argument, 'A Discourse upon Comedy', completes the volume.

The concept and the contents of the volume are derivative. The title itself, *Love and Business*, had been foreshadowed in other contexts. *A Flying Post, With a Packet of Choice new Letters and Complements* (1678), for example, contained a 'Variety of Examples of witty and delightful Letters, upon all Occasions both of Love and Business'.[2] John Norris's *A Collection of Miscellanies* (1687), the third edition of which appeared in 1699, contains a poem which begins:

> Thus ye good Powers, thus let me ever be
> Serene, retir'd, from *Love* and *Business* free. . . .

Nor were most of the materials new. Miscellanies at the turn of the century often comprised a collection of various kinds of materials seemingly culled from earlier occasions; Farquhar's volume exactly fits that description, and in fact many of the letters and poems can be dated to earlier times, either through their references to contemporary events or through earlier publication in other contexts. Only 'A Discourse upon Comedy' appears to be written specifically for the volume, to round out the contents and to provide some literary justification for its author's comedies, since they were regularly vilified by jealous playwrights and critics who aspired to neoclassical critical doctrine but whose plays failed to attract crowds to the theatre as Farquhar's did.

An examination of the works to determine their dates of composition indicates that with few exceptions the poems and letters were written during the period from Farquhar's arrival in town in 1697 or 1698 to the spring of 1701. These works are framed in the volume by earlier works, including the ode on Schomberg's death and a few early poems, placed at the beginning of the volume, and the 'Discourse', written after Farquhar signed the contract with Lintott, placed at the end.

The poem 'On the Death of General *Schomberg*' probably dated from Farquhar's school years or his days at Trinity College. There was little incentive for publishing it in 1702, more than a decade after the General's death. The elaborate hyperbole of the elegy 'On the Death of the late *Queen*' indicates that the youthful effort followed rapidly upon her death on 28 December 1694, when Farquhar was only sixteen or seventeen years old. 'An Epigram, on the Riding-House in

Dublin, made into a Chappel' was probably also written before Farquhar left Ireland. Neither would have been difficult to remember or reconstruct if he did not, in fact, bring copies with him to London. The two imitations and the Latin epigram probably also date from his student days, either before or during his time at Trinity College. But the other poems were written after his arrival in London. The poem to Catharine Trotter on *The Fatal Friendship* was undoubtedly written in 1698, for the play opened, probably in June, and was published on 7 July.[3] 'The Lovers Night' contains materials first printed in *The Adventures of Covent-Garden*, two lines of which were reused in *Love and a Bottle*; the poem, then, also dates from 1698, although Farquhar probably revised it specifically for publication in the miscellany. The 'Epilogue, spoken by Mr. *Wilks*' probably dates from autumn 1699, and the 'Prologue on the propos'd Union of the Two Houses' from 1701.[4]

Several of the letters or parts of them can be shown to date from the same period. For example, the letter headed '*Essex, Fryday Morning*' refers to 'the great Success of my Play', a reference to the first season of *The Constant Couple*, in 1699–1700. The poem 'Oh! cou'd I find (grant Heaven that once I may)', fourteen lines of which are reused in one of the love letters in *Love and Business*, first appeared in *Familiar and Courtly Letters, Written by Monsieur Voiture*, which was issued on 11 May 1700.[5] The letter which begins 'If I han't begun thrice to write' is a corrected copy of the original in the second volume of the Voiture collection, first published in 1701 (see p. 435 below). The volume had been announced in the *Post Boy* of 13–15 March 1701 and advertised as just published on 1–3 May 1701; it would have been fresh in Farquhar's mind when he contracted with Lintott in July.

Several of the love letters were written during a period in which Farquhar suffered from one of his recurring bouts with fever and painful inflammation of the joints. At least one of them was purportedly written on his trip to Holland. Although the first letter in 'A Collection of Letters and Other Miscellanies' requests return of his love letters, one cannot assume that these stylized, artificially witty letters were indeed actually sent to young women in the ardour of a ourning romance. Evidence for authenticity seems unobtainable because the love-letters lack the specificity of those from Holland. Certainly they are autobiographical, with references, for example, to Farquhar's rheumatism. At least two different recipients can be identified, the lady in mourning addressed in at least three of the letters, presumably his future wife Margaret Pemell, and Penelope, the pseudonym he apparently used for Anne Oldfield. And yet the letters are strewn with references to 'lady' and 'ladyship' that make them seem fabricated. Some are reused from the other miscellanies. They do not seem to be actual letters retrieved from the recipients, for they are neither concentrated on one or two romances nor organized into sequences comparable to those in miscellanies of the period, although a few give the impression of being sequential. Still, the very sloppiness and inefficiency with which the materials were amassed suggest that they were not created solely for the purpose of publication; had they been, one might have expected greater development and better organization. So they could conceivably be genuine.

Whenever they were written, they were probably intended for publication. If Farquhar indeed utilized them for the courtship of the moment, he doubtless kept a copy on hand for the day that a bookseller would deal with him for his miscellany. The titillation of guessing the original of Penelope and his other addressees was, of course, useful in selling the book, whether the letters were originally written to Oldfield and other famous women or not. But there would seem to be less compelling commercial reasons to invent a lady in mourning.

The three travel letters from the Netherlands must be genuine. No trace of Farquhar in London in August, September, and October 1700 has been found. The immediacy and autobiographical flavour epitomized by the obtrusive illness suggest an actual voyage. Farquhar speaks of 'a very tedious Fit of Sickness, which had almost sent your Friend a longer Journey than he was willing to undertake at present'; Farquhar's own health was plagued by illnesses, to one of which he refers in *Love and a Bottle*. But far more important, the letters are full of accurate detail that Farquhar could not have gleaned later in London without elaborate research, which of course he would never have considered. For example, his letter from the Brill speaks of Lyster, the envoy to the King concerning the death of the Duke of Gloucester, who actually sailed at this time: the King's arrival at the Hague from Het Loo on 22 October NS (11 October OS) and plans to sail on Wednesday, 27 October NS (16 October OS); his knowledge of the presence in Holland not only of Albemarle but of Westmorland, who, at seventeen years, was there for his education; the references to attempting to gain favour for the lady he wrote on 23 October NS, probably Margaret Pemell, who actually got a pension promised by King William as recompense for her husband's death in military service. The wealth and accuracy of detail strongly argues for the authenticity of the letters.

Rothstein argues from the dating that the letters are not genuine, pointing out that 10 August 1700 NS, the date of the letter from the Brill, was not a Saturday (it was a Tuesday) and that Farquhar could not have met 'an Express to the King, of the Duke of *Glocester*'s Death' so soon after the boy died on 30 July.[6] But indeed Martin Lyster or Lister (the 'L—r' to whom Farquhar refers in l. 26) was dispatched on 30 July.[7] The letter dated 23 October NS from the Hague, which mentions the King's arrival from Het Loo the night before, exactly coincides with Luttrell's account of the same events.[8] So although Farquhar called a Tuesday 'Saturday', the accuracy of his dates in terms of the events which occurred offers strong evidence that the letters were actually written during his travels in Holland.

If one can take references to contemporary events as evidence of the date of composition of *Love and Business*, again the period of 1698–1701 is pinpointed. For example, in one letter Farquhar records that he plans to take the recipient to the '*Entertainment of* Dioclesian', a reference to Betterton's operatic *The Prophetess; or, The History of Dioclesian*, an adaptation of Massinger and Fletcher's play, with music by Purcell. Although records of the period are sketchy, the play was performed at least three times during Farquhar's time in town, on 1 June 1700, 21 November 1700, and 4 December 1700. Farquhar may have been in London for the performances on 4 December 1697 and 15 January 1698 as well. John

Dryden's funeral service took place on 13 May 1700. The King's visit to Holland last from 4 July to 18 October 1700. The Duke of Gloucester died on 30 July 1700. None of the specific events mentioned in the correspondence occur outside the time frame of 1698–1701.

'A Discourse upon Comedy', however, was written specifically for publication by Lintott. Nichols records that in July Lintott purchased not only 'Love and Business; in a Collection of occasional Verse and Epistolary Prose, not hitherto published' but also 'A Discourse on Comedy, in reference to the English Stage. In Fourteen Letters. By George Farquhar.'[9] The ambitious scheme for the critical text was at some point abbreviated, for the 'Discourse' became a single 'Letter to a Friend' rather than the fourteen letters originally proposed. Abel Boyer doubted from the beginning that Farquhar could manage it. In a letter from 'Mr. *B—r* to *Astrea*', published in July 1701, he wrote:

> Mr. *F—* has not publish'd the Book he intended: Neither do I think he will ever any on that Subject.[10]

Connely (p. 110) argues that the book Boyer mentions was the correspondence between Emilia and Lord C— mentioned at the end of *The Adventures of Covent-Garden*, but Boyer clearly refers to the proposed full-length critical work. Moreover, in November 1701 Farquhar apparently had not completed the 'Discourse'; in *Letters from the Dead to the Living* (1702), 'Will. Pierre's Answer' to a letter from 'Julian', late secretary of the Muses, dated 'Lincolns-Inn Fields, Novem. 5, 1701', says that a new author 'that has wrote a taking Play is writing a *Treatise of Comedy*'. The description of the contents confirms Farquhar as the author:

> A new Author says one, that has wrote a taking Play, is writing *a Treatise of Comedy, in which he mauls the learned Rogues the writers to some purpose*; he shews what a Coxcomb *Aristotle* was and what a company of senceless pedants the *Scaligers, Rapines, Vossii, &c.* are; proves that no good Play can be regular, and that all rules are *as ridiculous as useless*. He tells us *Aristotle* knew nothing of Poetry (for he knew nothing of his fragments so extoll'd by *Scaliger*) and that common Sence and Nature was not the same in *Athens* as in *Drury-Lane*; that *Uniformity* and *Coherence* was *Green-sleeves* and *Pudding-pyes*, and that

irregularity and *nonsence* were the chief perfections of the *Drama.* . . .
but this *noble Treatise* being only yet in the *Embryo*, you may expect a
farther account of it in the next. . .[11]

The passage has been ascribed to Captain William Ayloffe,
although Boyer may have written it. The author was
obviously familiar with Farquhar's manuscript before publication. In early November, then, or slightly before, if the
date can be trusted, Farquhar was still struggling to complete
the ambitious full-length 'Discourse'; the 'Embryo' apparently
never matured to its intended size. Yet *Love and Business* was
published on 22 November; Farquhar must have ended his
struggles quickly. Resigned to a critical text of smaller scope
than he had originally intended, he incorporated the
'Discourse' into the 'Letters and Poems' for publication as
Love and Business.

One must conclude, then, that most of the materials in the
miscellany were written previous to the agreement with
Lintott and were at hand, to be corrected and improved in
some instances, but basically to be gathered together and sent
to the print shop. The 'Discourse' was new, probably
important to Farquhar, and very difficult to write. He claimed
in 'The Picture' (p. 352 below) that he could 'by Three Hours
Study live One and Twenty with Satisfaction my self, and
contribute to the Maintenance of more Families than some
who have Thousands a Year', but in the same portrait he
mentioned that he had 'so natural a Propensity to Ease, that I
cannot chearfully fix to any Study, which bears not a Pleasure
in the Application, which makes me inclineable to Poetry
above any thing else.' He was not, apparently, as inclinable to
criticism, for he struggled, as he had struggled with the
translation and adaptation of *The Stage-Coach*, for far longer
than usual to complete his 'Discourse'.

REPUTATION AND INFLUENCE

Dudley Ryder, 'a moderately well-to-do student of Noncom-
formist leanings', wrote in his diary for 29 June 1715 of
being diverted by Farquhar's miscellany, which displayed 'a
sprightly ready fancy and wit' that is sometimes 'a little too
refined and not natural'. He read the letters again the

following Monday and praised Farquhar's epistolary style:

He writes with that freedom and ease that you would think he was
talking with you. And at the same time shows he is a man full of wit
and good humour. . . . In short by all his letters it appears very plain
that he was a man' of a very agreeable conversation that made
pleasure his chief business and had a very quick and polite relish of
it. Could say the most shocking things with a good grace and make
them easily passed over by the humorous turn he gave them.[12]

Ryder's view probably reflected the opinion of many of
Farquhar's readers. However, there is little record of the
immediate reception of the poems and letters, and the
influence of these works must be considered altogether
inconsequential.

The 'Discourse', on the other hand, sent Farquhar's
detractors into a new frenzy of condemnation. One example of
virulent criticism occurred in *The English Theophrastus: or, The
Manners of the Age*, published in 1702. Abel Boyer, who signed
the dedication, is considered the author; however, the passage
concerning Farquhar closely echoes the quoted passage from
Letters from the Dead to the Living. Either Ayloffe or Boyer wrote
both pieces, or Boyer plagiarized Ayloffe.

Boyer had cause for offence at Farquhar's impudence in the
'Discourse', for he must have blamed the failure of his tragedy
Achilles; or, Iphigenia in Aulis, which opened in early December
1699, on the success of *The Constant Couple*. In the preface to
the printed version, published in January 1700, he says the
play laboured under the difficulty of being acted 'at a time
when the whole Town was so much, and so justly diverted by
the *Trip to the Jubilee*'. The 1714 edition of the revised play,
newly entitled *The Victim; or, Achilles and Iphigenia in Aulis*,
elaborates on the failure:

The following Tragedy . . . was acted with general Applause,
towards the End of the Year 1699, and Beginning of 1700. The
Reasons why this Excellent Play stopt, on a sudden, in a full Career,
are, in some Measure, accounted for in Mr. Boyer's Preface: To
which he might have added, That the Dutchess of Marlborough,
who at that Time bore an irresistable Sway, bespoke the Comedy
then in Vogue, during the Run of *Iphigenia in Aulis*. . . .

The author of *The English Theophrastus* harshly derided

Farquhar. Under the Plautine tag-name Curculio, meaning 'weevil', the author ridiculed the critical doctrine although he continued to praise the plays as Boyer had done in his preface to *Achilles*:

Curculio is a Semi-Wit, that has a great *Veneration* for the *Moderns*, and no less a *Contempt* for the *Ancients*; But his own ill Composures destroy the force of his Arguments, and do the Ancients full Justice. This Gentleman having had the good Fortune to write a very taking, *undigested medly of Comedy* and *Farce*, is so puff'd up with his Success, that nothing will serve him, but he must bring this new *fantastick way of writing*, into Esteem. To compass this Noble Design, he tells you what a Coxcomb *Aristotle* was with his Rules of the *three Unities*; and what a Company of Senseless Pedants the *Scaligers*, *Rapins*, *Bossu's*, and *Daciers* are. He proves that *Aristotle* and *Horace*, knew nothing of *Poetry*; that Common Sense and Nature were not the same in *Athens*, and *Rome*, as they are in *London*; that *Incoherence*, *Irregularity* and *Nonsense* are the Chief Perfections of the *Drama*, and, by a necessary Consequence that the *Silent woman*, is below his own performance. . . . It will be a hard matter for any Man to trump up any new set of Precepts, in opposition to those of *Aristotle* and *Horace*, except by following them, he writes several approv'd Plays. The great success of the *first Part* of the *T—p* was sufficient I must confess, to justifie the Authors *Conceit*; But then the *Explosion* of the *second* ought to have cur'd him of it. . . . Of all the modern Dramatick Poets the Author of the *Trip to the Jubilee* has the least Reason to turn into Ridicule *Aristotle* and *Horace*, since 'tis to their *Rules* which he has, in some measure followed, that he owed the great success of that Play. Those *Rules* are no thing but a strict imitation of Nature, which is still the same in all Ages and Nations. . . .

In the Prologue to *The Governour of Cyprus*, which opened at Lincoln's Inn Fields probably in January 1703, John Oldmixon, another of Farquhar's friends turned enemies over his success,[13] carped about the 'Farce and Fustian' that pleased audiences, specifically referring to Farquhar, although not by name:

> A few Loose Characters, a Lucky Name
> Brings a full House, and gets the Poet Fame.
> And he that has the art to fill the Pit,
> With us shall ever be the topping Wit:
> Nor will we think the Criticks Judgement true,
> Or that's irregular which pleases you.

> Pure Envy makes 'em talk of want of Rule,
> As if a man cou'd take and be a fool.

Oldmixon's remarks attack *The Constant Couple*; his lines on denying the truth of critics' judgment and choosing what is irregular and ungoverned by 'the Rules' suggests that he also wished to denigrate Farquhar's critical treatise.

Farquhar's denial of neoclassical tenets reflected actual theatrical practice but shocked the sensibilities of the critics. To base critical doctrine on contemporary theatrical practice seemed intellectually wayward and eccentric; to do so after having succeeded excessively in the theatre was brazen. Other voices were to echo Farquhar's strain later in the century: John Dennis in *Remarks upon Cato, A Tragedy* (1713) condemned the indiscriminate adherence to the 'mechanick' unities of time and place, which can render the action of a drama more improbable rather than less,[14] Dr Johnson in his 'Preface to Shakespeare' pursued the point; even in his time, speaking out against the concept was bold. Farquhar was not the first to attack the unities (Sir Robert Howard, for example, had preceded him in 1668); nevertheless, his critical stance was daring and disreputable in 1702. Whether he influenced such critics as Dennis and Johnson, he anticipated them in his critical remarks. In doing so, he antagonized many of his contemporaries, earning their ire with their attention. He did not convince them.

THE TEXT

Love and Business was first published by Lintott on 22 November 1701.[15] It was advertised as written by 'Mr. *George Farquhar* Author of the Trip to the Jubilee.' A second issue appeared on 28 February 1702. The advertisement in the *Post Man* for 26–8 February read, 'This day is published, A new Collection of Poems and Letters, &c. all Written by Mr. George Farquhar, Author of the Inconstant, or the Way to Win him. Printed for Bernard Lintott at the Middle Temple Gate in Fleetstreet.' In fact, the collection was not new; rather it was a reissue of *Love and Business* with a new title-page to which was added an advertisement, 'There is now in the Press, and will speedily be Publish'd, *Memoirs of the Court of* France, *and City of* Paris. . . .' to be printed for Tonson, Wellington, Strahan, and Lintott.[16]

Although second issues of works were often disguised as second editions, the rationale for a second issue in this case is questionable. Advertised as a new collection yet not labelled as a second edition on the title-page, the work is changed only by the addition of the advertisement on the title-page.

The identification of Farquhar in advertisements for the second issue as author of *The Inconstant* linked him to his most recent play, which had opened earlier that month and was scheduled for publication by Lintott and his partners a fortnight later. The advertisement for *Love and Business* in the *Post Man* of 21–4 March, when the theatres were closed in mourning for King William, again called him author of the *Trip to the Jubilee*. The miscellany was advertised in the *Daily Courant* throughout the year, as late as 23 December; the price was 2*s*.

That the second issue was the 'new' collection is the only logical explanation for the advertisement of 26–8 February 1702. Yet inexplicably the following advertisement appeared on a2ᵛ of Richard Wilkinson's *Vice Reclaim'd*, published with Lintott's imprint in the summer of 1703:

Love and Business; in a Collection of Occasionary Verse and Epistolary Prose, not hitherto publish'd. A Discourse likewise on Comedy in reference to the *English* Stage. In a familiar Letter. *Price* 2*s*. 6*d*.

A new Collection of Poems and Letters, *&c. Price* 2*s*. *Both these are Written by* Mr. George Farquhar, *Author of the* Inconstant, or way to win him.

For Lintott to advertise both issues, and at different prices, seems peculiar at best. Yet no 'new Collection' other than the second issue of *Love and Business* has been located.

The octavo volume of *Love and Business* has the collational formula A–L⁸. No running-titles were used. The pagination erroneously omits pp. 144 and 145; K8 bears the pagination 143 on the recto and 146 on the verso.

The first edition was the only one published during Farquhar's lifetime. As late as 20 October 1704, the *Daily*

Courant carried advertisements for the miscellany, now reduced in price to 1*s*. 6*d*. Copies may well have remained on hand long after that. When the first octavo edition of the *Comedies* was published on 27 March 1708, copies of the original octavo of *Love and Business* could still have been on hand; if so, the two works could have been issued bound together, although the pages of type in the *Comedies* are longer than those in *Love and Business*.[17] At any rate, I have located no first edition of the *Works*. A 'Second Edition' of the *Works* appeared on 18 January 1711[18] (title-page undated, but the individual plays dated 1711); in it the second printing of the 'Poems, Letters, and Essays', that is, *Love and Business*, was bound preceding a new printing of the *Comedies*, which has its own title-page as well as individual engravings and title-pages for each of the seven plays (*The Stage-Coach* was excluded). Farquhar, of course, had nothing to do with this edition, published four years after his death; therefore it can not be considered authoritative.

With the exception of the seventh edition, called *The Dramatick Works*, later editions of the *Works* included the 'Poems, Letters, and Essays' as the first item in the collection. The title *Love and Business* disappeared; consistently there was no title page for the miscellany but there was one for the *Comedies*. Editions appeared in 1714, 1718, 1721, 1728, 1742, ·1760, and 1772. An edition of the *Poems, Letters, and Essays, Of the late Ingenious Mr. George Farquhar* was published in Dublin in 1728, labelled 'The Sixth Edition. Corrected from the Errors of former Impressions'. The miscellany was republished in Dublin in the 'eighth' edition of the *Works* in 1755 and again in Thomas Wilkes's edition of 1775.

Three poems in *Love and Business* reappear in the *Poetical Courant*, a half-sheet broadside weekly publication issued by Benjamin Bragg in 1706. A fourth poem in the *Poetical Courant* has strong similarities to one in *Love and Business* and shares six lines but is largely rewritten. Bragg had published the London edition of *The Stage-Coach* in 1705, probably through his connection with Motteux rather than Farquhar (see Introduction, *The Stage-Coach*, vol. i. pp. 334–5). However, in October 1706 he published Farquhar's half-sheet broadside *Prologue Spoken by Mr. Wilks, At the Opening of the Theatre in the Hay-Market, October the 15th, 1706*, so one can assume that Farquhar knew Bragg.

According to the *Cambridge Bibliography of English Literature*, Samuel Philips was editor of the *Poetical Courant*.[19] Philips was the author of the prologue and epilogue to *The Stage-Coach* first published in 1718 but 'Spoken upon the revival of this Comedy at the theatre in Lincolns-Inn-Fields, some Years since, when acted for the Benefit of the Author',[20] probably in 1704. It seems likely, then, that Farquhar, who knew both the editor and the bookseller responsible for publishing the *Poetical Courant*, offered his poems for publication although they might indeed have been lifted from *Love and Business* by a desperate editor.

'To a Lady, being detain'd from Visiting her by a Storm. By G. F.' appeared in the *Poetical Courant*, No. 4, dated 16 February 1706. Although the accidentals are different, there are only four minor substantive revisions. The poem is printed in italic with roman used for emphasis of certain words, for example, 'Wind' and 'Waves' in l. 2, 'Tears' and 'Floods' in l. 3, etc.

'A Prologue on the Propos'd Union of the Two Play-houses' is reprinted in No. 22, dated 22 June 1706. Four insignificant substantive variants occur. 'A Song' ('Tell me Aurelia, tell me Pray') appears in the same issue: no substantive variants appear.

The fourth poem, 'To a Gentleman, that had his Pocket pick'd', is closely imitated in 'To a Gentleman who had his Pocket Pick'd of a *Watch* and *Money* by a Mistriss', published in the *Poetical Courant*, No. 2, 2 February 1706. The version in the *Poetical Courant* is addressed to Tony rather than Sam. It is very similar in content and tone, and six lines are identical or almost identical. The puns and word play are largely the same, even when the lines have been changed; many of the same rhyme words are used.

The chronology suggests that Farquhar rewrote 'To a Gentleman', perhaps with the intention of offering several poems to Philips. However, ten days after his first contribution was published, Lintott bought the rights to *The Recruiting Officer*, and the play was completed, rehearsed, and ready for the *première* by 8 April. Farquhar simply did not have time to dabble with bits of poetry, so he sent instead pieces he had already written and, indeed, published in *Love and Business*. The minor substantive revisions in 'To a Lady' and 'A Prologue' could have been his, since he was apparently responsible for the poems appearing, but there is no reason to assume that he, in fact, made these insignificant changes.

I have used the first edition of *Love and Business* as copy-text; no later text has been considered authoritative. I have examined copies at the British Library, the University of Texas, and the Huntington. I have collated copies at the Bodleian, the Folger, and the Library of Congress.

The substantive variants from *The Adventures of Covent-Garden* in 'The Lovers Night' and from *A Pacquet from Will's* in 'Madam, If I han't begun thrice to write' are recorded in Appendix A.

The substantive variants in two poems reprinted in the *Poetical Courant* are recorded in Appendix B. The second version of 'To a Gentleman' is printed in Miscellaneous Prose and Poetry.

NOTES

1. Nichols, viii. 296.
2. Cited in Rothstein, p. 106.
3. Advertisement, *London Gazette*, 4–7 July 1698.
4. 'George Farquhar and "The Bus'ness of a Prologue"', p. 153.
5. Advertisement, *Post Boy*, 7–9 May 1700.
6. Rothstein, pp. 112–13.
7. *State Papers Domestic* (SP 44, 101, p. 137).
8. See Luttrell, iv, 676, 696, 698.
9. Nichols, viii, 293.
10. No. 30 of the 'Original Letters of Love and Gallantry', in *Letters of Wit, Politicks and Morality*. The volume's dedication is dated 5 July 1701, and it was advertised in the *Post Man* on 24 July.
11. *Letters from the Dead to the Living*, by Mr. Tho. Brown, Capt. Ayloff, Mr. Hen. Barker, &c., 2nd. edn., (London, 1702?) i. 75.
12. *The Diary of Dudley Ryder, 1715–1716*, ed. William Matthews (London, 1939), pp. 44, 47.
13. 'Farquhar and "The Bus'ness of a Prologue"', pp. 143–5.
14. *The Critical Works of John Dennis*, ed. Edward Niles Hooker, 2 vols. (Baltimore, 1939–43), ii. 68.
15. On 18–20 Nov. 1701 the *New State of Europe* advertised that *Love and Business* would be published 'On Saturday next', i.e. 22 Nov. Both the *New State of Europe* and the *Post Man* advertised 'This Day is Publish'd, *Love and Business*. . . .' in the

issue of 22–5 Nov. The *New State of Europe* carried four additional advertisements 'There is now Publish'd', on 27–9 Nov., 2–4 Dec., 16–18 Dec. and 30 Dec.–1 Jan.

16. An advertisement for the published *Memoirs* appeared in the *Daily Courant* on 12 May 1702; Lintott's imprint appears in the advertisement and on the title-page; Tonson, Wellington, and Strahan are not listed.

17. 'George Farquhar', *TLS*, 17 Sept. 1971, p. 1119.

18. Advertisement, *Evening Post*, 16–18 Jan. 1711, 'This Day is Publish'd, The Works of Mr. George Farquhar, containing all his Poems, Letters, Essays and Comedies Publish'd in his Life Time.'

19. The CBEL lists the *Poetical Courant* in two places, once with the parenthetical statement 'Said to be ed. by S. Philips' (ii. 187) and again 'Ed Samuel Philips' (ii. 676).

20. 'The Mystery of Farquhar's Stage-Coach Reconsidered', pp. 234–5.

Love and Business:

IN A

COLLECTION

OF

Occasionary VERSE,

AND

Epistolary PROSE,

Not hitherto Publish'd.

A Discourse likewise upon COMEDY
in Reference to the *English* STAGE.
In a Familiar Letter.

En Orenge il n'ya point d'oranges.

TO
Edmond Chaloner, Esq.

SIR,

As it is the Business of Writing to transmit Vertue to Posterity, so 'tis the Policy of the Pen to make a Party for it's Productions, by engaging in their Cause some worthy Person universally Honour'd and Belov'd, whose admir'd and established Character may add a Value to the Work, and take off all Imputation of Flattery from the Author.

These Advantages I had design'd my self before, in a Piece of another Nature, had not your Modesty caution'd me the contrary; but I think it Injustice that one Part of your Character shou'd obscure the rest; and tho' I must despair of 10 your Consent for what they call a Dedication, yet I must beg your Excuse, if at present I consult what shall turn most to my own Honour, and the Interest of my Book, before your Approbation and Allowance. But I hope you will come to pardon the Presumption, when I assure you, that my Intention is not so much a *Panegyrick* upon you, as to compliment my self, and my own Modesty, not yours, shou'd take the Offence.

The great and vertuous Actions of Progenitors look with a twofold Aspect upon their Posterity; for when the Vices of the 20 latter appear in the same Degree of Opposition with the Merits of the first, the Praise of the Father becomes a Satyr upon the Son; and that *Coat of Arms* which was the Glory of one, turns to a severe Libel upon the t'other. But when the Bloud runs in the same Channel of Virtue, as of Consanguinity; when the Course of the Stream is as pure and lucid as the Fountain-head; then may the Memory of the past, and the Practice of the present Age come boldly Face to Face, where, by a just Resemblance of Features, the Forefather may joyfully own his Ligitimate Posterity. 30

This Advantage, Sir, is yours in Perfection, being sprung from an ancient and honourable Family, of which Merit laid the Foundation, and Vertue has cemented the Structure.

The known Bravery of your famous Ancestor Sir *Thomas Chaloner* added more Value to the *Order*, than he receiv'd by the *Knighthood*, not meanly dubb'd by a Court-Favourite, but on the Field of Battel, where the Voice of War declar'd him Noble, before the General made him a *Banneret*. Add to this, the Politick and Prudent Discharge of his honourable Embassy
40 from *Queen Elizabeth* to the *King of Spain*, and it will evidently appear how *Minerva* had an equal share with *Mars* in his Education; and that his Character left us by a Great Statesman, and his intimate Friend, the illustrious *Cecil*, was just to his Merit.

> ————*Pietas, Prudentia, Virtus*
> *Quæ divisa aliis, Chalonero juncta fuere.*

This Encomium, Sir, is lineally descended to his Posterity, but with all its Circumstances appears most visibly intail'd upon you. In Vindication of which I shall only appeal to the
50 Judgment of Mankind, and the Actions of your Life; and tho' your Modesty may quarrel with the World for doing you Justice, yet you cannot give your own Behaviour the Lye—Sir, there is not a Day of your Life but will rise up against you, and produce in legible Characters the constant Actions of your Piety, your Generosity, your Loyalty, Honour and Integrity, to convince you of your Merit whether you will or not.

So that you must give me leave to apply the Great *Burleigh*'s Versification to the present Opportunity, with the Alteration
60 only of a Word:

> ————*Pietas, Prudentia, Virtus*
> *Quæ divisa aliis, Chalonero juncta* supersunt.

Another part of your great Ancestour's Character I remember is thus describ'd by Mr. *Malim*—*Nam quamvis* πολυΐστωρ *ac variæ lectionis fuerat Chalonerus, utilitatem tamen potius veræ quam ostentationem variæ Eruditionis mihi quesivisse videtur.* These Colours, Sir, present you with your own Picture drawn to the Life; your Application to Books is qualify'd by an universal Knowledge in Mankind, and your Acquisitions by

Study are as far remov'd from Pedantry, as your Experience in 70
the World from the Foppery of a Traveller. The Qualifications
of Foreign Countries are so naturaliz'd in you, that they seem
rather a genuine Transmigration from your Ancestours, than
the Effects of your own Industry; and the Temperance of your
Life, with the modesty of your Conversation, makes not to
inform us that you have seen so much, but may convince the
World that you have chosen the best.

But we need not have Recourse to *France* or *Italy* for your
Improvements; your Alliance and daily Conversation with so
many of the most noble Families in *England* is sufficient to 80
authorise your Merit, and finish your Character, being
equally related to their Bloud, and their Vertues.

And now, Sir, I come about to my first Position, inferring
from this a Compliment upon my self; I have the Honour
sometimes of sharing some few Hours of that Conversation,
which is so much courted by my Superiours, and consequen-
tially do plume my Vanity in this Occasion of acquainting the
World with my Happiness.

From the mentioning of the Honourable Sir *Thomas
Chaloner*, I deduce this Advantage, That I make the most 90
Courtly Address imaginable to Poetry, by informing the
World, in Defence of that Art so much vilify'd by some, that
this great Statesman and Souldier, the trustiest Minister to
the greatest of Queens, and the intimate Friend to the wisest
of Politicians, was at the same time one of the greatest Poets
that ever *England* produ'd. His ten Books *de Republica Anglorum
instauranda* are sufficient Proofs that the Qualifications of *Virgil*
are consistent with those of *Cato*, and that a poetical Genius
has accompany'd the greatest Abilities both in Court and
Camp. 100

Thus, Sir, you see that I have avoided the current Forms of
Pieces in this Nature, not loading the Modesty of my Patron,
but heightning the Vanity of the Author; and by commending
you, I have flatter'd my self.

As the Form is new, pray Sir, let me entreat you to believe
the Design of it Novel, it being only sent in the Capacity and
Character of a familiar Letter, and therefore refuses to be

93 Statesman] Statesmen

receiv'd with the usual Formalities of a Mercenary Dedication. I am,

110
                              SIR,

                    Your most faithful, and
                    most Humble Servant,

                         G. Farquhar.

TO THE
READER.

SIR,

In this Collection of Letters, 'tis but reasonable that you shou'd have one among the rest; and tho' I may want the Honour of your Acquaintance, yet be assur'd, there is no Person in the World more willing to oblige you at present than your Humble Servant. I have heard such a Character of your Honour, your Wit, your Judgment, your Learning, and your Candour, that I'm in a perfect Rapture to think how happy I shall be in your Hands.

It was a good ancient Custom with our Forefathers, to begin their Prefaces with *Kind Reader*; I wou'd have reviv'd 10 that Fashion with all my Heart, and call'd you *Courteous* or *Gentle Reader*, as you very well deserve; but I thought the Stile a little too obsolete for a Book that I design shou'd be a *Beau.* For you must understand, Sir, that this Gentleman is Span new from Top to Toe, talks of every thing but Religion, admires Himself very much, and his greatest Ambition is, to please the Ladies. But to finish his Character, he is perfectly civil to every Body he meets, and with a more particular and profound Respect do's he run to kiss your Hands. He's none of those Bully-books that come bluff into the World, with 20 *Damme, Reader, you're a Blockhead if you don't commend me.* No, no, Sir—If you like him, why you have all the Sense that he thought you had—If you dislike him, you have more Sense than he was aware of, that's all.

Besides all this, he has more Manners than to come among Gentlemen with his Tailour's Bill in his Hand, and to entertain the Company with a long Preface or Inventory of his Equipments; as, such a thing cost so much, and such a thing is worth so much, the Work of such a part is excellent, the Fashion from *Paris*, and the Taylour a *Frenchman*; you must 30 pardon him for that, Sir, if you like the Suit, taking it all together; approve his Fancy, and allow it becomes him, he's your very humble Servant.

Moreover, Sir, I wou'd have you to know, that this Gentleman is of some Circumstance and Condition, and has not been ingag'd in the Shifts that some late Sparks are put to for their Habiliments, who ferret all the Wit-brokers in Town, taking up from several Places, and strut in a Second-hand Finery, patch'd up of the Scraps and Remnants of the *eminent*
40 *Men of the Age*. For I must tell you, Sir, tho' his Cloaths be but plain, yet they are his own, taken up handsomly at one Place, where he may have Credit for as much more, when these are worn out.

And now, Dear Sir, let me intreat you to receive him with the usual Forms of Civility; if you be a Courtier, you will show your Breeding, receive him with a sincere Smile, swear to do him all the Service you can, and you will certainly keep your Word—as you us'd to do. From the City he expects a more than ordinary Reception, because he is become one of their
50 Honourable Society, he is bound to Mr. *Lintott*, and ten to one may serve Seven Years in his Shop, if the Town don't club to purchase his Freedom; he expects good Quarter from the Wits, and Criticks, because he sets up for neither; besides, he has scatter'd some little Nonsense here and there, that they might not be disappointed of their Prey. But his greatest Concern is for his Entertainment with the Ladies, resolv'd however not to complain, thinking it a greater Honour to fall a Sacrifice to the Resentment of the fair, than to live by the Approbation of Men. Tho' he has some Grounds for a more
60 moderate Fate at their Hands, because a great Part of the Work was first design'd for one of that Sex without any farther Consideration of pleasing the World; and the Beauties of the Book, if there be any, was brought from a Ladies Cabinet to the Press; and if it can but from the Press get back again into the Ladies Closets, there may it rest, and Peace be with it.

Now, Sir, as we met good Friends, pray let us part so; I hate quarrelling mortally, and especially with a Person of your present Character and Condition; and as you like my Epistolary Stile, we shall settle a farther Correspondence.

ADVERTISEMENT

In the Discourse upon Comedy, I must beg the Readers Excuse for omitting to mention a certain Fragment of Poetry, Written by *Aristotle*. I thank *Scaliger* for his timely Discovery, but shou'd be much more obliged to any body that cou'd shew me the Piece.

On the Death of General Schomberg kill'd at the Boyn.

A Pindarick.

(1.)

What dismal Damp has overspread the War?
    The Victor grieves more than the Conquer'd fears;
The Streams of Blood are lost in Floods of Tears,
And *Victory* with dropping Wings comes flagging from afar.

(2.)

    The *Brittish* Lyon roars
    Along the fatal Shores;
The *Hibernian* Harp in mournful Strains,
Mixt with the *Eccho* of the Floud, complains.
Round whose reflecting Banks the grieving Voice,
    Shakes with a trembling Noise,
    As if afraid to tell   10
How the great, Martial, Godlike *Schomberg* fell.

(3.)

    Gods! How he stood,
    All terrible in Bloud.
Stopping the Torrent of his Foes, and Current of the Floud.
He, *Moses* like, with Sword, instead of Wand,
This redder Sea of Gore cou'd strait command;
But not like *Moses*, to secure his Flight,
But spight of Waves and Tides to meet, and fight.

(4.)

The labouring Guns oppos'd his Passage o're   20
    With Throws tormented on the Shore,
Of which delivered, they start back, and roar,
As frighted at the Monster which they bore.

The furious Offspring swath'd in curling Smoak,
　　And wrapt in Bands of Fire,
　　Hot with it's Parent's sulphurous Ire,
And wing'd with Death, flies hissing to the Stroak.

(5.)

　　Like some great rugged *Tower*,
　　The Ancient Seat of Power,
30　　Bending with Age it's venerable Halls,
　　With old and craggy Wrinkles on its Walls,
The Neighbours Terrour whilst it stands, and Ruin when it
　　falls.
　　Thus mighty *Schomberg* fell—
Spreading with Ruines o're the Ground,
　　With Desolation all around,
Crushing with destructive Weight
　　The Foes that undermin'd his Seat;
Whilst *Victory*, that always sped,
With towring Pinions o're his Army's Head,
40 Making his Banner still her Lure,
Like *Marius*'s Vultures, to make Conquest sure;
Seeing the spacious Downfal so bemoan'd,
Perch'd on the Ruines, clapt her Wings, and groan'd.

(6.)

Thus *Israel*'s Heroe 'twixt the Pillars sat,
The *Ne plus Ultra* of his Fate
These *Columns* which upheld his Name,
　　Much longer by their Fall,
Than those erected strong and tall,
The standing Limits of *Alcides*'s Fame.
50　　He sat depriv'd of Sight,
Like a black rowling Cloud involv'd in Night.
Conceiving *Thunder* in it's swelling Womb,
Big with surprising Fate, and rushing Doom:
No Flash the sudden Bolt must here disclose;
The Lightning of his Eyes extinguish'd by his Foes.

* *Sampson.*

His Foes, industrious in their juggling Fate,
    Him slavishly enchain'd we see,
    To what must set him free,
And them his cheated Keepers captivate.
He shook his Chains with such a Noise,   60
    The trembling Rout,
    Amidst their Joys,
    Gaz'd all about,
And heard the real *Sampson* in the Voice:
    They saw him too, 'twas *Sampson* all,
    Who by his thundring Fall
    Gave the loud dread Alarm,
Dragging a Train of Vengeance by each *Gyant* Arm.
Their chilling fears did such amazement Frame,
They seem'd all stiff and dead before the Ruin came.   70
The Ruine! only such unto his Foes;
From thence his glorious Monument arose;
But *Time*'s corroding Teeth in spight of Stone
Has eat thro' all, and even the very Ruine's gone:
But *Schomberg*'s Monument shall ne'er decay,
    The gliding *Boyn*
    Time never can disjoyn,
Nor on it's Flouds impose his Laws;
They slide, untoucht, from his devouring Jaws,
And always running, yet must ever stay.   80

(7.)

Hark! how the *Trumpets* hollow Clangours sound,
The Army has receiv'd an universal Wound;
    The Death of *Schomberg* hung
    Oh every faultring Tongue,
    Whilst pallid Grief did place
A sympathizing Death in every Soldiers Face.
    But hold, ye mighty Chiefs,
    Suspend your needless Griefs,
And let victorious Joy your Arms adorn;
    The mighty Warriour's *Ghost*   90
    Upon the *Stygian* Coast
Your Sorrows, more than his own Fate, do's mourn,

He scorns to be lamented so,
Moving in stately *Triumph* to the Shades below.
Behold the Sprites that lately felt the Blow
          Of his commanding warlike Arm,
They shivering all start wide, and even more fleeting grow
          As if the powerful Hand
That cou'd their Grossest Shapes alive command,
100 Had Power to dissolve their Airy Form.

(8.)

Then let not funeral Plaints his Trophies wrong;
Let Spoils and Pageants march his Hearse along,
And shout his *Conclamatum* in Triumphal Song.
All baleful *Cypress* must be here deny'd,
But Lawrel Wreaths fix in their blooming Pride
For as he conquer'd living, so he conquering dy'd.

Written on Orinda's Poem's, lent to a Lady, *in imitation of* Ovid.

Me *Damon* sends his amorous cause to plead,
Orinda must for *Damon* intercede:
Me has he chose to move your angry Mind,
Me the soft Favourite of the Softer Kind.
Me has he chose your rigorous Breast to move,
He knows my Force in Poetry and Love.
Me has he chose to tell his anxious Pain;
Read me, and read the Passion of the Swain.
Whatever Power of Love my Lines can show,
10   It falls far short of what he feels for you.
Where're *Orinda* melts in moving Strains,
Think, *Cælia* think, that *Damon* thus complains:
Whene're I grieve, think *Damon* grieves for you;
Pity the Swain that do's so humbly sue:
This *Damon* begs, *Orinda* begs it too.

99 Grossest] Grosses

To the Ingenious Lady, Author of the Fatal Friendship, *design'd for a Recommendatory Copy to her Play.*

Let others call the Sacred Nine to Aid,
Their moving Thoughts, in moving Numbers laid,
Invoke the fiery *God* with all the Throng
That ancient Bards implore to guide their Song;
Whilst I for nobler Inspiration sue,
Scorning their weaker Helps, invoking You.
You, who alone have Power our Thoughts to raise,
And wing our Fancy to attempt your Praise.
Nought but your charming Beauty can dispense
A Flame sufficient to describe your Sense.   10
Whilst so much Beauty in your Form is shown,
No Pen on Earth can reach it, but your own
Go on then *Daphne*, *Phœbus* will pursue,   ⎫
His chaster Fires are all enjoy'd by you;   ⎬
You are his fairer Nymph, you bear his Lawrel too. ⎭
Go on, thou Champion for thy Sex design'd,
And prove, the Muses are of Female kind;
Let distant Nations *English* Beauties prize,
As much for Charms of Wit, as Power of Eyes:
Your moving Scenes the ravish'd Audience drew,   20
Raptures we felt, as when your Eyes we view;
Such Arts were us'd to mix our Hopes and Fears,
You made Grief pleasing, and we smil'd in Tears.
Thus Lovers view a Mistresses Disdain,
And love to look, tho' sure to look in Pain.
Th' effects of labour'd Art your Work reveals,
Yet a superiour Art, that Art conceals.
Here Nature gains, tho' naked, thus display'd,
Like Beauty most adorn'd, when least array'd.
Go on then, doubly arm'd, to conquer Men;   30
Phœbus his Harp and Bow, you boast your Eyes and Pen
All to the first without Reluctance yield,
But your victorious Pen has forc'd the Field.

An Epigram, on the Riding-House in Dublin, *made into a Chappel*.

A *Chappel* of the Riding-House is made;
We thus once more see *Christ* in Manger laid,
Where still we find the Jocky Trade supply'd;
The *Laymen* bridled, and the *Clergy* ride.

To a Lady, *being detain'd from visiting her by a Storm*.

So poor *Leander* view'd the *Sestian* Shore,
Whilst Winds and Waves oppos'd his Passage o're;
More moist with Tears, because by Flouds restrain'd,
Than, in these Flouds had he his Wish obtain'd;
So drown'd, yet burnt within, upon the Banks he lean'd;
Lean'd begging Calms, and as he begging lay,
Implor'd with Sighs the Winds, with Tears the Sea.
One would have thought by all these Mixtures sent,
To raise a second greater Storm he meant.
10 Just so whilst kept from you by Storms, I weep;
The Winds my Sighs, my Tears augment the Deep;
With flowing Eyes I view the distant side,
The space that parts us doth my self divide.
Here's only left the poor external Part,
Whilst you, where're you move, possess my Heart.
Depriv'd of Love, and your blest sight, I dye,
Whilst you the first, and Storms the last deny.

The Lovers Night.

The Nights black Curtain o're the World was spread,
And all Mankind lay Emblems of the Dead,

A deep and awful Silence void of Light,
With dusky Wings sat brooding o're the Night,
The rowling Orbs mov'd slow from East to West,
With Harmony that lull'd the World to rest.
The Moon withdrawn, the Oozy Flouds lay dead,
The very Influence of the Moon was fled;
Some twinkling Stars, that thro' the Clouds did peep,
Seeming to wink as if they wanted Sleep,   10
All Nature hush'd, as when dissolv'd and lay'd
In silent Chaos e're the World was made;
Only the beating of the Lover's Breast
Made Noise enough to keep his Eyes from Rest;
His little World, not like the greater, lay
In loudest Tumults of disorder'd Day;
His Sun of Beauty shone, to light his Breast
With all its various Toils and Labours prest;
The Sea of Passions in his working Soul, ⎫
Rais'd by the Tempest of his Sighs did rowl ⎬   20
In towring Flouds, to overwhelm the whole, ⎭
Those Tyrants of the Mind, vain Hope and Fear, ⎫
That still by turns usurp an Empire there, ⎬
Now raising Man on high, then plunging in Despair. ⎭
Thus *Damon* lies, his Grief no Rest affords,
Till swelling full, it thus burst out in Words.
Oh! I cou'd curse all Womankind, but one,
And yet my Griefs proceed from her alone.
Was not our Paradise by Woman lost?
But in this Woman still we find it most: 30
Hell's greatest Curse a Woman if unkind,
Yet Heaven's great Blessing, if she loves, we find.
Oh! if she lov'd, no God the Bliss cou'd tell,
She wou'd be Heaven it self, were she not so much Hell.
Thus our chief Joys with most Allays are curst,
And our best things, when once corrupted, worst.
But Heaven is just; our selves the Idols fram'd,
And are for such vain Worship justly damn'd.
Thus the poor Lover argued with his Fate; ⎫
Emilia's Charms now did his Love create; ⎬   40
That Love repuls'd, now prompted him to hate. ⎭

Sometimes his Arms wou'd cross his Bosom rest,
Hugging her lovely Image printed on his Breast,
Where flattering Painter Fancy shew'd his Art,
In charming Draughts, his Pencil *Cupid*'s Dart.
The Shadow drawn so lively did appear,
As made him think the real Substance there.
Then was he blest, all Rapture, stunn'd with Joy,
Excess of Pleasure did his Bliss destroy;
50   He thought her naked, soft, and yeilding waste ⎫
Within his pressing Arms lay folded fast;   ⎬
Nay, by the Gods, she really there was plac'd; ⎭
Else how cou'd Pleasure to such Raptures flow?
Th' Effect was real—Then, the Cause was so.
What more can most substantial Pleasures boast
Than Joy when present, Memory when past?
Then, Bliss is real which the Fancy frames,
Or these call'd real Joys are only Dreams.

> *The Brill, August the* 10th. 1700.
> *New Stile.*

Dear Sam,

   To give you a short *Journal* of my short Voyage, on *Wensday* I
got to *Harwich* about Four in the Afternoon, and alighted at
one of the cleanest, best-furnish'd *Inns* in the Kingdom. My
Warrant for the Packet-Boat cost me *Half a Piece*, and to the
Officers for not executing their Duty *Half a Crown*. This Place,
like most Sea-Ports, we found extravagantly dear; but to ease
that inconvenience, we were advis'd to get aboar'd by Eleven
at Night; here I met a Gentlman, whose Company I was very
happy in, tho' extreamly concern'd for the occasion of his
10 Voyage, which was an Express to the King, of the Duke of
Glocester's Death. This was the first News I had of this publick
Loss, which I had not much time to reflect upon, being so
nearly touch'd on the Score of my Private Concern by a
violent Storm that immediately came upon us; you may guess
at our Circumstances, when I assure you, that our greatest
Comfort was the Lightning that show'd the Seamen their

4 Packet-Boat] Packet-Boot   4 cost] coast

Business, which otherwise they must have grop'd for; all
Intercourse of Speech being broken off by the loudness of the
Thunder: We had such warm Work, that I sometimes allow'd
it a Just Thought, that Satan shou'd be intitled *Prince of the* 20
Air; and again, why the Devil shou'd command the Artillery of
Heaven, I cou'd not so well comprehend. I supported my self
with the Thought, that Providence had no design upon me,
but that this Tumult of the Elements was their manner of
expressing their Grief for the Loss of his *Highness*; or that they
were angry at Mr. *L—r* for bringing such unwelcom News into
their Dominions, and for making a Property of them to spread
it abroad. By this kind of Poetical Philosophy I bore up pretty
well under my Apprehensions, tho' never worse prepar'd for
Death, I must confess; for I think I never had so much Money 30
about me at a time; we had some Ladies aboard, that were so
extreamly Sick, that they often wished for Death, but were
damnably afraid of being drown'd; but, as the Scripture says,
Sorrow may last for a Night, but Joy cometh in the Morning. The
Weather cleard up with the Day, the Wind turn'd Westerly,
and in a few Hours, I was going to say, we saw *England* out of
Sight; all *Thursday* we had a fresh Gale, and cold Chickens; our
Wine went about at a strange rate, for our Stomachs ebb'd
and flow'd like the Element. On *Friday* Morning we made the
coast of *Holland*, a stiff Gale, and the Sea runs high. I was 40
mightily pleas'd to view the Continent, you may be sure; but
as I stood upon the *Poop* perusing its first appearance with my
Perspective, I had such a Rebuke for my Curiosity, by a great
Sea, that took us *Fore and Aft*, that I was season'd for a *Dutch*-
man immediately. Whether this be a Compliment of Salutation
usually paid to Strangers, or that the *Batavian* Out-Guards
took me for a Spy upon their Frontiers, I shall leave the
Skipper to determine. In short, by working of a Staunch Ship,
and the influence of a Staunch *Proverb* in favour of the *Old
Bayly Bar*, we got over the *Bar* at the *Maese*; and the *Dutch* 50
Wave has clear'd my Eye-sight of an Errour that we *Brittains*
are very fond of, that the *Thames* is the finest River in the
Universe; for I can assure you, *Sam*, that the *Rhine* is as much
beyond it, as a *Pair of Oars* before a *Sculler*, let all the *Tritons*
between *Chelsea* and *Richmond* Argue never so loud to the
contrary; tho' in one sort of *Traffick* upon that part of the

Thames we exceed the whole World; both for the Quantity and Cheapness of the Commodity; and I believe the Storehouse for this kind of *Staple*, including the *Playhouse* and the *Rose*, may
60 contend with most *Marts* in *Europe*.

This Day at Eleven we landed at the *Brill*, and here I have a small Taste of this *Republick*, that makes such a noise in the World—My Fancy in respect of Expectation has generally been so fruitful, that the dearest Part of my Hopes have frequently ended in Disappointments; and I have seldom found things come up to answer the *Idea* that I have usually fram'd of their Excellence; but here I must confess the Reality exceeds the Shadow, and I am pleas'd once in my Life to find a thing that can afford me substantial Pleasure in the
70 Enjoyment. I have read much of this Place, fancy'd more, yet all falls short of what I see.

At my first Entrance into this Town, I made one Discovery, which I beleive has hitherto scap'd most Travellers, *viz*. That the *Dutch* are the greatest *Beaux* in the World, only with this difference from the Gentlemen at *White*'s, that their Finery is much more noble, and substantial; I never knew the fairest, finest, full-bottom Wig, most nicely fixt on the most beautiful Block in the Side-Box, look half so genteel as a *Dutch* Canal with a stately row of flourishing Trees on each side, and some
80 twenty beautiful Bridges laid a cross it, within sixty or seventy Paces one of another: I never knew a Valet and a Barber with Rasors, Twizers, Perfumes, and Washes, work half so hard upon a Gentleman's Face, that design'd a Conquest on a Birth-Night, as I have seen a lusty *Dutch* Woman with a Mop and warm Water scrub the Marbles and Tyles before the Door, till she has scour'd them brighter than any Fops Complexion in the Universe. No first Rate Beau with us, drawn by his Six before and Six behind, lolling luxuriously in his Coach, appears half so Gallant, as a jolly *Skipper* at the
90 Stern of his Barge, with a fur'd Cap like Rays about his Head, the Helm in his Hand, and his Pipe in his Mouth, with Liberty seated in one *Whisker*, and Property on t'other; and in this Splendour making the *Tour* of half a Dozen fine Cities in a Day, without either Qualm of the Spleen, or Twinge of the Gout. Such a Person I take for a Beau of the first Magnitude, who scorning to be lugg'd by Beasts as Fellows are to *Tyburn*,

can harness the Winds and Waves for his Equipage, and improving on the Works of Providence, makes the universal Elements, (Air and Water) submit to his private Composition of Advantage and Diversion, to see the Wind work in his Sails, 100 and play with his Pendants, must certainly afford more substantial and pure Satisfaction, than the Whinnee of a Horse, or the Crack of a Coachwhip.

In short, dear *Sam*, I am not so bigotted to Domestick Customs, as not to approve what is admirable here; and you must Pardon me that I have thrown up the Prejudice of Nativity with my Beef and Pudding as I came over; and 'tis no small part of my present Wonder, why we should call the *Dutch* a slovenly sort of People, since to the Eye, which must determine that Circumstance, they are much more gaudy 110 than that Nation we so mimick and admire; and with this Advantage that they are gay without Levity, and fine beyond Foppery. Why we shou'd mention the *Dutch* with Contempt, and the *French* with Admiration, is a severe Satyr upon the *English* Judgment, when the Bravery of the former attract the Admiration of Men, and the Pageantry of the latter draw only the Eyes of Women: But our *English* Ladies are so very fine, that we are very willing to please them, and thus are drawn into this unreasonable Prejudice; but we ought to take Care, that by being thus particular Slaves to our respective *Mistresses*, 120 we ben't drawn at last into universal Bondage to a *Master*. The *French* have taken no small Pains of late Years to render themselves agreeable; they treat us like a Mistress, do every thing that they fancy will please us, till they bring us at last to act whatsoever shall please them; but this is no News, and I think it a little improper to tell you an *English* Story from a Place where you may expect some Foreign Entertainment. I have no more to say at present, but that I am just going for *Rotterdam*, and departing from a *Scotch* House here, where nothing of that Country is to be found but the Landlord; for 130 the Rooms are a Paradise for Cleanliness, but the Host is a Rogue for his Reckoning. I have got such a heap of Silver out of a *Pistol*, as upon a hansom Counter might give Credit to a Banker; and I can assure you that while I have a Brother to that Pistol left, you shall not see

Your Freind and Servant.

Leyden. *October* the 15th. 1700.

Dear Sam,

The usual Excuse of Gentlemen abroad for neglecting their
Friends at home is, that new Setts of different Objects
continually entertaining us with Changes of Admiration, the
Idea's of our Old Acquaintance is by degrees worn out by the
Accession of the New: But this kind of Forgetfulness were too
severe a Charge upon the Merit of my Friends and my own
Gratitude, both which I will choose to maintain, and leave it
to your Charity to make me an Excuse for my Silence: The
Truth is, I have had a very tedious Fit of Sickness, which had
10 almost sent your Friend a longer Journey than he was
willing to undertake at present; but now being pretty well
recover'd, I can only inform you in general, that every day
surprises me with some agreeable Object or other; and I find
very much to my wonder, that the Accounts I have had of this
Countrey are very different from the Observations that may
be made upon the Place. Some general Remarks there are
undisputably certain, as that nothing can parallel the *Dutch*
Industry but the Luxury of *England*; and that the Money laid
out in the Taverns in *London*, in purchasing Diseases, wou'd
20 victual the whole *United Provinces* very plentifully at their
wholsom Course of Diet; that the Standing-Army maintain'd
by the *Dutch* for their Security against a Foreign Force, are not
half so expensive, as the fifty thousand Lawyers kept up by
our civil Factions in *England*, for no other use but to set us
continually by the Ears; People, like the *Jews*, that are
tolerated in all Governments for the Interest of the Publick,
while their main Drift is to enrich themselves; and who by
their Gettings and Cunning have brought their Riches and
Practice into a Proverb. The Lawyers here put the Question
30 only, Whether the thing be Lawful; and, upon Application to
the Statutes, the Controversy is immediately determin'd. But
our Casuists at *Westminster* dispute not so much upon the
Legality of the Cause, as upon the Letter of the Law, and
make more Cavils on the meaning of Words that shou'd
determine Justice, than upon the Equity of the Allegations
contended for by the Parties; and the bulk of our Laws have
loaded Justice so heavily, that 'tis become a Burthen to the

People, who in regard of their Sufferings in this kind shou'd
borrow an Appellation from Physick, and be call'd *Patients*
rather than *Clients*.

Another thing worth Consideration in respect of the Laws 40
in *Holland*, is this; None but honest Men make Estates by their
Practice; for the siding with the wrong Party brings the
Lawyer into Contempt, and lays him under a severe Repre-
hension, either of Ignorance in his Business, or Knavery to the
People: Hence it comes to pass, that Injustice, not finding a
Patron to support its Cause, is forc'd to remove to a
neighbouring Country, where the wrong Side was never
known to make its Assertor blush; where the Eloquence of
S—re, and the Impudence of *S—n* are plausible Pretences for 50
patronising Injustice, and abusing the Client: But there are
Bravo's in all parts of the World, that will take Money for
cutting of Throats, whether there be Grounds or not for the
Resentment.

So much for the Law, now for the Gospel, *Sam*. I think
Holland may contend for the Catholick Church with any part
in *Europe*, because 'tis more universal in its Religion, than any
Countrey in the Universe. 'Tis a pleasant thing to see
Christians, Mahometans, Jews, Protestants, Papists, Armenians and
Greeks, swarming together like a Hive of Bees, without one 60
Sting of Devotion to hurt one another; they all agree about the
business of this Life, because a Community in Trade is the
Interest they drive at; and they never Jostle in the Way to the
Life to come, because every one takes a different Road. One
great Cause of this so amicable a Correspondence and
Agreement, is, that only the Layety of these Professions
compose the Mixture; here are no Ingredients of Priestcraft to
sowr the Composition; Pulpits indeed they have, but not like
Hudibrass's Ecclesiastick Drums, that are continually beating
up for Volunteers to the alarming of the whole Nation. Here is 70
no Interest of Sects to be manag'd under the Cloak of gaining
Proselytes to the Truth; nor strengthning of Parties, by
Pretence of reclaiming of Souls; every Shepherd is content
with his own Flock, and *Mufti, Levite, Pope*, and *Presbiter*, are
all *Christians* in this, that they live in Unity and Concord.

'Tis a strange thing, *Sam*, that among us People can't agree
the whole Week, because they go different Ways upon *Sundays*:
This is to make the Lord's Day a Sower of Dissention, and
Religion, (which is call'd the Bond of Peace) to be the Brand
80 of Discord and Combustion: But we have some Preachers that
think themselves inspir'd with the Spirit, when they are really
possess'd by the Devil; the Fervency of whose Zeal dismisses
Congregations with Heats and Heartburnings of Spirit, and
blows up the Coals on the Altar to set their Neighbours
Houses on Fire; the Efficacy of the Pulpit is sufficiently shown
in the Practice of the Congregations. No People in the World
are so full of National Principles of Faith, and to what purpose
the following Instance shall shew you. Two Gentlemen of my
Acquaintance, one a Devout Hearer at *Common-Garden-Church*,
90 and the t'other a violent Zealot for Doctor *Burgess's* Meeting,
met one Evening at *Tom's Coffee-house*, and wou'd adjourn to
the *Fleece-Tavern*, to discourse upon some Point of Doctrine
manag'd that *Sunday* by their respective Ministers. The
Drawer brought in a Bottle of New *French*, and the Disenter
introduc'd Predestination: After two or three hearty Glasses,
the Dispute grew pretty warm, and the Quotation of the
Fathers and the Texts of Scripture made such a Noise, that
two Wenches that usually ply upon those Stairs, overhearing
the bustle, took them for a couple of *Levites*, and so made
100 account to bolt in, and sell their Mackerell. The fervency of
the Argument was presently abated upon the appearance of
the Ladies, and a Topick of a more Familiar Nature assum'd;
till both being pretty well convinc'd of their Opponent's Fire
and Fancy, the Whores were dismiss'd, and Predestination
reassum'd; the Argument grew warmer, as the Disputants
grew fudled: In short, they disputed themselves stark drunk,
drew their Swords to decide the Controversy; and, had not
Mr. *Fern* come in, 'twas great odds that Predestination had
sent one to the Devil, and t'other to the Gallows. But they
110 parted Friends at last, and said one to t'other, *I'm sorry at my
Heart, dear Friend, that you wont go to Heaven my Way.* And so
away he reel'd to a Bawdy-house. Now the Moral of the Fable
is this: If the Divines, instead of their Speculative Theology,

110 one] on

had preach'd that Day a thundring Sermon against Drunkenness and Fornication, 'tis probable that the *Faith* of these Gentlemen had been ne'er the less fortify'd, and their *Good Works* much more improv'd.

But I beg your Pardon for this Digression; I was going to say that, excepting a few general Remarks, some of which I have mention'd, the Accounts we have of this People are very lame, and sometimes exactly opposit to the Truth. I shall mention one or two Particulars that I found very obvious.

We have a Notion in *England*, that the *Dutch* are very great Drunkards; whether this Aspersion arise from some People's confounding the *High Dutch* with the *Low*, or that there is a Sottishness in their Miens and Complexions, I can't determine; but this I can assure you, that the Report is as false, as shou'd I aver, that the People in *London* are the most chast and sober Gentlemen in the World. 'Tis true indeed they will take off a toping Glass of Brandy, but that is only what is absolutely necessary to moderate the Moisture and Coldness of their Constitution, and us'd in such quantity by the meaner sort only, who living continually in the Water, must require an allowance to fortify themselves against the Chillness of their Habitations; for you must know, that whole Families, Men, Women, and Children, live continually in Boats, and have no more Tenement on Dry-land than a *Thames*-Salmon; but notwithstanding this incumbent necessity of their taking a Cup of the Creature, I never have seen since I came into this Countrey but one *Dutch*-man drunk; and altho his Impertinence was no more than is naturally incident to any Body in his Condition, yet the whole Boatful of People, to the number of sixty Persons, shew'd the greatest aversion imaginable to his Circumstances, except two or three Jolly *English* Men that made very good sport with his Humour; and had not we, with some *French* Gentlemen, protected his Carcass, his Countrymen wou'd have sous'd him in the Canal very heartily for his Debauch.

As the laborious Life of the inferiour sort requires an exhilerating Glass, so the same Necessity both as to Time and Charge secures them from Excess: And for the Gentry, they

132 meaner] [om.] The word 'meaner', catchword on p. 29, was omitted as the first word on p. 30 but clearly intended as part of the text.

are indeed sociable in their own Houses; but were it not for
Strangers, all Places of Publick Entertainment must consequently fall; which is the greatest Argument imaginable for
the Sobriety and Temperance of a People; whereas 'tis very
well known, that if the very Taverns in *London*, with Seven or
Eight handsom Churches, and one or two of our Inns of
Court, (all which we could well enough spare) were but
handsomly seated on the Banks of a River, they would make a
160 Figure with some of the most remarkable Cities in *Europe*. This
indeed is a Noble Argument of the Riches of *England*; but
whether our Luxury sprang from Plenty, or the Temperance
of *Holland* the Effect of Necessity, be the happier State, is a
question that I want leisure now to determine.

Another Account we have very current among us, That
there are no Beggars in *Holland*; That they are very careful in
employing their Poor, and that their Manufactures require a
great many Hands is most certain, but Ocular Demonstration
is too strong a Proof against all their Industry; and I'm apt to
170 believe, that the Order of Mendicants is of a very late
Institution, else so visible a Falsity cou'd never have put this
Trick upon Travellers. Whether their late expensive Wars
have ruin'd more People than their Manufactures can employ,
or that the Poverty of the *Spaniards* in the Neighbour
Netherlands, have by degrees infected the meaner sort, I shan't
be positive; but nothing is more certain, than that a well-
dispos'd *Christian* may find as many Objects of Charity here as
in any part of *England*, if we may judge of their Wants by the
Fervency of their Cries.

180 I do believe that the Charity of the *Dutch* is no great
Incouragement to Beggars; which is the Reason (I conceive)
why the Poor flock all to the High-ways and *Track-scouts*,
where the Opportunity is good for Application to Strangers.

From these, and some other such like Particulars, I found it
matter of some Speculation, how the generality of the *English*
Nation being so near Neighbours to this State, should be so
very short in their Knowledge of the Manners and Constitution
of this People, but this I may presume to proceed upon the
following Accounts.

190 Most of our *English* that visit this Place, are either young
Gentlemen that come aboard to Travel, or Merchants that

make a short Trip upon their own private Concerns.

'Tis the usual Way with the first of these to take *Holland En Passant*, either going or coming; and being youthful Sparks, are so fond of the Finery at *Paris*, and Delicacy of *Rome*, that they han't Leisure, forsooth, to dwell upon the Solidity of this Place. *France* and *Italy* are their Provinces, and *Holland* is only their Inn upon the Road; they lye for a Night, and away the next Morning.

They can tell you, perhaps, that the *Dutch* manner of Travelling is very commodious; that the *Hague* is a pretty Village, *Amsterdam* a fine City, and that the People are a parcel of heavy, dull, unconversable Creatures, and so they leave them. Nothing can relish more of old *England* than this peremptory Declaration; I wou'd willingly understand how Gentlemen can make a true Estimate of the Wit and Ingenuity of a People, when they don't stay to make one Acquaintance in the Countrey, nor can speak one Syllable of their Language.

Most of our young Nobility and Gentry travel under the Tuition of *French* Governours, who however honest in their Intentions of serving their Pupils, are nevertheless full of their *Moy Meme*; and from the Prejudice of Birth and Education, like all other People, are most inclinable to the Manners, Language, Dress, and Behaviour of their own Nation; and tho' perfectly skill'd perhaps in the Accomplishments that compose what we call a fine Gentleman, yet 'tis probable they may fall short in those Qualifications that are absolutely necessary to an *Englishman* in respect of the Interest of his Country, and of these I take the *Dutch* Language to be none of the most trivial. For at the present Juncture, which renders it not only ours, but the Interest of *Europe*, that we shou'd be well with these People, it were not unnecessary that our Amity shou'd be link't with private Friendships and Correspondence, as by publick Leagues and Alliances. An Instance of which is very visible to our Prejudice in the Habitudes and Familiarity contracted by our young Gentlemen at *Paris*, which, without all Dispute, is one great Reason for the Influence retain'd by that Court, not only over our Fashions and Behaviour, but which is extensive also to matters of more weighty Consequence, including even our Councils, Laws, and Government.

The second sort of People that make a turn into this

Country, are our Merchants, whose Speculation is limited by a few Particulars; their Affairs not extending to the Policies of State, nor the Humours of the People; they are satisfyed to mind their Business only, and to understand the Incouragement of Trade, the Prices and Customs upon Goods, the Value of Stock, and the Rates of Exchange. Their Conversation lies chiefly between the Store-house and the Board-side, and that in one or two Cities at most, where their Correspondents are

240 resident; so that all the Account we must expect from these Persons, must only relate to their Trade in General, or to some particular Branch of it, which is universally understood already thro' the Intercourse of our Dealing, and neither so improving to our Polity, nor satisfactory to the Curious. But even among their Incouragements of Trade so universally known and admir'd, as the advantageous Situation of their Countrey, their natural Propensity to Navigation, the lowness of their Imports, &c. yet by an odd accident I came to understand one Policy in their Trading Constitution, which I

250 have never hitherto met with in any verbal or written Account whatsoever. The matter was thus in all its Circumstances.

One Day upon the *Exchange* at *Rotterdam* I casually met a Gentleman, who some time ago liv'd one of the most considerable Merchants in *Ireland*, and about some four Years since by great Losses at Sea was forc'd to fly his Country in a very mean Condition. I put him in mind of his Misfortunes by a Favour he once confer'd upon me of a Bottle of Claret and a Neat's Tongue at Launching of a new Ship that he had built in *Dublin*, which Vessel, (Bottom and Goods all his own) was

260 unfortunately lost the very first Voyage. The Gentleman seem'd very sensible of his Misfortunes, but withal told me, That he still had a Glass of Wine and a Tongue at my Service, if I wou'd come and see him at his House that Evening. I made him a Visit, and found, to my no small Surprize, a handsome House, neatly furnish'd, excellent Meat, and as good *Burgundy* as every joy'd the Heart of Man. I took the Freedom to ask my Merchant how a Bankrupt shou'd come by all this; in answer to which he gave me the following Account of his Affairs.

270 The *Dutch*, Sir, (said he) have a Law, that whatever Merchant in any part of *Europe*, who has had any considerable

Traffick with this Countrey, whose Honesty is apparent by his
former Accounts, and can prove by sufficient Testimony, that
his Losses and Misfortunes are not chargeable upon his
Ignorance nor Extravagance, but purely those of unfortunate
Chance, above the reach of humane Prevention; that then
such a Merchant may repair to them, have the Freedom of
any Sea-port in the State; have a supply of whatever Money
he's willing to take up out of the Publick Revenue, upon the
bare Security of his Industry and Integrity; and all this upon 280
the Current Interest, which is seldom above Four *per Cent.*

Pursuant to this (continued the Gentleman) my Qualifications for this Credit being sufficiently testify'd, I took up
here two Thousand Pound Sterling, and in two Years have
gain'd Fifty *per Cent.* So that by God's Assistance, and my own
diligent Endeavours, I question not but in a few Years I shall
be able to show my Face to my Creditors, return to my
Countrey, and there live in *Statu quo.*

Here are two Points remarkable enough: A Charitable
Action to relieve distress'd Strangers, and a Policy of State for 290
the Interest of the Republick, which you may soon discover by
repeating the Conditions. His Honesty must be manifest from
his former Accounts, his sufficiency in Business apparent from
his precedent manner of Dealing, his Misfortunes such as
were above humane prevention, as by Storms, Pyrates, or the
like; but above all, he must have some considerable Traffick
with this Countrey, there's the Clincher; the *Utile,* the greatest
Incouragement imaginable for all Forreigners to Traffick with
this Nation; and for the most ingenious Traders, who are not
always the most Fortunate, to seek a Residence among them: 300
and what a Life and Vigour these two Circumstances may add
to the Trade of a Nation, the flourishing Condition of this
People is the most sufficient Witness.

Now, *Sam,* I have tir'd you most certainly; for I am weary
my self, and we are seldom the soonest tir'd with our own; the
Gravity of my Style you must impute to the Air of the
Country; and the Length of my Letter to a very Rainy Day
that has kept me within; and to excuse the Matter, it shall cost
you nothing, for I send it by a Gentleman, who can assure you

294 precedent] predecent

310 that what I have said is true. I shall at least conclude with a
Truth, that I am,

Dear Sir, Yours, etc.

An Epilogue, *spoken by Mr.* Wilks *at his first Appearance upon the* English *Stage*.

As a poor Stranger wreck'd upon the Coast,
With Fear and Wonder views the Dangers past;
So I with dreadful Apprehensions stand,
And thank those Pow'rs that brought me safe to Land.
With Joy I view the smiling Countrey o're,
And find, kind Heav'ns! an hospitable Shore.
'Tis *England*—This your Charities declare,
But more the Charms of *British* Beauties there.
Beauties that celebrate this Isle afar,
10   They by their Smiles, as much as you by War.
True Love, true Honour, here I can't fail to play.
Such lively Patterns you before me lay.
Void of Offence, tho' not from Censure free,
I left a distant Isle too kind to me.
Loaded with Favors I was forc'd away,
'Cause I wou'd not accept what I cou'd never pay.
There I cou'd please, but there my Fame must end,
For hither none must come to boast, but mend.
Improvement must be great, since here I find
20   Precepts, Examples, and my Masters kind.

A Prologue *on the propos'd Union of the Two Houses*.

Now all the World's tak'n up with State Affairs,
Some wishing Peace, some calling out for Wars.
'Tis likewise fit, we shou'd inform the Age,
What are the present Politicks of the Stage.

Two different States, ambitious both, and bold,
All Free-born Souls, the New House and the Old,
Have long contended, and made stout Essays,
Which shou'd be Monarch, absolute in Plays.
Long has the Battel held with bloody Strife,
Where many ranting Heroes lost their Life:
Yet such their Enmity, that ev'n the slain
Do conquer Death, rise up, and fight again.
Whilst from the Gallery, Box, the Pit and all
The Audience look'd, and shook its awful Head,
Wondring to see so many Thousands fall,
And then look'd Pale to see us look so Red.
By Force of Number, and Poetick Spell,
We've rais'd the ancient Heroes too from Hell
To lead our Troops; and on this Bloody Field,
You've seen great *Cæsar* fight, great *Pompey* yield.
Vast Sums of Treasure too we did advance
To draw some Mercenary Troops from *France*;
Light-footed Rogues, who when they got their Pay,
Took to their Heels—*Alons*—and run away.
Here have you seen great *Philip*'s Conquering Son,
Who in Twelve Years did the whole World orerun;
Here has he fought, and found a harder Jobb
To beat one Playhouse, than subdue the Globe:
All this from Emulation for the Bays;
You lik'd the Contest, and bestow'd your Praise:
But now, (as busie Heads love something new)
They wou'd propose an *Union*—Oh, *Mort-dieu.*
If it be so, let *Cæsar* hide his Head,
And fight no more for Glory, but for Bread.
Let *Alexander* mourn, as once before,
Because no Worlds are left to conquer more.
But if we may judge small from greater things, ⎫
The present Times may show what *Union* brings, ⎬
We feel the Danger of *United Kings*. ⎭
If we grow one, then Slavery must ensue
To Poets, Players, and, my Friends, to you.
For to one House confin'd, you then must praise
Both cursed Actors, and confounded Plays.
Then leave us as we are, and next advance
Bravely to break the Tye 'twixt *Spain* and *France*.

10

20

30

40

On the Death of a Lady's Sparrow, in Imitation of Catullus, for his Lesbia's.

Mourn all ye Muses, mourn ye Nymphs and Loves,
Mourn all ye Woods, mourn all ye Trees and Groves.
Weep all ye Streams, ye Forrests fade and mourn,
Your well-lov'd Bird must ne're again return.
Let the dull Air ne're be serene again,
Let all the Winds with loudest Sighs complain.
The once blest Winds, whilst they cou'd bear away
His charming Notes, and with his Feathers play.
How shall I grieve, or how bewail his Death?
None fit to sing that wants his tuneful Breath:
Like the melodious Swan prepar'd to dye,
He shou'd himself have Sung his Elegy.
Ye winged Choristers, come here, and sing,
Lament his Death; sweet Flowers and Blossoms bring,
To strew his Grave with Beauties of the Spring.
Sweet was his Voice, well were his Notes belov'd;
His careful Mistress with his Tunes he mov'd;
Oft has he sung upon the Flowry Plain,
But ne're, alas! like wretched me, in vain.
Round her alone the pretty Bird wou'd fly,
Chirp to the fair, and in her Bosom lye;
Her Bosom, fairer than the Silver Sky:
There did the Wanton Play, and there was blest,
And there alone he made his downy Nest;
All her Discourse to him he understood,
And kindly answer'd with what Voice he cou'd.
Upon her Head oft wou'd be fluttering move,
And spread a living Canopy above;
Ten thousand pretty things shew'd his officious Love.
Oft as she walk'd, when she began to sing,
With her own Breath he fann'd her from his Wing;
Then would he pluck the Daises here, and there,
And to her Hands the blushing Presents bear.
The Woods he scorn'd, and chose with her to dwell,
Her Fingers did all Boughs by far excell.

Ye winged Choristers, come here, and sing;
Lament his Death; sweet Flowers, and Blossoms bring, }
To strew his Grave with Beauties of the Spring.
For ah! he's gone, his pleasing Sports must cease,
He's gone, alas! and now no more can please;　　　　40
Still is his Voice, and still his stifning Wing,
He ne're again must to his Mistress Sing.
See his deep grave by mournful *Cupid* made, }
Himself close by in a sad Posture lay'd, }
Breaking his Golden Arrow, late his Spade. }
Around his Grave let circling *Fairies* play,
Dance the whole Night, and scarce depart by Day;
Let all things grieve, *Selinda*'s Sparrow's gone;
Selinda's Sparrow, so belov'd alone,
For him the tender Virgin Mourns and Cries, }
For her dear Sparrow she Laments and Sighs, }　　50
Sworn to be buried there, whene're she dyes. }
Then shall the winged Choire flock here, and Sing, }
Lament her Death, sweet Flowers and Blossoms bring, }
To strew her Grave with Beauties of the Spring. }

On the Death of the late Queen.

Whilst Heaven with Envy on the Earth look't down,
Saw us unworthy of the Royal Pair,
And justly claim'd *Maria* as its own,
Yet kindly left the Glorious *William* here:
The Heaven and Earth alike do in the Blessing share:
He makes the Earth, She Heaven our great Allies;
And tho' we mourn, she for our Comfort dyes;
Nor need we fear the rash presumptuous Foe,
Whilst she's our Saint above, and he our King below.

A SONG

(1.)

Tell me, *Aurelia*, tell me pray,
  How long must *Damon* sue;
Prefix the time, and I'll obey,
With Patience wait the happy Day,
  That makes me sure of you.

(2.)

The Sails of Time my Sighs shall blow,
  And make the Minutes glide;
My Tears shall make the Current flow,
  And swell the hastning Tide.

(3.)

The Wings of Love shall fly so fast,
  My hopes mount to sublime,
The Wings of Love shall make more hast,
  Than the swift Wings of time.

The Assignation, a Song.

(1.)

The Minute's past appointed by my Fair,
    The Minute's fled
    And leaves me dead
With Anguish and Despair.

(2.)

My flatter'd Hopes their Flight did make
    With the appointed Hour;
None can the Minute's past o'retake,
    And nought my Hopes restore.

(3.)

Cease your Plaints, and make no Moan,
    Thou sad repining Swain;   10
Although the fleeting Hour be gone,
    The Place doe's still remain.

(4.)

The Place remains, and she may make
    Amends for all your Pain;
Her Presence can past Time o'retake,
    Her Love your Hopes regain.

An Epigram.

Dans vitam panis, nobis dans gaudia vinum
Omnia dans aurum, sunt pretiosa nimis:
Nil commune bonum est, at res est flebilis altera,
Dans, est communis fæmina ubique, nihil.
          In *English*, thus:
Nature's chief Gifts unequally are carv'd;
It surfeits some, while many more are starv'd:
Her Bread, her Wine, her Gold, and what before
Was common Good, is now made private Store:
Nothing that's Good we have among us Common   10
But all enjoy the Common Ill—a Woman.

To a Gentleman, that had his Pocket pick'd of a Watch and some Gold by a Mistress. A Burlesque Letter.

I'm sorry, *Sam*, thour't such a Ninny
To Let a Wench rob thee of Guinea,
And thus to spend and lose your Cobbs,
By lavish opening both your Fobbs:
You're fairly fobb'd, to let her get all,
Both one, and also t'other Mettal.

Your Work was on a pretty Score,
You dug the Mine, she found the Oar; }
The Devil take the cunning Whore.
10 You slily laid her down to rest her,
And on the Bed she found a Tester.
Your Watch too, *Sam*, (these Men of Power
Must lye with Doxies by the Hour)
A Minute's time did that command;
Then her's, it seems, was Minute Hand.
She wound you up to her own liking,
Then stole the Watch, while you were striking:
Then think not, Sir, that you are undone;
What's wound so high, must next be run down:
20 In revelling time you thought no Sin,
To play a Game, at *In and In*.
I wonder tho' you did not win for't,
Since that you were so fairly in for't:
But what destroy'd you in a Trice,
She held the *Box*, you shook the *Dice*:
The Devil was in the Dice then surely, }
To loose when you plaid so securely, }
And *three* to *one* was lay'd so purely. }
But what's the worst of all Mishaps
30 You dread, they say, some After-claps:
If that be so, my dearest *Sammy*,
You'll curse, and bid the Devil dam ye:
The Fruit of *Wild Oats* which you scatter,
Is nothing else but *Barley-water*:
The Seed-time's good, you know my meaning,
But Faith, the Harvest's only gleaning.
Take Heart howe're, 'tis my desire, }
You will revive, the P—x expire; }
Then rise like Phænix from the Fire. }
40 The Mettal's stronger that's well souder'd
And Beef keeps sweeter once 'tis powder'd.
So farwell, *Sam*, and may you ne're want
Such a true faithful humble Servant.

May the 4th, from Temple Inner,
The Post's going out, I in to Dinner.

17 you] your

A
COLLECTION
OF
LETTERS
AND
Other MISCELLANIES.

Grays-Inn, Wensday.

T'is a Presumption to imagine, that you have thought my
Letters worth the keeping, and yet a greater Presumption to
expect you shou'd now return them if you have kept them so
long; but I hope the Design will partly excuse my request: I
have promis'd to equip a Friend with a few Letters to help out
a Collection for the Press, and there are none I dare sooner
expose to the World than those to you, because your Merit
may warrant their Sincerity, and because your Ladyship was
pleas'd to commend them: This makes me imagine, Madam,
that they have still secur'd a Place in your Cabinet, tho' the 10
unworthy Author cou'd merit no room in your Heart; whence
I may infer that they may be as acceptable to you in Print as
in my Manuscript; but if you have a Mind to secure Trophies
of so poor a Conquest, I shall be proud to return them as soon
as ever they are Transcrib'd, for which I now pawn my Word
and Honour, as sincerely, as I once did the Heart of,

MADAM,

Your most humble Servant

---

*Tuesday Morning, one Stocking
on, and t'other off.*

I have had your Letter, Madam, and all that I understand
by it, is that your Hand is as great a Riddle as your Face, and
'tis as difficult to find out your Sense in your Characters, as to
know your Beauty in your Mask; but I have at last conquer'd

the Maidenhead of your writing, as I hope one day I shall that of your Person; and I'm sure you han't lost your Virginity, if the Lines in your Complexion be half so crooked as those in your Letter. I return your Compliment of Advice in the same Number of Particulars that you were pleas'd to send me. First,

10 If you are not hansom, never show a Face that may frighten away that Admirer, which your Wit has engaged. Secondly, Never believe what a Gentleman speaks to you in a Mask, for while the Ladies were double Faces, 'tis but Justice that our Words shou'd bear a double Meaning—Lastly, You must never advise a Man against wandring, if you design to be his Guide. You tell me of swearing to a known Lye; I don't remember, Madam, that I ever swore I lov'd you, tho' I must confess that a little Lady in a half mourning Mantue and a deep Morning Complexion, has run in my Head so much

20 since *Monday* night, that I'm afraid, she will soon get into my Heart: But now Madam, hear my Misfortune.

> *The Angry Fates and dire Stage-Coach*
> *Upon my Liberty incroach,*
> *To bear me hence with many a Jog*
> *From thee my charming dear* Incog.
> *Unhappy Wretch! at once who feels*
> *O'returns of Hack, and Fortune's Wheels.*

This is my Epitaph, Madam, for now I'm a dead Man, and the Stage-Coach may most properly be call'd my Herse,

30 bearing the Corps only of deceas'd *F—r*; for his Soul is left with you, whom he loves above all Womankind; by which you may judge of the height of his Passion; for he cares not one Farthing for your whole Sex, as I hope to be saved.

Thursday, 11 *a Clock.*

Bopeep is Child's Play, and 'tis time for a Man to be tir'd of it; I went yesterday to *Bedlam* upon your mad Assignation, stay'd till Seven like a Fool, to expect one, who, unless she were mad, wou'd never come. I begin to believe that they are only wise that are there, and we possess'd that put them in; they at least have this advantage over us Lunaticks at Liberty, that they find Pleasure in their Frenzy, and we a Torment in our Reason; I was so tir'd with walking there so long, that I could not bear the Fatigue of putting off my Cloaths, but sat up all Night at the Tavern; so that your Letter is but just come to my Hands, when, like *Prince Prettyman*, I have one Boot on and t'other off, Love and Honour have a strong Battel, but here comes my Friend to claim my Engagement, so Love is put to the Rout, and away for *Essex* immediately; but a Word of Advice before we part. Pray consider, Madam, whether your Good or Ill Stars have usually the most Ascendant over your Inclinations, and accordingly prosecute your Intentions of corresponding with me or not; wou'd you be advis'd by me, you wou'd let it alone; for by the Uneasiness that my small Converse has already rais'd in me, I guess at the greater Disturbance of being farther expos'd to your Charms, unless I may hope for something which my Vanity is too weak to ensure. Fortune has always been my Adversary; and I may conclude that Woman, who is much of her Nature, may use me the same way; but if you prove as blind as she, you may, perhaps, love me as much as she hates me. My humble Service to your two Sister Fairies, and so the Devil take you all.

If you will answer this—you may.

Essex, Fryday Morning.

I have been a Horseback, Madam, all this Morning, which has so discompos'd my Hand and Head, that I can hardly think or write Sense; the Posture of my Affairs is a little extraordinary in some other parts about me; for my Saddle was very uneasy, the Hare we hunted put me in mind of a Mistress, which we must Gallop after with hazard of breaking our Necks, and after all our Pains, the Puss may prove a Witch at the long run. I have had no Female in my Company since I left the Town, or any thing of your Sex to entertain me; for your *Essex*-Women, like your *Essex*-Calves, are only Butcher's Meat; and if I must cater for my self, commend me to a Pit Partridge, which comes pretty cheap, and where I have my Choice of a whole Covy; how well I love this kind of

Meat, you may guess, when I assure you, that I have purely
fed upon your Idea ever since, which has stuck as close to me,
as my Shirt; which by the way I han't shifted since I came to
the Countrey; for Clean Linnen is not so modish here as a
Lover might require. I receiv'd just now an impertinent Piece
of Banter from an angry Fair, she says, I pawn'd my Soul to
20 the Devil for the great Success of my Play: But her Ladyship is
thus angry, because I wou'd not pawn my Body to the Devil
for another sort of Play, of which I presume the Lady to be a
very competent Judge; I shall disappoint her now, as
formerly; for I will set her raging mad with the Calmness of
my Answer: Besides, Madam, there is nothing can put me out
of Humour, that comes by that Post which brings me a Line
from you; tho' I must tell you in Plain Terms, that I begin to
have but a mean Opinion of your Beauty; for were it, in the
least, parallel to your Wit, the number of your other
30 Conquests wou'd raise your Vanity above any Correspondence
with a Person, whose chief Merit, is his indifference.

Grays-Inn, Wensday Morning.

The Arguments you made use of last Night for still keeping
on your Mask I endeavour'd to refute with Reason, but that
proving ineffectual, I'll try the Force of Rhime, and send you
the Heads of our Chat in a Poetical Dialogue between you and
I.

You.
Thus Images are veil'd which you adore;
Your Ignorance does raise your Zeal the more.

I.
All Image-Worship for false Zeal is held;
False Idols ought indeed to be conceal'd.

You.
10 *Thus Oracles of old were still receiv'd,*
The more ambiguous, still the more believ'd.

I.
But Oracles of Old were seldom true;
The Devil was in 'um—sure he's not in you.

You.

Thus masqu'd in Mysteries does the Godhead stand,
The more obscure, the greater his Command.

I.

The Godhead's hidden Power wou'd soon be past,
Did we not hope to see his Face at last.

You.

You are my Slave already, Sir, you know,
To shew more Charms wou'd but increase your Woe;   }
I scorn to insult a Conquer'd Foe.

20

I.

I am your Slave, 'tis true; but still you see
All Slaves by Nature struggle to be free:
But if you wou'd secure the stubborn Prise,
Add to your Wit the Fetters of your Eyes:
Then pleas'd with Thraldom would I kiss my Chain,
And ne're think more of Liberty again.

Sunday, after Sermon.

I came, I saw, and was conquer'd; never had Man more to
say, yet can I say nothing; where others go to save their Souls,
there have I lost mine; but I hope that Divinity which has the
justest Title to its Service has receiv'd it; but I will endeavour
to suspend these Raptures for a Moment, and talk calmly.

Nothing upon Earth, Madam, can Charm beyond your
Wit, but your Beauty; after this not to love you, would
proclaim me a Fool; and to say I did, when I thought
otherwise, would pronounce me a Knave: If any Body call'd
me either, I should resent it; and if you but think me either, I   10
shall break my Heart. You have already, Madam, seen
enough of me to create a Liking or an Aversion; your Sense is
above your Sex, then let your Proceeding be so likewise, and
tell me plainly what I have to hope for. Were I to consult my
Merit, my Humility would chide any Shadow of Hope; but
after a Sight of such a Face, whose whole Composition is a
Smile of good Nature, why should I be so unjust as to suspect
you of Cruelty: Let me either live in *London* and be happy, or

retire again to my Desart to check my Vanity that drew me
20 thence; but let me beg to receive my Sentence from your own
Mouth, that I may hear you speak, and see you look at the
same time, then let me be unfortunate if I can.

> *If you are not the Lady in Mourning*
> *that sat upon my Right Hand at*
> *Church, you may go to the Devil,*
> *for I'm sure you're a Witch.*

Madam,

If I han't begun thrice to write, and as often thrown away
my Pen, may I never take it up again; my Head and my Heart
have been at Cuffs about you these two long Hours—Says my
Head, You're a Coxcomb for troubling your Noddle with a
Lady, whose Beauty is as much above your Pretensions, as
your Merit is below her Love. Then answers my Heart, Good
Mr. Head, you're a Blockhead; I know Mr. *F—r*'s Merit
better than you; as for your Part, I know you to be as
whimsical as the Devil, and changing with every new Notion
10 that offers; but for my Share, I am fixt, and can stick to my
Opinion of a Lady's Merit for ever; and if the Fair She can
secure an Interest in me, Monsieur Head, you may go whistle.
Come, come, (answer'd my Head) you Mr. Heart, are always
leading this Gentleman into some Inconvenience or other;
was't not you that first entic'd him to talk to this Lady? Your
damn'd confounded Warmth made him like this Lady, and
your busie Impertinence has made him write to her your
leaping and skipping disturbs his Sleep by Night, and his good
Humour by Day: In short, Sir, I will hear no more on't; I am
20 Head, and I will be obey'd—You lie, Sir, reply'd my Heart,
(being very angry) I am Head in Matters of Love, and if you
don't give your Consent, you shall be forc'd; for I'm sure that
in this Case all the Members will be on my Side. What say
you, Gentlemen Hands? Oh! (say the Hands) we wou'd not
forego the tickling Pleasure of touching a delicious, white, soft
Skin for the World.—Well, what say you, Mr. Tongue?
Zounds, says the Linguist, there's more Extasie in speaking
three soft Words of Mr. Heart's suggesting, than whole

Orations of Seignoir Head's; so I am for the Lady, and here's
my honest Neighbour Lips will stick to't. By the sweet Power 30
of Kisses that we will, (reply'd the Lips.) And presently some
other worthy Members standing up for the Heart, they laid
violent Hands, (*nemine contradicente*) upon poor Head, and
knock'd out his Brains. So now, Madam, behold me as perfect
a Lover as any in *Christendom*, my Heart purely dictating every
Word I say; the little Rebel throws it self into your Power, and
if you don't support it in the Cause it has taken up for your
sake, think what will be the Condition of the Headless and
Heartless

Farquhar. 40

Monday, twelve a Clock at Night.

Give me leave to call you, dear Madam, and to tell you that
I am now stepping into Bed, and that I speak with as much
Sincerity as if I were stepping into my Grave; Sleep is so great
an Emblem of Death, that my Words ought to be as real, as if
I were sure never to waken; then may I never again be blest
with the Light of the Sun, and the Joys of *Wensday*, if you are
not as dear to me as my Hopes of waking Health to Morrow
Morning; your Charms lead me, my Inclinations prompt me,
and my Reason confirms me,

MADAM,   10
Your faithful and humble Servant.
My humble Service to the Lady, who, next to my Savour, must be chief
Mediatour for my Happiness.

Madam,

In Order to your Ladyship's Commands I have sent you
my Thoughts upon your two weighty Maxims of Amorous
Policy,—*If we fly, they pursue*; and *Enjoyment quenches Love*: But I
shall run a greater hazard of your Displeasure by my
Obedience, than I shou'd by the Neglect of your Commands,
these Subjects leading me into more Gravity than is well

consistent with my own Inclinations, or the perusal of a fair Lady. But to the Business.

To examine rightly how far these Female Maxims are in Force, we must dispose Mankind into a Division, which I think hitherto has scap'd the *Logicians*, *to wit*, the Men of Idleness, and Men of Business; under the first Branch of which Distinction is reduceable a great share of the World, and especially that which composes the Character of what we call the *Beau Monde*; for to make them all of a Piece, we must give them a *French* Name too.

The Practice of these Gentlemen, I must confess, has gone a great way to pass these Maxims for Authentick, and have sufficiently authoris'd the Ladies to stick so firmly to their Principles; but wou'd they consider a little upon what a Scurvy Foundation these Topicks are grounded, they wou'd damn the Doctrin for Sake of the Adorers.

These Idle Gentlemen (begging their Pardon for so familiar an Epithet) shou'd show the Ladies what a difference there is between modish intreaguing, and true Love; for these Sparks make intreaguing their Business, and Love only their Diversion. They visit their Mistress as they go to the Park, because it is the Mode, and continue to sollicit her Favour, not thro' the impulse of Passion, but because they have nothing else to do; some other Motives there are to engage these Sparks in the pursuit of a fair Lady; as for instance, upon the Survey of his Rent-Roll the Lover finds two or three thousand a Year still unmortgag'd sends down immediately to his Steward to screw up his Tenants to due Payments, and concludes with *Money conquers all things*; a Potent Proverb, I must confess, to back his Resolution. But here consider, Madam, what it is that pursue you, not the Gentleman, but Fidlers, Masquerades, Jewellers, Glovers, Milleners, hir'd Poets, with the confus'd Equipage of all their respective Trades, the Devil a Dart of Love is in the whole Bundle, no more than there is in the Straw and Oats that keeps a Horse for *New Market*; here are only two Beasts to be back'd, one for Pleasure and t'other for Profit; I will feed one for the Plate, and Pamper the t'other for my own riding.

A second Life to his pursuit is his Vanity; the Beau having receiv'd a Repulse over Night, steps to his Glass in the Morning, and surveying his charming Shape, 'Sdeath, (says he,) *why should I despair of Success? Bloud, I'm as pretty Fellow as another; but I think my Calves are a little of the largest. Ay, that's it, she did not like my Dress Yesterday—Here Boy, reach my blew Coat, I'll tye my Cravat with a double Knot to day, and wear the Buckles of my Garters behind.* Thus while his Foppish Fancy can invent any particular Change or Whimsey in his Dress, his Hopes are nourish'd by an abusive Presumption, that the Ladies are smitten by such *Bagatel* Impertinence. Here indeed, Madam the first Maxim, *If we fly, they pursue,* is in Force; but upon Scurvy Terms; for the Continuation of such a Coxcomb's Address is the greatesst Satyr upon the Sex; and a Woman of true Sense rather than be plagued with such a Follower, if there were no other way, shou'd give him her Person to be quit of his Company; for here I dare be sworn your second Maxim will hold, That *Enjoyment quenches Love.* For these Gentlemen love as they hunt, for Diversion, as I said before; and no sooner is one Hare snapt up, but they beat about for another. Besides, Madam, 'tis but a modest Presumption that these Men of Pleasure and Idleness must have an Ingredient of the Fool in their Composition, which cannot relish the true and lasting Beauties of a fine Woman, they cannot make a true estimate of her Sense, her Constancy, her several little kind and endearing Offices, which can only engage the Affections of a Man that truly understands their Value.

This brings into my Consideration how far these Maxims may be applicable to your corresponding with the latter part of the Distinction, which I call'd the Men of Business; by which I understand Men of Sense, Learning, and Experience, and call them Men of Business, because I wou'd exclude a parcel of flashy, noisy, rhiming, atheistical Gentlemen, who arrogate to themselves the Title of Wit and Sense, for no other Cause but the Abuse of it; such must be rank'd with the first sort of Lovers, for they are the Idlest of Mankind; neither do I confine the Character of a Man of Business to the Law, the Church, the Court, Trade, or any particular Employment; I intend it a farther Latitude, and inclusive of all those, who deriding the Fop, and detesting the Debauchee, have laid down to themselves some certain Scheme of Study, in any lawful Art or Science, for the benefit of the Publick, or their own private Improvement.

Upon this Foundation we may rationally conclude the Actions of such Men to flow directly from the Operations of their Reason. But here, Madam, without doubt the Ladies
90 will interrupt me—*Hold, Sir,* (say they) *we absolutely deny that Love and Reason are consistent.* From which it follows, that your Men of Business have no Business here.

I am very sorry, Madam, in the first Place, that the Qualification which must recommend a Man to a fair Lady, must debase him so near the Level of a Brute, and deprive him of that divine Stamp by which he is distinguish'd from the Beasts of the Field; what an affront is this to your Sex, that one must no sooner begin to admire a Woman, but he must cease to be a Man; and that the Glory which a Lady receives by the
100 plurality of her Adorers, shou'd depend only upon the Esteem of so many irrational Creatures! No, no, Madam, I am too much a Courtier to let this vulgar Calumny and severe Reflection upon your Sex pass unexamin'd.

I shall therefore make bold to say, that this very Opinion touching the Inconsistency of Love with Reason has cost the fair Sex more Tears, and have subjected Men to more Curses, than the worst Circumstances of Falshood and Perjury; for depending upon this Principle of the Ladies, the greatest Rascals have appeared the most passionate Lovers, because
110 the greatest Knaves make the best Fools; and the most usual Cloak for natural Villany is an artificial Simplicity.

But granting such Follies and Absurdities to be the Results of a real Passion, such Love ought not to gain one Grain the more weight in the Ballance of true Sense; for if the Lover be a Fool, this Extravagance is but what's natural to his Temper, and esposes it self as wildly in the effects of his other ordinary Passions, as in Anger, Fear, Joy, Grief, and the like; and must not properly be call'd the strength of his Love, but the Weakness of his Reason; and the same pitch of Passion that
120 may make a *Witall* appear Lunatick, wou'd scarcely be discernable in a *Dorimant*; but if the Force of Love raise a Man of true Sence to the pitch of Playing the Fool, 'tis then, if not more rediculous, at least much more dangerous in the Consequence; for be assur'd, Madam, that the bent of his Desire must be too violent to last long; and once it begins to decline, 'twill prove as violent in the Fall as in the Rise; and

the constant result of a sober Reflection, is the Hatred and Detestation of any thing that had made him guilty of Extravagance, and debas'd him below the Dignity of his Reason; and there is no Medium in this Case between the 130 extravagant Lover and the inveterate Enemy.

But begging your Ladyship's Pardon for this Digression, I shall return to my Man of Business, and see how far your Principle, *If we fly they pursue*, is applicable to a Person of this Character.

To the Examination of this Point, 'twill not be amiss to consider, the several Paces and Proceedings of such a Lover in his Amour. A Man of Business and Study has his Thoughts too round and compact within himself to have his Fancy sallying out upon the appearance of every Beauty that his 140 daily Conversation may throw in his way; but if once it lights upon that Fair, which can rouse him from his Indifference, raising a Pleasure in his Eyes when she's present, and an Uneasiness in his Heart in her Absence, 'tis no Imprudence to indulge the Thought; Love (he considers) is a Blessing; and since it depends so much upon a Sympathy of Natures, why mayn't I expect that the fair Creature, who has rais'd such Emotions in me, may in time perhaps be brought to have a mutual Concern upon her? The Happiness that I may expect from her Love, if her other Qualities be proportionable to her 150 Beauty, will infinitely reward the Pains of my inquiring into her Life and Conversation. Here is the Foundation of Love fairly laid; and now my Gentlemen goes to work upon the Structure; he first enquires into the Ladies Character, but that as a Man of Sense ought to do, without trusting the Malice of some that may be her Enemies, nor yet consulting the Partiality of her Friends; his Reason may make a tolerable good Ballance between both; and if perhaps some Slip in her Conduct has made the Scale of her Accusation the heaviest, he has some Grains of Love to throw into the other to 160 counterpoise it. His next Business is to gain admittance to her Company; here he may find a thousand Beauties to augment, or as many Failings perhaps to destroy his Passion; and to his Examination he must refer his Judgment upon the different Characters he might have heard of her before; for no reasonable Man will peremptorily conclude from the Mouth

of Common Fame; 'tis a notorious Lyar, and generally in Extreams: If he beleives it to the Lady's Prejudice, he may wrong her Innocence past Redress; and if he trusts flying
170 Report in her Favour, he may be impos'd upon himself: For the Vulgar (by which I mean the Lac'd Coat as well as the Hobnail) cannot enter into the nice Secrets of Female Behaviour, they sometimes mistake Levity for Freedom, ill Humour for Gravity, Noise and Tattle for Wit and Sense; sometimes they change Hands, and call an Air of good Breeding, Coquetry; they brand Affability and good Nature with the Name of Looseness; and, in short, there can be no such thing as a Woman in their Estimate, all must be Angels, or all Devils: Now my Lover shall find out all these
180 Distinctions, he shall, in spight of Female Dissimulation, search to the very Bottom, and discover the least Paint upon the Mind, as he does that upon the Face. Having found the Lady's Temper conformable to his own, or being at least assur'd that he can frame his own Humour to square with hers, having known her Sense and Understanding sufficient for a prudent Conduct, at least plyable to good Advice, he stands fixt in his Resolution, and resolv'd upon his Affection.

Thus the beautiful Edifice of Love is gradually and firmly rais'd, whereof Reason is still the Corner-stone; not like the
190 trifling Pomp of a Fop's Preparation, which like a Lord-Mayor's Pageant, is built in a Night, Glitters, and is gaz'd at for a Day, and the next dwindles into nothing. The Building thus finish'd, the next Business is to invite the fair Guest; 'tis impossible to confine the Rules of his Address to any particular Observation, because they may be so diversify'd by the Circumstances of the Lover, the Accidents of Time, Place, or according to some Humours and Inclinations in the Lady's Temper, which last have always prov'd the most effectual means of gaining a Heart: If the Lady's Disposition be
200 inclinable to Gayety, he makes the Muses speak a good Word for him; he can dispense in an Evening with a very dull Play, to have the Pleasure of acting the Lover himself; nay, he can comply so far, as to commend a very Dull Thing, if his Mistress is pleas'd to approve it; he can take a turn in the *Mall*

171 Lac'd] Laid. Farquhar clearly means to indicate a well-dressed man. 'Laid' would mean 'pawned'.

with his Hat off, tho' the Weather by very cold, and join with
her in railing at my Lord Such-a-one, or Mistriss Such-a-one,
tho' perhaps he understands the Quarrel to be no more than a
Pique, or a piece of Malice. If the Lady's Temper be more
Grave and Sedate, he can sit an Hour or two condemning the
Vices of the Town, and extolling the Pleasures of a Countrey 210
Life; nay, sometimes perhaps he may have a Fling at the
Government, and be a little *Jacobitish* to please her; he can
wait on her to Church, and hear a *Levite* thump Dust and
Nonsense out of a Pulpit Cushion for an Hour, and call it an
excellent Sermon, to humour her Approbation; with a
thousand other little foolish Fancies, which because they are
not very hurtful in themselves, and that Custom has brought
them into Play, must be born with upon this Occasion; and
when all is done, Ceremony looks as decently in Love, as in
Religion; and a Clown in an Intreague makes as awkard a 220
Figure as a *Quaker* in Church. Our Love therefore writes,
visits, sighs, declares his Passion with all Demonstrations of
Submission and Sincerity, all which is often repeated, to save
the Lady's Modesty, and to sooth a little pleasing Vanity,
incident to the Female Sex of seeing themselves admir'd. He is
satisfy'd also that the World shou'd know it, and submits to
the Censure of a whining Coxcomb, to favour the Lady's
yeilding by the plausible Excuse of a hard Siege; but if after all
this he finds his Pretensions to no Purpose, your Maxim,
Madam, *If we fly*, etc. will not be of force to detain him longer; 230
he has the same Thread of Reason to guide him out of the
Labarinth that led him in; he has not perhaps the same
Supports to his Hope, that every glittering Spark, with a
Coach and Six, can pretend; but were his Fortune ever so
considerable, he wou'd not affront the Lady's Honour, nor his
own Judgment so far, as to suppose her of a Mercenary
Temper; neither can he imagine that the Charming Fair,
whose Sense he has so much admir'd, shou'd be captivated
with the tying of his Cravat, or the Fancy of his Snush-box.
No, no, he is rather convinc'd, that there is something 240
disagreeable to the Lady in his Person, Behaviour, or
Conversation, which being a Defect of Nature, or Education,
he must patiently submit to, without cutting his Throat; and
he's the more willing to take up with his Failings, because

Time may perhaps produce some other Lady that may value him upon these very Circumstances, that made the first disdain him; so that in spight of your celebrated Maxim, he betakes himself to his Business, has the good Manners to free the Lady from his Impertinence, and the Prudence to
250 disingage himself of the Trouble; neither is he much distress'd to withdraw his Affections; for as the prospect of Happiness was the first Foundation of his Love, so the Progress of his Passion must have been nourish'd with Favours to keep it alive, and as naturally without this Fuel with the Fire go out of it self.

I have already, Madam, so far transgressed the Bounds of a *Billet-doux*, that I'm afraid to meddle with your second Maxim: But give me a Moment's Patience, Madam, and I'll make quick Work with *Enjoyment quenches Love*: One Simile,
260 Madam, and I take my Leave. What a strange and unaccountable Madness wou'd it appear in a Subject of *England*, a Gentleman that enjoys Peace and Plenty, Ease and Luxury, if he, discontented with his happy State, shou'd raise a Combustion in his Country, turn ambitious Rebel, make a Party against his Prince, and by Force and Treachery lay hold upon the Government, and all this for the bare Pleasure of being call'd King. I can assure you, Madam, did the Pleasures of a Monarch consist in nothing more than being plac'd in a Throne, with a Crown upon his Head, and the Scepter in his
270 Hand, we should have the upstart Prince use his Government as a Fool does a fair Lady after Enjoyment, he wou'd soon be cloy'd with his Desire, and uneasie till he got quit of it. But if our *Noll* understood the Policy of Government, the many Glories that attend a Crown, the Pomp of Dependencies, the Sweets of absolute Power, with the many Delights and Joys that attend his Royalty, he would maintain his Station to the last Drop of Blood. This is easily applicable to a Man of Sense gaining the Crown of Beauty, he can judge the Charms of his Possession, and values Enjoyment only as the Title to his
280 greater Pleasures, there are a thousand Cupids attending the Throne of Love, all which have their several pretty Offices and serviceable Duties to exhilarate their Masters Joy, and

262 Gentleman] Gentlemen

contribute to his constant Diversion, if he but understands
how to employ them.

How far, Madam, I have recommended to you the
Addresses of an ingenious Man I dare not determine; but I'm
afraid I have said so much against the Passion of Fools, that I
have ruin'd my own Interest; tho' you can't reckon me among
the Idle part of Men, being so happily imployed this Morning
by the Commands of so fair a Lady.   290

> *Your Ladyship's most Humble Servant.*

> *Friday Night*, 11 *a Clock*.

If you find no more Rest from your Thoughts in Bed than I
do, I cou'd wish you, Madam, to be always there, for there I
am most in Love. I went to the Play this Evening, and the
Musick rais'd my Soul to such a pitch of Passion, that I was
almost mad with Melancholy. I flew thence to *Spring-Garden*,
where with envious Eyes I saw every Man pick up his Mate,
whilst I alone walked like solitary *Adam* before the Creation of
his *Eve*; but the Place was no Paradise to me; nothing I found
entertaining but the Nightingale, which methought in sweet
Notes like your own pronounc'd the Name of my dear   10
Penelope—*As the Fool thinketh, the Bell chinketh*. From hence I
retir'd to the Tavern, where methought the shining Glass
represented your fair Person, and the sparkling Wine within
it, look'd like your lively Wit and Spirit: I met my dear
Mistress in every thing, and I propose presently to see her in a
lively Dream, since the last thing I do, is to kiss her dear
Letter, clasp her charming Idea in my Arms, and so fall fast
asleep.

> *My Morning Songs, my Evening Pray'rs,*
> *My daily Musings, Nightly Cares.*   20

> Adieu.

Here am I drinking, Madam, at the Sign of the Globe; and
it shall go hard but I make the Voyage of old Sir *Drake* by to
morrow morning: We have a fresh Gale and a round Sea; for
here is very good Company and excellent Wine; from the Orb

in the Sign I will step to the Globe of the Moon, thence make the Tour of all the Planets, and fix in the Constellation of *Venus*. You see, Madam, I am elevated already. Here's a Gentleman tho' who swears, he loves his Mistress better than I do mine, but if I don't make him so drunk that he shall disgorge his Opinion, may I never drink your Health again; the generous Wine scorns to lye upon a Traytor's Stomach, 'tis Poyson to him that profanes Society by being a Rogue in his Cups. I wish Dear Madam, with all my Heart that you saw me in my present Circumstances, you wou'd certainly fall in Love with me, for I am not my self, I am now the pleasantest foolish Fellow that ever gain'd a Lady's Heart, and a Glass or two more will fill me with such Variety of Impertinence, that I cannot fail to pass for agreeable. You Drawer, bring me a Plate of Ice—Ha! How the Wine whizes upon my Heart, *Cupid* is forging his Love-Darts in my Belly—Ice, you Dog, Ice—The Son of a Whore has brought me Anchoves. Well! This is a vexatious World, I wish I were fairly out of it, and happy in Heaven, I mean your dear Arms; which is the constant Prayer of your humble Servant, Drunk or Sober.

> *I design to Morrow in the Afternoon*
> *to beg your Pardon for all the ill*
> *Manners of my Debauch, and make*
> *my self as great as an Emperour*
> *by inviting your Ladyship to the*
> *Entertainment of* Dioclesian.

In pursuance to your Order, Madam, I have sent you here inclos'd, my Picture; and I challenge *Vandike* or *Kneller* to draw more to the Life. You are the first Person that ever had it, and if I had not some Thoughts that the Substance would fall to your share, I wou'd not part with my Likeness. I hope the Colours will never fade, tho' you may give me some Hints where to mend the Features, having so much Power to correct the Life.

The Picture.

My Outside is neither better nor worse than my Creator

made it, and the Piece being drawn by so great an Artist, 'twere Presumption to say there were many stroaks amiss. I have a Body qualify'd to answer all the Ends of its Creation, and that's sufficient.

As to the Mind, which in most Men wears as many Changes as their Body, so in me 'tis generally drest like my Person, in Black. Melancholy is its every Day Apparel; and it has hitherto found few Holydays to make it change its Cloaths. In short, my Constitution is very Splenatick, and yet very Amorous, both which I endeavour to hide, lest the former shou'd offend others, and the latter might incommode my self; and my Reason is so vigilant in restraining these two Failings that I am taken for an easy-natur'd Man with my own Sex, and an ill-natur'd Clown by yours.

'Tis true, I am very sparing in my Praises and Complements to a Lady out of a fear that they may affect my self more than her; for the Idols that we worship are generally of our own making; and tho' at first Men may not speak what they think, yet truth may catch them on t'other Hand, and make them think what they speak. But most of all am I cautious of promising, especially upon that weighty Article of Constancy, because in the first Place, I have never try'd the Strength of it in my own Experience; and, secondly, I suppose a Man can no more engage for his Constancy than for his Health, since I believe they both equally depend upon a certain Constitution of Body, and how far, and how frequently that may be lyable to Alteration especially in Affairs of Love, let the more Judicious determine.

But so far a Man may promise, that if he find not his Passion grounded on a false Foundation, and that he have a continuance of the same Sincerity, Truth, and Love to engage him; that then his Reason, his Honour and his Gratitude may prove too strong for all changes of Temper and Inclination.

I am a very great Epicure, for which Reason I hate all Pleasure that's purchas'd by excess of Pain; I am quite different from the Opinion of Men that value what's dearly bought, long Expectation makes the blessing always less to me, for by often thinking of the future Joy I make the Idea of it familiar to me, and so I lose the great Transport of Surprise;

9 Artist] Artists   20 restraining] restraing

'tis keeping the Springs of Desire so long upon the Rack, till at last they grow loose and enervate; besides, any one of a
50 Creative Fancy by a Duration of Thought, will be apt to frame too great an Idea of the Object, and so make the greater part of his Hopes end in a Disappointment.

I am seldom troubled with what the World calls Airs and Capriches; and I think it an Ideot's Excuse for a foolish Action, to say, It was my Humour. I hate all little malicious Tricks of vexing People for Trifles, or tiezing them with frightful Stories, malicious Lies, stealing Lapdogs, tearing Fans, breaking China, or the Like; I can't relish the Jest that vexes another in earnest; in short, if ever I do a wilful Injury,
60 it must be a very great one.

I am often Melancholy, but seldom angry; for which Reason I can be severe in my Resentment, without injuring my self: I think it the worst Office to my Nature to make my self uneasy for what another shou'd be punish'd.

I am easily deceiv'd, but then I never fail at last to find out the Cheat; my Love of Pleasure and Sedateness makes me very Secure, and the same Reason makes me very diligent when I'm alarm'd.

I have so natural a Propensity to Ease, that I cannot
70 chearfully fix to any Study, which bears not a Pleasure in the Application, which makes me inclineable to Poetry above any thing else.

I have very little Estate, but what lies under the Circumference of my Hat; and shou'd I by any Mischance come to loose my Head, I shou'd not be worth a Groat; but I ought to thank Providence that I can by Three Hours Study live One and Twenty with Satisfaction my self, and contribute to the Maintenance of more Families than some who have Thousands a Year.
80   I have something in my outward Behaviour, which gives Strangers a worse Opinion of me, than I deserve; but I am more recompenc'd by the Opinion of my Acquaintance, which is as much above my Desert.

I have many Acquaintance, very few Intimates, but no Friend, I mean in the old Romantick way; I have no Secrets so weighty, but what I can bear in my own Breast; nor any Duels to fight, but what I may engage in without a Second; nor can I love after the old Romantick Discipline; I wou'd have my

Passion, if not led, yet at least, waited on by my Reason; and the greatest Proof of my Affection, that a Lady must expect, is 90 this: I wou'd run any Hazard to make us both happy, but wou'd not for any transitory Pleasure make either of us Miserable.

> *If ever, Madam, you come to know*
> *the Life of this Piece, as well as*
> *he that drew it, you will conclude,*
> *that I need not subscribe the Name*
> *to the Picture.*

Well! Mrs. *V*— and my Charming *Penelope* are to lye together to Night; what wou'd I give now, to be a Mouse, (God bless us) behind the Hangings, to hear the Chat; you don't know, Madam, but my Genius which always attends you, may over-hear your Discourse; therefore not one Word of *George*; I'm resolv'd to have a Friend to lye with me to Night, that I may quit Scores with you; and it shall go hard but I prove as kind to my Companion, as you are to yours; tho' I must confess, that I had rather be in Mrs. *V*—'s Place, with all the little Pillows about me, or in that of Monsieur *Adonis* upon the 10 Chair.

> *My Rival is a Dog of Parts,*
> *That captivates the Ladies Hearts;*
> *And yet by* Jove, *(I scorn to forge)*
> Adonis *self must yield to* George.
> *I am a Dog as well as he,*
> *Can fawn upon a Lady's Knee;*
> *My Ears as long, and I can bark,*
> *To guard my Mistress in the Dark:*
> *I han't four Legs, that's no hard Sentence,*
> *For I can paw, and scrape Acquaintance.*   20
> *I am a Dog that Admires you;*
> *And I'm a Dog, if this ben't true.*
> *And if* Adonis *do's outrival me,*
> *Then I'm a greater Son of a Bitch than he:*
> *Reach my Wastcoat—but ne'er trouble it,*
> *I am already a Dog in a Doublet.*

9 be in] bein

Was ever such a poetical Puppy seen? But when my
Mistriss is sick, 'tis then *Dog Days* with me; tho' 'tis but a
30 Cur's trick, I must confess; but I wou'd be content to bark at
this Rate all my Life, so I might hunt away all Rats and Mice
from my fair Angel, whose fearful Temper is the only Mark of
Mortality about her. The Remembrance of the Water-Rat last
Night has inspir'd me with the following Lines.

> *Fair* Rosamond *did little think*
> *Her Christal Pond shou'd turn a Sink,*
> *To harbour Vermin that might swim,*
> *And frighten Beauties from the Brim.*
> *Henceforth, detested Pond, no more*
40 *Shall Beauties crown your Verdant Shore;*
> *Your Waves so fam'd for amorous League,*
> *Are now turn'd Ratsbane to Intreague.*

> *Now good Morrow, my fair Creature,*
> *and let me know how you are reco-*
> *ver'd from your Fright.*

Why shou'd I write to my dearest *Penelope*, when I only
trouble her with reading what she won't believe; I have told
my Passion, my Eyes have spoke it, my Tongue pronounc'd it,
and my Pen declar'd it; I have sigh'd it, swore it, and
subscrib'd it; now my Heart is full of you, my Head raves of
you, and my Hand writes to you; but all in vain; if you think
me a Dissembler; use me generously like a Villain, and
discard me for ever; but if you will be so just to my Passion, as
to beleive it sincere, tell me so, and make me happy; 'tis but
10 Justice, Madam, to do one or t'other.
Your Indisposition last Night when I left you, put me into
such Disorder, that not finding a Coach, I miss'd my way, and
never minded whither I wander'd, till I found my self close by
Tyburn. When blind Love guides, who can forbear going
astray? Instead of laughing at my self, I fell to pittying poor
Mr. *F—r*, who, whilst he rov'd abroad among your whole
Sex, was never out of his way; and now by a single She was led
to the Gallows: From the Thoughts of Hanging, I naturally
entred upon those of Matrimony. I consider'd how many

Gentlemen have taken a Hansom Swing to avoid some inward 20
Disquiets; then why shou'd not I hazard the Noose, to ease me
of my Torment? Then I consider'd, whether I shou'd send for
the Ordinary of *Newgate*, or the Parson of St. *Ann*'s; but
considering my self better prepar'd for dying in a fair Lady's
Arms, than on the Three Leg'd Tree, I was the most
inclinable to the Parish Priest; besides, if I dy'd in a fair
Lady's Arms, I shou'd be sure of *Christian* Burial at least, and
shou'd have the most beautiful Tomb in the Universe. You
may imagine, Madam, that these Thoughts of Mortality were
very Melancholy, but who cou'd avoid the Thoughts of Death, 30
when you were sick? And if your Health be not dearer to me
than my own, may the next News I hear be your Death, which
wou'd be as great a Hell as your Life and Welfare is a Heaven
to the most Amorous of his Sex.

> *Pray let me know in a Line, whether*
> *you are better or worse, whether I*
> *am Honest or a Knave, and whe-*
> *ther I shall live or dye.*

I can no more let a Day pass without seeing, or writing to
my Dear *Penelope*, than I can slip a Minute without thinking of
her: I know no body can lay a juster Claim to the Account of
my Hours than she, who has so indisputable a Title to my
Service, and I can no more keep the discovery of my Faults
from you, than from my own Conscience, because you
compose so great a Part of my Devotion; let me therefore
confess to my dearest Angel, how last Night I saunter'd to the
Fountain, where some Friends waited for me; one of 'em was a
Parson, who Preaches over any thing but his Glass had not his 10
Company and Sunday Night sanctify'd the Debauch, I shou'd
be very fit for Repentance this Morning; the searching Wine
has sprung the Rheumatism in my Right Hand, my Head
akes, my Stomach pukes; I dream'd all this Morning of Fire,
and waken in a Flame: To compleat my Misery I must let you
know all this, and make you angry with me. I design tho' this
Afternoon to repair to St. *Ann*'s Prayers, to beg Absolution of

10 any] [om.] The word 'any' appears as catchword on p. 92 of the first edition but
is omitted on p. 93.

my Creator and my Mistress; if both prove merciful, I'll put
on the Resolution of amending my Life, to fit me for the Joys
20 of Heaven and you.

Dear Madam,
    Now I write with my aking Hand the Dictates of my aking
Heart; my Body, and my Soul are of a Piece; both uneasy for
want of my dear *Penelope*. Excuse me, Madam, for troubling
you with my Distemper; but my Hand is so ill, that it can
write nothing else, because it can go no farther.

    Misfortunes always lay hold on me, when I forsake my
Love, or fall short of my Duty; your Coach was full, and
Mr. C—*r* was vanish'd; so I had no pretence left to avoid some
sober Friends, that wou'd haul me into a Cellar to drink
Syder; a dark, chilly, confounded hole, fit only for Treason
and Tobacco. Being warm with the throng of the Play-house,
I unadvisedly threw off my Wig, the Rawness of this cursed
Place, with the Coldness of our Tipple, has siez'd upon me so
violently, that I'm afraid I shan't recover it in a Trice; I have
10 got such a Pain in my Jaws, that I shan't be able to eat a Bit;
so now, Madam, I must either Live upon Love, or starve; for
Heaven's Sake then, dear Madam, send me a little Subsistance;
let not a hungry Wretch perish for want of an Alms. Your
Charity, for the Lord's Sake. Kind Words is all I crave; and
the most uncharitable Prelate will afford a Begger his
Blessing—Pity my Condition, fair Charmer, I have got a Cold
without, and a Fire within; Love and Syder do not agree; so
I'll have no more Cellars. If you don't send me some Comfort
in my Afflictions, expect to have a Note to this purpose—Be
20 pleas'd to Accompany the Corps of an unfortunate Lover, who
dy'd of an aking Chops, and a broken Heart.

    Your Verses, Madam, I have read, scan'd, and consider'd
over and over; I must still complain of the Difficulty of your
Characters, but your Sense is like a rich Mine, hard to come
at, but when found, an infinite Treasure. I wou'd answer you
in Verse, but for the Reason that follows.

Of all the specious Wiles and formal Arts
Us'd by our young intreaguing Men of Parts,
None can their Ignorance in Love express
So much, as whining Words in fawning Verse.
The Nymph, whose softer Breast soft Numbers gain,
Must have a Soul celestially serene,
Seraphically bright, and sparkling as her Mien.
But Women now that Character disown,
They are all Mortal, very Mortal grown.
By Verse was Beauty's Empire first ordain'd,
And stubborn Man to Love, by Verse, was chain'd.
Verse gave to Love his Quiver and his Bow,
Nay even from Verse he had his Godhead too.
And now ungrateful Beauty scorns that Aid,
By which its greatest Triumphs first were made.
A sordid Blockhead with an empty Scull
Shall have Access, because his Pocket's full.
Curse on thee, Gold—why Charmer, tell me why
Shou'd that which buys a Horse, bright Beauty buy?
O cou'd I find (Grant Heaven that once I may)
A Nymph fair, kind, poetical, and gay,
Whose Love shou'd blaze, unsully'd, and divine,
Lighted at first by the bright Lamp of mine.
Free as a Mistress, faithful as a Wife,
And one that lov'd a Fiddle as her Life;
Free from all sordid Ends, from Interest free,
For my own Sake affecting only me.
What a blest Union shou'd our Souls combine!
I hers alone, and she be only mine.
Free generous Favours shou'd our Flames express
I'd write for Love, and she shou'd love for Verse.
In deathless Numbers shou'd my fair one shine,
Her Love, her Charms shou'd blazon every Line,
And the whole Page be, like her self, Divine.
Not Sacharissa's self, great Waller's Fair,
Shou'd for an endless Name with mine compare
My Lines shou'd run so high, the World shou'd see
I sung of her, and she inspired me.
Vain are thy Wishes, wretched Damon, vain,
Thy Verse can only serve thee to complain:

10

20

30

40

Wealth makes the Bargain, Love's become a Trade,
Blind Love is now by blinder Fortune led.
Who then wou'd sing, or sacred Numbers boast,
Since Love, the just Reward of Verse, is lost?
50 *Of the soft Sex why were the Muses made,*
If in soft Love they can't afford us Aid?
No, Cupid, no, you have deceiv'd too long,
My Muse and Love have ever done me wrong; ⎱
Farewel, ungrateful Love, farewel ungrateful Song. ⎰

You see, Madam, that my Rhime has argu'd me out of
Love; but I'm violently suspicious that my Reason will
convince me, that I am still as much your Captive, as ever; for
I have the greatest Inclination in the World to intreat the
Favour of meeting your Ladyship in the Park to Morrow by
60 Six; if you tarry till Seven, you may find me at the End of the
Lover's Walk, hanging upon one of the Trees, which will be
the readiest way, for ought I see, to bring our Amour to a
Conclusion. I am an impudent Fellow; that's to prevent your
Reflection upon my presuming to appoint you a Place of
assignation.

If any thing shou'd come to your Hands, Madam, that I
writ last Night, I humbly beg that you wou'd pardon it's
Impertinence; for I was so fudled, that I hardly remember
whether I writ or not; you'll think perhaps that my Excuse
needs as much an Apology as my Fault; but you ought to
forgive me, when I assure you, that I shall never forgive my
self; I have vow'd this Morning never to taste Wine till I can
recover that Opportunity of seeing you, that Wine made me
loose; I went to the *Royal-Exchange* at Two, and stay'd in the
10 City till Twelve at Night; I din'd with Mr. *M—x*, who (by the
way) is a pretty Gentleman, but has a confounded Wife; such
Stories have I heard of her Persecution, and his long Suffering,
that he deserves to go to Heaven, and she to Hell for sending
him; and so much for a Citizens Wife. I come now from Mr.
Dryden's Funeral, where we had an Ode in *Horace* Sung,
instead of *David*'s Psalms; whence you may find, that we don't

10 *M—x*] ed.; *B—x* The intended reading was doubtless *M—x*, a reference to
Peter Anthony Motteux. See Commentary.

think a Poet worth *Christian* Burial; the Pomp of the Ceremony
was a kind of Rhapsody, and fitter, I think, for *Hudibras* than
him; because the Cavalcade was mostly Burlesque; but he was
an extraordinary Man, and bury'd after an extraordinary 20
Fashion; for I do believe there was never such another Burial
seen; the Oration indeed was great and ingenious, worthy the
Subject, and like the Author, whose Prescriptions can restore
the Living, and his Pen embalm the Dead. And so much for
Mr. *Dryden*, whose Burial was the same with his Life; Variety,
and not of a Piece. The Quality and Mob, Farce and
Heroicks; the Sublime and Redicule mixt in a Piece, great
Cleopatra in a Hackney Coach.

And now, Madam, for the Application; let us consider, that
we are all mortal, that neither Wit can protect a Man, nor 30
Beauty a Woman from the impertinence of a Burial: There is
but one way, let us joyn our Forces to disappoint it, as thus;
Beauty causes Love, Love inspires Poetry, and Poetry makes
Wit immortal: So in return, Wit is fir'd with Gratitude, that
extols your Charms, and so makes Beauty immortal. Now,
Madam, if your Beauty can make as mad work in my Head as
it has in my Heart, I will show the World such a Copy of your
Countenance, that you shall be as fair a hundred Years hence,
as you are at this Instant; all the Worms in the Church-yard
shall not have Power to touch one Feature in your Face; and, 40
for my part, if I am not more a Poet a hundred Years hence,
than I am now, I'll be damn'd. And I can assure you, that
Mr. *Dryden* had never dy'd, had he not grown too old to please
the Ladies; and if that be my Case already, the Lord have
Mercy upon me.

Your strange and unexpected Declaration of your unkind
Thoughts of me, has cast a Damp upon my Spirits that will
break out either in Melancholy or Rage; I wish it prove the
latter, for then I shall destroy my self the shorter way; in the
Fervency of my Passion, and diligence of Courtship, which
has allarm'd part of the World. To be accus'd of Coldness and
Neglect, is—but I'll say no more upon that Subject, 'tis too
warm; and if I touch it, will set me in a Blaze. I remember the
Cause of my Uneasiness t'other Day, and I remember that
Cause was repeated last Night; and in short, I remember a 10

thousand things that make me mad; and since you have taken so opportune a Time of telling me of the Coldness of my Love; give me leave to tell you, that my Passion is so violent, that 'twill give me Cause to Curse your whole Sex; nay, even you, tho' at the same time I cou'd stab my self for the Expression; now, Madam, I'll endeavour to sleep, for I han't clos'd my Eyes since I saw you.

Hague, October the 23rd, New Stile.

This is the second Post, dear Madam, since I have heard from you, which makes me apprehensive that you are not well, or that you have forgot the Person, whose Health and Welfare so intirely depends upon yours: I am proud to say, that all my Words, my Letters, and Endeavours, have unfeignedly run upon the strain of the most real Passion that ever possest the Breast of Man; and if, after all this, they shou'd all prove vain, I leave you to judge how poor an Opinion I shou'd have of my Understanding; which must be a very mortifying Thought for 10 a Person who is very unwilling to pass for a Fool. 'Tis true, I have laid out all the little Sense I had in your Service, and if it shou'd be cast away, I shou'd turn Bankrupt in my Understanding, and run stark mad upon the Loss. For God's sake, Madam, let me know what I have to trust to, that I may once more set up for a Man of some Parts, or else run away from my Senses as fast as I can; my Thoughts begin to be very severe Creditors, and I am perfectly tir'd of their Company. The *King* came hither last Night about Eleven from *Loo*; and if the Weather prove fair, designs for *England* next *Wensday*. 20 Providence has design'd my staying so long, out of his great Mercy to secure me from the violence of a terrible Storm, which has lasted here this Fortnight past, to that degree, that *Holland* is no more at present than a great Leaky Man of War, tossing on the Ocean, and the Mariners are forc'd to pump Night and Day to keep the Vessel above Water. I can assure you, without a Jest, that the Cellars and Canals have frequent Communication, and happy is he that can lodge in a Garret: There are Fellows planted on all the Steeples, with a considerable Reward to him that can make the first Land, tho' 30 they had more need to look out for a Rainbow, for without that I shall believe that God Almighty, in his Articles with *Noah* after the Floud, has excluded the *Dutch* out of the Treaty: I have transcrib'd your Letter to my Lord *A—le*, and will consult with Captain *L—oe* about your Affairs, whither it be proper to mention matters now, or defer it till we come over: My Lord *West—nd* treated us yesterday with a Pot of *English* Venison sent him by his Mother. But never was poor Buck so devour'd by hungry Hounds; we hunted him down with excellent *Burgundy*—Cou'd this Place afford as good Toasts as it does Wine, 'twere a Paradise. But we made a shift to call 40 you all over, every Beauty in *London*, from the D—ss of *G—n* to Mrs. *B—le*; and when we got drunk, we toasted the *Dutch* Ladies; and by the time we got thro' the whole Assembly, we were grown as dull and sottish as if we had lain with them. You must pardon my Breeding, Madam, and consider where I am; but I do blush a little, and can't say a Word more, but that I am,

MADAM,

Your faithful and humble Servant.

I receiv'd your Letter, Madam, with the strange Relation of your being robb'd. I can't tell whether my Grief or Amazement was greatest, it suspended the Pain of the Rheumatism for some Hours, tho' I gain'd little by that; for it only gave Place to a greater. All the Consolation I can afford in your Sorrow, is, that you have a Companion in your Afflictions that sympathizes in every Particular of your Grief. I consider my self a Lady robb'd of my fine things, strip'd of my best Cloaths, and what is worse, of all my pretty Trinkets that have cost me some Years in purchasing; tho' this be the greatest 10 Misfortune a fine Lady can sustain, yet am I still more troubled at the manner of the Action, than at the Greatness of my Loss, that in a House so well peopled as mine, in an Hour so early, when all the World was awake, that all my good Stars shou'd then be asleep, is very provoking.

By this, Madam, you may judge, whether my Heart be not

42 Mrs.] Mr.

tun'd to the very same Notes of Sorrow with yours; and as I
have the same Reasons of my Grief, so perhaps I shall agree
with your Ladyship as to the Thoughts which may afford you
20 most Consolation.

Religion teaches me, that nothing in this World is properly
our own, but borrow'd; and since I am oblig'd to resign even
my very Life without murmuring, when he that lent is pleas'd
to recall it, why shou'd I repine at parting with things of so
much less Importance? But to comfort my self after a more
worldly manner, I consider that my Cloaths had been worn
out in a Year or two, that my fine things had been out of
Fashion in a Year or two more, so that I have only lost the use
of those things which four or five Years wou'd have robb'd me
30 of without breaking a Lock, or opening a Window. Besides,
another thing which gives me no small Comfort is, a
Reflection on the Mercies of Providence in matters of greater
Moment, as in Relation to my Life, my Honour, &c. one
instance of which is pretty fresh in my Memory. I recollect
that some few Months ago, I was in a foreign Countrey, far
from my Relations to comfort me, or Friends to assist me; a
Stranger to the Place, more to the Language; like a Child
among Savage Beasts, I had no Companion but a Brute more
Savage than they, who betray'd me into the Hands of a
40 Villain, that wou'd have ruin'd me past Redemption, had not
Providence sent a Gentleman to my rescue, who is now at
Richmond dying for Love of me. This Deliverance, I think, may
make sufficient amends for the present Loss.

Now, Madam, that I have guess'd at your Thoughts upon
the matter, give me leave to present you with my own
Sentiments upon this Affair; and in the first Place I think that
if the Rogues had strip'd you of all that you enjoy in the
World, even the white Covering to your fair Nakedness, I
wou'd catch you in my Arms before any Dutchess in
50 *Christendom* set out in Brocade and Jewels.

I think, Secondly, that a Lady without a Husband lies very
much expos'd to all Abuses from the rude World; that the
Weakness of their Constitution is a sufficient Proof, that their
Maker design'd Man for their Guard. Now if a Lady will

26 worldly] wordly

neglect the Protection which Providence has design'd her, when there is one that begs so very earnesty, and has so long sollicited for the Honour of the Place, 'tis but just, I think, that she meet with some small rubbs to mind her of her insufficiency. I know, Madam, that your Ladyship has a very good and worthy Gentleman very near you; one, who is both a Friend and a Father to you; but yet a Husband is still the best *Guard-du-Corps*, and there are some Priviledges annex'd to his Place, which wou'd make Rogues more cautious how they invaded your Bed-Chamber. In the third Place, Madam, give me leave to ask you one Question: Don't you think this Thief that robb'd you to be a very barbarous Fellow? And wou'd you not be very severe upon him, if he were taken? Most certainly you wou'd. Then what must I think of a Person that has robb'd me of a Jewel, much more precious than any they have taken from you, I mean, my Ease and Quiet? A little Thief has stole my Heart out of my very Breast; the Loss of which has cost me more Sighs and Uneasiness than all the Wealth in the World cou'd have done. I have pursu'd this charming *Bandit* from Place to Place, from Town to Countrey, from Kingdom to Kingdom, yet all in vain—I beg you now, Madam, to consider this, and be not too severe upon the poor Rogues, tho' they shou'd be taken.

This is the first Service, my Hand has done me since I left *London*; and were not the Air too piercing for me to venture abroad after so much Bleeding, I wou'd have told you all this personally; but happen what will, three or four Days shall be the utmost Confinement I can lay upon my Desire of waiting on you; and that you have been so long releas'd from my Company, you are more beholden to the Force of my Illness, than the Strength of my Resolution, which is always too weak to encounter the Passion of,

MADAM,

Your most sincere, and humble Servant.

Madam,

'Tis a sad Misfortune to begin a Letter with an *Adieu*; but when my Love is cross'd, 'tis no wonder that my Writing shou'd be revers'd. I wou'd beg your Pardon for the other Offences of this Nature, which I have committed, but that I have so little Reason to Judge favourably of your Mercy; tho' I can assure you, Madam, that I shall never excuse my self my own share of the trouble, no more than I can pardon my self the Vanity of attempting your Charms, so much above the reach of my Pretensions, and which are reserv'd for some more worthy Admirers. If there be that Man upon Earth that can merit your Esteem, I pity him; for an Obligation too great for a Return, must to any generous Soul be very uneasy; tho' still I envy his Misery.

May you be as happy, Madam, in the Enjoyment of your Desires, as I am miserable in the Disappointment of mine; and as the greatest Blessing of your Life, may the Person you admire Love you as sincerely, and as passionately, as he whom you Scorn.

A
DISCOURSE
UPON
COMEDY,
In Reference to the
English Stage.
In a Letter to a Friend.

With Submission, Sir, my Performance in the Practical Part of Poetry is no sufficient Warrant for your pressing me in the Speculative; I have no Foundation for a *Legislator*, and the two or three little *Plays* I have written, are cast carelessly into the World, without any Bulk of *Preface*, because I was not so learn'd in the Laws, as to move in Defence of a bad Case. Why then shou'd a Compliment go farther with me, than my own Interest? Don't mistake me, Sir, here is nothing that cou'd make for my Advantage in either *Preface* or *Dedication*; no *Speculative Curiosities*, nor *Critical Remarks*; only some present

Sentiments which Hazard, not Study, brings into my Head, without any preliminary *Method* or *Cogitation*.

Among the many Disadvantages attending Poetry, none seems to bear a greater Weight, than that so many set up for Judges, when so very few understand a tittle of the matter. Most of our other Arts and Sciences bear an awful Distance in their Prospect, or with a bold and glittering Varnish dazle the Eyes of the weak-sighted Vulgar. The *Divine* stands wrapt up in his Cloud of Mysteries, and the amus'd *Layety* must pay Tyths and Veneration to be kept in Obscurity, grounding 20 their Hopes of future Knowledge on a Competent Stock of present Ignorance (in the greater part of the *Christian* World this is plain.) With what Deference and Resignation does the bubbled *Client* commit his Fees and Cause into the Clutches of the *Law*, where Assurance beards Justice by *Prescription*, and the wrong side is never known to make it's *Patron* blush. *Physick* and *Logick* are so strongly fortify'd by their impregnable Terms of Art, and the *Mathematician* lies so cunningly intrench'd within his *Lines* and *Circles*, that none but those of their Party dare peep into their puzling Designs. 30

Thus the Generality of Mankind is held at a gazing Distance, whose Ignorance not presuming perhaps to an open Applause, is yet satisfy'd to pay a blind Veneration to the very Faults of what they don't understand.

Poetry alone, and chiefly the *Dramma*, lies open to the Insults of all Pretenders; she was one of Nature's eldest Offsprings, whence by her Birthright and plain Simplicity she pleads a genuine Likeness to her Mother; born in the Innocence of Time, she provided not against the Assaults of succeeding Ages; and, depending altogether on the generous End of her 40 Invention, neglected those secret Supports and serpentine Devices us'd by other Arts that wind themselves into Practice for more subtle and politick Designs: Naked she came into the World, and 'tis to be fear'd, like its Professors will go naked out.

'Tis a wonderful thing, that most Men seem to have a great Veneration for *Poetry*, yet will hardly allow a favourable Word to any Piece of it that they meet; like your Virtuoso's in

44 World] Wold

Friendship, that are so ravish'd with the notional Nicety of the
50 Vertue, that they can find no Person worth their intimate
Acquaintance. The Favour of being whipt at School for
Martial's *Epigrams*, or *Ovid*'s *Epistles*, is sufficient Priviledge
for turning Pedagogue, and lashing all their Successors; and it
wou'd seem by the fury of their Correction, that the ends of
the Rod were still in their Buttocks. The Scholar calls upon us
for *Decorums* and *Oeconnomy*; the Courtier crys out for *Wit* and
Purity of Stile; the Citizen for *Humour* and *Ridicule*; the Divines
threaten us for Immodesty; and the Ladies will have an
Intreague. Now here are a multitude of Criticks, whereof the
60 twentieth Person only has read *Quæ Genus*, and yet every one is
a Critick after his own way; that is, Such a Play is best,
because I like it. A very familiar Argument, methinks, to
prove the Excellence of a Play, and to which an Author wou'd
be very unwilling to appeal for his Success: Yet such is the
unfortunate State of Dramatick Poetry, that it must submit to
such Judgments; and by the Censure or Approbation of such
variety it must either stand or fall. But what *Salvo*, what
Redress for this Inconvenience? Why, without all Dispute, an
Author must indeavour to pleasure that Part of the Audience,
70 who can lay the best claim to a judicious and impartial
Reflection: But before he begins, let him well consider to what
Division that Claim do's most properly belong. The Scholar
will be very angry at me for making that the Subject of a
Question, which is self-evident without any Dispute: For, says
he, who can pretend to understand Poetry better than we, who
have read *Homer, Virgil, Horace, Ovid*, &c. at the University?
What Knowledge can outstrip ours, that is founded upon the
Criticisms of *Aristotle, Scaliger, Vossius*, and the like? We are the
better sort, and therefore may claim this as a due Compliment
80 to our Learning; and if a Poet can please us, who are the nice
and severe Criticks, he cannot fail to bring in the rest of an
inferiour Rank.

I shou'd be very proud to own my Veneration for Learning,
and to acknowledge any Complement due to the better sort
upon that Foundation; but I'm afraid the Learning of the
Better Sort is not confin'd to Colledge Studies, for there is
such a thing as Reason without Silligism, Knowlege without
Aristotle, and Languages besides *Greek* and *Latin*. We shall

likewise find in the Court and City several Degrees, superiour
to those at Commencements. From all which I must beg the 90
Scholar's Pardon, for not paying him the Compliment of the
better Sort, (as he calls it) and in the next Place, inquire into
the Validity of his Title from his knowledge of *Criticism*, and
the Course of his Studies.

I must first beg one favour of the Graduate—Sir, here is a
Pit full of *Covent-Garden* Gentlemen, a Gallery full of Citts, a
hundred Ladies of Court-Education, and about two hundred
Footmen of nice Morality, who having been unmercifully
teiz'd with a parcel of foolish, impertinent, irregular Plays all
this last Winter, make it their humble Request, that you 100
wou'd oblige them with a Comedy of your own making, which
they don't question will give them Entertainment. O, Sir,
replies the *Square Cap*, I have long commiserated the
Condition of the *English* Audience, that has been forc'd to take
up with such wretched Stuff, as lately has crouded the Stage;
your *Jubilees* and your *Fopingtons*, and such irregular impertinence, that no Man of Sense cou'd bear the perusal of
'em: I have long intended, out of pure pity to the Stage, to
write a perfect Piece of this Nature; and now, since I am
honour'd by the Commands of so many, my Intentions shall 110
immediately be put in Practice.

So to work he goes; old *Aristotle*, *Scaliger*, with their
Commentators, are lugg'd down from the high Shelf, and the
Moths are dislodg'd from their Tenement of Years; *Horace*,
Vossius, *Heinsius*, *Hedelin*, *Rapin*, with some half a Dozen more,
are thumb'd and toss'd about, to teach the Gentleman,
forsooth, to write a Comedy; and here is he furnish'd with
*Unity of Action, Continuity of Action, Extent of Time, Preparation of
Incidents, Episodes, Narrations, Deliberations, Didacticks, Patheticks,
Monologues, Figures, Intervals, Catastrophes, Choruses, Scenes,* 120
Machines, Decorations, &c. a Stock sufficient to set up any
Mountebank in *Christendum*; and if our new Author wou'd take
an Opportunity of reading a Lecture upon his Play in these
Terms, by the help of a *Zany*, and a Joynt-Stool, his Scenes
might go off as well as the Doctors Packets; but the Misfortune
of it is, he scorns all Application to the Vulgar, and will please
the better Sort, as he calls his own sort. Pursuant therefore to
his Philosophical Dictates, he first chooses a single Plot,

because most agreeable to the regularity of Criticism, no
130 matter whether it affords Business enough for Diversion or
Surprise. He wou'd not for the World introduce a Song or
Dance, because his Play must be one intire Action. We must
expect no Variety of Incidents, because the Exactness of his
three Hours wont give him time for their Preparation. The
Unity of Place admits no variety of Painting and Prospect, by
which Mischance perhaps, we shall loose the only good Scenes
in the Play. But no matter for that, this Play is a regular Play;
this Play has been examin'd and approv'd by such and such
Gentlemen, who are staunch Criticks and Masters of Art; and
140 this Play I will have acted. Look'ee, Mr. *Rich*, you may
venture to lay out a Hundred and fifty Pound for dressing this
Play, for it was written by a great Scholar, and Fellow of a
College.

Then a grave dogmatical Prologue is spoken, to instruct the
Audience what shou'd please them; that this Play has a new
and different Cut from the Farce they see every Day, that this
Author writes after the manner of the *Ancients*, and here is a
Piece according to the Model of the *Athenian Drama*. Very well!
This goes off *Hum drum, So, so*. Then the Players go to work on
150 a piece of hard knotty Stuff, where they can no more show
their Art, than a Carpenter can upon a piece of Steel. Here is
the Lamp and the Scholar in every Line, but not a Syllable of
the Poet. Here is elaborate Language, Sounding Epithets,
Flights of Words that strike the Clouds, whilst the poor Sense
lags after like the Lanthorn in the Tail of the Kite, which
appears only like a Star, while the Breath of the Players Lungs
has Strength to bear it up in the Air.

But the Audience, willing perhaps to discover his ancient
Model, and the *Athenian Drama*, are attentive to the first Act or
160 two; but not finding a true Genius of Poetry, nor the natural
Air of free Conversation; without any Regard to his Regularity,
they betake themselves to other Work; not meeting the
Diversion they expected on the Stage, they shift for themselves
in the Pit, every one turns about to his Neighbour in a Mask,
and for default of Entertainment now, they strike up for more
diverting Scenes when the Play is done; and tho' the Play be
regular as *Aristotle*, and modest as Mr. *Collier* cou'd wish, yet it
promotes more Lewdness in the Consequence, and procures

more effectually for Intreague than any *Rover*, *Libertine*, or old
Batchelour whatsoever. At last comes the Epilogue, which 170
pleases the Audience very well, because it sends them away,
and terminates the Fate of the Poet; the *Patentees* rail at him,
the Players Curse him, the Town damns him, and he may
bury his Copy in *Pauls*, for not a Bookseller about it will put it
in Print.

This familiar Account, Sir, I wou'd not have you charge to
my Invention, for there are Precedents sufficient in the World
to warrant it in every particular; the Town has been often
disappointed in those Critical Plays, and some Gentlemen
that have been admir'd in their speculative Remarks, have 180
been ridicul'd in the practick. All the Authorities, all the Rules
of Antiquity have prov'd too weak to support the Theatre,
whilst others who have dispenc'd with the Criticks, and taken
a Latitude in the *Œconomy* of their Plays, have been the chief
Supporters of the Stage, and the Ornament of the *Drama*; this
is so visibly true, that I need bring in no instances to enforce
it; but you say, Sir, 'tis a Paradox that has often puzled your
Understanding, and you lay your Commands upon me to
solve it, if I can.

Lookee, Sir, to add a Value to my Complaisance to you, I 190
must tell you in the first Place, that I run as great a hazard in
nibling at this *Paradox* of *Poetry*, as *Luther* did by touching
Transubstantiation, 'tis a Mistery that the World has sweetly
slept in so long, that they take it very ill to be waken'd,
especially being disturb'd of their rest, when there is no
Business to be done. But I think that *Bellarmin* was once as
Orthodox as *Aristotle*; and since the *German Doctor* has made a
shift to hew down the *Cardinal*, I will have a tug with *ipse dixit*,
tho' I dye for't.

But in the first Place, I must beg you, Sir, to lay aside your 200
Superstitious Veneration for Antiquity, and the usual Expressions on that Score; that the present Age is illiterate, or their
taste is vitiated; that we live in the decay of Time, and the
Dotage of the World is fall'n to our Share—'Tis a mistake, Sir,
the World was never more active or youthful, and true
downright Sense was never more Universal than at this very
Day; 'tis neither confin'd to one Nation in the World, nor to
one part of a City, 'tis remarkable in *England* as well as *France*;

and good genuine Reason is nourish'd by the Cold of *Swedeland*
210 as by the Warmth of *Italy*, 'tis neither abdicated the Court
with the late Reigns, nor expell'd the City with the Play-house
Bills; you may find it in the *Grand-Jury* at *Hick*'s *Hall*, and upon
the Bench sometimes among the Justices; then why shou'd we
be hamper'd so in our Opinions, as if all the Ruins of
Antiquity lay so heavily on the Bones of us, that we cou'd not
stir Hand nor Foot: No, no, Sir, *ipse dixit* is remov'd long ago,
and all the Rubbish of old Philosophy, that in a manner
bury'd the Judgment of Mankind for many Centuries, is now
carry'd off; the vast Tomes of *Aristotle* and his Commentators
220 are all taken to pieces, and their Infallibility is lost with all
Persons of a free and unprejudic'd Reason.

Then above all Men living, why shou'd the Poets be
hoodwink'd at this rate; and by what Authority shou'd
Aristotle's Rules of Poetry stand so fixt and immutable? Why,
by the Authority of two Thousand Years standing, because
thro' this long Revolution of time the World has still continu'd
the same—By the Authority of their being receiv'd at *Athens*, a
City, the very same with *London* in every particular; their
Habits the same, their Humours alike, their publick Trans-
230 actions and private Societies *Alamode France*; in short, so very
much the same in every Circumstance, that *Aristotle*'s Criticisms
may give Rules to *Drury Lane*; the *Areopagus* give Judgment
upon a Case in the *Kings Bench*, and old *Solon* shall give Laws
to the *House of Commons*.

But to examine this Matter a little farther; all Arts and
Professions are compounded of these two parts, a Speculative
Knowledge, and a practical Use; and from an excellency in
both these any Person is rais'd to Eminence and Authority in
his Calling. The Lawyer has his Years of Student in the
240 Speculative Part of his Business; and, when promoted to Bar,
he falls upon the Practick, which is the Tryal of his Ability;
without all dispute the great *Cook* has had many a tug at the
Bar, before he cou'd raise himself to the Bench; and had made
sufficiently evident his Knowledge of the Laws in his
Pleadings before he was admitted to the Authority of giving
Judgment upon the Case.

The Physician to gain Credit to his Prescriptions, must
labour for a Reputation in the Cure of such and such

Distempers, and before he sets up for a *Galen* or *Hippocrates*, must make many Experiments upon his Patients. Philosophy 250 it self, which is a Science the most abstract from Practice, has its publick Acts and Disputations; it is rais'd gradually, and its Professour commences Doctor by degrees; he has the Labour of maintaining Theses's, Methodising his Arguments, and clearing Objections; his Memory and Understanding is often puzled by Oppositions couch'd in Fallacies and Sophisms, in solving all which he must make himself remarkable, before he pretends to impose his own Systems upon the World. Now if the Case be thus in Philosophy, or in any branch thereof, as in Ethicks, Physicks, which are call'd Sciences, what must be 260 done in Poetry, that is denominated an Art, and consequently implies a Practice in its Perfection?

Is it reasonable that any Person that has never writ a Distich of Verses in his Life, shou'd set up for a Dictator in Poetry; and without the least Practice in his own Performance, must give Laws and Rules to that of others? Upon what Foundation is Poetry made so very cheap, and so easy a Task, by these Gentlemen? an excellent Poet is the single Production of an Age, when we have Crowds of Philosophers, Physicians, Lawyers, Divines, every Day, and all of them competently 270 famous in their Callings. In the two learned Commonwealths of *Rome* and *Athens*, there was but one *Virgil*, and one *Homer*, yet have we above a hundred *Philosophers* in each, and most part of 'em, forsooth, must have a touch at Poetry, drawing it into *Divisions*, *Subdivisions*, &c. when the Wit of 'em all set together, wou'd not amount to one of *Martial*'s *Epigrams*.

Of all these I shall mention only *Aristotle*, the first and great Law-giver, in this Respect, and upon whom all that follow'd him are only Commentators. Among all the vast Tracts of this Voluminous Author, we don't find any Fragment of an Epick 280 Poem, or the least Scene of a Play, to authorise his Skill and Excellence in that Art: Let it not be alledg'd, that for ought we know he was an excellent Poet, but his more serious Studies wou'd not let him enter upon Affairs of this Nature; for every Body knows, that *Aristotle* was no *Cinick*, but liv'd in the Splendour and Air of the Court, that he lov'd Riches as much as others of that Station; and being sufficiently acquainted with his Pupil's Affection to Poetry, and his Complaint that he

wanted an *Homer* to aggrandize his Actions, he wou'd never
290 have slipt such an Opportunity of farther ingratiating himself
in the King's Favour, had he been conscious of any Abilities in
himself, for such an Undertaking; and having a more noble
and copious Theme in the exploits of *Alexander*, than what
inspir'd the blind Bard in his Hero *Achilles*. If his Epistles to
Alexander were always answer'd with a considerable Present,
what might he have expected from a Work like *Homer*'s upon
so great a Subject; dedicated to so mighty a Prince, whose
greatest Fault was his vain Glory, and that took such Pains to
be Deify'd among Men.

300 It may be objected, that all the Works of *Aristotle* are not
recover'd; and among those that are lost, some Essays of this
kind might have perish'd. This Supposition is too weakly
founded; for altho' the Works themselves might have scap'd
us, 'tis more than probable that some Hint or other, either in
the Life of the Conquerour, or Philosopher, might appear, to
convince us of such a Production: Besides, as 'tis beliv'd, he
writ *Philosophy*, because we have his Books; so, I dare swear,
he writ no *Poetry*, because none is extant, nor any mention
made thereof that ever I cou'd hear of.

310 But stay—Without any farther enquiry into the Poetry of
Aristotle, his Ability that way is sufficiently apparent by that
excellent Piece he has left behind him upon that Subject—By
your Favour, Sir, this is *Petitio Principii*, or, in plain *English*,
give me the Sword in my own Hand, and I'll fight with
you—Have but a little Patience till I make a Flourish or two,
and then, if you are pleas'd to demand it, I'll grant you that
and every thing else.

How easy were it for me to take one of Doctor *Tillotson*'s
Sermons, and out of the *Œconomy* of one of these Discourses,
320 trump you up a Pamphlet, and call it, *The Art of Preaching*. In
the first Place I must take a *Text*, and here I must be very
learn'd upon the Etimology of this Word *Text*; then this Text
must be divided into such and such *Partitions*, which Partitions
must have their hard Names and *Derivations*; then these must
be Spun into *Subdivisions*; and these back'd by Proofs of
Scripture, *Ratiocinatio Oratoris*, *Ornamenta Figurarum Rhetoricarum*;
and, *Authoritas Patrum Ecclesiæ*, with some Rules and Directions
how these ought to be manag'd and apply'd; and closing up

this difficult Pedantry with the *Dimensions of Time* for such an Occasion; you will pay me the Compliment of an excellent Preacher, and affirm, that any Sermon whatsoever, either by a *Presbiter* at *Geneva*, or *Jesuit* in *Spain*, that deviates from these Rules, deserves to be hist, and the Priest kick'd out of his Pulpit. I must doubt your Complaisance in this point, Sir; for you know the Forms of Eloquence are divers, and ought to be suited to the different Humour and Capacities of an Audience; you are sensible, Sir, that the fiery Cholerick Humour of one Nation must be entertain'd and mov'd by other Means than the heavy flegmatick Complexion of another; and I have observed in my little Travels, that a Sermon of three quarters of an Hour, that might please the Congregation at St. *James's*, wou'd never satisfy the Meeting House in the *City*, where People expect more for their Money; and having more Temptations of Roguery, must have a larger Portion of Instruction.

Be pleas'd to hear another Instance of a different kind, tho' to the same Purpose. I go down to *Woollich*, and there, upon a Piece of Paper I take the Dimensions of the *Royal Soveraign*, and from hence I frame a Model of a *Man of War*; I divide the Ship into three principal Parts, the *Keel*, the *Hull*, and the *Rigging*; I subdivide these into their proper Denominations, and by the help of a Saylor, give you all the Terms belonging to every Rope, and every Office in the whole Ship: Will you from hence infer, that I am an excellent Shipwright, and that this Model is proper for a *Trading Junck* upon the *Volga*, or a *Venetian Galley* in the *Adriatick* Sea?

But you'll object, perhaps, that this is no parallel Case; because that *Aristotle's Ars Poetica* was never drawn from such slight Observations, but was the pure effect of his immense Reason, thro' a nice Inspection into the very Bottom and Foundation of Nature.

To this I answer, That Verity is eternal, as that the Truth of two and two making four was as certain in the Days of *Adam* as it is now; and that, according to his own Position, Nature is the same *apud omnes Gentes*. Now if his Rules of Poetry were drawn from certain and immutable Principles, and fix'd on the Basis of Nature; why shou'd not his *Ars Poetica* be as efficacious now, as it was two Thousand Years ago? And why

shou'd not a single Plot, with perfect Unity of Time and Place,
370 do as well at *Lincolns-Inn-Fields*, as at the Play-house in *Athens*.
No, no, Sir, I am apt to believe that the Philosopher took no
such Pains in Poetry as you imagine. The *Greek* was his
Mother Tongue, and *Homer* was read with as much Veneration
among the Schoolboys, as we learn our *Catechism*: Then where
was the great Business for a Person so expert in Mood and
Figure, as *Aristotle* was, to range into some Order a parcel of
Terms of Art, drawn from his Observation upon the *Iliads*,
and these to call the Model of an *Epick Poem*. Here, Sir, you
may imagine, that I am caught; and have all this while been
380 spinning a Thread to strangle my self; one of my main
Objections against *Aristotle*'s *Criticisms*, is drawn from his Non-
performance in Poetry. And now I affirm, that his Rules are
extracted from the greatest Poet that ever liv'd, which gives
the utmost Validity to the Precept, and that is all we contend
for.

Look ye, Sir; I lay it down only for a Supposition, that
Aristotle's Rules for an Epick Poem were extracted from
Homer's *Iliads*; and if a Supposition has weigh'd me down, I
have two or three more of an equal Ballance to turn the Scale.
390 The great Esteem of *Alexander* the great for the Works of old
Homer, is sufficiently testify'd by Antiquity; insomuch that he
always slept with the *Iliads* under his Pillow: Of this *Stagirite* to
be sure was not ignorant; and what more proper Way of
making his Court cou'd a Man of Letters Devise, than by
saying something in Commendation of the King's Favourite?
A Copy of Commendatory Verses was too mean, and perhaps
out of his Element. Then something he wou'd do in his own
way; a Book must be made of the Art of Poetry, wherein *Homer*
is prov'd a Poet by Mood and Figure, and his Perfection
400 transmitted to Poesterity; and if Prince *Arthur* had been in the
Place of the *Iliads*, we shou'd have had other Rules for Epick
Poetry, and Doctor *B—re* had carry'd the *Bays* from *Homer*, in
spight of all the Criticks in *Christendom*; but whether *Aristotle*
writ those Rules to Complement his Pupil, or whether he
wou'd make a Stoop at Poetry, to show that there was no
Knowledge beyond the flight of his Genius, there is no Reason
to allow that *Homer* compil'd his Heroick Poem by those very
Rules which *Aristotle* has laid down: For granting that *Aristotle*

might pick such and such Observations from this Piece; they
might be meer Accidents resulting casually from the Com- 410
position of the Work, and not any of the essential Principles of
the Poem. How usual is it for Criticks to find out Faults, and
create Beauties, which the Authors never intended for such;
and how frequently do we find Authors run down in those
very parts, which they design'd for the greatest Ornament.
How natural is it for aspiring ambitious Schoolmen to attempt
matters of the highest Reach; the wonderful Creation of the
World, (which nothing but the Almighty Power that order'd
it, can describe) is brought into Mood and Figure by the
arrogance of *Philosophy*. But till I can believe that the Vertigo's 420
of *Cartesius*, or the Atoms of *Epicurus* can determine the
almighty *Fiat*, they must give me leave to question the
Infallibility of their Rules in respect of Poetry.

Had *Homer* himself by the same Inspiration that he writ his
Poem, left us any Rules for such a Performance, all the World
must have own'd it for Authentick. But he was too much a
Poet to give Rules to that, whose excellence he knew consisted
in a free and unlimited Flight of Imagination; and to describe
the Spirit of Poetry, which alone is the *True Art of Poetry*, he
knew to be as impossible, as for humane Reason to teach the 430
gifts of Prophecy by a Difinition.

Neither is *Aristotle* to be allow'd any farther Knowledge in
Dramatick than in *Epick Poetry; Euripides*, whom he seems to
Compliment by Rules adapted to the Model of his Plays, was
either his Contemporary, or liv'd but a little before him; he
was not insensible how much this Author was the darling of
the City; as appear'd by the prodigious Expence disburs'd by
the publick for the Ornament of his Plays; and 'tis probable,
he might take this Opportunity of improving his Interest with
the People, indulging their Inclination by refining upon the 440
Beauty of what they admir'd. And besides all this, the Severity
of *Dramatick* Rage was so fresh in his Memory in the hard
Usage that his Brother *Sophocles* not long before met with upon
the Stage, that it was convenient to humour the reigning Wit,
least a second *Aristophanes* shou'd take him to Task with as
little Mercy as poor *Socrates* found at the Hands of the first.

443 *Sophocles*] *Soph*

I have talk'd so long to lay a Foundation for these following Conclusions; *Aristotle* was no Poet, and consequently not capable of giving Instructions in the Art of Poetry; his *Ars*
450 *Poetica* are only some Observations drawn from the Works of *Homer* and *Euripedes*, which may be meer Accidents resulting casually from the Composition of the Works, and not any of the essential Principles on which they are compil'd. That without giving himself the Trouble of searching into the Nature of Poetry, he has only complemented the Heroes of Wit and Valour of his Age, by joining with them in their Approbation; with this Difference, that their Applause was plain, and his more Scholastick.

But to leave these only as Suppositions to be relish'd by
460 every Man at his Pleasure, I shall without complementing any Author, either Ancient or Modern, inquire into the first Invention of Comedy; what were the true Designs and honest Intentions of that Art; and from a Knowledge of the *End*, seek out the *Means*, without one Quotation of *Aristotle*, or Authority of *Euripides*.

In all Productions either Divine or Humane, the final Cause is the first Mover, because the End or Intention of any rational Action must first be consider'd, before the material or efficient Causes are put in Execution. Now to determine the
470 final Cause of Comedy we must run back beyond the material and formal Agents, and take it in its very Infancy, or rather in the very first Act of its Generation, when its primary Parent, by proposing such or such an End of his Labour, laid down the first Scetches or Shadows of the Piece. Now as all Arts and Sciences have their first rise from a final Cause, so 'tis certain that they have grown from very small beginnings, and that the current of time has swell'd 'em to such a Bulk, that no Body can find the Fountain, by any Proportion between the Head and the Body; this, with the Corruption of time, which has
480 debauch'd things from their primitive Innocence, to selfish Designs and Purposes, renders it difficult to find the Origin of any Offspring so very unlike its Parent.

This is not only the Case of Comedy, as it stands at present, but the Condition also of the ancient Theatres, when great Men made Shows of this Nature a rising Step to their Ambition, mixing many lewd and lascivious Representations to gain the Favour of the Populace, to whose Taste and Entertainment the Plays were chiefly adopted. We must therefore go higher than either *Aristophanes*, or *Menander*, to discover Comedy in its primitive Institution, if we wou'd draw 490 any moral Design of its Invention to warrant and authorise its Continuance.

I have already mention'd the difficulty of discovering the Invention of any Art in the different Figure it makes by Succession of Improvements; but there is something in the Nature of Comedy, even in its present Circumstances, that bears so great a Resemblance to the Philosophical *Mythology* of the Ancients, that old *Æsop* must wear the Bays as the first and original Author; and whatever Alterations or Improvements farther Application may have subjoin'd, his *Fables* gave 500 the first Rise and Occasion.

Comedy is no more at present than a *well-fram'd Tale handsomly told, as an agreeable Vehicle for Counsel or Reproof*. This is all we can say for the Credit of its Institution; and is the Stress of its Charter for Liberty and Toleration. Then where shou'd we seek for a Foundation, but in *Æsop*'s symbolical way of moralizing upon Tales and Fables, with this difference, That his Stories were shorter than ours: He had his Tyrant *Lyon*, his Statesman *Fox*, his Beau *Magpy*, his coward *Hare*, his Bravo *Ass*, and his Buffoon *Ape*, with all the Characters that 510 crowd our Stages every Day, with this Distinction nevertheless, That *Æsop* made his Beasts speak good *Greek*, and our Heroes sometimes can't talk *English*.

But whatever difference time has produc'd in the Form, we must in our own Defence stick to the *End*, and Intention of his *Fables*. *Utile Dulci* was his Motto, and must be our Business; we have no other Defence against the Presentment of the *Grand Jury*, and for ought I know it might prove a good means to mollify the Rigour of that Persecution, to inform the Inquisitors, that the great *Æsop* was the first Inventor of these 520 poor Comedies that they are prosecuting with so much Eagerness and Fury, that the first *Laureat* was as just, as prudent, as pious, as reforming, and as ugly as any of themselves. And that the Beasts which are lug'd upon the Stage by the Horns are not caught in the City, as they suppose, but brought out of *Æsop*'s own Forrest. We shou'd inform them besides, that those very Tales and Fables which they apprehend as obstacles to Reformation, were the main Instruments and Machines us'd by the wise *Æsop* for its Propagation; and as he would improve Men by the Policy of Beasts, so we endeavour to reform Brutes with the Examples of Men. *Fondlewife* and his young Spouse are no more than the *Eagle* and *Cockle*; he wanted Teeth to break the Shell himself, so somebody else run away with the Meat,—The Fox in the Play, is the same with the Fox in the Fable, who stuft his Guts so full, that he cou'd not get out at the same Hole he came in; so both *Reynards* being Delinquents alike, come to be truss'd up together. Here are Precepts, Admonitions, and Salutary *Innuendo*'s for the ordering of our Lives and Conversations couch'd in these *Allegories* and *Allusions*. The Wisdom of the Ancients was wrapt up in Veils and Figures; the *Ægiptian Hierogliphicks*, and the History of the Heathen Gods are nothing else; but if these pagan Authorities give Offence to their scrupulous Consciences; let them but consult the Tales and Parables of our *Saviour* in holy Writ, and they may find this way of Instruction to be much more *Christian* than they imagine; *Nathan*'s Fable of the poor Man's Lamb had more Influence on the Conscience of *David*, than any force of downright Admonition. So that by ancient Practice, and modern Example, by the Authority of Pagans, *Jews* and *Christians*, the World is furnish'd with this so sure, so pleasant, and expedient an Art, of schooling Mankind into better Manners. Now here is the primary Design of Comedy, illustrated from its first Institution; and the same end is equally alledg'd for its daily Practice and Continuance—Then without all Dispute, whatever means are most proper and expedient for compassing this End and Intention, they must be the *just Rules of Comedy*, and the *true Art of the Stage*.

We must consider then, in the first place, that our Business lies not with a *French* or a *Spanish* Audience; that our Design is not to hold forth to ancient *Greece*, nor to moralize upon the Vices and Defaults of the *Roman* Commonwealth: No, no—An *English* Play is intended for the Use and Instruction of an *English* Audience, a People not only separated from the rest of the World by Situation, but different also from other Nations as well in the Complexion and Temperament of the Natural

Body, as in the Constitution of our Body Politick: As we are a Mixture of many Nations, so we have the most unaccountable Medley of Humours among us of any People upon Earth; these Humours produce Variety of Follies, some of 'um 570 unknown to former Ages; these new Distempers must have new Remedies, which are nothing but new Counsels and Instructions.

Now, Sir, if our *Utile*, which is the End, be different from the Ancients, pray let our *Dulce*, which is the Means, be so too; for you know that to different Towns there are different ways; or if you wou'd have it more Scholastically, *ad diversos fines non idem conducit medium*; or Mathematically, One and the same Line cannot terminate in two Centers. But waving this manner of concluding by Induction, I shall gain my Point a nearer way, 580 and draw it immediately from the first Principle I set down: *That we have the most unaccountable Medley of Humours among us of any Nation upon Earth*; and this is demonstrable from common Experience: We shall find a *Wildair* in one Corner, and a *Morose* in another; nay, the space of an Hour or two shall create such Vicissitudes of Temper in the same Person, that he can hardly be taken for the same Man. We shall have a Fellow bestir his Stumps from *Chocolate* to *Coffee-house* with all the Joy and Gayety imaginable, tho he want a Shilling to pay for a Hack; whilst another, drawn about in a Coach and Six, is 590 eaten up with the Spleen, and shall loll in State, with as much Melancholy, Vexation, and Discontent, as if he were making the *Tour* of *Tyburn*. Then what sort of a *Dulce*, (which I take for the Pleasantry of the Tale, or the Plot of the Play) must a Man make use of to engage the Attention of so many different Humours and Inclinations: Will a single Plot satisfie every body? Will the Turns and Surprizes that may result naturally from the ancient Limits of Time, be sufficient to rip open the Spleen of some, and Physick the Melancholy of others, screw up the Attention of a Rover, and fix him to the Stage, in spight 600 of his Volatile Temper, and the Temptation of a Mask? To make the Moral Instructive, you must make the Story diverting; the Spleenatick Wit, the Beau Courtier, the heavy Citizen, the fine Lady, and her fine Footman, come all to be instructed, and therefore must all be diverted; and he that can do this best, and with most Applause, writes the best Comedy, let him do it by what Rules he pleases, so they be not offensive to Religion and good Manners.

But *hic labor*, *hoc opus*, How must this Secret of pleasing so many different Tastes be discovered? Not by tumbling over Volumes of the Ancients, but by studying the Humour of the Moderns: The Rules of *English* Comedy don't lie in the Compass of *Aristotle*, or his Followers, but in the Pit, Box, and Galleries. And to examine into the Humour of an *English* Audience, let us see by what means our own *English* Poets have succeeded in this Point. To determine a Suit at Law we don't look into the Archives of *Greece* or *Rome*, but inspect the Reports of our own Lawyers, and the Acts and Statutes of our *Parliaments*; and by the same Rule we have nothing to do with the Models of *Menander* or *Plautus*, but must consult *Shakespear*, *Johnson*, *Fletcher*, and others, who by Methods much different from the Ancients, have supported the *English* Stage, and made themselves famous to Posterity: We shall find that these Gentlemen have fairly dispenc'd with the greatest part of Critical Formalities; the Decorums of Time and Place, so much cry'd up of late, had no force of Decorum with them; the Æconomy of their Plays was *ad libitum*, and the Extent of their Plots only limited by the Convenience of Action. I wou'd willingly understand the Regularities of *Hamlet*, *Mackbeth*, *Harry the fourth*, and of *Fletcher*'s Plays; and yet these have long been the Darlings of the *English* Audience, and are like to continue with the same Applause, in Defiance of all the Criticisms that ever were publish'd in *Greek*, and *Latin*.

But are there no Rules, no Decorums to be oberv'd in Comedy? Must we make the Condition of the *English* Stage a State of Anarchy? No, Sir—For there are Extreams in Irregularity, as dangerous to an Author, as too scrupulous a Deference to Criticism; and as I have given you an Instance of one; so I shall present you an Example of the t'other.

There are a sort of Gentlemen that have had the Jaunty Education of Dancing, *French*, and a Fiddle, who coming to Age before they arrive at Years of Discretion, make a shift to spend a handsom Patrimony of two or three Thousand Pound, by soaking in the Tavern all Night, lolling A-bed all the Morning, and sauntering away all the Evening between the two Play-houses with their Hands in their Pockets; you shall have a Gentleman of this size upon his Knowledge of *Covent-Garden*, and a knack of witticising in his Cups, set up immediately for a Playwright. But besides the Gentleman's Wit and Experience, here is another Motive: There are a 650 parcel of saucy impudent Fellows about the Play-house, call'd Doorkeepers, that can't let a Gentleman see a Play in Peace, without jogging, and nudging him every Minute. *Sir, will you please to pay—Sir, the Act's done, will you please to pay, Sir.* I have broke their Heads all round two or three times, yet the Puppies will still be troublesom. Before gad, I'll be plagued with 'em no longer; I'll e'en write a Play my self; by which means, my Character of Wit shall be establish'd, I shall enjoy the Freedom of the House, and to pin up the Basket, pretty Miss—shall have the Profits of my third Night for her 660 Maidenhead. Thus we see, what a great Blessing is a Coming Girl to a Play-house: Here is a Poet sprung from the Tail of an Actress, like *Minerva* from *Jupiter's* Head. But my Spark proceeds—My own Intreagues are sufficient to found the Plot, and the Devil's in't, if I can't make my Character talk as wittily as those in the *Trip to the Jubilee*—But stay—what shall I call it first? Let me see—*The Rival Theatres*—Very good, by gad, because I reckon the Two Houses will have a Contest about this very Play—Thus having found a Name for his Play, in the next place he makes a Play to his name, and thus he 670 begins.

ACT I. Scene *Covent-Garden. Enter*
Portico, Piaza *and* Turnstile.

Here you must note, that *Portico* being a compound of Practical Rake, and Speculative Gentleman, is ten to one, the Author's own Character, and the leading Card in the Pack. *Piaza* is his Mistress, who lives in the Square, and is Daughter to old *Pillariso*, an odd out-o'the-way Gentleman, something between the Character of *Alexander* the Great, and *Solon*, which must please, because it is new.

Turnstile is Maid and Confident to *Piaza*, who for a Bribe of ten Pieces, let *Portico* in at the Back-door; so the first Act 680 concludes.

In the second Enter *Spigotoso*, who was Butler perhaps to the *Czar of Muscovy*, and *Fossetana* his Wife; after these Characters are run dry, he brings you in at the third Act, *Whinewell*, and *Charmarillis* for a Scene of Love to please the Ladies; and so he goes on without Fear or Wit, till he comes to a Marriage or two, and then he writes—*Finis*.

'Tis then whisper'd among his Friends at *Will*'s and *Hippolito*'s, That Mr. *such a one* has writ a very pretty Comedy; 690 and some of 'em to encourage the young Author, equip him presently with *Prologue* and *Epilogue*; then the Play is sent to Mr. *Rich* or Mr. *Betterton* in a fair legible Hand, with the Recommendation of some Gentleman that passes for a Man of Parts, and a Critick; In short, the Gentleman's Interest has the Play acted, and the Gentleman's Interest makes a Present to pretty Miss—she's made his Whore, and the Stage his Cully, that for the loss of a Month in Rehearsing, and a Hundred Pound in Dressing a confounded Play, must give the Liberty of the House to him and his Friends for ever after.

700 Now such a Play may be written with all the Exactness imaginable in respect of Unity in Time and Place; but if you inquire its Character of any Person, tho' of the meanest Understanding of the whole Audience, he will tell you 'tis intollerable Stuff; and upon your demanding his Reasons, his Answer is, *I don't like it*. Him Humour is the only Rule that he can Judge a Comedy by; but you find that meer Nature is offended with some Irregularities; and tho' he be not so learn'd in the Dramma, to give you an Inventory of the Faults, yet I can tell you, that one part of the Plot had no Dependance 710 upon another, which made this simple Man drop his Attention and Concern for the Event, and so disingaging his Thoughts from the Business of the Action, he sat there very uneasy, thought the time very tedious, because he had nothing to do. The Characters were so unchoherent in themselves, and compos'd of such Variety of Absurdities, that in his Knowledge of nature he cou'd find no Original for such a Copy; and being therefore unacquainted with any Folly they reprov'd, or any Vertue that they recommended; their Business was flat and tiresome to him, as if the Actors had talk'd *Arabick*.

720 Now these are the material Irregularities of a Play, and these are the Faults, which downright Mother-Sense can

censure and be offended at, as much as the most learn'd
Critick in the Pit. And altho' the one cannot give me the
Reasons of his Approbation or Dislike, yet I will take his
Word for the Credit or Disrepute of a Comedy, sooner
perhaps than the Opinion of some *Virtuoso*'s; for there are
some Gentlemen that have fortify'd their Spleen so impregn-
ably with Criticism, and hold out so stifly against all Attacks
of Plesantry, that the most powerful Efforts of Wit and
Humour cannot make the least Impression. What a Misfortune 730
is it to these Gentlemen to be Natives of such an ignorant, self-
will'd, impertinent Island, where let a Critick and a Scholar
find never so many irregularities in a Play, yet five hundred
saucy People will give him the Lie to his Face, and come to see
this wicked Play Forty or Fifty times in a Year. But this *Vox
Populi* is the Devil tho' in a Place of more Authority than
Aristotle, it is call'd *Vox Dei*. Here is a Play with a Vengeance,
(says a Critick) to bring the Transaction of a Years time into
the Compass of three Hours; to carry the whole Audience with
him from one Kingdom to another, by the changing of a 740
Scene; Where's the Probability, nay, the Possibility of all this;
the Devl's in the Poet sure, he don't think to put Contradictions upon us?

Lookee, Sir, don't be in a Passion, the Poet does not impose
Contradictions upon you, because he has told you no Lie; for
that only is a Lie which is related with some fallacious
Intention that you should believe it for a Truth; now the Poet
expects no more than you should believe the Plot of his Play,
than old *Æsop* design'd the World shou'd think his *Eagle* and
Lyon talk'd like you and I; which I think was very Jot as 750
improbable, as what you quarrel with; and yet the Fables
took, and I'll be hang'd if you your self don't like 'em. But
besides, Sir, if you are so inveterate against improbabilities,
you must never come near the Play-House at all; for there are
several Improbabilities, nay, Impossibilities, that all the
Criticisms in Nature cannot correct; as for instance; In the
part of *Alexander* the Great, to be affected with the Transactions
of the Play, we must suppose that we see that great
Conquerour, after all his Triumphs, shunn'd by the Woman
he loves, and importun'd by her he hates; cross'd in his Cups 760
and Jollity by his own Subjects, and at last miserably ending

his Life in a raging Madness; we must suppose that we see the very *Alexander*, the Son of *Philip*, in all these unhappy Circumstances, else we are not touch'd by the Moral, which represents to us the uneasiness of Humane Life in the greatest State, and the Instability of Fortune in respect of worldly Pomp. Yet the whole Audience at the same time knows that this is Mr. *Betterton*, who is strutting upon the Stage, and tearing his Lungs for a Livelihood. And that the same Person
770 shou'd be Mr. *Betterton*, and *Alexander* the Great, at the same time, is somewhat like an Impossibility, in my Mind. Yet you must grant this Impossibility in spight of your Teeth, if you han't Power to raise the old Heroe from the Grave to act his own Part.

Now for another Impossibility; the less rigid Criticks allow to a Comedy the space of an artificial Day, or Twenty Four Hours; but those of the thorough Reformation, will confine it to the natural or Solar Day, which is but half the time. Now admitting this for a Decorum absolutely requisite: This Play
780 begins when it is exactly Six by your Watch, and ends precisely at Nine, which is the usual time of the Representation. Now is it feazible in *rerum Natura*, that the same Space or Extent of Time can be three Hours, by your Watch, and twelve Hours upon the Stage, admitting the same Number of Minutes, or the same Measure of Sand to both. I'm afraid, Sir, you must allow this for an Impossibility too; and you may with as much Reason allow the Play the Extent of a whole Year; and if you grant me a Year, you may give me Seven, and so to a Thousand. For that a Thousand Years shou'd come
790 within the Compass of three Hours is no more an Impossibility, than that two Minutes shou'd be contain'd in one. *Nullum minus continet in se majus*, is equally applicable to both.

So much for the Decorum of *Time* now; for the Regularity of *Place*. I might make the one a Consequence of t'other, and alledge, That by allowing me any Extent of Time, you must grant me any Change of Place; for the one depends upon t'other; and having five or six Years for the Action of a Play, I may travel from *Constantinople* to *Denmark*, so to *France*, and home to *England*, and rest long enough in each Country besides: But
800 you'll say, How can you carry us with you? Very easily, Sir, if you be willing to go? As for Example: Here is a New Play, the

House is throng'd, the Prologue's spoken, and the Curtain drawn represents you the Scene of *Grand Cairo*. Whereabouts are you now, Sir? Were not you the very Minute before in the Pit in the *English* Play-house talking to a Wench, and now *Presto pass*, you are spirited away to the Banks of the River *Nile*. Surely, Sir, this is a most intolerable Improbability; yet this you must allow me, or else you destroy the very Constitution of Representation: Then in the second Act, with a Flourish of the Fiddles, I change the Scene to *Astrachan*. O 810 *this is intolerable*! Look'ee Sir, 'tis not a Jot more intolerable than the other; for you'll find that 'tis much about the same distance between *Egypt* and *Astrachan*, as it is between *Drury-Lane* and *Grand Cairo*; and if you please to let your Fancy take Post, it will perform the Journey in the same moment of Time, without any Disturbance in the World to your Person. You can follow *Quintus Curtius* all over *Asia* in the Train of *Alexander*; and trudge after *Hannibal* like a *Cadet* through all *Italy*, *Spain*, and *Africk*, in the space of Four of Five Hours; yet the Devil a one of you will stir a Step over the Threshold for 820 the best Poet in *Christendom*, tho he make it his Business to make Heroes more amiable, and to surprize you with more wonderful Accidents and Events.

I am as little a Friend to those rambling Plays as any body, nor have I ever espous'd their Party by my own Practice; yet I cou'd not forbear saying something in Vindication of the great *Shakespear*, whom every little Fellow that can form an *Aristus primus* will presume to condemn for Indecorums and Absurdities; Sparks that are so spruce upon their *Greek* and *Latin*, that, like our Fops in Travel, they can relish nothing but what 830 is Foreign, to let the World know, they have been abroad forsooth: but it must be so, because *Aristotle* said it; now I say it must be otherwise because *Shakespear* said it, and I'm sure that *Shakespear* was the greater Poet of the two. But you'll say that *Aristotle* was the greater Critick—That's a mistake, Sir, for Criticism in Poetry, is no more than Judgment in Poetry; which you will find in your Lexicon. Now if *Shakespear* was the better Poet, he must have the most Judgment in his Art; for every Body knows, that Judgment is an Essential part of Poetry, and without it no Writer is worth a Farthing. But to 840 stoop to the Authority of either, without consulting the

Reason of the Consequence, is an Abuse to a Man's Understanding; and neither the Precept of the Philosopher, nor Example of the Poet, shou'd go down with me, without examining the Weight of their Assertions. We can expect no more Decorum or Regularity in any Business, than the Nature of the thing will bear; now. if the Stage cannot subsist without the Strength of Supposition, and Force of Fancy in the Audience; why shou'd a Poet fetter the Business of his Plot,

850 and starve his Action, for the nicety of an Hour, or the Change of a Scene; since the Thought of Man can fly over a thousand Years with the same Ease, and in the same Instant of Time, that your Eye glances from the Figure of Six, to Seven, on the Dial-Plate; and can glide from the *Cape of Good-Hope* to the *Bay of St. Nicholas*, which is quite cross the World, with the same Quickness and Activity, as between *Covent-Garden Church*, and *Will*'s *Coffee-House*. Then I must beg of these Gentlemen to let our old *English* Authors alone—If they have left Vice unpunish'd, Vertue unrewarded, Folly unexpos'd, or Prudence

860 unsuccessful, the Contrary of which is the *Utile* of Comedy, let them be lash'd to some purpose; if any part of their Plots have been independant of the rest; or any of their Characters forc'd or unnatural; which destroys the *Dulce* of Plays, let them be hiss'd off the Stage: But if by a true Decorum in these material Points, they have writ successfully, and answer'd the end of Dramatick Poetry in every Respect, let them rest in Peace, and their Memories enjoy the Encomiums due to their Merit, without any Reflection for waving those Niceties, which are neither instructive to the World, nor diverting to Mankind;

870 but are like all the rest of Critical Learning, fit only to set People together by the Ears in rediculous Controversies, that are not one Jot material to the Good of the Publick, whether they be true or false.

And thus you see, Sir, I have concluded a very unnecessary Piece of Work, which is much too long, if you don't like it; but let it happen any way, be assur'd, that I intended to please you, which shou'd partly excuse,

SIR,

Your most humble Servant.

FINIS.

APPENDIX A

Love and Business contains a revised version of 'The Lovers Night', a poem first published in *The Adventures of Covent-Garden*, and of the letter headed '*Madam*, If I han't begun thrice to write', first published in *A Pacquet from Will's*. Farquhar was the authority for revisions in both cases. The substantive variants, which do not affect the printed text are recorded here. The reading from *Love and Business* precedes the bracket:

The Lovers Night

19 Passions] passion   20 Tempests] Tempest   26 full] high
29–30 Was not . . . most:] [not in original version] 33–34 Oh! if . . . much
Hell.] [not in original version]   41 repuls'd] replus'd   43 on]
in   48–49 Then was . . . Bliss destroy;] [not in original version]
51 lay] was   52 by the Gods,] in her Charms   54 Th']
The   55 Pleasures] pleasure   58 these] those

'*Madam*, If I han't begun thrice to write'

1 thrown away] laid down   3 these two long Hours] [om.]
5 Beauty] Wit   7 you're] You are   *F—r's*] *F—*'s   8 to be] are
10 Share] part   14 Inconvenience] Trouble   17 write [om.]]
~ twice   19 on't] of her   22 I'm] I am   25 forego the
tickling] want the   delicious white,] [om.]   27 Linguist] Tongue
Extasie] Pleasure   29 I am] I'm   30 stick to't.] stand by me
31 that] [om.]   32 worthy Members] considerable Parts   33
(*nemine contradicente*)] [om.]   36 throws] has thrown   38 [om.]
Condition] miserable ~   39 Heartless ∧] ~

APPENDIX B

Substantive revisions made in two poems from *Love and Business* republished in the *Poetical Courant*, apparently by Farquhar's authority (see Introduction, vol. ii., p. 295) included the following substantive variants. The reading from *Love and Business* precedes the bracket:

To a Lady, being detain'd from visiting her by a Storm

    4 these] *those*   13 that] *which*   doth] *does*   15 where're] *where e're*

A Prologue *on the propos'd Union of the Two Houses*

    4 of the] *o'th'*   10 Heroes] *Heroe*   36 are] *was*   38 Times] *Time*

PROLOGUES AND EPILOGUES

INTRODUCTION

COMPOSITION

SEVENTEEN of Farquhar's prologues and epilogues are known, eight written for *premières* of his own plays and nine for other occasions.[1] They include ten known prologues and seven epilogues. Eleven of those, six prologues and five epilogues, have been printed elsewhere in this edition; nine, including one written for a revival of *The Constant Couple*, are printed with the individual plays; two appear in *Love and Business*. The other six, four prologues and two epilogues, have been collected in this section.

During Farquhar's time in London, prologues and epilogues were a surprisingly important feature of the playhouse programme. Audiences clamoured for them, and consequently managers paid cash for them. Prologues and epilogues were deemed particularly important for *premières*. If one can judge from the doubtlessly exaggerated accounts of the period, playwrights eagerly accosted poets, other playwrights, managers of playhouses, and assorted friends, hoping they would write prologues to evoke a warm response from audiences. In particular, authors and managers hoped to bolster the audiences for weak plays by including prologues and epilogues by famous authors. Dryden, Steele, Addison, and Pope, for example, all wrote prologues and epilogues for other men's plays. Farquhar's own first play is a good example; it was framed by a prologue and epilogue by the popular comedian Joe Haines, famous for speaking epilogues from the back of an ass; Haines, dressed in mourning, also spoke the latter.

Authors could eke out some cash by providing these minor pieces. Dryden, in fact, profited rather handsomely; he contributed prologues and epilogues to lesser poets for a fee of four guineas; after 1682, he charged Thomas Southerne six. Peter Anthony Motteux, Farquhar's collaborator in *The Stage-Coach*, profited if not by high prices then certainly by volume; he wrote at least twelve for London theatres.

Farquhar was, of course, ever ready to write for cash. But his career as a prologist was unusual in that he only wrote for one company of actors, the troupe at Drury Lane, many of whom, including Wilks, moved in 1706 to the Queen's Theatre in the Haymarket. Moreover, his known prologues and epilogues all date from the years when he was actively producing his own plays; during the period 1704–6 when he served as an officer, he neither staged new plays nor contributed prologues and epilogues.

Although Farquhar was a close friend of Wilks and other Drury Lane actors, he never grew close to cliques of writers, either the Kit-Cats or hacks like Tom Brown and Abel Boyer, with whom he collaborated in miscellanies. His production of prologues and epilogues was clearly not related to his friendship with the authors of the plays. In several cases, in fact, he was actively feuding with the authors; in others he did not know them well; only Susanna Centlivre, who had reputedly been his mistress and the recipient of some of his letters later published in miscellanies, was a friend. He seems to have been drawn into prologue-writing by his acting friends and his financial exigencies rather than by the playwrights.

The six pieces printed here suggest periods in which he was busily engaged in writing prologues and epilogues. Two were written in 1700, two in autumn 1702, and two in autumn 1706. Only the last two, one written for Centlivre's play, one designed for Wilks to speak at the opening of the Queen's Theatre, bespeak any personal involvement with those for whom they were written. Only one indicates any knowledge of the play being performed.

The earliest, the Epilogue for John Oldmixon's *The Grove, Or, Love's Paradice*, was spoken at the *première* on or about 19 February 1700. The epilogue provides no internal evidence that Farquhar was familiar with the play which it adorned; in fact, either he or Motteux reworked part of it to provide the first six lines of the prologue to *The Stage-Coach* printed in Q2 in 1705 (see vol. i, p. 321). There is, however, evidence that Oldmixon needed help to make his opera a success. Oldmixon had written *Thyrsis*, a pastoral that serves as Act I of *The Novelty* by Motteux and others (Lincoln's Inn Fields, 1697) and later a full-length pastoral *Amintas* (Drury Lane, 1697 or 1698), a failure according to the author of *A Comparison Between the Two Stages*.[2] *The Grove* opened at Drury Lane in February 1700, perhaps on 19 February when Lady Morley attended. The *première* followed by only a couple of months the opening of *The Constant Couple*; the author of the season's record-breaking success would have been intensely desirable as epilogist for the opera. It also followed Farquhar's alleged discovery of Anne Oldfield, reading from *The Scornful Lady* in her aunt's tavern; Robert Gore-Browne speculates on a trade-off between Farquhar's writing the epilogue and Oldfield's acquiring the role of Sylvia.[3]

But despite the epilogue and despite music by Daniel Purcell, *The Grove* failed, as the rather bitter preface of the printed version indicates. Perhaps the audience's predilection for Farquhar's *Trip* was in part responsible for the failure; perhaps the blame must be placed squarely on *The Grove*. As Farquhar was soon to write in the prologue to David Crauford's *Courtship A-la-Mode*, if a play was good, it did not need the additional enticement of a prologue, 'If bad, no Prologue on the Earth can save it.' Oldmixon, to judge from his venomous attack on Farquhar in the prologue to Charles Gildon's alteration of *Measure for Measure* only a month later (see vol. i, pp. 131–2), felt no gratitude for the prologue but expressed considerable wrath at the indomitable attraction of *The Constant Couple*.

The composition of the Prologue for David Crauford's *Courtship A-la-Mode* a few months later gives an even clearer indication of Farquhar's *modus operandi*. If he conceivably knew Oldmixon—they soon published in the same miscellanies—he most likely did not know Crauford, a Scottish lawyer, later appointed Historiographer of Scotland by Queen Anne, and author of no previous plays (his second appeared in 1704). If Crauford drank at the Rose, there is no indication of it in Farquhar's references to that venerable establishment. Crauford had, in fact, as he explains in the preface to the printed play, first taken his play to Lincoln's Inn Fields, where the company dawdled for six weeks in 'sham Rehearsals' attended by six or seven actors rather than the requisite fifteen. Crauford reclaimed his manuscript and immediately offered it to Drury Lane. Rehearsals followed briskly, and in twenty days, according to the author, the *première* occurred. As a result of the delay, it opened on 9 July 1700, 'at a time when there were scarce Witnesses in Town of its Birth'. Farquhar was in town, however; either he wrote the prologue during those twenty days—his pattern as a prologist suggests he would not have written one for Lincoln's Inn Fields—or he had previously sold the prologue to the Drury Lane management to be used when needed. Nothing in the prologue suggests familiarity with or even knowledge of the play. George Powell, who played Sir John Winmore, spoke the prologue.

An odd difference exists between this prologue and the epilogue for *The Grove*. In the earlier piece, the word 'Whore' is used, rhyming with 'secure'; in the prologue to *Courtship A-la-Mode*, the word 'whores', rhyming with 'insures', is omitted, both in performance and in print; the following lines play on the omission:

> For Custom chiefly all our Ills insures;
> 'Tis Custom makes Men Knaves, and Women —s.
> You know the Rhime, if not, let each Man ask
> His pretty little Neighbour in a Mask.

Except for the innuendo of the couplet, there seems little explanation for the omission of a word used by Farquhar in other contexts.

Farquhar wrote the 'New Prologue to *The Constant Couple*' in answer to Oldmixon's prologue to *Measure for Measure* for a performance on 13 July 1700, only four days after the opening of *Courtship A-la-Mode*. Then he sailed for the Netherlands, and his period of theatrical activity ended for a few months. In April or perhaps May 1701 *Sir Harry Wildair* opened, and later in that year he must have written 'A Prologue on the propos'd Union of the Two Houses', published in *Love and Business*. But the next period of theatrical activity that can be more precisely traced occurred in the autumn of 1702, when the rehearsals and production of *The Twin-Rivals* were under way. During that period he composed a prologue for Francis Manning's *All for the Better*, which opened in late October or early November, and an epilogue for Charles Gildon's *The*

Patriot: or, The Italian Conspiracy, which opened in late November or early December.

Francis Manning had no connections with Farquhar that have been traced. He had given his first play, *The Generous Choice*, to Lincoln's Inn Fields in 1700. In an autobiographical poem written in 1737 Manning mentioned his literary friends at Will's, including Cheek, Moyle, Cromwell, Dennis, Rowe, Garth, Addison, and Pope,[1] but not Farquhar. Wilks, who took the role of Frank Woodvil, an English gentleman in Madrid, spoke the prologue, but the highly topical prologue, with its references to the fighting at Bellona and winter quartering of the troops, has no relationship to the character Wilks played.

Echoes of the prologue, but not specific borrowings, occur in the epilogue of William Walker's *Marry; or, Do Worse*, which opened at Lincoln's Inn Fields on 1 November 1703. For example, Farquhar's lines

> The Troops for Winter-quarters now come in,
> And now your brisk Campaigns at home begin.
> See there a Prospect of fair Wealthy Towns,
> Stor'd with strong Magazines of Look and Frowns.

are echoed in the passage:

> Now the Campaign Abroad draws near an End,
> And harrass'd Troops t'ward Winter Quarters bend,
> Now our young Heroe's, flush'd with new Renown,
> Return to fresh Engagements here in Town, . . .

However, the parallels are casual enough to suggest neither plagiarism nor Farquhar's authorship of the latter, possibilities diminished by the fact that the passage did not echo rhyme-words and the fact that Walker's play opened at Lincoln's Inn Fields.

A month later Charles Gildon's *The Patriot*, an alteration of Nathaniel Lee's *Lucius Junius Brutus*, opened at Drury Lane, with a prologue by John Dennis and an epilogue by Farquhar. This is perhaps the most surprising dramatic alliance of all, for Farquhar and Gildon were antagonistic on both personal and literary grounds. Gildon had mounted two earlier plays at Drury Lane, *The Roman Brides Revenge* (1696) and *Phaeton*

(1698), before switching to Lincoln's Inn Fields for *Measure for Measure* (1700) and *Love's Victim* (1701). Both Oldmixon's scathing prologue to *Measure for Measure* and the prologue to *Love's Victim* 'Written by a Friend' attacked *The Constant Couple*.⁵ Gildon may have been the author of *A Comparison Between the Two Stages*,⁶ published 14 April 1702, which also attacked Farquhar's play harshly. He steadfastly believed in neoclassicism, as did Dennis, whereas Farquhar had by then published his attack on the Rules in 'A Discourse upon Comedy'. If ever there was a marriage of convenience, it was this one between playwright and epilogist. Staring B. Wells speculated that Farquhar wrote it 'for the Drury Lane players to enhance *The Patriot*'s possibilities of success by the presence of an epilogue from the pen of Drury Lane's most popular playwright.'⁷

Yet for the first time in these prologues and epilogues, Farquhar's awareness of the play becomes evident in the epilogue, for he refers to 'Poor *Julio* slain', a reference to the tragic end of the son of Cosmo di Medici, portrayed by Wilks, in *The Patriot*. Farquhar knew the play perhaps from Wilks but most likely from the rehearsals that occurred even as the company prepared his own new comedy *The Twin-Rivals*, which opened about a fortnight later. The reference to Julio suggests that the epilogue was commissioned and written during the rehearsal period specifically for Gildon's play. Clearly Farquhar's proximity, his daily activity in the theatre at the time, rather than any friendship with Gildon, led to his composition of the piece.

The epilogue was spoken by the popular comedian Will Pinkethman, who was not in the cast of *The Patriot*. The choice of author and actor bespeak an attempt to increase the possibilities of success for the tragedy. But the effort apparently failed; the *London Stage*, with limited information available for the season, does not record the length of the first run, and it lists no later performances.

After the production of *The Twin-Rivals*, Farquhar's theatrical activities were curtailed, first presumably by his marriage to Margaret Pemell, then shortly after by his military service. He left his martial duties some time before March 1706 and returned to London; *The Recruiting Officer* opened in April. By autumn startling developments in the theatrical world had occurred. Vanbrugh entered an agreement with Owen Swiny to manage the new theatre. Christopher Rich, the manager of Drury Lane, to whom Swiny owed £200, surprisingly agreed to let him depart, taking with him most of Rich's best actors, including Farquhar's good friend Robert Wilks, Benjamin Johnson, John Mills, William Bullock, Theophilus Keen, Henry Norris, Henry Fairbank, and Anne Oldfield. The new policy at the Queen's Theatre was to favour good English plays as opposed to the foreign music that had dominated the London stage recently.

On 14 and 15 October 1706 the new company advertised in the *Daily Courant* a performance of Dryden's *The Spanish Fryer* to open the season; the advertisement defiantly proclaimed the performance 'Without Singing or Dancing'. The management planned hastily for the opening; Cibber remembered that the actors' scheme of desertion from Drury Lane was concerted and executed in a 'very few Days' before the season opened.[8] Farquhar's 'Prologue Spoken by Mr. Wilks, At the opening of the Theatre in the Haymarket, October the 15th, 1706', then, must have been composed at the eleventh hour. Conceivably it was written as late as 14 or 15 October, because it was not mentioned in the advertisement of 14 October, rerun on the day of performance. A prologue by Farquhar, who had regained his standing as most popular playwright with *The Recruiting Officer* the previous spring, would unquestionably have provided an inducement to attend the opening performance; the lack of mention of it in the advertisement strongly suggests that it had not yet been written or perhaps even commissioned. In the last-minute bustle of preparations, Farquhar devised a topical prologue which compares the theatrical battlefield of London to the European theatre of war, Rich to Louis XIV, the actors fleeing the 'Dramatick Prince of *Drury-Lane*' to Louis's subjects, specifically the Camisards, and the theatrical subscription of £100 each from thirty 'Persons of Quality' to the government loan which allowed Marlborough to campaign in Europe. The prologue was assigned to Wilks, an actor noted for his excellent memory and his efficiency in studying parts,[9] and doubtless altogether capable of memorizing it even if it was written on the eve or day of performance.

The prologue to Susanna Centlivre's *The Platonick Lady*, first performed about six weeks later, on 25 November, is the only prologue Farquhar wrote for an author who was also his friend. When Centlivre was still Susanna Carroll, widow (?) and strolling actress, she became Farquhar's mistress.[10] The evidence upon which scholars have assumed their affair is the correspondence published in *Familiar and Courtly Letters, Written by Monsieur Voiture . . . To which is added, A Collection of Letters of Friendship, and other Occasional Letters* (1700) and *Letters of Wit, Politicks and Morality* (1701), printed below. If a liaison did occur, as the publication of the letters encouraged the public to believe, it obviously predated publication of the correspondence. It would have been only one of Farquhar's romantic escapades, presumably brought to a halt by his marriage if Farquhar was as faithful a husband as his biographers have painted him. At any rate, by 1706 the affair had doubtless ended. Carroll met Joseph Centlivre, a cook at the court at Windsor, in 1706 and married him in 1707.

Such a close personal relationship and mutual interest in the theatre might have encouraged Farquhar to write earlier prologues for Mrs. Carroll, but such was not the case, even for the three of her earlier plays produced at Drury Lane. Farquhar was in Holland when *The Perjur'd Husband* opened there in September or October 1700, recently married when *Love's Contrivance* opened on 4 June 1703, and on duty as a recruiting officer in Lichfield or Shrewsbury when *The Basset Table* appeared on 20 November 1705. Three of her other plays were produced at Lincoln's Inn Fields in June and December 1702 and February 1705, and a fourth at Bath in 1706. The composition of the prologue to *The Platonick Lady* in 1706 may suggest some lingering esteem for a friend and mistress—there is no evidence. It certainly represented another effort for the theatre with which Farquhar was affiliated, now the Queen's Theatre in the Haymarket, where his prologue for Wilks was spoken in October and his final play was to open the following March. Once again the prologue reveals no knowledge of the play itself. It was the first one that Farquhar ever wrote for Betterton to speak, a result of the Drury Lane actors' new alliance with that grand old man of the theatre.

A few general conclusions can be drawn from the evidence of these prologues and epilogues. Farquhar seems to have written all his pieces for the Drury Lane Theatre until the actors deserted for the Queen's Theatre in autumn 1706. Whether he wrote and sold them to be used at will by the management or prepared them by special commission for individual plays, he clearly wrote by arrangement with the management rather than the authors, with only one of whom he conceivably had any cordial relationship (even the relationship with Centlivre may have proved, after his marriage, more an unfortunate echo from the past than a passion of the moment). He only once showed any awareness of the content of the play to be performed. This in itself was not singular since prologues and epilogues often had no direct relationship to the play. But combined with the other known facts about Farquhar's pieces, it suggests he did not know the plays unless they were in rehearsal while he was in the theatre on other business. He wrote for cash and had little concern for the quality of the performance he adorned. In fact, most of his poems were used in futile attempts to rescue bad plays from audience apathy or dislike. He probably did not care—he was paid his fee by the theatre, and thereafter he may well have been indifferent to the disposal of the pieces. The company took advantage of the arrangement to try to buoy lesser authors, to salvage some of the worst plays in the same seasons that Farquhar was writing some of the best.

THE TEXTS

Farquhar had nothing to do with actual publication of the prologues and epilogues, other than those which appeared with his own plays or in *Love and Business*; nor would he have profited from publication. All except the prologue on the opening of the Queen's Theatre were published with the plays for which they were written. Therefore a brief word concerning their publication history will be sufficient.

Oldmixon's *The Grove* was printed for Richard Parker and

published on 16 March 1700, according to an advertisement in the *Post Man* of 14–16 March. Crauford's *Courtship A-la-Mode* appeared probably in July 1700, issued by J. Barnes and E. Rumbal. Manning's *All for the Better* was advertised in the *Post Boy* of 7–10 November 1702 as published that day by Benjamin Bragg and the Booksellers of London and Westminster. The *Post Man* of 17–19 December 1702 advertised Gildon's *The Patriot* as published 'Yesterday'; William Davis and George Strahan issued it. Centlivre's *The Platonick Lady* was published 9 December 1706, with the date 1707, printed for J. Knapton and Egbert Sanger. In each case the prologue or epilogue accompanied the play in publication; in each it is ascribed to 'Mr. Farquhar' except for *The Platonick Lady*, which postdated Farquhar's military service, in which 'Captain Farquhar' is listed as the author.

Only the prologue on the opening of the Queen's Theatre was published separately. Benjamin Bragg issued it as a half-sheet broadside, an unusual form of publication for prologues or epilogues other than occasional ones.[11] The occasion doubtless prompted separate publication; Farquhar's prologue was most likely printed for immediate sale to play-goers. Perhaps it was ordered for distribution inside the playhouse on the night it was spoken,[12] as part of the extraordinary effort to create a celebratory aura for the opening of the season. If Farquhar did write it as late as 14 October, it could have been ready for distribution at the opening, since it was printed as a half-sheet broadside, the verso blank.

Two copies of the prologue survive. One resides in the Chatsworth House Library, Bakewell, Derbyshire; a variant date '5th' in the title has been corrected by hand to '15th'.[13] The other, preserved by a fluke of history, is now in the Houghton Library at Harvard University. It survived because it was backed in 1708 by a government list of the names of prisoners taken on board the *Salisbury* by Her Majesty's troops on the *Leopard* and brought to Newgate to trial on 21 April 1708. The list was printed not by Bragg but by Henry Hills.[14]

Three of the six prologues and epilogues, those for *The Grove*, *The Patriot*, and *The Platonick Lady*, were reproduced in Stonehill's edition. The other three are being printed with Farquhar's works in this edition for the first time.

NOTES

1 'George Farquhar and "The Bus'ness of a Prologue"', Appendix, pp. 152–3. Additional information which appears in that article will not be specifically cited.

2 *Comparison*, p. 18.

3 Robert Gore-Browne, *Gay was the Pit. The Life and Times of Anne Oldfield. Actress (1683–1730)* (London, 1957) p. 30.

4 'The Retrospect: or A Poetical Survey of the Author's Life and Fortunes. Written to — in 1737', published in *Poems Written at Different Times on Several Occasions. By a Gentleman who resided many Years abroad in the Two last Reigns with a Public Character* (London, 1752), pp. 254–5.

5 See. vol. i, pp. 131–2.

6 'Farquhar and The Bus'ness of a Prologue', p. 147.

7 Wells, p. 243 n. 42.

8 Cibber, p. 179.

9 Cibber, p. 133, says '. . . *Wilks* never lost an Hour of precious Time, and was, in all his Parts, perfect, to such an Exactitude, that I question, if in forty Years, he ever five times chang'd or misplac'd an Article, in any one of them.'

10 Connely, p. 107.

11 Survival of such ephemera is rare at best; Mary E. Knapp believes that prologues and epilogues were often printed separately in the Restoration and first two decades of the eighteenth century. See Knapp, *Prologues and Epilogues of the Eighteenth Century* (New Haven, 1961), p. 4.

12 This was the case for Nicholas Rowe's epilogue for *Love for Love* spoken by Elizabeth Barry at Thomas Betterton's benefit at Drury Lane on 7 Apr. 1709.

13 D. F. Foxon, *English Verse 1701–1750* (2 vols., Cambridge, 1977), i. 267.

14 For full details of this unusual print shop coincidence, see my article 'A Broadside Prologue by Farquhar', *Studies in Bibliography*, 25 (1972), 179–85.

John Oldmixon, *The Grove, Or, Love's Paradise*
February 1700

EPILOGUE.

Writ by Mr *Farquhar*.

Time was when Poets rul'd without disputes,
Turn'd Men to Gods, transform'd their Gods to Brutes.
Our Poets change the Scene, with mighty odds
Make Men the Brutes, make nothing of their Gods.
'Tis strange to see by what surprizing skill,
Things are transforme'd by Brothers of the Quill.
No more than this—high—*Presto*—pass,
Great *Jupiter*'s a Bull—Great Beaux's an Ass.
Whene'er they please to give their thoughts a loose,
10   *Jove*'s made a Swan, your Alderman's a Goose.
Things of most differing forms too we may find,
By spells of Poetry in one combin'd.
The blustering Face, which Red-Coats bear about,
Is the false Flag which Cowards still hang out,
And that shall huff, and rant, swear loud and ban,
Hector his God, and yet be kickt by Man.
They make the Villain look precise and grave,
And the poor harmless Cit, a thriving Knave.
Strange contradictions! reconcil'd we see,
20   They sometimes make even Man and Wife agree.
Poets of Old chang'd *Io* to a Cow,
But what strange Monsters Women are made now?
Females with us, without the Poet's fraud,
Change often to the worst of Beasts, a Bawd.
There are but two things from all change secure,
Nought can transform a Poet or a Whore.
Others for being chang'd, their Stars may blame,
Their punishment is this—still they're the same,
Like paint on Glass that's valu'd at such cost;
30   Poets ne're fade, although the Art be lost.

David Crauford, *Courtship A-la-Mode*
9 July 1700

PROLOGUE,

Written by Mr. *Farquhar*, and spoken by Mr. *Powell*.

The bus'ness of a Prologue, who can say?
I think it has no bus'ness in a Play:
For if the Play be good it need not crave it;
If bad, no Prologue on the Earth can save it.
But you plead Custom for this needless Evil,
Custom! why ay, this Custom is the Devil.
For Custom chiefly all our Ills insures;
'Tis Custom makes Men Knaves, and Women —s.
You know the Rhime, if not, let each Man ask
His pretty little Neighbour in a Mask.   10
Custom makes Actors, Poets keep a pother,
And Custom starves the one, and damns the other.
Custom makes Modern Criticks snarle and bite,
And 'tis a very evil Custom makes 'em write.
'Tis Custom brings the Spark to *Sylvia*'s Lap,
Custom undresses him, and Custom gives a Clap.
Why Poets write ill Plays, why Maids miscarry,
Ask why *Beaux* paint, they'll say 'tis Customary.
Custom makes modern Wives break Marriage Vows,
And Custom damns most Plays at t'other House.   20
'Tis Custom makes our Infant Author fear,
And we plead Custom for your Kindness here.

Francis Manning, *All for the Better*
October or November 1702

PROLOGUE.

By Mr. *Farquhar.*
Spoke by Mr. Wilks.

Rejoyce the Stage—All Rural Sports are fled,
Fields cast their Green, and Trees their Beauty shed.
Nature is chill'd abroad with Winter's Rage,
And now looks only pleasing on the Stage.
Rejoyce ye *Beaux*, for now the Season comes
To hush *Bellona*, and to Silence Drums.
The Troops for Winter-quarters now come in,
And now your brisk Campaigns at home begin.
See there a Prospect of fair Wealthy Towns,　　　[*To the Boxes.*
10 Stor'd with strong Magazines of Look and Frowns.
Of forreign Dangers let those talk who please, ⎫
We *Beaux* will swear no Town beyond the Seas ⎬
Has kill'd us half the Men, as one of These. ⎭
But, Ladies, have a care your time will come,
The Conquering *Venlo*-Sparks are coming home.
If on the jaws of Death at honour's Call
They bravely rush'd—No pillage, but a Wall:
How would they Storm such Fortresses as those,
Whence so much sweet and wealthy Plunder flows!
20 Trust me, ye Fair, no strength can their's withstand.
A Soldier is the Devil—with Sword in hand.
Rejoyce ye Sparks, that walk about and huff
From *Will*'s to *Tom*'s, and so take Towns—and Snuff.
Ye now Shall be employ'd, each have his Wench,
And so perhaps ye may engage the *French*.
Rejoyce ye *Criticks*, who the Pit do Cram,
For ye shall have a glut of Plays—to damn.

Charles Gildon, *The Patriot: or, The Italian Conspiracy*
November or December 1702

EPILOGUE:

Mr. *Mills* comes forward and makes an Apology for want of an
Epilogue; then Mr. *Penkethman* enters dress'd like a Beaux, and
says he has one by a Friend, Mr. *Farquhar.*

Something you may expect—I'm dash'd—I doubt
I ne'r, shall have the Face, to stand it out.
Something you may expect, to raise delight
Foolish enough at least, when Beaux do write.
Tho here we stand, and look Wit evermore,
We never ventur'd to talk Wit before
Our outward parts, each Night, we here expose,
But for our Inward, gad we nere shew those.
We dont pretend to write, with Wit, nor Care;
But only, as we Dance, we write, with Air;   10
With careless sliding Stile; just like our Gate;
But Gay, and Modish, Thoughtless, as our Pate;
A soft and flowing Number, fit for Song,
And that we write, just as we sing it, wrong.
Prologues and Epilogues, we often make 'um,
But then these Rogues, the Players, never speak 'um;
We, that support their House! alack a day!
We, make more Comedy, on the Stage, than they.
What draws the Ladies pray? but such as we ⎫
They bring not here, their lovely Eyes, to see ⎬   20
Poor *Julio* slain, but to kill Beaux, like me: ⎭
The Poets too, from us, draw all the Profit,
Tho' not their Wit, we make, the Subject of it;
But we, good-natur'd we, those things can smother,
As we put up Affronts, from one another.
I cou'd not for my Life, see this poor Rogue,
Have this Play lost, for want of Epilogue.
And therefore beg, you wou'd not damn it thus,
The Ladys, can't refuse, when ask'd by us;

30   You side-Box, Beaux, I've orders, to engage
     From all us, Brother Beaux, here on the Stage.
     You, Sir, and I, and you, and he that writes,
     Were all resolv'd, to meet, anon at *Whites*;
     There, spight of Criticks Malice, save the Play;
     And make a Party, for the Poets day.

THE

PROLOGUE

Spoken by Mr. WILKS,
At the Opening of the THEATRE in the *Hay-Market*,
October the 15th, 1706.

Great Revolutions Crown this Wond'rous Year,
And Scenes are strangely turn'd, abroad, and here;
A Year mark'd out by Fate's Supream Decree
To set the *Theatre*, and *Europe* free:
A Year, in which the Destinies Ordain ⎫
The Might Monarch *LEWIS* to Restrain, ⎬
And the Dramatick Prince of *Drury-Lane*. ⎭
Both boldly push'd, to make the World their Prey,
Beggar'd their Subjects to inlarge their Sway;
10   But here, we own, the Simile does break,
Our Prince ne're hurt us for Religion's sake.
     To you the Asylum of the Refugee,
Like Poor Distressed *Camisars* we flee;
Who Starv'd beneath our Vines, like those in *France*,
To feed those Damn'd Dragoons of Song and Dance.
The Muses Cause we own, here stand our Ground,
With Sense to Combate all the Power of Sound:
They take the Foreign; we the *Brittish* Law,
The Poets ours, and theirs the Fa, la, la.
20   You—whose Subscriptions rais'd this fair Machine, ⎫
Whose timely Loan recover'd lost *Turin*, ⎬
Declare for Action in this Glorious Reign. ⎭

A Female Reign gives Liberty to Man;
And Tyrants vanish at the Name of *ANNE*:
Our State, and Stage must Liberty pursue,
When Rul'd by *ANNA*, and Maintain'd by you.

Susanna Centlivre, *The Platonick Lady*
25 November 1706

PROLOGUE.

By Captain *Farquhar*.
Spoken by Mr. *Betterton*.

Rejoice, ye Fair, the *British* Warrior's come,
Victorious o're, to your soft Wars at home.
Each Conqueror flies, with eager Longing's fraught,
To clasp the Darling Fair, for which he fought.
He lays his Trophies down before those Eyes,
By which Inspir'd, he won the Glorious Prize.
Prouder, when wellcom'd by his Generous Fair,
Of dying in her Arms, than Conquering there.
O! cou'd our Bards of *Britains* Isle but write
With the same Fire with which our Hero's fight: 10
Or cou'd our Stage but represent a Scene,
To Copy that on great *Ramillis* Plain;
Then we with Courage wou'd assert our Plays,
And to your glorious Laurels joyn our Bays.
But our poor *Pegasus*, a Beast of ease,
Cares not for foraging beyond the Seas:
Content with *London* Provender, he flyes,
To make each Coxcomb he can find, a Prize:
And after trudging long, perhaps he may
Pick up a Set of Fools, to furnish out a Play.   20
To make him Eat, and you to Entertain,
That for his safety fought beyond the Main.
Your Courage There, but Here your Mercy show;
The Brave scorn to insult a Prostrate Foe.

[*Exit.*

MISCELLANEOUS PROSE AND POETRY

INTRODUCTION

INCLUDED in this section are letters from three collections to which Farquhar contributed in 1700–1, a poem published in the *Poetical Courant* in 1705, and *Love's Catechism*, a humorous romantic catechism very closely related to dialogue in *The Beaux Stratagem*, published in 1707. Other materials which may also have been miscellaneous contributions of Farquhar have been printed in Doubtful Attributions.

Because the materials in this section are varied and unrelated, separate introductory discussions precede the miscellaneous letters, the poem, and *Love's Catechism*.

MISCELLANEOUS LETTERS

THE CANON

FARQUHAR wrote and published letters; one need look no further than *Love and Business* for proof. Incontrovertibly he published in other miscellanies, sometimes under his own name. But with that statement, certainty ends, and the editor enters the half light of ifs and maybes.

Stonehill attributed to Farquhar letters that appeared in three collections, *Familiar and Courtly Letters, Written by Monsieur Voiture, etc.*, printed for Sam Briscoe and sold by John Nutt (1700); *A Pacquet from Will's*, printed by Briscoe and sold by Nutt (1701), published as part of the third edition of *Familiar and Courtly Letters* (1701); and *Letters of Wit, Politicks and Morality*, printed for J. Hartley, W. Turner, and Thomas Hodgson (1701). Altogether, Stonehill reprinted five letters from *Familiar and Courtly Letters*, twenty-one from *A Pacquet from Will's*, and twenty-four from *Letters of Wit, Politicks and Morality*. His proofs of Farquhar's authorship include two passages reused in *Love and Business*; the signatures 'Farquhar' and 'Wildair' found in some of the sequences; and the use of 'George' and 'Damon' in a sequence with Susanna Carroll, later Centlivre. Stonehill reprinted the entire sequences, so that the reader can read Farquhar's letters in context. Only Stonehill has seriously attempted to identify all Farquhar's contributions to these volumes.

John Wilson Bowyer, in his biography of Susanna Carroll Centlivre, attempted to identify the correspondents in her published epistolary sequences. Bowyer accepted as correspondence between Farquhar and Mrs. Carroll the first Celadon sequence in *A Pacquet from Will's* and the Astræa–Damon correspondence in *Letters of Wit, Politicks and Morality*. However, Bowyer claimed Captain William Ayloffe wrote the Celadon sequence in *Letters of Wit, Politicks and Morality*.[1]

The lack of scholarship on the problem is understandable,

for the problem itself is formidable, perhaps unanswerable. Some letters can be readily identified as Farquhar's works through internal evidence. But even in *Love and Business* Farquhar included letters that are so conventional and undistinguished that they are not readily recognizable as his; how, then, can one decide on such letters in the epistolary collections to which he contributed?

In establishing the canon, several kinds of evidence are acceptable. First of all, if lines are reused, as they stand or slightly revised, in one of his other works, the letters can comfortably be accepted as Farquhar's; the young author frequently reused his own lines in his early years although he apparently did not plagiarize from others. I have considered reused lines the best evidence for his authorship. Second, if the letters are identified as 'By Mr. Farquhar' in the first edition, a presumption of his authorship exists. Even if only subsequent editions identify Farquhar as author, one must consider his authorship carefully. Third, if the letters refer to the characteristic symptoms of his illness—long bouts of fever, exceedingly painful extremities, rheumatism—a strong suggestion of authorship exists. Farquhar was certainly unusual in referring to his debilitating illness in his love-letters. All other kinds of evidence have been considered less substantial.

A nagging problem is the possibility that Farquhar contributed to additional miscellanies, not yet recognized as part of his canon. He was, after all, supporting himself by his pen, and every little author's fee must have helped. I have been able to identify no additions to the canon in that category of materials, but the possibilities for additions seem to me strong. In rejecting materials in other miscellanies, I have used the criteria listed above.

FAMILIAR AND COURTLY LETTERS

The first volume of *Familiar and Courtly Letters, Written by Monsieur Voiture* was printed in octavo for Sam Briscoe and sold by John Nutt in 1700. It was advertised to be published in a few days in the *Post Boy* of 2–4 May 1700, and in the issue

of 7–9 May it was again advertised, to be published on
11 May. It was advertised as published in the *Post Man* of
14–16 May and the *Post Boy* of 8–11 June.

The volume contains translations of Voiture's correspondence
by Dryden, Thomas Cheek, John Dennis, Henry Cromwell,
Joseph Raphson, and others, if the title page can be trusted. It
includes epistles of Aristænetus, letters of Pliny the Younger
and Fontenelle translated by Thomas Brown, original letters
by Brown, and a collection of occasional letters by Dryden,
Wycherley, Congreve, Dennis, and others. Among the original
love letters is a series of five 'Love-Letters, written by Mr. — to
Madam —' followed by four letters 'To a young Lady. By
another Hand.' The first sequence of five letters can be
confidently attributed to Farquhar, and the next sequence of
four were probably his too. Stonehill reprinted only the first
five.

The most telling evidence for Farquhar's authorship of the
first sequence is fourteen lines embedded in the text of the
third letter reused in a slightly different sequence with some
revisions in a letter in *Love and Business*.[2] Corroborating
evidence includes his reference in the first letter to his
rheumatism and to himself as 'an unfortunate Man, who has
but one Hand', one of many references to his letters to the
pain of his rheumatic illness. To a lesser degree, his drunkenly
romantic letter from the Rose tavern and subsequent apology
the next day, a theme he pursued more than once, suggested
Farquhar's authorship.

The second sequence of four letters, not printed in
Stonehill's edition, can be attributed to Farquhar with less
certainty. Its placement following the first sequence suggests
the possibility of the same authorship despite the attribution
'By another Hand'. References to his indisposition and his
seeming expectation of fever in the first letter ('I find my self
tolerable, my Feavour, I think, did not think fit to visit me last
Night. . .') and to his health and his poor handwriting in the
fourth ('one wou'd guess by my Hand-writing, that I am just
at the point of Death. . . .') argue for his authorship; the
reference to his painful hand appears in both sequences as
well as in *Love and Business*.

A PACQUET FROM WILL'S

A Pacquet form Will's: Or a New Collection of Original Letters on Several Subjects, printed for Sam Briscoe and sold by John Nutt in 1701, contains its own title page and separate pagination, but it was bound and sold with volume II of *Familiar and Courtly Letters*, printed for Briscoe and sold by Nutt in 1701; the third edition of volume I was issued with it. Although the first volume had been dedicated to Sir Charles Duncomb by Briscoe, the second was dedicated to Henry Brett, to whom Farquhar later dedicated *The Twin-Rivals*. The second volume was first advertised in the *Post Boy* of 13–15 March 1701 to be published the following week, announced again on 15–17 April to be published a few days later, and advertised as published in the issue of 1–3 May. Curiously, another advertisement appeared in the *Post Boy* of 1–3 July saying the work would be published 'in a few Days', and on 14–16 August it was advertised as already published.

Stonehill printed twenty-one letters from *A Pacquet from Will's* in the *Complete Works*, including two '*By Mr.* Farquhar', a sequence of four '*To Mrs. C*—', one signed by 'Wildair', seven in a sequence between 'Celadon' and 'Mrs C—ll' (three of which are Mrs C—ll's answers), and 'Seven Passionate Love Letters written by *Celadon* to his Mistress'. Stonehill pointed out the use of a revised version of the first letter in *Love and Business* and argued that 'Wildair' is Farquhar and further that 'one would naturally suspect' the four letters between the Farquhar and Wildair letters were also written by the playwright. His argument for the correspondence of Celadon and Mrs. C—ll is that Schmid accepted them. He gives no rationale for accepting the 'Seven Passionate Love Letters'.

The first seven letters contain evidence of Farquhar's authorship. The first two are headed by 'By Mr. Farquhar'. The first of these, 'Friday', is republished in a revised form in *Love and Business*. Twenty-three substantive revisions occur in the version in *Love and Business*. Five are additions of words or phrases, one adjective is omitted, and many word changes occur: for example, 'Inconvenience' replaces 'Trouble', 'Beauty' is substituted for 'Wit', 'Linguist' for 'Tongue', 'Extasie' for 'Pleasure', and 'stick to't' for 'stand by me'. The second version ends with the author's arrangements for the letter's recipient to go to *The Constant Couple* so that he can see her ('I have sent you a Note for the Pit, to see the *Jubilee*, to morrow. . . .')

The next, '*To Mrs. C—*', and the next three, two 'By the same' and one 'By —', carry Farquhar's jaunty tone, and include a mention of the Rose and restoration of his cure. Internal evidence in these letters seems far less convincing than that in the second sequence in *Familiar and Courtly Letters*, but the placement of the four letters, between the two by Farquhar and the one signed 'Wildair' argues for their inclusion. The seventh letter, 'To a Masque on Twelfth-day', signed by Wildair, includes a reference to the *Jubilee* and seems to follow from the letter 'To a Lady, whom he never saw'. I have included all seven letters; the balance tips toward Farquhar's authorship in all, not just the first two.

However, I have excluded the other fourteen letters accepted by Stonehill. Stonehill based his attribution of the first Celadon sequence on that of Schmid, who had seen the 1718 edition. For full discussion of this sequence, see Doubtful Attributions, pp. 530–2 below.

Finally, the 'Seven Passionate Love-Letters written by *Celadon* to his Mistress' which follow have been attributed only by Stonehill. They did not appear in the 1718 edition, and Schmid, working from it, never saw them. Stonehill, one would assume, accepted them because of the logic of their proximity to the other Celadon letters and the reuse of Celadon as pseudonym. However since Celadon, a lawyer, was not Farquhar and was probably not even invented by Farquhar, there seems no reason to accept these texts as belonging to him. Again the tone is not characteristic of Farquhar, and there are no references to his plays, his illnesses, or his tavern. I can find absolutely no evidence for inclusion.

LETTERS OF WIT, POLITICKS AND MORALITY

Letters of Wit, Politicks and Morality was published 24 July 1701, according to the *Post Man* and *Post Boy* of 22–4 July, both of which advertised the octavo, under Abel Boyer's editorship, as published 'This day' to be sold for five shillings. It was printed for J. Hartley, W. Turner, and Tho. Hodgson, according to the imprint. The dedication by Abel Boyer to Lord Halifax is dated 5 July 1701.

The miscellany contains letters by Cardinal Bentivoglio, Aristænetus, Quevedo, Petronius, Count Bussy, Rabutin, Mme Maintenon, Fontenelle, etc., translated by the Hon. H— H—, Cheek, Richard Savage, and Boyer. To the translations is added 'a large Collection of Original Letters of Love and Friendship' written by such noteworthy literati as Granville, Cheek, Captain Ayloffe, Dr. G—(Garth), Mr. B—y (Burnaby), Mr. O—n (Oldmixon), Mr. B—r (Boyer), Mr. G—(Gildon), Mr. F—r (Farquhar), Mrs. C—l (Susanna Carroll) under the pseudonym Astræa, and Mrs. W—n (Jane Wiseman) under the pseudonym Daphne. Although Farquhar was not identified on the title-page of either of the other two collections, he is noted on that of *Letters of Wit, Politicks and Morality*.

Stonehill prints thirty-two letters from this collection. Fifteen are supposedly by Farquhar's hand, including thirteen by Celadon, one by Damon, and one by 'Mr. Farquhar to *Mr.* R— S—'; the other seventeen are letters by Astræa, Chloe, 'Mr. Ch. U—' (Charles Ustick), Mr. B—r (Abel Boyer), and B. (probably Boyer again). Stonehill identifies Chloe as possibly Anne Oldfield.

Of the three collections, this is the most confusing. The Damon–Astræa correspondence can be assigned with some assurance to Farquhar and Carroll, but one has the strong suspicion that it is primarily a creation of Carroll with unmistakable clues provided for the identification of Farquhar. Epistle XL is a poem '*To Mr.* Farquhar *upon his Comedy call'd* A Trip to the Jubilee'; presumably Carroll's 'Female Genius' (l. 3) was responsible for it. Astræa provides clues to the identification of the correspondents in Letter XLI from Astræa to Damon when she relates her sorrow over her pet rabbits: the one named George 'no sooner shar'd your Name, but all your inclinations follow'd, which made him grow indifferent to his *Suky*', and the next day after he left, Suky, 'bemoaning the loss of her belov'd *George*', also disappeared. The next letter is the only one in the sequence actually attributed to Damon (Farquhar). After some punning references to the rabbits and the false rumour of his marriage, in which he refers to the noose of marriage, as he does several times in other works ('I have ne're a Den to put my head in, much less a Noose to secure my Neck'), he continues,

You have heard, I suppose, Madam, how scurrilously I have been abus'd by Mr.— I am now busie about the vindication of my Honour, and endeavouring to answer him in his own Kind.

The remark has traditionally been assumed to refer to John Oldmixon's vicious attack on Farquhar in the prologue to Charles Gildon's adaptation of *Measure for Measure*, which opened in March 1700; Farquhar's 'answer' was his new prologue to *The Constant Couple*, first performed on 13 July 1700 and published on 20 August in the third edition of the play.[3] Damon's letter is followed by an epistle in verse from Astræa to Damon, which addresses him as 'My dearest G—'. Then come two copies of verses, one that is '*Astræa*'s Advice to *Cupid*, in the Box, when open'd by *Damon*' and the second '*Daphne*'s Complaint to Astræa'. A letter from '*Mr.*— to Astræa' is signed *B*. The next letter, No. XLVII, is labelled '*Mr.* Farquhar *to Mr.* R— S—' (probably Richard Steele), and can therefore be indisputably assigned to the playwright. The letter from Damon and the one from Mr. Farquhar, Nos. XLII and XLVII, then, are the only ones in the sequence of eight that are Farquhar's. I have printed No. XLI, the letter from Astræa to Damon (which introduces the melancholy leporine romance and therefore prepares for Damon's reply) as well as the two letters by Farquhar.

The Celadon letters, Nos. XV–XXXVII, however, have been omitted. The series follows fourteen letters from Captain Ayloffe; it is identified in the table of contents as '*Astræa* to *Celadon*, with *Celadon*'s Answers'. There are many indications that the correspondence belongs to Ayloffe rather than Farquhar. The Celadon in most of these letters bears little resemblance to the character of Farquhar that emerges from the letters in *Love and Business*. He speaks of himself as having no wit (and indeed he displays little), of having an 'out-of-Fashion Way of Plain-Dealing' with Astræa, of standing in awe of her. His tone is sententious and ploddingly serious

(Letter XVI). Moreover, he is passionately emotional, dwelling on the 'lingring Death' he suffers for want of her company, the torment which is too much to maintain silence, the pity he needs if she cannot give love to assuage his pains. He cries that 'I love you; I doat on you; my passion makes me mad when I am with you, and desperate when I am from you' (Letter XVII). Certainly this is not the Farquhar of *Love and Business*. His tone in Nos. XX–XXIII is far lighter and more bantering, but there is nothing in these letters that identifies the lover as Farquhar. Celadon speaks of a letter 'directed for me at *Chelsey*, and inclos'd by my Sister'. There is no evidence that Farquhar had either an address in Chelsey or a sister in town. Moreover, in No. XXVI, Astræa clearly speaks to Ayloffe:

> Your whole Sex is scarcely worth the trouble I have given my self about you, and now I dare boldly say, I know Mr. *A—e*.

Three of the letters concern a challenge from Charles Ustick and responses from Celadon dated 16 July and 18 August 1700, agreeing to meet him when he returns to town in October and agreeing on Aylesbury as the site of the duel. Farquhar himself strongly opposed the practice of duelling. Celadon returns to his groveling penance and remorse in Letters XXXII–XXXIV, and then turns to a lighter tone again in Nos. XXXV and XXXVI. All in all, the Celadon letters in the sequence reflect two personalities, the agonizing lover and the jaunty suitor. Although published sequences intentionally showed modulation of tone and mood as romances progressed, these letters do not convince a reader that a single author has written them. If they are truly a sequence from one writer, one must conclude that he is Ayloffe.[4]

The possibility exists that in fact Carroll combined two sets of letters in the Celadon sequence, or, for that matter, simply turned over her letters, which were then rendered sequential by Boyer or even a printshop employee. For despite the overwhelming evidence that Farquhar did not write the sequence, within the lighter letters are several clues that he could conceivably be the author, that his letters could have been combined with Ayloffe's and melded into the Celadon sequence; perhaps Carroll added a few creative strokes to make them seem his. There are minor echoes of other works by Farquhar—the mention of usquebaugh and talk of love and wine in No. XXII, the reference to the exquisite delight of imagining her in his arms all night. There are references by Chloe to 'his natural Indisposition' and suspicion by Astræa as to whether illness has truly kept him away from her; he once speaks of writing to her in pain, possibly a reference to his 'rheumatism' instead of his lovesick suffering. There are close relationships between the dates and places of Celadon's letters and the actual locations at which Farquhar resided during the same time. Specifically, Celadon in Letter XXXII, dated 16 July 1700, tells Astræa that he will be out of town fourteen weeks in 'an unsociable Country'; Farquhar left for Holland on 30 July. The same letter, however, mentions the sister in Chelsea. The letters concerning the duel agree to set it for his return in October; Farquhar returned from Holland some time after 12 October. When Astræa asks for the return of her letters in a letter dated 23 July, he points out that 'twill be some months before I shall be where they are'. Yet the same letter XXXIV is one of the passionate, serious ones that seem uncharacteristic of Farquhar's epistolary personality. Letter XXXVI, which returns to a lighter tone, on the other hand, is dated 11 August, after he had arrived in Holland, and speaks of difficulties of communicating about Chloe 'at this distance'.

Moreover, references to Chloe seem to echo the tradition that Farquhar found Oldfield in the Mitre Tavern, where she was reading from *The Scornful Lady*, and immediately recognized her talent for the stage. The details are slightly different:

I met her by chance a visiting, and heard her sing; the Devil tempted me to like her, . . .

He speaks of her as 'but a Girl, not eighteen', and indeed Oldfield was very young when, according to tradition, he discovered her.

All these seemingly biographical details plus the relationship to the Celadon letters in *A Pacquet from Will's* must have led to Stonehill's inclusion of the materials. But evidence suggests that Farquhar was indeed not the author of either set of

Celadon letters. Perhaps Carroll did intersperse a few of his letters with the others, but the weight of evidence suggests that Stonehill was over-generous in his attributions. Therefore, the Celadon letters are not included in Doubtful Attributions.

Letters XXXVIII and XXXIX in the same collection should be mentioned for their significant references to Farquhar; however, they relate to the sequence of Farquhar's letters that follows rather than the Celadon sequence which precedes them. The first of these, from Boyer to Astræa, speaks of trying to get Farquhar and Wilks to support her play at the theatre, and mentions Farquhar's difficulty in completing *Love and Business*:

I design to desire Mr. *F—* to peruse it [i.e. her play], for I have reasons to think both he and Mr. *W—* will stand your Friends in this affair. Mr. *F—* has not publish'd the Book he intended: Neither do I think he will ever any on that Subject. *Briscoe*'s Book [i.e. *Familiar and Courtly Letters*] is out, and your Letters in it, with Answers to the same, both which are no small Ornament to the Collection.

In the next letter, Astræa's answer to Boyer, Carroll praises Farquhar extravagantly:

If he who pleases best merits most, I am bold to say the Bays will fall to the *Hibernian* Bard: and were his vanity as great as his success, he would demand the Trophies of his Conquest, nor fear the Malice of his snarling critical Brethren, nor the ill-nature of the Town, who just even in the Grin of Laughter shall condemn the Play.

She encloses the poem in praise of *The Constant Couple*, printed as No. XL. Boyer believes the implication is that she knows Farquhar only by reputation but hopes Boyer will use the verse to catch his attention for the support of her play (p. 25).

The number of letters, then, accepted into the canon in this edition is very small. The possibility that Farquhar wrote other letters in this miscellany or others certainly exists, as does the possibility of his contributing minor poems to other miscellanies and periodicals. But only when strong proofs for his authorship exist have letters have accepted as his.

Of all Farquhar's literary contributions, these letters are the least significant. They were written in the period in which he had become a celebrity, if a harassed one, because of the success of *The Constant Couple*. He was eking out a living by creation of prologues and epilogues and other piecework, while engaged in the major projects of playwriting and assembling his own miscellany, *Love and Business*. He was twenty-two years old. Surely no one then or now should take them very seriously; they are a breezy attempt to enjoy a fashionable if inconsequential mode of publishing.

THE TEXT

The first edition of *Familiar and Courtly Letters, Written by Monsieur Voiture* (O1) is an octavo with the collational formula A–S^8 T^4(–T4) Aa–Gg^8 Hh^2 (–Hh2). Sig Hh1 must have been printed as T4; T2 is signed T3. The chainlines in gatherings A and S are horizontal, the others vertical. A second issue (O1a) appeared, with the same collation, using the same title-page; it included several changes. Sheet T is in a different setting of type; Hh1 seems again to have been printed as T4 and given the signature H instead of Hh; an errata list for Pliny's letters has been added to Hh1^v in the second printing. I have found no copy of a second edition.

The 'third edition' (O2), greatly expanded and printed in two volumes, was published in octavo a year after the first. Volume I has the collation A–F^8 G^4 Aa–Ll^8 Mm^4 Aaa^6 Aaa-Ggg^8 Hhh^2 (–Hhh^2). Hhh1 is missigned Hh; it was probably printed as part of the six-page additional Aaa gathering which contains the prelims to *Letters of Friendship, and several other Occasions*. The single letter signatures contain the first part, the double letter signatures the second, and the triple letter signatures and third; pagination begins afresh in each part, and each has a new title-page. Volume II has the collational formula A–L^8 Aa–Kk^8. The second volume contains *A Pacquet from Will's*, to which Farquhar contributed.

The text of the first volume of the 'third edition' is a new setting, but some pages of A and Aaa4–7 may be corrected standing type from the edition of 1700. The last leaf of the volume, signed Hh, also seems to be the same setting of type as the issue of 1700 which does not include errata, and was probably printed in the 'third edition' as Aaa7. The errors cited in the errata of O1a have been corrected.

When Farquhar submitted his letters for *A Pacquet from*

Will's, he must have revised for the 'third edition' of the first volume the poem which begins 'Oh! cou'd I find (grant Heaven that once I may)'. The poem was carefully reprinted; only three minor changes in accidentals occur: '*Nymph*' in the third edition replaces '*Nimph*' in the first, '*unsulli'd*' appears for '*unsullied*', and '*e'er*' for '*e're*'. Yet three lines have distinctive substantive revisions, which are clearly 'improvements' in the text, carefully considered by their author, not the careless errors of a compositor. The lines must have continued to bother Farquhar, for oddly enough when he reused them again in *Love and Business*, published the following year, he returned to the original version but tinkered yet again with the same couplets. For example, l. 25 has three versions:

First edition: *My Verse shou'd run so high, the World shou'd see,*
Third edition   *My Verse shou'd soar so high, the World shou'd see,*
Love and Business: *My Lines shou'd run so high, the World shou'd see*

Farquhar obviously thought well enough of the poem to recycle it, but he continued to seek improvements in it.

A third edition was also advertised in 1704 in Thomas Brown's *Stage-Beaux Toss'd in a Blanket*, in a list of books printed and sold by Nutt, as 'now much improv'd'. Perhaps this was the 1701 edition still being advertised.

Another edition of both volumes was published in 1705 (O3). The British Library copy of this edition, printed for Briscoe and sold by Nutt, is an octavo with the collational formula in volume I, A–F⁸ G⁴ Aa–Ll⁸ Mm⁴Aaa⁶ Aaa–Ggg⁸ Hh² and in volume II, A⁴ B–P⁸ Q⁶ Bb–Ff⁸. Some variants occur, for example, a line omitted from 'Friday' in *A Pacquet from Will's*; they are obviously compositorial errors. Farquhar was in military service outside London in 1705; there is no reason to believe he had any hand in this edition.

Then followed duodecimo editions of 1718 (D1) and 1724 (D2). The 1718 edition, which does not reproduce the whole text of the third edition, lists Farquhar's name on the title-page. It also indicates the possibility that two more letters were Farquhar's. For details, see Introduction, Doubtful Attributions, pp. 530–1 below. Briscoe is still on the imprint. The 1724 edition follows the 1718 text.

The only edition of *Letters of Wit, Politicks and Morality* was published in 1701. The collational formula is 8°: A–Z^8 Aa–Ee^8. There is no W gathering. D3 is missigned B3, and N4 is missigned M4. N3 is unsigned. Page numbers 157–76 are omitted and page numbers 327–35 repeated. The volume was still being advertised in 1706 in a list of books sold by William Turner, at the end of Thomas Betterton's play *The Amorous Widow*.

In each work, the first edition has served as copy-text. I have introduced the corrections of the poem 'Oh! cou'd I find (grant Heaven that once I may)' from the 'third edition', since Farquhar clearly seems to have made them. No other substantive revisions have been accepted from later editions of the two Voiture volumes.

I have examined copies of all the editions at the British Library and the first edition of each text plus O1a, O2, and the 1718 edition of both volumes of *Familiar and Courtly Letters* at the Folger.

NOTES

1. *The Celebrated Mrs. Centlivre*, (Durham, NC, 1952), pp. 15–31.
2. Stonehill identifies this sequence as Farquhar's on the basis of ten rather than the actual fourteen lines.
3. See Introduction, *The Constant Couple*, vol. i, pp. 131–2 above. Also 'George Farquhar and "The Bus'ness of a Prologue"', pp. 143–5.
4. John Wilson Bowyer believes Ayloffe is Celadon. See *The Celebrated Mrs. Centlivre*, pp. 20–1. See also F. P. Lock, *Susanna Centlivre* (Boston, Mass., 1979), pp. 124–5.

ABBREVIATIONS USED IN THE NOTES

O1   First edition. London: Briscoe and Nutt, 1700.
O1a First edition, second issue. London: Briscoe and Nutt, 1700.
O2   'Third' (actually second) edition. London: Briscoe and Nutt, 1705.
O3   Third edition. London: Briscoe and Nutt, 1705.
D1   Fourth edition. London: Briscoe, 1718.
D2   Fifth edition. London: Briscoe, 1724.

Familiar and Courtly
LETTERS,
Written by Monsieur *Voiture*
To Persons of the greatest Honour,
Wit, and Quality of both Sexes in
the Court of FRANCE.

Made English by

Mr. *Dryden*,
Tho. Cheek, Esq;
Mr. *Dennis*,
} {
Henry Cromwel, Esq;
Jos. Raphson, Esq;
Dr. —, & c.

10

WITH

Twelve Select *Epistles* out of *Aristænetus*:
  Translated from the *Greek*.
Some Select *Letters* of *Pliny*, Jun. and Monsieur *Fontanelle*.
  Translated by Mr. *Tho. Brown*.
And a Collection of Original *Letters* lately
  written on several Subjects. By Mr. *T. Brown*.

Never before Publish'd.

To which is added,
A collection of LETTERS of Friendship, and
  other Occasional LETTERS, written by
  Mr. *Dryden*,   Mr. *Congreve*,
  Mr. *Wycherly*,   Mr. *Dennis*, and
  Mr. —   other Hands.

20

LOVE-LETTERS,
WRITTEN

By Mr. — to Madam —

I had a Mind to know, *Madam*, whether you had quarrel'd with me t'other Night, at the — or not; and therefore, writing to you Yesterday, I find now that you are angry at something; but may I be *discarded*, if I know the Reason: If you have made a Quarrel on my approving —, I beg your *Pardon*, and shall henceforth do *Violence* to my own *Reason*, and contradict *Mankind* to agree with you: 'Tis hard to find any Simpathy in *Hearts*, where there's such *Contrariety* in Opinions. I shall therefore, *Madam*, henceforth square my Sentiments to yours in every thing; and if you will quarrel without a Cause, I will oblige you, and do so too. Your Uneasiness, *Madam*, wrongs either your own *Charms* or my *Sincerity*; either of which is a sensible Abuse to me. 'Tis a hard Fate, that you can't *love* and be *easie*, and I can't *desist* and *live*: but I can *die* to make you *happy*; an ill-natur'd Line or two does the Business; for I cannot bear the *Spleen*, the *Rheumatism*, and *your Displeasure* at once. So, *Madam*, strike now, and for ever quit your self of an unfortunate Man, who has but one Hand, which he thinks sufficient, since he can thereby ever own himself

Yours. 20

To the same.

Madam,   *Sunday-morning.*

Next to my *Prayers*, I must address my *Devotions* to you; to you whom I have offended, and to whom I must offer a *penitential Sacrifice*, if an Oblation of a *bleeding Heart* can make any Attonement for my *Sin*, I offer it freely. Heaven is merciful, and so shou'd you be; I dare not approach, without your Permission: If you will Sign my *Pardon* in a Line from your *dear Hand*, expect me with all the Joy of a repriev'd *Malefactor*. I am, *Madam*, *happy* or *miserable*, as you please to make me.

To the same.

What shall I say to the *dearest Woman* upon Earth! Were my
Thoughts common, how easily they be express'd! But the
Expression, like the Enjoyment in Love, is lost by a too ardent
Desire; my *Soul* plumes it self in the secret Pride of being
belov'd by you; and upon so just a Foundation of valuing my
self, who can accuse me of Vanity? I can no more *compliment*
what I *love*, than I can *flatter* what I *hate*; and therefore when I
tell you, that your *Charmes* are more and more engaging, and
my Love improving, believe it for a Truth; hear my *Wish*, and
10 then conclude me happy:

> *Oh! cou'd I find (grant Heaven that once I may)*
> *A Nimph fair, kind, poetical and gay;*
> *Whose Love shou'd blaze unsullied and divine,*
> *Lighted at first by the bright Lamp of mine:*
> *Free from all sordid Ends, from Interest free,*
> *For my own sake Affecting only me.*
> *What a blest Union both our Souls should joyn!*
> *I her's alone, as she was only mine;*
> *Blest in her Arms, I should immortal grow,*
> *Whilst in return, I made my* Celia *so.*
> *Sweet generous Favours shou'd our Loves express,*
> *I'd Write for Love, and she shou'd Love for Verse:*
> *Not* Sacharissa's *self, great* Waller's *Fair,*
> *Shou'd for an endless Name with mine compare.*
> *She shou'd transcend all that e're went before,*
> *Her Praises, like her Beauty shou'd be more:*
> *My Verse shou'd soar so high, the World shou'd see,*
> *I sung of her, and* Celia *smil'd on me:*
> *The World shou'd see that from my Love I drew,* ⎫
> *At once my Theam, and Inspiration too:* ⎬
> *Blest in my Wish, my Fair, I'm blest with you.* ⎭

20

30

I went abroad Yesterday morning about seven, and
return'd about one this morning, slept till past eight, then
arose to tell you, that I dreamt of you all the time, and that I
am your own.

17 *both*] Q2; *shou'd   should joyn*] O2; *combine*   27 *soar*] O2; *run*   28 Celia
smil'd on] O2; *she inspired*

To the same.

By Heavens and Earth (my Dearest) I am ty'd Neck and Heels with Wine, and Company! All the Spells of Love can't undo the *Charm*; besides, *my Dear*, I am almost fudled; I shall stay here at the *Rose* till towards eleven; it will be a tedious Walk to go home to Night, considering that you lie upon the same Floor with the Door: It is not impossible, methinks, for a Man of so much *Love* to slip in *Incognito*. Your — is with me, there will be a double Pleasure in deceiving him, and being happy in my *dear* One's Arms; I shall call at the Door, and see whether the Coast be clear: however, this, if it succeeds, will make me the happiest upon Earth—; however, my *Dear*, run no Hazard that may expose you; but consider, my *Dear*, the eager Wishes of the faithfullest, and most loving of Mankind.

To the same.

If I did not *Love*, I wou'd not beg, and if ever you *loved*, you'll grant my *Pardon*; your Letter, *Madam*, has tormented me more than all the *Favors* of your whole *Sex* besides can please *me*; if I have *lost you*, I have *lost* my *self, and* shall be lost to all *Womankind*: My Letter last Night was written in heat of *Wine*; so Men guilty of *Murder* in their *Drink*, repent it all their *Lives*; mine is a greater *Crime*, for I have *stab'd* my self, pierc'd my own *Heart*, and now it bleeds with *Anguish* and *Despair*.

Stab'd my own Heart, and pierc'd your *Image*, there the Remembrance of the Happiness I have enjoy'd, will now prove the greatest *Curse*; the melting Sighs, the moving Tears, the Joys, the Raptures that mounted me to Heaven, now cast me down to Hell: I shall now turn *Poet* in good earnest;
And like poor Ovid, *banish'd from his* Rome,
Curse that destructive Art, that caus'd his Doom.
In short, *Madam*, I am *Mad*, and if I think farther, I shall let the World see it. Revoke that word, *eternal Silence*, or you make me eternally *Miserable*, for I am now the most Disconsolate of Mankind.

To a young Lady.
By another Hand.

My Dearest Madam,

For so I must ever think you, I hope you got safe to *London*, and that your Indisposition is abated, which will be the Means to make mine the more tolerable, since I can more easily bear mine own than yours; You expect I should tell you, how I am; and excepting a little Melancholy, the Reason of which you know, I find my self tolerable, my Feavour, I think, did not think fit to visit me last Night; I ramble out of one Room into another, now and then I let fall a Tear. I design to come to *London*, on *Sunday* next, that my Heart and I, may be 10 in the same Place; till then, believe me most entirely

Yours.

To the same.

I cannot help telling my Dearest, how much I am hers, what Pleasure I have in her Company, what Pain in her Absence; to love her, is but to see her; and to value her, is only to know her: But pray, my Dear Mrs. —, forget not to drink some Chocolate with me to Morrow, that I may once say, I spent a *Sunday* well; I am sure I shall have some good Thoughts in the Morning, because I shall think of you; and when I do so, I shall think of one that I passionately Love, and that I hope is not unmindful of

Hers.

To the same.

To convince you, I am not given to Change, regard but this Piece of Paper, 'tis torn like my Heart at taking leave, and is such a Scribble as I usually write; I am harsh in my Stile, negligent of my Ink, and not too exact in fashioning up my Letter; and cannot have the least Esteem for my self, but when I reflect that I have the Honour to be lookt upon as,

Madam, your most Humble.

To the same.

Dear Madam,

Tis to you, I must always address to tell me how I do; 'tis no matter, tho' I shou'd find my self in Health, if your Frowns shou'd tell me otherwise; know then, Madam, I languish, or revive, as you smile or look out of Humour; and though, at present, one wou'd guess by my Hand-writing, that I am just at the point of Death; yet, I doubt not, but I shall live tell to Morrow Evening, if you wou'd but promise, at that time, to come to

Yours.

Familiar and Courtly
LETTERS,
TO
Persons of Honour and Quality,
By Mons. *VOITURE*,
A Member of the Royal Academy at *Paris*.

The Third Edition with Additions.

To which is added,
A Collection of LETTERS of Friendship, and
other Occasional LETTERS, written by
Mr. *Dryden*,   Mr. *Congreve*,
Mr. *Wycherly*,   Mr. *Dennis*, and
Mr.—   other Hands.

A
Pacquet from *Will*'s:
Or a New
COLLECTION
OF
Original Letters
ON
SEVERAL SUBJECTS;
Containing
Pleasant Memoirs, Intrigues and Adventures that lately hapned

AT

London, Hampton Court, Tunbridge, Epsom, North Hall and the *Bath.*

WITH

Several Satyrical Characters, both of Ladies and Gentlemen, in Prose and Verse, with *Original Letters* by King *Charles* II. and the late Q. of *Sweden.*

10

Written and Collected by several Hands.

20

FRIDAY.
By Mr. Farquhar.

If I ha'nt begun thrice to write, and as often laid down my
Pen, may I never take it up again. My Head and my Heart have
been at Cuffs about you. Says my Head, 'You're a Coxcomb
for troubling your Noddle with a Lady, whose Wit is as much
above your Pretensions, as your Merit is below her Love.
Then answers my Heart, 'Good Mr. Head, You are a
Blockhead: I know Mr. *F*—'s Merit better than you. As for
your part, I know you are as whimsical, as the Devil, and
changing with every new Notion that offers: but for my part, I
am fixt, and can stick to my Opinion of a Lady's Merit for 10
ever; and if the Fair she can secure an Interest in me,
Monsieur Head, you may go whistle.—'Come, come, (answer'd
my Head) you, Mr. Heart, are always leading this Gentleman
into some Trouble or other. Was't not you that first enticed
him to talk to this Lady? Your damn'd confounded Warmth
made him like this Lady; and your Busie Impertinence has
made him write twice to her: Your Leaping and Skipping
disturbs his Sleep by Night, and his good Humour by Day. In
short, Sir, I will hear no more of her.—I am Head, and I will
be obey'd.—You lye Sir, replied my Heart (being very angry) 20
I am Head in Matters of Love. And if you don't give your
Consent, you shall be forced: For I am sure, that in this Case,
all the Members will be on my side. What say You,
Gentlemen Hands? Oh! (say the Hands) we would not want
the Pleasure of touching a soft Skin for the World—Well, what
say You, Mr. Tongue—Zounds, says the Tongue, there's
more Pleasure in speaking three soft Words of Mr. Heart's
suggesting, than whole Orations of Seignior Head's;—So, I'm
for the lady, and here's my honest Neighbour Lips will stand
by me. By the sweet Power of Kisses, we will (replied the 30
Lips:) And presently some other considerable Parts standing
up for the Heart, they laid Violent Hands upon poor Head,
and knock'd out his Brains. So, now Madam, behold me as
perfect a Lover as any in *Christendom*, my Heart purely
dictating every Word I say. The little Rebel has thrown it self

into your Power; and if You don't support it in the Cause it
has taken up for your sake, think what will be the miserable
Condition of the Headless and Heartless,

Farquhar.

To a Lady, *whom he never saw: Being a true Relation of a* Saturday Night's Adventure. *By Mr.* Farquhar.

I have now, Madam, had time to reflect on *Saturday* Night's
Adventure: and if I have reflected on any thing else since that,
may I never be blest with such an Adventure again. A Lady in
a Masque, with a pretty Hand, that presently got hold of my
Heart, desires to know where she shall see me after the Play:
At the *Rose*, Madam, said I. There the Lady calls, like a
Woman of Honour, where I was found, like a Man of Honour,
and without much Ceremony, leaves three honest Gentlemen,
and two roasted Fowls, to venture my self, Neck, and Gizard,
with two strange Ladies in a Coach. Compliments (which, by
the way, were pretty plain on my side) being past on both
sides; the Ladies would do nothing under the Rose, but must
drive to the *Fountain* in the *Strand*. If the Ladies had inform'd
me of their Quality, I had called for *Burgundy*; but seeing
nothing about them that promised beyond *Covent-Garden*, I
thought a Bottle of New *French* might be suitable. They both
were in love with me; but one a little further gone than t'other;
their Discourse was Modest, and they drank like Women of
Quality; for our Bottle was soon out. I was then impatient to
return to my Fowls; for I could not feed upon Covered Dishes.
The Lady that was most in love with me, promised to take off
her Mask, if I should see her home. I promised to wait on her
home, if she would let me lie with her all Night. I was a
Blockhead for that: for the Lady was angry, not with the
Matter, but the manner of the Expression: But I thinking still
of *Covent-Garden*, was not so very nice in my Phrase; but at last,
away we drove, and set down one Lady, the Lord knows
where: The t'other (relying, I suppose, more upon my
Modesty than her own) had the Courage to stay alone with
me in the Coach; which, after several Turnings, stopt where

we lighted, in *Golden-Square*; she advised me to make the Coach wait; which I thought a very good hint to discharge it. She conducted me up Stairs to a *very stately Apartment*; and she, according to her Promise, took off her Mask; but pull'd her Hoods so about her Face, that I was as far to seek for her Beauty as before. After some foolish Chat, in comes a Maid, with a red-hot Warming-Pan, and retires into a Bed-Chamber; and returning presently, told her *Lady*, that her Ladiship's Bed was ready; dropt a modest Curtesie, and made her *Exit*: the *Lady* told me, 'twas time for me to go to Bed. Madam, said 40 I, with all the Speed I'm able; and began to unbutten: but in spight of all my haste, she was a-bed before me. Our Conversation was free, natural, and pleasant, till ten a-clock next Morning. The Chamber was so dark, that I could not see the *Lady*'s Face; so was forc'd to depart as great a Stranger to that, as when I met her first; tho' I know every other part about her so well, that I shall never forget her. I hope Your Ladiships will pardon my Familiarity: For, by Heavens, I can no more forbear whispering my past Joys to my self, than I could abstain repeating them with You, would you bless me 50 with a second Opportunity. I have sent you a Note for the Pit, to see the *Jubilee*, to morrow, tho' I would rather try the Power of my Love, by finding you out in the Front Boxes. I'm sure you can't be handsome; for Nature never made any thing entirely Perfect. In short, if I can't find you out by Instinct, never trust me, when I say I love, which must be as great a Curse, as your Favour will prove a Blessing to, Madam,

Your most humble Servant.

To Mrs. C—

Madam,

   I am got to the *Rose*, whence I send to know how my Dear is. Bless me with a Line, my Dear. If I durst, I would visit You.

> *'Tis a cold frosty Night,*
> *My Desires are warm:*
> *My Love makes a Fire*
> *To keep me from Harm.*

> *But should you prove Cruel,*
> *And your Favours with-hold,*
> *My Fire goes out*
> *For want of its Fuel,*
> *And I, poor I, must perish with Cold.*

10

So much for Rhime; now for Reason. I love you, my Dear, and I have a thousand Reasons for it: And if you don't believe me, by Heaven, you wrong the faithfullest Man on Earth.

Pray Madam, don't put me to the Expence of Vows and Oaths. I hate swearing under my Hand. I love you, in plain downright Terms. But what sort of Love, I can't tell you, till I have the Honour and Happiness of seeing and conversing with you once more. You have Art enough to engage my
20 Friendship, and Beauty enough to engage my Love; You shall make a Friend of me, and I'll aspire to make a Mistress of You; but if You will bless me with the Knowledge of Time and Place of waiting on you, you shall make a Friend, Lover, Fool, or what you please of, Madam,

Your Admirer.

By the same.

Madam,

You were so engaged with Wits last Night, Madam, that an honest Man could not be happy; and I'm so engaged with Wits now, that I can't write Sense. I am very uneasie, and I don't know for what. I can drink no Health that can restore my Cure. I am stupid and Lifeless; for my Love is where,—Gad damme, Madam,—I wish I had never seen You. You made a turn in the — to Night, that has changed the Scene of my Happiness.—Now 'tis out—and I good Company again,—Sir, my humble Service to you; and I am this *Lady*'s

most humble Servant.

---

26 Admirer. [om.]] O3; ~, Gad Damme. The 1705 edition omitted the curious and surely unintended pseudonym.

By the same

Madam,

When I left You, my Dear, I went to the *Play*; from thence to Wit and Wine; which detained me till Four this Morning: Then I went to bed, and dreamt of her, whose Health I came from Drinking. 'Twas Yours, by Gad.—Now, Madam, I've given you an Account of my mis-spent Hours, for such I must reckon those that I throw away in any Company but Yours; but Love and Fortune cannot be reconciled. They are both blind, and therefore can never meet; but You and I can see: for we love one another. I'll answer for You, and You shall do the same for me.

10

Witness my Hand.

By —

Madam,

'Tis a hard Case, that you should disturb a Man of his Natural Rest at this rate. If I have slept one Wink to Night, may I sleep to all Eternity. The very Thoughts of You made me wakeful, as if I had had your dear self in my Arms. Zounds, Madam, what d'ye mean? Consider, I'm a Man; a mortal, wishing, amorous Man.

> *My Heart is Wax, your Eyes are Fire.*
> *You are all Charms, and I all o'er Desire.*
> *I'm start staring mad*
> *In Mind be gad.*
> *To day I languish with sorrow.*
> *But since I can't crown it,*
> *I'll drink till I drown it,*
> *And make my self well by to morrow.*

10

Madam, I am,

Your most—what you please by Jove.

To a Masque on Twelfth-day.

To be a Man, and honourable, You'll say, Madam, are Contradictions. But to be a Man, and not curious, were a greater Contradiction. Now, Madam, amidst all these Contradictions, I'll say one thing *very reasonably*. Your Letter is very *Witty*; You may be very handsome, and I have a Mistress already: she has Charms enough to secure my Heart hitherto, but can't well tell whether they are of force to maintain their Ground against Yours. If You think the *Victory* worth your Trouble, 'twill be the best way to take a Garrison possest by 10 so powerful an *Enemy*. You may at last come and view the Fortifications; and if you be an Ingineer worth a Farthing, you may presently guess whether the Fort be impregnable or not. Though this be the last Day of *Christmas*, it may prove the first of my *Jubilee*, if Your Ladiship please to honour me with your Commands where I shall wait on You. I am, Madam,

Your most humble Servant,

Wildair.

LETTERS
OF
Wit, Politicks and *Morality*.

To which is added a large Collection of
ORIGINAL LETTERS
OF
Love and Friendship.
WRITTEN,
By several Gentlemen and Ladies, particularly,
the Honourable Mr. *Granville, Tho. Cheek,* Esq; ₁₀
Capt. *Ayloffe*; Dr. *G*— Mr. *B*—*y*; Mr. *O*—*n*, Mr.
B—*r*, Mr. *G*—, Mr. *F*—*r*, Mrs. *C*—*l*, under the
name of *Astræa*; Mrs. *W*—*n* under the name of
Daphne, &c.

LETTER XLI.
Astræa to Damon.

I am extremely concern'd at my ill Fortune in being absent when *Damon* design'd me a visit: Could I have known by instinct that your visits were pretty well over, and that I should come again in my turn, I would have waited with pleasure. I am going into mourning, for I have lost my Rabbits, which makes me as melancholly as a Cat. As soon as I brought them home, I christen'd them, the Male *George* and Female *Suky: George* no sooner shar'd your Name, but all your inclinations follow'd, which made him grow indifferent to his *Suky*; and on *Sunday* whilst I was at Church he scamper'd 10 away, and left his poor Female over-whelm'd with Grief. At my return, I made strict inquiry in the Neighbourhood, but nothing can be heard of him. The next day I was reading Mr. *Asgill* (which you lent me) and *Suky* by me, in a very melancholy posture, bemoaning the loss of her belov'd *George*, when of a sudden I mist her, and notwithstanding all diligent search, she's no where to be found. She's, I suppose, bent upon Pilgrimage, till she finds her Mate; except *Asgill's* Doctrine had effect upon her, and mounted her to the Heavens, to provide a feat for her *quondam* Master and 20 Mistress. Thus I have given you an account of my unhappy fate, by which you see that nothing of Male cares long for

SIR,

Humble Servant,
ASTRÆA.

LETTER XLII.
Damon to Astræa.

Did I think, Madam, that my visits were as agreeable to your inclinations as to my own, I would repeat them oftener: but I can't imagine, Madam, that a person whom you make a perfect *Rabbit* of, should ever employ your thoughts, either

with hopes or disappointments. Some think me a Rabbit in another case, because they imagin I have been digging a Cunny-burrow in the Country, and have saluted me with joy upon my Marriage; but they should rather think me a Fox, for I care not for Earthing too long in the same hole, for fear I
10 should be found out by the Huntsmen. But, Faith, Madam, I am at present more unhappy than the Beasts of the Field, for I have ne're a Den to put my head in, much less a Noose to secure my Neck. You have heard, I suppose, Madam, how scurrilously I have been abus'd by Mr. — I am now busie about the vindication of my Honour, and endeavouring to answer him in his own Kind. Had the Rabbit staid I had perhaps expected your Prayers for my increase of ill-nature, to qualifie me for so kind an office; but now I beg only you would not think me so fickle as my name's-sake, since I am with as
20 much Truth as ever,

Ingenious Astræa, *yours*, &c.

LETTER XLVII.
Mr. Farquhar *to Mr.* R— S—

SIR,

Having been in company with Mr. *Johnson* just now, he inform'd me that you were in Love, and that you desir'd the advice of your Friends upon that Subject; I have long wish'd, Sir, for an opportunity of serving you, and I thank fortune which has now presented me so fair an occasion; for *Love* being very often of the same importance with an affair of Life and Death, the tryal of a friend may be well enough prov'd in it.

I have had some hints in that Folly from my own Experience and general Observation: but I have found it like
10 Chymistry, a knowledge very chargeable in Experiments, and worth nothing in the Enjoyment. 'Tis a misfortune, Sir, that Love can only be nourish'd by *ingenious* Men, yet Women should admire none but *Fools*; for which reason, I'm afraid, your success will prove but indifferent. If your passion can make you a Coxcomb, something may be done, but be assur'd, that the affection which can have so much power over

one of your parts, is much too violent to last; and the sober
reflections of a Man of Sense, will certainly at the last incline
him to a hatred and detestation of whatsoever could throw
him into extravagance, or abase him below the dignity of his 20
Reason. Had my experience extended only to one Woman, I
should not have concluded so peremptorily to the disadvantage
of the whole Sex; but, Sir, I have known several, and they all
wear blacker Masks on their minds, than on their Faces. They
are as fickle as Fortune; and like her, favour none but Fools.
The nature of a Woman's composition is exactly opposite to
the frame of a man's; for their Bodies are heavenly, but their
Souls are Earth; and therefore their corporeal parts I like well
enough, but their Minds let them bestow on sordid Souls of an
equal size in understanding. If a Woman's Beauty if extra- 30
ordinary, she is only qualified for a Whore, if her Sense be
above the common level, she is equip'd, and sets up for a Jilt.
Some will say that a Woman has a thousand irresistible Arts
and Tricks: not half so many as a Monkey, nor half so witty
and surprizing. Whence comes it then that they please us so.
Why 'tis our fancy that pleases, which like a flattering Glass
creates the Beauties, and therefore should be broke for telling
so damn'd a lye, as to make a Devil an Angel. When once
Love comes to be heighten'd by thought, 'tis like the study of
the black Art, which after long pains and application raises 40
the Devil to run away with the Conjurer. 'Tis the freedom of a
friend, Sir, to communicate his thoughts; and to be yet more
free, you must know that I have at this instant a Mistress that
I love dearly, but all as a reasonable man ought to do. My love
is a down-right Syllogism; her Beauty and Wit are major and
minor, and my Passion is the conclusion; but if I find either of
the Premises false, (which ten to one I shall) I have the same
thread of reason to guide me out of the Labyrinth which led
me in. Some will say that a Mistress is a pretty amusement in
a man's studies, but my observation can allow it no less than 50
the ruin and distruction of study, for a man must make it his
business to gain her, and afterwards she will make it her
business to disturb him. You may perhaps, find innocency in
the Country, but remember, Sir, that *Eve* lost her Maidenhead
in a Garden. Advice, I know, is a very impertinent thing, but
any thing upon so dear a Subject is agreeable to a Lover. If I

can be so happy as to be serviceable to you in any other respect, Pray, Sir, Command.

Your humble Servant

60

G. FARQUHAR.

TO A GENTLEMAN WHO HAD HIS POCKET PICK'D

THIS poem was published anonymously in *The Poetical Courant*, No. 2, 2 February 1706. The weekly halfsheet paper was edited by Samuel Philips, who had written the prologue and epilogue for *The Stage-Coach* 'for the Benefit of the Author', probably in 1704. (See Introduction, *The Stage-Coach*, vol. i, p. 326.) In all, Farquhar contributed four poems to the periodical; one was published on 16 February and two more on 2 June.

An earlier version of this poem as well as the other three poems had appeared in *Love and Business*. The first version. 'To a Gentleman, that had his Pocket pick'd of a Watch and some Gold by a Mistress', was a forty-five line poem addressed to Sam rather than Tony. Four lines are almost identical, and four others are close enough to leave no doubt of the close relationship of the two poems. Other verbal echoes include use of the same puns, rhyme words, and *double entendres*.

The poem seems to be another example of Farquhar borrowing from his own earlier work. He was in London at the time, knew Philips and perhaps owed him a favour to recompense the prologue and epilogue to *The Stage-Coach*, and may well have agreed to submit poems. He apparently took some care in revising the first one he contributed. However, ten days after it was published, he contracted with Lintott for publication of *The Recruiting Officer*, an indication that he was already at work on the comedy that opened on 8 April. Perhaps he wrote other unidentified poems for Philips as well. However, concentration on the play may explain the fact that the three other known poems were reprinted practically verbatim from *Love and Business*.

The characteristic reshaping of materials, the timing, the familiarity with Philips, and the publication of three other poems in the *Poetical Courant* all argue strongly for Farquhar's authorship of the poem.

To a Gentleman who had his *Pocket* Pick'd of a *Watch* and *Money* by a *Mistriss*.

You know the Ancient Writings say,
That Men shou'd *Watch* as well as *Pray*;
Had you but *Watch'd* your *Fob*, dear *Tony*,
You'd not been rob'd of *Watch* and *Money*;
However, *Friend*, to leave off punning,
I much admire the *Doxy*'s cunning,
Who was resolv'd to make all sure,
And of your *Mettal* be secure;
But faith, I think, it was a crime
Basely to rob you of your *Time*,
Sly Devil! she knew her *Minute* Hand
Cou'd in a *Moment Hours* command,
So *wound* you up to her own liking,
And stole the *Watch* while you were *striking*.
 Well, since 'tis gone, ne'er fret and vex,
Necessitati non est Lex;
You say, for your *lost Time* you grieve,
Why, *Money* can your *Time* retrieve?
But then, which is the worst *Mishap*,
You say, you fear some *After-clap*;
Suppose the worst, your *Old Friend CASE*,
Still Practices in the same place,
Send him but word, he'll send you down
A *perfect Cure* for half a Crown,
Therefore take Heart, your Courage rouze,
Things aren't so bad as you suppose;
And tak't from me—
The *Mettal*'s stronger that's well souder'd,
And *Beef* keeps sweeter once 'tis powder'd.

LOVE'S CATECHISM

THE device of the catechism, not to rehearse church doctrine but for the benefit of the new religions of politics or social life, became popular in pamphlet publications at the turn of the eighteenth century. In 1703 the fad of mock catechisms produced *The Ladies Catechism, The Beaus Catechism,* and *The Town-Misses Catechism.* Octavo pamphlets of eight pages, they used the speech prefixes 'Q.' and 'A.' rather than names. The pamphlets were satires on fine ladies and beaux, but they did not display the wit of *Love's Catechism.*[1] In 1704 more mock catechisms were published, including *The Player's Catechism, The Atheist's Catechism, The High Flyers Catechism,* and *The Ladies Catechism for Paint and Patches.*[2] In 1706, Benjamin Bragg, who had published the London edition of *The Stage-Coach,* issued a religious one, *The Historical Catechism,*[3] and other serious catechisms continued to be published. For example, the corrected fourth edition of *The Art of Catechizing* appeared in 1707.[4]

A tradition of secular catechisms also existed on stage, particularly in love scenes in comedies. In Wycherley's *The Country Wife,* for example, Sparkish catechizes Harcourt in Act III Scene ii:

Spar. . . . answer to thy Catechisme: Friend, do you love my Mistriss here?

Har. Yes, I wish she wou'd not doubt it.

Spar. But how do you love her?

Har. With all my Soul.

Alith. I thank him, methinks he speaks plain enough now.

Spar. You are out still.   [*to* Alithea.

But with what kind of love, Harcourt?

Har. With the best, and truest love in the World.

Spar. Look you there then, that is with no matrimonial love, I'm sure.

Alith. How's that, do you say matrimonial love is not best?

Spar. Gad, I went too far e're I was aware: But speak for thy self *Harcourt,* you said you wou'd not wrong me, nor her.

Har. No, no, Madam, e'n take him for Heaven's sake.

Spar. Look you here, Madam.
Har. Who shou'd in all justice be yours, he that loves you most.

*Claps his hand
on his breast.*[5]

In *The Constant Couple*, Wildair considers himself catechized by Angelica and Lady Darling:

Angelica. Now Sir, I hope you need no Instigation to Redress our Wrongs, since even the Injury points the way.
Lady Darling. Think Sir, that our Blood for many Generations, has run in the purest Channel of unsully'd Honour.
Wildair. Ay, Madam. (*Bows to her.*)
Angelica. Consider, what a tender Blossom is Female Reputation, which the least Air of foul Detraction blasts.
Wildair. Yes, Madam. (*Bows to t'other.*)
Lady Darling. Call then to mind your rude and scandalous Behaviour.
Wildair. Right, Madam. (*Bows again.*)
Angelica. Remember the base price you offer'd me.

Exit.

Wildair. Very true, Madam, was ever Man so Catechis'd.

Many other examples exist in the dramatic literature of the period. Cherry's catechism in *The Beaux Stratagem*, then, is by no means unique although it is notable for its delightful wit.

Love's Catechism echoes the catechism scene between Archer and Cherry. Altogether it reuses fifty-nine lines from *The Beaux Stratagem*, including dialogue between Archer and Aimwell as well as Mrs. Sullen and Dorinda. The multiple borrowings, as opposed to a single source, would argue for Farquhar's authorship of the insignificant little pamphlet; Farquhar characteristically reused prized lines, although he eschewed plagiarizing from other authors. Moreover, the title, *Love's Catechism: Compiled by the Author of the Recruiting Officer, for the Use and Benefit of all Young Batchelors, Maids, and Widows, that are inclinable to change their Condition*, argues for Farquhar's authorship on two counts: first, because of the reference to the author of *The Recruiting Officer*, and second, because of the inclusion of 'Widows' in the beneficiaries, a surprising choice that might well have been a gentle reference to the widow who had brought him to the '*Matrimony Nooze*' (l. 157).

The only major doubts concerning Farquhar's authorship

are that (1) it was published in 1707, the year of his death, and (2) Lintott was apparently not the publisher, although he was then consistently issuing Farquhar's works. Lacking the evidence of printed advertisements for publication, I should suspect that *Love's Catechism* was written and even published before *The Beaux Stratagem* opened and that it was so insignificant a work that Lintott was not interested or perhaps not consulted. Farquhar was in exceedingly bad health, expecting death, in the spring of 1707, and trying to provide for his family. Even small publication profits would have helped.

The reasons I suspect publication preceding the final play are several: (1) Farquhar had borrowed from himself in earlier plays, notably in the lines, plot devices, and characters from *The Adventures of Covent-Garden* reused in *The Constant Couple*. Ill when he wrote *The Beaux Stratagem*, he might well have resorted to such economy again. (2) It seems unlikely that the materials in *Love's Catechism* could be recycled in the year *The Beaux Stratagem* appeared without arousing cries of plagiarism, but so few people would have read the inconsequential pamphlet that if the play appeared second, it might well reuse materials from the pamphlet without complaint from the critics, as had happened when *The Constant Couple* borrowed from *The Adventures of Covent-Garden*. (3) Finally, had the pamphlet postdated *The Beaux Stratagem* and reused its materials, the title-page would probably have read 'By the Author of the Beaux Stratagem' instead of 'the Recruiting Officer'. Although the early performances of *The Beaux Stratagem* were advertised as 'Written by the Author of the Recruiting Officer', by 17 April 1707 the Drury Lane advertisement of *The Recruiting Officer* boasted 'Written by the Author of the Beaux Stratagem' (*London Stage*, Part 2, i. 142, 144).

Another possibility to be considered is that Farquhar wrote the piece and after his death his widow retrieved it, as she did the text of *Barcellona*, and arranged for it to be published. But if it were printed after his death, one would have expected the authorship to be identified by *The Beaux Stratagem*, not *The Recruiting Officer*. Evidence suggests, then, that Farquhar wrote the piece before his final play opened.

THE TEXT

The only edition has served as copy-text. I have collated copies in the British Library, Bodleian, and Folger. I have not regularized speech prefixes.

NOTES

1. Copies at the Folger Shakespeare Library.
2. Advertisements, *Post-Man*, 17–19 Oct. and 2 Nov. 1704; *Daily Courant*, 8 Dec. 1704.
3. *Daily Courant*, 14 Oct. 1706.
4. *Ibid.*, 27 Feb. 1707.
5. Quoted from Friedman, *The Plays of William Wycherley*, pp. 295–6.

LOVE'S CATECHISM:

Compiled by the Author of the

Recruiting Officer,

FOR THE

USE and BENEFIT of all Young
Batchelors, Maids, and Widows,
that are inclinable to change their
CONDITION.

Love's Catechism, &c.

Tom. Come, my Dear, have you con'd over the Catechise I taught you last Night?

Betty. *Come, Question me.*

Tom. What is Love?

Betty. *Love is I know not what, it comes I know not how, and goes I know not when.*

Tom. Very well, an apt Scholar. But where do's Love enter?

Betty. *Into the Eyes.*

Tom. And where goes it out?

Betty. *I won't tell ye.*

Tom. What are Objects of that Passion?

Betty. *Youth, Beauty, and clean Linnen.*

Tom. The Reason?

Betty. *The two first are Fashionable in Nature; and the third at Court.*

Tom. That's my Dear; what are the Signs and Tokens of that Passion?

Betty. *A stealing Look, a stammering Tongue, Words improbable, Designs impossible, and Actions impracticable.*

Tom. That's my good Child, Kiss me. But what must a Lover do to obtain a Mistress?

Betty. *He must adore the Person that disdains him, he must bribe the Chamber-maid that betrays him, and court the Footman that Laughs at him; he must, he must.*

Tom. Nay, Child, I must Whip you if you don't mind your Lesson; he must Treat his—

Betty. *O, ay, he must treat his Enemies with Respect, his Friends with Indifference, and all the World with Contempt; he must suffer much, and fear more; he must desire much, and hope little; in short, he must embrace his Ruine, and throw himself away.*

Tom. Had ever Man so hopeful a Pupil as mine? Come, my Dear, why is Love call'd a Riddle?

Betty. *Because being Blind, he leads those that See; and tho' a Child, he governs a Man.*

Tom. Mighty well. And why is Love Pictur'd Blind?

Betty. *Because the Painters out of the Weakness, or Privilege of their Art chose to hide those Eyes that they could not Draw.*

Tom. That's my dear little Scholar, Kiss me agaen. And why shou'd Love, that's a Child, govern a Man?

40　*Betty.* *Because that a Child is the End of Love.*

Tom. What are the Hindrances of Love?

Betty. *A mean Habit and no Money.*

Tom. Why?

Betty. *Because 'tis a Maxim now a-days, that there's no Scandal like Rags, nor any Crime so shameful as Poverty.*

Tom. How must a Man remedy this?

Betty. *Why the World's wide enough, let Men bustle; for Fortune has taken Fools under her Protection, but Men of Sense are left to their Industry.*

50　*Tom.* But what say you to those amorous Puppies that can't counterfeit the Passion of Love without feeling it?

Betty. *'Tis true, tho' the whining part be out of Doors in Town, yet 'tis in force with the Country Ladies.*

Tom. S'death, *Betty*, you have a delicate pair of Eyes, pray what d'ye do with'm?

Betty. *Why,* Tom, *don't I see every Body?*

Tom. Ay, but if some Women had 'em, they wou'd kill every body.

Tom. Well, what say you to a good Husband?

60　*Betty.* *That's a Rarity; and truly there are so many bad ones now, which give me such an Impression of Matrimony, that I shall be apt to condemn my Person to a long Vacation all its Life.*

Tom. Why then I find your Inclinations are for a silent, solitary sort of a Man.

Betty. *O, by no means; for if ever I Marry, I'll beware of a sullen, silent Fool, one that's always Musing, but never thinks: There's some Diversion in a talking Blockhead; and if a Woman must wear Chains, I wou'd have the Pleasure of hearing 'em Rattle a little.*

Tom. But what say you to my Lady what d'ye call'ums
70　Page that was here to Day? I observ'd by his sweet Addresses to you, that he's up to the Head and Ears in Love.

Betty. *Do you think that I am so weak as to fall in Love with a Fellow at first Sight.*

57–9 No reply by Betty intervenes between Tom's two consecutive speeches.

62 *Vacation*] Vacation　　　72 *in*] in in

Tom. Pshaw, now you spoil all; I warrant you the young Whipster has got to some of his boon Companions already, has avow'd his Passion, toasted your Health, call'd you ten thousand Angels, has run over your Lips, Eyes, Neck, Shape, Air, and every thing in Description that warms their Mirth to a second Enjoyment.

Betty. Well, as much as you Banter, I'll have you to know there are 80 *some of your Sex have prais'd me for Wit and Beauty before now, and wou'd be my humble Servant when I please.*

Tom. You're in the right, *Betty*, for Pride is the Life of a Woman, and Flattery her Daily Bread; and she's a Fool that won't believe a Man there, as much as she that believes him in any thing else.

Betty. I own my self a Woman, full of my Sex, a gentle, generous Soul, easie and yielding to soft Desires; a spacious Heart, where Love and all his Train might Lodge in a chast Inn.

Tom. Why then you pretend as if you would not pluck the 90 Fruits of Love without Marriage?

Betty. Truly, I must acknowledge that as the weak Frailty of Flesh and Blood, will not give one leave to Swear to an absolute Resistance of a Temptation, yet I can safely promise to avoid it; and that's as much as the best of us can do.

Tom. Right, right, *Betty.*

Betty. But suppose, Tom, *now that you had a fancy for a young Woman, in what manner would you address her?*

Tom. I would throw my self at her Feet; speak some Romantick Nonsense or other; address her like *Alexander* in the 100 height of his Victory; confound her Senses; bear down her Reason; and away with Her.

Betty. That's the right way of those who have a Design upon a Woman's Virtue; but my Chastity shall ne'er submit to Cupid*'s Arms without Marrying, and that too with one whose Temper and mine may agreeably make one another happy; for,*

> *Wedlock we own ordain'd by Heaven's Decree,*
> *But such as Heaven ordain'd it first to be,*
> *Concurring Tempers in the Man and Wife.*
> *As mutual Helps to draw the Load of Life.*

110

View all the Works of Providence above,
The Stars with Harmony and Concord move;
View all the Works of Providence below,
The Fire, the Water, Earth, and Air, we know, }
All in one Plant agree to make it grow.
Must Man, the chiefest Works of Art Divine,
Be doom'd in endless Discord to repine?
No, we shou'd injure Heaven by that Surmise,
Omnipotence is just, were Man but wise.

120 *Tom.* Nay, Madam, if you are for Verse, I'll at you presently.

Betty. *As soon as you please.*

Tom. Why dost thou all Address deny?
    Hard-hearted, pretty *Betty*, why?
    See how the trembling Lovers come,
    That from thy Lips expect their Doom.

Betty. Thomas, *I hate them all, they know,*
    Nay, I have often told them so,
    Their silly Politicks abhorr'd;
130   *I scorn to make my Slave my Lord.*

Tom. But *Richard*'s Eyes proclaim his *Love*
    Too brave, tyrannical to prove.

Betty. *Ah, Thomas! when we lose our Pow'r,*
    We must obey the Conquerour.

Tom. Yet where a gentle Prince bears sway,
    It is no Bondage to obey.

Betty. *But if like* Nero, *for a while,*
    With Arts of Kindness he beguile,
    How shall the Tyrant be withstood,
140   *When he has writ his* Laws *in Blood.*

Tom. Love (pretty *Betty*) all commands,
    It fetters Kings in charming Bands;
    Mars yields his Arms to *Cupid*'s Darts,
    And Beauty softens savage Hearts.

Betty. *If nothing else can pull the Tyrant down,*
    Kill him with Kindness, and the Day's your own.

Tom. Well, *Betty*, now we are got into a Discourse of *Love*
Affairs, I'll sing you the Batchellor's Song.

Betty. *With all my Heart.*

150 *Tom.* Now for it.

The Batchelor's SONG.

Like a Dog with a Bottle, fast ty'd to his Tail,
Like Vermin in a Trap, or a Thief in a Jail,
Or like a Tory *in a Bog,*
Or an Ape *with a Clog;*
Such is the Man, who when he might go free,
Does his Liberty lose,
For a Matrimony Nooze,
And sells himself into Captivity.
The Dog he do's howl, when his Bottle do's jog;
The Vermin, the Thief, and the Tory *in vain*   160
Of the Trap, of the Jail, of the Quagmire complain.
But welfare poor Pug, *for he plays with his Clog;*
And though he would be rid on't rather than his Life,
Yet he lugs it, and he hugs it, as a Man do's his Wife.

FINIS.

BARCELLONA

INTRODUCTION

Epic poetry was not Farquhar's genre. Even elegiac odes to military heroes proved too much: witness the Pindaric on the death of General Schomberg, included in *Love and Business*. Yet Farquhar chose to print that embarrassing effort, and perhaps he would have sought to publish *Barcellona* as well, had he lived until the time that publication of his epic could conceivably have proved profitable. But the Earl of Peterborough, its hero and dedicatee, fell from royal favour before the poem was published and did not return to the Queen's good graces until after Farquhar died. It was, therefore, Farquhar's impoverished widow instead who thrust the poem into print in 1710. By doing so, she did Farquhar's posthumous reputation no good, but perhaps she managed to gain a few pounds from the Queen and from Peterborough.

In brief, the siege of Barcelona proved a triumph for Charles Mordaunt (1658–1735), third Earl of Peterborough. After a complicated relationship with William and Mary, Mordaunt, who stood in Anne's favour, was appointed general and commander-in-chief of an expeditionary force to Spain on 31 March 1705, and on 1 May he received an additional commission as admiral and commander-in-chief jointly with Sir Clowdisley Shovell; the fleet arrived in Lisbon on 9 June. In Spain, Mordaunt and Shovell met the Archduke Charles, whom the English recognized as King of Spain, Prince George of Hesse-Darmstadt, the Earl of Galway, and other leaders. The leaders debated in one council of war after another; some argued for landing at Valencia and heading for Madrid, others, including Peterborough, for joining Prince Eugene of Savoy in Italy. Finally they agreed on Barcelona as their target. The troops left the river Tagus on 17 July and anchored east of Barcelona on 11 August. Another lengthy series of councils took place as the leaders continued to disagree over strategy. On 30 August the generals formally agreed to march on 4 September against Tarragona and then Valencia. But on 1 September, when Mordaunt learned that Montjuich, a hillfort less than a mile from Barcelona, was poorly defended, its fort still unfinished, he decided to attack it.

The battle itself could be described as a tragedy of errors. A thousand men marched on 2 September and arrived at the foot of the hill the next day. Unfortunately, the scaling ladders proved too short, and other problems arose. The garrison at Montjuich began shouting 'Viva el Rey', a defiant cry misinterpreted by the English as surrender. The English troops leapt from their breastworks into the ditch, thus exposing themselves to the fire of two bastions. Many were killed; two hundred surrendered. A musket shot severed an artery in Hesse-Darmstadt's leg, killing him, and Colonel Allen was taken prisoner.[1] Mordaunt spurred the troops to hold the outworks regardless of the tragic mistake, and on 6 September the English captured the garrison. The next day 3,000 men and heavy guns arrived at Barcelona; Mordaunt's determination, bravado, and self-aggrandizement are all reflected in a letter he wrote to Godolphin from the castle of Montjuich on 9 September.

> . . . our affaire is brought att Barcelona to this passe, it must prove the most amazing action perhaps that Ever was heard off, or we must suffer extreamly in itt. . . .[2]

By 22 September a large breach had been made in the city walls, and by 28 September Barcelona capitulated; if it was not 'the most amazing action' in military history, it was indeed acclaimed a great victory for Peterborough and the English troops.[3]

Yet there was a grimly distasteful inside view of the whole military enterprise as far less heroic and more contemptible than the wisdom and valour described in laudatory accounts of the battle. Peterborough himself complained to Godolphin, while preserving his patriotic stance:

> The meannesse, the Fatigues, the dificulties I have mett with are inexpressible, if I have the least satisfaction it has been in this that I

am certain, I shall have your aprobation, I can now say her Majestys Arms will gaine no disrepute under my command. . . .[4]

The constant wrangling of the admirals and generals did not arise from a group of brilliant strategists debating military strengths and weaknesses, but from headstrong, wilful men, such as the Archduke Charles, intent on having their own way, protective of their own interests, and thoroughly contemptuous of one another. The leaders never built a consensus based on reason and probability; instead, the decision to strike at Barcelona was finally dictated by the impossibility of moving the Archduke Charles, who was determined to be monarch of Spain, or of getting the other commanders to agree on anything.

An undated, unsigned letter to Richard Hill, envoy to Savoy, gives a first-hand assessment of the situation; the author is apparently Peterborough himself, who, according to Colin Ballard, may have designed a scheme to sabotage Charles's efforts in order to enable Prince Eugene of Savoy to become King of Spain.[5] In the letter he laments the failure to go to the aid of Prince Eugene in Italy although the land generals had agreed to quit the 'almost impossible siege of Barcelona for the more pressing and probable Support of the Duke of Savoy'. But the Archduke Charles prevailed over the 'Salt water Politicians' through the solicitations of Hesse-Darmstadt and Prince Anthony Lichtenstein. Yet, the author asks, what would the success have mattered if Eugene had been sacrificed and the war in Italy lost? He continues with a revealing passage concerning the decision to attack Fort Montjuich:

It's true our Successes here have been beyond hopes & expectation, but not the measures of those that kept us here, who would have lost our little Army, render'd those mixt attempts of Sea & Land contemptible wch I am sure will prove of consequence I pretended when rightly managed, for so vain & mad an Attempt as the Prince of Hesse always insisted upon could have ended in nothing but ruine, so ignorant he was (tho he had been so long in the place) of the proper way of attacking itt (how desperate so ever itt might seem the only way that could succeed was the Attack of Montjui, which I undertook without the knowledge of the King of Spain, and of his Ministers, of the Prince of Hesse, or any of our own Officers, for I was weary of doing nothing & of Councills of war, the copy of two of which I send to you.[6]

Despite these remarks, historians have tended to agree that Hesse-Darmstadt, not Peterborough, was the wiser and braver officer. Clearly they disagreed with each other, as all the officers did. Moreover, some of the greatest problems were not strategic but financial. John Methuen had advanced £20,000 and Peterborough was forced to pay the local troops called Miquelets from his own stock. The problem of finances was to plague Peterborough throughout his military career, as indeed it plagued the military establishment as a whole.

Other less passionate participants felt equally exasperated at the endless bickering. As early as 2 June 1705 Methuen wrote from Lisbon to Secretary of State Godolphin:

My Lord Gallway complains not only of the want of ye things necessary for ye enterprise of Alcantara but of ye confusion all things are in by ye incapacity of him who commands in cheif but what is yet worse there are partyes & factions there that hinder every thing. The Almirante continues his desire to go into the Kingdom of Leon as last year Monsr. Fagel then & Mons^4. Schonenbergh crosse every thing my Lord Gallway proposes as being proposed by him & Monsr. Schonenbergh on all occasions opposes whatever I mention at any time relating to ye cooperating with our fleet with all ye violence & greater than you can imagine. . . .[7]

Farquhar's epic reflects not only the victorious conclusion of often ignominious proceedings, but also the pettiness, the stupidity, and the self-serving obstinacy that marked the councils of war. His poem is more than an enamelled façade; he portrays the ignoble and untalented as well as the noble.

Farquhar's epic concludes with Peterborough's triumph at the first siege of Barcelona. Had he chosen a greater span of events, he could have recounted the triumphal entry of Charles into Barcelona as King of Spain on 12 October, Parliamentary praise of Peterborough as the hero of Barcelona, Peterborough's becoming the nominal governor, and later renewing quarrels with his allies, Charles himself, the German ministers, and others. Peterborough captured Valencia on 24 January 1706 and stayed there until 27 March; his delayed return once again endangered Barcelona, by then under threat from the French. The second siege of Barcelona raged from 4 April to 11 May, with the allied fleet under Admiral Leake trying to protect the city. On 11 May, the French beat a retreat, and Peterborough once again reaped praise. But that high esteem was not to last, for he continued his quarrelsome relationships with everyone including King Charles, until finally he received orders to return home. He returned, but by an exceedingly indirect route through Europe, not arriving in England until 20 August. He then fell into even greater disgrace: asked to render account of his military money, he could not do so, and therefore his property was attached until he took care of his pay-lists. Then followed personal disasters, his wife's death in March 1709, his two son's deaths from small-pox the next year. However, with the new ministry in 1710, his years of Job-like suffering ceased. He was brought into Harley's circle of friends. He was restored to a military commission, as general of marines and first lord of the admiralty, and on 2 November 1710 he became captain-general of the marines. In December he became ambassador extraordinary to Vienna. The publication of Farquhar's poem in 1710, then, coincided with Peterborough's restoration to respectability; he might well have been ready to reward the author's widow for any aid to his campaign for return to grace.

Although Farquhar was in the army at the time of the siege of Barcelona, he was not among the troops in Spain. He was probably still in Dublin in September, when fighting raged in the Spanish campaign. Jordan argues convincingly that before the end of October Farquhar had probably left for the recruiting duty in Lichfield that provided the location for *The Beaux Stratagem*; in October authorizations to recruit more men went out to officers including Orrery, and by 1 November Farquhar's name no longer appeared on the Dublin court-martial lists.[8] The preface to *Barcellona*, presumably written by Margaret Farquhar, says that although Farquhar was an officer at the time, he was not in Barcelona but received the information from 'an ingenious Friend' who fought there. Indeed such a possibility exists, for the accurate detail with which Farquhar refers to various officers and their troops suggests astonishing familiarity. His description of the relationships of the commanders, as reflected in the councils of war, matches to an incredible degree the attitudes reflected in the extant letters written by the principals before and during the siege. For a lieutenant stationed in Ireland and England to have acquired such accurate detail suggests personal contact with someone who witnessed the events at first hand, perhaps a staff officer. The descriptions are too precise to have derived from journalistic accounts. Newspaper accounts did occur, of course, but Farquhar must have relied on additional information, for many details in the poem cannot be traced to contemporary journalistic endeavours. A number of volumes were published on Peterborough's exploits in Spain, some giving far greater detail than the newspapers; however, most of these were published after Farquhar's death. The most detailed and significant one, *An Account of the Earl of Peterborow's Conduct in Spain* with a dedication signed by John Freind, first appeared on 1 December 1707; in it details such as the names of officers and the accounts of councils of war appear; Farquhar, however, had died before it was published. Therefore, Margaret's statement that a friend recounted the events seems most probable.

The date of composition can be assigned with some confidence to the period between the end of November, when word of victory arrived in England, and 30 May 1706, when news of Peterborough's successful second siege of Barcelona reached London.[9] At least part of it was written after the Earl of Donegal's death on 21 April 1706, mentioned in Canto VI; Henry Conyngham's death on 15 January 1706 is also noted in the same canto. No later events are cited. Had composition occurred after the English learned about the successful outcome of the second siege, Farquhar probably would not have ended at the moment of victory in the first siege without even a hint of the later triumph. Since Farquhar probably left his regiment before the end of January 1706, it seems most likely that he began a draft of *Barcellona* at least by December or January, perhaps while still on military duty. On 2 February he published a poem in the *Poetical Courant*. On 12 February he contracted with Lintott to print *The Recruiting Officer*, which opened on 8 April. Perhaps Farquhar left military service by February, with his new play in mind or perhaps even drafted, and brought it to the playhouse at least a month to six weeks before opening night. He might have had time to return briefly to the epic in March during rehearsals and certainly in April and May, after the opening; but he probably did not make major additions after that time. He certainly did not revise to include the second siege.

Farquhar did not immediately contract for publication of *Barcellona*. He returned to the life of the theatre, writing prologues, seeing new editions of *The Recruiting Officer* go into print, and drafting *The Beaux Stratagem*. Although one treatise on Peterborough's behalf, *An Exact and Full Account of the Siege. By Way of Journal, from the 2d. of April to the 11th of May 1706 (London: Benjamin Bragg, 1706)*, a far less detailed account than Freind's, appeared in 1706, most of Peterborough's defenders did not publish until 1707. By March 1707, Peterborough had once again headed for trouble with his quarrelsome ways and was ordered home. *The Beaux Stratagem* opened that month, as Farquhar lay ill and dying and, by several accounts, looking for ways to provide for his wife and children.

On 31 March 1707 Benjamin Bragg, who had published the London quarto of *The Stage-Coach*, published the second edition of *The History of the Triumphs of her Majesty's Arms both by Sea and Land in and about Spain during this War; More particularly under the Conduct of his Excellency Charles Earl of Peterborough and Monmouth*.[10] Clearly, then, in Farquhar's last few months a poem honoring Peterborough, even one celebrating his penultimate victory, might have proved publishable. But Farquhar, consumed with his illness and having just given his best efforts to *The Beaux Stratagem*, did not market his modest attempt at epic.

He died in May, and his wife embarked on a fiercely intense series of attempts to make money from her husband's reputation. On 25 May 1708, Drury Lane staged a benefit performance of *The Constant Couple* on behalf of her and her children, doubtless at her behest. In January or February 1709 she petitioned the Queen for redress for her two husbands, Pemell and Farquhar, both military men who had died. In a letter to Harley asking for his intervention, she mentioned that she 'never yet receiv'd a farthing from her Matie, except ten Guinneys by ye hands of y^c Dutchess of

Devonshire upon ye^c presentation of my husband's poem.'[11] If
the poem was *Barcellona*, as seems likely, Farquhar's widow
probably presented it to the Queen soon after his death, before
Mordaunt fell from favour in the summer of 1707. Margaret's
petition to the Queen through Harley was accompanied by
certificates from Orrery, dated 26 January 1708/9, and
Ormonde, dated 28 January 1708/9, both attesting to
Farquhar's faithful service and good character.[12] The exasperated tone of the widow's letter to Harley ('I have bin S^r a
celisitriss to her most gracious majesty ever since she came to
her crown and have spent all my fortune upon dependance. . . .')[13] is understandable if she had tried to gain the
Queen's bounty for several years but had progressed no
further than the receipt of ten guineas.

Margaret's financial strain led her to petition the Queen
as it caused her to squabble with the theatre over the
house charges for Farquhar's benefit performance of *The
Beaux Stratagem*. Then in 1710 she hit upon the notion
of publishing *Barcellona*. She worked from an imperfect
manuscript; in fact some of the pages must have been lost.
Canto II, considerably shorter than any of the other four,
stops abruptly in the middle of the Lisbon council of war,
following the lines:

> He spoke: They talk'd a while. *Guiscard* withdrew,
> And shew'd himself again to publick View.

The next canto opens with the allied fleet approaching
Barcelona. Clearly an important passage which finished the
debate and prepared the audience to sail in Canto III never
reached the print shop. The widow Farquhar had good cause
to apologize in the Preface for the lack of a corrected version of
the poem. But that lack did not deter her from publishing the
decidedly inferior epic.

THE TEXT

Two issues of the first and only edition of *Barcellona* were
published. The imprint of one reads: '*London*| Printed for *John
Smith* at the *Post-House* in *Russell-*|*street*, *Covent-Garden*, and
Richard Standfast in *West-*|*minster-Hall*, Booksellers. Price 1 *s.*'

The collational formula is A–G^4, with the prelims unpaginated and the text paginated 1–48. There are no running-titles for the text. The prelims of this issue include: A1 title-page; A2^r–A3^v the dedication 'To|The Right Honourable|Charles| Earl of *PETERBOROUGH* | AND | *MONMOUTH*'; A4^{r-v} contains the preface (copies at the British Library, Bodleian, Huntington, and Yale).

The other issue bears the same type on the title-page except for the imprint, which reads: '*Publish'd for the Benefit of the Author's* | *Widow and Children*, 1710.' No price is listed on the title-page. The dedication does not appear in the prelims; the A gathering includes the title-page on A1 and the preface on A2^{r-v}, (copies at the British Library, Bodleian, National Library of Scotland, Williams College, New York Public Library).

The two issues are printed on two different papers, both described by Foxon as of poor quality. The one with Smith and Standfast's imprint contains a watermark with a fleur-de-lys and the initials FH; the one printed for the widow and children has a grape watermark.[14]

The Smith and Standfast issue was advertised in the *Tatler* on 11 May 1710. Peterborough had reached his nadir with the death of his wife and sons, the second son only a month earlier, and his fortune was beginning to change. It was a time in which Peterborough, extolled in many pamphlets in 1707, then having suffered great disgrace and misfortune, might well have welcomed an epic, even a bad epic, praising his strengths and service to his country.

The two issues are difficult to explain. The fact of different paper suggests either that they were printed at separate times or that some were printed on a finer stock for presentation copies. The grape paper appears to me somewhat finer, although Foxon describes it as poor. If the issues were printed at separate times, the printing house might simply have finished one lot of paper and started another; yet the poem was not reset, so it is unlikely that much time elapsed between the two printings. If presentation copies were made, one would certainly expect them to go to the Earl of Peterborough and his friends; yet oddly enough those printed for the widow and children do not contain the dedication to Peterborough.

Perhaps a clue to the mystery lies in one version of Margaret Farquhar's letter to Harley.[15] Margaret begins by thanking Harley for returning her book by her daughter and later says, '. . . her Majesty was pleased to give me ten guineas for ye book wch you did me ye hon^r to receive. . . .' The 'book' is probably the 'poem' previously mentioned as honoured by ten guineas from the Queen, although the other letter speaks of the Duchess of Devonshire as the one who interceded. Since the letter was accompanied by copies of the certificates written early in 1709, it probably predated the advertisement for *Barcellona* in the *Tatler* by more than a year. Could that book, in fact, have been *Barcellona*, prepared without the dedication to Peterborough as a way to test the waters with the Queen?

No later editions were ever printed, nor was *Barcellona* ever included in editions of Farquhar's works until Stonehill's edition of 1930.

I have collated the following copies: British Library (two copies), Bodleian (two copies), Huntington.

NOTES

1. Colin Ballard, *The Great Earl of Peterborough* (London, 1929), p. 149.
2. British Library, Add. MS 39 757 f. 117^v.
3. Sources of information for this short account include Ballard; *DNB*; John Freind, *An Account of the Earl of Peterborow's Conduct in Spain. Chiefly since the raising the Siege of Barcelona, 1706. To which is added the Campaign of Valencia. With Original Papers.* (2nd edn. corrected, London, 1707); *Impartial Remarks on the Earl of Peterborow's Conduct in Spain. Written by a Gentleman who was an Eye-Witness of his Lordship's Transactions in that Kingdom* (London, 1707); *The Earl of Peterborows Vindication: With an Account of His Lordships Conduct in Spain* (London, n.d.).
4. British Library, Add. MS 39 757, f.116".
5. Ballard, p. 183.
6. British Library, Add. MS 28 057, f. 25^{r-v}.
7. British Library, Add. MS 28 056, f.273^r. For yet another contemporary account of the disagreements, see ff. 309–10.
8. Jordan, p. 261.
9. Ballard, p. 186.
10. Advertised in the *Daily Courant*.
11. British Library, Loan 29/32.
12. British Library, Loan 29/32. A third certificate, from Bolton on Pemell's character, is dated 4 February 1708/9.
13. British Library, Loan 29/194, f.108^r.
14. Described in D. F. Foxon, *English Verse 1701–1750* (Cambridge, 1977), p. 267, F62, F63.
15. British Library, Loan 29/194. f.108^r.

BARCELLONA.

A
POEM.

OR,

The Spanish Expedition,
Under the COMMAND of
CHARLES Earl of *Peterborough.*

UNTIL

The Reduction of the City of *Barcellona*
to the Obedience of *Charles* III. King of
Spain.

TO

The Right Honourable
CHARLES
Earl of *PETERBOROUGH*
AND

MONMOUTH.

My Lord,

My Presumption in Dedicating to Your Lordship this Poem (found among my dear Deceas'd Husband's Writings) will I hope obtain not only Your Lordships Pardon, but favourable Acceptance, for to whom should this Address be made, but to that Hero who is the glorious Subject of the Song, Happy, could it by Art represent what was really done by Your Lordship in that Expedition, so surprising, as not only surpasses all Poetick Description, but makes even *Truth* it self Romantick. The Difficulties Your Lordship had to encounter in the different Interest and Opinions of your Confederates 10 was not the least part of that Undertaking, You were to convince before you engag'd, and Your invincible Reason was to confirm assured Conquest to Your Sword. *Monjuich* beyond *Obilisks* and *Pyramids* will be the Eternal Monument of your Fame, whereupon the Fall of that great tho' unhappy Prince of *Darmstad*, Your Lordship Heroically interpos'd, turn'd and assured the Fate of the *Austrian* Monarchy; *Barcellona* became the Rival of Madrid, and *Madrid* it self had received its natural Lord. And had not Envy it self blasted the sure laid Design, my Lord *Mordaunt* had rival'd the Glory of the Black Prince 20 himself on the Theatre of *Spain*. Accept, Great Sir, these Lawrels planted by your transcended Valour and reap'd by your Victorious Arm. Accept that Tribute which is here offer'd by an humble but sincere Hand, to that magnificent Vertue which hath restored the Foundation of the *Austrian*

Spanish Monarchy, which none but our great Queen can establish and confirm.

That Your Lordship may live to see the noble Effects of so glorious an Undertaking ratify'd in a sure and lasting Peace, ₃₀ the *West-India* Trade flowing into the *British* Channel, and the good Wishes of all good Men, deriv'd into lasting Blessings upon your Lordship and noble Family is the hearty Prayer of

My Lord,

Your Lordships
Most Devoted
Humble Servant,

Marg. Farquhar.

THE
PREFACE.

The Author of this Poem, (tho' an Officer that Time in the Army,) was not imbark'd in the *Spanish* Expedition, but was oblig'd to an ingenious Friend for his Informations, wherein he himself was actually engag'd till the Reduction of the City of *Barcellona*, which afforded the Author Matter for the Composition of this Poem.

The Author's tedious Sickness whereof he dy'd, hinder'd him from making such Corrections which he design'd, especially in the Two last Canto's, and some considerable Time elaps'd since his Death before the Original was produc'd under his own Hand, nor indeed had it been now publish'd, but at the Instance of some of his ingenious Friends, though doubtless had he liv'd it wou'd have appear'd much more correct, which 'tis hop'd may be pleaded as a justifiable Excuse for its present Defects, especially in curtailing the Names of such Officers of whom he gives such deserving Characters, which the Publisher wou'd not presume to fill up for fear of Mistake, but judges it not very difficult to come to the Knowledge of 'em by viewing the Lists of such Regiments and Officers which compos'd that Army who were at the Reducing the City of *Barcellona*.

As the Author has been very fortunate in pleasing the Ingenious of both Sexes in his Comedies, so it may be hop'd this posthumous Work of his may not be unacceptable, and that the Criticks in Poetry may not be too severe in their Censures.

Barcellona.
A
POEM.

CANTO I.

Now had those Fleets *once* Rivals in dispute,
Had battle'd often, for a bare Salute
Own'd the same common Cause; their Squadrons meet
And yield a Prospect formidably great,
With loosen'd Sails before the Winds they go,
Here English Flags, *there Belgick* Stremers flow.
Those in the Van, with awful Pomp appear,
And *these*, lie by, to guard the lagging Rear;
Capacious Transports, big with warlike Force,
Sail safe between, and keep the middle Course.   10
While on their Wasts the chearful Soldiers stand
And long to stretch their Joints on welcome Land.
For Preparation both in Men and Store,
No Expedition run so high before,
United firm the Nations frankly vote,
To carry Terrors off to Lands remote;
Close the Design—the *differing* People guess,
And all impatient, wait the great Success,
Tho' eager for th' Event, yet much they dread,
A *brave* and *pushing* General at their Head.   20
Loud Murmurs ran, and with a sawcy Voice,
Arrain the best of Sovereigns in her Choice.
  Some in Experience tardy Measures make,
First, by fresh Errors, rectifie Mistake,
Improv'd at last, they mend as they decay,
Their Judgments rise, as they rise in Pay:
By dint of lingring time slow Captains made,
They work upon the War, as on a Trade.

Such have we seen on the *Alsatian* Plain,
30 Make mighty Conquests to retire again.
For Contributions strenuous they excell,
No Hero's ever canton'd Troops so well;
They spin the War in cuning dull delay,
By Night unravel what they wove by Day,
With lingring Steps, o'er difficulties climb,
And wait Peace issuing from the Womb of Time.
Not such the *Heroes*, whom the *Gods* create
Expressly for the War with Martial Heat,
Who dart like Sun Beams to the utmost Line,
40 At *once* set out, and reach the grand Design.
Thus *Philip*'s *Son* had half the World o'er run
Before the *astonisht* World perceiv'd his Course begun.
   Such *Mordaunt* was, on whom this Business lay,
Mourdaunt had Fire to o'er inform his Clay,
But not superfluous;
The *Hero* glowing at his Army's Head,   ⎫
The Soldiers caught the Sparkles as they fled, ⎬
Which made each Man a *Mordaunt* that he led. ⎭
From the *First Light* his active Judgment flows,
50 Almost by Intuition *Mordaunt* knows
War not his Province; yet the *Hero* knew,
To take in long Experience at a View,
Stood in his Ken, and with a bold Essay,
Mark'd all the *Heights* and *Distances* of Sway,
Chalk'd *Nassaw*'s Steps at *Namur* and the *Boyn*,
And *Marlborough*'s larger Strides on *Bleinhem*'s Bloody Plain.
Early the *Hero* in the Senate stood
A *Daring Champion* for his Country's Good,
Brought all its past Miscarriages about,
60 And lash'd *within*, the Errors made *without*.
The listning *Peers* an awful Silence guard.
Their strickt Attention he could well reward,
When siding Parties strong Debate had warm'd,
And just *perswasive Warmth* had *Mordaunt* arm'd,
Gods! how he spoke—
His *Eloquence* like some full Bosom'd Flood,
With native Surface undistain'd with Mud,

Not broke by abrupt Banks, nor sunk in Holes,
But thro' the Plain, rather *declines* than *rowls*,
With an Impetuous, but unbroken Sway, 70
O'er the weak bending Reeds does gently play;
But if some Dike oppose its Barrier Side, ⎫
The *Torrent* swells, grows rapid in its Pride, ⎬
And forces all with Arbitrary Tyde. ⎭

   Long had he waited for a bold Command,
To stretch his *Soul* and executing *Hand*,
It offers now—the Royal Seals ordain, ⎫
To *Mordaunt*, Power supream upon the Plain, ⎬
And *Shovell* post his Partner on the Main. ⎭
Shovell had oft' the *British* Squadrons led, 80
Oft' frighted *Thetis* from her wat'ry Bed;
The Nymph agast, starts from her Coral Throne,
Wak'd with *his* Tempest louder than her *own*.
With him, the Nations knew their Fleet secure,
And Seamen fought because of Conquest sure.
From two such Chiefs united in Employ,
The Coward shakes with *Fear*, the Brave with eager Joy;
The People feel alternate *Hopes* and *Fears*,
And Mothers melt in antidated Tears.

   Now, from the kinder *North* a Gale is sent, 90
That streins each Concave Sail to stiff Extent,
Southward they steer and shun that hostile Place,
Where *Tourville* lost his Ships and found Disgrace,
Press'd hard by *Russel* with impetuous Shocks;
Some drive on *Shoals*, some strike on couchant *Rocks*.
Monstrous Deformities the *Surges* bore,
And scatter'd *Ruins*, thick emboss the Shore.
Unhappy *Tourville* from the Deep retires,
And mourns his Fleet consum'd by foreign Fires,
Mourns his *Sun Royal*, now an Orb of Flame, 100
As if there were an Omen in the Name.
Forward they sail and pass that boisterous Bay,
Where deadest Calms ne'er influence the Sea,
Where unprovok'd by Winds the Billows roar,
Rowl Mountain high and dash the humble Shoar.

   Next they proceed by *Bayonne*'s verdant Isles;
Not distant far, inrich'd with foreign Spoils

Stand *Vigo Bay*—within, the flota lies,
From *India*'s rifled Stores, a wealthy Prize.
110 The Ships of Force range in a Line before,
Boom'd in, and fenc'd with Batteries from the Shore,
In vain—for now the dreadful Engins play,
Ormond by Land, and *Rook* attacks by Sea.
The Boom flies short, the abandon'd Forts begin
To turn their Fire, and pour fresh Vengeance in,
Confederate Horrors of the Land and Sea,
In thick Obscurities involve the Day;
The adverse Elements compound the Spoil,
And share the Profits of the Warrior's Toil.
120 They sooth each others *Enmity* and *Rage*,
In joint Destruction o'er the purpl'd Stage,
What e'er escap'd th' Extreams of Fire and Sea,
Became a *British* or a *Belgick* Prey.
This was Great *Ormond*'s valiant Feat of Arms,
Who's martial Presence *animates* and *charms*,
Mars the great God of War frowns in his Eye,
And *Cupid*, God of Love, sits smiling by;
A Friend he is to all, that's *just* and *brave*,
And equally hates the *Coward* and the *Knave*.
130 Whilst others *basely* scorn the humble Crowd,
And strive to climb, because they wou'd be proud.
His graceful Presence is to none denied,
For he's too great to stoop to slavish Pride;
His Veins has often shed a purple Flood,
And like the Sea, his precious vital Blood
Has flow'd, and always ready is to flow,
To guard this *British* Island from the Foe.
'Twas *here* he seiz'd the Plate of *France* and *Spain*,
And burnt their Naval Strength upon the Main,
140 And thus return'd loaded with *Indian Pelf*,
He *all* enrich'd, except it was *himself*.
Hence where rich *Tagus* by *Lisbona*'s Side,
Pays Oceans Tribute with his golden Tide,
They bend their Course—Unhospitable Ground!
Where *little* Faith, and *less* of Friendship's found,
Where scanty Gains reward the Labourer's Toil,
Choak'd by the Clergy, Weeds that load the Soil;

What Seeds of Good thou gain'st by foreign Aid,
By thy *unkindly* Sands are ill repaid!
For *Albion*'s Blood which widow'd Tears lament, 150
What canst thou pay? For *Albion's* Treasure spent;
What canst thou pay? poor parch'd ungrateful Coast,
For that brave Hand which *great Ruvigni* lost.
That *giving* Hand, felt by his Friend and Foe,
Which Favours *there*, are *here* did Fate bestow.
    Again they sail, and thro' some hazy Frets,
Steer from *resisting Gales*, and gain the *Streights*,
Where an old *Hero* of immortal Fame,
Ceas'd from his Labour and inscrib'd his Name,
Here, a stupendious Promontory stands, 160
The Southern Point of *European* Lands,
Its Eastern Front a Steep of ridgy Rocks,
On its *dull Base* sustains *Levantine* Shocks,
Along the Western Side the Hill decays,
In Hills alternate, and rough abrupt Ways,
And where so e'er the Interspaces fill,
Botanick Nature shews her utmost Skill,
Here *Æsculapius* trac'd the simpling Path,
And *here* Instructed left his Art to *Garth*.
Extending on the coasting Plain below, 170
Where Eastern Winds with fragrant Murmurs blow,
There stands a Town, under a Growth of Fame,
To which its Passage owed its modern Name,
This Place was first by *British* Fleets possess'd,
With *Galick* Fury since with Danger prest,
Sustaining every Hardship that befell,
Six Months besieg'd, six Months defended well.
    Now *Mordaunt*'s Frigat hasts this Bay to gain
Whence *Ponti* run from *Leak*, but run in vain.
The *Hero* thence descends, and pusht to Land, 180
Where *Darmstadt* meets him on the crowded Sand;
Darmstadt who twice the dubious Place sustain'd,
Sav'd by his *Conduct*, by his *Counsel* gain'd;
Him Mankind owns temper'd with lawful Sway, ⎫
Pious and Prudent, watchful, just and gay, ⎬
He govern'd Hearts—spontaneous Hands obey. ⎭

157 *Gales*] *Cales*

He ne'er gave Mandate with an idle Hand,
His *own* Example was his first Command;
Prompt to relieve, none left him unredrest,
190   Or by his *Smiles* deceiv'd, or *Frowns* opprest,
In Peace and War so known to govern well,
He ne'er was Cause of Grief untill he fell,
Then all Men griev'd.
Some time elaps'd, the Heroes walk and view
Where *threatning French* their first Approaches drew,
Here now in spight of Opposition made,
A Royal Battery on the Breach was laid,
All wrought to raise the Breast and Terrace high,
Nor did the Prince himself stand idly by;
200   *There* lay a Bulwark gaping on the Side,
A practicable Breach, but never tried,
The doubtful Foe durst no Attack begin,
They knew that *Death* and *Darmstadt* lodg'd within,
Hence they ascend, and to that Battery came,
Which to its first Projector owes its Name;
Here they observe, nor did refuse their Praise,
The *French* surmount impracticable Ways;
Thick panting up the craggy Mount they crawl,
And *Giant like*, storm rugged Nature's Wall,
210   Like Emmets, in promiscuous Swarms they creep,
Cling to the Rocks and graple with the Steep.
    The Summit gained, their *trembling* Eyes they cast
With Horror back upon the Danger past;
Scarce dare their giddy Brains the Distance take
Which *now* their mangled Carcasses must make,
For *now* the Prince attacks—the *Gallick* Foe, ⎫
From custom'd Fate in Fire no Weakness show, ⎬
But shiver at the Thought of untry'd Death Below. ⎭
Horrid the Sense—from Steep to Steep they bound,
220   At last with frightful Smash they daub the Ground,
Some stuck half way, on pointed Rocks complain
And cry for Death to ease their wretched Pain,
The Prospect lengthen'd, for *below* are seen
Promiscous Arms, Brains, Legs, and Trunks of Men,
Some by the Sword chose Death's profound Abyss,
Rather than leap this dreadful Precipice.

O! faithless Rock that bore the warm Embrace
Of Champions courting thee in Glory's Race!
That stretch'd thy treacherous Arms to help the Brave
With eager Toil, only to find a Grave! 230
Thus Mortals at Ambition's louder Call,
With Labour gain the Top, with Ruin *thence* to fall.
Now having view'd the Incampment of the Foe,
And by what Oblique Lines the Trenches go.
Where every Chief his Prize of Glory won,
Where *Ajax* fought, and where *Thyrsites* run,
They with the Lesser Circumstances end,
And both the *Heroes* to the Fleet descend.
　　Now by *Europa*'s Point they stretch away,
Quiting the *Streights*, and gain the *Midland* Sea, 240
A Native Barrier, serving to restrain,
The *Moorish* Enmity and Rage of *Spain*,
Then towards that Place, were by the Current set
Where *Rook*'s rough Squadron with *Tholouse*'s met;
Where wasted Stores, Fatigue and haizy Weather
Parted the Fray, and gave the Odds to neither;
Thus when *Ulysses* on the *Trojan* flew,
And interposing *Pallas* stood in View,
Both Parties toil'd, compounded the Offence,
And thank'd the Gods for giving a Pretence. 250

BARCELLONA.

CANTO II.

'Twas Summer now, and heavy Calms begun
To *clog* their Course, and *hang* upon their Run;
Then the Commanders in a thick Resort,
Hasten on Board the Flag, the *Naval Court*
This goodly Ship o'er all the Seas renown'd,
Shew'd like an *Island* with the *Forrest* crown'd
In it's Autumnal Dress, when Winds forbear
To strike the Bosom of the Balmy Air,
And sickly Leaves hang fading o'er the Place,
Meet no Disturbance but decay in Peace.   10
    Here waiting Crowds obsequiously draw near,
For *Interest*, makes Men *Courtiers* even here.
In Tempests, born, those Children of the Main ⎫
Compose their ruffled Looks with little Pain, ⎬
And *soft* as Calms can *sooth* and *cringe* for Gain. ⎭
Now whilst the num'rous Cheifs themselves address
To Entertainments proper for the Place,
Mordaunt retires, by busie Crowds unseen,
And with him takes the Stranger *Guiscard* in.
Somtime elaps'd—*Mordaunt* desires to know ⎫   20
What Fate had caus'd the courteous *Gaul* forgoe ⎬
His Native Land, to join a foreign Foe. ⎭
Then *Guiscard* thus—from near the Banks of *Rhosne*
I lately fled, whose bleeding People groan,
Beneath a *Tyrant*'s Rage, no Rods before,
Was e'er so sharp, no Land such *Lashing* bore,
In vain the labouring Hind manures the Soil
Destruction reaps the Harvest of his Toyl,
All that from foreign Shoars the Merchant gains,
Extracted out of Industry and Pains,   30
Oppression grasps at once, and in a Day,
The Labours of a Life are snatch'd away;

The *Poor* and *Weak* are always in the wrong,
Nor is there *Property*, but in the Strong;
In vain the Houshold Gods they all invoke,
Their Gods are snatch'd away, *their* Altars broke,
The *Free born Mind* is now no longer free,
Nor *Reason* acts but by the King's *Decree*.
Strange Arbitrary Sway that thus commands
A Forfeiture of *Sense* as well as *Lands*;
Religion to the Gown becomes a Sport,
Priests like Dragoons, take Order from the *Court*;
No sacred Mission from *their* God they bring,
Their Gospel is a Warrant from their King;
By *that*, these ghostly Villains preach and pray, ⎫
Draw forth Confessions, privately betray,   ⎬
And make all Seals of Secresy give way.   ⎭
Hence, Patriots unheard are doom'd to feel
The *lasting Rigours* of the dark *Bastile*,
Sudden and *Sure* as the Arrests of Fate   ⎫
Are *those*, for that close *Limbo* of the State, ⎬
Hard to repass, as *Hell*'s infernal Gate. ⎭
Here, lusty Youth, whose light aspiring Soul,
The wide capacious World could scarce controul,
In vain laments his darling Freedom crost,
And his whole Brood of noble Pleasures lost.
There aged Truth to Walls may plead his Cause,
The *Walls* his Judges, and his *Chains* the Laws;
Tortur'd by private Racks, the Wretch sometimes
Is forc'd to own some ne'er committed Crimes,
Condemn'd by false Confessions he must bleed,
And private Murder expiates the Deed.
Unknown to Parents, *here* may Children die
Unknown to Friends, *there*, dearest Freinds may lie.
The Lover doubly chain'd may *here* expire,
And th' unconscious Maid still hope with warm Desire.
  Such is the Tyrant's Vengeance on the Land,
But where his hostile Fleets the Seas command,
A fresher Scene of Misery succeeds,
Where many a poor *Cevennian* Captain bleeds;
Where *those*, that in soft Plenty liv'd before, ⎫
Now chain'd in Couples, naked, gaul'd and sore, ⎬
Jerk at each Lash, and *lug* the bended Oar. ⎭

40

50

60

70

Thus long enslav'd, they no Resistance made,
But bore what Burdens their Oppressors laid;
At length *Religion* rous'd him in her Cause,
And *Nature* urging to assert her Laws,
Wide *Interests* join in the vindictive Scene,
Opinions close and leave no Chasme between,
80   But like descending Branches, all agree
To centre in the Root of Liberty.
'Twas *then* the lusty Youth together crowd,
Each *catching* at what Arms his *Fury* shew'd;
At first, with generous Rage they firmly stand,
Till veteran Force o'er run the harrast Land,
Then to the Woods and Wilds for Refuge go,
There they remain and wait the Tyrant's Blow.
Such is the wretched Case of *those* for whom
To supplicate Releif, I abandon Home;
90   To *Anna*, the Asylum of Distress,
Whose great Endeavours distant Nations bless,
To *Anna*, the Afflicted all must sue;
Thither my Course, when I fell in with you.
And hope, great Sir, this powerful Fleet I see,
For our Assistance may appointed be.
     Then *Mordaunt* thus—I own most courteous *Gaul*,
Your *pressing Wants* for *speedy Succours* call,
Cevennian Troubles reach remotest Land,
And may expect Relief from *Anna*'s Hand;
100   But *now* her Armies bend a different Course,
He paused—and then continued his Discourse.
Scarce had that *Villain Priest* of working Brain,
Betray'd to *France* the *Civil Rights* of *Spain*,
When thro' the several Nations that compose
That Empire, Discontents and Fears arose,
Of these, a People vigorous fierce and tall,
Who from *Valentia* reach the Bounds of *Gaul*.
Early assert their *Native Rights*, and Show
What ever *Zeal*, depriv'd of Power can do;
110   In broken Troops, they scower the Neighbouring Plain,
Then fly for Refuge to their Hills again.

86 harrast] harrest. Stonehill emends to 'harrast'.

Then like fell Hawks descending low, to bear ⎫
Their ravish'd Prey, soon quit the Danger there; ⎬
Mount out of Sight, and hide themselves in Air. ⎭
   This rash Attempt to surer Bondage leads:
Here were the *Hands*, but destitute of *Heads*.
The Nobles challeng'd by their injur'd Laws,
Receive a moving Call t'assert their Cause;
Yet *prudence* louder calls, to arm forbear,
Without a Prospect of Protection near,   120
The bleeding People, thus oppress'd complain,
Look on their Cheifs for Help but look in vain;
Of Leaders destitute, and warlike Stores,
Thus humbly sue to those Confederate Powers,
Who, the third *Charles* protect, and in his Choice
Preserve the *Scale* of *Europe* in a Poize.
Albion, the first of these, a wealthy Land,
Stretching to distant Shoars her wide Command,
Now rul'd by *Anne*; the Blessing of her Age,
The *Scourge* of Tyranny and *lawless* Rage;   130
Justice at her Command keeps even Course,
And *her* Example gives her Precepts Force;
These join'd, suppress all Evils in their Growth,
None can withstand the Unity of both;
Her, every Art, does for its Patron chuse,
The *Theme* of Wit and *Subject* of the Muse.
Converted Malice owns her Rightful State,
And proselited Faction shuns Debate;
Under so just a Management we live,
Subjects, secure of Application, *give*;   140
In Glory, she does all those Kings succeed,
Which former Times transcrib'd for *her* to read.
Her Predecessor, of immortal Fame,
In the full Tyde of *France* had stopt the Stream;
But *she*, by her Lieutenants has done more,
And urg'd the *Stream* back, to the *Spring* of Power.
Albion had often bled in Hopes of Ease,
Engag'd in War, only to purchase Peace.
Oft push'd her Squadrons thro' th' embattl'd Way,
And drove the *panting* Monster to a Bay: 150

While no Advantage she propos'd to find,
Beyond the common Safety of Mankind.
Her, *Darmstad* serv'd at th' *Hibernian* Flood,
And urg'd her Troops thro' *Deluges* of Blood,
On *Belgick* Plains, while still the Hero trod
His Father's Steps in Worship of his God.
And now in *Albion* shews himself again,
To press the Rescue of *Revolting Spain*:
Where with *strong Reasons*, and a *graceful Mien*
160　　He mov'd the *Senate* and the *sacred Queen*.
Shows *Catalonia* ready to declare,
Invokes Assistance, and *demands* the War;
How the three Kingdoms, on the Midland Sea,
Oppress'd with Wrongs, but by Constraint obey:
How a small Force sent outwards might insure
Men prompt for Vengeance, for Revolt mature:
Enough disgusted at a Foreign Line,
To *oust* the *French* and bring the *Austrian* in.
Then having urg'd the Profits that must rise
170　　From *France*, strip'd naked out of all Allies;
He shew'd those great Advantages, that are
To recompence the Charge of such a War.
How intercepted Trade, that moves but slow,
Will cease to stagnate, and begin to flow.
How Eastern Commerce must begin to thrive,
When *Spanish* Harbours their Protection give.
And *Indian* Drugery encourag'd thus,
Must leave th' Elixir of its Toil for us.
Whilst *France* crampt up, and stop'd in its Supplies,
180　　Must *fall* by Steps that *raise* the Great Allies.
His Reasons carry a prevailing Force,
And *Catalonia* ends our present Course.
He spoke: They talk'd a while. *Guiscard* withdrew,
And shew'd himself again to publick View.

153 *Hibernian*] *Herbernian*　　　　168 *oust*] *out*

BARCELLONA.

CANTO III.

At *Mordaunt*'s Prayer stiff Gales their Canvass fill,
And bring their Fleet in Sight of *Monjuich Hill*:
Next, from the Mountain to the roulling Main,
Appears that spacious, that delightful Plain,
Where *Barcelona* stands: A fruitful Ground,
Where Natures Plenty is spontaneous found.
Thick studded on the Vale fair Structures lay,
Like Daizies on young Meadows set in *May*.
At length the City opens to the Sight,
Aspiring Churches make th' unequal Height;   10
Tall Steeples o'er the Buildings proudly rise,
Whose pointed Spires menace the lofty Skies.
Eastward, some Furlongs off the Town, they stretch,
And drop their Anchors, out of Cannon Reach;
Th'impatient Soldiers, after three Months Stay,
With Longings, wait on Board the Rise of Day,
Some nodding, in dry Battle spend the Night,
And safely rush into the thickest Fight.
Some fix their Arms, *some* brace the sullen Drum,
Some dream of Conquest, and of Plunder *some*.   20
Now Light ascending gilds the Eastern Skies,
The *Shades* sink downwards as the *Beams* arise.
The Birds of Darkness with the Night retires,
And Stars decreasing wink away their Fires.
When every Warriour with bright Arms in Hand,
Stand active for the expected Word to land.
Around, throng'd Troops does in the Boats appear
With Colours loose, and all the Sounds of War
The Sailors Shouts, and Soldiers chearful Cries,
Percussive shake the Shoars and pierce the Skies.   30
Mordaunt himself the *Signal*, leads the Van,
The Gods lookt down and blest the Godlike Man;

The *Tritons* proud, their favourite Burden bore,
And Winds Confederate, waft him to the Shoar.
The Chiefs with active Bounds, their Boats forsake,
Possess the Land, *there*, firmer Stations take:
The Soldiers tread the Glebe with eager Joy,
Whilst mutual Welcomes, Tongues and Hands employ;
Transported, *some* upon their Captains call
40 To be led streight to *Barcellona*'s Wall,
While *some* supine, upon the Welcome Strand,
With Limbs extended, print the passive Sand:
Thence view the Fleet, and thence Remembrance take
Of their past Hardships on the boistrous Lake;
Recount their tedious Voyage o'er and o'er;   ⎫
What Oaken Beds, what Sickness, Thirst they bore, ⎬
When thank'd the Gods that brought them safe to Shoar. ⎭
Some climb the neighbouring Summits to descry ⎫
The Approach of adverse Troops; and *some* to spy, ⎬
50 If any Hope of Booty might be nigh.   ⎭
To *these*, descending from the Hills afar,
Appear the dusty Clouds of marching War:
The moving Cohorts, in a dubious Mien,
Now, Friends to *France, now*, seem'd to *England*'s Queen:
Till *Darmstad*'s Ken, the wide Conjecture ends,
And *Catalonian* Shouts confess'd 'em Friends;
All arm'd and well appointed for the Fight,
And firmly bent to vindicate their *Right*:
The Priests and Nobles own their *Austrian* King,
60 And Acclamations thro' both Armies ring.
The Country thus declar'd, remain'd alone,
To fix their Conquest, the proud *Barcelone*.
A Town large, wealthy, populous and strong,
Fit for a Stay to Empire, yet whilst young.
Where old *Velasco* in Command grown Grey,
With his Confederate Strength, collected lay;
The *Chiefs* in Counsel sat, the general Voice,
Votes for a Siege, great *Mordaunt*'s hardy Choice,
Which push'd successful, forcibly must gain
70 A powerful Influence on the Fate of *Spain*.
Thus bold, they thus determine, and their Care
Succeeds to disimbark the Stores of War.

Mordaunt's Example urg'd his Orders on,
Refresh'd the *Faint*, and made the *Tardy* run:
Deaf to the Calls that clamorous Nature makes,
He restless moves, nor craving Slumber, wakes.
Here confluent Crowds with animating Voice,
Tug to the creeking *Machines* grating Noise;
By firm Endeavour, and prevailing Hands,
Their ponderous Wheels plough thro' the sinking Sands: 80
On lofty Carriages erected stood
The weighty Guns, late Burdens to the Flood:
The Ships, now lighter made, amaze the Foe,
Put on new dreadful Forms, and taller grow:
Upward the lofty Pines are seen to shoot,
As when they sprouted from their Mountain Root.
The thronging *Catalans* with Care supply
Materials for erecting Batteries high.
All labour'd—All must labour to be Great,
Or, *Mordaunt* like, make such a Work compleat.   90
      Above the Tops of lofty Mountains, where
Æther, releas'd from Storms, breaths balmy Air,
The *Genij* dwell intelligent, and show
Respective Care o'er Provinces below.
Of *these*, a *Spright*, fierce, bloody, hugely tall,
Subtle, and vigilant, protected *Gaul*,
Of Strength, and Stature, equal to his Care,
Tyrannically Proud, *Majestically* Fair.
His Native Lillies on his Cheeks were spread,
And martyr'd Blood laid on the blushing Red: 100
His Temples, ravish'd *Crowns* and *Rights*, adorn,
And at his Feet, lay Heaps of Treaties torn.
      Long had *he* toil'd, nor were his Labours lame
To fetter *Europe* and make *France* Supream.
Strong his Efforts, he aw'd declining *Spain*,
Inspir'd old *Richlieu*, and spur'd on *Turenne*.
The *former*, Leagues occasional to make,
With antidated *Purpose*, Leagues to break.
Decisive Sword, the casuist Warriour draws,
And Success pleads, and justifies the Cause.   110
Hence, the proud *Genius* saw the ancient Bounds
Of *France* abscond'd, in Tracts of conquer'd Grounds.

Hills set on Hills, and Rivers thro' the Plain,
Met Rivers, to *oppose* his *Troops* in vain.
In vain, the *Pirenees* point chilling Snows,
Currents, in vain, Banks limitting expose:
The rapid *Rhine*, smooth'd his indignant Wave,
And *Lewis* trod upon the *murmuring* Slave.
Progressive *thus*, he turn'd his haughty View,
120 *Iberia*'s Proud Dominion to Pursue;
Soon gave Pretence to his ambitious Aims,
And *Priest-craft* brib'd, young *Bourbon, there* Proclaims.
Then who remain'd the sinking World to save,
Great *Nassau* fell—the *Spright* Insults his Grave;
Thence cries aloud, my labouring Task is done,
Proceed *Gran Lewis*, boldly now go on;
Now, I have stamp'd thy Victories compleat,
And leave thy Force an over-match for Fate.
This said—the *Genius* with past Cares *opprest*,
130 His Lillies folded in, and sunk to rest.
Mistaken Spright! thy *Bourbon* to forsake,
And idely Sleep, when most requir'd to Wake.
Anna's denouncing Trumpet, that defies
Thy Perjur'd Prince, and fills the conscious Skies,
Awakes thee not, not *Europe*'s louder Voice,
Blessing Auspicious *Anna* in her Choice
Of *Marlb'rough*'s Sword—nor *Blenheim*'s dreadful Plain,
Ten thousand Cries invoke thy Help in vain;
In vain, thy Favourite *Lewis* Raves and Weeps,
140 His *Angel* calls in vain, his *Angel* sleeps.
And slept secure; till the big Trump of Fame,
Fill'd with the lofty Notes of *Mordaunt*'s Name,
Shook the *Iberian* Hills with Ecchoing Blast,
And pierc'd the *Demons* sloathful Ear at last.
  Agast he rose, and casting round his Eyes,
Ye Gods! it cannot be—the *Demon* cries,
Or I have Ages slept—
Such wondrous Change in *Gallia*'s Face I see,
No less than Work of *Ages* it can be.
150 Whence rears the *Danube* thus his crested Flood,
And swells his *Sanguine* Banks with Tides of Blood.

How came those reeking Heaps of *Gallick* slain,
That *tall*, that *monumental* Spire on *Hockstet* Plain;
What heavenly Form, serene, augustly Fair,
Adorns the Top, and lights the ambient Air?
The *Genius* here, with dubious Wonder prest,
First *Juno* fancy'd, then *Minerva* guest,
Till downwards looking, *Bourbon*'s prostrate Mien,
Confess'd the greater Goddess, *England*'s *Queen*.
The *Spirit* starts, shock'd with a wild Surprise,   160
Strain'd hard to look, but his affrighted Eyes
Ake at the Object, then falls sinking down
At the bare Shadow of *Great Anne*'s Renown;
His dire Regards far thence the *Demon* sends,
But no Place finding that his Prospect mends;
Dispair and *Grief* his hardned Silence broke,
Oh! had I never slept, or ne'er awoke,
Inrag'd, he cries—*where*, tell ye Furies, *where* ⎤
My present Aid, and my late dormant Care   ⎬
Is wanted most, my *Gallia* to repair.   ⎦   170
There, Marlb'rough drives us thro' the dusty Plain,
Yonder, we fly from conquering *Eugene*.
Haughty stands *Baden there*, at sullen Bay;
Yonder, *Ruvignies* Squadrons push the Day.
Here, *Mordaunt*'s Cohorts vex the heated Plain,
And formidable *Shovell* awes the Main;
From *Marlb'rough*'s Arms, I much had Cause to fear,
But against *those*, strong Bulwark'd Towns appear;
Baden he knew, for want of Quota's, *slow*;
His Ally wou'd retard *Ruvigne*'s Blow.   180
Eugene his rapid March thro' Seas of Blood
Urg'd on, but *Vendosme* and the *Po* withstood.
But *Mordaunt*, yet a Stranger in the War,
With sharp descerning Ken, he views afar;
Well mark'd his early Toil, and midnight Care,
His easie Access, and determin'd Air.
Then cries aloud—this Man, this wondrous Man,
Unless prevented, turns the Fate of *Spain*.
Mine it must be to frustrate his Design,
The Work is worthy me—the Work be mine.   190

This said—he darted thro' the yielding Air;
A Train of Light, like Comets blazing Hair
Pursu'd his Course; poor frightful Mortals gaze,
And from the Sight, strange wild Conjectures raise.
The *stairing Rustick*, his wise Sentence past,
Beware our Grain, he crys, *this* bodes a Blast.
Well, I remember—then begins a Tale
Of Blazing Star, and prophesying Whale;
Another brings a Story to reply
200　　Some old, and long, successive lineal Ly
Which, had like Gout. or such Traditions run
I'th' Blood, from *Father* to the infected *Son.*
The *Zealous Priests*, whose Province 'tis to pry ⎫
Into *Celestial* Secrets, hence descry　　　　　⎬
The *Church* in Danger, and no Buckets nigh. ⎭
The busy *Polytician* in Disgrace,　　　　　　⎫
The Portent views with penetrating Face　　　⎬
Foretells a Change at Court, himself a Place. ⎭
Some *Philomaths*,, the Comets Rage explain,
210　　In Storms at Land and Tempests on the Main.
The *Pedlars*, hence, much dread cold rainy Fairs,
And *Sailors* think of going oft to Prayers;
Some fatal Fevers livid Plagues confess,
Physicians bow, and the fair Omen bless.
　　But now, their laging Sight pursues in vain,
The *Spright* had now reach'd the subjacent Plain,
From States to Kingdoms, *there*, he roves about
To search his darling Mistress, *Discord*, out;
Thro' his whole Progress, every where he saw
220　　The deep Impressions of the Fury's Paw.
In Cities, *wildly* did the *Fury* range
Her Footsteps plainest, on the Crowded Change:
Here in a murmuring Whisper, she pursues
The Merchants open Ear, with factious News:
With all her Arts, the tedious War decries,
Shews *Funds* exhausted, and no more Supplies.
Here in a Wager or stockjobbing Face,
With knavish Lyes she buzzes round the Place.
Inspir'd by *Her*, Sedition to excite
230　　Rehearsals *here*, *there*, Observators write;

At Night, *She* to some Lordly Mansion flies,
And, *there* 'twixt Man and Wife the *Fury* lies.
Nor was the *Church* from her Impressions free,
Prelates and *Convocations* disagree.
Their ancient Province, *now* lies far remote, ⎫
Not who converts a *Soul* adorns his *Coat*,   ⎬
But who converts a *Burgess* for his *Vote*.   ⎭
Opinions different, different Heat express
And *Doctors* leave the *Pulpit*, for the *Press*.
Much read in Books, but ignorant in Men,   240
The learned Graduate draws his pusling Pen
Disturbs the Moths, old Notions to translate,
In *Logick* good, impertinent in *State*.
Half studdy'd in *prophane*, half *sacred* Writ,
'Twixt *Heaven* and *Hell* he hangs, for neither fit:
   Fair *Albion*'s Court *once* had the Fury seen,
There left Impressions deep, but *Albion*'s *Queen*
Had lately from the Place the Fury chas'd,
With some few *Friends*, that *Discords* Cause embrac'd.
Reluctant, she forsook the *sacred* Ground,   250
But at the *Bar*, the Compensation found;
Triumphant *there*, she puzzled every Cause,
And left to *Fees* or *Bribes*, the Power of *Laws*;
Then, from the noisy Hall the *Fury* burst,   ⎫
And as she flew, the Neighbouring *Senate* curst, ⎬
Touch'd at the *Lobby*—but no farther durst.   ⎭
Thus far the *Gallick Guardian* past the Throng.
Marking the Fury as she went along.
To a fair *Colledge* he at length ascends,
A new Foundation laid for pious Ends,   260
Where first to the *Library* he bends his Pace,
Hoping to find her in the old *Recess*.
Here Order stood in level Ranks arraid,
The *Dusty* Shelves with *Paper* burthens spread,
Books pil'd on Books, the greatest downward tend,
And Vellum Authors to the Roof ascend,
In Volums, open on the Board, was seen,
Here something blotted out, *there* foisted in.
Here, in the Margin, were large Glosses plac'd,
And *there* whole *Paragraphs* intirely raz'd.   270

Now, *Genius* searches every Nook with Care,
The *recent* Ink betray'd her lately *there*,
But late withdrawn—he trac'd her blasted Road,
And found her Speeching to a list'ning *Crowd*,
There in a Garb, that suits the *Mission* well,
Her distant Feats, she does with Pleasure tell.
In *British* Lands what hopeful Mischiefs stir,
Behind a Mask of *Zeal* inspir'd by her:
What *Indian* Wonders she had seen and done,
280   Both at the *Setting* and the *Rising* Sun.
What Work while she far Northward made her Stay,
But not a Word of *Sweden* by the Way.
    When now the Fury, lifting up her Eyes,
Well knew the mighty *Genius* by his Size,
Their Glances meet—the *Demons* gastly Air,
Declare his pressing Wants and Business there;
She took the *Signal*—vanish'd from their Sight,
And left the *Fathers* in a doubtful Fright;
Who straight repairing to the *sacred Shrine*,
290   Own it a *Miracle*, and bless the Sign.
    The *Gallick Guardian* led the Fury still,
Nor stopt untill they came to *Montjuich Hill*:
Here on a Summit of a Cliff they Stand,
Which awes the Sea, and brows the Neighbouring Land.
    Then *Genius* thus—behold on yonder Tide,
The *Brittish* Fleet with awful Terrour ride,
Lo! Their *Battalians* on the Plains appear,
Here, *English* Troops, *there*, *Belgick* Cohorts war,
By *Spanish* Rebels joyn'd on every hand,
300   *Here* flank'd by Hills, and *Yonder* by the Strand.
Observe the working Crowd move up and down,
See how their Preparations brave the Town.
If *Barcellona* drops, the *Province* falls,
And carries Ruin to the Neighbouring Walls,
Which our young *Bourbon* own—the care be thine
To ride my *Fears*, and baffle their *Design*.
    Play *Sergius* close in *him* is lodg'd the Care
Of all their *Train*, and all their Stors of War.
His Councel must have Force; thy Task is hard,
310   But on—and listen to thy great Reward.

Thy Friend *Albani* sends a scarlet Hat,
And *Poland*'s *Prymacy* shall be thy Lot;
Three banish'd Princes, whom our *Cause* and *Care*
Have rendred wretched, shall attend thy Chair;
Old speeching *Nestor* shall his Offerings bring,
And *Margaretta* shall thy Praises sing.
  He spoke; the Fury with a horrid Smile,
Confess'd the *Price* well suited to her *Toil*;
Then lash'd her Sides, that swell'd to meet the Blow,
Her flaming Eyes with Lust of *Mischief* glow   320
Tumult and *Faction* cloud her anxious Face,
And crested Snakes erect, hiss round the Place.
Enough, my *Darling Spright*, enough; she cries ⎫
Before the Sun can measure thrice the Skies,   ⎬
I'll blast their *Hopes*, and gain my glorious *Prize*. ⎭

BARCELLONA.

CANTO IV.

She spoke descending, and her self convey'd
Swift, as a Shot below its Level made;
To *Sergius* Quarter she directs her Way,
Sergius all Night in broken Slumbers lay,
He thought th' Access impracticably Steep,
And doubt of Success interrupted Sleep:
In Form of *Galba* she approach'd his Bed,
Just as the Morning had her Blushes spread
On Eastern Hills; this *Galba* dealt in Mines,
In Angles, Traverses and oblique Lines;
By *one*, he safely cou'd th' Approach compleat,
And by *another*, fortify Retreat.
In taking Aim he felt an odd Delight,
But levell'd low, and seldom hit the White.
Thro' a clear Perspective wou'd often look,
And Danger still in full Proportion took;
But when to Success a fair Passage lay,
He turn'd the *Glass*, and drove the *Means* away.
Thus, in this borrow'd Form, the Fiend intends
To mould unstable *Sergius* to her Ends.
To *you*, whose Years have yielded length of Course,
To judge of promising Designs with Force.
To *you*, who early with the War begun,
Who *much* have seen, and *much* have made your Own.
Your *Galba* comes, to know with what Pretence
Of Judgment, Reason, or Experience,
This Work, this fatal Work is thus begun,
Without sufficient Force to push it on.
Our Warriours grant, such as full greatly dare,
A Siege as *ours* is the toughest Tug of War:
This calls for Numbers and stupendious Stores,
Neither of which, you know, my Friend, are ours;

Three Moons, these Walls, sustain'd *Vendosm*'s Attack,
Oft push'd his veteran Legions bleeding back:
Our living Thousands rang'd upon the Plain,
Amount not here to *Vendosm*'s Thousand slain:
Our General wants—what? among other things,
Councels, and thousand Advantages it brings;
The Leaders, strong in Opposition grown,
Distrust a Conduct wiser than their own.   40
   Man in the common Course of Causes gains
To judge of probable Events by Means,
When *Marlb'rough* fights, *Fate* Victory decrees,
And *Prior*'s Song can never fail to please;
Great *Anna*'s Reign, her Subjects grateful Sence
Follows but as the *Cause* and *Consequence*.
Aurora's Dawn the Sun must follow still,
And *G—ns* Eyes retain their Power to kill.
The Bolts confess the angry Gods; no less
Dejected Swains *M—ns* Frown confess: 50
From flowry Meads, we guess the Climate mild,⎤
The general Joy, speaks Nations reconcil'd; ⎬
Or rather says,, that *S—nd* has smil'd.   ⎦
Who doubts of Wine on *Gallia*'s happy Coast,
Or *Nectar*, when fair *C—sh* is the Toast;
When frighted Virgins *weep* and *pray*, we know,
A—le's abroad and *O—ry* must go;
When Poets write,inspir'd with sacred Rage,
We're sure that *Ormond* fills the mighty Page;
And when the listning Souls wound up to hear,   60
Wise *Harley* speaks, or *Cooper* charms the Ear.
   Again from gross Defects we're sure to meet,
Designs as short, Miscarriages as great.
When Hackney Scriblers for a Party write,
Erected Justice retributes their Spight.
Or thoughtless *C—r* rises from his Place,
The Cause he urges, sinks in his Disgrace.
Thus *Projects* ill design'd, can ne'er prevail,
And without needful Funds, are sure to fail;
But *here* are Wants peculiar more to you,   70
The Trains unfurnish'd, and the Gunners few:

Us will they charge, and tho' we want Supplies,
Allow no Credit for Deficiencies;
Thus must we labour, destitute of Means,
And without *Unites* multiply our *Tens*.
    If Victory shou'd on our Side take Post,
Things are inverted, and their *Order* lost.
Causes, no longer, their Effects can gain,
And many Links are broke in Natures Chain.
80   The heavenly People must in Crowds come down,
Range on our Side, and make the Cause their own;
Or we, to Chance must in Procession go,
As to the greatest *Deity* below.
Desist in Time, least by sinister Fame,
These Works unfinish'd, shou'd preserve your Name,⎫
Assert your *Folly* and record your *Shame*.   ⎭
    Then *Sergius* thus—O *Galba* your Discourse,
Bears me before it with convincing Force;
I own, my *Reason* urg'd the same before,
90   But yours has fixt and rooted it the lower;
My Resolution mounts, and is made good,
By Help of Numbers and of Neighbourhood;
A single Oak shock'd with an angry Blast,
Nods, bends and totters, and falls flat at last:
But when rough Tempests thro' the Forrest roar,
One Poplar serves an other to secure.
Thus 'gainst this rash Attempt we'll boldly stand,
And combat Opposition Hand in Hand.
    He ceas'd—the *Fury* thus—whilst yet you have
100   Redemption in your Power, make hast to save:
When surly *Death* has made his Conquest sure,
Not *Celsus*, tho' he strove, cou'd work a Cure.
Celsus who sees th' Extent of humane things,
And with that Softness cures with which he sings,
Whose Numbers might suspend the Tyrant's Strife,
And stop the listning Soul upon the Verge of Life.
    To Day the Chiefs in Council sit, upon
The safest *Methods* how to be undone:
Your Arguments will shock the thinking few,
110   They'll sway the rest—she finish'd and withdrew.

107 sit] sits

Now she disrobes her self of her Disguise,
And stands a Fury in her former Size,
Then takes another Vehicle of Air,
Compress'd into the Form of *Cordelier*,
A *Canting Tool* that *Mordaunt* had employ'd
To preach the zealous *Crowd* to *Austria*'s Side;
He knew that o'er the vegetative Throng,
No *Reason* cou'd prevail, to *Right* or *Wrong*;
But *Conscience*, if well manag'd by the Gown,
And *Hell* well threatned, *gives* or *takes* a *Crown*.   120
  In this Disguise the Fury hastes away,
To shed the Influence of her Spight at Sea;
From Ship to Ship, incessantly she goes,
And plies the principal *Commanders* close,
Insinuates, shifts her Subjects oft, and makes
Her Language sute the Man, to whom she speaks;
She *Phocas* moves with Magisterial Mien,
All *Confidence* without, and *none* within;
In Speech decisive, partial in his Choice,
Of shallow Sense, and arbitrary Voice.   130
Blest with these Talents, Darlings of the Crowd,
The forked Fabrick stalk'd and talk'd aloud;
Swell'd like a Billow, blustering wou'd he stand ⎫
Upon his Wooden Province, there command   ⎬
Tyrant at Sea, and Spaniel on the Land.   ⎭
To some she is cautious, and with wonderous Skill,
Utters some *Good*, with Aspect fixt on *Ill*,
To *some* more free she hinted, and cou'd show
Time swiftly running, and the Works but slow,
The Question next with labouring Doubt she chose,   140
How weak *Beginnings* prosperous *Ends* shou'd close?
How far Success may without Means advance,
Or how far Causes may be rul'd by Chance?
How far the Nation cou'd the Loss sustain
Shou'd their Fleet perish on the groundless Main?
Show'd, if they longer on these Coasts shou'd wait, ⎫
Approaching Winter, their returning late,   ⎬
Then told the wretched tale of *Wheeler*'s Fate.   ⎭

To which great Point having pursued her Drift;
150 Tho Poison she to Operation left,
Sergius, mean while assiduously beset
The Land Commanders, and of *those*, he met
Men, who in spight of Nature will be wise, ⎫
Labour and sweat, and make a mighty Noise, ⎬
If *Councells* are not stampt with their Advice. ⎭
But now they sit, where Silence first was broke
By *Mordaunt*; who th' Assembly thus bespoke:
   According to the *Resolutions* made
By you, upon the last Debate we had,
160 The Preparations for the Siege are gone
As far as Circumstance can push 'em on.
'Twas then, indeed, concluded best to make
Th' Impression on *this Side* for an Attack?
But later Observations, say it will
Do better, to begin with *Montjuich Hill*.
This Strength commands the Town, with all its Lines,
And opens its weaker Sides to our *Designs*.
Here we our Batteries may with Safety raise,
And carry our Approaches on with Ease:
170 While, by the help of *fast* and *Hilly* Land,
Sustaining Soldiers will be still at Hand.
To this Opinion, *Darmstadt* has come in;
And *yours* is only wanting to begin.
He ceas'd—
Dissenting Sounds thro' th' Assembly ran,
And several rose; but *Serpion* thus began,
True, I concurr'd in the *Debate* before,
To act against the Town with all our Power,
Because I thought the Country wou'd attend,
180 With proper Means to serve so great an *End*.
Our Expectations were prepar'd t' have seen
Defection all without, *Revolt* within,
By secret Correspondencies; we thought,
Supplies from *Vich* and *Doris* had been brought:
But this Assistance wanting on our Side,
By the Condition, the Decree's destroy'd.
For as the Man no wilful Madness feigns.

160 Preparations] Preparation

Who thinks to hit without the Help of Means;
So is his Frenzy ne'er a jot the less,
Who leans on Fortune only for Success.   190
And he who blindly sticks to his first Decree,⎫
When *Seasons* change, or *Causes* cease to be? ⎬
Is yet the greatest Madman of the three.   ⎭
But with your Favour, I may further go,
And say we han't an equal Chance to throw:
Abate their Odds of Walls? *their* Wings wou'd stretch
In open Plains, as far as *ours* can reach.
For say in Foot, we are a superior Force,
Yet all allow they out number us in Horse.
Then what Advantage could we hope to get,   200
Were their Walls down and levell'd to a Flat.
Here with decreasing Numbers we might come
Yet still want Hands to push the Business home.
Yet say, revolting Crowds themselves disclose,
How far with Safety we may lean to those.
If artless Numbers cou'd the War abide,
Issum had bounded *Alexander*'s Pride:
In Sun shine these appear; but shady Night
Conveys 'em out of *Danger*, out of *Sight*.
Then left th' expending Nations should complain   210
That Expeditions still are made in vain,
I humbly offer *This*; that we pass o'er
With utmost hast to the *Italian* Shore.
Savoy our great Ally is sore distress'd,
And his *Metropolis* with Danger press'd:
This Force too small for a Diversion *here*,
Will *there* toss up the Ballance of the War.
And 'twill be an Action worthy great Success,
To save such a Confederate as *This*:
By which important piece of Service, *You*,   220
Your Orders in the second Branch pursue.
He spoke, and several back'd him; when they'd done
Thus *Darmstad*, with a Godlike Grace begun.
    The Reasons that induc'd Assent before,
Are still the *same*; but in their Vigour more:
The Correspondence mention'd in the Town,
Goes its own Pace; tho' not so publick known.

Some things too tender are a Touch to bear;
And others lose their Vertue in the Air.
230　But when they to a ripen'd State attend,
They work with Certainty and gain their End.
　　Say you there's no Defection to our Side?
How are our Wants so willingly supplied?
Whence all those Hands that with incessant Care,
Provide things needful for th' incountring War?
Who made *Torto*'s and *Lerida* our own?
And who on t'other side blocks up the Town?
If nothing cures your Infidelity
But *Sense*; pray ride a little out and see:
240　*There* you'll find Numbers, such as ill can stay
In one united Body without Pay.
If they be rude and artless in the War,
Lay no more Strength upon them than they'll bear.
Yet will you find 'em struggle with their Hold;
Rough, patient, hardy, vigilant and bold.
　　But the great Difficulty yet remains
You're call'd to work without the Help of Means,
That's wanting; but the Want proceeds from you;
For *Resolution* would the Business do:
250　'Tis this will all Deficiencies make good.
Had *Alexander* at the *Granick* Flood,
Stumbled at every Doubt that cross'd his Way,
His *Tears* had swell'd the River to a Sea:
Nor with small Numbers bafled wou'd aspire
T'have finish'd the stupendious Work of *Tyre*.
But what are th' Doubts you cross your self withall
They cannot whistle Armies at a Call.
The Walls you grant may easie be lain flat
And I'll pronounce the Business done with *that*,
260　To make a Breach allow sufficient Hands,
And with th' *Ascent* we'll close up our *Demands*.
An Enemy of course will keep the Field,
Until he has a fair Pretence to Yield.
　　But one Word more, the first *Decree* you made
Has drawn ten thousand People to your Aid:

---

235 incountring] incounting

Wou'd you to *Gallies, Gibbets Racks* and *Shame*
Betray those Men that to your *Succour* came.
An Act so foul, would fill the World with Cries,
And startle Nature into a *Surprise*.
   Pinch'd hard with such Remonstrances as these,   270
Your *Arguments* can have but little Ease:
Then close with mine, and think the Fate of *Spain*
Lies all at Stake. He spoke, but spake in vain:
For the malignant Influence had got
Too deep Impression to be routed out.
   Then *Mordaunt* thus: Since so Affairs must be
Give your Subscription to your own Decree.
This they immediately consented to,
And in Dissatisfaction all withdrew.
Thence to the Fleet he goes, where having found   280
No Lenitive to mollify his Wound,
Back he returns on the Approach of Night,
And clog'd with anxious Thoughts retir'd from Sight.

BARCELLONA.

CANTO V.

Now *Mordaunt*, walking in his Tent cou'd find
No Rest amidst the Hurries of his Mind:
His present *Crosses* met his *Troubles* past;
And all Misfortunes center in the last.
Then striving to expectorate his Grief,
In this Soliloquy he sought Relief.
    Alas what's *Power*, what's *Glory, Conquest, Fame*;
Things we call Blessings, but mistake the Name.
Can they be happy who are forc'd to tread
Those slimy Paths where Snakes their Venom shed.
Life's but a glittering Bait, for if it run
In a calm Mind thro' ease and Plenty on,
Its due to Constitution, or to *Chance*;
And thus is only good by Circumstance.
But what's all this to numerous Crowds that bear
Its pressing Loads, 'midst *Wants, Distrust* and *Care*;
Who strive against the *Steep* of Life to crawl
And lose their footing on the slippery Ball.
Oft when our Joys are in full Prospect seen,
Some sullen Disappointment comes between,
The fleeting Pleasure into Shadows go,
And th' Landskip changes to a Scene of Woe.
Yet *still* we drive the fruitless Chace; and still
The Fugitive deceives us with a Smile:
Nor tho' thus treated have we Power to make
Th' Advantage rising from our own Mistake:
Again we sink into the soft Embrace,
Again we're jilted, and lose all our Peace:
Again we trust the flatt'ring Calms, and toss
The Seas uncaution'd by our former Loss.
O Hope, thou great Deceiver of the Mind,
What e'er we lose, by *thee* we expect to find:

Thou flatt'rest Mankind with Delight at last,
Shews them the Golden Fruit and bids them tast:
But when *Desire*, with greatest Force inclines;
You shew the *Impotence* of our *Designs*.
Thou, thou *Seducer*, makes us seek for Ease
On rugged Paths, and on tempestuous Seas;
But tost and rambling in a Maze of Care,
Y' abandon us a *Prey* to wild *Despair*;   40
Then prompt us on, by fresh Deceits again,
T' expect Relief in an Exchange of Pain.
   How happy is the Man of moderate Store
Who is by another's Toil provided for:
Fortune purveys for *him*, he lives at rest,   ⎫
Is of his own *Felicity* possest,   ⎬
Which if he understands, he's truly blest.   ⎭
And by exporting Hazards, hope to raise
Immense Returns of profitable Praise.
Thus while our Ease is at our own command,   50
We love to wade, tho' there's a Bridge at Hand,
He ceas'd; and for some time with Thought opprest,
Reclin'd himself upon his Bed to rest.
His Spirits softly thro' their Channels creep;
And straight he sunk into a downy Sleep.
When *Lo!* a Form *irregularly* fair
Of frank *Address*, and of alluring *Air*
Approach'd his Sight: Her Age was in the Bloom
Of blushing Virgins just to Ripeness come;
Easie her *Mein*, and what appear'd to be   60
In all her Shape, was *volatil* and *free*.
No Girdle bound her *Wast*, no Knots her *Hair*,
This play'd and wanton'd with the sportive Air:
And all her Blandishments seem'd *such* as move
The trembling Needle to its Point of *Love*.
Now pensive *Mordaunt*, wondring as he lay,
To see a Form so irregularly gay;
Was *thus* by her addrest: *Me* mortals know   ⎫
By Name of *Fortune*; and where e'er I go,   ⎬
Regard me as a *Deity* below.   ⎭   70
Where now, great *Marlb'rough*, near the *Belgick* Stream
Treads *Nassau*'s Steps in the Pursuit of Fame,

Lies my *abode*, with Wreaths of Laurels crown'd,
He has the Fulness of my *Favours* found.
The *Brave* ask big, nor can I close my Hand
To *Vertue*, when she makes a bold Demand.
No arm e'er *his*, was strong enough to stretch
The *British Glory* to so wide a Reach.
Nor need our *Hero* now look back as far
As *Rome* or *Greece* for Presidents in War:
Much greater Masters less remote they find,
Nassau's enough to fire the Warriour's Mind:
In *Marlb'rough* and *Nassau* collected meet
The scatter'd Vertues of the ancient *Great*.
Be these your Patterns in th' Affairs of War,
So shall the Nations bless your pious Care
By their just Methods, that *Design* pursue
Which then you clos'd your Eyes you had in View.
And think the Admonition you receive
Is, what the Genius of the Land wou'd give.
⠀⠀⠀With that, th' admonish'd Hero rais'd his Head,
Look'd round, and full of the *Idea*, said;
It must be so; did not the *Vision* name
Nassau and *Marlborough*, as my Guides to *Fame*?
Did it not bid me that *Design* pursue,
Which when Sleep clos'd my Eyes, I had in View.
My busie Thoughts, did e'er I slumber'd, stray
O'er the expected Turns of Yesterday:
How obstinately bent the Leaders were
To abandon *Spain*, and lose good Footing *here*;
And how to gloss their dark Intentions o'er,
They urg'd our Passage to th' *Italian* Shore.
How, when on Board the Fleet I told the News,
The Sea Commanders their Assent refuse.
Urging the Dangers met by those that roam
In stormy Seasons, and so far from Home.
Considering next, how by inquiring Laws,
The *Consequence* might here involve the *Cause*:
And satisfy'd, this *Choice* was still my own,
To fall in Company, or rise alone,
I purpos'd in my self, no more to be
Encounter'd by an opposite *Decree*;

But by an Attack on *Montjuich Hill*, to have
Or certain *Glory*, or a certain *Grave*.
   Now had *Aurora* usher'd in the Light,
And conquering Morning chas'd the Troops of Night;
When th' *Hero* bow'd to his *Creator* thrice;
Then to good *Darmstad* hasten'd for Advice.
Highly the great Design did *Darmstad* please;
Who fortified it by such Words as these.   120
   By *tim'rous Minds* made fearful by Complaints,
Councils are call'd to justifie *Events*:
It's true, the *Brave* are rid of half their Cares,
When *other* Mens Assents come in with *theirs*:
But where *Dispatch* and *Vigour* shou'd be great,
The *Enterprize* grows cool beneath *Debate*.
   This Action you're upon, affords no less
Then a fair View of probable Success.
Their Force is bent on *This*, on t'other Side
They fear no Danger; and 'tis ill supply'd.   130
To render 'em securer, seem to make
A Stop; and let your Preparations slack:
Then give it out, that tir'd in an Affair,
Which yields no *Prospect* but of foul *Despair*;
You'll rise from *Barcellona* and sit down
Before th' important Town of *Tarragon*.
   In *War* Amusements are of wond'rous Pow'r;
But *This* is useful on a double score;
'Twill lull your Foes; and while none knows your Ends,
Bind up the *Laxity* of babling Friends.   140
Thus Secrecy the Business will ensure,
And make the Blow both *sudden* and *secure*,
Your Foes, like Men where Magazins take Fire,
Shall see one *Glance* of Ruin, and *expire*.
   The Fort, the Hill and Passages thereon,
To *Me* of old, familiarly were known.
Therefore, when things are ripe for the Design,
With your Consent, the Conduct shall be mine.

---

144 *Glance*] *Glace* 'Glance', meaning a sudden flash or gleam of light, best fits the
context. 'Glace' can mean a swift or glancing blow or wound. The words are
etymologically related and may have been used interchangeably, but the *OED* does
not list the meaning of 'flash of light' for 'glace'.

Then *Mordaunt*, thus: Be yours the sole Command;
150   The Business calls for a well manag'd Hand;
Therefore, *in Justice* must devolve on you,
Ulysses Arm best bends *Ulysses* Bow.
But you must give me Leave t'attend you *There*.
Tho' but as a Companion in th' Affair.
A while their mutual Friendships they renew
By fresh *Civilities*; and so withdrew.
As soon as the *Decree* in Councel made,
Had thro' the Limits of the Army spread,
The Face of things put on an Air of Woe,
160   And Warriours in dejected Postures go:
Dreading the Scandal of a base Return,
They greive, and with Desire of Action burn.
Th' *Italian* Expedition, once made known,
Gave them a *Spring* of Hope, that wither'd soon:
For *this*; but shew'd it self, and pass'd away,
Shock'd by th' Encounter which it met at Sea.
At length, the News of *Terragona* rings;
Which seem'd to fix th' unsettled State of *Things*:
This Way, the Preparations all incline,
170   As Evidences of a true Design.
Again, the Guns, the wounded and the Weak,
With all th' Incumb'rances of War which make
A Length of lagging March, are sent away;
As if design'd for *Terragon* by Sea:
While the glad People chearfully prepare,
All necessaries for the moving War.
Now *Things* approach'd ne'er to their ripen'd State;
And forward Preparations seem'd to wait:
When Orders swift, were thro' the Camp convey'd,
180   That a Detatchment should be quickly made:
A Thousand Men of War; a chosen Band;
At th' Head of which, the leading *Hero*'s stand,
All ready for the Fight. C—d in place
The first; a Noble of the *Hibernian* Race;
Who thought to encounter *Death* with Gallantry,
Was to live well, and be prepar'd to die.
A—n with Age and large Experience blest,
Whose *Soul* denies his *Body* needful rest.

S—*l* whose Youth must plead in his Excuse
Of over Warmth; sprung from an ancient House   190
Ne'er *Senus*'s Banks; where forc'd by adverse Fates,
Hibernian Youth embark'd for foreign Seats.
Nor must the Warriours of inferiour Post,
By the recording Muse be entirely lost:
All pressing to look Danger in the Face,
And in a larger Volume worth a Place.
    The Appointed Party ready for Command,
At *Darmstad*'s Quarter in *Battalia* stand.
Who at their Head march'd off in open Day;
And on to *Terragon* directs his Way.   200
His Friends in Town, with rough Oppression, *sore*,
Expect Relief of *Grievances* no more:
They think of nothing now, but how to make
The Yoke sit light, and easie to the Neck.
Thus greiving inward at th' unprosp'rous Day,
Their *Sorrows* double, as their Hopes Decay.
    With stern *Volasco* otherwise it far'd;
As Grief in *them*, so joy in *him* appear'd:
He from his Walls beholds 'em as they go,
And thanks his Stars for scaping such a Foe.   210
Spontaneous *Terror* does his Mind employ,
And as he looks, he *shivers* in his Joy.
For threatn'd *Terragon* he shews his Grief;
Still pleas'd to hav't the Cause of his Belief:
So some lament their Neighbours House pull'd down,
Joyful it stood 'twixt Danger and their own.
    Mordaunt, who with the Army yet had stay'd,
Order'd another Party should be made,
To march by Noon of Night a shorter Way,
And be at the sustaining Place by Day.   220
Then privately, by secret Ways he went,
And overtook the *Prince* e'er Day was spent.

194 þe] b'

BARCELLONA.

CANTO VI.

Sunk deep, below the Level of the Sight,
The Sun had left no Remnant of his Light;
The Flocks upon their resting Places lie,
And the dim Clouds skim o'er the azure Skie.
The Stars thick studded with a glitt'ring Shew,
Reflect themselves upon the Seas below.
Relaxing Nature had her self undress'd,
Disposing all things to a State of Rest;
But th' *Hero*'s disobedient to her Call,
10 Refuse that *Tender* which she makes to all.
Forward the Soldiers rush without a Stop;
None lag but such as kill'd or wounded drop.
From Post to Post they press and drive down all,
Nor stop until they reach the Castle Wall:
Where they for Passage search on every side;
But search in vain, then scatter and divide.
    As whilst the surly Waves disturb the Main
No Opposition can their Force restrain;
But when, to shoar, they roul their Fury Home,
20 They waste their Strength, and dash themselves to Foam.
Amongst the Rocks and Oase a Covert have;
Or, the *leading* forc'd upon the *following* Wave.
    The Soldiers thus pursue their driving Course
Up to the Walls but thence recoil with Force:
Then lodge themselves behind the Rocky Ground;
Or any Shelter nearest to be found.
    When *Darmstad* saw the staggering Troops give back,
He swiftly hasten'd to the left Attack,
There rally'd 'em, and said: What is't I see! ⎫
30 You combat an inferior Enemy: ⎬
But, if you're *Englesh Men*, you'll follow me. ⎭

With that, he urg'd thro' Dangers, louder far
Then raging Seas, or Elements at War:
From level Engins, thick Irruptions broke,
Involving all the Plain with Sheets of Smoke;
But as the *Hero* negligent of Life,
Urg'd on his Warriors thro' th' important Strife,
Death hit him low, the broken Ballance drop'd:
A *while* Life ran, and *then* for ever stop'd.
   Thus *Darmstad* (like to great *Gustavus*) set   40
To ask the Success of the Day by Fate.
   Stun'd by their Leader's Loss they left the Attack,
Staggers again, and *once* again gives back.
Things promise but a doubtful Consequence;
And *Success* seem'd to totter in *Suspence*;
When watchful *Mordaunt*, hastens from the *Right,*
Confirms the *Cohorts*, and renews the Fight:
He rais'd his Sword up lifted in the Air,
And dash'd the *Terrors* of the sulph'rous War;
Leading thro' all the *Dangers* that oppose,   50
He gain'd their former Ground, and lodg'd 'em close.
Then, the sure Instruments of Death, begin
To turn, and pour associate *Horrors* in:
In Central Lines the Guns discharge their *Ire,*
And Bombs assist with supplimental Fire:
A blast of ruin follows: and from th' Walls,
Loudly the astonish'd Foe for *mercy* calls.
   The Fort thus gaind, and Success now no more
Seeming to totter as it did before;
All faintness soon went of, a large supply   60
Of zeal succeeds, and every pulse beat high.
Encouraged *thus* the confluent Numbers press,
And work ith' great Vocation with success:
By Indefatigable, and an active, toil,
The Guns are forc'd along the rugged soil;
With much constraint up every Steep they go;
But from the top a willing Motion show:
At length, from fifty Mouths, of largest size,
They belch forth sulph'rous Flames, and gape surprize:
Soft rouls of Thunder with unequal pace,   70
Thickning to hoarsness give each other Chase.

The higher *Batteries*, with incessant pain,
Dismount their *Cannon*, and dislodge their *Men*,
While those, erected nearer to the Town,
Hurl ponderous ruin at the Massy Stone:
Pounded by *Horizontal* Stroaks, *some* flow
In dusty Torrents, and assist below:
Others in abrupt Lumps role piece by piece,
Whilst tumbling rubbish follows by Degrees:
80   With intermitting Peals the Engins play,
To humble the assent, and clear the way:
At every *shock*, a slice of *Terras* falls;
Till a fair pause is opened in the Walls.
    Affairs thus forward; they proceed to make
A disposition for the Grand attack:
The Joyful Leaders struggle for the Fight,
But *Con—m* demanded it of Right:
One without any affectation grave,
Watchful, and indefatigably *brave*.
90   A Lineage destin'd *Glories* race to run,
Thus fell the *Father* and so fell the *Son*.
Blest with a large and plentiful Estate,   ⎫
Possest of *Beauty* and in *Honours*, Great;   ⎬
He pushed for *Fame*, but was attack'd by *Fate*. ⎭
Spain, with a *Cales* or with a *Gibraltar*,
May recompence the Nations for the War:
But Oh *Belbastro*, thou canst nothing give
To make the beautious Mourner cease to grieve.
Pirenian Hills, the Silver *Cinca*'s Flood
100   Behold him fall; and mourn'd in trails of Blood.
    Next *D—l*; who for the dusty Fields
Bartered those softnesses that plenty yields:
To *him* (a Noble of th' *Hibernian* Isle)
Quiet was drudgery and *ease* a toil.
The mournful *Montjuich* saw the *Hero* slain,
Where he dy'd *Saving*, what he thought to *gain*.
    G—s was next, inflam'd with martial heat,
The adventerous *Hero* left his native Seat,
In the pursuit of *Glory*, urging far:
110   Where he fought well, and was himself a War.

L—*n*, who early with the war began,
Er'e yet his downy Chin confess'd him Man;
Though great in *Title*, greater yet in *fame*,
But greatest in the Lustre of his *Name*.
  Now Muse proceed—
To *S—l—g*, and *S—a—d* doe right,
Who led the *Belgick Cohorts* to the fight.
These Hero's, long, on the *Batavian* plain,
Had urg'd their Squadrons o'er the reeking slain,
Under a *State*, which in last Age, began   120
T'assert the native *liberty* of Man.
The City gain'd, *one* makes his last Retreat,
And leaves the *Other* to sustain it's fate.
  Nor does obscurity to those belong,
Whose Names are unrecorded in our Song:
Their rank secures our silence: but desert
Justly to *each*, demands his Name apart:
With Resolutions noble and sublime,
These the *Deliv'ry* wait of pregnant time;
And as the Action struggles to get forth,   130
Exert their utmost Strength t'assist the Birth.
  Whilst Fate stood *thus* with lifted Arm, the Foe
Shrinks at the Apprehension of the Blow;
As *Dangers* press, their *Constancy* retires,
And *Resolution*, in a Fright, expires.
They saw th' Attack prepar'd; and knew the Fate
Of *Leige*, that call'd for Mercy when too late,
Thence, dreading such a terrible Event,
Clos'd with the Welcome Summons *Mordaunt* sent.
  Stanhope the Treaty manag'd with Address,   140
As *they* ask more, *he*'s in *Concession* less,
In *Courts*, he made peace his incessant Care,
But glow'd in *Camps*, with Ardour of the War.
Swift in Design and Execution was;
Thus be became both first and second Cause.
  In the mean while *Hostility* retires,
The Soldiers *Anger* with its *Cause* expires;
They mix in freindly Parle, and every Night
Conveys revolting Crowds to *Mordaunt*'s Sight.

150   But *now* from Eastern Skies the Morning shone
       That was to look on the surrender'd *Town*;
       Th' appointed Troops arm'd with a martial Grace
       Stand ready for Possession of the Place:
       When, from *within*, tumultuous Sounds they hear;
       Like *those*, that rise from *Riots* in a Fair.
       Odd scattering Shots from every Quarter stray'd,
       Such as oft straggle when a Volley's made
       Fleeting *Disorders* thicken up and down,
       And Shouts of *Popular Fear* involve the Town.
160   This was the Tumult in its Infant State;
       But *strong* with Age, and by *Resistance* great,
       The Sounds grew feircer then they were before,
       And Peals of War, in rolling Thunders roar.
       On Churches level Roofs, thick Crowds of Men
       Are in a Mingle of Confusion, seen:
       While *Priests* and *Women*, crowding on the Wall,
       In shuddering Horrour, *Help* and *Vengeance* call.
       When *Mordaunt* found the Uproar thus increase,
       The Troops were order'd to surround the Place.
170   *Some*, by th' unguarded Breach ascend; *some* gain
       The Walls, where most accessible, with Pain;
       The *Spaniards* careful of their Friends within,
       To shew their Zeal, with early Aid begin.
       By one anothers Help they quickly climb;
       Lay Ladders to, and lose but little time.
       Mean time great *Mordaunt*, with an active Speed,
       To *Angel Port* a chosen Cohort led.
       The *Brittish* Guards possess the *Ravelin*;
       But were not Masters of the Gate within.
180   Hither the *Hero* comes; and first of all
       Demanded Entrance with an awful Call,
       But *this* refus'd, the Danger prompts him on
       With Instruments of Force to beat it down.
       Ope flies the Gate, warm'd with a martial Fire,
       He drives thro' Deluges of fluid Fire:
       From either Side the *Missive* Lightning broke
       Mingle half way and mounts in Hostile Smoke
       Till urging thro' the crowded Danger, *on*
       Th' opposing Party fac'd about and run.

Now as the *Hero* rais'd his Voice to grant   190
A loose to *Rage* and military *Want*;
The Goddess *Peace*, descended o'er the *Throng*,
And stop'd the fault'ring *Order* on his Tongue.

Unseen to th' Crowd she stood: *He* only there,
Undazled, cou'd the Shine of *Glory* bear:
All soft she seem'd, all affable and kind,
Like what in painted *Cherubins* we find.
Her Mien was *lovly, chearful*, full of *Grace*:
And smiles of *Gladness* dimpled all her Face.
Diffusive of themselves her *Beauties* were;   200
And shed their Influence on the ambient Air.
A flowry *Garland* deck'd her Brows; and thence,
With grateful *Odours* struck the ravish'd Sence.
Her *Golden Locks* fell curling every way;
Bright, as a Sun Beam at the Noon of Day;
With a soft Motion round her Shoulders flew;
And hid the *Beauties* of her Neck from View.

Over a Garment, white as *Alpine* Snow,
Loosly did her embroiderd *Mantle* flow:
This shews a stately Oak, the Forrests grace,   210
Deep furrow'd by the *Ivy*'s close Embrace;
That, how the *Hop*, the *Briony and Vine*
With clasping Tendrills round their Standards twine.
A num'rous *Senate*, in profound Debate,
Sat brooding *here* o'er an Affair of *State*:
Their *Councels*, cent'ring in the Peoples Good;
Receive their Sanction from *a Regal Nod*.
Hist'ries of Friendship, in another Place,
Are mixt with *Emblems* of *Concord* and *Peace*:
And *Lovers* clasp'd in one anothers Arms,   220
Show *Love* and *Freindship* in united Charms.

The *Hero* thus surpriz'd into a stand,
She rais'd an Ivo'ry *Scepter* in her Hand;
And *thus* began—Let *Rage*, let *Slaughter* cease;
And *here* erect a Monument to *Peace*.
Enough of War—By gent'lest Means go on,
T'appease the bleeding Tumults in the Town,
Velasco arm'd with Arbitrary Sway,
Forces th' imprison'd *Citizens* away;

230 Guiltless of *Error*, to submit their Cause
Before a *foreign* Judge, to *foreign* Laws,
To stop whose Progress in its early Course,
The Town prepares t'oppose it self with Force
Add if it shou'd be sack'd or sink in Flames: ⎫
All Help from *thence* th' Alliance vainly claims, ⎬
'Twill stop the Fountain, or cut off the Streams. ⎭
    Then be't your Care t'interpose, and bar
The Mischeifs rising from th' intestine War:
    Thus having said—The *Goddess* mounted high
240 Into the Upper *Regions* of the Skie,
And soon all *Tumults* in the Town did cease,
And *War* was turn'd into a State of *Peace*.
    Thus *Discord*, *Envy*, *Malice*, strove in vain,
T'eclipse the *Glory* of great *Mordaunt*'s Fame.

FINIS.

DOUBTFUL ATTRIBUTIONS

INTRODUCTION

THE materials included as doubtful attributions have been so culled that only those attributed to Farquhar by eighteenth-century literary colleagues, biographers, and, in the case of *A Pacquet from Will's*, editors or printers, have been included. Although Stonehill expanded Farquhar's supposed canon by inclusion of the Celadon letters from *A Pacquet from Will's* and *Letters of Wit, Politicks and Morality*, I have printed only the two Celadon letters from *A Pacquet from Will's* marked as his in the 1718 edition. There is no significant or convincing internal evidence in the other letters included in the Stonehill text of Farquhar's authorship, and indeed there is considerable internal evidence to the contrary.

In the future, more additions to the canon may appear. When Farquhar was in London, he probably spread his talents rather broadly by writing prologues, epilogues, poems, and letters for publication. However, incontrovertible proof of Farquhar's authorship will prove extremely difficult since evidence is slight and many of the works that seem likely possibilities are exceedingly conventional. The materials in this section, although suspect, are indicative of inconsequential 'hack' works that may or may not have been written by Farquhar.

Because this section is so eclectic, the introductory discussion precedes each item or group of items.

ONE OF HIS JUVENILE PRODUCTIONS

THIS short poem was originally published in 'Some Memoirs of Mr. George Farquhar', the biographical sketch in the 1728 edition of *The Works of the late Ingenious Mr. George Farquhar*, printed for the Knaptons, Lintott, Strahan, and Clark. The biographer claims that Farquhar wrote it before he was ten:

As they who are bless'd with a Poetical Genius always shew some Glimmerings of their Fancy in their Youth, so he, e'er he arriv'd at his Tenth Year, gave several Specimens of a peculiar Turn that way. One of his Juvenile Productions I shall here mention, in which he discover'd a way of Thinking, as well as an Elegancy of Expression, far beyond his Years. (I.3)

The memoirs, including the poem, were reprinted in the seventh (1735), eighth (1742), and ninth (1760) editions of the *Works*, as well as the 'sixth edition' of the *Poems, Letters, and Essays* (i.e. *Love and Business*), printed by S. Powell for George Risk and William Smith in Dublin in 1728. Theophilus Cibber also included the poem in his biography of Farquhar in *The Lives of the Poets of Great Britain and Ireland* (iii. 124).

One of his Juvenile Productions

I.

The Pliant Soul of erring Youth,
  Is like soft Wax, or moisten'd Clay,
Apt to receive all Heavenly Truth;
  Or yield to Tyrant Ill the Sway.

II.

Slight Folly in your early Years,
  And Manhood may to Virtue rise;
But he, who in his Youth appears
  A Fool, in Age will ne'er be wise.

LETTER TO MRS. COCKBURN

The letter, partly paraphrased and partly quoted, appears in the biographical sketch published in *The Works of Mrs. Catharine Cockburn, Theological, Moral, Dramatic, and Poetical. . . . With an Account of the Life of the Author*, by Thomas Birch (2 vols., London: J. and P. Knapton, 1751). Catharine Trotter, later Cockburn, (1679–1749) wrote five plays; the first, *Agnes de Castro*, was performed at Drury Lane in December 1696, before Farquhar came to London. The second, *Fatal Friendship*, opened at Lincoln's Inn Fields probably in May or June 1698 before *Love and a Bottle* appeared in December. Birch wrote that Farquhar was so 'highly pleased' with *Fatal Friendship* that he 'soon after took the opportunity of sending to her his first comedy, called *Love and a Bottle*' with a letter in which he complained of the ladies' aspersions and formulated an elaborate epistolary compliment (I, pp. viii–ix).

Stonehill printed a version of the letter, quoting from Birch, but changing a few words ('I send' for 'he sent', for example), adding the signature 'G. Farquhar' and the date '[Dec. 20, (?) 1698]'. The letter was not published in any of the miscellanies to which Farquhar contributed.

Even if there was an actual letter available for Birch's perusal, there is no reason to believe the wording is accurate; Birch clearly paraphrases parts and perhaps all of the letter.

Farquhar's poem 'To the Ingenious Lady, Author of the *Fatal Friendship*, design'd for a Recommendatory Copy to her Play', probably composed in 1698 or 1699, was printed in *Love and Business*. He obviously sought the writer's favour, although one must be dubious about the authenticity of the letter Birch described.

Letter to Mrs. Cockburn

... *Love and a Bottle* has been scandalously aspersed for affronting the ladies ... as an argument of its innocence, [he sends] it to stand its tryal before one of the fairest of her sex, and the best judge. Besides, Madam, it is an offering due to the favour and honour shew'd me, in your appearance of my third night; and a stranger cannot be denied the privilege of shewing his gratitude. But humbly to confess the greatest motive, my passions were wrought so high by representation of *Fatal Friendship*, and since raised so high by a sight of the beautiful author, that I gladly catched this opportunity of owning myself, your most faithful and humble servant.

A PACQUET FROM WILL'S

Two letters from *A Pacquet from Will's* have been printed in this section, the first and third of the seven-letter sequence between Celadon and Mrs C—ll (Carroll). Celadon is listed as author of letters one, three, five, and seven of the sequence, Mrs C—ll of the other three. Stonehill, following Schmid, attributed the Celadon letters to Farquhar on the basis of the 1718 edition. He also printed the following 'Seven Passionate Love-Letters' between Celadon and Celia based on the 1718 and 1724 editions. But both textual and internal evidence suggest the strong possibility that Farquhar wrote the first two Celadon letters and none of the others.

Both the 1718 and 1724 editions were printed for Sam Briscoe, the entrepreneur of the first edition, and the bookseller mentioned by Farquhar in the new Prologue to *The Constant Couple*, in which he claimed enigmatically that he had no hand in 'Bankrupt Brisco's Fate'. Conceivably Briscoe or someone else could have, in fact, accurately remembered that Farquhar wrote the two letters.

Ordinarily one would assume that a compositor rather than a knowledgeable editor was responsible for the attribution to Farquhar in the 1718 edition, but there are unusually insistent indications of his authorship. In the 1718 edition, the first letter, which immediately follows Farquhar's '*To a Masque on* Twelfth-day', is labelled 'By the Same' and the third, 'By the same Hand'. Not only does the byline suggest his authorship, but the running-titles for the pages on which the first and third letters begin read '*Mr. FARQUHAR*'. The same running-title appears on the versos of Ii5–Ii10 of a twelve-leaf gathering. The letter I have identified as Farquhar's and printed in Miscellaneous Prose and Poetry appear on Ii5^r–Ii8^r. The first Celadon letter appears on Ii8^v–9^r and the second, labelled Letter II but published as the third in the series after Mrs C—ll's reply, on Ii9^v–Ii10^v. Ii11 carries the running-title '*Mrs* C—ll's *Answer*.' and Ii12^v, '*Celadon to Mrs.* C—ll.' Kk1^v

repeats the running-title of Ii12ᵛ, 'Celadon to *Mrs.* C—ll.' Hence the running-titles support the case for attribution to Farquhar, because they accurately reflect the contents of the individual pages rather than merely being used for the entire gathering.

The table of contents also supports the attribution of the first letter. Of the original seven letters identified as Farquhar's, the first two are listed in the 1718 edition as by 'Mr. George Farquhar' and the next five 'By the same'. The first of the Celadon letters is also identified as 'By the same'; however, the third is not.

Internal evidence in the sequence supports attribution of the first and third letters to Farquhar; however, internal evidence strongly argues that he did not write the fifth and seventh. The first letter refers to 'a trembling Disorder', not one of his usual symptoms, but conceivably a problem caused by his ill health as well as his love for Mrs C—ll. The third letter claims that the fine words she has written of him in her poem 'become him as ill as the Jubilee Beau's Cloaths do a Porter', a reference to *The Constant Couple* certainly intended to point to Farquhar as author. Her poem, to which this letter serves as reply, might well be '*To Mr.* Farquhar upon *his Comedy call'd* A Trip to the Jubilee', printed three months later as Epistle XL in *Letters of Wit, Politicks and Morality*.

But in the fourth letter Mrs. C—ll speaks of Celadon as a lawyer rather than a playwright:

If I remember, *Truth* and *Sincerity* (which ought to be cloath'd in *Modesty*) were the Principles you profest, and seem'd to defend. But I find those are Points as far out of a *Lawyer*'s way, as good Manners from a *Dutchman*; especially a *Templer*'s.

Celadon, obviously, is a lawyer, for he replies:

Certainly You have been very ill used by some of the Gown [i.e. lawyers], which provokes you to condemn us all for Monsters, Creatures void both of good Morals, and common Civility.

Mrs C—ll refers yet again to Celadon as a member of the legal profession in her next reply:

I will not insert the Particulars, the better to disarm your Defence:

For one of Your Profession knows how to defend a bad Cause as well as a good one.

Celadon at least from the fourth to the sixth letter, is a lawyer, not a playwright.

It seems likely, then, that Farquhar wrote the first and third letters but not the fifth and seventh. The tenor of these letters and the relationship of Mrs Carroll to Boyer and others involved in the project suggest the possibility that the lady of the correspondence, not the gentleman, may have been responsible for submitting the letters for publication. If she did, she might well have mixed letters from two different suitors in the Celadon sequence or, indeed, invented some. It is, of course, possible that Farquhar was responsible for none of the letters; certainly he did not write the fifth and seventh since he never studied or practised law. Capt. William Ayloffe,[1] a lover and correspondent of Mrs Carroll who was admitted to Gray's Inn, is a far likelier candidate. Therefore, I have included the first and third letters, for which there is a body of positive evidence, but not the fifth and seventh.

Stonehill also printed the next sequence in *A Pacquet from Will's*, 'Seven Passionate Love-Letters written by *Celadon* to his Mistress', in this case Cælia rather than Astræa, probably because the pseudonym Celadon is reused. There is no textual or internal evidence to suggest Farquhar's authorship.

The Celadon sequence in *Letters of Wit, Politicks and Morality* (Letters XV–XXXVII) most likely belong to Carroll and Ayloffe, although some of them show some ambiguous internal evidence that might conceivably point to Farquhar. Stonehill without explanation attributed them to him, probably by analogy with the Celadon letters in *A Pacquet from Will's*. These letters have not been included in Doubtful Attributions because there is no strong evidence that Farquhar had a hand in them.

NOTE

1. In Letter XXVI, Astræa refers to Celadon as 'Mr. *A—e*'.

A PACQUET FROM WILL'S

Celadon *to Mrs.* C—ll.

You may be assured, *Astræa*, that neither Grief nor Love will break the Heart of any Man, since neither of them have killed me, though I have been forc'd to be two Days without the Honour of seeing You. When I parted from you, to begin this tedious Separation, I remember you promised me a Letter; the Expectation of which was a Comfort to me in my Absence: But when I came to Town this Morning, and found none; if ever you saw or could fancy a Man wild with Despair, just such a thing was I: The mildest of my Thoughts was, that I was forgotten and deservedly slighted; that something of Disadvantage to me had occurr'd since I saw you; and that some body, I don't know who, has been doing, I don't know what, to ruine me in your Esteem: For You are in your Nature generous, and a strict Observer of your Word. Sure therefore, it must be something extraordinary that could provoke you to be at once both unkind and unfit to

Yours,

CELADON.

P.S.

I would have wrote more; but I find my self in a trembling Disorder, as you may perceive by my manner of writing, which I can no more give an Account of, than You can, why you are pleas'd to admit of Letters from

Your Humble Servant.

Letter II.

Celadon *to Mrs.* C—ll, *in answer to a Copy of Verses she sent him.*

Madam, by making such a Pother,
Of being tost this way and t'other,

Methinks 'tis plain you want a Rudder:
Which, if my Counsel might prevail,
You'd get, and fasten to your Tail
The next time you resolve to sail.
Then you'd not fear a Storm or Quick-sand,
When once your Ladiship is mann'd.
And should you touch my Rock of Wit,
Why should you be afraid of it?
For I shall sink and you shall split.
But to descend to Phrase of Land,
And speak what both may understand.
You say you ventur'd a Surprize,
And went much wounded from my Eyes:
And when recover'd and grown better,
There came a parlous witty Letter,
Which bound your Heart fast as with Fetter.
Madam, all Women must submit
To my joint Force of Eyes and Wit.
Where e'er I come, I make sure Slaughter:
But were you dead, dead as Dish-Water,
I have a Cordial Infection,
Will cause a speedy Resurrection,
A blessed Medicine ne'er failing
Those that, like you, are giv'n to sailing.
Three Doses does it; sometimes more,
According as I am in store.
But shou'd it fail, pray what of that?
Though I have kill'd you like a Cat,
As I shall find, 'ere I have done,
You have alas more Lives than one.
But one thing more, and I have ended:
Your two last Lines have much offended.
You seem unkindly to suspect
I shou'd my glorious Prize neglect;
Or else mis-use the Pow'r you gave,
And frown ungently on my Slave.
But did you know your Man throughout,
You'd be asham'd of such a Doubt:
For I'm as merciful as stout.

10

20

30

40

No more *Poetry*, I beseech you: 'Tis too chargeable a way of writing to be pleasant to a Man that's forc'd to hire: So unlucky am I too at this Juncture, that my Hackney's at Grass, which must seem, both for a Reason why your Answer has been delayed so long, and for the Faintness of his Performance. Give me leave to tell you with as much good manners as I can, that not one of those fine Sayings, you would flatter your humble Servant with, sits easie on him. They become him as ill as the Jubilee Beau's Cloaths do a 50 Porter; or as fine Trappings would an Ass: Let me intreat you therefore to believe that I know my self, and can't bear being laugh'd at by one I would make my Friend. Immoderate undeserv'd Praises, are the severest Lampoons; and you must have a very mean Opinion of him you give 'em to, if you think he'll take 'em: Let Example instruct you. I check my Pen when I find it inclines to any thing that can be wrested to a Compliment, tho' all I could say, would be less than you truly deserve. Oblige me with more Truth and less Wit, as you value the Friendship and Conversation of Your Humble 60 Admirer,

> *CELADON.*

P.S. Send me word if I may have leave to visit you to morrow.

LAST LETTER TO ROBERT WILKS

THE only source for this letter is 'The Life of George Farquhar' in Thomas Wilkes's edition of the *Works*, published in Dublin in 1775. According to Wilkes's inaccurate account, Farquhar died on the third night of *The Beaux Stratagem*, in the last week of April. The letter to Robert Wilks was found among his papers after he died.

Actually, *The Beaux Stratagem* opened 8 March and ran twelve times the first season, with interruptions for previous stage commitments. Farquhar received benefits on the third, sixth, and eleventh nights. The third benefit occurred on 29 April; Farquhar was buried 23 May. The stories of his death were obviously romanticized. He did have two daughters; his widow Margaret, in her petition to Queen Anne, probably in February 1708, records that 'after a lingring and Expensive Sickness it pleasd God to take him from y^r Petitioner, leaving 2 little babes Wholly unprovided' (British Library, Loan 29/32). Apparently, the actor Wilks looked after the girls. 'Menander' discusses Wilks's kindness to them in a critique of *The Inconstant*, in *Pasquin* No. 75, dated 22 October 1723:

... I cannot pass over in Silence the Humanity of that Person [Wilks] towards his [Farquhar's] two Orphan-Daughters, who have by his Gratitude been defended from Shame and Want, the Snares of Wickedness and Folly; the dreadful Apprehension of which was the last sad Thought which afflicted their expiring Parent.

Farquhar's first biographer, in the 'Memoirs' published in the 1728 sixth edition of the *Works*, also mentioned his having two daughters. The biographer continues:

... his Fortune being too slender to support a Family, led him into a great many Cares and Inconveniencies; for I have often heard him say, *That it was more Pain to him in imagining that his Family might want a needful Support, than the most violent Death that cou'd be inflicted on him.* But his Wife being long since dead, his good Friend Mr. *Wilks* has been highly instrumental in setting his Children above Want.

However, the biographer tells another often repeated tale of Farquhar:

He left no other Papers behind him [besides his published plays]; for, three Hours before his Death, he flung several Fragments into the Fire, declaring at the same time, that he had no Remains worth saving.

The early biographer doubtless refers to literary papers, omitting the kind of papers to which Wilkes refers in 1775; otherwise the story of finding the letter contradicts the traditional tale of Farquhar's having thrown his papers into the fire. Indeed none of his holograph papers have been found.

Whether the letter is apocryphal or not, the tradition of Wilks's caring for his friend's daughters seems to represent a genuine and continuing commitment. Moreover, the theatre managers must have felt some obligation. On 29 May 1717 a performance of *The Recruiting Officer* at Drury Lane benefited 'the Orphan Children of the late Mr. Farquhar'. After Wilks's death, other benefits occurred on 14 May 1737 (*The Beaux Stratagem*, Drury Lane, 'Benefit Boman and the Daughters of the late Mr Farquhar'); 1 April 1741 (*Oroonoko*, Covent Garden, 'tickets for Dan French and the late Farquhar's Daughter'); 19 December 1750 (*The Stratagem*, Drury Lane, 'Tickets deliver'd out by a Daughter of Mr Farquhar's in great distress, will be taken this night'); 8 June 1756 (concert, Haymarket, 'Benefit for the daughter of the late Mr Farquhar, now under Misfortunes'); 13 May 1757 (*Merope*, Drury Lane, Miss Farquhar was one of several beneficiaries); and 23 December 1758 (*Much Ado about Nothing*, Drury Lane, 'Tickets deliver'd by a Daughter of the late Mr Farquhar will be taken') (*London Stage, passim.*) Whether only one daughter survived by 1741 is unclear.

Wilkes's inaccuracies on matters such as death date and first run cast some doubt on the authenticity of the Wilks letter, published 68 years after Farquhar's death. But the contents of the note reflect a relationship that previous biographical materials support.

Last Letter to Robert Wilks

Dear Bob,

I have not any thing to leave thee, to perpetuate my memory, but two helpless girls; look upon them sometimes, and think on him that was to the last moment of his life thine,

G. FARQUHAR

LAST LINES

According to William Chetwood, this couplet was Farquhar's last: 'Even the two last Lines he ever wrote, seem'd to be playing with Words.'[1] There is no corroborating evidence that Farquhar wrote these lines.

NOTE

1. W. R. Chetwood, *A General History of the Stage From its Origin in Greece down to the present Time* (London, 1749), p. 152.

Last Lines

Death now appears to seize my latest Breath;
But all my Miseries will end in *Death*.

APPENDIX

THE Dedication of the *Comedies* to John Eyre, published in 1708 and subsequent editions, was signed by Bernard Lintot. Obviously Farquhar had nothing to do with it, for he had died before the *Comedies* appeared. It is reprinted here for informational purposes.

TO
JOHN EYRE, Esq;

SIR,
Most of the following PLAYS are inscrib'd to Persons of greatest Worth and Honour: And one, not less successful than the rest, to the Gentlemen of *Shropshire*, than which there are few Counties in *England* that can make a Figure more distinguishable.

Yet still there is one Play, and the whole Collection as now made, which want a Patron.

As *Ben Johnson* shew'd the several Humours of his Time, with a Stroak so masterly, that they still do and may please hereafter: And as Mr. *Shadwel* was allow'd to have excell'd in that Strain of Writing, so it is my Hopes, that Mr. *Farquhar*'s Comedies will not have less Approbation in future Ages, than they have had in the present. My Reason is, because we still desire to know what our Fore-fathers did: And he that in late Posterity would look for the Humours of this Age, must search Mr. *Farquhar* for them as much as he would *Vandike, Vario, Lilly*, or Mr. *Howard*, for their Personages or their Habits.

There is a Liveliness and Vigour runs through the whole, and therefore these following Pages may sometimes divert you in your Retirements, when freed from the accustom'd Fatigue of serving your Friends.

As it is my Interest to wish these Scenes, may divert to late Posterity, so my utmost desire of being grateful is, that you wou'd Patronize this Collection, and receive the small Acknowledgement of my Duty, as from one that would take all Opportunities of testifying to the World how much he is,

SIR,

Your most Obedient,
Humble Servant,

BERNARD LINTOTT.

COMMENTARY

The Recruiting Officer

Title-page

[motto] Virgil, *Aeneid*, ii, 196, contains the phrase 'captique dolis lacrimisque coactis', translated by H. Rushton Fairclough as 'we were ensnared by wiles and forced tears' (*Virgil* with an English translation by H. Rushton Fairclough, Loeb Classical Library, 2 vols. [Cambridge, Mass. and London, 1940], pp. 307–9). Farquhar's version could be translated 'ensnared by wiles and gifts'. The motto refers to the wiles of recruitment.

Dedication

0.4 Wrekin] an isolated hill that dominates the countryside near Shrewsbury. Farquhar uses a familiar toast:

> The Wrekin, the central point of the county, the *motif* of the county toast, 'To all Friends round the Wrekin' (the rallying cry, as it might almost be called of North and South), has been imagined to be the work of a baffled giant. He wanted to dam up the Severn and drown out the people of Shrewsbury. . . .

But the giant was fooled by a cobbler, according to the old folks tale (Thomas Auden, *Memorials of Old Shropshire* [London, 1906], p. 125).

9 order'd some time ago] Farquhar served a stint in Shrewsbury as a recruiting officer, possibly in 1704 when he was on duty raising a regiment of foot soldiers under the command of the Earl of Orrery (Jordan, p. 253).

23–34 Some little . . . short of his own.] Rightly or wrongly, Shrewsbury citizens have been identified as models for Farquhar's characters. Kite was supposedly based on an actual Sergeant Jones, and Ballance on a local citizen, Mr. Berkeley. (See Introduction, vol. ii, pp. 4–6.)

36 Mr. *Rich*] Christopher Rich, manager of Drury Lane.

40 Mr. *Durfey*'s Third Night] D'Urfey's *The Wonders in the Sun*; or, *The Kingdom of the Birds* opened 5 April 1706 at the Queen's Theatre. On 8 April, the third night of its run and presumably the author's benefit, *The Recruiting Officer* opened. D'Urfey's extravaganza lasted only five nights, and, according to Downes, lost a lot of money (see Hume, p. 479). The Queen's company must have blamed the timing of Farquhar's opening for the lack of success. However, an opening even as late as 8 April meant a short season, interrupted by benefits and other committed evenings. Farquhar and the management obviously felt that to wait longer would shorten the run of the comedy.

43–4 huge Flight of frightful Birds] In the last act of D'Urfey's comic opera, the characters visit the Kingdom of the Birds of the sub-title, encountering many strange birds.

62 Duke of *Ormond*] James Butler, Duke of Ormond (1665–1745) succeeded to his grandfather's titles in 1688. In 1702 he became generalissimo of the forces against Spain and Lord Lieutenant of Ireland in 1703. With Sir George Rooke, he captured Cadiz and Vigo Bay. He was Farquhar's general. Some ambiguity surrounds the question of whether Ormonde or Orrery was responsible for the award of Farquhar's commission (Jordan, pp. 251–4).

63 Earl of *Orrery*] Charles Boyle, Earl of Orrery (1676–1731) raised a regiment of foot soldiers in 1704. Farquhar's lieutenancy was in Orrery's regiment; he travelled to Shrewsbury and later to Ireland on the business of the regiment. Boyle, who had written *As You Find It* for Lincoln's Inn Fields in 1703, was perhaps considered a literary arbiter since his approval is noted.

i.i

0.3 *Granadeer-March*] Ross identifies the tune as one first printed in John Playford's *The Dancing Master*, 7th edn., published in 1686 (Ross, p. 11), not 'The British Grenadiers'.

0.4 Kite] J. C. Hotten in *The Slang Dictionary* (1859) lists 'Sergeant Kite' as a colloquialism for a recruiting sergeant from *c*.1850. It was obsolete by 1920. The usage testifies to the popularity of the play in the nineteenth century.

6 the *Raven*] an establishment in Castle Street (Ross, p. 11 n.).

12 Granadeers] Each foot regiment commanded by a colonel, consisted of one battalion, divided into a headquarters and ten to twelve companies, one of which was a company of grenadiers (Scouller, p. 97). Grenadiers were defined in the *Military Dictionary* as 'Soldiers arm'd with a good Sword, a Hatchet, Fire-lock slung, and a Pouch full of Hand-Granadoes. Every Batalion of Foot, of late Years, has generally a Company of Granadeers belonging to it, or else four or five Granadeers belong to each Company of the Batalion, and upon occasion form a Company of themselves. There are Horse and Foot Granadeers, and they have often been found very serviceable.'

14–15 in the drawing of a Tricker] quickly; in the time it takes to pull a trigger.

29–30 the great Bed of *Ware*] an enormous bed from the Crown Inn in Ware, Hertfordshire; it was also mentioned by Shakespeare in *Twelfth Night* and Jonson in *The Silent Woman*.

57 humming Ale] '*Hum*, or *Humming Liquor*, Double Ale, Stout, Pharaoh' (*NDCC*).

73 Banks of the *Danube*] Plume is presumably returning from the great British victory at the Battle of Blenheim on 13 August 1704.

81 the strong Man of *Kent*] William Joy or Joye. See Commentary, *The Constant Couple*, Prologue, l. 35, vol. i, p. 599.

81–2 King of the Gypsies] 'the Captain, Chief, or Ring-leader of the Gang, the Master of Misrule' (*NDCC*).

87–9 I will have . . . discharge him.] Boswell tells of dining in 1762 with Thomas Sheridan, who felt bishops deplored merit: 'If a man could write well, they were of Captain Plume's opinion about the attorney: "A dangerous man; discharge him, discharge him"' (*Boswell's London Journal, 1762–63*, ed. Frederick A. Pottle [New York, 1951], p. 91).

118 the *Buss*] an obsolete form of Bourse, perhaps referring to the Bourse at Antwerp. Buss was also a term for a kind of ship used in the Dutch herring fishing industry; the name 'Van-Bottomflat' is a reference to the wide flat boats and the broadly built, short women Dutch were known for.

125 Chopping Boy] bouncing boy (*NDCC*).

129 Subsistence] Subsistence rates, the amount allotted for food and clothing for each man, as set in the 1704 Mutiny Act (Ann. 3 and 4, c. 5), allowed 6*s*. for each sergeant in the foot regiments, 4*s*. 6*d*. for corporals and drummers, and 4*s*. for privates. At the end of every two months, the commanding officer was held accountable for 'the remainder of the subsistence', 1*s*. per sergeant, 2*d*. per drummer or corporal, and 6*d*. per private (Scouller, Appendix H, p. 381). The practice of 'allowing and mustering' fictitious men occurred often, sometimes to help support widows, pay for loss of clothing or burial expenses, cover the losses due to desertion, and in other ways bolster the subsistence figures (Scouller, p. 142). Plume is, of course, bribing Kite with the promise falsely to list the newborn baby as 'Francis Kite', on leave so that Kite can make a profit. The scheme was neither legal nor moral; Farquhar satirizes the chicanery in military finances at a time when the cost of the army was a matter of grave concern to taxpayers.

151–2 safe from *Germany*, and sound I hope from *London*] Plume was not injured in the Battle of Blenheim, and he did not catch a venereal disease in London. The loss of a nose refers to the effects of syphilis.

201 dy'd upon the Breach] a sexual pun.

303 *Barcelona*] Because of the exorbitant duties on French wines, the wine trade with Spain was growing in this period.

I.ii

43–4 *And there's a Pleasure sure, in being mad.* | *Which none but Mad-men know.*] Silvia gives lines from *The Spanish Fryar*, Act II:

>. . . There is a Pleasure sure
>In being Mad, which none but Madmen know!

Dryden's play opened probably in 1680 and remained popular on stage. In Farquhar's time, it played in repertory at both houses. When Estcourt, the original Kite, first came to Drury Lane in October 1704, he opened in *The Spanish Fryar*, and he played in it often. Dryden's play had run with *The Stage-Coach* at Lincoln's Inn Fields in 1704. It played at both houses in 1705–6.

66 He's my Aversion] another allusion to *The Plain Dealer*, in which the hypocritical Olivia refers to everything she finds interesting as her 'aversion' (II. i). See Commentary, *The Constant Couple*, I. ii. 107, 134–5, vol. i, p. 603.

II.i

1–9 [comments on the war] After the Battle of Blenheim on 13 August 1704, in which Marshal Tallard was captured, the British felt considerably heartened. The comedies of Farquhar's era are full of references to specific battles. Although the periodicals reported news from the battlefield rather quickly, the plays continued to talk about battles that were several years old. Kite accurately reflects attitudes toward the British forces in action, both before and after Blenheim.

14–19 Battle of *Hochstet*] Battle of Blenheim. Blenheim is a village on the Danube near the town of Höchstädt, where the French were garrisoned. The allied forces, outnumbered by the French, won through the brilliant generalship of Marlborough. Estimates indicate the Allies had approximately 12,500 casualties, including 4,500 dead, and 8,000 wounded; of these, the English casualties were approximately 2,200. Franco-Bavarian casualties have been estimated at 38,000 (C. T. Atkinson, *Marlborough and The Rise of the British Army* [New York, 1921], pp. 235–6). Churchill (iv. 128) sums up the importance of the battle:

> Blenheim is immortal as a battle not only because of the extraordinary severity of the fighting of all the troops on the field all day long, and the overwhelming character of the victory, but because it changed the political axis of the world. This only gradually became apparent. Even a month after all the facts were known, measured, and discounted, scarcely any one understood what transformations had been wrought.

70–1 the Evening before the Battel of *Blenheim*] Outnumbered as the allied forces were, thoughts and deeds on the eve of battle must have been sombre indeed. Churchill reports that Marlborough spent some of the night in prayer and received the sacrament (iv. 85). Plume would doubtless not have been alone in spending time composing his will.

II.ii

33 magotty] freakish (*NDCC*).

41 Prince *Prettyman*] Actually, Prince Volscius rather than Prince Prettyman in *The Rehearsal* ponders his conflict between love and honour in terms of which boot to pull on (III.v). Farquhar made the same error in *Love and Business*, 'Bopeep is Child's Play', ll. 11–12, vol. ii, p. 337.

46 Pad] 'an easy Pacing Horse' (*NDCC*).

121 a hank upon] advantage over, or ascendency over.

II.iii

1–9 [SONG] A full text of this song, with somewhat different lyrics, was published in *Wit and Mirth: or Pills to Purge Melancholy* in 1706 (iv. 102–4)[7]. See Appendix.

18–19 pressing Act] The Mutiny and Impressment Acts of 1703, 1704, and 1705 allowed justices of the peace to 'raise and levy' able-bodied men who had no lawful employment or visible means of support (Scouller, p. 106). Costar, therefore, believes justices of the peace have more power than emperours.

33 *Broad Pieces*] The broad-pieces, originally worth twenty shillings, were coined during the reigns of Charles II and James II; they were broader and thinner than guineas. Ross (p. 39) believes that the coins Kite foists on the 'recruits' were probably hammered unites struck between 1660 and 1672, since they show a beardless Charles II, whose image could conceivably be mistaken for the Queen's. Recruits were given twenty shillings levy-money; Kite attempts to entrap Costar and Thomas with the broad-pieces.

80 St. *Mary*'s Clock . . . St. *Chads*] two venerable churches in Shrewsbury. St Mary's is said to have been founded in the tenth century; it was described by Thomas Harral as 'altogether the noblest and the handsomest in the country, that of Ludlow alone excepted' (*Picturesque Views of the Severn* [2 vols., London, 1824], i. 162). St. Chad's was named after a bishop of the Mercians (Auden, p. 66).

164 Firelock] 'a Piece that is fir'd with the Flint that is fast'ned to the Cock, whereas formerly Match-locks were more in use, fixing a Match to the Cock' (*Military Dictionary*). Carried by foot soldiers, firelocks had a barrel about 3 ft. 8 in. long and a stock about 4 ft. 8 in.; the bore fitted a lead bullet weighing an ounce (*The Gentleman's Dictionary* [London, 1705]).

168 two Guineas] Each volunteer was supposed to receive a bounty of forty shillings for three years' service; the bounty was raised to £4 by the Recruiting Act of 1707.

III.i

22–38 SONG] Farquhar presumably wrote the lyrics, which were set to music by Richard Leveridge. Wilks himself sang.

93 *Hussars*] Kite is, apparently, inventing war stories about the fierce Hungarians.

93 Ravelin] 'the Point of a Bastion, with the Flanks cut off, as consisting of only two Faces, which make an Angle Saillant. It is plac'd before a Curtin, to cover the opposite Flanks of the two next Bastions; or to cover a Bridge and Gate, being always beyond the Moat' (*Military Dictionary*).

94 Palisado] 'Great Wooden Stakes, or Spars, 6 or 7 Inches Square, and 8 Foot long, whereof 3 Foot are let into the Ground. They are planted on the Avenues of all Places that may be carry'd by Assault, and even by regular Attack' (*Military Dictionary*).

129 Halbard] The weapon was the mark of a sergeant.

137 a Garret in the *Savoy*] The Savoy was a refuge for debtors, inhabited also by many miscreants. Misson (p. 224) describes the Savoy as one of the privileged places 'which are nothing but Dens of Thieves and Bankrupts. There are in these Places inaccessible Nests of such Vermin: Nothing can be more easy or common at *London* than to turn Bankrupt; and three Steps from their own Houses, there is a sacred *Asylum* ready to receive them.'

138 Garrison] 'either the Place into which Forces are put into Winter-

Quarters, or the Troops themselves put into a fortify'd Place to defend it, being strong Holds, as are generally along Frontiers' (*Military Dictionary*).

169–70 the *Hungarians . . .* and the *Irish*] Kite has created war tales. Prince Eugene had been imperial general against the Turks in Hungary. He won a victory at Zenta in Hungary, and in 1699 the first definitely victorious peace that the Christians ever wrested from the Turks was signed (G. N. Clark, *The Later Stuarts 1660–1714* [Oxford, 1934, rept. 1947], p. 185). In the summer of 1703, Eugene was in Hungary trying to deal with a rebellion against the Emperor (Churchill, ii. 241). The Irish were not involved.

233 Battel of *Landen*] a disastrous battle in 1693. See Commentary, *The Constant Couple*, i. i. 174, vol. i, p. 602.

218 *Chevaux de Frise*] the French term for turnpikes, spars 12 or 14 feet long and 6 or 8 inches in diameter, with six sides. On every side, holes were bored and pickets 5 or 6 feet long, with iron points, fitted. Turnpikes were used in a breach or camp entrance to stop the enemy (*Military Dictionary*).

258 the *India* Company] the East India Company.

259 *Tongue-Pad*] 'a smooth, Glib-tongued, insinuating Fellow' (*NDCC*).

278–9 the Tombs and the Lions] The tombs of the famous in Westminster Abbey and the lions kept in the Tower of London were two tourist attractions.

283 *Mechelin*] The lace brought home by military men was the finest quality Flemish work.

287 *Turky*-shell Snuff-box] The snuff habit had become popular after the victory at Vigo Bay in 1702, in which large quantities were captured by the English. Snuff-boxes of gold, silver, tortoiseshell, agate, ivory, and other precious materials became very fashionable (Cunnington, *Eighteenth*, p. 102).

288 *Mangeree*] expensive snuff. See Commentary, *Love and a Bottle*, ii. ii. 37, vol. i, p. 586.

303–7 [SONG] 'The Milke-maids Life', a song first written by Martin Parker in 1634, was reworked by Thomas D'Urfey in 1694 for *Don Quixote*, Part II, with new music by John Eccles (Ross, pp. 132–3). The lyrics printed in *The Recruiting Officer* most closely resemble D'Urfey's version, which is reprinted in the Appendix.

iii.ii

6 Pinners] See Commentary, *Sir Harry Wildair*, i. i. 150, vol. i, p. 615. The term was used not only for headwear but also for a modesty piece pinned to conceal a decolletage.

52–4 *Flanders . . . Moors*] Brazen brags of serving on all fronts, in Flanders in the War of the Spanish Succession, in Hungary with Prince Eugene in 1697–9 against the Turks, and in Tangier before 1683 when the English garrison was withdrawn. Charles II had acquired Tangier when he married Catherine of Braganza; as his financial troubles increased, he found it increasingly difficult to repel the Moors and finally withdrew the garrison (G. N. Clark, p. 58).

64 Stove] a sexual *double entendre*.

84 the Raven] I have not been able to trace a tavern called the Raven at Shrewsbury. On the Wrekin was a natural hollow called the Raven's Bowl, which gathered water; the tasting of the water there became a local ritual (Auden, p. 35).

92 close Pinners for a Punk in the Pit] modesty pieces worn by a prostitute in the pit at the theatre.

93 Vessel] woman. Farquhar also used nautical puns for women in *Love and a Bottle*.

106 Platoon] 'A small square Body of Musketeers, such as is us'd to be drawn out of a Batalion of Foot, when they form the hollow Square to strengthen the Angles. The Granadiers are generally thus posted' (*Military Dictionary*).

108 kneel, stoop and stand] Soldiers were trained to fire from all three positions so that in warfare a platoon could fire at different heights.

176 Field-Officer] the commander of the regiment.

197 Banes] Plume uses the metaphor of marriage banns.

224 C fa ut flat] The notation indicates C flat.

IV.i

13–14 Drum-Major] From 1700 every regiment was authorized to have a drum-major. They were paid 1*s.* 6*d.* per day, whereas private foot soldiers received 8*d.* (Scouller, pp. 99, 376).

54–5 an ugly Song of Chickens and Sparragus] 'The Jovial Companions, or, the Three Merry Travellors', a ballad, printed probably *c*.1685, told a bawdy tale of three travellers at an inn run by a young widow:

> Both Chickens and sparrow grass she did provide,
>> *with a hye down, ho down, Lanktre down derry.*
> You're Welcome kind Gentlemen, welcome (she cry'd)
>> *without ever a stiver of Mony.*

Pills to Purge Melancholy (1714, v, 17–19) includes the words and music to the old ballad and also another bawdy poem (p. 202) to be sung to the tune of 'Chickens and Sparrow-grass' (Peter Dixon, '"Chickens and Sparrow Grass" in Farquhar and Pope', *N&Q*, NS 26 (1979), 541–2).

82 furbuloe Scarf] Furbaloes or ruffles were used as trimming for scarves.

95–6 send *Ruose* to the *West-Indies*] that is, transport her as punishment for prostitution.

118 Listing-money] the levy money paid to volunteers.

29–30 the best Security for a Woman's Soul is her Body] Boswell quoted this phrase in describing his love affair with Louisa (*Boswell's London Journal*, p. 140).

IV.iii

18 *Tycho*] Kite's fortune-telling assistant is undoubtedly named after Tycho Brahe and his system of astronomy.

19 cunning Man] a man who possesses magical powers or skills.

21 *Coppernose*] extremely red nose (*NDCC*).

33–4 *Furns, Dixmude, Namur, Brussels, Charleroy*] references to various military campaigns. Furns or Furnes was a minor fortress near Dunkirk, which fell in the campaign in the Netherlands in 1693. The Allies also took Charleroi in 1693. After losing at Landen, King William's army retired to Brussels and the French took Charleroi. In 1694 the Allies had captured Dixmude, but in 1695 Major General Ellenburg surrendered nine British battalions and a regiment of dragoons at Dixmude to Villeroi. When Boufflers capitulated at Namur, Villeroi was asked to return the garrison at Dixmude, but refused and was arrested (G. N. Clark, pp. 165–8; Stephen B. Baxter, *William III* [London, 1966], pp. 329–30). All the names Kite invokes had long been associated with foreign battles in which the British often lost, sometimes won.

42 Arrears] Pay was divided into subsistence plus arrears for officers or off-reckonings for other ranks. The Army was notoriously bad about underfunding the payment due to military men, and arrears were often long overdue (Scouller, p. 127).

49 Agent] Army pay agents profited by charging exorbitant percentages to advance pay (Fortescue, i. 383).

61–2 a Cane hanging upon his Button] Canes, used from 1700 on, were either carried by hand, tied or attached by a ring to a coat button, or slung by a loop to a finger. Cane heads were often fashioned of gold, silver, agate, or amber (Cunnington, *Eighteenth*, pp. 100–2).

77 *Tom a Lincoln*] From Richard Johnson's *The most pleasant History of Tom a Lincolne* (1599) and *The Second Part of the Famous Historie of Tom a Lincolne* (1607). A thirteenth edition of both parts was published in 1704. Son of King Arthur and Angelica, Tom o'Lincoln became a knight of the Round Table, married the daughter of Prester John, and was eventually murdered.

78 *Tom o' Bedlam*] Although the *OED* defines the term as a deranged person discharged from Bedlam and licensed to beg, the *NDCC* defines it as an Abram-man, 'the seventeenth Order of the Canting-crew. Beggers antickly trick'd up with Ribbands, Red Tape, Foxtails, Rags, &c. pretending Madness to palliate their Thefts of Poultrey, Linnen, &c.'

172–3 the Justices can't press me] As a butcher, Pluck has a visible means of employment.

179–80 Guineas for Claps] Cures for venereal disease were a staple of some medical practices outside the military; Kite is suggesting that army doctors not only treat many patients with the 'French disease' but also profit by it apart from their regular pay. London newspapers advertised cures for venereal disease regularly. For example, *The Flying Post* advertised on 18–20 January 1704:

A Present Remedy after Misfortune: Or, an immediate Cure for the Fr. Disease and Clap; and all other its numerous Attendents, which often times produce other grievous and lasting Distempers, to the utter ruin of many, besides frequently untimely Death, procured by them thro' grand Abuses, committed by the base and irregular Methods and Medicines of foolish & unskilful Pretenders. Good Medicines and Advice may be had of a Physician of 40 Years Practice, living at the Blue Ball in Whale-Bone-Court, the lower end of Bartholomew-lane behind the Royal Exchange. His Pills prepared for the French Disease and Running of the Reins, may be had in Boxes of several Prizes, with other Venereal Arcanas as occasion requires, with Directions.

The *Daily Courant* advertised on 30 November 1706:

Dr. Harborough's Pills, which perfectly cure all the Degrees and Indispositions in Venereal Persons by a most easie, safe, and expeditious Method; they also prevent the Disease if taken soon after the Danger fear'd . . . They are dispos'd of at a Coffee-house over against the Doctors late Dwelling-house in great Knight-Rider-Street, near Doctor's Commons Back-gate, with Directions for their Use.

246 *Cacodemon del Fuego*] Cacodemon means an evil spirit. Kite plays on the word 'cacafuego', of Spanish derivation, used for a braggart.

v.ii

34 Goose-Cap] fool.

40–1 threw the Stocking, and spoke Jokes by their Bed] By folk tradition, men threw the bride's stockings backwards toward the couple in bed and women threw the groom's stockings in the same way; to hit the man with his stockings or the woman with hers gave a prognosis of early marriage for the hurler (see Misson, pp. 352–3). The friends of the bride and groom traditionally tucked them into bed on their wedding night, a ritual that also aided in verification that the marriage had been consummated.

65–6 a Martial Twist in my Cravat] a reference to a steinkirk, a cravat loosely twisted in front, with the ends threaded through a button-hole or pinned to one side to the coat. The style, originally created for battle-action and named after the Battle of Steinkirk, became fashionable in London (Cunnington, *Eighteenth*, p. 75).

66 a fierce Knot in my Perriwig] The campaign wig had knots on each side and sometimes one at the back to keep the hair out of the way during battle (Corson, p. 284; Cunnington, *Eighteenth*, pp. 91, 94).

69 cock my Hat with a Pinch] another military style, also worn by fashionable beaux. Hat brims were turned up high in 'the fierce trooper's cock' and the front peak was usually given a 'smart pinch' (Cunnington, *Eighteenth*, p. 85).

v.iv

12 the Canonical Hour] the time at which marriages could legally be performed in parish churches.

19–20 I have spent twenty times as much in the Service] The hyperbolic statement not only suits Brazen's tendency to exaggerate; it also comments on the enormous costs that sometimes accrued to military officers who did not receive the pay they were due for their men and, in particular, for the costs of recruiting. Farquhar himself lost a considerable sum in his recruiting venture (Sutherland, p. 171), so much that Jordan believes the resultant poverty may have led to his relinquishing his commission (Jordan, p. 262).

21 a Privateer or a Play-house] The dialogue satirizes the new Queen's Theatre in the Haymarket, designed by John Vanbrugh. The theatre, while beautiful, had notoriously poor acoustics and was therefore considered 'ill built'. Because there were so many complaints about the management, it might also be considered 'ill mann'd'. It ran upon the shallows because financial difficulties became intense. There were complaints that the management was growing rich by clandestine sharing while not settling with all who were owed money. The three actors Betterton, Barry, and Bracegirdle, the senior sharers, apparently skimmed profits to the dismay of those in the company thus cheated (see Judith Milhous, *Thomas Betterton and the Management of Lincoln's Inn Fields 1695–1708* [Carbondale and London, 1979], pp. 151–70). Meanwhile, the shareholders at Drury Lane were complaining about Rich's financial manipulations and failure to pay his actors. He was accused of keeping double books in order to avoid paying dividends to the shareholders (Price, pp. 116–17, p. 275 n. 30).

46 *wear my Mask till after the Ceremony*] a common device in comedies with tricked marriages. Marriages behind masks occur, for example, in Dryden's *Sir Martin Mar-all* (1668), Shadwell's *The Humorists* (1671), and Congreve's *The Old Batchelour* (1693). According to canonical law, such marriages could be declared invalid, since an *Error Personae* dissolved the contract (John Ayliffe, *Parergon juris canonici Anglicani* (1726), pp. 362–3, quoted in Alleman, pp. 61–2).

48 her own hand] Robert L. Hough sees a logical inconsistency in the fact that Lucy has sent Brazen two letters in her own hand ('I've had two Letters from a Lady of Fortune that Loves me to Madness . . .', IV. iii. 348–50), but in V. iv she has used Melinda's signature, which she acquired at the fortune-teller's. He points out that there is no reason for her to switch signatures since she does not think her plot is suspected, and Brazen might now notice the difference in the two signatures. The use of Melinda's signature is, of course, necessary to the plot because it misleads Worthy. Hough believes that the inconsistency demonstrates that Farquhar wrote *The Recruiting Officer* hurriedly ('Farquhar: "The Recruiting Officer"', *N&Q*, NS 1 (1954), 474).

v.v.

93–4 no visible means of a livelihood] Farquhar is suggesting that chicanery occurred in the enforcement of the Impressment Acts. Constables profitted by ten shillings for each recruit so impressed (Scouller, p. 106).

143 read the Articles of War] A man recruited by justices through the Mutiny and Impressment Acts had the Articles of War read to him and then, on receipt of twenty shillings as levy money, was 'deemed a listed soldier' (Scouller, p. 106).

150 a Horse] The Wooden Horse, formed of planks at an acute angle vaguely to resemble the shape of the animal, was often used for military punishment; it was, for example, the normal punishment for drunkenness.

The prisoner was mounted on it, his hands tied, and his feet weighted with muskets, shot, or other weights (Scouller, p. 268).

152–3 Captain *Huffcap*] *NDCC* defines Captain Huff as 'any noted Bully, or Huffing Blade'.

v.vi

32 *Rose* Tavern] a favourite haunt, mentioned in several of Farquhar's plays. See Commentary, *The Constant Couple*, Epilogue, l. 4, vol. i, p. 610.

v.vii.

137 a pickled Dog] arch or waggish fellow (*NDCC*).

142–3 a Cruiser under false Colours, and a *French* Pickaroon] another instance of the nautical metaphor for women. Cruisers were 'nimble Friggats Coasting to and fro for Prizes' (*NDCC*). Picaroons were very small privateers and the term was also used for brigands. The term 'French' suggests the possibility that Brazen has not only been duped by a prostitute, but conceivably by one with syphilis.

175–7 *the Recruiting Trade . . . I gladly quit*] Farquhar himself had quit the recruiting trade shortly before writing the play. He had personal knowledge of the '*lasting Plague, Fatigue, and endless Pain*' and perhaps some regrets for serving his country in Shrewsbury and Lichfield rather than on '*the active Field, Where Glory full reward for Life does yield*'.

Epilogue

8 *Musick chiefly do's delight ye*] Increasingly the theatre companies strove for audiences via expensive musical entertainments. *Arsinoe* opened at Drury Lane on 16 January 1705 and became a great popular favourite. The new Queen's Theatre was inaugurated with a production of an Italian pastoral opera, *The Loves of Ergasto*, which did not prove a success. The companies also encouraged *entr'acte* musical entertainment. In the season of 1705–6, Drury Lane's roster included thirteen singers, two notable musicians aside from the band, and thirteen dancers; the Queen's Theatre had at least seven singers and fifteen dancers.

14–15 *Vigo, Schellenberg, and Blenheim*] all victories over the French. The storming of Schellenberg occurred on 2 July 1704.

21 *Bonancini's*] Giovanni Bononcini's opera *Camilla* is credited as 'the catalyst which triggered a permanent change in the position of music on the London stage'. It was the first full-length, heroic Italian opera in London; it was sung entirely in English, mostly by English performers (Price, p. 116). Its success was a subject for comment for years. *Camilla* opened at Drury Lane just nine days before *The Recruiting Officer* opened at the same theatre. Farquhar's attack on its soporific qualities is interesting in the light of the fact that it was offered at the same theatre.

28 the present Subscription] *Camilla* was regularly performed by subscription.

The Beaux Strategem

Advertisement

5–6 the friendly and indefatigable Care of Mr. *Wilks*] presumably a reference to Robert Wilks's friendship during Farquhar's terminal illness. Wilks is reputed to have encouraged Farquhar to write a play and then taken it to the theatre for performance. See Introduction, vol. ii, pp. 132–3.

Prologue

3 Plain-Dealer] William Wycherley, addressed under the name of his play; Wycherley also earned the nickname 'Manly' Wycherley after the titular character.

6 *Active Fields*] that is, the battlefields.

7 Union] The Act of Union between England and Scotland received royal assent on 6 March 1707, two days before the opening of *The Beaux Stratagem*.

19 *Simpling*] collecting simples, that is, herbs or plants used for medicinal purposes.

I

16 the *Lyon* and the *Rose*] Rooms in inns were named rather than numbered.

27 *Litchfield*] Jordan believes that Farquhar served on a recruiting mission in Lichfield some time after the beginning of August 1705 (Jordan, p. 261).

36 Number 1706] Presumably the ale is recently brewed (in 1706), not fourteen years old.

64 Tympanies] tympanites, or abdominal distention and discomfort due to gas.

67 Lady Bountiful] In *Pilgrim's Progress*, ii, Mercy says 'I had a sister named Bountiful that was married to one of these churls. But he and she could never agree because my sister was resolved to do so she had began, that is, to show kindness to the poor.'

69–77 [Lady Bountiful's cures] Books concerning home remedies were published for housewives, with recipes for cures for the kinds of ailments mentioned here. For example, Charles Carter's *The Compleat City and Country Cook: or, Accomplish'd Housewife* (London, 1732) listed the following recipe for the green sickness: 'Take of Aloes and Rhubarb four Ounces each, pound them and sift them fine; mix with them your Drams of prepared Steel, mix them with a little Claret Wine, make them up into twenty-seven Pills, take three of them every Morning for nine Days, drink a Glass of Claret after them, and use Exercise' (2nd edn. [London, 1736], p. 317). *Mr. Boyle's Receipts* gave the following recipe for fits of the mother: 'Dissolve store of *Sea-Salt* in the best *Wine-Vinegar*, and in this dip a soft Linnen Cloth, which being folded so as to make 3 or 4 Doubles, is to be applied somewhat warm to the

Soles of the Patient's Feet, and kept on till the fit be over' (3rd edn. [London, 1696], i. 24). The newspapers also carried advertisements of cures for many ailments; for example, the *Daily Courant* on 17 January 1704 advertised: 'Pills for the Green Sickness, which eradicate that Distemper tho' never so inveterate, opening the Obstructions, carrying off by their purging Quality all the vitious offending Humours, and by their altering Property renovates the Blood and Juices, and changes sickly pale Countenances into healthy florid Complexions; removes Sickness at Stomach, creates Appetite, and causes the Patient to be Active and Lively that Before was Dull and Slothful, not caring to stir about. To be had only of the Author (Practitioner in Physick and Surgery) at the Golden Head in *Bridgewater-Square* near *Aldersgate-street*, at 4s. per Box with Directions.' However, most people and certainly the poor still relied on home remedies such as those Lady Bountiful dispatched.

75 Chin-Cough] hooping cough.

88–9 he's a Man of a great Estate, and values no Body] This speech may be shaded by Farquhar's own experience. The traditional story, perhaps apocryphal, relates that Farquhar relinquished his commission with the understanding that a great man would help him get a captaincy but his supposed patron abandoned him, and he resided in poverty until illness overtook him. Daniel O'Bryan recounts the tale poignantly:

> Such was the unhappy Fate of this Gentleman, that upon his Application to the late Duke of *Ormond* for Preferment, he promised him a Captain's Post that was then vacant, and ordered him to dispose of his Lieutenancy. Mr. *Farquhar* not doubting the Duke's Sincerity, sold his Commission, and summoning his Creditors, paid off their Bills. By this honest Action he had left himself almost pennyless, and waiting daily on the late Duke to remind him of his Promise, his Grace told him one Morning, that the Commission had been given to another Gentleman at the Instigation of the Colonel; but added, that if he would attend him to *Ireland*, for he was then made Lord Lieutenant of that Kingdom, he would give him the first Company of Foot, or Troop of Horse or Dragoons that should become vacant. Mr. *Farquhar*, who was naturally of a tender Constitution, laid the Duke's Words so near his Heart, that they occasioned his Death soon after.

(*Authentic Memoirs; or, The Life and Character of That Most Celebrated Comedian Mr. Robert Wilks* [London, 1732], p. 23; rept. in Jordan, pp. 262–3.) Jordan believes through other evidence that Ormonde did promise Farquhar a commission in 1706 but did not follow through. In Mary de la Riviere Manley's *The Secret Memoirs and Manners of Several Persons of Quality* (1709), the following passage occurs:

> [Adario's] now favourite Mistress is a Woman of exalted Birth; he purchas'd her of her Mother, (and that was most abominable) by a considerable Sum to her self, and a Settlement of Two thousand Crowns a Year upon her Daughter; the reverent Matron did not blush to sell the Prince's Favour to all that would purchase; (a wretched Principle) she was not asham'd to take sixty Pieces of a poor

Poet, (all the Profit that his Brains had ever been able to present him) to make him only a *Subaltern* (p. 166).

132–3 no Scandal like Rags, nor any Crime so shameful as Poverty] Farquhar was again, no doubt, speaking from his own immediate experience. The accounts of his life tell that he was living in a garret, suffering not only his illness but his worries about his family, when Wilks, who had missed him at the theatre, found him and implored him to write his last comedy to relieve his debts. The dialogue in ll. 132–58 suggests the intensity of Farquhar's feelings about his present destitution.

142 *Marrabone*] Marylebone Gardens, an entertainment spot during the latter part of the seventeenth and most of the eighteenth century, boasted a notable bowling-green, its chief attraction, where persons of quality tried the sport. However, the road to it was beset by highwaymen at times and had to be protected. The gardens were situated in the fields behind the manor-house of Marylebone (Wheatley, ii. 511–13).

160–1 I am a Man of Quality, and you my Servant] The disguise of one friend as servant and the switching of roles is borrowed from Steele's *The Lying Lover*, in which Bookwit and Latine try the same scheme:

But *Jack*, you know we were talking in *Maudlin* Walks last Week of the necessity, in Intrigues, of a faithful, yet a prating Servant.—We agreed therefore to cast Lots who should be the other's Footman for the present Expedition (*Steele*, p. 119).

248–71 [discussion of the menu] The scene is highly reminiscent of a scene in Cibber's *She Wou'd and She Wou'd Not* (1702), as Richard Hindry Barker points out:

Flo. . . . What have you in the house now that will be ready presently.

Host. You may have what you please Sir.

Hyp. Can you get us a partridge?

Host. Sir, we have no partridges; but we'll get you what you please in a moment. We have a very good neck of mutton Sir; if you please it shall be clapped down in a moment.

Hyp. Have you no pigeons or chickens?

Host. Truly, Sir, we have no fowl in the house at present; if you please you may have any thing else in a moment.

Hyp. Then prithee get us some young rabbits.

Host. Upon my word, Sir, rabbits are so scarce they are not to be had for money.

Flo. Have you any fish?

Host. Fish Sir! I drest yesterday the finest dish that ever came upon a table; I am sorry we have none left Sir; but if you please you may have any thing else in a moment.

Trap. Pox on thee! hast thou nothing but any thing else in the house?

Host. Very good mutton Sir.

Hyp. Prithee get us a breast then.

Host. Breast! don't you love the neck Sir?

Hyp. Ha'ye nothing in the house but the neck?

Host. Really, Sir, we don't use to be so unprovided, but at present we have nothing else left.

Goldsmith created a similar scene in *She Stoops to Conquer* (1773):

Hastings. . . . But let's hear the bill of fare.

Marlow. (*Perusing*) What's here? For the first course; for the second course; for the desert. The devil, Sir, do you think we have brought down the whole Joiners Company, or the Corporation of Bedford, to eat up such a supper? Two or three little things, clean and comfortable, will do.

Hastings. But, let's hear it.

Marlow. (*Reading*) For the first course at the top, a pig, and pruin sauce.

Hastings. Damn your pig, I say.

Marlow. And damn your pruin sauce, say I.

Hardcastle. And yet, gentlemen, to men that are hungry, pig, with pruin sauce, is very good eating.

Marlow. At the bottom, a calve's tongue and brains.

Hastings. Let your brains be knock'd out, my good Sir; I don't like them.

Marlow. Or you may clap them on a plate by themselves. I do.

Hardcastle. (*Aside*) Their impudence confounds me. (to them) Gentlemen, you are my guests, make what alterations you please, Is there any thing else you wish to retrench or alter, gentlemen?

Marlow. Item. A pork pie, a boiled rabbet and sausages, a florentine, a shaking pudding, and a dish of tiff—taff—taffety cream!

Hastings. Confound your made dishes, I shall be as much at a loss in this house as at a green and yellow dinner at the French ambassador's table. I'm for plain eating.

Hardcastle. I'm sorry, gentlemen, that I have nothing you like, but if there be any thing you have a particular fancy to—

293 to be chosen Parliament-man] a jibe at candidates who buy votes.

354 *tight*] neatly.

377 St. *Martin*'s Parish] Farquhar's own parish. He was buried at St. Martin's in the Fields in May.

II.i

6 a Form of Law in *Doctors-Commons*] Doctors Common housed the ecclesiastical courts that could decide to dissolve a marriage. Annulments could be given on grounds of pre-contract to someone else, bigamy, consanguinity, impotence, or mutual consent in child marriage after the parties reached the age of consent (Alleman, pp. 125–6.)

13–14 a Case of Separation] Legal separation by mutual consent was a far simpler process than divorce. A couple could decide to live separately without any legal procedure; the property settlement might bring the matter into court, however. If the couple wished to reunite they could do so without legal process (Alleman, p. 107).

34 Diet-drinks] drinks with curative or restorative powers.

35 stilling Rosemary-Water] distilling the medicinal potion made from rosemary. A recipe was given in *The Family-Dictionary; Or, Household Companion*, by J. H. (London, 1695):

> Take the Flowers and Leaves of Rosemary when they are at their best, half a pound, of the Root of Elicampame four ounces, Red Sage

a handful, Cloves three ounces, and a like quantity of Mace, Aniseeds twelve ounces; beat the Spices separately, and the Herbs together; put to them four gallons of Whitewine: and having infused them for the space of seven Days, distil them.

This Water greatly comforteth the Heart, removeth Pains of the
. Stomach, creates a good colour, and gently purgeth the Blood by breathing Sweats.

40–1 Poets and Philosophers] Praise of the pastoral life was fashionable in poetry of the period. Pomfret's *The Choice*, for example, published in 1700, had gone into a third edition (labelled the fourth) by 1701.

47 weekly Bills] the weekly bills of mortality.

86 *Scrub*] The tag name indicates stunted-growth, as in a tree. The part was written with the physically small actor Henry Norris in mind. Strap in Smollett's *Roderick Random* arrives in London sporting a 'short crop-eared wig that very much resembled Scrub's in the play' (see Thomas R. Preston, 'The "Stage Passions" and Smollett's Characterization', *Studies in Philology*, 71 [1974], 105–25).

II.ii.

47 at the Coronation] Queen Anne's coronation had occurred five years earlier, on 23 April 1702; Archer is not a regular church-goer.

70–1 mourning Rings] Undertakers had made the funeral trade a profitable business. Mourners had to be dressed properly for the occasion. Mourning rings were given to friends of the deceased, sometimes bought by bequests in the will. The accounts of Pepys's funeral in 1703 show a total of forty-three mourning rings at 20s. each, sixty-six at 15s., and sixteen at 10s., a total of 125 rings at £100.10s. (see Ashton, pp. 441–4).

76 the Arms] the coat of arms.

80 elop'd from her Husband] ran away from her husband with a lover.

86 Cereuse] Ceruse was white lead paint used as a cosmetic to whiten the complexion.

86–7 a Lady's under Pocket] Ladies' pockets were flat, pear-shaped bags, usually with a central vertical slit as opening, joined by a tape that tied around the waist under the dress. The pockets were accessible through the plackets (Cunnington, *Eighteenth*, pp. 177–8).

95 Gentlemen o' the Pad] highwaymen.

100 smoak 'em] smell them out.

108–9 as dirty as old *Brentford* at *Christmas*] Brentford was notorious for the mud in its streets.

114 at the Bar] Archer's skill at evading questions convinces Gibbet that he had been hauled into court before.

128 a contrary way] he will go upwards, via the hangman's noose.

142 whip'd out Trooper] Soldiers could be whipped for offences, cashiered, or both.

239 *Don Quixote*] Farquhar's friend Motteux had published a four-volume English edition of *The History of the Renown'd Don Quixote* in 1700–3. D'Urfey's *Don Quixote*, with both parts made into one, continued to play on

stage occasionally; it had played at the Queen's Theatre as recently as August 1706.

248 *Pride saves . . . Woman too*] In v. ii. 78 Mrs Sullen calls for her 'Sex's Pride' to assist her in resisting Archer's temptation.

III.i

71–2 Tops to his Shoes, up to his mid Leg] Shoes with very high tongues were worn by military men, and as with other martial fashions were emulated by stylish beaux (Cunnington, *Eighteenth*, p. 79).

72–3 a silver headed Cane dangling at his Nuckles] See Commentary, *The Recruiting Officer*, IV. iii. 61–2, vol. ii, p. 554, for details of fashionable canes.

74–5 Perriwig ty'd up in a Bag] Bag wigs had the queue enclosed in a square black silk bag tied by a string which was hidden by a black bow at the nape of the neck (Cunnington, *Eighteenth*, p. 94).

III.ii

5 *Oroondates, Cesario, Amadis*] heroes from romances. The adventures of Oroondates are related in the romance *Cassandra*. See Commentary, *The Inconstant*, II. i. 10, vol. i, p. 629. Cesario, the son of Caesar and Cleopatra, appears in the romance *Cleopatra* by Gautier de Costes, Seigneur de la Calprenède. Sent to Hydaspes, Cesario fell in love with Candace. The romance was first translated into English in parts, beginning in 1652, under the title *Hymen's Praeludia, or Love's Masterpiece*. A complete edition in English appeared in 1687. For *Amadis de Gaul*, an early Spanish or Portuguese romance, see Commentary, *The Inconstant*, IV. iv. 57, vol. i, p. 634.

23 *brazen Engine hot*] the warming pan.

23 *Quoif clear starch'd*] The round-eared cap, slightly bonnet-shaped, curving round the face to the ears and frilled in front, was sometimes called a coif (Cunnington, *Eighteenth*, p. 156).

25 a Touch of Sublime *Milton*] Archer's Miltonics resemble those of John Philips's *The Splendid Shilling*, a parody first published in 1701. That Farquhar was, in fact, reading Milton, however, is clear from his discussion of divorce in Acts III and V.

34 Do my *Baisemains*] pay my respects.

36 *Toftida*] The very popular singer Katerine Tofts was singing with the Drury Lane company during the 1706–7 season.

85 in the Plantations] Gibbet has been transported for his crimes.

93–4 *Will's* Coffee-house] See Commentary, *Love and a Bottle*, II. i. 343, vol. i, 588.

95 *White's*] See Commentary, *The Twin-Rivals*, III. i. 161, vol. i, p. 642.

170–1 What King of *Spain* . . . I cannot tell you yet.] In 1706 negotiations were conducted concerning the partitioning of the Spanish monarchy between Prince Philip of Bourbon and Archduke Charles of Austria. The Allies were offered the choice of which part each should reign over, except that Philip was to have the province of Guipúzcoa and Charles the Spanish Netherlands. Max Emmanuel was to be restored to Bavaria, and he, followed by his son, was to govern the Netherlands as a vassal of Charles, who had been and still was a bitter foe. Marlborough, finding the negotiations very harmful to English military interests, disrupted the negotiations, refusing to sign the French counter-proposals (Churchill, v. 168–9). Therefore, Foigard's comment reflects the current state of affairs.

III.iii

54 Pressing Act] Able-bodied men without employment or a visible means of support could be conscripted into the army by the decision of three justices of the peace. See Commentary, *The Recruiting Officer*, II. iii. 18–19, vol. ii, p. 550.

64 dings] dashes, bounces, or flings herself about.

184–5 I had a Lieutenancy offer'd me . . . but that is not Bread] These lines seem to emerge from Farquhar's military experience. His lieutenancy as a recruiting officer had proved costly, to the disadvantage of his family (Sutherland, p. 171).

275 upon the Tapis] upon the table-cloth; that is, under discussion.

284–8 I was ever so . . . a dead Body] One of many verbal echoes from Milton's *Doctrine and Discipline of Divorce*:

> Nay, instead of being one flesh, they will be rather two carcasses chained unnaturally together; or, as it may happen, a living soul bound to a dead corpse.

320 a Ransom may redeem me] For prisoners not exchanged with the French, ransoms could purchase freedom. The ransom was approximately one month's pay, although the British preferred a higher sum (Scouller, p. 312).

408 Dorinda *the Opera Tune*] The lyrics of 'Fair Dorinda', a song from *Camilla*, I. ix, was written by Owen Swiny:

> *Fair* Dorinda, *happy, happy,*
> *Happy may'st thou ever be:*
> *The Stars that smile on happy Days.*
> *May they all now smile on thee.*

420–30 shou'd I lie groaning . . . upon Antipathies.] As Larson demonstrates, 'Here are echoes of Milton in every word'. Milton deplores the suffering that results from ill-matched couples, particularly those with mental incompatibility. Like Mrs Sullen he deplores legal interference in such matters; God, he says, did not 'authorize a judicial court to toss about and divulge the unaccountable and secret reason of disaffection between man and wife, as a thing most improperly answerable to any such kind of trial' (Milton's *Doctrine and Discipline of Divorce*; see Larson, pp. 177–8).

431–6 They never pretended . . . first Lawgiver.] Verbal as well as ideological echoes from Milton occur in this passage:

> Natural hatred, whenever it arises, is a greater evil in marriage than the accident of adultery, a greater defrauding, a greater injustice. . . . They would be juster in their balancing between natural hatred and *casual adultery*. this being but a *transient injury*, and soon amended . . . but that other being an unspeakable and unremitting sorrow and offence. . . . To forbid dislike against the guiltless instinct of nature is not within the province of any law to reach. (See Larson, p. 178.)

432 Uncleanness] infidelity.

436–8 when she ... keep 'um fast.] Again Farquhar verbally echoes Milton:

> To couple hatred, therefore, though wedlock try all her golden links, and borrow to her aid all the iron manacles and fetters of the law, it does but seek to twist a rope of sand.

IV.i

4 where Women rule] Farquhar's reference to England as a country 'whose Women are it's Glory' is part of an elaborate compliment to Queen Anne. Although or perhaps because the Queen did not favour theatrical endeavours, many compliments were paid her on stage, particularly in prologues and epilogues of the period.

27 the Graips] The gripes or griping of the guts was a common ailment. Recipes were offered in housewives' manuals, for example, *The Compleat City and Country Cook*:

For the Gripes.

> Warm a Glass of Canary, dissolve in it as much *Venice* Treacle or Diascordium as an Hazel Nut; drink it off going to bed, and keep warm.

An approved Remedy for the Griping of the Guts.

> Make a Toast of Bread (that is not too fine or white) put it very hot into a quartern of Brandy, and when it is thoroughly soaked, take it out immediately and eat it hot. This may be repeated two or three times a Day, if need require.

70 Asse's Milk] often prescribed as a restorative for persons in ill health; Pope, for example, underwent a course of ass's milk. Ashton (p. 148) reports that it sold for 3*s*. 6*d*. a quart.

121.1–138 [Aimwell's 'fit'] Steele used the same trick in *The Conscious Lovers*, in which Myrtle, dressed as old Sir Geoffrey Cimberton, fakes a fit, and uses the pretence to squeeze Lucinda and pull Cimberton's ear (v. i. 76–93, in *Steele*, p. 368).

231 *Cedunt Arma togæ*] Cicero, *De Officiis*, i. 77. Actually 'Cedant arms togæ', 'Let the sword give way to the gown'.

253 *Logicè*] in logic.

257 *Gra*] dear; an Irish term of endearment.

285 *Le Brun*] Charles Le Brun (1619–90) was 'first painter' to Louis XIV of France. He created a series of paintings on the life of Alexander the Great, including The Passage of the Granicus, The Battle of Arbela, Alexander and Porus, and The Entry of Alexander into Babylon. Three of the paintings measured more than forty feet in length.

285–6 greater Battles, and a greater General] an elaborate compliment to Marlborough, whose victories at Blenheim and Ramillies outshine the triumphs of Alexander the Great, according to Archer's speech.

291 poor *Ovid* in his Exile] He acknowledged two reasons for his exile, his *Ars Amatoria*, considered subversive, and an unspecified indiscretion or error. One frequent explanation of the latter is that he was an accomplice in

some way in sexual misconduct involving Augustus' granddaughter Julia the younger, who was banished at the same time.

320 *Salmoneus*] Impiously arrogant, Salmoneus, the son of Aeolus, competed with Zeus for glory. To prove his greatness he drove his chariot through the city, dragging hides and bronze kettles to imitate thunder and throwing torches skyward for lightning. Zeus destroyed with a bolt of lighting Salmoneus and the entire city he had founded and named after himself.

390–1 beg that Fellow at the Gallows-foot] According to an ancient custom the life of a criminal might be spared if a woman begging for his release promised to marry him.

413–29 What did your Fellow . . . Arrow in his Quiver] The dialogue is studded with *double entendres*.

iv.ii

11 *Tom's*] Tom's Coffee-house at no. 17 Russell Street in Covent Garden, on the north side by Button's, was named after Captain Thomas West. John Macky's *A Journey Through England* (1714) relates:

> After the Play the best company generally go to Tom's and Will's Coffee Houses near adjoining, where there is playing at Picket, and the best of conversation till midnight. Here you will see blue and green ribbons and Stars sitting familiarly, and talking with the same freedom as if they had left their quality and degrees of distance at home (quoted in Wheatley, iii. 384).

14 Drabs] sluts.

18 *Morris*] presumably the owner of Morris's Coffee-house, listed by Ashton (p. 450) for Essex Street, the Strand. Wheatley does not mention it.

19 *Bohee*] a fine black tea, associated with the luxury of the idle rich.

23 sneak into the side-Box] Beaux sneaked from one side-box to another, evading the box-keeper and thus not paying for their tickets. Archer suggests 'stealing' an act at one house without paying, then going to the other house to catch an act of some other play without paying. See Commentary, *The Constant Couple*, Epilogue, l. 23, vol. i, p. 610.

55–6 Death by our Law] Desertion and mutiny were offences punishable by the death penalty.

60 Bogtrotter] 'Scotch or North Country Mols-troopers or High-way Men formerly, and now Irish Men' (*NDCC*). Here the term implies an Irish ne'er-do-well.

124 Plate] silver.

135 half seas over] almost drunk.

154 *Tyburn*] the site of public executions.

156 the Household] the royal household.

v.i

58–64 are not Man and Wife . . . the Body] The passage echoes Milton's conviction that 'There is no true marriage between them who agree not in true consent of mind' and 'The solace and satisfaction of the mind is regarded and provided for before the sensitive pleasing of the body'. See Larson, p. 176.

87 *All-fours*] a two-handed card game involving sets of the highest card, lowest card, Jack, and 'Game'. See *The Compleat Gamester*, in Hartman, pp. 111–13, for very complicated details. All-fours is said to have been invented at Kent; like whist, it was a rural or servants' pastime rather than a city pleasure such as piquet or basset.

v.ii

32 *Alcmena*] Zeus tricked Alcmene, the wife of Amphitryon, into lying with him. Their union resulted in the birth of Heracles, a twin to Amphytrion's son Iphicles.

54 *Ingineer*] Army engineers were responsible for undermining enemy fortresses.

159 *a Chaplain*] the prison chaplain.

168 *to save my Life at the Sessions*] He will save his life by bribery, presumably of the justices.

v.iii

38 *Alexander*] Nathaniel Lee's *The Rival Queens* (1677) still ran regularly; it played several times at the Queen's Theatre during the season that *The Beaux Stratagem* opened. Alexander's oratory was, therefore, known from the stage presentation. In *The Constant Couple*, v. i, Wildair uses lines from *The Rival Queens*.

92 *the Edistone*] The Eddystone lighthouse off the Cornwall coast was destroyed on 27 November 1703 by a violent storm.

v.iv

5 *The Sweets of Hybla*] the finest honey.

194 *consent*] Milton's theory was that mutual consent should be all that was required for divorce. The scene of mutual consent between the Sullens (ll. 211–54) and Archer's tag-lines at the end of the scene all exemplify Milton's beliefs.

202 *Charles*] Archer calls Aimwell 'Tom', not 'Charles', in II. ii.

244–5 *Is there on Earth . . . To part.*] These lines are reminiscent of Motteux's *The Loves of Mars and Venus*.

275 *Escritore*] An escritoire was a writing desk.

296 *Consent is Law enough to set you free.*] Milton says 'There can be nothing in the equity of law, why divorce by consent may not be lawful' (quoted in Larson, p. 176).

Epilogue

0.4 *Mr. Smith*] Edmund Smith, author of *Phaedra and Hippolitus*, which opened at the Queen's Theatre on 21 April 1707.

2 *its expiring Author*] Either the prologue was written after the opening performance, a strong likelihood since it is labelled 'Design'd to be spoke'

rather than 'Spoke', or Farquhar's imminent death was apparent even at the beginning of the run. If Wilks, who spoke many of Farquhar's prologues, gave this one, the pathos is intensified, for Wilks, a true friend, was attempting to help his impoverished, dying friend with money and production of the new comedy.

9 Leuctra] At the Battle of Leuctra the Theban patriot Epaminondas devised a new arrangement of the phalanx that allowed Thebes to triumph over Sparta. Epaminondas again fought the Spartans at Mantinea, nine years later, and he was killed there, not at Leuctra. One would expect Smith, educated at Oxford and author of *Phaedra and Hippolitus*, to have the facts straight.

14 *Serjeant* Kite] *The Recruiting Officer* played immediately before and during the first run of *The Beaux Stratagem*, with simultaneous performances at both houses on 17 April.

15 *Sons of* Will*'s*] coffee-house critics and literary men, who frequented Will's.

The Adventures of Covent-Garden

Title-page

Scarron's City Romance] In 1671 Furetière's *Le Roman bourgeois* was .ranslated under the title *Scarron's City Romance, Made English* and published by Henry Herringman.

Et quorum pars Magna fui] Virgil, *Aeneid*, ii. 5–6, 'and in which I was myself greatly involved'. The lines in sequence read:

> Quaeque ipse miserrima vidi
> Et quorum pars magna fui.

This is one of several indications that either the material was autobiographical or at least the anonymous author wished it to appear so.

Dedication

1 all my Ingenious Acquaintance at *Will's Coffee-House*] Farquhar's lack of words for his acquaintance at Will's, the coffee-house of the literary wits, is not surprising. He was not accepted as a notably playwright even after his success with *The Constant Couple*; critics condemned him as an upstart Irishman. William Walker, in the Preface to *Marry, or Do Worse* (1704) describes the ambience:

> ... I am sensible, by Experience, that there's a great deal of Artifice and Accomplishment requir'd in a Gentleman, that will Write for the *Theatre*;—And 'tis a mighty Presumption in any one, to Attempt it, who has not Ingratiated himself among the *Quality*, or been Conversant at *Wills*; for, 'tis to be presum'd, there is a kind of Unity among the *Great Ones*, to preserve the Commerce of the *Stage* to themselves, as our *Companies* do their *Trade* to *Guinea*, and the *Indies*;

and that they treat any *Upstart*, who Barters his Wit there, like an *Interloper*.

To the Reader

6–7 the greatest Critick of our Age] Perhaps a reference to Dryden, who was the reigning wit at Will's Coffee-House. Dryden had dedicated *Annus Mirabilis* to the metropolis of London, yet Sir Robert Howard rewarded him for the poem.

18–19 *Collierist* nor *Poet*] Farquhar's first play *Love and a Bottle* clearly ignored Collier's strictures on the theatre; like other playwrights, he was later to be affected by the new morality represented by Collier's *Short View*. He did not publish any pamphlets against Collier as did other poets, including Vanbrugh and Congreve. However, like many other theatrical writers, he made references to the stage reform movement within the context of prologues, prefaces, and other materials printed with the plays. In *A Discourse Upon Comedy* he became more outspoken.

19 *Æsop of Tunbridge*, nor *Æsop of Bath*] In 1698 a series of Æsop poems were published, including *Æsop at Tunbridge*, *Æsop at Bath*, *Æsop of Epsom*, *Æsop Return'd from Tun-bridge*, and several others. *Æsop at Tunbridge* argues the Tory stance, favouring peace with France and reducing the size of the Army; *Æsop at Bath* favoured continuation of the war. Farquhar is claiming to be neither Whig nor Tory on the war issue.

19–20 the *Dragon of Bow*, nor the *Grashopper at the Exchange*] *A Dialogue between Bow-Steeple Dragon, and the Exchange Grashopper*, published in 1698, contained an argument between the Dragon, representing the Church of England, and the Grasshopper, representing the Catholics. The Dragon of Bow is an ornament on the spire of Bow Church, or St Mary Le Bow, the church that houses Bow bells. Although it appears small, it is, according to Wheatley, 8 feet 10 inches tall. The reconstruction of the church after the Great Fire is one of Wren's great works, completed in 1677 (Wheatley, ii. 497–9). Although the church was again destroyed in World War II, the spire and dragon still stand, and the church has again been restored. The Grasshopper, which surmounted the clock tower at the east entrance to the Royal Exchange, was the emblem of Sir Thomas Gresham, who had initiated the building of the Exchange.

25 Unity of Time] In both the *Adventures* and *A Discourse Upon Comedy*, Farquhar gave irreverent arguments against the classicists' insistence upon the three unities.

29–30 perhaps I was very Young when I writ it, or Recovering from a fit of Sickness] Farquhar was indeed very young when he wrote the *Adventures*, for he was no more than twenty-two when it was published. It is probable that he had suffered an illness, for Roebuck in *Love and a Bottle*, in a seemingly autobiographical passage, also refers to a month's 'violent Fit of Sickness' at Coventry. The autobiographical hints in this passage suggest that Farquhar was indeed author.

30–1 great Climacterick] the age of sixty-three.

31–2 my first Essay] If Farquhar again speaks autobiographical truth, he wrote the *Adventures* before composing *Love and a Bottle*.

38 fight Dog, fight Bear] a reference to the sport of bear baiting. 'Their Combates between Bulls and Dogs, Bears and Dogs, and sometimes Bulls and Bears, are not Battels to Death, as those of Cocks: Any Thing that looks like Fighting, is delicious to an *Englishman*' (Misson, p. 304).

52–3 the Act against *Immorality and Profaneness*] On 24 February 1698 the King issued a proclamation declaring 'our resolution to discountenance and punish all manner of vice, immortality and profaneness in all persons, from the highest to the lowest . . .'. The proclamation commanded that judges, mayors, sheriffs, and justices of the peace be vigilant in prosecuting and punishing offenders and that they read the proclamation repeatedly in open court, that ministers read it at least four times a year, that military officers make their men cognizant, and that the publication of pernicious books be avoided (*State Papers Domestic*, [S.P. 45. 13. No. 161]).

54–5 whether the New Lord M—r is *Dragon, Grashopper*, or what other Animal] Sir Francis Child (1642–1713), a banker, was elected Lord Mayor for 1699 on 29 September 1698, and his inauguration occurred on 29 October. Child was a Tory and a Church of England man, who served as an MP for Devizes in 1698. His inauguration was costly and elaborate; Elkanah Settle prepared a pageant, paid for by the Company of Goldsmiths, which was published in folio as 'Glory's Resurrection, being the triumphs of London revived, for the Inauguration of the Right Honourable Sir Francis Child, Kt., Lord Mayor of the City of London'. Members of the Privy Council, judges, and 'Persons of Quality' attended. Farquhar, newly in London, may well have witnessed this grand occasion. For details of the event see the *London Gazette*, 27–31 October 1698.

66–7 a *Rowland for her Oliver*] equivalent (*A Classical Dictionary of the Vulgar Tongue by Captain Francis Grose*, ed. Eric Partridge, 3rd edn. [London, 1963], p. 291). Rowland and Oliver were two famous paladins from the Charlemagne cycle of legends, who in achievements were equal only to each other, as they demonstrated in a perfectly matched single combat.

The Adventures of Covent-Garden

1–2 A Young Gentleman somewhat addicted to Poetry and the Diversions of the Stage] This description, along with the reference to 'another Kingdom' (i.e. Ireland) in l. 7, suggests either autobiographical elements in the *Adventures* or an attempt to make the novella appear autobiographical. Since its authorship remained a well-kept secret for 140 years, one suspects the former.

15 Peregrine] Stonehill (i. p. xiv) and Rothstein (p. 18) both speculate on whether Farquhar intended any connection between either Peregrine or Lord C— in the *Adventures* and Peregrine Osborne, second Marquess of Carmarthen, to whom he dedicated *Love and a Bottle*, published two weeks later. Since the *Adventures* was published anonymously, he could have done so without great risk of arousing ire. However, it is difficult to understand why he should have chosen to do so except perhaps that he was, after all, not yet twenty, and high spirits might have encouraged him. The use of the names does seem oddly coincidental.

30 *Bow-Street*] The street was often mentioned in plays of the period. Wycherley lived in Bow Street, as did William Longueville (see Preface, *The Twin Rivals*) and later Robert Wilks. Will's Coffeehouse was at the corner of Bow-Street and Russell Street.

69 his Club at the *Rose*] his drinking partners. A minor irony exists in the use of the term, since the term would more properly be used for the club of wits at Will's than the actors and other theatrical personnel who frequented the Rose and with whom Farquhar himself 'clubbed'.

71 Bumpers] full glasses (*NDCC*).

74 Scarlet] red coat.

95 a Lac'd Coat and Feathers] A laced coat, that is, one trimmed with metallic lace or braid, and feathers worn on the hat were marks of a fashionable man, appropriate clothing for an attractively dressed military officer.

125–6 to Raffle] to play a game of chance in which three dice were thrown; the player who threw three alike won, or if no one threw three, the one with the highest pair became winner.

128 the *Cloysters*] Prostitutes and gamblers stalked their prey in the Cloisters of St Bartholomew. The *Observator* complained (21 August 1703): 'Does this market of lewdness tend to any thing else but ruin the bodies, souls, and estates, of the young men and women . . . in the Cloisters (those conscious scenes of polluted amours) in the evening, they strike the bargain to finish their ruin . . .' Raffling was one of the amusements of the Cloisters (James Peller Malcolm, *Anecdotes of the Manners and Customs of London during the Eighteenth Century* [London, 1808], pp. 313–14). Luttrell noted that on 10 October 1705 the grand jury 'found bills of indictment against all those persons who kept rafling shops in the cloysters during Bartholomew fair' (v. 600).

182 *Montague* House] The town house of Ralph Montagu (1638–1709), Earl of Montagu in 1698, made Duke in 1705. In 1753 the house was purchased by the government to become the British Museum. The fields behind Montague House were the most frequent scene of duels for many years.

206 convicted] convinced; brought to the conviction.

248 only a Porter] The incident of the Captain escaping dressed as a porter was reused in *The Constant Couple*, III. iii, in which Clincher Senior and Tom Errand change clothes after Standard has spotted Clincher on Lurewell's balcony.

356 liquor'd his Buff] literally, dressed, i.e. lubricated, his buff leather coat; figuratively, beat him.

359 off the Laughing pin] 'Upon a merry pin' meant 'in a pleasant Mood' (*NDCC*). The Captain was out of humour.

382–3 Justice *M*— in *Drury-lane*] Probably William Mathew or Mathews, whose name appears in a commission dated 30 August 1699 (PRO, C231/8, p. 413). The document is not a complete commission of the peace for Westminster, so conceivably other justices with the initial M were also commissioned. Justices were recommissioned annually. (I am indebted to

Professor James Cockburn of the Department of History, University of Maryland, for this information.)

394 Mr. *W*— Mr. *H*— Mr. *M*—] Possibilities are numerous, and identification cannot be certain. Farquhar's reference to these gentlemen 'with others of that Club' suggest wits from Will's. Mr. W— was probably William Walsh (1663–1708), a friend of Dryden and later Pope. Mr. H— may be Bevil Higgons (1670–1735), who had contributed to Dryden's *Examen Poeticum* in 1693 or conceivably Anthony Henley (d. 1711), 'the poetical squire', who later collaborated with Richard Steele, Arthur Maynwaring, and John Oldmixon in the *Medley*. Mr. M— could be Maynwaring (1688–1712) or Francis Manning, author of panegyric poems and plays, to one of which Farquhar contributed a prologue. All these writers have been linked with Dryden and most with the attack on Blackmore but not with pamphlets concerning the Collier controversy. From the measured response in the conversation described in this scene, it is clear these men were not participants in the fray.

397 the Battel between the Church and the Stage] Jeremy Collier's *A Short View of the Morality and Profaneness of the English Stage* was published on 21 April 1698. From April to December there were at least twenty publications dealing with the controversy, including seven which attack the stage, twelve which attack Collier and defend the stage, and one by Dryden which falls on neither side (Sister Rose Anthony, *The Jeremy Collier Stage Controversy 1698–1726* [New York, 1966], p. 293). The controversy was, of course, mentioned in many theatrical pieces, including the Epilogue to *Love and a Bottle*. Farquhar's disputants reflect Dryden's views expressed in his poetical epistle to Motteux published with *Beauty in Distress*, condemning Collier for being too harsh and unforgiving, admitting that the theatre has been too loose and that his own plays can stand correction, and at the same time condemning the lack of wit in the controversy.

408 Captain *Va*—] Playwright and military officer John Vanbrugh (1664–1726) was one of those found guilty by Collier. On 8 June 1698 he published. *A Short Vindication of the Relapse and the Provok'd Wife, from Immorality and Prophaneness (Flying Post*, 6 June 1698, cited in Anthony, p. 97).

410 Mr. *C*—'s] William Congreve's (1670–1729) *Amendments of Mr. Collier's False and Imperfect Citations, etc. From the Old Batchelour, Double Dealer, Love for Love, Mourning Bride. By the Author of those Plays* appeared on 12 July 1698 (*Post Boy*, 12 July, cited in Anthony, p. 108). Congreve's 119-page response reveals his anger and indignation over the attacks on him.

411 Mr. *S*—*le*] Ten anonymous replies to Collier had been published before the *Adventures*; Mr. *S*—*le* presumably wrote one of them. His identity remains a mystery. Presumably he is not Settle, who is contrasted with Mr. S—le later in the sentence. Richard Steele (1672–1729) would have been known as Captain Steele after attaining his commission in 1697 (Calhoun Winton, *Captain Steele, The Early Career of Richard Steele* [Baltimore, 1964], p. 46). He was in London by 1698, but had not begun publishing any literary works. A reference to Thomas Shadwell (1642?–92) is possible, since he was viewed as lacking Vanbrugh's wit as much as Settle's gravity, but the spelling seems unlikely.

412 Mr. *Settle*'s gravity] Elkanah Settle (1648–1724), a rival of Dryden, was noted for his tragedies and heroic plays.

413 the two Answers to Mr. *C*—] Presumably the pamphlets written by Vanbrugh and Congreve. John Dennis also entered the fray, with *The Usefulness of the Stage, to the Happiness of Mankind, To Government, and to Religion* published 6 June 1698 (*Post-Man*, 6 June 1698, cited in Anthony, p. 92). He had not been abused in Collier's work as Vanbrugh and Congreve had.

417 Mr. *Dryden*, or Mr. *Wicherly*] Although Dryden and Wycherley were both among Collier's victims, neither had published a counterattack.

419–20 the last Peace] The cripple in Act I of *Love and a Bottle* also refers to the disbanding of the army after the Peace of Ryswick in 1697. See Commentary, *Love and a Bottle*, i. i 29–30, vol. i, p. 582.

425–6 *Indian Emperour*] Dryden's *The Indian Emperour; or, The Conquest of Mexico by the Spaniards*, first acted in 1665, remained a repertory staple. *The London Stage*, very sketchy for this period, lists no performances in 1698–9.

430–1 *exactness of Plot, unity of time, place, and I know not what*] Selinda's views of the unities, the purpose of plays, and other critical matters prefigure Farquhar's critical stance in *A Discourse upon Comedy*, published in *Love and Business* in 1702.

455 Double Dealer] When Congreve's *The Double Dealer* opened in fall 1693, it was successful; Dryden noted on 12 December 1693 that it had been performed eight times (*London Stage*, Part I, 428). It played on 4 March 1699 and perhaps earlier that season, before the *Adventures* was published. When the play was revived in 1699, Dryden commented that it 'was never very takeing'. He also mentioned that the playbills announced it would be acted with 'Several Expressions omitted'—presumably immoral and prophane ones (*London Stage*, i. 509).

455 Plot and no Plot] John Dennis's *A Plot and No Plot* opened in spring 1697 at Drury Lane; the only known performance was 8 May. Noted in *A Comparison Between the Two Stages* for its regularity ('a very regular Farce', p. 18), it was apparently not very successful on stage. Dennis said in his preface that the audience was not as numerous as it might have been had the heat not been so oppressive but that he 'never saw the Company there in better humour'. The play was never revived.

458 Beauty in Distress] Peter Motteux's tragedy was first performed probably in April 1698, and was, according to the author of the *Comparison*, damned. It lasted only during the first run, never being revived.

459 *Scene-Drawers*] The men who pushed the moveable scenery on and off the stage.

460–1 *a commendatory Copy from Mr.* Dryden] Dryden's poetical epistle 'To my Friend, the Author', published with the play, praised Motteux's classical regularity. See Cunningham, pp. 135–6.

468 Guyomar] According to tradition, Farquhar gave up his acting career at Smock Alley after he almost killed a man on stage because he forgot before the performance to change his sword for a foil. Farquhar was playing the role of Guyomar in *The Indian Emperour*, and the accident occurred at the point in Act V at which Guyomar kills Vasquez (T. Cibber, iii. 127). Farquhar must have been quoting these lines from memory, for he slightly misquotes.

469–70 *That Love . . . longer stay.*] *The Indian Emperour*, i. ii. 165–6. Odmar ends his speech (l. 164):
> That Love tooke deepest roote, which first did growe.

Then Guyomar (the character Farquhar acted) answers:
> That Love which first was set will first decay,
> Myne of a fresher date will longer Stay.

(Quoted from *John Dryden, Four Tragedies*, ed. L. A. Beaurline and Fredson Bowers, [Chicago and London, 1967], p. 44).

531–84 [poem] This poem was revised and six lines added for publication as 'The Lovers Night' in *Love and Business*. For the revisions, see *Love and Business*, Appendix A, vol. ii, p. 387.

574–5 *He thought . . . folded fast,*] In *Love and a Bottle*, Roebuck uses almost identical phrasing to describe his wedding night:
> When her soft, melting white, and yielding Waste,
> Within my pressing Arms was folded fast, (v. iii. 25–6).

596–9 *From Wit . . . Libera nos,*] Peregrine parodies the Litany. His 'prayer' is based on Cranmer's version (1544) which 'combined a number of petitions together under one response' (Francis Procter, rev. Walter H. Frere, *A New History of The Book of Common Prayer* [London, 1961], pp. 415–16). The Latin '*Libera nos*', of course, comes from the Roman Catholic litany.

Love and Business

Dedication

0.2 *Edmond Chaloner*] Once again Farquhar chose as dedicatee a good friend of no very great political or financial note. In 1699 Chaloner was a commissioner of appeal of the Treasury (listed in *An Account of the Principal Officers Civil and Military of England in the Year 1699*). Whether Chaloner was able to reward Farquhar for this dedication immediately or not, he proved a devoted friend after Farquhar's death. By his own account, for several years he prevented Margaret Farquhar's being sent to debtor's prison, 'to ye costs of severall hundred of pounds' (letter to Harley, British Library, Loan 29/129). When his own fortunes declined, he continued to write to Harley for help for the distressed family (British Library, Loan 29/34, 129). Margaret, in an undated letter to Harley, described Chaloner as a man 'who has been a father to me and mine for some years past' (British Library, Loan 29/135). After Margaret's death, Chaloner continued to care for her children. Discovering that 'so soon as her breath was out of her body, her house was seizd on, all her goods, her poor children put out', he brought the four children to London and again petitioned Harley in their behalf (British Museum, Loan 29/129). The *Calendar of Treasury Books* shows he had some success, with payments of £20 through him for her children on 23 December 1713, 12 August 1715, 18 May 1716, and 25 August 1718. Chaloner died in October 1730.

7–8 *a Piece of another Nature*] Apparently Farquhar offered to dedicate

The Adventures of Covent Garden or one of the early plays to Chaloner but was rejected.

34–5 Sir *Thomas Chaloner*] Considered a distinguished warrior, Sir Thomas Chaloner the Elder (1521–1565) accompanied Somerset to Scotland in 1547 and fought at the battle of Musselburgh. Elizabeth's government sent him to Brussels to arrange with Philip II for a peaceful treaty with England. He later became ambassador to Spain. Sir Thomas was a learned man, who published four books during his lifetime, including a translation of Erasmus' *The Praise of Folly*.

43 *Cecil*] William Cecil, first Baron Burleigh (1520–98), Elizabeth's chief advisor, was a friend of Sir Thomas who helped his son, Sir Thomas the Younger, get an education after his father died. Sir Thomas published as his fourth work *De Republica Anglorum Instauranda decem libri*, with a Latin panegyric on Henry VIII as well as Latin epigrams and epitaphs on notable persons. Burleigh and his friends prefixed Latin verses in praise of Chaloner to the work.

45–6 *Pietas . . . fuere.*] Piety, prudence, virtue, which are divided in others, were united in Chaloner.

61–2 *Pietas . . .* supersunt.] Farquhar changed the verb to *supersunt* to indicate that the qualities of the ancestor survive in the living Chaloner.

64 Mr. *Malim*] *De Republica Anglorum Instauranda decem libri* was published by William Malim, master of St Paul's School. The passage may be translated, 'For however learned and widely read Chaloner was, he seems to me none the less to have sought the utility of true, rather than the ostentation of varied erudition.'

On the Death of General Schomberg *kill'd at the* Boyn.

1–106 [poem] Crum lists a manuscript of the Pindaric ode in the Rawlinson poetical manuscripts, vol. 172, fol. 131. The work is attributed to Farquhar (*First-Line Index of English Poetry, 1500–1800 in Manuscripts of the Bodleian Library, Oxford.* [2 vols., Oxford and New York, 1969], ii, 1034 W432).

0.1 *General* Schomberg] Friedrich Hermann Schomberg, first Duke of Schomberg (1615–90), was a German soldier of fortune who fought in the service of Portugal and France before joining William III and assisting him in the Glorious Revolution, for which he was created duke. Well past seventy, Schomberg commanded the English forces, apparently rather ineffectively, in Ireland at the battle of the Boyne in 1690; he was fatally wounded during the fighting. Sutherland claims that Farquhar was a volunteer under Colonel Hans Hamilton at the battle of the Boyne; he would have been twelve or thirteen. If this were true, Farquhar would have witnessed, at a very tender age, the scenes described in this poem ('New Light on George Farquhar,' p. 171).

15 Stopping the Torrent of his Foes] According to Baxter, a group of perhaps thirty Jacobites tried to cross the river, and the few who made it managed to kill Schomberg before they were killed (p. 265). The *London Gazette* of 7–10 July 1960 described his death thus:

. . . the greatest loss we have had is that of the Duke of *Schomberg*, who being pressed upon by a Party of the Enemies Guard du Corps, (not having then about him above 30 or 40 Horse) was by one of them shot in the Neck, with which Wound, having likewise received 3 Cuts over the Head, he fell from his Horse. Captain *Foubert*, who was next to him, and had likewise received a wound in the Arm, got from his Horse to help the Duke, but he dyed immediately without speaking a word.

41 *Marius*'s Vultures] Gaius Marius (*c.* 157 BC–86 BC) was a Roman general who fought heroically against Jugurtha and the Germans. A rival of Sulla, he seized Rome and ruthlessly murdered his opponents. Rome was plunged into civil war from which Sulla emerged victorious. Julius Caesar, Marius' wife's nephew, was greatly influenced by him.

Thomas Otway wrote a play called *The History and Fall of Caius Marius*, which opened at Dorset Garden in the fall of 1679 and became a repertory staple. It played, for example, on 11 November 1699 and again on 4 December 1701 at Drury Lane. In Act IV Scene ii, Marius speaks to Martha, the Syrian prophetess that had brought him good fortune until she was banished from Rome:

> I know thee now most well. When thou wert gone,
> All my good Fortune left me. My lov'd Vultures,
> That us'd to hover o're my happy Head,
> And promise Honour in the day of Battel,
> Have since been seen no more. Ev'n Birds of prey
> Forsake unhappy *Marius*:

(Quoted from the 1680 edition.)

49 *Alcides*] Hercules.

Written on Orinda's *Poem's*

1–15 [poem] Margaret Crum identifies a manuscript copy of the poem in the Rawlinson Poetical Manuscripts, vol. 172, fol. 132. The manuscript version reads 'vigorous' rather than 'rigorous' in l. 5. (Crum, i. 560, M262).

0.1 Orinda's *Poem's*] The *Poems* of Katherine Philips (1632–64), 'the matchless Orinda', were published posthumously in 1664 and reprinted in 1667, 1669, 1678, and 1710.

1 *Damon*] Damon is a pseudonym used by Farquhar in his correspondence with Astræa (Susannah Carroll) in *Letters of Wit, Politicks and Morality*, published the year before *Love and Business* appeared.

To the Ingenious Lady

1–33 [poem] A manuscript version of the poem appears in the Rawlinson Manuscripts, vol. 172, fol. 132ᵛ, with only a few minor substantive variants ('implor'd' for 'implore' in l. 4; 'was' for 'is' in l. 11; 'lovers' for 'love to' in l. 25; 'results' for 'effects' in l. 26). The poem is attributed to Farquhar (Crum, i, 514, L 265).

0.1–2 *Author of the* Fatal Friendship] Catharine Trotter, later Cockburn (1679–1747), was the author of five plays which opened between 1695 and 1706. Although all her other plays opened at Drury Lane, *The Fatal Friendship* opened at Lincoln's Inn Fields, probably in June 1698.

Farquhar's poem may have been intended to be published in the only edition (1698), which included three commendatory poems to the author. See also 'Letter to Mrs. Cockburn', Doubtful Attributions, vol. ii, pp. 527–9.

An Epigram

1–4 [poem] Crum lists a manuscript of the epigram in the Rawlinson Manuscripts, vol. 116, fol. 90. The work is not attributed to Farquhar in the manuscript (Crum, i. 3, A52).

To a Lady, being detain'd from visiting her by a Storm

1–17 [poem] This poem was reprinted in the *Poetical Courant*, No. 4, dated 16 February 1706, with the notation 'By *G. F.*'

The Lovers Night

1–58 [poem] The poem, except for the addition of three couplets, was first published in *The Adventures of Covent-Garden* in 1698; accidentals in this version are remote enough from those of the novella to suggest that a printed copy was not the copy text used for *Love and Business*. By recognizing the recycling of the poem, Leigh Hunt identified Farquhar as the author of the *Adventures* (Hunt, p. lxv).

50–1 He thought . . . folded fast] In *Love and a Bottle*, (v. iii. 25–6), Roebuck uses a variant on the couplet. See Commentary, *The Adventures of Covent Garden*, ll. 574–5.

The Brill, August the 10th 1700. New Stile.

0.1 *The Brill*] Den Briel must have been Farquhar's first stopping place on his trip to Holland.

0.3 Sam] One can only guess at Sam's identity, if indeed the letters were actually written to a 'Sam'. We know Farquhar knew Sam Briscoe, the bookseller, at least slightly, and conceivably he could have aimed at publication of these letters. (See Commentary, *The Constant Couple*, A New Prologue, vol. i, pp. 611–12.) Sam Bagshaw, to whom the London edition of *The Stage-Coach* was dedicated, was probably a friend of Motteux rather than Farquhar. (See Introduction, vol. i, p. 321.) Samuel Philips did not come to London until 1704. At any rate, the familiar heading, along with the wealth of detail, suggests these letters were indeed written from Holland during Farquhar's sojourn there.

10 the King] Suffering from illnesses and swelling in his legs, King William left England for Holland and arrived at The Hague on 27 July 1700 NS (16 July OS) He was there at the time that Farquhar sailed.

10–11 the Duke of *Glocester*'s Death] Princess Anne's son, having celebrated his eleventh birthday on 25 July OS, fell ill, and despite (or perhaps because of) the efforts of several doctors who 'bled, blisterd, and cup't him, tho to no purpose' (Luttrell, iv. 672), he died on 30 July. The playhouses were closed for six weeks for mourning. The little Duke was buried on the night of 10 August, with great state and ceremony. On 13 August, Luttrell reported that King William, according to letters from Holland, was in perfect health but deeply grieved by news of his nephew's death, and 'confin'd himself to his chamber from company two dayes' (iv. 676).

11 first News I had] If Farquhar had come from London, he would surely have known of the Duke's death. He was probably in London on 13 July, when the new prologue to *The Constant Couple* was performed, or shortly before, when he wrote it.

26 Mr. *L—r*] Martin Lyster or Lister (1638–1712) carried the news of the young Duke's death to the King (*State Papers Domestic* [SP 44, 101, p. 137]). James Vernon wrote from Whitehall to Edisbury on 30 July, indicating that he had left, 'Mr. Lyster carrying the letters he should have done to the king, you are to stop the mail till he comes.' Farquhar's awareness of the fact that Lyster was messenger suggests that the letter actually was written from Holland at the time. Apparently Farquhar boarded the ship at 11 p.m. on 30 July OS along with Lyster.

Lyster was a member of the Royal Society, a physician and fellow of the Royal College of Physicians. In 1698 he accompanied the Earl of Portland on his embassy to Paris (*DNB*), and in 1699 published *A Journey to Paris*. He also published several medical treatises including *De fontibus medicatis Angliae* (1682) and *Exercitatio Anatomica* (1694).

43 *Perspective*] optical instrument, such as a spy-glass.

49–50 *Old Bayly Bar*] The Old Bailey sessions house was the site of criminal proceedings for Middlesex. Prisoners being prosecuted stood in a small enclosure on bar.

50 the *Bar* at the *Maese*] the sandbar at the entrance to the Maas River.

78 Block] 'a silly Fellow' (*NDCC*).

133 *Pistol*] pistole, gold coin.

Leyden, October the 15th. 1700.

9 a very tedious Fit of Sickness] one of Farquhar's many references to his recurring bouts of illness. The letter from The Hague, dated 23 October, which accurately describes the King's arrival at the Hague as occurring 'yesterday' does not mention the illness described here, but speaks of Farquhar's attendance at social events.

50 *S—re* and *S—n*] I have not identified these two lawyers.

69 *Hudibrass*'s Ecclesiastick Drums] In Canto One of Samuel Butler's *Hudibras*, the pulpit is described as a 'Drum Ecclesiastick':

> When *Gospel-trumpeter, surrounded*
> *With long-ear'd rout, to Battel sounded,*
> *And Pulpit, Drum Ecclesiastick,*
> *Was beat with fist, instead of a stick:*

(*Quoted from Hudibras*, ed. John Wilders [Oxford, 1967], p. 1.)

89 *Common-Garden-Church*] a reference, probably slightly derisive, to Covent Garden Church, one of the most fashionable congregations of the day. Grose (p. 99) says Covent Garden was 'vulgarly called Common Garden'. Lillywhite also notes that references to Covent Garden sometimes appeared as Common Garden (p. 172). 'Common garden-gout, or rather Covent-Garden' is defined as the pox in *NDCC*.

90 Doctor *Burgess*'s Meeting] Daniel Burgess (1645–1713), a Presbyterian minister with a spellbinding oratorical style, preached in a meeting house in Russell Court, Drury Lane, at this time. His terse, epigrammatical style was described by Tom Brown as a 'pop gun way of delivery'.

91 *Tom's Coffee-house*] Although there were several coffeehouses with that name, Farquhar probably refers to the one at No. 17 Russell Street, Covent Garden, the one most mentioned in literature. Other Tom's Coffee-houses existing in 1700 include one at Ludgate Hill, where library sales occurred; another in St Martin's Lane, important in the insurance industry; and perhaps others, for which dates have not been established (See Lillywhite, pp. 580–96).

92 *Fleece-Tavern*] According to Wheatley (ii. 51), Fleece Tavern was located on the west side of Brydges Street, Covent Garden. The tavern had a bad reputation. Aubrey wrote in 1692 that it 'was very unfortunate for homicides; there have been several killed there in my time.'

94 New *French*] Since importation of French wine had been forbidden, the religious discussion, conducted over illegal wine, is ironically presented.

99 *Levites*] priests or parsons.

100 sell their Mackerell] 'Mackerel' was slang for a bawd. Obviously these prostitutes were hawking their wares.

108 Mr. *Fern*] presumably the owner of the Fleece Tavern. A Henry Fern was involved in a customs case about a decade later. According to the *Manuscripts of the House of Lords 1712–1714* (x. 218), John James David bought 82 hogsheads of 'French prize wines taken by the Ramelly Galley' from Henry Bray and John Bowden on or about 20 August 1708. They accepted bills of exchange drawn on them payable to Henry Fern 'for customs due for the same'.

182 *Track-scouts*] boatways. A scout (*schuit*) was a flat-bottomed Dutch boat, used in the river trade.

238 Board-side] ship's side.

An Epilogue, *spoken by Mr.* Wilks

0.1–2 *his first Appearance*] Robert Wilks had performed in London during the season of 1693–94, although Farquhar may not have been aware of it since he did not meet Wilks until he joined the Smock Alley company in Dublin in 1696. This epilogue was written for Wilks's return to the London stage, probably in autumn 1699. There are no listings for Wilks in London before that season; moreover, had he been there, he would probably have taken the part of Roebuck in *Love and a Bottle*. Chetwood suggested that his first role in London was Palamede in Dryden's *Love à la Mode*, but there is no record of this performance.

14 a distant Isle too kind to me] Ireland. Wilks had begun acting at Ashbury's Smock Alley theatre in Dublin in December 1691 and had returned with Ashbury after his season in London. Clark lists him in the Dublin company in 1698–9, another indication that the proper date for this prologue is autumn 1699.

A Prologue *on the propos'd Union of the Two Houses*

0.1–45 [prologue] The prologue was reprinted in the *Poetical Courant*, No. 22, for 22 June 1706.

0.1 *A* Prologue *on the propos'd Union*] The possibility of reuniting the two companies, who were engaging in disastrously bitter competition, arose early in 1701. Betterton made discreet enquiries about whether Drury Lane would be interested (Judith Milhous, *Thomas Betterton and the Management of Lincoln's Inn Fields 1695–1708* [Carbondale, Ill., Edwardsville, Pa., London, and Amsterdam, 1979], p. 119). The possibility was mentioned in the prologue to Catharine Trotter's *The Unhappy Penitent*, which opened on 4 February 1701, and in the epilogue to Mary Pix's *The Double Distress*, which opened in March. Farquhar's prologue probably dates from March or conceivably late February (he mentions performances of *The Rival Queens* that occurred 20 and 22 February).

For a description of the competition between the Drury Lane and Lincoln's Inn Fields theatres, which Farquhar describes in the prologue, see 'Theatrical Warfare', pp. 130–45.

6 New House and the Old] Lincoln's Inn Fields, where Betterton and many of the best actors set up, was the New House, established in a tennis court. Drury Lane, where the few remaining actors were assisted by many neophytes, was the Old.

22 some Mercenary Troops from *France*] Jean Balon and Anthony l'Abbé were imported from France to dance. (Mlle Subligny followed early in 1702.) Cibber describes the situation:

> . . . they [Betterton's company] were reduc'd to have recourse to foreign Novelties; *L'Abbee, Balon*, and Mademoiselle *Subligny*, three of the, then, most famous Dancers of the *French* Opera, were, at several times, brought over at extraordinary Rates, to revive that sickly Appetite, which plain Sense, and Nature had satiated. (*Apology*, p. 170).

See Commentary, *Sir Harry Wildair*, v. vi. 119, vol. i, p. 619.

25 great *Philip*'s Conquering Son] *The Rival Queens; or, The Death of Alexander the Great* by Nathaniel Lee, which had first opened in 1677, continued to play. Drury Lane performances of the play, sometimes called *Alexander*, occurred on 20 and 22 February and 5 April 1701. Apparently the play did not succeed at Drury Lane although it was popular at Lincoln's Inn Fields. According to Cibber, Betterton remained popular in the role as long as he played it, but when he quit, the popularity of the play declined (*Apology*, pp. 63–5).

39 *United Kings*] On 16 November 1700, Louis XIV announced that the Duke of Anjou, his grandson, would become King of Spain. Early in 1701, Philip V of Spain, at the age of eighteen, entered the country he would rule. The English and Dutch recognized the new King, but demanded some safeguards. The fear of 'United Kings' led to the creation of the second Grand Alliance within the year.

45 the Tye 'twixt *Spain* and *France*] The allied interests of Spain and

France were considered so threatening that they led to the War of the Spanish Succession.

On the Death of a Lady's Sparrow

1–55 [poem] This translation of Catullus' poem III may well have dated from Farquhar's university days. Another translation of the same poem appeared in *Miscellany Poems and Translations By Oxford Hands* (London, 1685), pp. 85–6.

On the Death of the late Queen

0.1 *Death*] Queen Mary died 28 December 1694. One can only surmise that the poem dates from that period, when Farquhar was sixteen or seventeen.

A SONG

0.1–13 [song] The song was reprinted in the *Poetical Courant*, No. 22, 22 June 1706, with no substantive variants.

1 *Aurelia*] Anne Oldfield played the role of Aurelia in Susanna Centlivre's *The Perjured Husband*, which opened at Drury Lane, probably in October 1700 (published 22 October).

To a Gentleman, that had his Pocket pick'd

1–43 [poem] A similar poem, entitled 'To a Gentleman who had his *Pocket* Pick'd of a *Watch* and *Money* by a *Mistriss*', addressed to Tony rather than Sam, was printed in *The Poetical Courant*, No. 2, 2 February 1706. See Miscellaneous Prose and Poetry, vol. ii, pp. 447–8.

3 Cobbs] money. Cob was slang for a Spanish dollar used in Ireland (*NDCC*). It was worth about 4*s*. 6*d*. (Grose, p. 88).

4 both your Fobbs] his breeches and his watch pocket.

5 fobb'd] robbed.

6 Mettal] a pun, referring to his watch and his semen. The later version in *The Poetical Courant* contains a reference to the doxy's cunning in being secure 'of your *Mettal*' (l. 8).

11 Tester] another pun, referring to the bed's canopy and the slang term for a sixpence.

15 Minute Hand] a pun on the minute hand of a watch and the precise, accurate hand of the prostitute/pickpocket. The pun was also used in l. 11 of the second version.

16–17 She wound . . . striking:] reused in the second version (ll. 13–14), with the substitution of 'So' for 'She' and 'And' for 'Then'.

21 *In and In*] copulation.

25 *Box*] a woman's genitals. The reference is to the dicebox used in gambling, but boxing the dice was also slang for tricking or swindling.

29–30 But what's . . . After-claps:] These lines appear, with slight revisions, as ll. 19–20 in the second version. An after-clap was an unexpected happening after something was supposed to be ended, for example, another demand after business was seemingly discharged. Farquhar utilizes a pun, of course, on 'clap' or gonorrhea.

40–1 The Mettal's . . . powder'd] reused in the second version, ll. 28–9.

41 Beef] prostitutes' flesh.

41 powder'd] treated for syphilis. A powdering-tub was a heated tub used in the treatment. *NDCC* lists the '*Powdring-Tub*, the pocky Hospital at *Kingsland* near *London*'.

Tuesday Morning

13 were] i.e. wear.

18–19 a little Lady in a half mourning Mantue and a deep Morning Complexion] This may be a reference to the widow Margaret Pemell, who was to become his wife. No evidence has been found to indicate when the two met.

22 *Stage-Coach*] a reference to composition of the farce by that name. See vol. i, pp. 319–20.

Thursday, 11 a Clock.

11 *Prince Prettyman*] Farquhar also refers incorrectly to this scene from *The Rehearsal* in *The Recruiting Officer*, II. ii. 41. Prince Volscius rather than Prince Prettyman actually decides between love and honour by debating whether to don his second boot (III. v).

Essex, Fryday Morning.

2 Hand and Head] Presumably this is a reference to Farquhar's recurrent illness, for horseback-riding otherwise should not have 'discompos'd' his hand. The references to pain in his hands recur in his letters.

20 the great Success of my Play] a reference to the record-breaking run of *The Constant Couple* in 1699–1700.

Sunday, after Sermon.

2–3 where others go to save their Souls, there have I lost mine] Farquhar was to use the same motif of love at first sight during church services when he wrote *The Beaux Stratagem*. In Act III Scene i, Mrs Sullen and Dorinda discuss her instantaneous amorous feelings for the fellow she saw at church; in Scene ii, Aimwell describes similar palpitations.

23 *the Lady in Mourning*] Possibly another reference to Margaret Pemell.

'Madam, If I han't begun thrice to write'

[letter] This is a corrected version of the letter headed 'Friday' in *A Pacquet from Will's*, vol. ii, pp. 435–6.

'Madam, In Order'

120 *Witall*] the foolish, cowardly knight, Sir Joseph Wittol, in Congreve's *The Old Batchelor*.

121 *Dorimant*] the attractive, rakish hero of Etherege's *The Man of Mode*.

172 Hobnail] rustic lout, a metonymy based on hobnail boots worn by farmers and ploughmen.

273 *Noll*] Oliver, meaning any man; also an off-handed reference to Oliver Cromwell.

Friday Night, 11 a Clock.

5 *Spring-Garden*] Wheatley lists three Spring Gardens. Dating from the reign of James I and located near St. James's Park and Whitehall, the 'Old Spring Garden' was built around a spring 'which sprung with the pressure of the foot, and wetted whoever was foolish or ignorant enough to tread upon it'. There was a pond, pheasant-yard, and bowling green. The 'New Spring Garden' was at Lambeth, and later became Vauxhall. A third, developed in the early eighteenth century at Knightsbridge, was also a popular public resort (Wheatley, iii, 293–7).

'Here am I drinking'

1 the Sign of the Globe] The Globe Tavern, mentioned as early as 1629, was at No. 133 on the north side of Fleet Street. Toward the end of the eighteenth century, it became a coffeehouse (Lillywhite, p. 234).

22 Anchoves] Anchovies were served in taverns to make guests thirsty.

31 *Entertainment of Dioclesian*] Betterton's operatic adaptation of Massinger and Fletcher's play, *The Prophetess; or, The History of Dioclesian*, with music by Purcell, played at least three times in 1700.

'In pursuance to your Order'

2 *Vandike* or *Kneller*] Sir Anthony Van Dyck (1599–1641) had painted James I in 1620 and returned to England in 1632 as court painter to Charles I, painting more than 350 portraits. Sir Godfrey Kneller (1646–1723) became court painter to Charles II and was the most prominent portrait painter in Farquhar's time.

'Well! Mrs. *V*—'

1 Mrs. *V*— and my charming *Penelope*] Critics have assumed Farquhar wrote of Susannah Verbruggen (1667?–1703), actress and wife of John Verbruggen, and Anne Oldfield (1683–1730), actress and alleged mistress of Farquhar. Theophilus Cibber discussed the identification:

> Whether this mistress [i.e. the one to whom he addressed the letter from the Hague] was the same person he calls his charming Penelope, in several of his love-letters addressed to her, we know not, but we have been informed by an old officer in the army, who well knew Mr. Farquhar, that by that name we are to understand Mrs. Oldfield, and that the person meant by Mrs. V— in one of them, said to be her bedfellow, was Mrs. Verbruggen the actress, the same who was some years before Mrs. Mountford, whom Mrs. Oldfield succeeded (when Mrs. V— died some years after in child-bed) with singular commendation, in her principal parts; and from so bright a flame it

was no wonder that Farquhar was more than ordinarily heated (T. Cibber, iii. 129).

Both actresses performed with the Drury Lane company during the period 1699–1702.

33 Rosamond] a reference to Rosamond's Pond in St. James's Park, usually associated in literature of the period with star-crossed lovers rather than water-rats. The pond was also mentioned in *The Twin-Rivals*, v. i. 17.

'Why shou'd I write'

18 Hanging] Farquhar links hanging and matrimony more than once, such as '. . . if I marry my Woman, I shall hang myself . . .' (*The Constant Couple*, v. i); '. . . Hanging and Matrimony are so much alike. . . .' (*The Inconstant*, ii. i); etc. The epistolary debate between marriage and hanging is reminiscent of Wildair's debate on the same subject in *The Constant Couple*, v. i.

23 the Ordinary of *Newgate*] the prison chaplain charged with the duty of preparing prisoners for death.

23 St. *Ann's*] The church in Wardour Street and Dean Street was consecrated in 1686. The parish was taken out of St. Martin's-in-the-Fields by act of Parliament (Wheatley, i. 49–50). The church was an appropriate choice if indeed, as seems likely, Farquhar was addressing Anne Oldfield. He refers in another letter ('I can no more let a Day') to praying there for absolution from 'my Creator and my Mistress.'

25 Three Leg'd Tree] gallows.

'I can no more'

9 the *Fountain*] According to Lillywhite, at least seven 'Fountains' are known in and off the Strand, most of them taverns. Farquhar may well refer to the Fountain Tavern in Fountain Court, identified as extant from 1685 to 1742 (Lillywhite, p. 213).

12 searching] keen, sharp, seeking out weaknesses.

13 Rheumatism] This letter and the next two refer to another bout of Farquhar's recurring illness with fever and 'rheumatism' of the hands and jaw.

'Misfortunes always lay'

3 *C—r*] Colley Cibber.

'Your Verses, Madam'

25–8 *O cou'd . . . mine.*] These four lines are the first of fourteen within the poem derived with slight revisions from the third of Farquhar's letters in *Familiar and Courtly Letters*, printed vol. ii, p. 428. These four lines contain no substantive revisions.

31–6 *Free from . . . Verse.*] These six lines also derive from the poem in the third Farquhar letter in the Voiture volume. In l. 33 the Voiture version reads 'as she was' instead of 'and she be'. Two additional lines appear in the original between ll. 33 and 34 of the *Love and Business* version. In l. 34, the earlier version reads 'Sweet' for 'Free' and 'Loves' for 'Flames.'

40–3 *Not* Sacharissa's . . . *inspired me.*] These four lines also derive from the earlier text, although the two couplets are separated in the original by another couplet. The Voiture version has 'Verse' for 'Lines' in l. 41 of the *Love and Business* text.

40 Sacharissa's *self*] Edmund Waller's poetry often addresses and praises Sacharissa, his pseudonym for Lady Dorothy Sidney.

'If any thing shou'd come'

0.1 [date] This letter should be dated 13 May 1700, the day of Dryden's funeral.

10 Mr. *M—x*] Peter Anthony Motteux, a merchant notorious for his thriftiness, collaborated with Farquhar on *The Stage-Coach*, probably during 1700 (see the Introduction to that play, vol. i, pp. 317–22).

11 a confounded Wife] Motteux had married his second wife, Priscilla, after his first, Elizabeth, died in 1694. Although the exact date of the marriage is not known, Priscilla gave birth to a daughter on 8 August 1699 (Cunningham, p. 179). Motteux's biographer does not record that he was henpecked.

14–15 Mr. *Dryden*'s Funeral] Dryden died on 1 May 1700; after being embalmed, he lay in state for almost a week at the College of Physicians in Warwick Lane. A grandiose funeral was planned, and plans made to bury him in Westminster Abbey. Invitations were printed to ask people to accompany his corpse from the College to its final resting place on Monday, 13 May, at 4 p.m., 'it being resolved to be moving by Five a clock. And be pleased to bring this Ticket with you.' The pomp of the funeral was apparently quite extraordinary, even for a time of ostentatious funeral ceremonies. Accounts of the funeral were carried in the *Post Boy*, *Post Man*, and *Flying Post*. (Charles E. Ward, *The Life of John Dryden* [Chapel Hill, NC 1961] pp. 317–18).

15 an Ode in *Horace* Sung] Horace's ode iii. 30, was sung to 'mournful music', according to the newspaper accounts.

17 the Pomp of the Ceremony] Ned Ward in the *London Spy* found the ceremony grander than that accorded an 'Ambassador from the greatest Emperor in all the Universe, sent over with a Welcome Embassy to the Throne of England' on his entry to court.

19 the Cavalcade was mostly Burlesque] According to the newspaper accounts, recorded in Ward, p. 318, mourners on horseback preceded the hearse, mourners on foot followed it, and more than one hundred coaches 'of the chief of nobility and gentry' attended. The hearse itself, bearing the arms of his and his wife's families and carrying the double coffin necessitated by Dryden's girth, was pulled by six white horses with velvet plumes and housings. Eight men in black played black-draped instruments as the procession moved.

22 the Oration] Dr Garth gave the funeral oration in Latin (Ward, p. 318).

23 the Author] Garth was both physician and writer.

Hague, October the 23rd.

1 dear Madam] possibly Margaret Pemell, who sought a pension from William III (see Sutherland, 'New Light on George Farquhar,' p. 171). Farquhar's attempt to interest Albemarle in the affairs of the addressee may well have been an attempt to secure a pension.

18 The *King* came hither last Night] Luttrell noted on Saturday, 12 October (23 October NS), 'That the king of Great Brittain was to come as yesterday from Loo to the Hague, and, if the wind serve, will embark on Fryday next for England. . . .' (iv. 696). Farquhar says he will leave on Wednesday. The King actually sailed, according to Luttrell, on Thursday, 17 October, from Oranje Polder (iv. 698).

33 Lord *A—le*] the first Earl of Albemarle, who travelled with the King to Holland. Farquhar may well have met Albemarle in Holland, for he dedicated *Sir Harry Wildair* to him the following spring and mentioned having access to him. (See Commentary, *Sir Harry Wildair*, Dedication, vol. i, p. 612.)

For many years Margaret Pemell sought royal compensation for the loss of her two husbands, Pemell and later Farquhar, both military men. She claimed in a petition to Queen Anne *c.*1708 that William III had promised her a pension, but he died before she received it (British Library, Loan 29/32). Albemarle would have provided the channel; as Farquhar said in the dedication to *Sir Harry Wildair*, 'the Nation has voted you their *Good Angel* in all Suits and Petitions to their Prince. . . .' No one has found evidence of when Pemell died, when Farquhar met the widow, or when they married; the identification of Margaret as recipient of the letter is therefore incapable of proof. But if Margaret did petition William, she may well have been a widow by 1700, and Farquhar may well have been her messenger, through Albemarle.

34 Captain *L—oe*] I have not been able to indentify the Captain.

36 Lord *West—nd*] Thomas Fane, twelfth Earl of Westmorland (1683–1736) studied at the Hague from 1699 until 1702. His brother, the eleventh Earl, had died on 19 May 1699. Westmorland had just turned seventeen when this letter was written; Farquhar was twenty-two or twenty-three.

41 D—ss of *G—n*] probably the Duchess of Grafton, (1667–1723), 'whose sweetness and beauty were universally commended', according to the *DNB*. She had married Henry Fitzroy, first Duke of Grafton and second son of Charles II; he died in 1690. The Duchess married Sir Thomas Hanmer in 1698.

42 Mrs. *B—le*] A number of possible ladies identified as 'Mrs. *B—le*' might have been intended. Farquhar might have referred to Juliana Boyle (1672–1750), wife of Charles Boyle, second earl of Burlington and Cork, or to Arethusa Boyle, Charles Boyle's half-sister; both these are mentioned as members of the fashionable St James's congregation in Arthur Mainwaring's poem, 'The Brawny Bishop's Complaint' (see *Poems of Affairs of State, vi: 1697–1704*, ed. Frank H. Ellis [New Haven, Com., and London, 1970],

p. 41). Charles Boyle, fourth Earl of Orrery, did not marry until 30 March 1706, so his wife could not have been intended.

'I receiv'd your Letter'

  35 a foreign Countrey] presumably the Netherlands.

A Discourse upon Comedy

  3–4 two or three little *Plays*] Farquhar had written *Love and a Bottle*, *The Constant Couple*, and *Sir Harry Wildair*, and had probably completed *The Stage-Coach* before he wrote the *Discourse*.

  5 without any Bulk of *Preface*] Only *The Constant Couple* had a Preface to the Reader, and it was brief.

  106 *Jubilees*] comedies like *The Constant Couple*.

  106 *Fopingtons*] characters like Vanbrugh's Lord Foppington, in *The Relapse*, an extension of Cibber's Sir Novelty Fashion in *Love's Last Shift*, acted by Cibber to the great amusement of audiences.

  169–70 *Rover*, *Libertine*, or old *Batchelour*] Aphra Behn's *The Rover* (1677), Thomas Shadwell's *The Libertine* (1675), and William Congreve's *The Old Batchelour* (performed at least by 1693 but probably as early as 1689) were bawdy, rowdy plays that continued popular long after their first runs.

  174 *Pauls*] St Paul's Cathedral, around which many booksellers clustered.

  196 *Bellarmin*] The Italian cardinal (1542–1621) whose published polemics against the Protestants made him greatly influential in the Counter-Reformation.

  212 *Hick's Hall*] the Sessions House of the County of Middlesex.

  242 the great *Cook*] Sir Edward Coke (1552–1634), the greatest of all English legal minds.

  288 his Pupil] Alexander the Great.

  318–19 Doctor *Tillotson*'s Sermons] The 254 sermons of John Tillotson (1630–94) were first published in 1694. They were republished in fourteen volumes between 1695 and 1704.

  341 the Congregation at St. *James*'s] St James's Church, Westminster, a masterpiece of Sir Christopher Wren's, was a fashionable, elegant place of worship. It was often mentioned in literature of the period, for example, in Vanbrugh's *The Relapse*, Cibber's *The Non-Juror*, and Defoe's *A Journey through England*.

  400 Prince *Arthur*] Richard Blackmore (d. 1729) was continuously and heavily criticized for his epics, in particular *Prince Arthur*, published in 1695. Dryden was intensely critical, and Dennis published *Remarks on a Book Entitled, Prince Arthur, An Heroick Poem* in 1696. Dennis argued that the poem 'has neither unity, nor integrity, nor morality, nor universality' and that the narration 'is neither probable, delightful, nor wonderful'. Farquhar has chosen to illustrate with a modern work generally derisible to the critics.

  402 Doctor *B—re*] Blackmore was physician to Queen Anne.

  421 *Cartesius*] Latinate form of Descartes.

  445–6 as little Mercy as poor *Socrates* found] a reference to Aristophanes' satire of Socrates in *The Clouds*.

524–5 the Beasts which are lug'd upon the Stage by the Horns] cuckolded husbands, characters condemned by the Collierists.

528 Reformation] The Society for the Reformation of Manners in the Cities of London and Westminster was established in 1696. The Society published an annual report of their progress 'in suppressing profaneness and debauchery'. In 1703 they published a list of 858 persons who had been convicted of lewd behaviour in 1702, the year *Love and Business* was published.

532 *Fondlewife* and his young Spouse] The foolish banker Fondlewife is cuckolded by his young wife Laetitia in *The Old Batchelour*, one of the plays attacked by Collier.

547 *Nathan*'s Fable] In 2 Sam. 12, Nathan told David of the rich man with many flocks and herds who took the poor man's one little ewe lamb. David, infuriated, said the rich man deserved to die. Then Nathan pointed out that David was that man, for he had caused Uriah the Hittite to die so that he could take his wife Bathsheba. David then realized he had sinned.

584 *Wildair*] the hero of *The Constant Couple*.

585 *Morose*] Jonson's self-centred bachelor who cannot abide noise, in *Epicoene, or The Silent Woman* (1609), a play that remained very popular on stage during Farquhar's lifetime.

592–3 making the *Tour* of *Tyburn*] going to be executed at the gallows at Tyburn.

613–14 Pit, Box, and Galleries] the three seating areas in the theatre, metonymically used for the audience. Farquhar makes the point that all the audience, not just the educated, must be pleased.

620–1 *Shakespear, Johnson, Fletcher*, and others] Selinda refers to Shakespeare, Jonson, and Dryden as being 'irregular' poets who please audiences.

625 Decorums of Time and Place] Farquhar had earlier criticized the unities of time, place, and action through Selinda's critical remarks in *The Adventures of Covent Garden* (ll. 429–64).

644 soaking] toping, drinking copiously.

652 Doorkeepers] Doorkeepers collected the money for theatrical attendance. For an explanation of the trickery of young men to avoid paying, see Commentary, *The Constant Couple*, Prologue, l. 30, vol. i, p. 599.

682–3 the *Czar of Muscovy*] *The Czar of Muscovy* by Mary Pix was published on 15 April 1701. Avery assumed the play opened in March (*London Stage*, Part ii, i. 8); it ran at Lincoln's Inn Fields.

688–9 *Will*'s and *Hippolito*'s] These two fashionable coffeehouses were also mentioned in Farquhar's plays: Will's, the meeting place of the wits, in *Love and a Bottle* and *The Beaux Stratagem* as well as *The Adventures of Covent-Garden*, Hippolito's, frequented by fashionable young gentlemen, in *The Constant Couple*.

691 *Prologue* and *Epilogue*] Friends, literary acquaintances, and paid authors frequently wrote prologues and epilogues for other people's plays. For Farquhar's own contributions in this genre, see Prologues and Epilogues and 'George Farquhar and "The Bus'ness of a Prologue"'.

692 a fair legible Hand] Professional scribes were hired to make fair copies of plays for the theatres.

697 a Month in Rehearsing] Three or four weeks was the standard time between casting and opening night. During that time, the actors rehearsed for several hours daily. See *London Stage*, Part i, pp. cliii–cliv.

697–8 a Hundred Pound in Dressing] Although not all new plays featured new costumes, the theatres spent large amounts on costumes and advertised when a play was 'new dressed'. Sometimes new costumes and sets could justify elevating the price of tickets.

756–7 the part of *Alexander* the Great] Betterton assumed the role of Alexander in Nathaniel Lee's *The Rival Queens* after William Mountfort's death in 1692. Cibber's description in the *Apology* of Betterton's acting in the role corroborates Farquhar's comments:

> There cannot be a stronger Proof of the Charms of harmonious Elocution, than the many, even unnatural Scenes and Flights of the false Sublime it has lifted into Applause. In what Raptures have I seen an Audience, at the furious Fustian and turgid Rants in *Nat. Lee's Alexander the Great*! . . . When these flowing Numbers came from the Mouth of a *Betterton*, the Multitude no more desired Sense to them, than our musical *Connoisseurs* think it essential in the celebrate Airs of an *Italian* Opera. . . . If I tell you, there was no one Tragedy, for many Years, more in favour with the Town than *Alexander*, to what must we impute this its command of publick Admiration? Not to its intrinsick Merit, surely, if it swarms with Passages like this I have shewn you! . . . When this favourite Play I am speaking of, from its being too frequently acted, was worn out, and came to be deserted by the Town, upon the sudden death of *Monfort*, who had play'd *Alexander* with Success, for several Years, the Part was given to *Betterton*, which, under this great Disadvantage of the Satiety it had given, he immediately reviv'd, with so new a Lustre, that for three Days together it fill'd the House; . . . This I mention, not only to prove what irresistable Pleasure may arise from a judicious Elocution, with scarce Sense to assist it; but to shew you too, that tho' *Betterton* never wanted Fire, and Force, when his Character demanded it; yet, where it was not demanded, he never prostituted his Power to the low Ambition of a false Applause. And further, that when, from a too advanced Age, he resign'd that toilsome Part of *Alexander*, the Play, for many Years after, never was able to impose upon the Publick . . . (pp. 63–65).

Betterton's company performed it on January 1699, right after *Love and a Bottle* opened in December. His last performance may well have occurred before this reference to his acting. At least three performances occurred at Drury Lane from February to April 1701, when *Sir Harry Wildair* was being prepared for its April opening, so Farquhar would certainly have been aware of them. No cast list exists, but once Betterton was at the other house, the role of Alexander may well have fallen to Wilks, who performed it in 1704. Others who tried the part in the next few years included Verbruggen, Powell, and Thurmond.

854–5 *Bay of St. Nicholas*] St Nicholas Bay was on the north side of Java 'in the eastern ocean'. It was noted for 'a convenient rivulet of fresh water; and at the village near shore provisions and vegetables may be had', according to *The Naval Gazetter; or, Seaman's Complete Guide* of 1801.

856 *Covent-Garden Church*] the church of St Paul's, Covent Garden, on the west side of the square, is the parish church, attributed to Inigo Jones. Robert Wilks, among other theatrical luminaries of the time, was later buried there.

Prologues and Epilogues

Epilogue, *The Grove. Or, Love's Paradice*

1–8 Time . . . Ass.] Lines 1–4 and 7–8 were reused with slight variations at the first six lines of the Prologue printed in the 1705 London edition of *The Stage-Coach*. Motteux rather than Farquhar may well have been responsible for the borrowing (see *The Stage-Coach*, Introduction, vol. i, p. 321). For the revisions that were made, see Commentary to Appendix A of that farce, vol. i, p. 622.

21 *Io*] the princess of Argos who, in Greek mythology, was turned into a heifer and persecuted by Hera.

Prologue, *Courtship A-la-Mode*

20 Custom damns most Plays at t'other House] By summer 1700, Drury Lane had clearly gained the upper hand over Lincoln's Inn Fields, thanks in large part to Farquhar's *Constant Couple*. The play had opened in December and played fifty-three times during the season. Betterton tried nine more *premières* at Lincoln's Inn Field before the end of the season, but none of them succeeded. Even Congreve's *The Way of the World* had only five known performances. Farquhar's glee at Drury Lane's success is reflected in this line. (See 'Theatrical Warfare,' p. 137.)

Prologue, *All for the Better*

6 *Bellona*] the Roman goddess of war.

7 Winter-quarters] The troops wintered in England before resuming warfare when the weather improved.

15 *Venlo*-Sparks] Venlo capitulated to the Allies in September 1702. See *The Twin-Rivals*, Commentary, Prologue, l. 28, vol. i, p. 638.

17 a Wall] The Allies had stormed the ramparts and parapets of Venlo.

23 *Will's* to *Tom's*] From Will's, the coffeehouse of the wits, in Bow Street, to Tom's, another fashionable coffeehouse in Russell Street, Covent Garden. The juxtaposition of Will's and Tom's was not uncommon. For example, the Epilogue to Rowe's *Tamerlane* in 1702 mentioned:

> *With careful Brows at* Tom*'s and* Will*'s they meet,*
> *And ask, who did Elections lose or get—*

25 engage the *French*] i.e. the pox, known as the French disease.

27 a glut of Plays] Most *première* performances occurred in the late fall and early winter. Manning's *All for the Better* was the first *première* of the season; in all, Drury Lane performed nine new plays, including *The Twin-Rivals*, and

Lincoln's Inn Fields, five. Of those, we have records of only a few playing as many as three or four nights.

Epilogue, *The Patriot: or, The Italian Conspiracy*

0.2 Mr. *Mills*] John Mills played the role of Cosmo di Medici in *The Patriot*.

0.3 Mr. *Penkethman*] The comedian William Pinkethman did not have a role in the mainpiece; nevertheless, he spoke the epilogue.

21 *Julio*] The role of the hero Julio, Cosmo's son, was played by Farquhar's good friend Robert Wilks.

33 *Whites*] Farquhar mentioned this chocolate house in *Love and a Bottle*, *Sir Harry Wildair*, and *The Twin-Rivals*.

Prologue, At the Opening of the Theatre in the Hay-Market

1 Great Revolutions Crown this Wond'rous Year] The central design of the prologue is a comparison of the European theatre of war and London's theatrical warfare. This line speaks of the 'revolution' against Louis XIV and the actors' 'revolt' against Drury Lane manager Christopher Rich when they moved to the new theatre in the Haymarket.

4 To set the *Theatre*, and *Europe* free] The Haymarket actors had declared their independence from Rich, a notably tight-fisted and eccentric manager. In Europe, the Allies had defeated the French troups in Ramillies, elsewhere in Belgium, in Turin, and in Spain.

6 *LEWIS*] Lewis XIV of France.

7 Dramatick Prince] Christopher Rich.

12 you the Asylum of the Refugee] that is, the Queen's Theatre in the Haymarket.

13 *Camisars*] Camisards, the French Protestant insurgents from the Cévennes, who rebelled against the persecution which followed the revocation of the Edict of Nantes by Louis XIV in 1685.

15 Dragoons of Song and Dance] The musical performers at Drury Lane had increased in numbers and importance. Thirteen singers, two musicians (Gasparini and Paisible), and thirteen dancers are identified in *The London Stage* for the season of 1705–6; twenty-five actors and actresses are listed for the same season. In other words, the musical entertainers outnumbered the dramatic performers.

20 Subscriptions] Farquhar compares the subscription of £100 each from thirty 'Persons of Quality' to build the theatre to the loan issued by the government which enabled Marlborough to campaign in Europe in the spring and summer of 1706 and thereby conquer Turin and Ramillies. For details of the government loan see P. G. M. Dickson, *The Financial Revolution in England, A Study in the Development of Public Credit 1688–1756* (London, 1967), pp. 59–60.

Prologue, *The Platonick Lady*

2 Victorious] The summer of 1706 had been a truly triumphant year for

the allied forces, who had prevailed at Ramillies, Belgium, Spain, and finally Turin. Farquhar expresses the elation of victory.

12 *Ramillis*] Marlborough had won the battle of Ramillies on 23 May 1706. Churchill describes the battle dramatically: 'Thus, in the space of four hours, between three and seven o'clock, the entire magnificent French army was shattered and scattered into utter rout and ruin' (Churchill, v. 128).

MISCELLANEOUS PROSE AND POETRY

Familiar and Courtly Letters

Title-page

8 *Henry Cromwel*] Cromwell, a wit about town, moved in Dryden's circle and was a friend and correspondent of Dennis and Pope, among others. Cromwell had earlier contributed poems to Gildon's *Miscellany Poems* (1692). (For fuller discussion of his literary connections, see Hooker, ii. 442–3.)

9 *Tho. Cheek*] Cheek, one of the wits that gathered at Will's, also contributed to *Letters of Wit, Politicks and Morality*.

9 *Jos. Raphson*] Joseph Raphson (1648–1715) wrote mathematical works including *A Mathematical Dictionary* (1702).

By Mr.— to Madam—

16 *Rheumatism*] The references to Farquhar's rheumatism in the period from 1698 to 1702 are thickly strewn in his correspondence. He was apparently having considerable pain in his extremities, as he suggests by his reference to having 'but one Hand'.

'What shall I say to the *dearest Woman*'

ll. 11–18, 21–4, 27–8 *Oh! cou'd I . . . smil'd on me*] These fourteen lines were used by Farquhar in *The Adventures of Covent-Garden* and reused in slightly revised form in a letter in *Love and Business*. For details of revision, see Commentary, *Love and Business*, vol. ii, pp. 584–5.

A Pacquet from Will's

FRIDAY

1–39 [letter] This letter, with 23 revisions, most of them minor, was reused in *Love and Business*. For details of the revisions, see *Love and Business*, Appendix A, vol. ii, p. 387.

To a Lady, whom he never saw

13 *Fountain* in the *Strand*] The Fountain Tavern after which Fountain

Court was named. (Lillywhite, p. 213; Wheatley, ii. 74).

20 Covered Dishes] i.e., ladies in masks.

31 *Golden-Square*] Golden Square, Regent's Street, was an exceedingly elegant part of town, inhabited by aristocrats and other fashionable people.

51–2 a Note for the Pit, to see the *Jubilee*] that is, free entrance to the theatre for his play *The Constant Couple*. He chose to give her entry to the pit, where the other masked ladies would have been rather than the front boxes with ladies of her own quality, in order to allow her to co 'inue her anonymity.

To Mrs. C—

0.1 *Mrs*. C—] Susanna Carroll, later Centlivre.

To a Masque on Twelfth-day

0.1 Twelfth-day] This poem should be dated 6 January 1700 or 1701. The references to *The Constant Couple* ('*Jubilee*' in l. 14, and the pseudonym 'Wildair') suggest that it probably appeared in 1700, during the first run of the popular play.

17 Wildair] The name of Farquhar's most popular character, Sir Harry Wildair in *The Constant Couple*, is here obviously used to indicate the author. Later it became a name pampleteers accorded the actor Robert Wilks, who played the role.

Letters of Wit, Politicks and Morality

Title-page

10 Mr. *Granville*] George Granville (1667–1735), created Lord Lansdowne, Baron of Bideford, Devon, in 1711, author of four plays as well as published poetry and prose. Two plays, *The She-Gallants* (1695), a comedy, and *Heroick Love* (1698), a tragedy, as well as his adaptation of Shakespeare, *The Jew of Venice* (December 1700 or January 1701), had all been performed at Lincoln's Inn Fields before *Letters of Wit, Politicks and Morality* appeared.

11 Capt. *Ayloffe*] Captain William Ayloffe (d. 1706) was a contributor to various miscellanies. He was probable the Celadon in the published correspondence with Astræa (Susanna Carroll) in this volume. See Introduction, vol. ii, pp. 417–20.

11 Dr. *G*—] Sir Samuel Garth (1661–1719), a physician, published the mock-epic *The Dispensary* in 1699. This remained his most popular work. He and Granville were early friends of Pope. Like the other contributors to this and other miscellanies, he was a wit about town.

11 Mr. *B—y*] William Burnaby (1672 or 1673–1706) had published two of his four comedies, *The Reform'd Wife* in 1700 and *The Ladies Visiting-Day* in January or February 1701. He had also translated *The Satyr of Titus Petronius Arbiter* in 1694, and contributed to *Commendatory Verses, on the Author of the Two*

Arthurs, the volume in which Dryden and the wits at Will's responded to Sir Richard Blackmore's *Satyr against Wit* (Winton, p. 53).

11 Mr. *O—n*] John Oldmixon (1673–1742) wrote miscellaneous works, including plays, pamphlets, miscellanies, poems, and periodical pieces. Farquhar wrote an epilogue for his opera *The Grove, Or, Love's Paradice* in January or February 1700. Oldmixon attacked Farquhar within a month or two in his prologue to Charles Gildon's alteration of *Measure for Measure*, and Farquhar retaliated in his 'New Prologue to *The Constant Couple*' that July. In *Letters of Wit, Politicks and Morality* Farquhar complained in Letter XLII about Oldmixon's attack on him, but omitted his name.

11–12 Mr. *B—r*] Abel Boyer (1667–1729), compiler of *Letters of Wit, Politicks and Morality*, was another of the second tier of wits, who contributed to the miscellanies at the turn of the century. His translation of Racine's *Iphigénie* as *Achilles, or, Iphigenia in Aulis* opened shortly after *The Constant Couple*, probably in December 1699; according to the preface, one of the difficulties it laboured under was 'being acted at a time when the whole Town was so much, and so justly diverted by the *Trip to the Jubilee*'. (Quoted in *London Stage*, Part I, p. 519). The prologue of the play was written by Cheek, the epilogue by Motteux. Boyer later published histories of the reigns of William III and Anne, *The Political State of Great Britain*, historical works, political tracts, translations, a French–English dictionary, and other miscellaneous works.

12 Mr. *G—*] Charles Gildon (1665–1724), a prolific writer of the period, had published numerous critical writings, staged four of his five plays, edited several miscellanies and editions of works by other authors, for example, Aphra Behn and the Earl of Rochester, and contributed to a number of miscellanies. His adaptation of *Measure for Measure*, which opened in or around February 1700 at Lincoln's Inn Fields while audiences were flocking to Drury Lane to see *The Constant Couple*, occasioned Oldmixon's prologue attacking Farquhar. The prologue to his *Love's Victim*, which opened in April or early May 1701, shortly before publication of his miscellany, condemned *The Constant Couple* as farce. Yet Farquhar later contributed an epilogue to his *The Patriot*, an adaptation of Nathaniel Lee's *Lucius Junius Brutus*, which opened late in 1702. (See 'George Farquhar and the "Bus'ness of a Prologue"', pp. 143–8).

12 Mr. *F—r*] Farquhar.

12 Mrs. *C—l*] Susanna Carroll, later Centlivre (1669–1723). Only one of her nineteen plays had been published at this time; however, she had contributed to the three collections containing letters by Farquhar. Tradition holds that Carroll and Farquhar were romantically linked, and the correspondence supports that theory.

13 Mrs. *W—n*] Jane Wiseman (dates unknown) wrote *Antiochus the Great*, which opened at Lincoln's Inn Fields, probably in November 1701, that is, after the publication of the miscellany.

Letter XLI

0.2 *Astræa to Damon*] Pseudonyms for Susanna Carroll and Farquhar.

13–14 reading Mr. *Asgill*] John Asgill (1659–1738) published a pamphlet on 13 June 1700 (Luttrell, iv. 656), arguing that death is not obligatory to Christians. The work was entitled *An Argument Proving, That According to the Covenant of Eternal Life revealed in the Scriptures, Man may be translated from hence into that Eternal Life, without passing through Death, altho the Humane Nature of Christ himself could not be thus translated till he had passed through Death*. In Ireland the House of Commons ordered that the hangman burn the pamphlet.

Letter XLII

7–13 Cunny-burrow . . . Neck] This passage is full of sexual innuendo. Farquhar often used the image of the noose ('a Noose to secure my Neck') to indicate marriage.

14 Mr. —] Oldmixon, who had abused Farquhar in his prologue to Gildon's *Measure for Measure*.

Letter XLVII

0.2 *Mr. R— S—*] probably Richard Steele, although Steele was already being addressed as 'Captain' during this period (Winton, p. 41). He was a minor figure in London literary circles at the time, having contributed to *Commendatory Verses, On the Author of the Two Arthurs*. Later in 1701, his first play, *The Funeral*, opened at Drury Lane. It seems likely that the two playwrights were acquainted. A less likely possibility is Richard Swan, a noted punster, who published in various miscellanies including *A Pacquet from Will's*.

1 Mr. *Johnson*] Charles Johnson (1679–1748), author of numerous plays. The first, *The Gentleman Cully*, published in January 1702, opened at Lincoln's Inn Fields in summer 1701.

2 in Love] According to Winton, 'Richard Steele before his marriage was Cupid's faithful follower' (p. 48). He pursued amours, wrote verses, and fathered two illegitimate children; Farquhar was not the only one to ridicule his amorous propensities.

9–10 like Chymistry, a knowledge very chargeable in Experiments] In the late 1690's Steele backed with John Tilly, Mary de la Riviere Manley, and William Burnaby an alchemical enterprise of Sir Thomas Tyrrel. As Manley described the results in the *New Atalantis*,

> . . . the young Soldier's little ready Money immediately flies off, his Credit is next staked, which soon likewise vanishes into Smoke . . . his Credit was stretched to the utmost; Demands came quick upon him, and grew clamorous; he had neglected his Lord's Business and even left his House, to give himself up to the vain Pursuits of Chemistry. . . .'

See Winton, p. 52. The reference to chemistry strongly points to Steele as the recipient of the letter.

To a Gentleman who had his Pocket Pick'd

Explanations of the puns and *double entendres* can be found in the Commentary, *Love and Business.*

11–12 Sly Devil . . . command,] These lines are revised from ll. 14–15 of the version in *Love and Business.*

13–14 So *wound . . . striking.*] These lines were borrowed from ll. 16–17 of the earlier version. 'She' was revised to 'So' and 'Then' to 'And'.

19–20 But then . . . *After-clap*;] These lines are revised freely from ll. 29–30 of the earlier version.

21 *CASE*] Dr Case, an astrologer who set up as a doctor and added 'MD' to his name, was satirized more than once in the contemporary miscellanies. For example, in No. 14 of the *Poetical Courant*, 27 April 1706, '*Sanus ab Insano*: Or, the Doctor cur'd by his Patient' appears:

> The Quack with learned Nonsense stuffs his Bills,
> Pretending mighty Cures for mighty Ills,
> The Mobb, gull'd by his Rhet'rick, flock apace
> To see their *Friend* and *Servant* Doctor C—
> The Patient wants his *Health*, the Quack his *Fees.* ⎫
> And tho his Med'cine gives the Sick no Ease,   ⎬
> His healing Money cures the Quack's Disease.   ⎭

28–9 The *Mettal*'s . . . powder'd.] This couplet is repeated verbatim from the earlier poem, ll. 40–1.

Love's Catechism

1–40 *Tom.* Come . . . *End of Love.*] The first forty lines of text derive almost verbatim from the catechism scene in *The Beaux Stratagem.* Only two minor substantive variants occur in the text, although the speech prefixes are changed from Archer and Cherry to Tom and Betty.

44–5 '*tis a Maxim . . . Poverty*] Archer says to Aimwell in *The Beaux Stratagem*, 1. 131–3, 'tis still my Maxim, that there is no Scandal like Rags, nor any Crime so shameful as Poverty.'

47–9 *the World's . . . Industry*] Archer says to Aimwell in *The Beaux Stratagem*, 1. 156–8, 'the World's wide enough, let 'em bustle; Fortune has taken the weak under her Protection, but Men of Sense are left to their Industry.'

50–3 But what . . . *Country Ladies*] *The Beaux Stratagem*, 1. 233–7:
Archer. Ay, you're such an amorous Puppy, that I'm afraid you'll spoil our Sport; you can't counterfeit the Passion without feeling it.
Aimwell. Tho' the whining part be out of doors in Town, 'tis still in force with the Country Ladies;—

61–2 *which give . . . Life.*] 'your Example gives me such an Impression of Matrimony, that I shall be apt to condemn my Person to a long Vacation all its Life.' Dorinda to Mrs. Sullen in *The Beaux Stratagem*, II. i. 10–12.

65–8 *if ever . . . little*] 'if ever you marry beware of a sullen, silent Sot, one that's always musing, but never thinks:— There's some Diversion in a talking Blockhead; and since a Woman must wear Chains, I wou'd have the Pleasure of hearing 'em rattle a little.' Mrs. Sullen to Dorinda in *The Beaux Stratagem*, II. i. 58–62.

72–9 *Do you . . .* Enjoyment] *The Beaux Stratagem*, III. i. 6–14:

Dorinda. But do you think that I am so weak as to fall in Love with a Fellow at first sight?

Mrs. Sullen. Pshaw! now you spoil all, why shou'd not we be as free in our Friendships as the Men? I warrant you the Gentleman has got to his Confident already, has avow'd his Passion, toasted your Health, call'd you ten thousand Angels, has run over your Lips, Eyes, Neck, Shape, Air and every thing, in a Description that warms their Mirth to a second Enjoyment.

Barcellona

Title-page

7 *CHARLES* Earl of *Peterborough*] Charles Mordaunt (1658–1735), the third Earl of Peterborough, assumed duties as general and commander in chief of naval forces on 31 March 1705. On 1 May he received a further commission, jointly with Sir Clowdisley Shovell, as admiral and commander-in-chief. He became a hero at Barcelona and Valencia but later fell into disgrace, first through a defiant delay of his return when summoned to England and then more seriously through difficulties in answering enquiries into his military pay-lists. In 1709 his wife died, and early in 1710 his two sons also died. The poem was published about a month after the death of the second, when his fortune was beginning to rise again; by 2 November 1710 he had been commissioned captain-general of the Marines as well as First Lord of the Admiralty. In December of that year, his reputation restored, he became ambassador extraordinary to Vienna. Peterborough has remained a controversial figure. Although Colin Ballard praises him, Winston Churchill paints a less admirable picture:

> Everybody hated Peterborough, and Peterborough struck at all. His differences with 'the Germans', or 'the Vienna crew', as he described Charles III and his Imperialist advisers, soon made even formal relations difficult. (Churchill, v. 65.)

His contemporary John Methuen, English envoy at Lisbon, however, welcomed his selection to command the forces:

> . . . beside the life spirit & resolution which indeed I expected ther appears in him a great temper calmness which seem the effects of a strong judgement. (British Library, Add. MS 28 056, f. 293.)

10 *Charles* III] Archduke Charles of Austria (1685–1740) was proclaimed King of Spain by the allied forces. After the battle of Barcelona, he came to the throne.

Dedication

0.6 MONMOUTH] King William, who held Mordaunt in high esteem, named him Earl of Monmouth in 1689. Monmouth had been the title of Mordaunt's mother's family. There has been some scholarly speculation that in giving Mordaunt the title, William meant to indicate he would not revive it for the late Duke of Monmouth's son.

2 found among my dear Deceas'd Husband's Writings] Margaret Farquhar had probably been trying to peddle the poem ever since Farquhar's death. See Introduction, vol. ii, pp. 469–70.

10 the different Interest and Opinions of your Confederates] The squabbling between the leaders of the allied forces had become well known. In John Freind's *Account of the Earl of Peterborow's Conduct in Spain*, published, after Farquhar's death, on 1 December 1707, and issued in a second edition on 9 December, the various councils of war evoked in the poem are recorded in considerable detail.

15–16 Prince of *Darmstad*] Prince George of Hesse-Darmstadt (1669–1705), reputed by both contemporaries and historians to be one of the best military leaders of the allies in Spain, but scorned by Peterborough (see Introduction, vol. ii, pp. 454–6), was described by Trevelyan as 'the wisest head among the allied chiefs in Spain', (George Macauley Trevelyan, *England Under Queen Anne*, ii. *Ramillies and the Union with Scotland* [London, 1932], p. 73). He was mortally wounded during the attack on Monjuich. A musket shot severed an artery in his thigh, and he bled to death. Ballard records Lord Mahon's description of how Peterborough had Hesse-Darmstadt's body laid in state in a convent, dressed not only in his usual clothes and boots, but adorned with a wig, a hat, a sword in one hand, and a cane in the other (pp.150–1).

16 Your Lordship Heroically interpos'd] when the disaster at the hill-fort Montjuich (described in the Introduction, vol. ii, p. 464 above) occurred, Viscount Charlemont's troops were retreating in disarray till Peterborough galvanized them. He grabbed a half-pike—some say from Charlemont's hands—and led the troops back to regain the outerworks. His conspicuous bravery proved successful because the Spanish army, believing the allied troops were far more numerous than they were, retreated to Barcelona. (Ballard, pp. 149–50; Churchill, v. 62–3.)

17 assured the Fate of the *Austrian* Monarchy] by the accession of Charles III to the throne of Spain.

18–19 *Madrid* it self had received its natural Lord] On 27 June 1706 the Earl of Galway entered Madrid and declared Charles King of Spain and the Indies. But Charles took a circuitous route, going first to be declared King of Aragon, and the allies had to retreat again from Madrid.

19 had not Envy it self blasted the sure laid Design] Peterborough's relationships with the other allied commanders and with the ministers in England were at best stormy. Margaret Farquhar attributes the difficulties and the resultant lost military opportunities to the envy of the other leaders. Scholarly interpretations of the problems vary widely: Ballard defends Peterborough; Churchill finds him capricious and even at times malicious.

Preface

1 an Officer that Time] Farquhar was on duty in Dublin at the time of the siege. Jordan shows that he was in Dublin on 27 July, and that on 23 October Orrery was authorized to beat for new recruits (pp. 260–1); Farquhar would have left for recruiting duty after that date.

3 an ingenious Friend] The precision of the descriptions of internal conflict and of the events of battle support Margaret Farquhar's assertion that Farquhar got his facts from someone who was present.

7 The Author's tedious Sickness] Symptoms, recorded in works throughout his writing career, suggest that Farquhar suffered and died from a rheumatic ailment, probably rheumatic fever.

9–10 some considerable Time elaps'd] Actually this may be an excuse rather than fact. A letter from Margaret Farquhar to Harley, in the Portland manuscripts, suggests that she had sent a copy of 'my husband's poem', probably *Barcellona*, to the Queen; she received ten guineas. The letter to Harley was sent early in 1709, and the poem must have been forwarded to the Queen earlier.

Canto I

32 canton'd] quartered.

41 *Philip's Son*] Alexander the Great.

51 War not his Province] Mordaunt's appointment to high military command was most unusual in the light of his lack of experience at lower levels. Farquhar claims in this passage that he learned from observing the strategies of William III at Namur and the Boyne (the latter being a battle in which Margaret claimed Farquhar himself fought), and those of Marlborough at Blenheim.

57 Early the *Hero* in the Senate stood] Peterborough entered the House of Lords in 1680, when he was twenty-two years old.

58 A *Daring Champion*] Mordaunt sided with Shaftesbury, signed the petition against the Oxford Parliament in January 1681, and in other ways made himself heard. After the accession of James II, he protested at the increase in the standing army and the appointment of Catholics as officers.

60 lash'd *within*, the Errors made *without*] Louis XIV had revoked the Edict of Nantes, and Huguenots were pouring into England. The terrors described by the refugees made King James's determination to maintain the standing army and abolish the Test Act seem a grave threat to Protestants.

66 His *Eloquence*] Mordaunt's maiden speech in Parliament was marked by boldness and passion:

> ... A standing army exists. It is officered by Papists. We have no foreign enemy. There is no rebellion in the land. For what then is this force maintained, except for the purpose of subverting our laws, and establishing that arbitrary power which is so justly abhorred by Englishmen?

So impressive was the speech that the French Ambassador quoted at length from it in his letter to Paris (Ballard, p. 43). Mordaunt was one of the earliest Englishmen to consider bringing Prince William of Orange to the British throne.

78 Power supream upon the Plain] Mordaunt became commander-in-chief, Shovell admiral.

79 *Shovell*] Sir Clowdisley Shovell (1650–1707) had been rear admiral in the battle of Beachy Head in 1692. He was a respected naval commander with far more experience than Mordaunt. The two men had some personal difficulties in their joint leadership. Peterborough, writing from the Castle of Montjuich on 9 September 1705, soon after the capture of the fort, described his compatriot thus:

> . . . Sr Clowdesly Shovell is a man possest of many good qualityes, those things in which we have differd I can not reproach him for, He has had grounds for his opinions, I can only say I thought I should have acted other wise if it had been in my power. He is Brave if I may say to a fault, and in matters he does not understand thinkes yt whatever is directed him must be begun, and when begun must be carryed on, what accidents soever occur or whatsoever improbabilityes come in the way, He sticks to what he calles orders an will conceive no Latitude in such instructions that I think were calculated for the greatest. He is a man under that rough case of the greatest good nature and can be imposed upon that way, but my Lord He is entirely Governed by one Norris Capt of the Brittania a man of whom I can say no good. . . . (British Library, Add. MS 39 757, f. 116^v.)

93 *Tourville*] French Admiral Anne Hilarion de Tourville (1642–1701), who had defeated the English forces at Beachy Head in 1690, was soundly trounced in the naval battle of Cape La Hogue in 1692. This decisive victory established the supremacy of the English over the French at sea.

94 Press'd hard by *Russel*] Admiral Edward Russell, Earl of Orford (1653–1727), commanded the English at both Beachy Head and Cape La Hogue. Russell commanded ninety-nine ships to Tourville's forty-four. Russell and the Anglo-Dutch navy pursued the enemy into French harbours and totally destroyed the fleet.

100 *Sun Royal*] The flagship *Le Soleil Royal*, named after Louis XIV, was an appropriate symbol of the French defeat. Russell's forces first shattered the ship, then burned it. One scholarly view is that Tourville's unwillingness to abandon the flagship was an important element in the defeat of the French by the Anglo-Dutch troops. (Frank Fox, *Great Ships: The Battle Fleet of King Charles II* [London, 1980], p. 170.)

108 *Vigo Bay*] The victory of Vigo Bay, a port in Galicia, on 23 October 1702 was considered by the British one of the most illustrious of the War of the Spanish Succession. Sir George Rooke's ships forced the boom and entered the bay while the Duke of Ormonde's land forces took the fortifications overlooking the bay. The destroyed fleet included fifteen French warships and two frigates, as well as three Spanish galleons and thirteen trading vessels. The British brought home a booty estimated at more than £1,000,000. Although Spanish merchants suffered severe losses, according to recent evidence King Philip V profited enormously by

confiscating from the ships the silver bullion which belonged to English and Dutch merchants (Henry Kamen, *The War of Succession in Spain 1700–15* [Bloomington, Ind., and London, 1969], pp. 179–80). Contemporary British lore about Vigo Bay, however, celebrated the total, glorious victory of the Anglo-Dutch fleet.

109 *India's* rifled Stores] riches from the West Indies. The cargo ships in Vigo Bay had arrived from Vera Cruz. (George Malcolm Thomson, *The First Churchill, The Life of John, 1st Duke of Marlborough* [New York, 1980], p. 104.)

113 *Ormond*] James Butler, second Duke of Ormonde (1665–1745), had fought at the battle of the Boyne, at Steinkirk, and at Landen where, in 1693, he was taken prisoner. He commanded the land forces sent on the expedition to Cadiz in 1702, and his troops captured the fortifications during the battle of Vigo Bay. In 1709 Ormonde stated, in his certificate for Margaret Farquhar, that he had given the lieutenant's commission to Farquhar; however, scholars have argued that the Earl of Orrery in fact commissioned him. In either event, Ormonde, was Lord Lieutenant in Ireland during Farquhar's service there; moreover, he not only gave permission for Farquhar to play in *The Constant Couple* in Dublin during his service but, according to tradition, also attended the performance. Finally, there is some evidence that Ormonde was the officer who encouraged Farquhar to give up his lieutenancy, then never followed through with the captaincy that had been promised; Farquhar's disappointment has traditionally been given as a cause for his death (see Jordan, *passim*). If Farquhar indeed drafted *Barcellona* before he left his regiment early in 1706, and if the traditional account of his relinquishing his lieutenancy is true—and there is evidence to support both conclusions—he wrote the laudatory passage on Ormonde when he was banking his hopes on the nobleman to commission him captain.

113 *Rook*] Sir George Rooke (1650–1709) was made vice-admiral and Lieutenant of the Admiralty in 1702. As commander of the British fleet, he stormed Vigo Bay, destroyed the fleet, and captured the treasure to bring back to England.

114 The Boom flies short] Rooke's troops broke the boom and entered the Bay as Ormonde's troops captured the fortifications and turned their weapons against the Spanish.

123 a *British* or a *Belgick* Prey] The looting of the allies has been estimated at more than a million pounds sterling.

127 *Cupid*, God of Love, sits smiling by] Lady Mary Vere, Ormonde's mistress, was trying to solicit Ormonde's favour for Farquhar's captaincy, if we may believe the scandalous gossip of Mary de la Riviere Manley's *The New Atalantis; or The Secret Memoirs and Manners of Several Persons of Quality* (1709) and the printed key published in 1720. Manley, in the *roman à clef*, implies that Lady Mary took money ('sixty Pieces') from the poet, presumably Farquhar, 'to make him only a Subaltern' (p. 166). If she was in fact interceding for Farquhar, he might have been eager to include a smiling Cupid in his praise of Ormonde.

128 A Friend he is to all] Ironically, if the traditional account is accurate,

Ormonde proved no friend to Farquhar, although Farquhar was depending on his amity when he wrote his passage.

138 *here*] Vigo Bay.

138 the Plate of *France* and *Spain*] The ships were laden largely with a cargo of bullion.

142 rich *Tagus* by *Lisbona*'s Side] the river at Lisbon. On 24 May 1705 Peterborough and Shovell headed to Lisbon with sixty-six British and Dutch battleships, many smaller ships, and 6,500 troops (Churchill, v. 58).

153 *great Ruvigni*] Henri de Massue, second Marquis de Ruvigny (1648–1720), was deputy-general of the French Huguenots; he was raised first to Viscount (1692) then Earl of Galway (1697) by William III. He received the earldom for his service as general of horse in Ireland. He later fought heroically at Landen. Supposedly he was at one point captured by the French at the battle of Neerwinden, but they so admired his courage that they released him to continue his heroic protection of the retreating army. He became commander of the English forces in Portugal in 1704. He was known as a brave man, modest and honorable, with a good mind as well as a courageous spirit. He lost his hand and lower arm in the battle of Badajoz on 20 October 1705, when he was struck by a cannonball (David C. A. Agnew, *Henri de Ruvigny, Earl of Galway* [Edinburgh, 1864], *passim*.)

157 *Streights*] Strait of Gibraltar. The forces sailed from Lisbon, through the Straits, to the eastern coast of Spain.

159 his Name] a reference to the Pillars of Hercules.

168 *Æsculapius*] a reference to the tradition that the famous physician of mythology gathered herbs at Gibraltar.

169 *Garth*] Sir Samuel Garth was famous not only for his medical practice but also for his burlesque poem *The Dispensary* (1699). Farquhar was not particularly friendly with the Kit-Cats, of whom Garth was one; the somewhat surprising compliment to him embedded in the military epic suggests some personal acquaintance.

174 by *British* Fleets possess'd] Gibraltar fell to the English in August 1704. Rooke and Shovell joined forces on the Atlantic side of the Straits of Gibraltar with the intention of attacking Cadiz, but Hesse-Darmstadt proposed that they strike Gibraltar instead. They attacked on 1 August, and by 6 August Hesse-Darmstadt occupied the city in the name of Charles III (Kamen, p. 13).

177 Six Months besieg'd] Mans-Jean-Baptiste René de Frouley, comte de Tessé, Marshal of France (1651–1725), was sent to Spain to lead the Franco-Spanish army against the allied troops at Gibraltar. He arrived in Madrid in November and at Gibraltar by February 1705. As many as 50,000 men were deployed under his command. However, by April he had still not recovered the town, and since there was little hope for success, the troops left.

179 *Ponti* run from *Leak*] Admiral Sir John Leake (1656–1720) served as second in command to Shovell. Jean Bernard Desjeans, Baron de Pointis (1645–1707), was the French commander of a squadron attempting to retake Gibraltar Bay. On 10 March 1705 Leake destroyed five French ships, including the flagship; Pointis, recognizing defeat, fled with his remaining

ships to Toulon (David Hannay, *A Short History of the Royal Navy: 1217–1815* [2 vols, London, 1909], ii. 67).

181 *Darmstadt*] Hesse-Darmstadt had been instrumental in cutting off the Franco-Spanish garrison at Gibraltar from their supply lines and thus an important contributor to the victory there; on 6 August he had claimed the city in the name of Charles III. He remained at Gibraltar during its six months' siege.

185 Pious and Prudent] Contemporary accounts from the scene of the battle indicate less admiration for Hesse-Darmstadt than Farquhar expresses. With the promise of a commission as Viceroy of Catalonia, Hesse-Darmstadt, siding with Charles in the councils of war, clung to the idea of fighting at Barcelona. Peterborough found him rigidly determined to attack Barcelona and, when the battle came, shockingly ignorant, considering he had lived there, of the proper way to attack it.

238 both the *Heroes* to the Fleet descend] Peterborough and Hesse-Darmstadt met with admirals including Shovell and Leake at Lisbon.

240 the *Midland* Sea] The councils at Lisbon led to a decision to assault Barcelona; the allies sailed from Lisbon through the Strait of Gibraltar to the Mediterranean.

244 *Rook*'s rough Squadron with *Tholouse*'s met] The battle of Málaga, the biggest naval battle of the war, pitted Rooke's fleet against the French fleet headed by Louis Alexandre de Bourbon, comte de Toulouse (1678–1737), on 23 August 1704. The French, according to Kamen, had ninety-six vessels, the Allies sixty-eight (p. 13). Neither side suffered any destroyed or captured vessels, but many ships were damaged and many officers killed. Toulouse himself was one of the thousands wounded. Neither side actually could claim a victory, but the battle was so costly to both sides that there were no further major naval battles during the course of the Peninsular war.

246 gave the Odds to neither] Neither side could boast a victory, although Toulouse, who had left for Toulon next morning, claimed he had won.

Canto II

19 *Guiscard*] The Marquis Antoine de Guiscard, Abbe de La Bourlie (1658–1711), who had been expelled from France and come to England, was colonel of a regiment of French Huguenot refugees. Although Farquhar portrays him as fleeing tyranny, as his published *Memoirs* indicated, his rakishness may have necessitated his flight from France. A tall, handsome man, he was accused of various excesses, including gluttony, killing a butcher over a dog-fight, seduction and abduction of a young girl, sexual licence with boys, heavy gambling, promiscuity, riotous living, and ravishing nuns. He got in considerable trouble when he and his brother eloped with a hatter's wife (Peter Jones, 'Antoine de Guiscard, Abbé de la Bourlie, Marquis de Guiscard, *British Library Journal*, viii [1982], 97).

Guiscard had married Prince Eugene's sister in 1704, but she died the next year; he was introduced to the Archduke Charles by Eugene. Guiscard traveled then to Barcelona, and from there Charles wrote to Marlborough on 24 September 1705 in his behalf (Jones, pp. 101–3).

Yet Guiscard was not a vital participant in the battle of Barcelona; it is odd that Farquhar included this long passage concerning him. The author may well have been influenced by the publication in London in 1705 of the self-righteous *Memoirs of the Marquis de Guiscard. Or, an Account of his Secret Transactions in the Southern Provinces of France, Particularly in Rouergue and the Cevennes, to Rescue the Nation from Slavery.* The volume was printed and sold by Bragg, who published the London edition of *The Stage-Coach* in 1705.

The *Memoirs* vividly describe the misery of the Cévenols. Guiscard hoped that battalions of Huguenots, reinforced by British troops, would land in the Bay of Biscay; then the allies would raise troops from the Cévennes and reactivate the Camisards to carry rebellion into the area. Five regiments of Huguenots and nearly a dozen British batallions assembled at Portsmouth near the end of 1705. The concept of the 'descent on France' continued under consideration for several years.

In 1711 Guiscard met an ignominious death. When Harley reduced his government retainer, the Frenchman began to sell British military secrets to the French. An incriminating letter was intercepted, and Guiscard was arrested for questioning. In the Privy Council session, he attacked Harley with a small knife; St John and others then attacked him with swords. He died three weeks later in Newgate.

23 *Rhosne*] Rhône.

25 *Tyrant*'s Rage] Louis XIV's tyranny.

36 *Their* Gods are snatch'd away] a reference to the treatment of the Huguenots. Guiscard is careful in the preface to the *Memoirs* to deny Catholicism, thus appealing to the English to help their Protestant brethren in France.

42 *Priests* like Dragoons] In the *Memoirs*, Guiscard condemns 'the cruel Instruments of the Prince's Passion', including curates, bishops, and missionaries, noting that 'these unworthy Ministers of the Altars were the most barbarous Executors of the Prince's Cruelty, whose Proceeding was detested by all sober Roman Catholicks' (p. 9).

70 *Cevennian* Captain] Guiscard hoped to join British troops with renewed Céveno forces for the 'descent on France'.

89 To supplicate Releif, I abandon Home] Guiscard's *Memoirs* conclude:
I shall always chuse rather to Sacrifice my Life for the Safety, Glory, and Liberty of my Native Country, than Sacrifice this to a vile and sordid Interest, and by that means contribute to the Upholding of one of the most Tyrannical and Unjust Governments upon the Face of the Earth (p. 56).

90 To *Anna*] Guiscard dedicated his *Memoirs* to Queen Anne, 'the Protectrix of the Liberty of EUROPE, and a professed Enemy to the Unjust Maxims of a Despotick and Arbitrary Power' (Sig. A2).

102 *Villain Priest*] At the time of the marriage treaty between the French King and the Infanta María Teresa, eldest daughter of Philip IV of Spain, in 1659, the French supposedly renounced the Spanish throne. But Cardinal Mazarin made the agreement dependent upon the infanta's dowry, and when that was not paid, the French did not consider themselves bound by the renunciation agreement. In fact, the French probably never committed

themselves to the agreement very seriously. Out of the marital agreement grew the causes of the War of the Spanish Succession.

106 a People] The people of Catalonia were separatists, who, with the Aragonese, resented the favoured position of Castile. Moreover, they did not welcome Philip's rule, although they did not openly protest. The Catalans greatly admired Hesse-Darmstadt, who had been their last Habsburg viceroy and who had defended Barcelona against the French in 1697. Hesse-Darmstadt was influential in the decision to attack Barcelona because of his good relations and strong contacts with the Catalans. However, Peterborough was gravely disappointed in Hesse-Darmstadt's lack of strategic insights and in the number of Catalans who joined the allies in the battle.

143–4 Her Predecessor . . . had stopt the Stream] A reference to William III's numerous encounters with the French, culminating in the Treaty of Ryswick in 1697. Stephen B. Baxter assesses Williams success thus:

> . . . for the first time in living memory France had lost a war. . . . Almost all the credit belonged personally to William III. He had planned the alliance, planned the war of attrition, conducted its battles in person, shared the losses but the victories too. His position as the greatest man in Europe could not be contested in 1697 or indeed for the rest of his life (*William III and the Defense of European Liberty 1650–1702* [New York, 1966], p. 358).

146 urg'd the *Stream* back] a reference to such victories as Vigo Bay, Blenheim, and Barcelona.

153 *Hibernian* Flood] Hesse-Darmstadt supported King William at the battle of the Boyne, a battle in which Margaret Farquhar claimed Farquhar fought, although he would have been only twelve years old at the time. Trevelyan reports that Hesse-Darmstadt was at William's side when the king was grazed by a cannon-ball during a tour of inspection; another shot felled Hesse-Darmstadt's horse.

155 *Belgick* Plains] Hesse-Darmstadt became an ally of William in 1688.

163 the three Kingdoms] Valencia, Catalonia, and Aragon.

165–6 a small Force sent outwards might insure | Men prompt for Vengeance] Hesse-Darmstadt maintained that the Catalans would fight with the Allies to oust the French. However, his estimates of their willingness to join forces proved highly exaggerated. Although there had been talk among the Allies of 12,000 Catalan troops, in fact only 1,500 Miquelets, local mercenary guerrillas, joined them in battle. Their number was desperately disappointing to the Allies, but the Miquelets proved invaluable.

182 *Catalonia* ends our present Course] The assembled leaders who met at Lisbon finally agreed to march on Barcelona.

Canto III

53 The moving Cohorts] Farquhar suggests that the Catalans vacillated politically between Philip and Charles, but their warm affection and gratitude toward Hesse-Darmstadt swayed them strongly to the allied position.

57 All arm'd and well appointed] Actually, the allies were gravely disappointed at the lack of military support from Catalan nobles although they did welcome Charles as King. The Miquelets, however, proved invaluable allies to the British troops.

65 *Velasco*] Don Francisco de Velasco (d. 1716), the unpopular viceroy of Barcelona, described by Churchill as a resolute, vindictive champion of the Bourbons', commanded about 3,200 foot and 800 horse (Ballard, p. 139).

68 great *Mordaunt*'s hardy Choice] Peterborough had, in fact, argued for going to Eugene's aid in Italy until he realized it was useless to try to change Charles's mind.

106 *Richlieu*] To the British, the name of Cardinal Richelieu (1585–1642) was synonymous with French duplicity and monomaniacal misuse of power.

106 *Turenne*] Henri de La Tour d'Auvergne, viscount de Turenne (1611–75) marshal under Louis XIV. His military skill was legendary.

122 *Priest-craft* brib'd] In July 1700 the Pope declared for the French succession as least threatening to peace (Kamen, pp. 3–4).

124 Great *Nassau* fell] William III died on 8 March 1702.

137 *Blenheim*] Marlborough's great victory at Blenheim had occurred in August 1704, thirteen months before the battle of Barcelona.

150 the *Danube*] The battle of Blenheim was fought near the Danube.

153 that *monumental* Spire on *Hockstet* Plain] Höchstädt is the town near the village of Blenheim. The battle was interchangeably identified as Blenheim or Höchstädt. Perhaps Farquhar refers here to the notable church spire at Blenheim.

172 conquering *Eugene*] Eugene of Savoy fought along with Marlborough at Blenheim. The Tories emphasized the role of Eugene; the Whigs, Marlborough. Farquhar here gives credit to both commanders.

173 *Baden*] Prince Louis, Margrave of Baden, an Austrian general, joined Eugene and Marlborough in June 1704 and engaged in several battles along with them. At Schellenberg in July 1704 he was instrumental in preventing disaster. However, he went to fight at Ingolstadt, Bavaria, in August 1704 and consequently missed the battle of Blenheim. There was great tension in the relationship of Marlborough and Baden. The decision for Baden to march to Ingolstadt has been seen as possibly reflecting his own unwillingness to engage in the battle of Blenheim or perhaps Marlborough's reluctance to have him there.

174 *Ruvignies* Squadrons] Allied troops under Lord Galway were victorious at Valencia de Alcántara on 8 May 1705, and Albuquerque on 20 May 1705.

175 *Mordaunt*'s Cohorts] Many of the leaders who fought at Barcelona had come from the conquest and defence of Gibraltar. These included Hesse-Darmstadt, the Portuguese Marquês das Minas, and others. Therefore the French sprite might well worry about the battle of Barcelona.

176 *Shovell* awes the Main] Shovell, Leake, Rooke, and two Dutch admirals led the sea-battle at Gibraltar. Now they prepared for the attack on Barcelona.

179 *Baden*] In the spring of 1705, Baden commanded his troops on the Rhine. Marlborough planned to progress into France with more than 90,000

men in two armies, the larger led by him from the Moselle, the smaller led by the Margrave from the Landau area. But Baden was slow to join battle, seemingly in part because of an infected injury to his foot, in part because of a palace he was building in Rastadt, in part because he felt his command was weak and ill supplied (Churchill, iv. 182–3). Finally, after Marlborough personally visited him in May, he agreed to join the English commander's troops at Trier, but his forces were so depleted that he could bring less than half the men Marlborough had expected.

180 *Ruvigne*'s Blow] The Earl of Galway was in Portugal with 15,000 men. The indecision and disagreement first of Baden, then of the allied leaders, led to advice that it was too late in the season for battle; these arguments may well have deplayed action. Moreover, the troops waited for the arrival of the Marqués das Minas and Count Atalaya. Nevertheless, Galway took the field on 20 September 1705, and marched to Badajoz on 2 October; there he was wounded on 11 October. (See Agnew, pp. 114–15.)

181 *Eugene*] Prince Eugene commanded 30,000 men in Italy that spring.

182 *Vendosme*] Prince Eugene met Louis Joseph, duc de Vendôme (1654–1712), great-grandson of Henry IV of France, on the river Po at the battle of Cassano on 16 August 1705. Vendôme held his position.

187 this Man] Peterborough.

226 Shews *Funds* exhausted, and no more Supplies] The general election of 1705 focused on the war and its costs, as well as problems of the Church. The Tories felt the war was too costly, in men and money, and the benefits were not sufficient to justify it; the Whigs supported the war effort.

230 Rehearsals *here*, *there*, Observators] John Tutchin founded a Whig periodical, the *Observator*, in 1702. The journal apparently inspired Charles Leslie to found a Tory periodical, *The Rehearsal* (1704–9), which attacked the *Observator* and other Whig publications.

233 the *Church*] The Tories, fiercely antagonistic to Dissenters as well as reluctant to continue the war, managed to tack the Occasional Conformity Bill to the main supply bill. This action breached the tradition that internal political strife should not interfere with the war-effort. Therefore the church issues became inextricably woven into the electioneering of 1705.

239 *Doctors* leave the *Pulpit*, for the *Press*] The clergy participated in pamphleteering and journalism, publishing not only sermons but tracts on contemporary issues. For example, Dr James Drake attacked Marlborough and Godolphin as responsible for the nation's desertion of the Church in a pamphlet called *The Memorial of the Church of England* and continued to abuse them in the anti-Government Tory periodical *Mercurius Politicus*, begun in 1705.

241 pusling] puzzling, in the sense of confusing or groping for something.

249 some few *Friends*] The fierce battling between Whigs and Tories in spring 1705 caused considerable turmoil and upheaval within the administration. The Duke of Buckingham, who had close personal ties with Queen Anne, was asked to reliquish the Privy Seal because of his entanglements with the Tory leaders; the Duke of Newcastle assumed his responsibilities as Lord Privy Seal. Admiral Rooke lost command of the fleet. Several of the Lords Lieutenants were replaced.

250–1 she forsook the *sacred* Ground, | But at the *Bar*, the Compensation found] The Tories, blocked in numerous ways in spring 1705, raised the cry that the Church was in danger because of the Act of Security, which authorized the Scottish government to arm the peasantry, who were anti-episcopalian. Moreover, the Occasional Conformity Bill continued to be rejected. The Church controversy was complicated by discussions of the succession should Anne die childless: the Tories proposed to bring the Electress Sophia from Austria to England. Both the Lords and Commons declared that the Church was 'in a most safe and flourishing condition' and that anyone who suggested or insinuated otherwise was an enemy to Queen, Church, and country and could be prosecuted (Churchill, v. 34–36).

280 *Setting* and the *Rising* Sun] that is, in both the West and East Indies.

282 *Sweden*] The youthful Charles XII of Sweden was winning victories on every side; no armies could withstand him. Therefore there was no room for Discord.

307 *Sergius*] Conceivably Charles Sergison (1654–1732), commissioner of the Navy during the War of the Spanish Succession. The passage which follows, to the end of Canto III and throughout Canto IV, in which allusive pseudonyms are applied to the allied commanders, employs a mode not used elsewhere in the poem. The references are obscure. Because identifications are so tenuous, for the most part they are left unannotated.

Canto IV

7 *Galba*] Servius Sulpicius Galba (3 BC–AD 69) became emperor of Rome at Nero's death, but died soon after in a rebellion.

15 Perspective] spy glass.

28 Without sufficient Force] Paul Methuen reported that in a council on 5 September the engineers said they needed more men in order to attack Barcelona, 1,000 'men of the Country' and 1,500 seamen to work daily (British Library, Add. MS 28 056 f. 325ᵛ). The allies had no regular siege train and had to plan to land guns from the ships to blow a breach. Moreover, marshy ground further complicated field operations (Trevelyan, *Ramillies*, p. 68). Therefore, the engineers' concerns were well justified.

33 *Vendosm*'s Attack] In 1697 Hesse-Darmstadt had withstood an attack by Vendôme, leading an army of 26,000 men, for almost two months (Trevelyan, *Ramillies*, p. 67).

35 Our living Thousands] Eugene was mightily outnumbered in these battles, his men ill, poorly clothed, and lacking in necessaries. Luttrell records that at the action at the Adda, Eugene lost 3,000 men and Vendôme 6,000 (v. 589).

44 *Prior*'s Song] Matthew Prior (1664–1721) was a statesman, diplomat, and poet. There is no evidence that Farquhar knew him personally.

48 *G—ns* Eyes] Henrietta Churchill, Marlborough's eldest daughter, married Francis, Lord Godolphin's son, in 1698, thus becoming the Countess of Godolphin. She was beautiful and accomplished, the subject of much poetical praise.

50 *M—ns* Frown] Perhaps Lord Mohun's wife, who indeed seldom

frowned on any suitor. She was drowned while crossing to Ireland with one of her gallants.

53 *S—nd*] Marlborough's second daughter, Anne Churchill, married the Earl of Sunderland's heir, Lord Spencer, in 1700 and thus became the Countess of Sunderland. A Lady of the Queen's Bedchamber from 1702, she too was frequently toasted by the rhymesters.

55 *C—sh*] Lady Henrietta Cavendish, daughter of the Duke of Newcastle, became daughter-in-law to the Duke of Devonshire.

57 *A—le's*] The Earl of Albemarle. (See Commentary, *Sir Harry Wildair*, Dedication, vol. i, p. 612.) After William's death, Albemarle sat in the States-General and fought in the War of the Spanish Succession.

57 *O—ry*] Charles Boyle, fourth Earl of Orrery (1676–1731), was commander of the regiment in which Farquhar held his commission. A patron of the arts, Orrery was not a distinguished military figure. In the summer of 1705, his regiment took part in the annual encampment in Ireland, at the Curragh of Kildare in June and early July (Jordan, p. 259). In this line Farquhar manages to compliment Orrery although he was not even involved in the Spanish campaign.

59 *Ormond*] The Duke of Ormonde was in England at the time of the battle of Barcelona. Here Farquhar manages another compliment to his prospective benefactor (see Canto 1. l. 113).

61 *Harley*] Robert Harley, first Earl of Oxford and Earl Mortimer (1661–1724), Anne's Tory secretary of state, had helped defeat the 'tack'.

61 *Cooper*] Sir William Cowper (d. 1723), a moderate Whig and a distinguished lawyer noted for his oratory, was made Lord Keeper in place of the Tory Sir Nathan Wright on 11 October 1705.

66 *C—r*] Perhaps a reference to Charles Caesar, who, on 20 December 1705, made ill-advised allusions in Commons to Godolphin's widely known relationship with Mary of Modena, surely a tasteless topic for discussion in Parliament. Caesar went to the Tower for his offence (David Green, *Queen Anne* [New York, 1970], p. 147). Only the fact that Farquhar was writing the poem contemporaneously would have encouraged him to include this minor incident.

102 *Celsus*] Aulus Cornelius Celsus (fl. AD 14) was a Latin encyclo-paedist. Eight of his books, on medicine, are extant.

114 *Cordelier*] The word 'cordelier' refers to the knotted cord that Franciscan monks wear around their waists; here the reference is to a Roman Catholic. Peterborough was very close to Colonel John Richards, a Roman Catholic artillery officer. Unable to hold a British commission because of his religion, he had served in Venice and Poland and was now in the Portuguese army. Trevelyan claims he was not only a loyal Englishman but also a man of strong abilities, good linguistic skills, and 'a calm and excellent judgment' (*Ramillies*, p. 71).

127 *Phocas*] Probably a reference to Shovell, who opposed the attack.

147 Approaching Winter] The delays caused by the councils of war aroused concerns that the decision would come too late for battle before winter. The possibilities of going to Eugene's aid in Italy and of attacking Madrid via Valencia were finally ruled out because the decisions were too

late to allow time for such operations. At one point the Dutch fleet agreed to stay for only seventeen days more, for the leaders felt that if they were to winter in Valencia, they needed to leave at once. Paul Methuen expressed the general view when he wrote to Godolphin on 13 September, 'I do not conceive how it will be possible for us to do so many things in so little time' (British Library, Add. MS 28 056, f. 327).

148 *Wheeler*'s Fate] Sir Francis Wheler (1656?–1694) served as an admiral in the War of the Grand Alliance. In February 1694, he sailed from Cadiz to pass through the Straits of Gibraltar, but hurricane-force winds dispersed his ships. Sailing at night, he mistook Gibraltar Bay for the Straits, sailed into it and was driven ashore. One ship, the Cambridge, broke against the shore; the flagship Sussex also foundered there. Of 550 people on board, only two escaped; Wheler's body was washed ashore two days later. Sir Clowdisley Shovell was one of the trustees of Wheler's will.

157 th' Assembly] the council of war. Freind records several councils, one aboard the *Britannia* on 16 August, others on 22 August (in Major-General Schratenbach's quarters in the camp), 25 August, 26 August (Peterborough's quarters), and 28 August (Major-General Henry Conyngham's quarters). This 'Assembly' conflates several of the councils, as recorded by A. Furly and reported in Freind's *Account*.

158 who th' Assembly thus bespoke] Actually Peterborough remained very secretive about his plan to attack Montjuich:

> . . . the only way that could succeed was the Attack of Montjui, which I undertook without the knowledge of the King of Spain, and of his Ministers, of the Prince of Hesse, or any of our own Officers, . . . (British Library, Add. MS 28 057 f. 25ᵛ).

According to Trevelyan, Peterborough, Colonel Richards, and Hesse-Darmstadt met; the English and German commanders then agreed, but no one else was informed. At the last moment, as the troops prepared to march away, Charles was brought into the secret (*Ramillies*, pp. 70–2).

165 better, to begin with *Montjuich Hill*] The difficulties of mounting an attack on Barcelona were intensified by the fortifications that must be faced and by the marshy land that militated against an attack from the north-east, the only feasible line of attack. Peterborough decided to march around the city to attack the Montjuich fort instead. The '*fast* and *Hilly* Land' leading to the fortress would make such an approach preferable.

176 *Serpion*] Perhaps a reference to Lichtenstein, who argued consistently for heading toward Italy. He hoped to become viceroy of Naples.

184 *Vich* and *Doris*] Vich is a town thirty-five miles north-east of Barcelona. The mention of Doris is either allusive or erroneous, for Doris is an area in ancient Greece, containing the sources of the Cephisus river.

207 *Issum*] At Issus Alexander defeated Darius in 333 BC although he was greatly outnumbered.

236 *Torto*'s and *Lerida*] Tortosa and Lérida are two towns in Aragon strategically important in times of war. Tortosa is a port on the river Ebro; Lérida at the foot of the central Pyrenees is in a key spot for land attacks on Aragon and Catalonia. Both declared for Charles III when Barcelona fell

(*Memoirs of Captain Carleton*, ed. Cyril Hughes Hartman [New York, 1929], p. 110).

251 the *Granick* Flood] Alexander fought at the Granicus in 334 BC.

255 *Tyre*] Alexander captured Tyre in 333–2 BC.

277 your own Decree] On 4 September and again on 5 September the council voted to sail to Italy. On 8 September, having received instructions from the Secretaries of State and the Treasury to go to Eugene's succour in Italy, the council voted yet again for that action (British Library, Add, MS 28 056, ff. 325^r–326^v). Peterborough, Methuen, and others claim in their letters to have believed all along that the Italian project would have been far more important and valuable than the Spanish one.

Canto V

3 his *Troubles* past] Mordaunt had experienced political troubles. Having been made First Lord of the Treasury in 1689 by William III, he was removed from office in 1690. In January 1697 Mordaunt was committed to the Tower of London because of his role in the contrivance of letters delivered to the House of Lords concerning Sir John Fenwick, a Jacobite conspirator. He was released at the end of March.

71 great *Marlb'rough*, near the *Belgick* Stream] In July 1705 Marlborough pierced the Lines of Brabant which had deterred the allies from challenging the French in the northern theatre. The allied forces crossed the river called the Little Geet by rushing the stone bridge at Elixem and by merely wading through the shallow stream in other places.

72 Treads *Nassau*'s Steps] William III had fought heroically at the battle of Landen near the Geet in 1693.

104 The Sea Commanders their Assent refuse] The naval officers favoured the battle of Barcelona rather than going to help Prince Eugene because they were worried about impending weather if they sailed for Italy. They agreed to send naval personnel ashore to help in the battle.

118 to good *Darmstad* hasten'd for Advice] In fact Peterborough did not propose the attack on Montjuich to the council but spoke secretly to Hesse-Darmstadt.

119 the great Design] The councils of war continued almost daily as the generals and admirals debated the best action. The decision was complicated by the fact that storming Barcelona would mean killing or damaging the property of Catalans, who favoured the cause of Charles III and who admired and befriended Hesse-Darmstadt. Peterborough's idea to take the Montjuich fort rather than attacking Barcelona directly solved very serious problems for the Allied troops. According to Churchill, Hesse-Darmstadt was struck with the brilliance of the suggestion (v. 61). Neither of them told Charles III or the admirals until the troops set off.

136 *Tarragon*] Hesse-Darmstadt recommends the ruse of pretending to despair of taking Barcelona and seemingly setting off for Tarragona, fifty miles south-west down the coast.

159 an Air of Woe] Word was passed that there would be no attack on

Barcelona. The news was believed within Peterborough's camp as well as by Velasco. As Ballard says, by deceiving his own men he had chosen 'the very best way of deceiving the enemy'. Ballard records that in Barcelona on 13 September a night of triumphal rejoicing was designated, while allied troops grumbled about 'first coming like fools and then going away like cowards' (p. 147).

167 the News of *Terragona*] The word of a march on Tarragona engulfed the camp. A group of men led by Peterborough and Hesse-Darmstadt were to leave as an advance party, followed by Stanhope's men. The rest of the militia was to follow.

171 the Guns] The guns borrowed from the navy and brought to land, along with the heavy baggage, were restored to the ships as part of the ruse.

174 *Terragon* by Sea] On 13 September 1705, Hesse-Darmstadt and Mordaunt led British and other troops as if marching toward Tarragona and then Valencia. Stanhope followed with more men; in all, about 2,200 participated. By a circuitous route, the men, marching all night, gained position to attack Montjuich by the next morning.

181 A Thousand Men of War] the troops led by Hesse-Darmstadt and Mordaunt.

183 *C—d*] William Caulfield, second Viscount Charlemont (d. 1726), like Farquhar an Irishman, distinguished himself in the battle. He led 400 grenadiers under Hesse-Darmstadt (Ballard, p. 147). Promoted to brigadier general on 25 August 1705, he was one of the first to enter Montjuich; he received the King's commendation.

187 *A—n*] Lieutenant Colonel Thomas Allen commanded 600 musketeers marching with Hesse-Darmstadt to Montjuich. Allen and his troops jumped from the breastworks into the ditch, exposing themselves to fire. Allen himself was taken prisoner (Ballard, p. 149). Allen succeeded Gorges as colonel of the regiment on 15 April 1706.

189 *S—l*] William Southwell (1669–1719), younger brother of the first Baron Southwell, obtained a commission in Colonel Hamilton's regiment on 1 September 1693. Wounded at Namur, he rose to captain, then major, and on 1 January 1704 became lieutenant-colonel, second in command to Colonel James Rivers. He commanded 400 grenadiers. Southwell particularly distinguished himself in the siege of Barcelona (Dalton, iii. 325, n. 13). He was leading the troops when the scaling-ladders proved too short. Four days later, he was the first officer to enter the breach and gain the surrender. He was made temporary governor of Montjuich, and on 6 February 1706 he was once again promoted.

218 another Party] According to Ballard, Churchill, and Trevelyan, Peterborough and Hesse-Darmstadt marched together, and Colonel James Stanhope brought up the reserves. Farquhar's account differs slightly.

Canto VI

11 Forward the Soldiers rush without a Stop] The troops marched all night in order to circle the city and surprise the fort.

21 Oase] obsolete spelling of ooze; mud or muddy, boggy ground.

38 *Death* hit him low] Hesse-Darmstadt was wounded by a bullet in the thigh; he bled to death.

40 *Gustavus*] King Gustavus Adolphus II of Sweden (1594–1632) became a military legend in his lifetime. Allied with the Danes and French in the Thirty Years War, he was spectacularly victorious at Breitenfeld, the Lech, and finally Lützen, where he died in battle.

46 *Mordaunt*] Mordaunt was lionized for rushing into battle as the troops scattered in disarray. As Churchill describes it, 'Seizing a half-pike and declaring he would conquer or die, he rallied his surviving soldiers and led them back to the outworks' (v. 62).

87 *Con—m*] Henry Conyngham, also spelled Connyngham or Cunningham, (d. 1706), was Peterborough's major general.

91 Thus fell the *Father* and so fell the *Son*] Sir Albert Conyngham, Henry's father, commanded a regiment of dragoons later given over to his son's command. He was appointed Lieutenant General of the Ordnance in Ireland in 1660, and fought with William III at the battle of the Boyne, Limerick, etc. He died in battle with the Rapparees near Colooney, Co. Sligo. His son Henry perished in the battle of San Esteban in Spain in January 1706.

95 *Cales*] Cadiz.

97 *Belbastro*] the seat of a diocese in the area of Teruel.

99 *Cinca*] river in northern Spain.

100 Behold him fall] Conyngham was killed in a battle with Marshal Tessé's men as they approached Lérida on 26 January 1706. After the general's death, Colonel Wills continued the battle, holding the line until the French fell back (Ballard, p. 173).

101 *D—l*] Arthur Chichester, third Earl of Donegal (1666–1706), fought at the battle of Barcelona. He was the first person in the allied forces to set foot in Catalonia. He became Governor of Girona in 1705. (Dalton, iii. 339, n. 1). On 21 April 1706 he was killed when he tried heroically, with a garrison of seven hundred redcoats, to protect Montjuich from a massive attack by the French. In Churchill's words, 'Donegal, refusing all quarter, and striking down his foes on every side, perished gloriously, sword in hand, with the greater part of his men' (v. 80).

107 *G—s*] Brigadier Richard Gorges (d. 1728), of Kilbrew, Co. Meath, was adjutant-general of the forces in Spain. He had served throughout the Irish campaign (see Dalton, III, 75, n. 11). At the Council of 25 August, he had voted against the attack on Barcelona, as had Conyngham, Donegal, and others. All fought bravely in the war.

111 *L—n*] Prince Anthony Lichtenstein, one of Charles's 'Vienna crew' of advisers and officials. A great enemy to Peterborough, he was prone to assume 'most horrible ayrs' at the councils of war, and at one he allegedly threw a stool at Peterborough's secretary's head (Trevelyan, *Ramillies*, p. 70).

116 *S—l—g*, and *S—a—d*] a confusing and perhaps inaccurate reference. Lieutenant-Admiral Gerard Callenburgh led the Dutch fleet; Lieutenant-Admiral Filips van Almonde replaced him in 1705. Lieutenant-General François Nicolaus Fagel was commander of the army, and General

Schratenbach attended councils of war. I am indebted to Gerard Raven for information from the Royal Netherlands Navy.

137 *Leige*] The battle of Liege in October 1702 had been marked by unusual ferocity and bloodshed. When the governor refused Marlborough's offer of honourable terms for immediate surrender, the fighting became intensely bloody. About a third of the defenders fell casualties to the British, and the troops ravaged and pillaged following the invasion of the city (Churchill, iii. 151).

140 *Stanhope*] James Stanhope, first Earl Stanhope (1673–1721), brigadier in the Spanish expedition, was praised by Freind for his 'great Zeal, Vigilance, and very wise Conduct' (p. 47). In the vote of 25 August, he sided with Peterborough for the attack on Barcelona. He commanded the reserve in the attack on Monjuich. He was sent into Barcelona as a hostage. When Barcelona capitulated, he went into town and treated effectively with the inhabitants. He was also the person who brought the news of victory back to England.

228 *Velasco*] When an anti-Bourbon riot surged in Barcelona, Velasco was whisked off to an English ship (Kamen, pp. 15–16). The threat of a veritable bloodbath was deterred by strong English action.

Doubtful Attributions
A Pacquet from Will's

Celadon *to Mrs.* C—ll.

20–1 a trembling Disorder] Farquhar often complained of his inability to write well because of the rheumatic pain in his hand. The 'trembling Disorder' could be a reference to his illness, although the symptom is not mentioned elsewhere in his canon.

Letter II

0.1 *in answer to a Copy of Verses she sent him*] conceivably this is a response to Epistle XL, '*To Mr.* Farquhar *upon his Comedy call'd* A Trip to the Jubilee', published in *Letters of Wit, Politicks and Morality* a few months later. The text reads:

> SIR,
> Amongst the many friends your Wit has made,
> Permit my humble Tribute may be paid;
> My Female Genius to too weakly fraught
> With learn'd Expressions to adorn my Thought.
> My Muse too blush'd, when she this Task began,
> To think that she must Compliment a Man.
> She paus'd a while—at last she bid me say,
> She lik'd the Man, and I admir'd the Play.

For since the learned *Collier* first essay'd
To teach Religion to the Rhiming Trade,
The *Comick* Muse in *Tragick* posture sat,
And seem'd to mourn the Downfall of her State;
Her eldest Sons she often did implore,
That they her ancient Credit would restore.
Strait they essay'd, but quickly to their cost
They found that all their industry was lost.
For since the *Double Entendre* was forbid,
They could not get a Clap for what they did.
At last *Thalia* call'd her youngest Son,
The Graceful and the best beloved one:
My Son, said she, I have observ'd Thee well,
Thou doest already all my Sons excell;
Thy Spring does promise a large harvest Crop,
And Thou alone must keep my Glory up.
Go, something Write, my Son, that may atone
Thy Brethren's Faults, and make thy virtues known.
I'll teach Thee Language in a pleasant stile:
Which, without Smut, can make an Audience smile.
Let fall no word that may offend the Fair;
Observe Decorums, dress thy Thoughts with Air;
Go—lay the Plot, which Vertue shall adorn;
Thus spoke the Muse; and thus didst Thou perform.
Thy *Constant Couple* does our Fame redeem,
And shews our Sex can love, when yours esteem.
And *Wild-Air*'s Character does plainly shew,
A man of sence may dress and be a Beau.
In *Vizor* many may their Picture find;
A pious Out-side, but a poisonous Mind.
Religious Hypocrites thou'st open laid,
Those holy Cheats by which our Isle is sway'd.
Oh! mayst thou live! and *Dryden*'s Place supply,
So long till thy best Friends shall bid thee die;
Could I from bounteous Heav'n one wish obtain,
I'd make thy person lasting as thy Fame.

11 *For I shall sink and you shall split.*] These verses are full of *double entendre* but without the use of puns and slang that was characteristic of Farquhar.

50 the Jubilee Beau's Clothes] The reference to the exchange of clothes in *The Constant Couple* is the best argument for considering this letter the work of Farquhar, for he often referred to the *Jubilee* in other works, including letters.

EMENDATIONS OF ACCIDENTALS

THE RECRUITING OFFICER

Title Page. *dolis*] Q1 errata; *eolis*

Dedication. 0.4 WREKIN] Q1 errata; REKIN   22 *Wrekin*] Q1 errata; *Rekin*
66 *Wrekin*] Q1 errata; *Rekin*

II. i. 76 methinks] Q2; ~-|~

II. ii. 36 Gravel-walks] ed.; ~-|~   49 *Silvia*—] ed.; Q2 reads 'Ho *Silvia*!'
131 upon] Q2; ~-|~

II. iii. 37 Here's] Q2; Her'es   125 downright] Q2; ~-|~

III. i. 83 Gentleman] Q2; ~-|~   227–8 Side-|saddle] ed.; ~-~

III. ii. 168 Gentlemen] Q2; ~-|~   225 so,] Q2; ~∧

IV. i. 2 Preferment] Q2; Prefermeat   10 *Cartwheel*] ed.; ~-|~
161 something] Q2; ~-|~   169 something] Q2; ~-|~   189 Bedfellow]
ed.; ~-|~

IV. ii. 3 without] Q2; ~-|~   37–8 Bosom-|favorites] ed.; ~-~
65–6 Fortune-|teller] ed.; ~-~   94 upon] O1; ~-|~

IV. iii. 18 *Tycho*] ed.; *Ticho*   77–8 *Tom-|tit*] ed.; ~-~   203 Handkerchief]
ed.; Hand-|kerchief   372 I'm] ed.; 'Im

V. i. 21 off.] ed.; ~∧   The] ed.; the

V. ii. 26 without] O1; ~-|~   27 Gentleman] Q2; ~-|~

V. v. 98–9 under-|ground] ed.; ~-~

V. vii. 106 How!] Q2; how   157 Under-bred] ed.; ~-|~

THE BEAUX STRATAGEM

Dramatis Personæ. 16–17 Gentle-|woman] ed.; Gentlewoman

I. 12 overturn] ed.; ~-|~   36 1706,] O1; ~.   235 without] ed.; ~-|~
291 Gentleman] ed.; ~-|~   293 Gentleman] ed.; ~-|~   351 within] ed.; ~-|~

II. i. 35 Rosemary-Water] O1; Rose-|mary-Water

II. ii. 41 upon] ed.; ~-|~   71 Silver-hilted] O1; ~-|~   169 Footman]
ed.; ~-|~

III. i. 29 methought] O2; ~-|~ 34 Better] Q2; better 63 Because] Q2; because

III. ii. 86 into] O1; ~-|~ 116 upon] O1; ~-|~ 165 Foreigners] O1; Foregners 178 Landlord] O1; ~-|~

III. iii. 71 without] ed.; ~-|~ 347 Heart,] Q2; ~. 351 Hold] Q2; hold 430 upon] ed.; ~-|~

IV. i. 44 Ha] Q2; ha 56–7 Diet-|drink] ed.; ~-~ 68 Death's-door] ed.; ~-|~ 120 within] O1; ~-|~ 127–8 some-|what] ed.; somewhat 204 Gentleman] O1; ~-|~ 220–1 Common-|people] ed.; ~-~ 260 for a] O1; fora 288 and] Q2; aud 389 Gentleman] O1; ~-|~

IV. ii. 28 outliv'd] ed.; ~-|~ 76 *Mack-shane*] ed.; ~-|~ 115 Wind-pipe] O1; ~-|~

V. i. 12 Exciseman] O1; ~-|~ 79 Venison-pasty] O1 [~-Pastry]; ~-|~ 109 Godmother] O1; ~-|~

V. ii. 19 Bridegroom,] O1; ~. 32 *Alcmena*] Q2; *Alimena* 55 without] ed.; ~-|~ 86 What] O1; what 166 Rascal?] Q2; ~;

V. iv. 41 shannot] Q2; ~; 57 propos'd] Q2; popos'd 96 Now] O1; now 157 *make*] Q2; *maake* 277 Marriage] Q2; Marrriage 282 celebrate] Q2; celebaate

THE ADVENTURES OF COVENT-GARDEN

[Note: All emendations are made by the editor; therefore no siglum appears.]

Dedication. 3 am,] ~.

Preface. 21 *Englishman*] ed.; English-|man 46 Line,] ~. 48 Neighbours] Nieghbours 55 *Grashopper*] Gras-|hopper

Text. 31 *Peregrine*] *Pereg.* 59 looking] loooking 80 look] loook 100 Afternoon] ~-|~ 101 upon] ~-|~ 194 himself] ~-|~ 254 (answered Peregrine,)] ∧ ~-~, ∧ 258 (replied Emilia,)] ∧ ~~, ∧ 285 (said she;)] ∧ ~~; ∧ 312 Womankind,] ~-|~ 327 *Damon*] Damon 340 *Peregrine*'s] *Peregrin's* 351 something] some-|thing 352 without] ~-|~ 355 immediately] *immediately* Upon] ~-|~ 358 Coffeehouse] ~-|~ 362 himself] ~-|~ 385 *Newgate*] ~-|~ 433 (she continued,)] ∧ ~~, ∧ 472 without] ed.; withour 485 something] ~-|~ 539 Stars] Sars 555 *Damon*] Daman 557 Womankind] ~-|~ 629 hereafter] ~-|~ 636 Nightgown] ~-|~ 658 ∧ I] (~ 663 Upon] upon 668 *Peregrine* was . . . Discourse!] [italics reversed] 680 Utmost,] ~. 710 Methinks] Methirks 757–8 *What Tryal . . . a Porter*] [no italics]

Stop-press corrections. 401 wit,] University of Iowa, Harvard copies; ~; Bodleian, British Library copies Poets;] University of Iowa, Harvard copies; ~, Bodleian, British Library copies

LOVE AND BUSINESS

Title page. Epistolary] Eipistolary

Dedication. 0.2 Esq.] ~;   43 *Cecil*] *Cicil*   52 cannot] can-|not
62 *Prudentia*] *Prudenta*

To the Reader. 21 *Damme*] *Dam-|me*   me.] me∧

The Brill, August the 10th. 1700. 44–5 *Dutch-|man*] Dutch-man   58 Storehouse]
~-|~   103 Coachwhip] ~-|~   123 themselves] ~-|~
130 Landlord] ~-|~

Leyden, October the 15th. 1700. 27 themselves] ~-|~   85 themselves] ~-|~
83 Heartburnings] ~-|~   91 *Coffee-house*] ~-|~   106 themselves] ~-|~
146 Countrymen] Conntrymen   206 Gentlemen] ~-|~   226 without] ~-|~
229 weighty] wieghty   Consequence] Consquence   238 Board-side] ~-|~
250 hitherto] ~-|~   260 unfortunately] unfortuntely   298 Forreigners]
Forriegners

A Prologue on the propos'd Union of the Two Houses. 23 their] thir

Letter *Thursday,* 11 *o'clock.* 22 something] ~-|~

Grays-Inn, Wensday Morning. 6 *veil'd*] *viel'd*

'*Madam,* If I han't begun thrice to write'. 33 upon] ~-|~

Monday, twelve a Clock at Night. 3 into] ~-|~

'*Madam,* In Order'. 2 weighty] wieghty   37 Gentleman] Genteman
70 understands] ~-|~   172 Hobnail] ~-|~   240 something] ~-|~

'Well, Mrs. *V—*'. 4–5 over-|hear] ~-~

'Your Verses, Madam'. 26 *Nymph*] *Nymyh*

'Your strange and unexpected'. 10 remember a] remember

Hague, October the 23rd. 26 without] ~-|~

'I receiv'd| your letter|'. 42 Deliverance] Deliverace   51 without] ~-|~

A Discourse upon Comedy. 5 without] ~-|~   44 Professor] Professiors
102 question] quustion   120 *Choruses*] Chorusies   125 Misfortune]
Misfortuue   146 Day,] ~∧   179 Gentlemen] ~-|~   255 Understanding]
~-|~   270 Lawyers,] ~∧   275 *Subdivisions*] ~-|~   307 *Philosophy*]
Philo-|phy The word spans two pages; although the catchword *sophy* appears on
p. 127, p. 128 begins with *phy*   325 *Subdivisions*] ~-|~   363 certain] cetain
374 Schoolboys] ~-|~   381 Non-|performance] ~-~   391 insomuch]
in-|somuch   416 Schoolmen] ~-|~   482 Offspring] ~-|~
495 something] ~-|~   503 *agreeable*] *ageeeable*   511 nevertheless]
never-|theless   521 prosecuting] prosecucing   562 Commonwealth] ~-|~

579 cannot] connot   629 understand] ~-|~   *Mackbeth*] ~-|~
649 Playwright] ~-|~   652 Doorkeepers] ~-|~   676 out-o'th-way]
out-lo'th-way   747 believe] belive   756 cannot] ~-|~
845 examining] examing

MISCELLANEOUS PROSE AND POETRY

Familiar and Courtly Letters

'I had a Mind to know'. 2 therefore] ~-|~   19 himself] ~-|~

'By Heavens and Earth'. 10 however] ~-|~

A Pacquet from Will's

Friday. Quotation marks are standardized throughout. 13 Gentleman] ~-|~
23 What] what   32 upon] ~-|~   38 Heartless,] ~∧

To a Lady, whom he never saw. 37 red-hot] ~-|~

Letters of Wit, Politics and Morality

Letter XLI. 6 As soon] Assoon   7 brought∧] ~,   16 notwithstanding]
not-|withstanding

Letter XLVII. 0.1 R— S—] *R— S—*   14 If] if   30 If] if   63 him.
You] ~. you

LOVE'S CATECHISM

30 *himself*] ~-|~   107–49 *Wedlock . . . Heart.*] Italics are regularized, despite
irregularities of the original.

BARCELLONA

Dedication. 25 *Austrian*] *Austriam*

Preface. 16 such] snch

Canto I. 185 *Pious* and] ~ ond

Canto III. 304 Walls,] ~.   320 *Mischief*] *Miscief*

Canto V. 157 As soon] Assoon   158 spread,] ~.   187 blest,] ~?

Canto VI. 69 unequal] ~,   78 abrupt] abrumpt   121 T'assert] Tassert
228 *Velasco*] *Volasco*

DOUBTFUL ATTRIBUTIONS

A Pacquet from Will's

Celadon *to Mrs.* C—ll. 1 *Astræa*] *Astrea*

Letter II. 7 *Quick-sand*] ~-|~   39 throughout] ~-|~

INDEX